Understanding and Using

dBASE IV™

Rob Krumm

Brady

New York

Brady

Simon & Schuster, Inc.
15 Columbus Circle
New York, New York 10023

Distributed by Prentice Hall Trade

Manufactured in the United States of America

2 3 4 5 6 7 8 9 10

Library of Congress Cataloging-in-Publication Data

Krumm, Rob, 1951-
    Understanding and using dBASE IV
        p.   cm.

    1. Data base management. 2. dBASE IV (Computer program)
I. Title. II. Title: Understanding and using dBASE 4. III. Title: Understanding and using dBASE
Four.
QA76.9.D3K795 1989
005.75'65--dc20   8922244
                                                                CIP

ISBN 0-13-945056-4

For Carolyn

Lighten up...
Don't Panic ...
One page at a time...
And a Partridge in a pear tree...
Now you're set for life!

Trademarks

dBASE II, dBASE III, dBASE III Plus, dBASE IV, Rapidfile, Framework II, Framework III are trademarks of Ashton-Tate.
The Norton Utilies, The Norton Editor and The Norton Commander are trademarks of Peter Norton Computing.
Lotus 1-2-3 is a trademark of Lotus Development Corporation.
PFS File and PFS Professional File are trademarks of Software Publishing Corporation.
VisiCalc was a trademark of Visicorp.
MSDOS, Excel and Multiplan are trademarks of Microsoft Corporation.

Contents

Introduction   xv

Part I Database Management in dBASE IV

Chapter 1 The dBASE IV System   3

The Philosophy of dBASE IV   3
Dual Character   4
A Programming Language   4
Data Management or Programming?   5
Three Levels of Operation   6
Network Operations   7
SQL   7
Changes From dBASE III   8
Getting Familiar   11
Moving the Highlight   13
Selection   14
The Menu Bar   16
The Help System   23
Catalogs   26
Creating a New Catalog   27
Switching Catalogs   29
Quitting the Program   29
Summary   30
Exercises   32

Chapter 2 Creating a Database File   33

Creating a Structure   34
Entering a Field   38
Memo Fields   42
Activating a Database   46
Adding a File Description   48
Printing the File Structure   50
Ejecting the Page   50
Adding Records   52
Adding Another Record   56
The Ditto Key   57

Displaying Previously Entered Records   58
Adding More Records   63
The Browse Display   64
The Fields Menu   68
Freezing a Column   70
Unfreezing a Column   72
Undoing Changes   72
Closing a Database File   73
Setting Conditions   75
Getting Help   79
Summary   82
Exercises   83

Chapter 3 Retrieving Data   85

Listing by Index Order   86
Creating Additional Indexes   91
Using the Natural Order   98
Query by Example   98
Controlling Fields   99
Moving a Field   104
Selection of Records   106
Selecting by Characters   107
List Processing   111
Date Queries   112
Ranges   114
Logical Combinations   116
Sequencing Displays   120
Saving a Query   123
Saving a Query as a File   124
Removing Files   126
Summary Displays   127
Subtotal Groups   131
Unique Lists   132
Find   133
Calculated Fields   135
Query Variable Names   136
Date and Character Calculated Fields   138
Condition Boxes   141
Summary   145
Exercises   146

Chapter 4 Command Level Operations   149

What Is the Command Language?   149
The Dot Prompt Mode   150
Entering a Command   152
Syntax and Structure   153
Capitalization   154
Four Letter Abbreviations   155
File Lists   155
Adding Data   156
Selection and Sequencing   158
Fields Selection   159
Selecting Records   161
Command Shortcuts   162
Correcting Mistakes   163
Special Edit Clauses   164
Logical Selection   166
Display Versus Full Screen   168
Displaying Fields and Records   171
Selecting by Date   172
Using Date Functions   173
Selecting by Character Fields   175
Case Insensitive Expressions   176
Selecting by Number Values   177
Calculation by Expression   179
Clearing the Display   180
Memo Fields   180
Memo Width   181
Selecting by Memo Fields   183
Memo Field Functions   185
Summary Calculations   189
The Calculate Command   191
Listing by Index Order   194
The Status Display   196
Returning to the Natural Order   198
Search Index Fields   198
Printing Lists   201
Set Commands   201
Ending a Dot Prompt Session   205
Summary   205
Exercises   207

Chapter 5 Basic Column Reports   209

Report Forms   210
Creating a Column Report   213
Column Headings   219
Page Numbers and Dates   221
Templates   222
Adding Summary Calculations   225
Printing a Report   229
Saving a Report Form   232
Ordering reports   234
Revising a Report   237
Inserting a Field   237
Memo Fields   241
Changing Field Width   242
Quick Reports   244
Customizing a Quick Report   247
Creating Reports From Query Files   250
Calculated Columns   251
Numeric Calculations   255
Logical Fields   255
Memo Fields   257
Selecting Records For a Report   259
Summary   262
Exercises   264

Chapter 6 Custom Screen Forms   267

Creating a Screen Form   268
Adding Text   269
Drawing a Box   271
Placing Fields   272
Adding Non-field Information   279
Adding a Record Number   282
Creating a Graphic   286
Copying a Screen From a File   291
Deleting Fields   292
Logical Fields   293
Memo Fields   294
Working With Memo Displays   297
Field Options   299
Forms With Multiple Pages   306
Returning to the Default Display   311
Summary   312
Exercises   314
Work Around   314

Chapter 7 Putting Queries, Forms and Reports to Work   317

Adding Deposits	318
Creating the Input Screen	319
Entering the Deposits	325
The Checks Query	329
Renaming a File	331
The Checks Query	332
Creating Reports	335
Calculating the Balance	335
The IIF Function	337
Summary Reports	345
The Group Summary Band	351
Closing a Band	353
Reconciling Band Statements	355
Update Queries	356
Totaling Deposits and Checks	358
The Reconcile Report	361
Using the System	365
Summary	367
Exercises	369

Chapter 8 Labels, Mailmerge and Printed Forms   371

Creating a New Catalog	371
Labels	376
Printing Labels	385
Printing Three-Across Labels	386
Suppressing Blank Fields	389
Database Operations in the Dot Prompt Mode	393
Using Catalogs in the Dot Prompt Mode	393
Creating a Database—Dot Prompt Mode	396
Entering Data	398
The Replace Command	401
Form Reports	403
The Detail Band of a Form Report	407
Inserting Page Breaks	408
Printing Reports and Labels From the Dot Prompt	410
Selecting Records for Labels and Reports	410
Setting a Filter	410
Indexing Reports and Labels	411
Using the ? Option	412
Quitting From the Dot Prompt	415
Summary	415
Exercises	417

Chapter 9 Using and Relating Multiple Databases   419

Linking Databases	420
Alias Names	423
Create the Master Database	424
Linking the Products Database	431
Calculating Using Linked Databases	436
Selecting Records	438
Sorting	438
Multiple Links	440
Column Reports Using Multiple Databases	441
Mailmerge Reports	445
A Mailmerge Report Layout	447
Wraparound Text	453
Data Entry With Multiple Databases	457
Database Work Areas	458
Setting Relations	463
Editing Fields	467
Creating a Multiple Database Field List	469
Custom Screen Forms With Multiple Databases	473
Creating a Query From the Environment	480
Summary	482
Exercises	485

Chapter 10 Housekeeping, Maintenance, and Configuration   487

dBASE IV Files and File Operations	488
File Operations From the Control Center	492
Deleting Files	498
Copy and Backup Files	502
Repeating Operations With Macros	504
Macros With Pauses	508
Modifying a Macro	510
Saving Macros	515
File Operations From the Dot Prompt	515
Listings Directories	518
Duplicates Databases	520
Dividing a File	523
Combining Files	524
Summary Files	524
Deleting Records	527
Special Memo Operations	531
Exchanging Data	533
Summary	536
Exercises	537

Part II Programming

Chapter 11 Automating Tasks With Program Files   541

If You Have Written dBASE III Programs   542
Deferred Execution   543
Programs, Routines and Subroutines   544
The dBASE IV Compiler System   545
Your First Program   546
Linear Programs   547
Controlling the Screen Display   550
Memory Variables   553
Formatting Displayed Items   556
Horizontal Location   558
Adding More Information   560
Printing on the Same Line   561
Compiling Errors   563
Vertical Spacing   567
Replicating a Character   568
Centering Items   570
Programs That Carry on a Dialog   572
Full Screen Formatting   572
The Status and Scoreboard Displays   576
Input Area With Get   577
Initialization of Variables   578
Character Input Areas   580
Multiple Input Areas   581
Cursor Movement   583
A Full Screen Calculation Program   584
Input Area Options   587
Decimal Places   589
Lines and Boxes   591
Summary   596
Program Listing   599

Chapter 12 Structures In Programs   601

Pop-up Menus   601
The Pop-up Menu Toolbox   602
Pop-up Selection and Procedures   605
Writing a Procedure   606
The DO CASE Structure   607
Special Pop-up Menu Features   611
Scanning and Loops   615
Counters and Accumulators   619

User-Defined Functions   623
Structure of a User-Defined Function   624
Summary   626
Program Listings   627

Part III Networking

Chapter 13 Using dBASE IV on a Network   633

About Networks and Databases   633
Security   636
Establishing a Protection System   638
Logins   646
Forced Logins   647
File and Field Protection   648
Using Protected Files   652
Modifying a Protected Database   654
Field Protection   656
File Operations on a Multi-user System   659
Listing Users   663
File Versus Record Locks   667
Set Lock   670
Exclusive Access   672
Summary   675

Chapter 14 Programming on a Network   677

Editing on a Network   678
Explicit Record Locking   680
Turning off the Lock Message/pause   684
Unlocking a Record   684
Program With Explicit Record Locking   685
Alternative Actions   690
File Locks   697
Error Handing   701
Lock Function System   705
Converting File   706
User ID Messages   708
Lksys( )   710
Change( )   714
Summary   719
Program Listing   720

Part IV SQL

Chapter 15 Using SQL   731

What Is SQL?   731
Why Use SQL?   732
The SQL Approach   732
What SQL Does and Does Not Do   735
SQL Terminology   735
Starting SQL   736
Creating an SQL Database   737
SQL Tables   738
Entering SQL Commands   739
Data Entry   741
Displaying Data   744
Loading Data From a File   745
Using dBASE IV For SQL Data   747
Importing Databases   749
Selecting Data From Tables   750
Column List   751
Expressions In Column List   751
The Where Clause   752
Logical Operators   753
Getting Database Information   756
Sequencing Selections   757
Indexes In SQL   759
Unique Indexes   761
Distinct Selections   762
Summary Queries   763
Indirect Totals   765
Multiple Table Selections   766
Summaries With Multiple Tables   770
Views   772
New Tables   774
Deleting Rows   776
Dropping Tables   776
Programs Using SQL Databases   776
Printing SQL Information on Pages   783
Summary   784
Program Listings   786

Part V Configuration

Chapter 16 System Configuration and Customization 789

Temporary Changes 790
Set Commands 791
Permanent Changes 797
The SET( ) Function 797
DBSETUP 799
Editing the CONFIG.DB File 804
CONFIG.DB Only Settings 806
Starting dBASE IV 809
Summary 809

Index 811

Introduction

Why Read This Book?

If you are reading this introduction you are probably in a bookstore trying to select one of many books on dBASE IV. This book was written with a very specific purpose in mind and it uses a very specific approach to achieving that purpose.

The purpose of all of the books is to provide an educational text to aid users in learning both the techniques and the underlying concepts of dBASE.

To my way of thinking a book with this goal must use a special type of structure. It is not enough to create a reference book, i.e. one that provides information about features, functions, and technqiues similar to the way in which it is provided in the dBASE IV documentation.

In order to make the information a learning experience, all of that information must be placed into the context of a specific example that the reader can duplicate on his or her own system. This book is really an example which takes the reader through the various areas and stages in dBASE IV use. The information is sequenced in a learning progression from basic concepts to advanced.

All of the operations and commands are described within the context of a concrete example. The book contains all the commands and keystrokes needed to reproduce the same operations on your computer. The book contains over 400 screen images so that you can check the results on your computer with the book.

The book also covers the five major areas of dBASE IV:

1. Database Operations
2. Programming
3. Networks
4. SQL
5. System Configuration

This appraoch has been the heart of the 24 computer books that I have written. This is the fourth revision of a series of books that began with *Understanding and Using dBASE II* published in 1984.

The approach has proven to be popular and effective and I am proud of the fact that the edition has reached a wider audience.

If you have read any of the previous books in this series you will note that this book is quite a bit larger than *Understanding and Using dBASE III Plus* so that Networking and SQL could be covered in detail within a single book. The reader can thus learn the basic concepts that cover the entire range of dBASE IV activities.

Rob Krumm
Martinez, CA

Part I

Database Management in dBASE IV

1

The dBASE IV System

dBASE IV is the latest release in the dBASE software series that began with dBASE II. This book is, likewise, the latest in a series of books about dBASE, beginning with *Understanding and Using dBASE II*, published in 1983.

Although this is a new book, its purpose and methods remain the same. Its goal is to provide a structured series of lessons that teaches the reader how to use various parts of the dBASE IV system. Beyond the goal of mere knowledge about dBASE IV, this book instructs the reader in such a way as to gain insights into understanding how the elements in dBASE IV can be used to solve practical database problems.

The Philosophy Of dBASE IV

Since dBASE IV is the latest in a series of products, there are two questions you are likely to ask:

1. What do all the dBASE versions have in common?
2. How is this product different from previous versions?

The answer to the first question is interesting to users who have had experience with previous versions, as well as to those who are new to dBASE IV. The second question is primarily addressed to users who have had some experience with previous versions of dBASE.

The answers are useful because they establish the basic themes around which all the specific details included in this book are organized. To begin, let's look at what all the dBASE products have in common, i.e., their basic philosophy.

3

Dual Character

dBASE IV, like earlier versions, is a program with two related, but different characters. On the one hand, dBASE IV is a database management program; on the other hand, it is a database application-programming environment.

A database-management program is used to store information in a structured way so it can be retrieved using logical commands at some later time. The two important words in the previous definition are structured and logical. Almost every program running on a computer stores and retrieves information of some type. Even a computer game often stores information, such as the names of players and their highest scores. Word-processing programs store and retrieve large amounts of text.

Database management programs differ from other types of applications because they require you to organize information into a specific structure, in order to store and retrieve it. Suppose you enter the words *Mr. Walter LaFish* into a program that stores the information on the computer's disk. You could accomplish this task with any number of applications, i.e., word-processors, spreadsheets, data managers, etc. But if you want to retrieve the *last* name of the person—*LaFish*—the program needs some way of recognizing that *LaFish* is the last name, while *Walter* is not. Storing the letters *L a F i s h* is not sufficient to answer the question that has been posed. The information must be entered so that each item is classified, based on its significance.

In essence, database management requires that information be classified, as well as simply stored. The classifications enable the program to seek out information in a *logical* way. Thus the second characteristic of a database is the ability to retrieve information based on a logical request. By asking for just the last name, you are asking the program to draw a distinction between the different data items that have been stored.

In database management, it's necessary to store data in a structured way so each element can be manipulated according to its logical classification. This type of structure is in contrast to word-processing programs that treat all words, characters, and numbers, as indistinguishable parts of sentences, paragraphs, and pages. In Chapter 2 you will learn the details of how dBASE IV creates the structure files it uses to store data, and in Chapter 3 you will learn how this data is retrieved. What is important to remember is that database management deals with information in a structured, logical way, and that it manipulates the information based on logical classifications.

A Programming Language

The second part of dBASE IV's dual character is the programming language. In most computer applications the command structure allows you to enter commands in a *real-time* or *immediate execution* mode. When a command is issued, the application responds immediately by trying to carry out the task as quickly as possible. If the task creates a delay, you must wait until the task is finished before entering another command. The term *real-time* refers to entering commands processed in the same time frame they are entered.

However, instructions can also be processed in a *deferred execution* mode. In this mode, one or more commands are entered and stored, but not executed. At a later time, the command or commands are processed by telling the program to read and execute the entire group of stored commands. The deferred execution mode has two primary advantages. First, you can replay a single set of commands as many times as you like. If the command carries out a task that needs repetition periodically, you benefit each time the commands are replayed. Second, if the list contains more than one command, the entire sequence can execute without your intervention. The computer is on automatic pilot while the program instructions are executing. Deferred execution can take many forms. One of the most popular kinds is called *keystroke macros.* This type of macro command is created by recording a sequence of keystrokes and replaying those keystrokes at a later time. dBASE IV supports this type of macro.

However, true programming languages have another distinguishing element—they allow you to create structures inside the program. Structures are groups of commands that do more than function as a simple list of operations. A structure can cause a series of commands within a program to repeat many times, or to skip certain commands when the proper conditions do not exist. In the dBASE IV languages, there are special structures for creating menus, printing reports, and handling errors.

The main reason for working with a programming language is to create a customized version of the dBASE IV environment that closely addresses your particular circumstance. Keep in mind that a tool like dBASE IV must inherently be a *generalized* tool. The programming language allows you to create specialized routines within dBASE IV that reflect and respond to the types of tasks needed in your work, or the work of others in your organization. Programming is also a way to share your experience and knowledge about dBASE IV with other people who do not know how to control and use the program. By using the programming language, you can make dBASE IV appear in terms familiar to your colleagues so they can use its power without having an in-depth knowledge of the command structure.

Data Management or Programming?

Which part of dBASE IV should you learn—data management or programming? Both parts are conceptually linked to each other. Programming—the ability to defer execution of some commands—is integrated into many of the commands accessed through the dBASE IV menus. Ideally, you should know both parts of the program so you can take full advantage of its potential. In practice, many of you will find you can do all your tasks without creating programs. This book begins with data management in Part I, then Part II teaches you how to write programs. If you have tried to learn dBASE III or dBASE III Plus programming and have become discouraged, you will find the dBASE IV language is considerably improved and you can create very good looking applications with rather simple program structures. If you have used dBASE III or dBASE III Plus menu commands, you will find dBASE IV allows you to accomplish much more without programming than dBASE III or dBASE III Plus did.

Three Levels Of Operation

The dBASE IV environment is divided into three modes of operation.

Menu System Level

The menu system refers to the command structure in dBASE IV, which consists of a series of bar and pull-down menus. dBASE IV is automatically set to operate in this mode when you load the program. The master screen from which all menu system activities are carried out is called the Control Center.

The menu system is referred to as the Assist mode or the Assistant, because dBASE III used these names for its menu system. The advantage of the menu system is you can select actions from menus. The menus are organized to group together related commands and specification, making it easier to carry out a task that requires several related operations.

Command Level

The command level is different from the menu system in that operations are executed, not by picking commands from lists displayed on menus, but are entered as command sentences. The command level is similar to DOS in which a prompt is displayed and you must enter the full command next to the prompt. In dBASE IV the prompt is simply a period character called the *Dot Prompt.* The command level is often called the *Dot Prompt mode.*

The Dot Prompt mode is significant for two reasons. First, it provides access to more than 95% of dBASE IV's programming language commands. The command sentences entered at the Dot Prompt are exactly like the command sentences you would include in actual dBASE IV programs.

Second, the Dot Prompt allows you to enter quickly a series of commands that carry out specific tasks. As you become familiar with the command sentence structure you will find that you can carry out many tasks more quickly than you can by picking options for the menu system. The Dot Prompt mode is a bridge between the menu system and the programming language.

Program Level

The program level is different from the command mode in two small, but significant ways. Firstly, although the Dot Prompt mode provides access to 95% of the commands used in the program level, the remaining 5% create programming structures, and as such, represent a further dimension in the way you can control dBASE IV operations. Secondly, the program level requires you to store your instructions before they can be executed. This means you are working in a deferred execution mode.

This book provides details on all three modes, their relative strengths and weaknesses, and how, when taken together, they combine to offer you a vast amount of database management power. The key problem in dBASE IV, as in any full-powered application, is learning how to choose and control the large number of commands, options, and functions provided by the program. One of the primary goals of this book is to help the reader understand how all these individual pieces fit together to make a coherent data management system.

Network Operations

With the popularity of local area networks, it is important to discuss the features provided by dBASE IV for operations across a multi-user network. Many of the basic operations of dBASE IV remain the same in a network environment as they do in a stand-alone environment. However, dBASE IV does include special features allowing users at different work stations to carry out operations on the same data files.

Network features revolve around the need to avoid having two users simultaneously change the same part of the same database. This potential conflict always exists when more than one user has access to the same files. dBASE IV is equipped with automatic file and record protection mechanisms. You can also use the dBASE IV programming language to develop your own multi-user systems and create your own customized means of controlling access to files available on the network.

SQL

dBASE IV also offers an alternative method of database management called SQL. SQL stands for *Structured Query Language* and is modeled after IBM's popular mainframe and minicomputer language, DB2. SQL is provided as an alternative way of managing data to the standard structure used in dBASE III and dBASE IV.

The primary difference between dBASE IV and SQL is that dBASE IV is a process-oriented database, while SQL is a set-oriented database. For example, in dBASE IV most operations require a series of commands and options to extract the desired data. In SQL most data retrieval operations take place with a single command. The advantage of SQL is that a few different commands carry out all the different types of processing. In SQL you describe the type of data you need and SQL determines how to extract the data. SQL is designed to insulate or hide the processing from the user.

In dBASE IV the user must specify the processing commands for the program to carry out. In some ways this is more complicated because it requires you to enter a series of commands in the proper sequence. The advantage of dBASE IV's method is you can select how the data is retrieved. For example, there are usually many ways to achieve the same result. In dBASE IV you can select the approach that you feel is most efficient.

SQL is included within dBASE IV to enable users who are familiar with

SQL operations to use dBASE IV databases by entering commands in familiar SQL format. However, since all the information in SQL is eventually translated into some form of dBASE IV operation (the translation process is automatic), SQL will generally perform slower than standard dBASE IV. In Part IV of this book you will learn how to use and program SQL operations in the dBASE IV implementation of SQL.

Changes From dBASE III

If you have used dBASE III or dBASE III Plus it may interest you to learn about some changes and modifications made in dBASE IV before getting into the program's details.

dBASE IV can read dBASE III DBF and NDX files. It is also compatible with most of the dBASE III and dBASE III Plus commands, expanding their capabilities and adding many new commands to the dBASE system. The following information summarizes some of the most important changes in dBASE IV.

File Structure

While dBASE IV can read dBASE III and dBASE III Plus files, the dBASE IV file format is different from earlier versions. A database file can now contain up to 255 fields, in contrast to dBASE III Plus, which had a limit of 128 fields per database.

In addition, the dBASE IV file structure has an Index option. You can select fields for automatic indexing within the file structure. This option prompts dBASE IV to create an index file that is automatically updated each time the database is modified. You do not have to manually open the index file each time the database is placed into use.

The Control Center

The ASSIST mode menus found in dBASE III Plus have been replaced with a much more sophisticated system called the Control Center. The Control Center consists of bar and pop-up menus, along with lists of databases, query files, report forms, labels forms, and automatically generated applications.

The Browse and Edit modes have been modified to work together as part of the new Query by Example system. Both the Browse and Edit modes have pull-down menus that enhance your options.

Indexing

dBASE IV introduces multiple index files. A single multiple index file can contain up to 47 different index orders in a single file. Thus by opening one index file you can have access to several different index sequences. In dBASE III Plus you were required to create a separate index file for each index order. This created a complicated situation in which the user needed to remember which index files related to which database files. Using a single multiple index file that can contain many index orders simplifies the use of indexes.

Catalogs

The Control Center makes use of catalog files to keep lists of related databases, queries, labels, reports, and applications.

Memo Fields

The use of memo fields is enhanced by the addition of commands and functions that work directly with the information stored in memo fields. The word **memo** in the memo field display appears in uppercase letters when the field actually contains data. In addition, there are a set of functions that operate directly on memo information. For example, you can use the $ operator to test the contents of a memo field just as you would a character field. The COPY and APPEND commands have been modified to permit the importing and exporting of ASCII text files to or from memo fields making it possible to exchange memo field data with other applications.

Forms, Labels and Reports

The Screen Form, Label Printing, and Report Generation Design mode have been redesigned. All these modes include greater ability to integrate dBASE IV functions and formatting options, such as picture templates and functions, into the layout. For example, you can specify the use of commas in numeric data printed on reports.

If you program, you will find that all the screen, label, and report forms are generated as dBASE IV programs so they can be modified or integrated into dBASE IV programs.

Query By Example

The Query By Example mode provides a new way of designing data retrieval specifications. Queries are created by working with file skeletons, making it easier to create multiple database relations.

? Option

Commands used at the Dot Prompt that refer to files accept a ? argument. When used, the ? displays a pop-up menu from which you can select files by highlighting.

Alias Support

Many commands and functions accept alias designations so you can perform operations on the unselected databases without changing the current work area selection.

Relations

dBASE IV supports multiple relations between several databases. This means a specified database can be linked to more than one supporting database at the same time.

Printing

dBASE IV introduces a new printing system called the *streaming print* system. This system provides new ways to control printing, including the use of special printer drivers that contain special codes needed to implement printing effects on specific types of printers. The streaming print system maintains a special set of system variables specifically related to printing operations.

Macros

dBASE IV supports keystroke-type macros. Note that keystroke macros are different from macro substitutions carried out with the & in programs.

Programming

The dBASE IV programming language has been expanded to include commands that duplicate the Control Center environment. These commands make it possible to easily design bar and pull-down menus, windows, file lists, and other elements that appear as part of the Control Center, for use in your own customized programs.

    The new commands make it possible to develop a sophisticated series of customized menus in a fraction of the time previously used, with less program writing.

    dBASE IV uses a form of compiler to create object-code files from your

PRG source code files, speeding up the execution of dBASE IV programs. In addition, the compiler flags syntax errors as the programs are compiled.

The use of procedures is expanded so any program can contain one or more procedures. The program and procedures can be executed with a DO command.

Arrays

dBASE IV supports the use of one- or two-dimensional arrays. The arrays extend the ability of the programming language and can also be combined with standard dBASE commands, such as COPY and APPEND, to transfer information to and from memory variables in blocks, rather than one at a time.

Math Calculation

dBASE IV includes functions and commands carrying out financial and mathematical calculations, such as sine, cosine, tangent, logarithms, standard deviations, variance, future and present value, and monthly loan payment calculations.

Setup Program

You can make changes to the dBASE IV setup file, CONFIG.DB, by using a menu-driven program called DBSETUP.

Getting Familiar

The first part of this book is dedicated to the use of dBASE IV as a database management program. There are two ways to use the database management functions of dBASE IV: The Control Center menu system—the easiest way to use dBASE IV—and the Dot Prompt command mode, which is more difficult to learn than the menu system. However, once understood, the Dot Prompt command mode enables you to carry out specific tasks more quickly than the menu system.

This chapter familiarizes you with the organization of both the Control Center and Dot Prompt modes. You will also see how instructions and command sequences will be presented in the following chapters.

Begin by loading dBASE IV. The program can be loaded by accessing the directory where the program is stored and entering **dbase.** If you installed dBASE IV on the C: hard disk in a directory called **\DBASE,** you would enter a CD (Change Directory command) to access the correct directory.

```
cd\dbase ⏎
```

Then load and run the dBASE IV program by entering

    dbase ⏎

The installation process configures dBASE IV to automatically start in the Control Center menu system. When you load dBASE IV your screen should look like Figure 1-1.

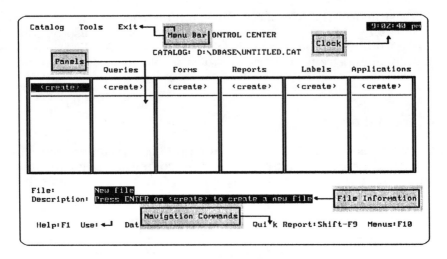

Figure 1-1. Control Center display.

Installing dBASE IV

dBASE IV is supplied with a program called DBSETUP. This program is automatically executed when you carry out the install procedure described in the dBASE IV documentation. The disk labeled 1* contains a batch file called INSTALL.BAT, which includes the command DBSETUP -d. This command runs the DBSETUP program in the Installation mode.Besides placing the dBASE IV files on the hard disk, the DBSETUP program creates a file called CONFIG.DB, which holds information about how your specific dBASE IV system should be set up. The file contains a command that reads COMMAND=ASSIST. This line causes dBASE IV to automatically enter the Control Center mode whenever you load the program.

The CONFIG.DB file can be altered in two ways. First, because it is a text file, you can change the commands within it by using a text editor or word-processor to alter the text of the file, which is the method used in dBASE III and III Plus. With dBASE IV you can use the DBSETUP program to make changes to the CONFIG.DB file. The advantage of the DBSETUP program is in its menu driven options, which allow you to change the configuration of dBASE IV without knowing the command syntax required when you manually edit the CONFIG.DB file.

The Control Center display is divided into several different parts. At the top of the screen is the Menu Bar that lists command options. The clock is located in the upper-right corner of the screen.

In the center of the screen are a series of columns with the words Data, Queries, Forms, Reports, Labels and Applications, at the top of each column. These columns (referred to as panels) are used to list the files you create while working with dBASE IV. If you are just starting with the program, the panels appear empty as they do in Figure 1-1. If you have been working with dBASE IV, the panels may contain the names of one or more files you have already created.

The file information display appears below the panels. At the very bottom of the screen are the navigation commands, telling you how to activate commands and move around the screen display.

The highlight is positioned on the <create> symbol in the Data panel.

Moving the Highlight

The most basic operation you can perform in the Control Center is to change the position of the highlight. There are several ways to do so.

Arrow Keys

The left, right, up and down arrow keys can be used to move the highlight one item in the direction of the arrow. Note that based on the number and arrangement of items, you can move only in a direction where there is actually an item to highlight. For example, if there are no files listed in a panel, you canno use up or down arrow.

[Tab], [Shift-Tab]

The [Tab] and [Shift-Tab] keys move the highlight one item to the left or right, respectively.

[F3], [F4]

These keys operate in a similar manner to [Tab] and [Shift-Tab]. In a multi-row display, these keys move up to the previous line, or down to the next line if they reach the end of the current row.

Move the highlight to the next panel to the right by entering

```
[right arrow]
```

The highlight is now in the Queries panel. Enter

```
[Tab]
```

The [Tab] key advances the highlight to the Forms panel. Move back to the Data panel by entering

```
[F3] (2 times)
```

Selection

The purpose of highlighting an item is to indicate which item you want to use. When an item is highlighted, you can select that item by pressing the ↵ key. The ↵ key is sometimes labeled Enter or Return, depending on the style keyboard you are using. (It is also possible that your keyboard has two Enter or Return keys, one of which is located on the numeric keypad. You can use either of these keys when the ↵ key is indicated.)

Currently, the <create> symbol in the Data column is highlighted. If you press ↵ it will be selected. In effect, you will be telling the program you want to create a data file. Enter

```
        ↵
```

When you select the option, the program changes the entire screen display. The menu bar now shows five new options, and the panels have been removed and replaced with a different display. At the bottom of the screen a line is displayed in enhanced video that provides information about the current activity. This is called the Status line.

In dBASE IV the term enhanced video refers to information displayed in a video different from regular text. On a monochrome monitor, enhanced video uses black letters on an amber, green, or white background. On a color monitor, the enhanced video is usually yellow letters on a red background. The user can select different color combinations if he desires.

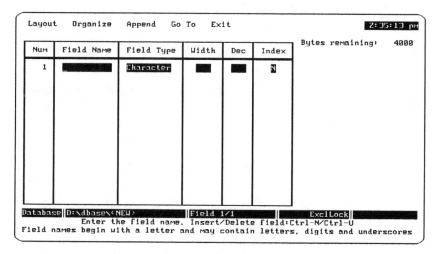

Figure 1-2. Database Design mode activated.

When you selected <create>, dBASE IV changed from the Control Center mode to the Design Database mode. The term mode is used to describe a change in the way the program behaves. For example, the Design mode displays a different set of menus than the Control Center mode does. The commands and keystrokes used in the Control Center mode may have a different effect in the Design mode. (In Chapter 2 you will learn how to use the Design Database mode.)

Assume you have accidentally entered a mode, such as the Design Database mode, and wish to return to the Control Center display. You can exit the mode by using the [Esc] key. Enter

        [Esc]

The program displays a box covering part of the screen. Such boxes are called windows and are used to display messages and warnings. Here, the window contains the message "Are you sure you want to abandon operation?". Below the message are two words, Yes and No. The word No is highlighted.

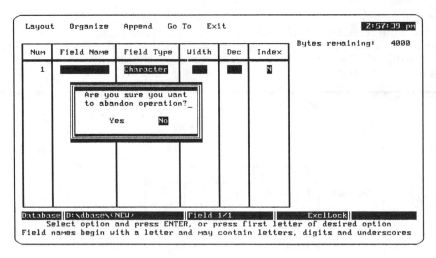

Figure 1-3. Abandon operation window.

The words represent your options. You can select the option you want to execute, in one of two ways.

1. You can use the left arrow or right arrow keys to move the highlight to the option you desire. Then press ⌐.
2. The options always begin with a unique first letter. You can directly select an option by entering the first letter of the option you desire. Here, you could enter y for Yes, or n for no. Enter

            y

The program exits the Design Database mode and returns to the Control Center display. When you abandon a mode, all the operations entered into that mode are lost. Later, you will learn how to save items created in the various work modes.

The Menu Bar

At the very top of the screen is the menu bar, as seen in Figure 1-4. The menu bar is provided to allow you access to dBASE IV commands. dBASE IV changes the menu bar to reflect the operational mode you are in. The first menu bar that appears when you load dBASE IV consists of three items.

Catalog

A catalog is a collection of related files. Catalogs enable you to group together all the files needed for a specific project or task. Conversely, you can use catalogs to separate files so you do not get confused about what files can be used with other files. You can create as many catalogs as you need.

IIIBradyLine

Insights into tomorrow's technology from the authors and editors of Brady Books.

You rely on Brady's bestselling computer books for up-to-date information about high technology. Now turn to BradyLine for the details behind the titles.

Find out what new trends in technology spark Brady's authors and editors. Read about what they're working on, and predicting, for the future. Get to know the authors through interviews and profiles, and get to know each other through your questions and comments.

BradyLine keeps you ahead of the trends with the stories behind the latest computer developments. Informative previews of forthcoming books and excerpts from new titles keep you apprised of what's going on in the fields that interest you most.

- Peter Norton on operating systems
- Jim Seymour on business productivity
- Jerry Daniels, Mary Jane Mara, Robert Eckhardt, and Cynthia Harriman on Macintosh development, productivity, and connectivity

Get the Spark. Get BradyLine.

Published quarterly, beginning with the Summer 1988 issue. Free exclusively to our customers. Just fill out and mail this card to begin your subscription.

Name _____

Address _____

City _____ State _____ Zip _____

Name of Book Purchased _____

Date of Purchase _____

Where was this book purchased?   *(circle one)*

    Retail Store   Computer Store   Mail Order

F R E E

Mail this card for your free subscription to BradyLine

Tools

Use the Tools menu to create keystroke macros, import or export data to other applications, run DOS commands, create password protection for information, or change the current configuration. (Note that changes made with the Tools menu affect only the current session. The next time the program is loaded, the settings will return to the default settings. To change the default settings you must run the DBSETUP program.)

Exit

Exit is used to exit from the Control Center or from dBASE IV.

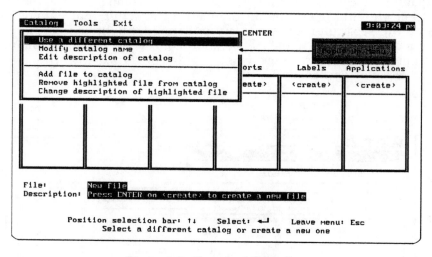

Figure 1-4. Menu bar(shaded).

Each of the items on the menu bar is related to a pop-up menu. The pop-up menus list specific operations you can carry out. In order to display the pop-up menus, you must activate the menu bar. The menu bar can be activated in two ways.

[F10]

The [F10] key is the menu key. When pressed, it causes the program to display one of the pop-up menus associated with the menu bar items. By default the pop-up menu displayed is the one corresponding to the leftmost item on the menu. Once you have activated the menu bar, the left arrow and right arrow keys move you to the other menu items and display the pop-up menus associated with each one.

[Alt-character]

The items on the menu bar are constructed in such a manner that no two items begin with the same first character. You can select a menu item by entering a keystroke combining the first letter of the menu item with the [Alt] key. For example, the Control Center menu consists of the items Catalog, Tools, and Exit. You can activate the menu items by entering [Alt-c] for Catalog, [Alt-t] for Tools, or [Alt-e] for Exit.

Activate the menu bar by using the menus key, [F10].

[F10]

The program displays the catalog pop-up menu, listing six different operations that can be carried out. The menu is divided by a line that is used to separate the commands into groups of related commands.The highlight is placed on the first operation on the menu, Use a different catalog. If you press ↵ the program begins to carry out the highlighted operation, here, using a different catalog of files.Don't be concerned if the meaning of the operation is unclear. For now, you are only concerned with the use of the menu system in general.

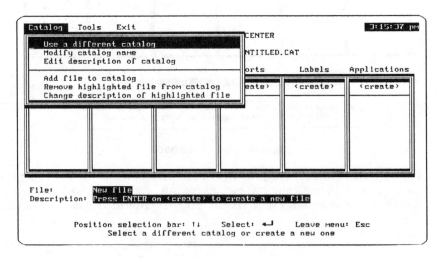

Figure 1-5. Catalog menu displayed.

If you look carefully at the five operations listed below the highlighted operation, you will see there are actually two different types of video used. The bottom two options are displayed in normal video, while the others are in bold video. This is no accident. While the catalog menu contains six operations, it is not always possible or logical to carry out all of them. The operations listed in bold video are the ones you can carry out at this time. The ones appearing in regular video cannot be executed now. This is because each dBASE IV operation requires specific conditions in order to operate. For example, you may have options for creating, editing, or removing a file. But it would not be possible to remove a file if none exists. If there are no files of the specified type, the program will display the Remove operation in normal video because the proper conditions for carrying it out do not exist.

At the very bottom of the screen is a message line that displays an explanation of the function of the highlighted operation. The message changes as you move to different options. Place the highlight on the next operation in this menu.

      [down arrow]

The message at the bottom of the screen changes to Change, the name of this catalog, indicating the purpose of the operation. Continue moving the highlight down the menu.

      [down arrow](3 times)

When the highlight reaches the last available command, i.e., the commands displayed in bold video, the highlight recycles to the top of the menu. The highlight skips any commands in normal video because they cannot be executed at this time.

When a pop-up menu is displayed, the left arrow and right arrow keys display the pop-up menu for the menu item to the left or right of the current pop-up. Enter

      [right arrow]

The Tools menu is displayed, Figure 1-6. The display on the Tools menu reveals another item on some pop-up menus, a submenu. A submenu is indicated by the triangle character in front of the menu operation. Items indicated in this manner display another pop-up menu if selected. For example, the currently highlighted operation is Macros. Since Macros is a submenu operation, selecting this option displays another pop-up menu.

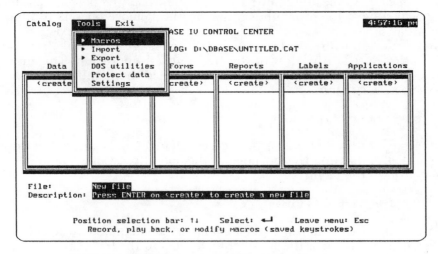

Figure 1-6. Pop-up menu with submenu operations.

Display the submenu by entering

⏎

The submenu under Macros is displayed. Observe the submenu itself displays selections that are submenus of the submenu. Menu systems that branch one submenu off another submenu, are tree-structured menu systems.

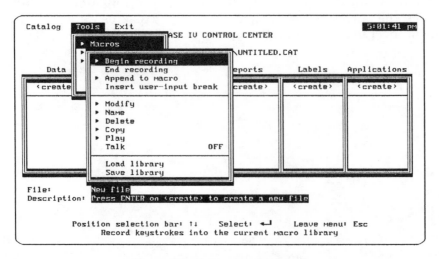

Figure 1-7. Submenu displayed.

When you are positioned in a submenu, even one several levels deep, the left arrow and right arrow keys can be used to return to the previous submenu level. In most cases, either left arrow or right arrow performs the same function. Enter

    [left arrow]

The sub-submenu is removed from the display, placing the highlight in the previous submenu.

   You can exit the current menu or submenu at any time by using the [Esc] key. Enter

    [Esc]

The menus are removed from the screen and the highlight returns to its normal position within the display.

   In addition to the [F10] key, menus can be activated by using the [Alt] key in combination with the first letter of the menu item.

The [Alt] or [Ctrl] keys are always used in combination with another letter key. When you combine the [Alt] or [Ctrl] keys with a letter key, [Alt] or [Ctrl] is always pressed and held down before you press the letter key you want to combine with it. You should not attempt to press both keys simultaneously because this produces inconsistent results. Keep in mind once [Alt] or [Ctrl] is held down, you can take as long as you like to select the letter key. There is no need to feel hurried in making the selection of a letter key, as long as you hold down [Alt] or [Ctrl] while you are deciding. Once you have pressed the letter key, you can release both keys. The [Shift] key is used just as the [Alt] or [Ctrl] keys are. In effect, this creates four possible ways to use every key on the keyboard: by itself, combined with [Shift], [Alt], or [Ctrl].

The advantage of this method is you can access the specific menu you want to work with, instead of having to browse through the other menus to get to the one you want. The current menu bar has three items beginning with the letters C, T, and E. To activate the Exit menu, enter

    [Alt-e]

The Exit menu is displayed. Exit the Exit menu by using [Esc].

    [Esc]

Activate the Tools menu. Try this on your own. The correct command is at the end of the chapter under Ex-1.

   dBASE IV also provides key shortcuts for the operations listed on a menu. Like the items on the menu bar, no two items on a pop-up menu begin with the same first letter. You can select an operation or submenu by entering the first letter of the menu item. It is not necessary to combine the letter with [Alt] because you have already activated the menus with the [Alt-e] command.

Activate the Export submenu by entering

e

The program displays the Export submenu.

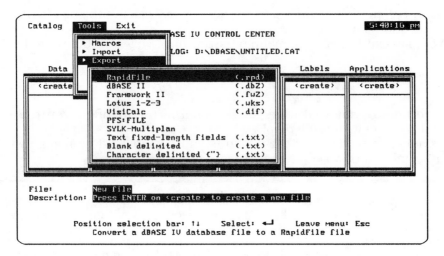

Figure 1-8. Sub-menu activated by first character.

Exit the menus by entering

[Esc] (2 times)

Using the first letters to select a menu option creates a system in which each command on a menu is activated by a unique sequence of characters. For example, the Export command is activated by the keystroke sequence [Alt-t]e. In a book such as this, the simplest and least confusing way to write a command you should enter is in the keystroke shortcut form. However, you always have the option of using the arrow keys to highlight the options if you prefer.

There is another reason instructions, such as those written in this book, are best written in the keystroke shortcut form. When the [F10] command is used to activate the menus, dBASE IV returns to the last menu used. Enter

[F10]

Instead of highlighting the Use a Different Catalog command, the first command on the first menu, dBASE IV highlights the Export command on the Tools menu because it was the last menu and operation selected. When you use [F10] to activate a menu, the position of the highlight is dependent upon the last action you took while the menus were active. This is a handy feature, because it allows you to repeat the previous command by pressing [F10]. However, when writing instructions, confusion can occur if your last operation was different from the sequence of operations laid out in this book. For this reason all menu operations are specified in terms of the keyboard shortcuts.

Exit the menu by entering

        [Esc]

The Help System

The instructions in this book contain every keystroke and command needed to carry out the operations discussed here. However, if when working on your own, you find the need for information about specific operations or commands, dBASE IV contains a complete, on-line, context-sensitive help facility. The Help system can be activated at any time by pressing [F1]. The program attempts to display a help topic corresponding to the current mode or operation. This is called context sensitivity, because the help screen displayed is related to the current activity.

For example, you are currently in the Control Center display. Activate help by entering

        [F1]

The Help system displays a window containing information about dBASE IV operations. Here, because the highlight was positioned on the <create> symbol in the Data column, the program displays information under the topic heading Create Database Files.

When a topic contains more information than you can fit into a single window, you will see the note <MORE F4> in the lower-right corner of the window. Pressing [F4] will display the next window of information stored for the current topic. Enter

        [F4]

Pressing [F3] displays the previous window. Enter

        [F3]

If there are no more screens for the current topic, [F3] displays the last screen in a previous topic. [F4] displays the first screen in the next topic. Using these keys, you can browse through all the screens in the Help system.

At the bottom of the window, there are four special commands for use in the Help system.

Contents

This option displays an alphabetical list of topics in the Help window. You can select a topic from the list, and display its contents in the Help window.

Related Topic

This option provides a list of help topics related to the currently displayed topic. This list is shorter than the Full-Contents list because only those items logically related to the current topic are displayed.

Backup

This option helps you go back to a previously displayed help screen.

Print

This option command sends a copy of the current help topic to the printer, providing you with a hard copy of the information stored in the help file. Keep in mind this command prints the entire Help topic, not just the portion appearing within the window.

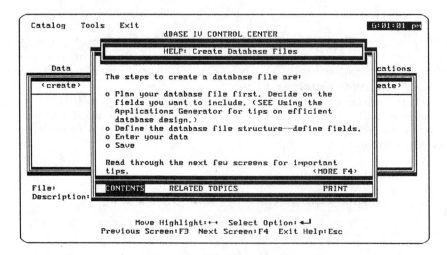

Figure 1-9. Help system window.

You can select one of the four Help operations by moving the highlight with the left arrow or right arrow keys. Pressing the [space] key performs the same function as the right arrow key. You can also type c, r, b, or p, to activate the respective commands. Display the related topics list by entering

r

The list of related topics is displayed in a window that overlaps the Help topic.

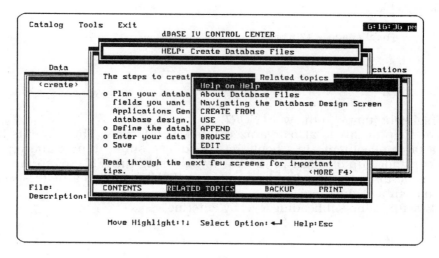

Figure 1-10. Related topics list.

Select the USE command from the list.

        [down arrow](4 times) ⏎

The help screen for the USE command is displayed. Display the Full-Contents list by entering

        c

The Full-Contents list is much longer than the related topics list. You can select a topic by scrolling through the list using the up arrow and down arrow keys. If you know the name of the topic you want displayed, dBASE IV performs a speed search of the list. The search is automatically activated when you type a letter. Suppose you want to display the help information for APPEND. Enter

        a

The program jumps the cursor to the first topic on the list that begins with the letter *A*, in this case, the ACCEPT command. Notice the letter A at the beginning of the word appears in normal video, while the rest of the topic is highlighted. The normal video indicates the characters used in the speed search. Enter the second letter in the word for which you are looking.

        p

The highlight jumps to the first topic on the list that matches the search characters, shown in normal video, *AP*. You can remove characters from the speed search if you make a mistake. Imagine that you now decide to look for information on sorting. Erase the current search characters using the [backspace] key.

        [backspace]   (2 times)

Enter

            so

The highlight jumps to the word *SORT*.

The Help facility is also organized into several levels. The contents list, like a table of contents in a book, has headings, subheadings, and topics. You can move up or down in the list levels using the [F3] key to move to more general topics (i.e., headings, etc.) or [F4] to move to a more specific level (i.e. subheadings, etc.).

Move up to the subheading level by entering

        [F3]

The window now shows the subheadings under the heading Dot Prompt Commands and Functions. Move up another level.

        [F3]

You have now reached the top level of the Help system. All the Help topics are divided among the five major topics:

1. Dot Prompt Commands and Functions
2. Control Center
3. SQL Main Topics
4. Help on Help
5. Reference

To exit the Help system, enter

        [Esc]

You return to dBASE IV at the point where you accessed the Help system. The Help system can provide useful information in a timely fashion. Remember that [F1] can be used at any time while you are working with dBASE IV.

Catalogs

Centered above the panels of the Control Center is the name of the current catalog. Catalogs are used by dBASE IV to maintain lists of files. The use of catalogs is optional in the sense that it does not directly affect the commands, procedures, and techniques discussed in this book. Catalogs are useful when you want to maintain separate lists of files created for different purposes.

The DOS operating system treats all files stored in the same directory as equals. The dBASE IV catalog system allows you to separate files into groups, even though they reside in the same DOS directory. The catalog system applies only to dBASE IV, and it does not affect the way DOS or other applications work with files stored in the DBASE directory.

When you first start dBASE IV, the catalog is automatically assigned the name UNTITLED.CAT. If you have yet to work with dBASE IV, your UNTITLED catalog will look like the one in the figure, i.e., blank with no files listed under the panels. If this is the case with your computer, begin working with the UNTITLED catalog.

However, if you have started to work with dBASE IV, the panels in the catalog will probably have files listed under the various panel headings. If this is so in your case, you may want to avoid confusing the data created while working through these chapters, with the files already existing on your computer. You can do so by creating a new catalog specifically designed to hold the files you create while working though this book.

Keep in mind that there is no harm in adding the files you create for this book, to files already created. Remember, the figures in this book will show only those files that would occur if you began with a blank catalog. Otherwise, all other operations remain the same.

If you want to create a separate catalog for this book, the next section guides you through the creation of a new catalog called LEARN. If you want to continue working with UNTITLED, you can skip this section.

Creating a New Catalog

To create a new catalog, begin with the Use a Different Catalog command found on the Catalog menu. Enter

    [Alt-c]u

When you select this command, dBASE IV displays a list of all the current catalogs in a window in the upper-right corner of the screen. There should be at least one name on the list, UNTITLED.CAT. dBASE IV assigns a CAT file extension to all catalog files.

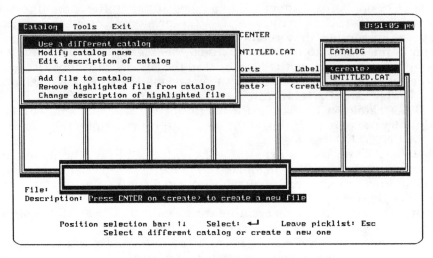

Figure 1-11. Catalog files listed.

At the top of the list is the <create> symbol, which is selected when you create a new catalog. Since it appears at the top of the list, it is automatically highlighted. Select <create> by entering

⏎

dBASE IV displays another window asking you to enter the name of the catalog. Do not be confused by the size of the window. Catalog names are restricted to the standard DOS filename size of eight characters, without any embedded spaces. The name of the new catalog is LEARN. Enter

learn ⏎

The new catalog is created. The Control Center panels appear empty and the name of the new catalog, LEARN.CAT, appears above the panels.

Keep in mind that dBASE IV remembers which catalog was the last one used in the previous session. Thus if you quit dBASE IV while working with the LEARN catalog, the program automatically reloads that catalog the next time you load dBASE IV.

Keeping track of catalogs

You may wonder how it is that dBASE IV remembers the name of the catalog last used in the previous session. All catalogs are actually database files containing file information. The catalog files have a CAT extension instead of a DBF extension, but are DBF files. The catalog files have seven fields, 1. Path, 2. File_name, 3. Alias, 4. Type, 5. Title, 6. Code and 7. Tag. The program records information about the files contained in the catalog in this database, which is then read when you activate the catalog. If you wish, you can open the catalog file with a command, such as USE LEARN.CAT. You can then treat this file like any other database.

Besides the individual catalog files, dBASE IV also maintains a master catalog file called CATALOG.CAT, that functions as a "catalog of catalogs." Whenever you quit dBASE IV, the list of catalogs stored in this file is rewritten, and the current catalog name becomes the last name in the file. When the program is re-loaded, it reads the catalog list and automatically activates the last catalog.

It is interesting to note that in dBASE IV, all the commands, menus, and functions needed to create the dBASE IV catalog system are available in the programming language. This means you can create a program that duplicates the catalog function. In Part II, the techniques needed to create programs having the look and feel of the Control Center are discussed in detail.

Switching Catalogs

If you are using the LEARN catalog for data related to this book, you should know how to activate other catalogs, so you can switch back and forth as necessary. The LEARN catalog is currently active. To reactivate the UNTITLED catalog, enter

    [Alt-c]u

Move to the name UNTITLED.CAT by using the down arrow to advance the highlight one name at a time, or use the speed search facility by entering the characters in the catalog name. Enter

    u ↵

The UNTITLED catalog is activated again, and the files listed as part of that catalog, if any, appear in the panels.

Reverse the process and activate the LEARN catalog. Try this on your own. The correct command is at the end of the chapter under Ex-2.

Quitting the Program

The last step in getting familiar with the Control Center is learning how to exit dBASE IV. You can exit the program from the Control Center display by using the Exit menu. Enter

[Alt-e]

The Exit menu has two options.

Exit to Dot Prompt

This option exits the Control Center and activates the dBASE IV Dot Prompt mode. Exiting to the Dot Prompt mode does not quit dBASE IV. You can return to the Control Center from the Dot Prompt mode by entering the command ASSIST, or by pressing the [F2] key.

Quit to DOS

This option terminates the dBASE IV program and returns to the operating system. Once you have exited dBASE IV you must re-load the program to use it again.

___

You can speed up the loading of dBASE IV by suppressing the graphic display of the Ashton-Tate logo, when the program is loaded. This is done by adding the text switch, /t, to the loading command, dbase. Example: dbase/t ↵

___

To exit, select the Quit to DOS command by entering

q

dBASE IV terminates and DOS is now active.

Summary

This chapter served as an introduction to the fundamental concepts employed in dBASE IV, as well as an introduction to the organization of the Control Center.

- **The Control Center.** The dBASE IV installation program configures dBASE IV to automatically start in the Control Center mode. The Control Center consists of a number of special operational modes, each of which displays lists of information and menus listing operations to be performed on data. The Control Center coordinates all the operations to be carried out through the dBASE IV menu system. In the Control Center, you can select to use or create a data file, query, form, report, label, or application.

- **Panels.** The Control Center display shows panels listing files stored in the current catalog, classified by category.

- **Menus.** Each of the menu system's modes displays a menu bar at the top of the screen. Each item on the bar represents a pop-up menu, listing operations related to that topic. The menu bar can be activated by pressing [F10]. You can activate a specific menu bar item by entering the first letter of the item, combined with the [Alt] key, e.g., Exit = [Alt-e]. You can select operations from the pop-up menus by highlighting the name of the operation and pressing ↵, or by typing the first letter of the operation name (without the [Alt]). Pressing [Esc] exits the menu and returns you to the current display.

- **Modes.** The dBASE IV menu system operates in a series of modes. Each mode activates a specific set of information and commands designed to work together to accomplish certain tasks. Modes make work easier because they limit the commands or information to only those needed for particular tasks. Each mode can be exited by using the Exit command on the menu bar.

- **The Dot Prompt.** In addition to the dBASE IV menu system, the program can be operated in a command-driven mode, in which instructions are entered as command sentences, rather than selected from menus. The Dot Prompt provides users with direct access to 95% of the commands in dBASE IV's programming language. Because the Dot Prompt is not part of a specific operation mode, you can enter commands in any sequence you desire. Of course, you must make sure your sequence is logical, or dBASE IV will not be able to carry out the operations.

- **Programming.** dBASE IV allows you to create program files. These files contain sequences of commands that can be executed at any time. Programs allow you to defer and repeat the execution of the commands, saving you time and effort in repeating commonly-used procedures. Programs have the added advantage of containing program structures that can build flexibility into the command sequences.

- **Catalogs.** A catalog is a list of files. dBASE IV allows you to create catalogs to organize files into related groups.

Exercises

Ex-1, activate Tool menu

```
[Alt-t]
```

Ex-2

```
Alt-c]u
1 ↵
```

2

Creating a Database File

The goal of this chapter is to teach you how to create a database in dBASE IV, using the Control Center menus. The first database you will create, CKBOOK (check book database), is the basis of all the operations discussed in the ensuing chapters, beginning with the simplest operations, up to and including the sections on dBASE IV programming and dBASE IV SQL programming.

By using a single example, all the techniques and procedures explained will be unified, and thereby be easier to understand.

The assumption is made that you have loaded dBASE IV and are looking at the main Control Center display, as discussed in Chapter 1.

If you are working on a network version of dBASE IV, there are some slight differences between the way dBASE IV operates and appears on your screen, and the information included in this book. When making modifications to a file in a network environment, you will need to have *exclusive* access to the database. In addition when you attempt to edit a record, a beep will sound and a message will ask you to press the spacebar. This initiates a record lock so that other users cannot edit the record while you are working with it. A network screen will show **RecLock** on the status line, while a non-network program will show a blank. These small differences, once understood, should not interfere with the instructions included in these chapters. For the most part, these functions will take place in the background automatically, while you are working in the Control Center. If you need more information about network operations, see Part III of this book on networking dBASE IV.

Creating a Structure

The goal of any computer database program is to help you organize information, in order to take advantage of the power the computer offers. The first step in this process requires entry of data into the database system. Data are the raw material the database program uses in its processing operations.

In order for the computer to process information, it must be able to understand what the structure of the information is like. Such structured information used in a database is in contrast to randomly-entered information used in a word-processing program, where any sequence of characters typed is accepted by the program. The program is not designed to interpret the information, therefore it makes no difference whether you enter *See Jane run* or *See Dick run*. Because the word-processor simply records the sequence of characters entered, there is no requirement to enter the information in any specific structure.

In a database program on the other hand, each item of information has a specific meaning. A database is used to record information about objects, such as products in inventory, or clients, such as patients in a hospital, or of events, such as financial transactions or a student's grades. When you want to record such information, you describe the event or object in terms of qualities. A database consists of information about a series of objects or events, having the same general qualities.

For example, all the checks you write have a check number, a date, an amount, and a payee. In addition, the check is written for a certain purpose, either to pay a bill or to purchase an item. From an income-tax point of view, the amount might be deductible or taxable, and so on. When you fill out the register in your checkbook, you are recording the specific details about each check. It is important to note that in doing so, you do not place the information randomly on the page, but in a specific place. For example, all the check numbers appear on a certain line, or in a certain column. The same is true for the check amounts. When you look at the register, it is clear whether a number represents a check number, or a check amount, based on the line or column into which it has been entered. The information is structured information because it is not just a sequence of characters, but forms groups of related pieces of information, each of which falls into a unique classification.

In order to enter information of any sort into a database program you must begin by explaining to the program how the information will be structured. Because dBASE IV has no preconceived notions about the type of information you enter, before entering a single piece of information you must go through the process of describing the qualities you want to enter information under. dBASE IV uses the term *field* to describe each such quality.

The term *field* may seem an odd word to describe a quality in a database structure. The word derives from the early days of computers when data was entered onto paper-punch cards. *Field* referred to the space on each card that could be used for data entry. Beginning with dBASE II, the term became part of the dBASE lexicon. Note that in dBASE IV SQL, the term for a database quality is column, not field. If you use dBASE IV and dBASE IV SQL, remember both terms refer to the same concept.

To begin the database creation process you must select <create> from the Data column on the Control Center. When dBASE IV is first loaded, the highlight is automatically positioned to create a database, and you can simply enter

⏎

dBASE IV changes the screen display from the Control Center to the database structure display.

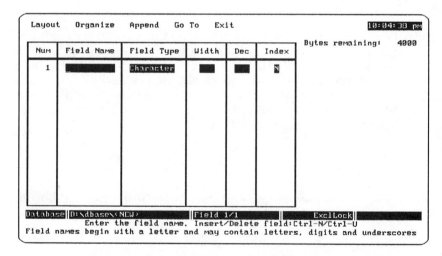

Figure 2-1. Database Structure Display.

Because you are about to create a new database, the current display is empty. The display is divided into six columns, each column representing the information you must enter to create a field.

Num

This is the field number. It is automatically generated by dBASE IV as you enter the fields. You can have up to 255 different fields in each database you create.

Field Name

The field name can be between 1 and 10 characters. You can use any letter or numbers in a field name, as long as the first character is a letter. It is important to note you cannot use a space as part of a field name. To present the appearance of a multi-word name, you are allowed to insert an underscore. Example: DATE_BIRTH

Field Type

The field type determines the type of information stored in the field. The two most common types of data are characters (text information) and numeric (numeric values). In addition, dBASE IV has field types used for specialized types of data: date, floating point, memo, and logical fields. You will learn more about field types later in this chapter.

Width

In dBASE IV it is necessary to enter the maximum width for each field you create. The limits of the field width depend upon the type of field you are creating. A character field can have a length of 1 to 254 characters. A numeric field can have a width of 1 to 20 characters. Other field types have predefined lengths. For example, date fields are *always* eight characters, logical fields use one character, and Memo fields use ten characters. More information about memos appears later in this chapter.

Dec

This specifies the number of decimal places for numeric or floating point fields. It is not used by other field types.

Index

Index is used to determine if dBASE IV should create an index based on the field's contents. Indexes allow you to display or print the database in a logically sequenced order. For example, if you want to list the checks in alphabetical order by payee, you must create an index for the payee field before you can display or print the list. If you select index in the database structure, the index is automatically generated. If you do not choose Y for index, dBASE IV still allows you to manually create indexes at some later point. It is not necessary to decide about indexes when you create a database if you are unsure exactly how the data will be used. You can always add indexes at some later point. Indexes are discussed in detail in Chapter 4.

If you place a Y in the index column of any field, dBASE IV creates an index file called the *production* index. This index is different from other index files in that it is automatically assigned the same name as the database file. Also, it is automatically opened whenever the database is opened. The production index is a dBASE IV innovation, designed to solve a problem common in previous versions, in which the user was required to remember the name of the index file and remember to specifically open that index file each time the database was placed in use.

How Databases are Structured

The database structure display tells you something about how dBASE IV works. There are two basic ways databases can be organized: by fixed length structure or delimited structure.

In a *fixed length* structure, each field is allocated a specific amount of space in the file structure. When you enter data, any allocated space not filled with characters is stored as blank space. This ensures all fields, regardless of the data entered, take up the same number of characters in the database file. For example, in a fixed length file you might allocate 10 characters for first name, and 20 for last name. The file would store data like this:

John   Smith
Walter LaFish

The other commonly-used structure is a *delimited* file. A *delimiter* is a character used to mark the end of each field. Typically, a comma serves as the delimiter, although any character will perform the same function. A delimited file would store data in this manner:

John,Smith
Walter,LaFish

The advantage of a delimited file structure is you can store data fields varying in length because it does not require fixing the number of characters in each field, in advance. This also means there is no need to store the blanks that pad the space between fields.

At first glance, the delimited file structure seems a better choice than the fixed length structure. However, dBASE IV uses a fixed length approach because it allows faster access to the data. When you look for data in a delimited file structure, you have no way of knowing in advance how many characters are in each field. To determine this, the computer must look at each character in the record and test to see if the character is part of the text or the field delimiter character. On the other hand, in a fixed length structure, you know in advance if the first field has a length of 10 characters, the next field begins as character 11. The program can simply move to the 11th character without having to check each character along the way.

In dBASE IV (and previous versions of dBASE II and dBASE III) the fixed length approach is used because it offers better overall performance than delimited database structures.

dBASE IV can, however, convert fixed length files to delimited files, or delimited files to fixed length files. This allows dBASE IV to use data from, or send data to, other applications. For details about these procedures see Importing and Exporting data, Chapter 10.

Entering a Field

The next step is to enter the information about the fields you need for the database. The database you are currently creating will keep a chronicle of checks. Each field in the database will record some information that contributes to a full description of the thing or event you are chronicling.

To begin, each check you write has a date. Since this is usually the first item you enter on a check, it seems logical for it to be the first field, although the order of the fields is up to you. To create the field you must enter a name for the field. Remember, the name can be from 1 - 10 characters long, and the first character should always be a letter from A - Z. The other nine characters can be A - Z or 0 - 9. You *cannot* use a space as part of a field name. If you wish to use a field name more than one word in length, an underscore character is typically used. Example: ACCOUNT NO would be written as ACCOUNT_NO.

It is also recommended that you avoid using single letters as field names. Letters A - J are used by dBASE IV to designate database work areas. Field names A - J can cause dBASE IV to become confused about the meaning of some commands that use both field and work area names.

The first field in this database is the DATE field. Enter

```
date ⏎
```

Notice the field name appears in upper-case letters regardless of how you enter the characters. Next, the cursor advances to the Field Type column. The Field Type determines the type of information you are going to place into this field. Field types are necessary because the information entered is interpreted differently, depending upon the Field Type you select.

dBASE IV has 6 types of fields:

Character

Character information is simply text you want to store in the database. Information such as names, and addresses, etc., are character information because they are composed of text. Also notice some sequences of characters thought of as numbers in common usage, are more appropriately classified as character information. For example, phone numbers, social security numbers, and zip codes, etc., are composed of number characters but have no arithmetic meaning or value. In general, these number sequences should be entered into character fields, not number fields. For example, the social security number 000851212 used in a numeric field would have a numeric value of 851,212. The 000 would be removed since they have no arithmetic significance. Character fields can be 1 to 254 characters in width.

Numeric

This field is used for numeric values having arithmetic meaning. dBASE IV interprets numbers entered into a numeric field in such a way that calculations can be performed upon these values. Monetary values are typically stored in numeric fields. Numeric fields can be up to 20 characters in length. When you select a numeric field, you have the option of specifying the number of decimal places.

Float

This is another type of numeric field, which interprets numeric values in a slightly different manner than in a *Numeric* field. This allows it to make faster calculations when performing complex combinations of multiplication and division, such as in scientific or engineering applications. For more information, see the Number Type sidebar. *Float* fields can be of up to 20 characters. When you select a float field, you have the option of specifying the number of decimal places.

Date

Date fields are used to store chronological values. It is possible to store dates in character fields by simply writing the date in any format you wish: Sept 13, 1951, 09/13/51 or 13 Sep 51. However, dBASE IV would not be able to relate all these different formats to actual chronological dates. The date field *requires* that you enter all dates in the form mm/dd/yy, e.g., 09/13/51. dBASE IV then stores the date in a special numeric sequence, e.g., 19510913. The advantage of this format is that dBASE IV can perform special operations, based on the chronological value of the date. These operations include calculating the number of days between two dates, or calculating the day of the week for a specified date. Date fields are automatically set at eight characters.

Logical

Logical fields are limited to two values: true or false. True values are entered with the characters T(rue) or Y(es). False values are entered with the characters F(alse) or N(o). Logical fields are useful when you want to record a true or false fact about an item or event. The advantage of the logical field is that you cannot accidentally enter some other character—e.g., A, B, C—into them. Another advantage is that logical fields are simpler and faster to test for than character or number fields. Logical fields are automatically restricted to one character in length.

Memo

Memo fields are the most complicated of the field types. Because character fields are restricted to 254 characters, Memo fields are used when you want to store a large amount of text. In fact, the data entered in Memo fields are stored in a format different from the fixed length structure used by dBASE IV. The data is stored in a variable length record file related to, and associated with, the database file that contains the Memo fields. Each memo can contain up to 64,000 characters in 1,024 lines. The entire Memo field, i.e., all the records containing memos, can contain up to 524,000 characters. Later in this chapter you will learn how Memo fields operate.

Number Types

A change in dBASE IV from previous versions is the inclusion of two types of numeric data fields: numeric and floating point.

The numeric type field stores numbers as *binary coded decimal* numbers. This term refers to a basic reality about how computers work internally. Computers must, in one form or another, translate all data, including decimal numbers, into a binary number representation. There are several techniques that accomplish this. The key issue is the degree of *precision* used in storing and calculating values.

Precision is an issue because in the process of converting numbers to and from binary form, small changes in the value can take place due to the rounding required when decimal numbers do not convert exactly to their binary code equivalents.

In most applications, these small changes are not significant. However, in complex financial applications, e.g., annuity calculations, which require calculated values to balance exactly, the numeric type fields offer precision up to 20 digits, as opposed to Float type fields that offer precision up to 15.9 digits.

In most cases, the numeric type field is used in financial database operations, such as addition, subtraction, and counting.

The Float type field is included as an option for fields used in complicated scientific or engineering calculations, where exact balancing is not required. Because Float fields are slightly less precise, dBASE IV can perform the complicated multiplication and division operations faster on Float fields than on numeric fields.

There are two methods by which a field type can be selected.

Spacebar

Pressing the <spacebar> causes dBASE IV to change the field type to the next type. Each time the spacebar is pressed, the type changes. When all six types have been displayed, the list repeats.

First Letter

If you know the type you want to select for the field, you can press the first letter. C= character, N= numeric, F= Float, D= Date, L= logical and M= memo
Enter

        d

The type column shows Date and the length is automatically set at eight characters. The cursor jumps to the last column, Index. Since checks are probably entered in the chronological order they are written, it may not be necessary to have the computer automatically index the database by date. In this case, leave the Index setting as it is, N, by entering

        ⏎

You have now completed the definition of the first field in the database.

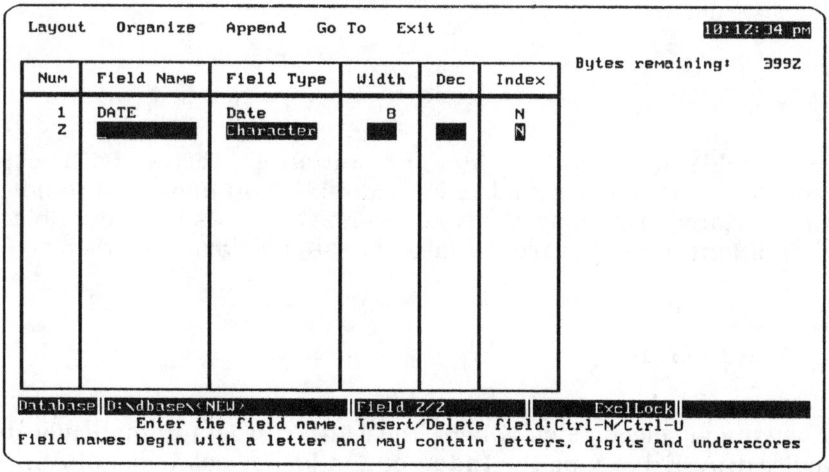

```
 Layout    Organize    Append    Go To    Exit                  10:12:34 pm

                                                         Bytes remaining:   3992
 ┌─────┬─────────────┬─────────────┬───────┬──────┬────────┐
 │ Num │ Field Name  │ Field Type  │ Width │ Dec  │ Index  │
 ├─────┼─────────────┼─────────────┼───────┼──────┼────────┤
 │  1  │ DATE        │ Date        │   8   │      │   N    │
 │  2  │ █████████   │ Character   │  ██   │  █   │   N    │
 │     │             │             │       │      │        │
 │     │             │             │       │      │        │
 │     │             │             │       │      │        │
 │     │             │             │       │      │        │
 │     │             │             │       │      │        │
 │     │             │             │       │      │        │
 │     │             │             │       │      │        │
 │     │             │             │       │      │        │
 └─────┴─────────────┴─────────────┴───────┴──────┴────────┘
 Database  D:\dbase\NEW           Field 2/2              CxclLock
             Enter the field name. Insert/Delete field:Ctrl-N/Ctrl-U
 Field names begin with a letter and may contain letters, digits and underscores
```

Figure 2-2. Field defined in database structure.

The next field is the check number. This item can be either a numeric or a character field, because check numbers are not usually used as numeric values. In this instance, make this field a numeric field. Enter

        check_num ⏎
        n

Numeric fields require you to enter the width, 1 to 20, and the number of decimal places. It should be noted the width is the total width of the numeric field, including a character for the +/- sign and the decimal place, if any. For example, if you want to enter numbers from -999.99 to 9999.99, you would need a numeric field seven characters wide with two decimal places.

In this case, the check numbers will be four digits with no decimal places. Enter

```
4 ↵
  ↵
  ↵
```

The next field will be PAYEE, a character field. Enter

```
payee ↵
      ↵
25 ↵
```

Here, it may be useful to accept the option to sequence the database by payee. Select this index by entering

```
y
```

The fourth field records the amount of the check, a numeric field. Enter

```
amount ↵
n
10 ↵
2 ↵
  ↵
```

Logical fields are useful to show the status of a record, with respect to some condition either true or false. For example, you may want to note if the check has cleared. You may also want to mark checks as deductible items. These conditions are either true or false. Create two logical fields by entering

```
cleared ↵
L
deductible
L
```

Notice when you select a logical field, the width of 1 is automatically entered. Also notice dBASE IV skips the **Index** option for logical fields. dBASE IV will not index records on a logical field.

Memo Fields

The next field to add to the database structure is a Memo field. A Memo field is used for storing text of up to 1,024 lines and 64,000 characters.

While character and Memo fields both store text, there are several important differences between the them other than capacity (character fields are limited to 254 characters). Text entered into a Memo field is not entered through dBASE IV editing screens. Instead, it is entered through the dBASE IV Editor program. When entering records into a database, Memo fields appear only as the word MEMO on the screen. When you want to enter text into the Memo field, the [Ctrl-Home] command loads the dBASE IV Editor.

where you can enter the text of the memo. The dBASE IV Editor is a simple but useful text editor, similar to a word-processing program.

The text entered into the Editor is not stored in the database file along with the rest of the data, but is stored in another file with a DBT (database text) extension. The Memo field serves as a link between the database records and the text stored in the DBT file.

As discussed earlier, fixed length record databases have the advantage of enhanced performance. Memo fields operate in a manner similar to delimited databases in that they allow you to enter a *variable* amount of information. They use only as much space as is needed to hold the text (i.e. Memo fields are not padded with blanks).

Memo field operations in dBASE IV have been considerably improved over dBASE III and dBASE III+. dBASE IV provides commands and functions making the data in Memo fields accessible to searches and other operations not possible in dBASE III. One of the most powerful commands is APPEND FROM *file* TO *memo*. This command allows you to import text from standard DOS text files, to dBASE IV Memo fields. This means you can import the text created with many of the most popular word-processing programs, into a dBASE IV Memo field without having to manually re-enter the text. The COPY MEMO command reverses the process by copying the text from a Memo field into a standard text file, so it can be used by applications, such as word-processing programs.

Create a Memo field called REMARKS, to hold any additional information you may want to record about the checks. Enter

```
remarks ↵
m
```

Notice Memo fields are automatically set to a length of 10 characters. This length has nothing to do with the amount of text you can enter into the Memo field. The 10 characters are used internally by dBASE IV to keep track of the text belonging to this record. The value of these 10 characters is hidden from view. Also notice Memo fields are not subject to indexing.

The file's structure is now complete.

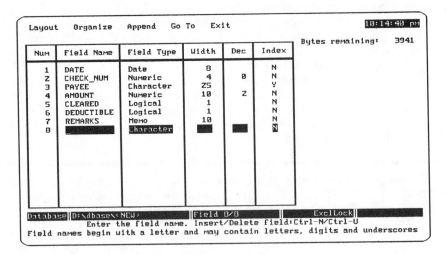

Figure 2-3. Database structure completed.

dBASE IV allows you to enter up to 255 fields totalling up to 4,000 characters for each database. Because dBASE IV is a relational database, you will find the 255 field limit does not place practical restrictions on database operations.

Notice in the upper-right corner of the screen dBASE IV displays the number of bytes remaining; here, the value is 3931. This means the current database structure can have another 3,941 characters added to it.

The term *byte.* refers to the amount of computer storage needed to store a single character. In most cases, one byte equals one character.

Now that you have specified the fields necessary to record the checkbook data, you can create the actual database file by saving the structure just outlined. There are three ways to do this:

Exit-Save

You can use the Exit-Save command found on the menu bar at the top screen. You can use the menu shortcut command [Alt-e]s.

[Ctrl-End], [Ctrl-w]

These keystroke commands also signal dBASE IV to save the structure and create a database file. These commands perform the same function as the

menu command. [Ctrl-w] maintains compatibility with dBASE II and [Ctrl-End] maintains compatibility with dBASE III.
Enter

       [Ctrl-End]

dBASE IV displays a small box in the center of the screen with the prompt Save as :.

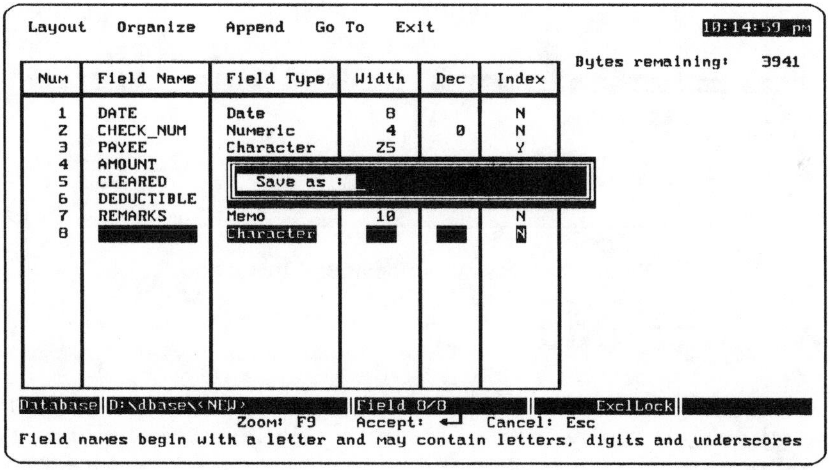

Figure 2-4. Save database as box.

The name you enter into this box becomes the name of the database. The name must conform to DOS filename rules: begin with a letter A - Z, between 1 and 8 characters, and contain no spaces. Enter

       ckbook ⏎

dBASE IV creates the database file with the DOS filename CKBOOK.DBF. The DBF (database file) extension is automatically appended onto the filename. In addition to the DBF (database) file, two other files are created. The Memo field REMARKS requires a file called CKBOOK.DBT, which will contain the text of the memos, if any. Also, an index file is created because you selected indexing for the PAYEE field. The index file will have the name CKBOOK.MDX (multiple index).

At the bottom of the display, the prompt "Input data records now? (Y/N)" appears. Entering Y places you into the Append mode. Entering N returns you to the Control Center. In this case, enter

       n

The Control Center now shows the name of the database file, CKBOOK, in the Data column of the Control Center display. CKBOOK is automatically added to the current catalog, UNTITLED.CAT.

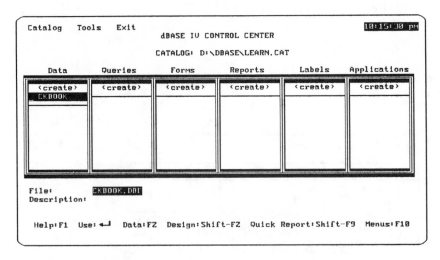

Figure 2-5. Database file added to catalog.

Activating a Database

Notice the name CKBOOK above the line in the Data column, indicating the database file is currently *active.* The active database is the one *open* for input and output. Since it is possible to have many database files, activating a given database selects it for use with the entry and output operations.

In this case, the CKBOOK file is activated automatically after it is created. This makes sense because you will probably want to use the file structure to enter data.

The ┘ key is used to change the status of a database file listed in the Data column. To use the ┘ command, you must use the up arrow and down arrow key to position the highlight on the database you want to work with.

In this instance, the CKBOOK database is highlighted. Enter

┘

dBASE IV displays a box in the center of the screen with three options.

Close file

Since the database is currently active, this option will deactivate it, (i.e. close the database). A closed database is one in which all new information has been written to the disk and is unavailable for further input or output, unless reopened.

Modify Structure/Order

This option returns you to the file structure menu. You can then modify the field structure of the database by adding new fields, deleting fields, or editing field specifications. You can also add more field indexes, as well. The Control Center provides a shortcut key for this option, Shift-[F2].

Display Data

This option allows you to display, edit, and append data to the database. The Control Center provides a shortcut key for this option, [F2].

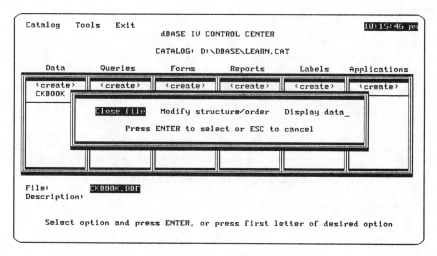

Figure 2-6. Activate database box.

The left-most option, Close file, is highlighted. To close the database file, enter

          ⏎

The database file is closed. You can tell because two parts of the Control Center display are changed. The CKBOOK file name moved below the line in the Data column, indicating it is no longer an active file.

Below the Control Center columns are two lines labeled File: and Description:. These two lines display information about the highlighted database file. Because the highlight is on the <create> symbol, the lines read "New File" and "Press ENTER on <create> to create a new file".

Move the highlight to the CKBOOK database by entering

     [down arrow]

The name next to the file reads CKBOOK.DBF, which is the full DOS filename of the highlighted database. To activate this database, enter

⏎

The activate database box appears again. This time, because the file is currently closed, the left option reads "Use file".

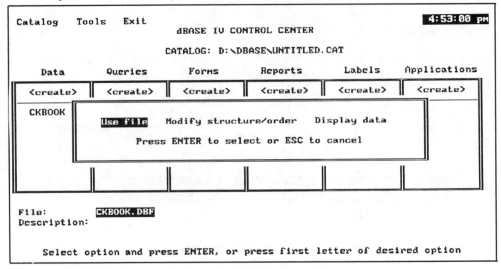

Figure 2-7. File use dialog box.

To activate the database file, enter

⏎

The file is activated. The active status of the file is indicated by the movement of the filename, CKBOOK, above the line in the data column.

Adding a File Description

You may have noticed the file description line for CKBOOK is empty. When you create a database file, the filename you select must conform to the DOS limitations on filenames. This means the database names are limited to eight characters. Applications running under DOS must conform to the existing limits on DOS filenames. In order to help you remember the purpose of the files, dBASE IV permits you to add a description to each database file.

File descriptions are added from the Design display you previously used to create the file's structure. Use the shortcut key to activate the Design mode by entering

    [Shift-F2]

When you enter the Design mode with the key, dBASE IV automatically displays the Organize menu.

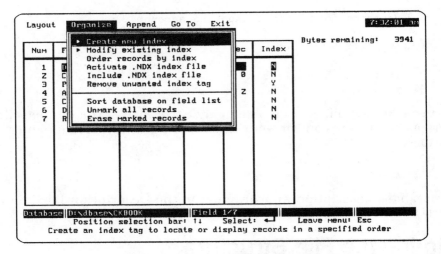

Figure 2-8. Organize Database menu.

However, the command you are looking for is found in the Layout menu. To display the Layout menu, enter

    [left arrow]

The second option on the Layout menu is Edit Database Description. To select this option, type the first letter of the option, in this case, the letter *e*.

    e

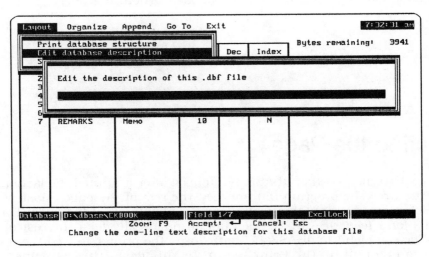

Figure 2-9. Enter a Database Description.

You can enter a one-line description of the database.

       `Database for business checking account` ⏎

Exit the design screen by entering

       `[Alt-e]`
       ⏎

Because you have made a change in the structure of the database, the program asks you to confirm your intention. Do so by pressing enter one more time.

       ⏎

The database description appears next to the Description label on the Control Center Display.

Printing the File Structure

Sometimes it is handy to have a description of a database, to which to refer. You can print a copy of the structure from the Design display. Activate the Design display by entering

       `[Shift-F2]`

Display the Layout menu by entering

       `[Alt-L]`

The first option on the menu is Print Database Structure. Enter

       ⏎

dBASE IV displays the Print Options menu. To begin printing, enter

       ⏎

dBASE IV prints the structure information.

Ejecting the Page

You may have noticed that dBASE IV stopped after it printed the last line of the structure. The program did not feed the rest of the page. Most word-processing programs automatically feed the remainder of the page. This is called a *form feed.* dBASE IV does not automatically feed the rest of the form. The command in dBASE IV that causes the printer to feed the rest of the form is found on the Print menu. In this case, the Print menu is accessed through the Print Database Structure command. To feed the rest of the form, you must use Print Database Structure to gain access to the Print menu. Enter

       [Alt-L] p

The Eject Page Now command prompts the printer to feed the remainder of the form. Enter

       e

You can now exit the menu by using the Esc command.

       [Esc] (*3 times*)

dBASE IV displays a box in the center of the screen that asks "Are you sure that you want to abandon operation?" This box is displayed each time you use the [Esc] key to exit a Control Center mode. In this case, you can safely enter Y because you have not made any additions, deletions, or changes to the file structure; you have only printed the information you had previously stored as the file's structure. Enter

       y

You have now printed a copy of the file's structure. The printout should look like this:

```
Structure for              E:\DBASE\CKBOOK.DBF
database:
Number of data             0
records:
Date of last update   :    01/12/89

Field  Field Name  Type        Width  Dec  Index
1      DATE        Date        8           N
2      CHECK_NUM   Numeric     4           N
3      PAYEE       Character   25          Y
4      AMOUNT      Numeric     10     2    N
5      CLEARED     Logical     1           N
6      DEDUCTIBLE  Logical     1           N
7      REMARKS     Memo        10          N
       ** Total **             60
```

The printout reveals several pieces of information about the database. First, dBASE IV keeps track of the number of records in the database—at this moment 0—and the date on which the last change was made to the file. This date will be updated any time changes are made to the file. If the database is output only (i.e. printed or displayed without making changes) the date is left as is.

At the bottom of the display the total number of characters in the database is calculated. The total for the CKBOOK file is 60. However, you may have noticed if you add together the values of the fields as they appear in the listing, (8+4+25+10+1+1+10), they total 59, not 60. Why is the total larger than the sum of all the fields?

The answer is dBASE IV automatically reserves an additional character for each record. This character is used to hold the deletion marker of the record. When you enter a record, the deletion marker is stored as an additional blank space. You will learn in Chapter 10 how this blank space can be changed to mark records for deletion from the database. The total number of characters in each record is always one greater than the sum of all the fields.

Adding Records

Now that you have created the database, you can begin to add actual data to the file. You can enter the Data Entry mode in two ways.

Display Data

Pressing ↵ allows you to select the Display Data option from the box.

        [F2].

This shortcut key immediately activates the Data Entry mode.
    Enter

        [F2]

dBASE IV enters the Data Entry mode. In this mode, you can enter new records and edit existing data. dBASE IV automatically generates a data form on the screen, based on the fields in your database structure. This form lists the names of the fields down the left side of the screen. Next to each field name is an input area, displayed in reverse video.

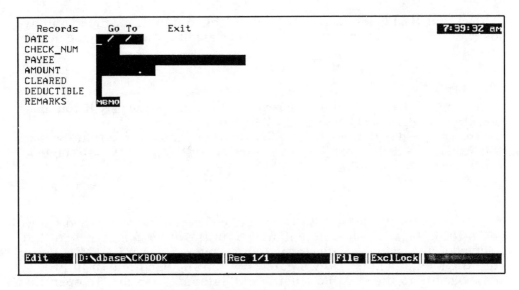

Figure 2-10. Data Entry Mode Display.

Begin by entering information about the first check, starting with the date. Notice it is not necessary to enter the forward slash marks (/). dBASE IV automatically inserts these marks into the field. Enter

010389

When the date is entered, dBASE IV beeps, warning you have filled the entire field. The cursor is then advanced to the next field, CHECK_NUM. Enter

1000

Next, enter the payee.

Allied Office Furniture ↵

Notice that because the entry did not fill the entire field, it is necessary for you to enter ↵ to complete the entry and move on to the next field. Now enter the amount of the check.

750.5 ↵

In the instance of the numeric field, you are required to enter only the significant figures. In this case, the last zero is not mathematically significant. Because the field is defined as having two decimal places, dBASE IV inserts the last zero automatically. This saves you from typing an additional keystroke. However, you *must* enter the decimal point if you want to enter a number with a decimal portion.

The next field is for cleared checks. In this example, assume you have just written the check, meaning it has not cleared the bank. Skip the field by entering

⏎

Keep in mind that by default all logical fields evaluate as false. If you make no entry in a logical field, its value will be false.

The next field is the DEDUCTIBLE field. Here, enter a true value because this expense is deductible. You can enter either T, t, Y, or y into the field. Enter

y

dBASE IV converts the entry to T. Finally, you reach the Memo field named REMARKS. It is clearly differentiated from the other field types in that, instead of displaying a blank entry area, it shows the word *MEMO*. Recall that the Memo field is really a gateway from the fixed-length dBASE IV database file to the variable-length field database text file. To open this gateway and actually enter data into the REMARKS field you must use a special command keystrokes, [F9] or [Ctrl-Home]. [F9] is the Zoom key in dBASE IV. [Ctrl-Home] maintains compatibility with dBASE III command keystrokes. Enter

[F9]

This command prompts dBASE IV to load and display the dBASE IV text Editor screen. The data entered into the previous fields is no longer visible because the editor has temporarily taken over the screen display.

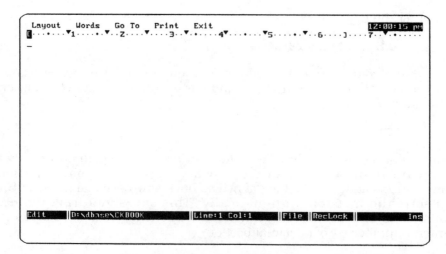

Figure 2-11. Editing a Memo field.

You can enter text into a Memo field in a manner similar to a standard word-processing program. The dBASE IV editor also allows you to print a copy of the Memo field text by using the Print command on the menu bar. The Editing Command sidebar lists the commands available in the dBASE IV Editor.

Del	Delete character
Ins	Toggle insert/typeover
End	End of line
Home	Beginning of line
Backspace	Delete previous character
Ctrl-Backspace	Delete previous word
Tab	Next tab
Shift-Tab	Previous tab
↵	Start New Line
Esc	Abandon text
Ctrl-right arrow	Move word right
Ctrl-left arrow	Move word left
PgDn	End of text
Ctrl-PgUp	Beginning of text
Ctrl-End	Save and exit
Ctrl ↵	Save and continue
Ctrl-t	Delete to end of line
Ctrl-y	Delete line

Enter the following text for the memo:

```
Office Furniture Purchased:  ↵
↵
1 - desk 36" by 48 "  ↵
1 - swivel chair  ↵
2 - side chairs  ↵
1 - computer desk  ↵
1 - printer stand  ↵
```

The memo looks like this:

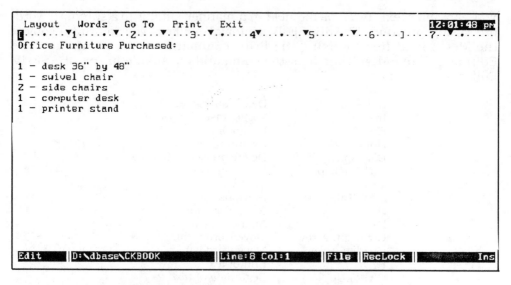

Figure 2-12. Text of memo entered into editor.

Save the memo text by using the Zoom key to return to Field Entry screen.

        [F9]

The cursor is still positioned in the Memo field. You can check to see that the text is correctly saved by entering

        [F9]

The dBASE IV editor displays the memo text once again. Return to the Field Entry display.

        [F9]

Notice when a Memo field contains text, the word *MEMO* (in upper-case letters) appears in the normal record display. If the Memo field is empty, the word appears in lower-case letters, in the normal record display.

Adding Another Record

The cursor is now positioned in the first field in the current record. To add another record you must either enter ↵ in the last field, or press [PgDn], if you are not positioned in it. Enter

        [PgDn]

dBASE IV displays another blank form in which more data can be entered. If you look at the center of the status line, you will see that the activity location area reads "Rec 2/2". The first number in the fraction indicates the current record, while the second tells you the total number of records in the database.

The Ditto Key

Sometimes consecutive records contain information in common. For example, when entering check book information, there may be several checks with the same date.

dBASE IV assigns the Shift-[F8] key combination the Ditto function. Pressing this combination prompts dBASE IV to copy the data from the same field of the previous record, to the current record.

In this instance, you can copy the date entered into the first record by entering

```
[Shift-F8]
```

The date *01/03/89* is copied into date field of Record 2. Note that the cursor still remains at the beginning of the field, after the date has been inserted. Move to the next field by entering

```
⏎
```

The Ditto function can be of use when the data is similar to, but not exactly the same as, the previous record. For example, the check number for Record 2 is 1 greater than the previous check number. You can save a keystroke or two by using Ditto to copy the data, then manually edit any characters needing change. Enter

```
[Shift-F8]
[End]
1
```

Enter the rest of the information about this check, as follows:

```
Central Office Supplies  ⏎
97.56
⏎
y
[F9]
envelopes  ⏎
manila folders  ⏎
hanging files
[F9]
⏎
```

It is a subtle point, but you may have noticed that the ⏎ key was not pressed for the last line of text. Instead, [F9] was used to save the memo. The program automatically inserted ⏎ for you at the end of the line.

You have now entered two records and have a third blank record displayed on the screen. Note that check 1002 is skipped, assuming that it was voided. Enter the following information into this blank record.

```
010689
1002
Western Telephone  ⏎
101.57
```

You don't want to add any more data to this record. To skip the rest of the fields and move to the next blank record, enter

```
[PgDn]
```

Fill a fourth record with the following data. The entry process below uses the Ditto command, [Shift-F8], to copy similar data from the previous record.

```
[Shift-F8]  ⏎
[Shift-F8]  [End] 3
United Federal Insurance  ⏎
590 ⏎
⏎
⏎
[F9]
business insurance  ⏎
Policy number: 10012002AF
[F9]
```

You have now entered four records into the database.

Displaying Previously Entered Records

The current screen display is the Edit display. The word **Edit** appears on the left end of the status line, indicating it as the current operational mode. In this mode, dBASE IV displays information on the screen from *only one record* at a time. The [PgUp] and [PgDn] keys flip forward and backward in the file, showing the next or previous records. Suppose you wanted to check Record 2. You would move backward in the file twice. Enter

```
[PgUp]   (2 times)
```

The data for Record 2 appears on the display. To move to Record 3, enter

```
[PgDn]
```

Record 3 is displayed. In addition to [PgUp] and [PgDn] keys that move one record at a time through the database, dBASE IV provides additional commands on the Goto menu. Display the Goto menu by entering

    `[Alt-g]`

The Goto menu lists eight commands, broken into two groups. They are used to locate individual records. The group of commands in the top section of the menu locate records by their physical position in the file, as well as their record numbers. The record numbers are consecutively assigned to the records as they are entered.

Top Record

Display the first record in the current database.

Last Record

Display the last record entered into the current database.

Record number

Use this command to display a specific record. You must know the number of the record you want to display.

Skip

Use this command to skip a specified number of records from the record currently displayed. The default value is to skip 10 records. The value determines the direction of the movement in the database. If the skip value is positive, the command moves towards the end of the database. If the value is negative, the command skips in the direction of the top of the database. For example, entering a skip value of 2 has the same effect as entering [PgDn] two times. Entering a skip value of -2 has the same effect as entering [PgUp] two times.

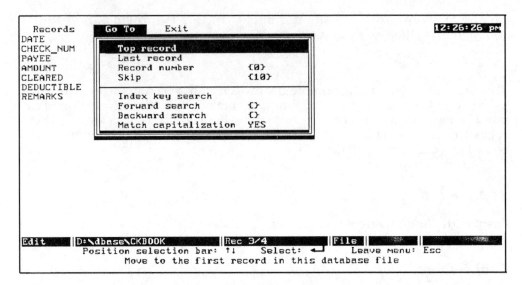

Figure 2-13. Goto record menu.

The commands in the bottom portion of the window locate records based on the contents of the fields. These commands search the field in which the cursor is currently positioned, for a record that contains a matching value.

Index key search

This option performs an index key search. An index file or tag must be active in order to use this option. You will learn more about indexes in Chapter 4.

Forward search

Searches forward in the file for the next record, if any, that matches the search item.

Backward search

Searches backward in the file for the next record, if any, that matches the search item.

Match capitalization

When set to YES, requires matching capitalization for a match. When NO, allows matches when capitalization differs. Example: when YES, *ALLIED* will not match *Allied* or *allied*; when NO, *ALLIED*, *Allied* or *allied* will be treated the same.

To move to the top of the file, select the Top Record command by entering

    t

The first record in the database is displayed. Move to the end of the database by entering

        [Alt-g]
        L

Move backward two records using the Goto Skip command instead of the [PgUp] key. Enter

        [Alt-g]
        s
        -2 ⏎

The display moves backward to Record 2. Return to the top of the database. Try this on your own. The correct command is at the end of the chapter under EX-1.

The commands in the bottom portion of the Goto menu allow you to search for records, based on their content, not their physical location. In general, this is a much more useful way of locating records. Suppose you wanted to display the record for check 1002.

The first step is to place the cursor in the field you want to search—in this case, the CHECK_NUM field. In addition to the arrow keys, [F3] moves the cursor one field back, and [F4] moves the cursor one field forward.

[F3] and [F4] act differently from the arrow keys in one respect. If [F3] or [F4] is used to move to a Memo field, the Memo field is automatically activated and the dBASE IV Editor is displayed with the text contained in the field. The arrow keys position the cursor on the Memo field, but they do not automatically activate the Editor. You must use [F9] or [Ctrl-Home] to activate the Editor.

Enter

        [F4]

With the cursor positioned on the field you want to search, you can enter the Search Forward or Search Backward command. In most cases, it is best to begin a search either at the first or last record in a database, to be sure you have not skipped the record you are looking for. Since you are at the top of the database, search forward by entering

        [Alt-g] f

Enter the information you are searching for.

        1002 ⏎

The program locates Record 3 as containing the desired information, and displays that data.

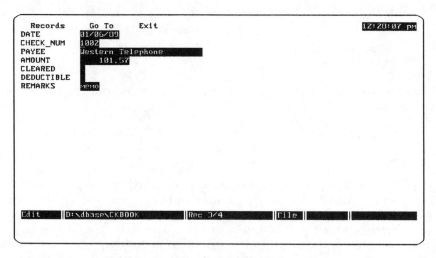

Figure 2-14. Record located by the search.

Suppose you wanted to locate the check written to United Federal Insurance. The first step is to move to the top of the file. Try this on your own. The correct command is found at the end of the chapter under EX-2.

Next, place the cursor in PAYEE field by entering

        [F4]   *(2 times)*

Enter the command to search forward in this field.

        [Alt-g] f

Notice that the previous search item, 1002, remains in the entry box. The cursor is automatically positioned at the end of the entry so you do not have to enter the search item again if you want to continue the previous search. In this case, you want to erase the existing item and enter a new one. Move the cursor to the beginning of the entry line by entering

        [Home]

To delete an entire line of text, use the command keystroke [Ctrl-y]. Enter

        [Ctrl-y]

Now enter the text you want to find. You cannot search for partial matches. For example, if the field contains *United Federal Insurance*, searching for United Federal will not work. The search text must match the information stored in the field, exactly and completely. You will learn in Chapter 3 how more flexible searches can be implemented using the Query By Example mode. Enter the text you want to locate. Keep in mind that when the default setting, Match Capitalization, is ON, the capitalization of the characters will count toward determining a matching record. Make sure you enter the following text with the exact capitalization shown.

    United Federal Insurance

Because the entry is longer than the input area inside the box, dBASE IV scrolls the text to make room for the additional characters. If you want to see the entire entry, you can use the Zoom command, [F9], to enlarge the display. Enter

    [F9]

The text now appears both inside the box and at the bottom of the screen, just above the status line.

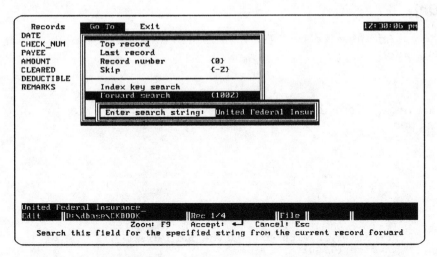

Figure 2-15. Entry boxed zoomed for larger display.

To initiate the search, enter

    ↵

dBASE IV locates the matching record and displays the information on the screen.

Adding More Records

Suppose you wanted to stop looking through the database and begin entering new records once again. There are two ways to get back to the Append mode.

[PgDn]

If you are positioned on the last record in the database and enter [PgDn] or ↵ in the last field of this record, dBASE IV displays a message at the bottom of the screen that reads "===> Add new records? (Y/N)." If you enter Y, you enter the Append mode.

[Alt-r] a

The Records menu contains the Add new records command, which automatically places dBASE IV into the Append mode. The advantage of this command is you do not have to position the display to the last record in order to enter the Append mode.

Because you are currently positioned in the last record in the database, either method will work the same. Enter

[PgDn]

The "===> Add new records? (Y/N)" message appears at the bottom of the screen. Enter

        y

You are now presented with a blank record, 5, for entry. Enter the following information.

```
010189
1004
Computer World ↵
2245.5 ↵
↵
y
[F9]
286 Computer with 40 megabyte hard disk↵
Invoice #75001
[F9]
```

The Browse Display

The Edit mode, in which you have been working, is characterized by a screen-display layout that shows one record at a time. This mode treats each of the records in the database file as if it were a 3 by 5 card. The [PgUp] and [PgDn] commands allow you to flip back and forth between the cards.

dBASE IV has another way of viewing a database—the Browse mode. In the Browse mode, dBASE IV presents the database as a table in which each row is one record, and each column is a field. You can toggle between the Edit and the Browse modes by using the [F2] key. Enter

        [F2]

The display changes to the Browse mode.

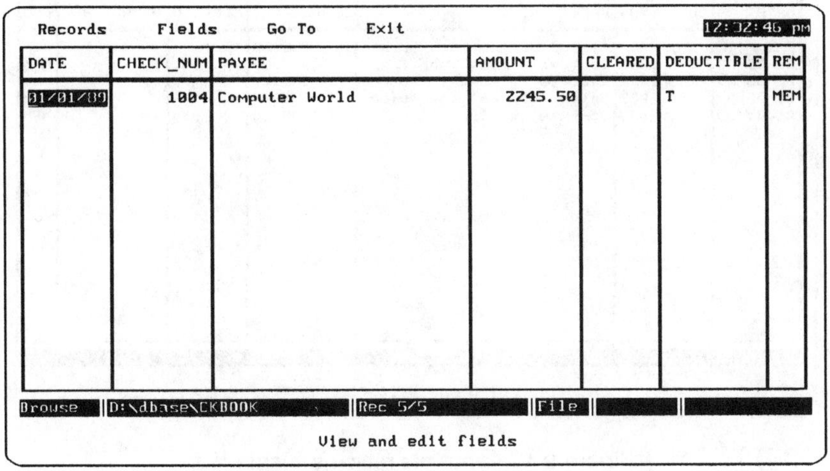

Figure 2-16. Browse mode display.

To reveal the previous records in the database, move to the top of the database by entering

[Alt-g] ↵

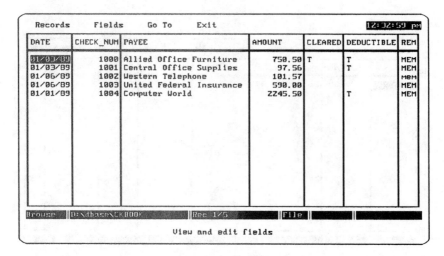

Figure 2-17. Multiple records displayed.

In the Browse mode the fields are displayed horizontally. In many cases, this means all the fields cannot be displayed at one time. The Browse mode *pans* to the right and left, to reveal additional columns. The following keys are used in the Browse mode.

down arrow	Next record
up arrow	Previous record
Tab	Next field
Shift-Tab	Previous field
F4	Next field
F3	Previous field
Home	First field in record
End	Last field in record
PgDn	Next screen full of records
PgUp	Previous screen full of records
↵	Next field
Ctrl-PgDn	Last record
Ctrl-PgUp	First record

Move to the last field in the record by entering

[End]

The display scrolls to the right, to make room for the last field, REMARKS.

```
  Records     Fields     Go To     Exit                    12:33:17 PM

 CHECK_NUM PAYEE                      AMOUNT   CLEARED DEDUCTIBLE REMARKS
      1000 Allied Office Furniture    750.50 T         T          MEMO
      1001 Central Office Supplies     97.56           T          MEMO
      1002 Western Telephone          101.57                      memo
      1003 United Federal Insurance   590.00                      MEMO
      1004 Computer World            2245.50           T          MEMO
```

```
Browse    D:\dbase\CKBOOK          Rec 1/5          File
                       View and edit fields
```

Figure 2-18. Browse display scrolled to the right.

This display shows all but one of the records contains a memo in the REMARKS field; all but Record 3 have the word *MEMO* in upper-case.

You can edit any of the records appearing in the Browse mode by moving your cursor to the record and field you want to edit.

You can also add new records in the Browse mode. You can append records by using the [Alt-r]a command, or entering down arrow in the last record. The primary advantage of entering data in the Browse mode is you can see the data from a number of surrounding records, while you are adding or revising new records. For example, the entries in the check-number field ought to be consecutive. The Browse mode makes it easier to see what the next number ought to be. In the Edit mode, only one record is displayed; you cannot see the previous record and cannot use it as a point of reference.

The primary disadvantage of the Browse mode is you may not be able to view as many fields at one time as you can in the Edit mode. In dBASE IV, you can switch between display modes at any time by pressing [F2].

Add a new record to this database in the Browse mode. Enter

        [Alt-r] a

Enter the following data:

        [Shift-F8] ⏎
        1005
        Fathead Software ⏎
        99.95
        down arrow

Add another record.

```
011489
1006
The Bargin Warehouse ⏎
145.99
⏎
t
```

Memo field data is entered the same way in the Browse mode as in the Edit mode.

```
[F9]
waste paper baskets ⏎
copier paper ⏎
computer paper ⏎
smoke alarm
[F9]
```

Place the cursor back at the top of the database. This time, use the cursor movement keystroke commands, rather than the GoTo menu command. [Ctrl-PgUp] moves you to the top of the database. Enter

```
[Ctrl-PgUp]
```

The cursor moves to the top of the database, but the field position remains the same. To move to the first field in the record, enter

```
[Home]
```

The Fields Menu

The menu bar in the Browse mode contains an additional option, *Fields*. The Fields menu provides commands that allow you to control aspects of the Browse mode display. Display the Fields menu by entering

```
Alt-f
```

The Fields menu contains four commands.

Lock fields on left

This option is used to prevent the scrolling of one or more of the fields. For example, suppose the current database contains additional fields that would not fit on the screen at the same time as the date and check number fields. When you scrolled to the right, you would no longer be able to see which date and check number matched the other data. By locking two fields, you would make sure the first two fields on the display will always show date and check numbers, no matter how far to the right you scroll.

Blank field

This command erases the contents of a field so you can re-enter new data. It performs a similar function to the [Ctrl-y] command keystroke.

Freeze field

This option is used to restrict the cursor to vertical movement in a single column. Use this option to quickly move from record to record, editing the same field in each record. This is a useful procedure when you need to update a particular field. When a column is locked, ⏎, down arrow, and Tab, all have the same effect—move to the next record, same field.

Size field

This option allows you to set the width for a field column. dBASE IV automatically sets the column width to the field width, or the width of the field name, whichever is the larger.

To learn more about the Fields menu commands try using them. Begin by locking the DATE field column. Enter

```
L
1 ⏎
```

Nothing appears to have changed. The setting takes effect when you move to a column that requires the screen to scroll to the right. Move to the last field by entering

```
[End]
```

The DATE column remains locked on the left side of the screen. Rather than scrolling this column off the display when you scrolled to the right, the first unlocked column, CHECK_NUM, was scrolled instead. The locking command creates row *headings* by locking the data in one or more columns, so they are always displayed, no matter how far to the right the screen is scrolled.

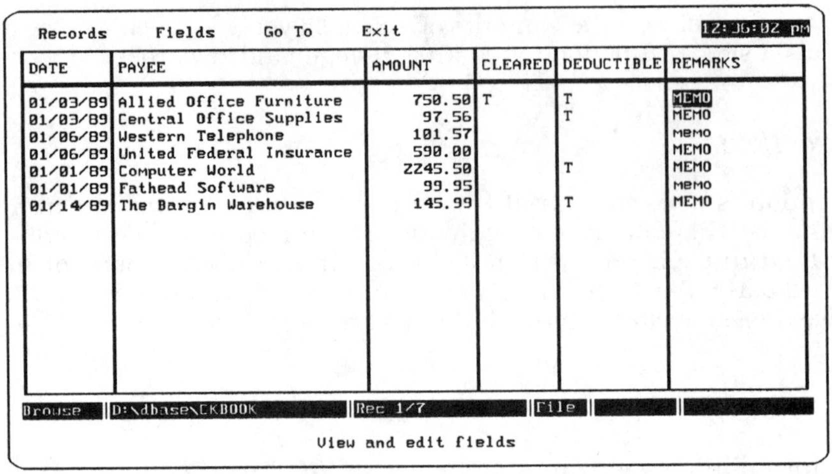

```
 Records      Fields      Go To      Exit                       12:06:02 pm
┌──────────┬────────────────────────┬─────────┬────────┬──────────┬─────────┐
│DATE      │PAYEE                   │AMOUNT   │CLEARED │DEDUCTIBLE│REMARKS  │
├──────────┼────────────────────────┼─────────┼────────┼──────────┼─────────┤
│01/03/89  │Allied Office Furniture │  750.50 │T       │T         │MEMO     │
│01/03/89  │Central Office Supplies │   97.56 │        │T         │MEMO     │
│01/06/89  │Western Telephone       │  101.57 │        │          │memo     │
│01/06/89  │United Federal Insurance│  590.00 │        │          │MEMO     │
│01/01/89  │Computer World          │ 2245.50 │        │T         │MEMO     │
│01/01/89  │Fathead Software        │   99.95 │        │          │memo     │
│01/14/89  │The Bargin Warehouse    │  145.99 │        │T         │MEMO     │
│          │                        │         │        │          │         │
└──────────┴────────────────────────┴─────────┴────────┴──────────┴─────────┘
 Browse    D:\dbase\CKBOOK              Rec 1/7          File
                            View and edit fields
```

Figure 2-19. DATE column locked.

To free the columns to scroll normally, simply set the locked value to zero.
Enter

        [Alt-f] L 0 ⏎

Freezing a Column

Another useful feature provided on the Fields menu is the ability to freeze a
column. Freezing causes the cursor to move vertically only, in the selected
column. Freezing is useful when you want to update the information in a
specific field, and you don't want to accidentally move into some other field
in the database.

   For example, the CLEARED field is one that is probably not going to be
filled out at the time you enter the check information. This field will be used
later, when you receive your bank statement and wish to mark the checks
that have cleared.

   This is exactly the kind of entry task the Fields Freeze command was
designed for. Begin by freezing the CLEARED field. Enter

        [Alt-f] f

Enter the name of the field you wish to freeze. Keep in mind you cannot
enter a number, only the exact spelling of the fieldname.

        cleared ⏎

The cursor moves to the CLEARED field. When a field is frozen, all
movement commands advance the cursor to the next or previous record, in

the same field. You cannot move horizontally until you unfreeze the column.

You cannot enter a series of values. Because this is a logical field—a width of one character—the cursor, in effect, automatically advances to the next field. This makes it easy to enter a series of values into consecutive records. Enter

> t
> t
> t
> f
>
> t
> t
> f

The last entry advances the cursor past the last record, prompting the program to ask "===> Add new Records? (Y/N)". Because you do not want to add more records at this time, enter

> n

When you have a column frozen and you need to edit one of the other fields in that record, you have two options:

Unfreeze

You can use the Fields Freeze command to unfreeze the column and return to the normal Browse mode.

Edit mode

Use the [F2] command to switch to the Edit mode display.

The Edit mode option has the advantage of not cancelling the column freeze. By switching to the Edit mode display you have access to all the fields in that record. When you switch back to the Browse mode, the column freeze is still in effect and you can continue with the column entry. Enter

> [F2]

The cursor appears in the DATE field of the active record. Enter

> [F4] *(2 times)*

The cursor moves to the next field in the record, unaffected by the column freeze executed in the Browse mode. Return to the Browse mode by entering

> [F2]

The cursor is now positioned in the CLEARED column. Enter

>   [F3]   *(2 times)*

The cursor moves up the column, demonstrating the column freeze is still active. The ability to use the [F2] command to switch between the Browse and Edit modes provides a great deal of flexibility in entering and editing data.

Unfreezing a Column

Unfreezing a column allows you to return to the normal Browse mode operation. Unfreezing requires you to remove the name of the field from the Freeze command. Enter

>   [Alt-f] f

To erase the contents of the box, enter

>   [Home]
>   [Ctrl-y] ⌐

The cursor is now free to move horizontally, as well as vertically. Enter

>   [Home]

The cursor moves to the DATE field in the current record.

Undoing Changes

When you are editing a record, dBASE IV does not record the changes you enter until you move to the next record, forward or backward in the file. *While the record is current*, you can restore the record to its original data by using the Records Undo command. Keep in mind the limitations of this command. If you move to another record in either the Browse or Edit modes, *you cannot restore the old data* with Records Undo.

Memo fields are an exception to this rule, since their data is saved when you close the Memo field editing window.

As an example of what the Records Undo command can do, enter the following into the current record.

>   123187

Because your cursor is still in the same record, the Records Undo command restores the date to its original value. Enter

>   [Alt-r] u

The date is returned to its original value of 01/10/89. On the other hand, moving to a new record negates the ability of the Records Undo command to restore edited data. Enter

```
2000
[down arrow]
```

The down arrow causes the cursor to move to the next record in the database. This means the original check number in the previous record cannot be recovered. You can attempt to do so by moving back to the previous record and using the Records Undo command. Try this on your own. The correct command is found at the end of the chapter under EX-3.

The record remains unchanged. The original check number, 1005, cannot be recovered once you have moved to another record in the database. The same principle applies to editing in the Edit mode, where the Records Undo command operates in exactly the same manner.

Replace the correct check number by entering

```
1003
```

Closing a Database File

When you are finished editing and appending records, you can exit the Edit/Browse modes by using the menu command, Exit, [Alt-e]e, or the command keystroke, [Ctrl-End]. Enter

```
[Ctrl -End]
```

You have now returned to the Control Center.

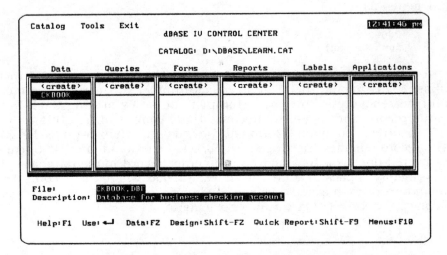

Figure 2-20. Control Center display following editing.

Closing a database ensures that all changes and additions have been written to a disk file. (See Memory Vs. Disk in the Sidebar below). This ensures that a power failure will not cause a loss of data. Enter

⌐

The file operations box displays the options *Close File,* *Modify Structure/Order*, and *Display Data.* Close the file by entering

c

The file is closed. The Control Center display confirms this by placing the name of the file, CKBOOK, below the line in the DATA column.

Memory Vs. Disk

Computers have two types of memory. The most obvious form is the information stored on disks—both hard and floppy. You are aware of disk operations because you can usually hear the disk drives working and/or see the disk activity lights on the computer flash, while the disk is in operation.

However, all the actual computing work takes place in the internal memory of the computer, which most users never actually see. To see the internal memory you must remove the cover from the computer and inspect the circuit boards.

The entry and editing of database records involves both these types of memory. When you add new records, or edit existing records, the information is stored in the internal memory of the computer, not the disk. The internal memory can lose data when the power is turned off accidentally.

dBASE IV eventually transfers the data from the internal memory to a file on the disk—hard or floppy. Once transferred, a power failure will not affect the stored data, because disks retain information after the computer is turned off.

The important question is, at what point does this transfer take place? Ideally, dBASE IV would transfer the data to the disk after you have entered or revised each record. This is not the case. Because transferring data to the disk is a slower operation than storing data in the internal memory, dBASE IV holds the data in a special area of the memory called a *buffer* area. When you fill the buffer area with a sufficient amount of data, dBASE IV writes the entire block of data to the disk. This method of holding data until a sufficient amount is accumulated is used to cut down the number of disk writing operations and improve the performance of dBASE IV.

dBASE IV provides a special SET command, SET AUTOSAVE, which changes the way memory buffers are used. When set to AUTOSAVE, dBASE IV saves each record as it is added or revised. On slow computers, e.g., IBM and compatible XT's, AUTOSAVE ON may cause a significant change in performance because of the increased number of disk operations performed. On 286 or 386 machines with hard disks that perform with 28 ms average access time, the change in performance may be negligible.

The default setting for AUTOSAVE is OFF.

Setting Conditions

dBASE IV provides a wide range of commands modifying the way many of its operations work. These are called SET commands. Some of the most commonly—used SET commands can be accessed directly from the Control Center by using the Tools Settings command.

---

dBASE IV contains 78 SET commands, of which only 16 can be accessed from the Control Center.   The remainder of the commands must be accessed through the Dot Prompt or Command modes.   These operations are covered in Chapter 16.

The Settings menu is found on the Tools menu. Display the Settings menu by entering

[Alt-t] s

dBASE IV displays the Settings menu. The menu has three items on its menu bar.

Options

This item lists sixteen optional settings that effect data entry, searches, and output.

Display

Use this to change the colors on the screen display.

Exit

This item returns you to the main Control Center display.

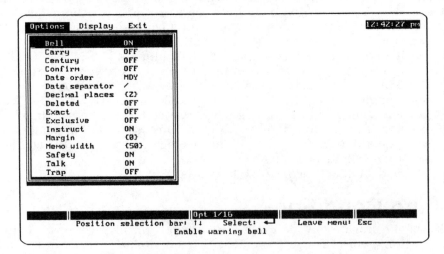

Figure 2-21. Settings display.

The items listed in the Options box are the ones directly affecting operations in the Control Center. The commands affecting data entry or editing in the Edit/Browse mode are:

Bell

When ON, a beep is sounded each time a field is filled. OFF suppresses the beep. The default is ON.

Carry

When ON, automatically "dittos" all fields when a new record is added. When OFF, "ditto" fields must be manually requested using [Shift-F8]. The default is OFF.

Century

When ON, the date fields are displayed with 4-character values for the year, e.g., 1989. When OFF, 2-character years, e.g., 89, are displayed. The century is assumed to be the 20th (i.e. 19). The default is OFF.

Confirm

When ON, requires a ↵ or [F4], in order to advance to the next field. When OFF, the cursor is automatically advanced to the next field if the current field is filled. The default setting is OFF.

Date Order

This option has three settings. The default, MDY, displays dates in the mm/dd/yy format. The DMY setting displays dates in dd/mm/yy format. The YMD option displays dates as yy/mm/dd. The default is MDY.

Date Separator

This option has three settings. The default, /, uses the / character as the separator for date fields. The other options are - or . for date separators.

You can change the way the Edit/Browse modes operate by making selections from this box. For example, turn off the beep for full fields by entering

↵

The bell is now set for OFF. Turn on the Century and Confirm settings by entering

```
[down arrow] (2 times)
 ↵
[down arrow]
 ↵
```

To see the effect these selections have on the Edit/Browse modes, exit the settings menu and enter the Append mode.

```
[Ctrl/End]
down arrow
[F2]
```

The DATE field now displays the dates with a 4-digit years component. Keep in mind the setting commands *do not change the contents* of the fields, but only the way they are displayed. If you choose to change the date separator or display order, you have not actually changed the contents of the date fields. The fields return to their original appearance if you change the settings back to the default values. This automatically happens the next time you load dBASE IV.

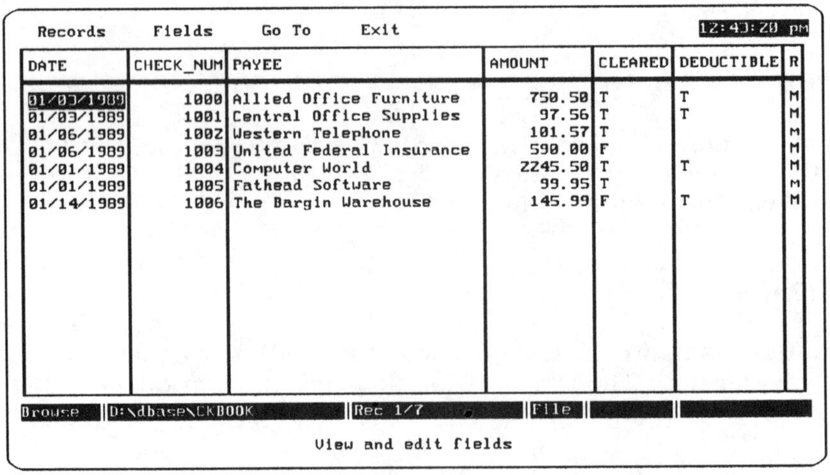

```
 Records      Fields      Go To      Exit                          12:43:20 pm
┌────────────┬──────────┬────────────────────────┬─────────┬────────┬─────────┬──┐
│ DATE       │ CHECK_NUM│PAYEE                    │ AMOUNT  │ CLEARED│DEDUCTIBLE│R │
├────────────┼──────────┼────────────────────────┼─────────┼────────┼─────────┼──┤
│01/03/1989  │     1000 │Allied Office Furniture  │  750.50 │T       │T        │M │
│01/03/1989  │     1001 │Central Office Supplies  │   97.56 │T       │T        │M │
│01/06/1989  │     1002 │Western Telephone        │  101.57 │T       │         │M │
│01/06/1989  │     1003 │United Federal Insurance │  590.00 │F       │         │M │
│01/01/1989  │     1004 │Computer World           │ 2245.50 │T       │T        │M │
│01/01/1989  │     1005 │Fathead Software         │   99.95 │T       │         │M │
│01/14/1989  │     1006 │The Bargin Warehouse     │  145.99 │F       │T        │M │
│            │          │                         │         │        │         │  │
│            │          │                         │         │        │         │  │
└────────────┴──────────┴────────────────────────┴─────────┴────────┴─────────┴──┘
 Browse    D:\dbase\CKBOOK          Rec 1/7            File
                         View and edit fields
```

Figure 2-22. Dates displayed with 4 digit years.

Enter a new record.

```
[Alt-r] a
01151989
```

Notice that when you entered the date no beep sounded, even though the field was filled. This is the result of setting the BELL to OFF. In addition, the cursor did not automatically advance to the next field. This is what happens when the CONFIRM is set ON. The confirmation requires a ↵ or [F4], to indicate you do want to move to the next field. Enter

```
        ↵
        1007 ↵
```

Complete the rest of the record by entering the following data. Notice with the BELL set to OFF and the CONFIRM set to ON, the entry process has a slightly different feel to it.

```
        Central Office Supplies ↵
        67.45 ↵
```

Return to the Control Center display by entering

```
        [Ctrl-End]
```

It is very important to understand that the settings selected on the Settings menu stay in effect only for the current dBASE IV session. If you exit dBASE IV and then re-load the program, the settings return to the default settings.

If you want to use a certain group of settings each time you load dBASE IV, there are two possible solutions. One is to use the dBASE IV macro feature to create a macro that automatically executes the setting you want to use. The other solution is to edit the CONFIG.DB file and enter the keywords for the settings into that file. (See Chapter 16 on dBASE IV Configuration).

Getting Help

dBASE IV provides a context-sensitive help feature. You can access the dBASE IV Help by pressing the [F1] key. dBASE IV displays the Help window closest to the activity you are performing. Because the specific screen displayed depends on what you are doing, the Help is called context sensitive.

At this point, you are at the main Control Center display. Activate Help by entering

```
        [F1]
```

The Help window is displayed in the center of the screen.

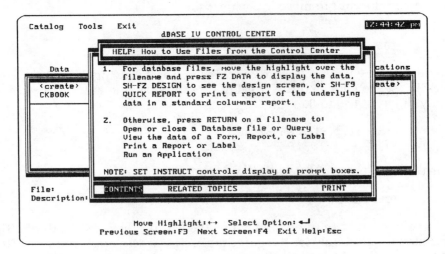

Figure 2-23. Help window display.

The name of the topic dBASE IV selected, appears in a box at the top of the Help window. Here, the topic is How to Use Files from the Control Center. This makes sense because the highlight is located in the Data column.

At the bottom of the Help window are three command options:

Contents

Displays a list of topics.

Related Topics

Displays a list of topics specifically related to the displayed topic.

Print

Prints the text of the displayed topic.

In addition, the [F3] and [F4] keys are assigned special functions in the help system.

[F3]

When a Help topic is displayed, [F3] scrolls the display up to the previous screen or topic. When a list of topics is displayed, [F3] moves up a level to a more general list of headings.

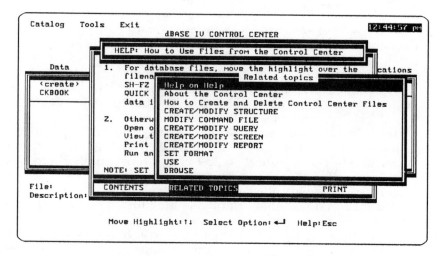

Figure 2-24. Related topics displayed.

[F4]

When a help topic is displayed, [F4] scrolls the display to the next screen or topic. When a list of topics is displayed, [F4] moves down a level to a more specific list of headings.

To display a list of topics related to the current topic, enter

        r

The Related Topics box appears. You can display the related topics by moving the highlight with the arrow keys to the topic you want to read, and pressing ⌐.

Chapter 1 contains more details about the dBASE IV Help system.

To exit Help, enter

        [Esc]   *(2 times)*

Exit the dBASE IV program by entering

        [Alt-e] q

Summary

- **Database Structure.** All databases begin with the creation of a database structure. The structure is a list of the fields used to hold data. A field definition requires you to specify a field name, field type, length, and decimal places for number fields. You also have the option of creating an Index Key file to speed data searches. A database can have up to 255 fields. The total number of characters in all fields cannot exceed 4000 characters.
- **Field Types.** dBASE IV supports six different types of fields: character, number, floating point, date, logical, and memo. Character fields can be 1 to 254 characters; number and floating fields from 1 to 20 characters. Date (8), Logical (1), and Memo (10) fields, are automatically set to default lengths.
- **Database Names.** Each database file must be assigned a name. The names must start with a letter, and can be up to 8 characters in length. Do not create files with single letter names. Such filenames can confuse the program. You can also add a one-line file description that will appear in the Control Center display.
- **Entering Data.** The [F2] keystroke command is used to enter or revise data. You must open a database file in order to use this command. dBASE IV has two Data Entry/Data revise modes: Edit and Browse.
- **Edit Mode.** The Edit mode shows the fields of one record at a time. The fieldnames are listed on the left side of the screen and input areas are placed next to the fieldnames.
- **Browse Mode.** The Browse mode displays data from several records at the same time. The records are displayed as rows in a table. Each column is a field. Fields that cannot fit onto a single screen can be displayed by scrolling to the right or left.
- **Locating Records.** In both the Browse and Edit modes the Goto menu provides methods of locating specific records. You can position the cursor to the top, or bottom of a specific record number. The Forward and Backward search commands will locate records with specific contents in the selected field.
- **Settings.** Settings are commands that affect the way dBASE IV operations are carried out. They effect such things as the method of date display and the movement of the cursor while editing. They do not change the actual data stored in the database file.
- **Help.** The [F1] key command prompts the display of context-sensitive help. You can browse the help display, use a list of contents, ask for a list of related topics, or print the text of the current topic.

Exercises

Ex-1
Return to the top of the database:

        [Alt-g] t

Ex-2
Return to the top of the database:

        [Alt-g] t

Ex-3
    Use *Records Undo* command:

        up arrow

        [Alt-r] u

3

Retrieving Data

The previous chapter demonstrated basic operations by which a database of information is established. As an example, you created a database called CKBOOK to keep track of information generated by a small business checking account. Even though a small amount of information about a few checks was entered, the database will serve as an example of how databases of all sizes are organized with dBASE IV.

This chapter demonstrates how data is retrieved from database files. Retrieving data is more than simply viewing the data previously entered. When a database is small, like CKBOOK, you will find you can analyze the data by simply looking at the information as listed in the Browse or Edit modes. However, as the volume of data grows, this approach does not work. Listing many records and fields, quickly outstrips your ability to comprehend what the data mean. The most meaningful way to look at data is to select groups of information logically related in some way.

For example, you may ask for a list of only the non-deductible expenses for the month of January. On the other hand, you may ask to find checks written to all businesses with the word *telephone* in their name.

These questions enable you to focus your attention on specific characteristics of the database. By retrieving only the data related to the question, you arrive at a list of information that is understandable. In database operations these questions are called *queries*.

This chapter shows how queries are made and used in dBASE IV.

Begin by loading dBASE IV in the usual manner.

You can speed up the loading of dBASE IV by suppressing the time-consuming graphics display showing the Ashton-Tate logo. This is done by starting dBASE IV with the command **dbase/t**. The **/t** is called a switch; it tells dBASE IV to skip the graphics logo and display a simpler text logo, instead.

Listing by Index Order

When you created the structure of the CKBOOK file, you designated the PAYEE field as an indexed field. An advantage of an indexed field is it can be used to display the sequenced records by the data in that field. In the CKBOOK file, you can use the index field PAYEE to list the records in alphabetical order by PAYEE.

When you select a database from the Data column list, dBASE IV opens the file in the *natural* order. The natural order is the order in which the records are entered. In this order, the first record is always Record 1; the records are listed consecutively by record number.

However, if you designate one or more fields as index fields, you can use those indexes to list the records in order based on any one of the indexed fields.

Begin by displaying the data in the CKBOOK database in the natural order. Do this by placing the highlight on the CKBOOK database and entering the Data command [F2]. Enter

        [down arrow]
        [F2]

The records are listed in the natural order—exactly the order in which they were entered.

The next task is to *activate* the PAYEE index so the records are listed according to PAYEE name. This operation is carried out using the Database Design mode—the same mode you used to create the database's structure. Exit the Browse display and return to the main Control Center display by entering

        [Ctrl-End]

Activate the Database Design mode by entering

        [Shift-F2]

The Database Design mode is activated. By default, the Organize menu is displayed.

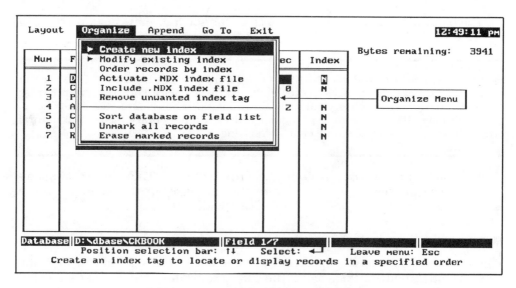

Figure 3-1. Organize menu displayed.

The Organize menu is divided into two sections. The top section contains commands allowing you to create, activate, and remove indexes.

Indexes in dBASE IV

The operation of index files in dBASE IV has been significantly changed from dBASE III and dBASE II, where the index concept remains basically the same. dBASE IV introduces a new form of index file called a *multiple* index. A multiple index file can contain up to 47 different index orders. Each order is called a *tag.*

Multiple indexes overcome a problem that created confusion in previous versions. In those versions, each index order required a unique filename. For example, if you had a file called CKBOOK and you wanted to index the PAYEE field, you could call the index CKBOOK. An NDX extension was added to the index file so it could be distinguished from the DBF (database) file of the same name. The problem occurred when you wanted to create a second, third, or fourth index. Each of those indexes would have to have a unique name. The only way you would know which index files were related to which databases was to remember the names of the index files. If another person wanted to use your data they would have no way of knowing which index files stored on the disk should be used with a given file.

Multiple index files allow you to use a single filename, usually the same as the database file, to store up to 47 different index orders. This makes it simpler to remember which database and index files go together.

dBASE IV fully supports dBASE III NDX indexes, as well as the new multiple index file (MDX). The Control Center menus using the word index refer to dBASE IV multiple indexes, unless they specifically show **.NDX**, indicating these options use dBASE III single index files.

The bottom portion of the menu is used for sorting, marking, and erasing records.

Sorting in dBASE IV (and dBASE III) is a different process from indexing. Sorting creates actual physical changes in the database. Thus, after a sort, the natural order of the database is changed permanently. Indexing does not change the database. It merely displays the records in a particular order on a temporary basis. The natural order of the database is *never* affected by indexing.

The command you want is Order Records by Index. This command allows you to select an existing index order for the database. In this example, there is only one index order, that for the PAYEE field. Enter

o

The program displays two boxes on the right side of the screen. The first box lists the index names, the second the index key value. Index orders created from the file's structure take a name and key value derived from a fieldname. Here, the name is PAYEE.

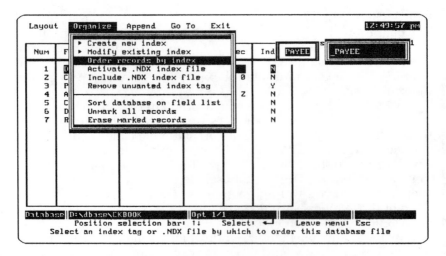

Figure 3-2. Index options displayed.

You can select the PAYEE order by entering

⌐

To see the effect of the index order, enter the Browse mode by pressing

[F2]

The Browse mode appears, showing the records listed in PAYEE order, not the order in which they were entered. Move the cursor to the top of the database by entering

    [Ctrl-PgUp]

You can now see all the records listed alphabetically by PAYEE name.

```
   Records      Fields     Go To      Exit                        12:52:14 pm
  ┌────────┬─────────┬────────────────────────┬────────┬───────┬──────────┬───┐
  │ DATE   │CHECK_NUM│PAYEE                   │AMOUNT  │CLEARED│DEDUCTIBLE│REM│
  ├────────┼─────────┼────────────────────────┼────────┼───────┼──────────┼───┤
  │01/03/89│    1000 │Allied Office Furniture │ 750.50 │T      │T         │MEM│
  │01/03/89│    1001 │Central Office Supplies │  97.56 │T      │T         │MEM│
  │01/15/89│    1007 │Central Office Supplies │  67.45 │       │          │mem│
  │01/01/89│    1004 │Computer World          │2245.50 │T      │T         │MEM│
  │01/01/89│    1005 │Fathead Software        │  99.95 │T      │          │mem│
  │01/14/89│    1006 │The Bargin Warehouse    │ 145.99 │F      │T         │MEM│
  │01/06/89│    1003 │United Federal Insurance│ 590.00 │F      │          │MEM│
  │01/06/89│    1002 │Western Telephone       │ 101.57 │T      │          │mem│
  │        │         │                        │        │       │          │   │
  └────────┴─────────┴────────────────────────┴────────┴───────┴──────────┴───┘
   Browse   D:\dbase\CKBOOK         Rec 1/8          File
                            View and edit fields
```

Figure 3-3. Records listed by PAYEE.

It is important to realize when a file is indexed, the top and bottom of the file are not necessarily the same as the first and last records in the natural order.

When a file is indexed, you have an additional search option in the Browse/Edit modes, Index key search. Enter

    [Alt-g] i

The index key search box appears. Index key searches have two advantages. First, there is no need to position the cursor to a specific field. Because the index key is logically related to a specific field—here the PAYEE field—the cursor can be positioned in any field while you perform this search. The second advantage is more subtle. Searching an index key is much faster than searching a non-indexed field. In a small database such as in this example, the difference in indexed and non-indexed searches is negligible. However, in larger databases, a few hundred records and up, the time saved by indexed searches is extremely significant. The larger the database, the longer the delay caused by a non-indexed search.

For this reason, non-indexed searches in large databases should be avoided whenever possible. Indexed searches, on the other hand, remain fast even when the database grows to a very large size. The size of the database has only a small impact on indexed searches; for this reason they are more desirable. (See sidebar on Search Techniques.)

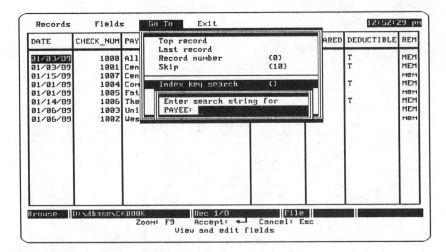

Figure 3-4. Index key search.

Enter the name of the payee you want to find. Notice partial matches *are* permitted in an indexed search. For example, if you are looking for *Fathead Software*, entering *Fat, Fathead, Fathead Soft,* would all find the correct records. Note, however, that *case* is significant. Entering *fathead* or *FatHead* will not match *Fathead Software.* Also keep in mind the matching starts with the first character. For example, entering *Software* for an indexed search would not match *Fathead.*

Finding *Software* with *Fathead Software* is called a *sub-string* match. You can perform this type of search using the Query mode operations, discussed later in this chapter.

Enter

```
Fat ⏎
```

The cursor moves to Record 6. Notice the field location of the cursor remains the same, on the DATE field. If more than one record exists with the same index key value, the search locates the first matching record. Because the file is indexed, all similar records are grouped together. Enter

```
[Alt-g] i
[Home]
[Ctrl-y]
Central ⏎
```

The cursor is moved to Record 2. The two records containing the same payee, 2 and 8, are grouped together by the index file.

Search Techniques

Non-indexed searches proceed with the first record in the database. Each record is examined to see if the field being searched has the desired information. If no match is found, the program moves to the next record. This means as the database grows larger, the amount of time needed to perform the search increases. This type of search is called a *sequential* search because each record is examined in the sequence in which it was entered.

In order to overcome the time delay caused by sequential searches, dBASE IV provides an alternative method called an *indexed* search. Indexed searches require the existence of an index for the field you are searching. An index is a file that maintains a list of the values in a specific field, arranged in alphabetical or numeric order. When you perform an indexed search, dBASE IV does not search the database file. Instead, it looks into the active index file and searches its list of key values. The index file is a highly structured file in which information is organized, not as a sequential list, but as a *binary tree*. The term *tree* implies data is grouped into branches of related information. When you search an index, the program locates the information by searching for the branches most closely matching the information you are looking for.

For example, when you perform an index search for *Fat*, the program skips to the branch, if any, containing records beginning with an *F*. This immediately eliminates all the records beginning with other letters. With a tree-structured file, a record can be located in a fraction of the time it takes to locate a record by sequentially searching the database file.

Keep in mind the actual tree structure of a dBASE IV index file is more complicated than the example given here. However, the basic principle remains the same. As a general rule, non-indexed searches of any but the smallest databases, is tedious. An occasional sequential search is tolerable, but if you intend to look for a large number of records, indexed searching is strongly recommended.

Creating Additional Indexes

In the current sample database, you have designated only one field as an indexed field. dBASE IV permits you to add other indexes whenever you desire. Suppose you wanted to index the AMOUNT field, as well as the PAYEE field. This is accomplished using the Database Design mode. Activate the Database Design mode by entering

```
[Ctrl-End]
[Shift-F2]
```

The simplest way to add an index to a database is to change the structure by entering a Y in the Index column of the field you want to index. By default, the Organize menu is displayed. Remove this menu by entering

> [Esc]

Move the cursor to the AMOUNT field by entering

> [down arrow] *(3 times)*

Jump the cursor to the last column, the Index column, by entering

> [End]

Create an index for this field by entering

> **y**

In addition, you may want to create indexes for DATE and CHECK_NUM. The reason for doing so is different from the reason for selecting PAYEE and AMOUNT as index fields. Ideally, the checks entered will always be entered in the correct date and check number sequence. However, by accident you may enter checks out of the correct order. Indexes on DATE and CHECK-NUM fields ensure a listing in which date or check number order will be correctly listed. But, the most significant reason for indexes on these fields relates to searching. Even if your records are entered in correct date order, dBASE IV still performs a sequential search if the DATE field is not indexed. The only way to perform a rapid search on a field is to have an index for it. This is true even if the natural order of the database is the same as the indexed order for the field.

Change the index settings for the DATE and CHECK_NUM fields. Try this on your own. The correct command is found at the end of the chapter under EX-1.

The first four fields are now set as indexed fields. The actual indexes are created when you save the modifications made to the file's structure. The [Ctrl-End] command is the simplest way to save a structure modification. Here, however, you do not want to Save and Exit because you will activate a new index after it is created. The Layout menu contains a command that saves the structure *without* exiting the Database Design mode. Enter

> [Alt-L] s

The name of the file is displayed to provide you with an opportunity to save the changes as a new file, leaving the previous file as it was. In this case, accept the filename by entering

> ↵

Another box is displayed, warning that you have made changes to the file's structure. A change in a file's structure is a significant change, so dBASE IV wants to make sure you really intend to make this change. Enter

> ↵

dBASE IV displays a series of messages in a box, which flash by too quickly to read. They are not significant and you need not be concerned with them.

These messages are called *talk*. dBASE IV displays talk to confirm certain operations are taking place. For example, when a file is indexed, dBASE IV displays a talk message showing what percentage of the database records have been indexed. When 100% have been indexed, the process is complete. In a small database, such as the current example, the indexing takes place so fast you hardly have time to read the talk before it disappears from the screen. However, in large databases, the talk appears for quite some time. The purpose of talk is to confirm to the user that the operation is being carried out successfully. If the screen were to show no changes as a long operation took place, you would begin to wonder if the computer is working properly, or at all. Talk has no actual affect on the operation, but it helps the user keep track of what the computer is doing.

You can select the index you want to activate. Enter

> **[Alt-o] o**

dBASE IV displays a list of four index choices.

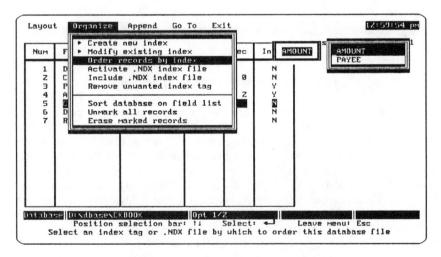

Figure 3-5. Indexes listed in box.

Select the first one on the list, the AMOUNT index, by entering

⏎

Display the records in the AMOUNT order by entering

[F2]

The records appear, ordered by the AMOUNT, from lowest to highest.

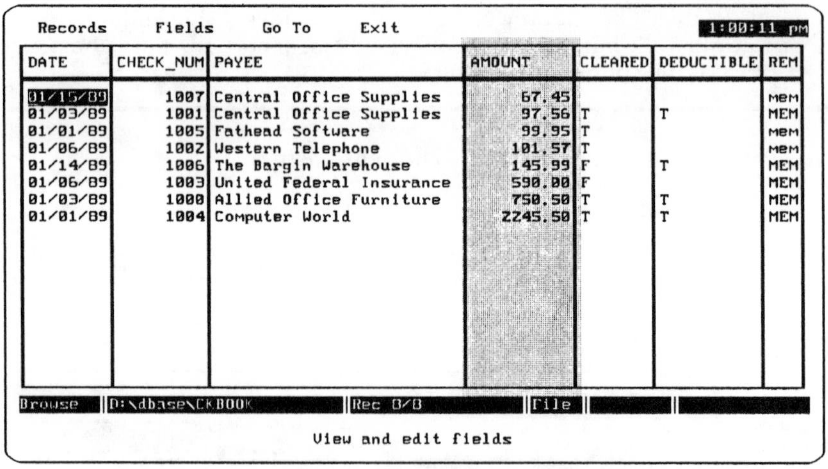

```
   Records      Fields      Go To      Exit                        1:00:11 pm
  ┌────────────┬──────────┬──────────────────────────┬────────┬────────┬─────────┬───┐
  │ DATE       │ CHECK_NUM│ PAYEE                    │ AMOUNT │CLEARED │DEDUCTIBLE│REM│
  ├────────────┼──────────┼──────────────────────────┼────────┼────────┼─────────┼───┤
  │ 01/15/89   │    1007  │ Central Office Supplies  │  67.45 │        │         │mem│
  │ 01/03/89   │    1001  │ Central Office Supplies  │  97.56 │ T      │ T       │MEM│
  │ 01/01/89   │    1005  │ Fathead Software         │  99.95 │ T      │         │mem│
  │ 01/06/89   │    1002  │ Western Telephone        │ 101.57 │ T      │         │mem│
  │ 01/14/89   │    1006  │ The Bargin Warehouse     │ 145.99 │ F      │ T       │MEM│
  │ 01/06/89   │    1003  │ United Federal Insurance │ 590.00 │ F      │         │MEM│
  │ 01/03/89   │    1000  │ Allied Office Furniture  │ 750.50 │ T      │ T       │MEM│
  │ 01/01/89   │    1004  │ Computer World           │2245.50 │ T      │ T       │MEM│
  │            │          │                          │        │        │         │   │
  └────────────┴──────────┴──────────────────────────┴────────┴────────┴─────────┴───┘
  Browse    D:\dbase\CKBOOK          Rec 0/0         File
                              View and edit fields
```

Figure 3-6. Records ordered by amounts.

The order from lowest to highest value is called *ascending* order. *Alphabetical* order is an ascending order because it begins with the lowest letter (A) and moves to the highest letter (Z). Listing records from highest value to lowest is called *descending* order. When you create an index order by selecting the index column in the file structure, the index is always in ascending order.

Suppose you wanted to create an index different from the default-type indexes. For example, you may want to have the amounts listed in descending order. This could be accomplished from the Database Design display, using another of the commands on the Organize menu.

Return to the Database Design mode by entering

    [Ctrl-End]
    [Shift-F2]

Here, you will create an index using the Create New Index command. This command is used to create an index that differs from the ones that are automatically generated by the Index column setting in the file structure. Select the Create New Index command by entering

    ⏎

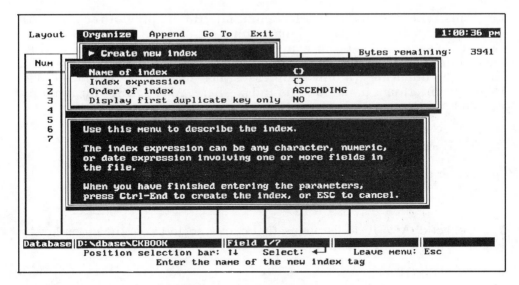

Figure 3-7. Create new index menu.

This command displays a menu with four options.

Name of Index

This is a 1 to 10 character name for the index order. It is probably a good idea to avoid creating an index having the same name as a field, unless you are sure you will not use the Index column option for that field.

Index expression

This option allows you to enter a field name or character expression that will be used as the key value for the index. You should not use a field having a length of more than 100 characters, as the index key. Character expressions allow you to create complicated index keys using advanced dBASE IV expressions. This is covered in detail in Chapter 4.

Order of Index

You can select ascending or descending order for the index.

Display First Duplicate Key Only

This option creates a *unique* index. In a unique index, records having the same key value appear only *once,* no matter how many records contain that key. This type of index is used to eliminate the display of records with duplicate keys. For example, you may want a list of states from a mailing list. Since each state could appear many times, you want only a single record for each state, because duplicates would be confusing. This option does not remove the duplicates; it only suppresses their display in the index order. Begin by entering a name for this index—here, AMT_DESC for (amount descending). Enter

    ⌐

    amt_desc ⌐

Next, enter the index key expression—here, the field AMOUNT.

    ⌐

You can get dBASE IV to list items that can be included in the index key by using the [Shift-F1] command. Enter

    [Shift-F1]

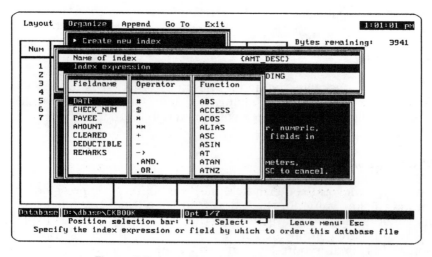

Figure 3-8. Items listed for index expression.

Select the AMOUNT field by highlighting the name of the field you want, and press ⌐. Enter

    [down arrow] *(3 times)*
    ⌐
    ⌐

The default setting for order is ASCENDING. Change this to DESCENDING by entering

⏎

You have now entered the specifications needed to create the index. To carry out the command, enter

[Ctrl-End]

dBASE IV generates the index according to your specifications. One more step remains. In order to see the records displayed in the order selected, you must activate the new index. Try this on your own. The correct command is found at the end of the chapter under EX-2.

Return to the Browse mode to see how this index effects the records.

[F2]

The records are now listed in descending order of amounts.

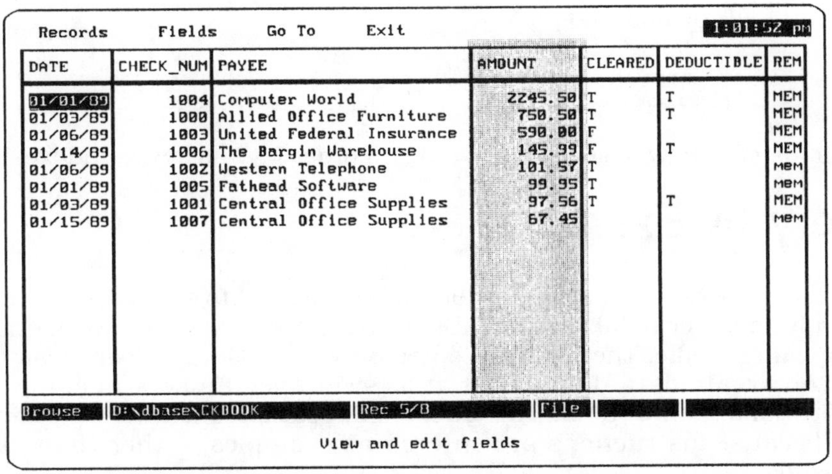

Figure 3-9. Records listed in descending order by amounts.

When you search an indexed file on a number field, you must use the exact numeric amount, in order to locate a record. Enter

[Alt-g] i
97 ⏎

dBASE IV displays a message box saying "** Not Found **". A record exists with the value of 97.56 in its AMOUNT field. But unlike a character field, a number field will match only the exact amount. Try the search again, this time entering the exact amount you are looking for.

```
[Esc]
.56 ↵
```

The cursor is positioned on Record 2 because it contains an exact match for the search key.

Using the Natural Order

When you are finished working with specific indexes, you may want to use the database in its natural order. The simplest way to accomplish this is to close, and then reopen, the database. When a database is closed, all indexes for that database are also closed. When it is opened again, the default setting is to display the records in the natural order. Close the file by entering

```
[Ctrl-End]
↵  (2 times)
```

Reopen the file by entering

```
[down arrow]
↵  (2 times)
```

The database is now open with the natural order (i.e. no active indexes).

Query by Example

This chapter began with a discussion about the need to select specific groups of data from larger databases. dBASE IV has several ways of extracting data from a database file. The Control Center provides a Query mode, designed to help you create data displays that answer specific sets of conditions, qualifications, and criteria. The Query mode is called a *Query by Example* mode because instructions are entered as examples, rather than explicit commands.

dBASE IV allows you to work with queries in two ways. The first is via an Interactive mode where you can design, display, revise, and re-display data, based on queries. If you create a query you want to use again, you can save it in a *query file* and retrieve it at some later point. A query file contains a set of qualifications and examples that dBASE IV uses to retrieve sets of database records.

To begin working with the Query mode, place the highlight into the Queries column and select <create>.

```
right arrow
↵
```

The Query mode display appears.

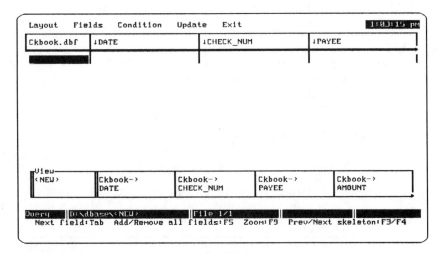

Figure 3-10. Query mode display.

The Query mode display consists of three parts. At the top of the screen is a menu bar with the items Layout, Fields, Condition, Update, and Exit. Below the menu bar is a series of boxes and lines. These boxes and lines are a *model* of the active database. The first box on the left contains the name of the open database file, in this case, Ckbook.dbf. The subsequent boxes represent the fields in the database. Below each box is a blank area. It is into this area you enter the examples used by the Query mode to select data for display. dBASE IV calls this model of the database a *skeleton*. The skeleton at the top of the screen is called a *file skeleton* because it lists all the fields in the current database file.

The bottom section of the screen shows another series of boxes, i.e., another skeleton. This is called the *view skeleton*, because it shows the fields that will be displayed when data is retrieved, and the order in which they will appear.

If there are more fields than can be displayed on a single screen width, the Query mode display scrolls horizontally to accommodate as many fields as exist.

When you first activate the Query mode, the view skeleton contains all the fields shown in the file skeleton. If you look at the file skeleton, you see a down arrow character before each field name, indicating the field is part of the view skeleton.

Controlling Fields

The Query mode provides a means of controlling many aspects of the data display, for example, the number of fields and the order in which they are displayed. When records are displayed in the Browse mode, one column for each field can be seen. The columns are arranged in the same order as they were entered into the file structure.

Suppose you wanted to simplify the data display to show only the DATE, PAYEE, and AMOUNT fields. To do this you must remove all fields from the view skeleton, except the three you want to display.

In this example, the first field to remove is the CHECK_NUM field. Place the highlight in the CHECK_NUM column.

[Tab]   *(2 times)*

To remove the current field from the view, enter

[F5]

Pressing [F5] makes two things happen. First, the down arrow marker in the CHECK_NUM field is removed. Second, the CHECK_NUM box is removed from the view skeleton, indicating it will not be included in the data display.

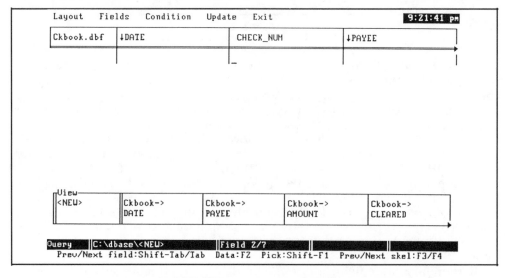

Figure 3-11. CHECK_NUM field removed from view skeleton.

The [F5] key operates as a toggle. If you press it a second time, it will re-insert the field into the view skeleton. The only difference is that it will be placed at the end of the view skeleton, not in its original location between the DATE and PAYEE fields.

Next, remove the CLEARED, DEDUCTIBLE, and REMARKS fields from the view. Enter

```
[Tab]  (3 times)
[F5]
[Tab]
[F5]
[Tab]
[F5]
```

The view skeleton at the bottom of the screen contains only three fields.

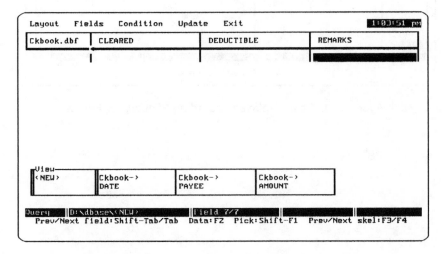

Figure 3-12. View skeleton contains three fields.

The purpose of the skeleton is to act as a control for the data display. Activate the data display by entering

```
[F2]
```

dBASE IV takes a few moments to process the query. Processing refers to the operations required to construct the view, based on the example shown in the Query mode. The data display appears with only the three specified fields displayed.

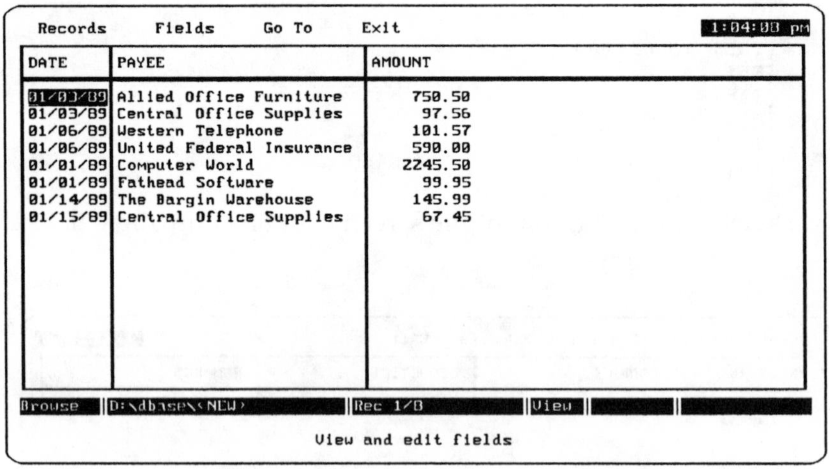

```
  Records      Fields     Go To    Exit                        1:04:00 pm
 ┌────────────┬───────────────────────────┬──────────────────────────────┐
 │ DATE       │ PAYEE                     │ AMOUNT                        │
 ├────────────┼───────────────────────────┼──────────────────────────────┤
 │ 01/03/89   │ Allied Office Furniture   │   750.50                      │
 │ 01/03/89   │ Central Office Supplies   │    97.56                      │
 │ 01/06/89   │ Western Telephone         │   101.57                      │
 │ 01/06/89   │ United Federal Insurance  │   590.00                      │
 │ 01/01/89   │ Computer World            │  2245.50                      │
 │ 01/01/89   │ Fathead Software          │    99.95                      │
 │ 01/14/89   │ The Bargin Warehouse      │   145.99                      │
 │ 01/15/89   │ Central Office Supplies   │    67.45                      │
 │            │                           │                              │
 │            │                           │                              │
 │            │                           │                              │
 │            │                           │                              │
 │            │                           │                              │
 │            │                           │                              │
 └────────────┴───────────────────────────┴──────────────────────────────┘
  Brouse    │D:\dbase\NEW>          │Rec 1/8        │View │
                        View and edit fields
```

Figure 3-13. Data displayed according to query skeleton.

How Queries Are Processed

When you execute or save a query, you will probably notice that the computer is busy doing something that causes a delay before the data can be displayed.

During the delay, the program creates two files that are used to process the query. The first file is the Query by Example file that is stored on the disk with a QBE extension. This file contains two separate items combined into a single file. One section is the Query by Example setup you created in the Query mode, including the skeletons and query items. The second is actually a dBASE IV program, based on the specifications entered into the Query mode display.

The QBE file is then converted into a dBASE IV *object-code file.* An object-code file is used to speed execution of dBASE IV programs. The use of object-code file is new in dBASE IV. For more information, see Part II of this book, Programming dBASE IV.

The object-code file produced from the QBE file is given a QBO extension. It is this file that is actually used to carry out the instructions stored in the QBE file.

The production of these two files, plus the time it takes to execute the commands, create the delay encountered when you execute a query.

If you are familiar with the dBASE programming language you can, in theory, look at or modify the commands that are used to execute a query. The *in theory* caveat has to do with the composition of the QBE file. If you load this file into a text editor, such as the dBASE IV editor, the non-text portion of the file will be truncated when it is saved. The file is thus converted from a QBE file to a dBASE IV program file. The disadvantage is that you can no longer use the file with the Query mode display. If you want to edit a QBE file, you should make a copy before editing.

If you examine the files created by the QBE mode, you may find that the QBE mode has not generated the most efficient way of accomplishing the task. For example, when you select sort orders in the Query mode, a SORT command is used to execute the sequence request. Generally, it is faster to INDEX a database to obtain a sequenced database because SORT involves copying all the records to a new database.

All these factors contribute to the delay experienced when you are executing a query.

Note that once a query is saved, the program will not generate new object-code files each time it is used. The QBO file will remain in force until modifications are made to the query file.

When a query is used to activate the Browse or Edit modes, you can edit or add records, just as you would in the normal Browse or Edit modes. The only restriction is you cannot enter data into fields not currently displayed.

Change from the Browse to the Edit mode by entering

[F2]

The Edit mode display is also restricted to the selected fields.

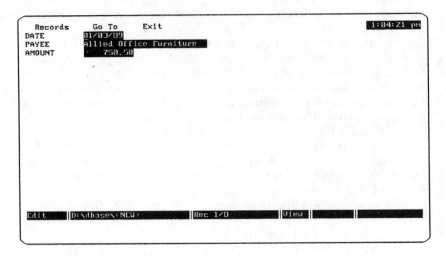

Figure 3-14. Edit modes display restricted to three fields.

You can return to the Query mode to modify the current query by entering

[Shift-F2]

Moving a Field

In addition to removing fields from a view, you can also change the order in which they appear. Suppose instead of the current order of the fields, you wanted to change them to PAYEE, DATE, and then AMOUNT. dBASE IV permits you to move a field or group of fields within the view skeleton.

To move fields in the view skeleton you must move the highlight down to the next skeleton on the display. Enter

[F4]

The highlight moves from the file skeleton to the first field in the view skeleton. Two keys are used in moving a field.

[F6]   This is the select key. When pressed, it is used to mark the field or fields to be moved or removed.

[F7]   This key activates the Move mode. When active, the left arrow and right arrow keys change the position of the selected field or fields. Keep in mind [F7] can only be used after [F6] is used to select the field or fields to be moved.

Select the DATE field by entering

[F6] ⏎

The DATE box is changed to indicate it is the selected field.

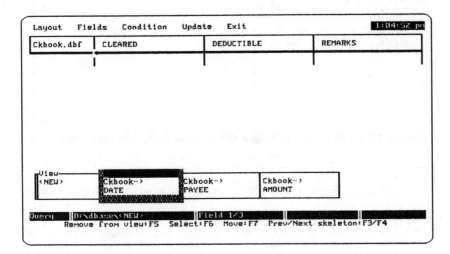

Figure 3-15. Date field selected for moving.

To move the field, enter

[F7]

You can use left arrow or Shift-Tab to move the field to the left, or right arrow or Tab to move the field to the right. Enter

[right arrow]

The DATE field is now positioned between PAYEE and AMOUNT. To fix the position of the field, enter

⏎

Display the data by returning to the Edit/Browse mode.

[F2]

Notice the last active mode, in this case Edit, is automatically re-displayed when processing the query. The fields are displayed in exactly the order you selected in the Query mode. Change to the Browse display by entering

[F2]

This display also conforms to the query specifications.

```
 Records      Fields      Go To     Exit                      1:05:27 PM
 ┌────────────────────────────┬──────────┬──────────────────────────────┐
 │ PAYEE                      │ DATE     │ AMOUNT                       │
 ├────────────────────────────┼──────────┼──────────────────────────────┤
 │ Allied Office Furniture    │ 01/03/89 │    750.50                    │
 │ Central Office Supplies    │ 01/03/89 │     97.56                    │
 │ Western Telephone          │ 01/06/89 │    101.57                    │
 │ United Federal Insurance   │ 01/06/89 │    590.00                    │
 │ Computer World             │ 01/01/89 │   2245.50                    │
 │ Fathead Software           │ 01/01/89 │     99.95                    │
 │ The Bargin Warehouse       │ 01/14/89 │    145.99                    │
 │ Central Office Supplies    │ 01/15/89 │     67.45                    │
 │                            │          │                              │
 │                            │          │                              │
 │                            │          │                              │
 │                            │          │                              │
 │                            │          │                              │
 └────────────────────────────┴──────────┴──────────────────────────────┘
 Browse    D:\dbase\NEW          Rec 1/8            View
                        View and edit fields
```

Figure 3-16. Fields rearranged according to query specifications.

Selection of Records

Another control provided by the Query mode concerns the records displayed. Suppose you wanted to list only the checks not yet cleared. You can create just such a list by entering an *example* into the query skeleton. In this case, the example is used to *filter* records. Filtering means only those records matching the example will be displayed.

Return to the Query mode by entering

[Shift-F2]

Place the highlight on the file skeleton.

[F3]

Suppose you wanted to filter the data so only records not cleared are displayed. In terms of this database, this means displaying those records with a **false** value in the CLEARED field. Move the highlight to the CLEARED field by entering

[Shift-Tab] *(2 times)*

dBASE IV uses special symbols to represent true and false values. These symbols are used only for logical fields or values.

True symbols   .T., .t., .Y., .y.

False symbols   .F., .f., .N., .n.

Here, you want to enter a false value as the example. Enter

.**N**.

Process the query to see the results.

[**F2**]

Only three records are displayed—the records not marked as cleared. You may have noticed because the CLEARED field was not included as part of the view, it was not displayed. This query may make more sense if CLEARED was included. Return to the Query mode and add this field. Then re-process the query. Try this on your own. The correct command is found at the end of the chapter under EX-3.

When finished, the display should look like this:

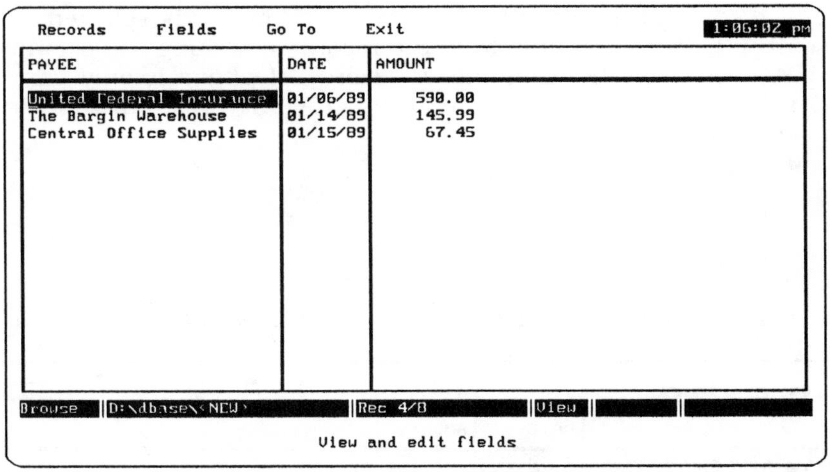

Figure 3-17. Field added to view.

Keep in mind that when a field is added to the view, it is automatically placed at the end of the view. If you desire a different placement, you have to use the Move command to re-arrange the fields.

Return to the Query mode by entering

[**Shift-F2**]

Selecting by Characters

The logical fields are the simplest to use for selection purposes because they are, by definition, either false, the default value, or true. Other field types allow greater variety of entry and require a different type of selection process. Suppose you wanted to display checks written to a certain payee. You would place an example of the payee under the PAYEE box in the file skeleton.

Before you do so, you must *remove* the example from the CLEARED field so the selection selects from all the checks, not just the uncleared ones. Enter

        [Ctrl-y]

Move to the PAYEE field.

        [Shift-Tab]   *(2 times)*

To find the check or checks written to the telephone company, enter an example into the skeleton. Remember, character skeletons *must* be enclosed in quotation marks. Enter

        "Telephone"
        [F2]

dBASE IV displays a message box telling you "No records selected". This is because dBASE IV was unable to locate records matching the example you entered. It is probably the case that the word *Telephone* is only part of the PAYEE entry. You may recall the actual PAYEE entered was *Western Telephone.* Try the selection again.

        ⌐
        [Ctrl-y]
        "Western Telephone"
        [F2]

This time dBASE IV is able to locate the record that you are looking for.

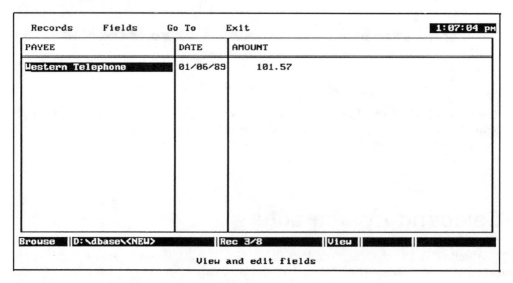

Figure 3-18. Record selected from text example.

Return to the Query mode by entering

        [Shift-F2]

Suppose you did not recall the exact text entered for that record. Try entering

        [Ctrl-y]
        "Western"
        [F2]

Once again, dBASE IV cannot match the example with any of the records. This is because the match must be an exact match, including all the characters entered into the record.

It is likely you will not recall exactly what was entered into the record. There are several ways to attempt to find information when you are not sure of the exact contents of the field you are searching.

One method is to use a Like operator. Like allows you to enter a partial example that can match fields containing that part. The characters *, asterisk, and ?, question mark, are used to indicate *wildcard* characters that will match any characters in the field. The ? is a wildcard for a single character and the * is a wildcard for a group of characters. See the sidebar below for details.

Wildcards
A wildcard is a symbol used to allow you to enter text examples that match records without their having to be an exact duplicate of the original entry. dBASE IV uses the * and ? wildcards in a way similar to the filename wildcards recognized by DOS.

The ? is a *place specific* wildcard. It matches any character appearing at the same relative position. For example, a wildcard *h?t,* will match words such as h*a*t, h*i*t and h*o*t. It will not match *hitter* or *hotter.* The wildcard *h?t* limits matches to three character words beginning with h and ending with t.

The * wildcard will match any group of characters. The wildcard *h*t* will match *height,* *habit* or *halt.*

Note that unlike DOS wildcards, dBASE IV queries are case sensitive; *h*t* will not match *Hot* because of the difference in case.

Enter a Like operator to search for any payees beginning with *West.*

        ⏎
        [Ctrl-y]
        Like "West*"
        [F2]

This search locates the record without requiring you to know the exact entry made for the payee.

Return to the Query mode by entering

        [Shift-F2]

The previous search looked for a payee matching the first word in the example. You can also use the * to match the last word. For example, you can search for all the payees ending with *Telephone*. To do so, you would place the wildcard character, *, in front of the text. Enter

```
[Ctrl-y]
Like "*Telephone"
[F2]
```

Doing so also locates the record because it correctly contains the last word in the field.
    Return to the Query mode by entering

```
[Shift-F2]
```

What if you are not sure the key word you are looking for is either the first, or last word in the field? To find the desired record, place two * wildcards in the example, one before, and one after, the text. Enter

```
[Ctrl-y]
Like "*Tele*"
[F2]
```

This method locates the record by matching the four characters, *Tele*, with any part of the PAYEE field. This example is called a *sub-string* match. *String* is computer terminology for text, i.e., a string of characters. A sub-string is any group of characters within a larger string.
    Return to the Query mode by entering

```
[Shift-F2]
```

A sub-string example can be expressed in another way. Instead of using the Like operator, a dollar sign, $, can be used. Enter

```
[Ctrl-y]
$"Tele"
[F2]
```

The $ used in a query has a similar function, but different implementation from the $ operator used in a logical expression. The dBASE IV expression "Tele"$payee is the equivalent of the query $"Tele". Notice the $ is shifted to the left side of the example text, when used in a query. In all other instances the "Tele"$payee form is correct. This form is also compatible with dBASE III and dBASE II.

This query retrieves the same record. Return to the Query mode by entering

```
[Shift-F2]
```

Use the sub-string examples to locate data based on keywords, when you are not sure where in the field the text will occur. Enter

```
[Ctrl-y]
$"Office"
[F2]
```

This time, three records containing the word *Office* in the PAYEE field are selected.

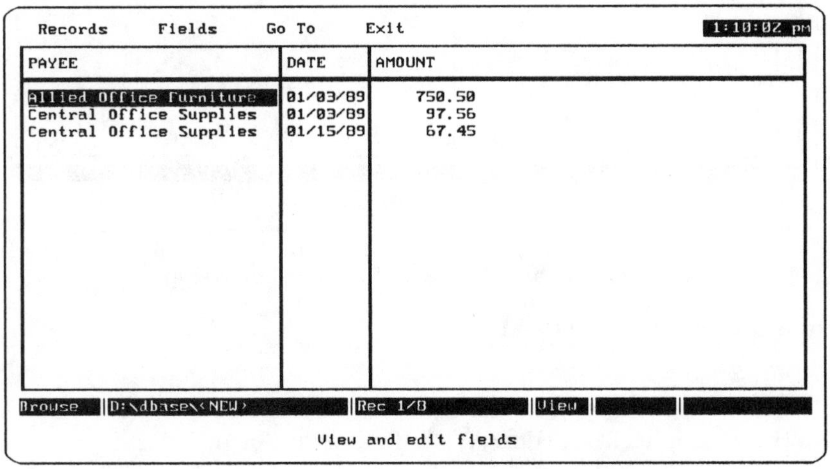

Figure 3-19. Records selected by sub-string example.

Return to the Query mode by entering

```
[Shift-F2]
```

List Processing

Another way to retrieve data is by entering a list of examples. You can search for records by listing possible entries. On the other hand, you may want to retrieve several items by listing several examples.

The current example is **$"Office"**. Add another example to the list. To add and not replace an example, simply press down arrow, then enter the next example below the first.

```
down arrow
Like "*Tele*"
[F2]
```

The resulting display retrieves records matching *either* one of the examples. The effect is that four records are displayed, representing three matches of the first example, and one match of the second.

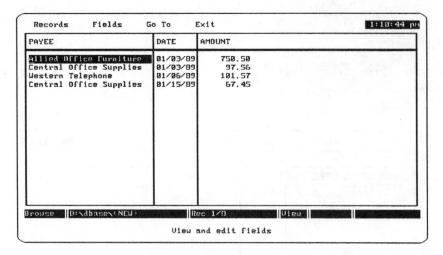

Figure 3-20. Records retrieved from a list of examples.

Return to the Query mode by entering

```
[Shift-F2]
```

Remove the examples from the PAYEE field by entering

```
[Ctrl-y]
up arrow
[Ctrl-y]
```

Date Queries

Information stored in date-type fields requires some special syntax. Place the highlight in the date field by entering

```
[Shift-Tab]   (2 times)
```

When you enter a date as a selection example, it must be surrounded in curly brackets, {}. Enter

```
{01/06/89}
[F2]
```

The records on this display are selected because they both contain the date 01/06/89.

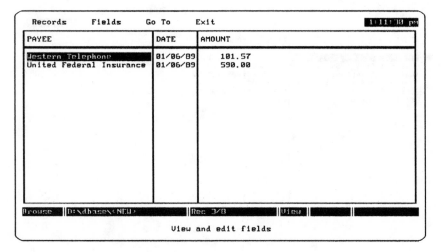

Figure 3-21. Records selected by date examples.

Return to the Query mode by entering

```
[Shift-F2]
```

You can add dates to the list. Enter

```
[down  arrow]
{01/15/89}
[F2]
```

This time, records containing either date are included in the listing.
Return to the Query mode by entering

```
[Shift-F2]
```

dBASE IV dates are subject to logical operations. For example, you can use
the concepts of greater than, or less than, to list dates falling before or after a
specific date. Suppose you wanted to list all the checks written before the
10th of January. First remove the current examples.

```
[Ctrl-y]
[up  arrow]
[Ctrl-y]
```

Use the <= (less than or equal to) symbol in combination with the date
01/10/89. Enter

```
<={01/10/89}
[F2]
```

dBASE IV displays all the records with dates on or before 01/10/89.

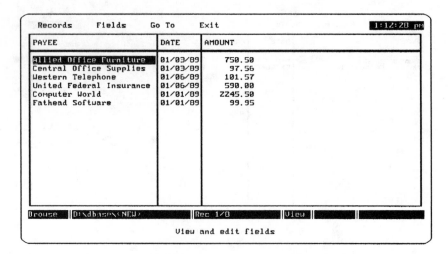

Figure 3-22. Dates selected by less than date example.

Return to the Query mode by entering

    [Shift-F2]

Ranges

A common selection task is to select a group of records falling between a beginning and ending date. In date and numeric fields you can select a range of values by entering two examples on the same line, separated by a comma.

When selecting records, dBASE IV allows you to use the standard mathematical inequality symbols:

Symbol	Meaning
>	Greater than
<	less than
=>	greater than or equal to
<=	less than or equal to
<>	not equal to
#	not equal to

To select for a range of dates, you would enter one example that sets the bottom of the range, and another that sets the upper limit of the range. For example, suppose you wanted to select all the records from January 5th to January 10th, 1989. Enter the following examples. Remember, you need to erase the current example before entering a new example.

```
[Ctrl-y]
>={01/05/89},{01/10/89}
```

Notice dBASE IV scrolls the entry to allow you to enter a longer example than can fit into the skeleton box. If you want to see the full text of the example, use the Zoom key, [F9].

```
[F9]
```

The DATE example box is expanded to a full screen display.

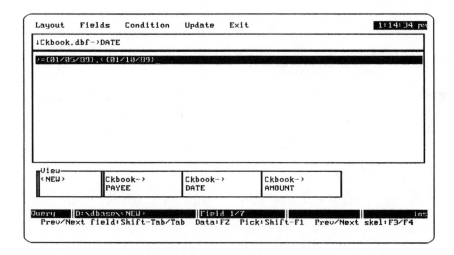

Figure 3-23. Examples box expanded.

You can execute the query directly from the expanded example box.

```
[F2]
```

The records displayed have dates falling within the selected range.
    Return to the Query mode by entering

```
[Shift-F2]
```

Delete the current example by entering

```
[Ctrl-y]
```

Ranges can be applied to number fields in the same way dates can be selected by ranges. This type of selection usually makes sense for numeric values that otherwise require exact matches. Suppose you wanted to select records with AMOUNT values from 50 to 100. Place the highlight in the AMOUNT example box by entering

```
[Tab]   (3 times)
```

Enter the range example.

```
>=50,<=100
[F2]
```

The example selects three records from the database having amount values that fall within the selected range.

Return to the Query mode by entering

```
[Shift-F2]
```

Clear the current example by entering

```
[Ctrl-y]
```

Logical Combinations

The Query mode allows you to combine the effects of examples in several fields, to create a single selection condition. Logical combinations come in two basic forms.

AND Relationships

An AND relationship is one in which a record must match all the examples, in order to be included in the display. For example, if you want to select all the deductible expenses between 01/05/89 and 01/10/89, you need an AND relationship because the records must qualify for both DATE and DEDUCTIBLE, in order to be part of the selection. AND relationships exclude more records because each record must meet several qualifications.

OR Relationships

An OR relationship selects records that meet any one of several examples. For instance, to select records that have cleared or are deductible, use an OR relationship. Several records can qualify if they meet either one of the examples. OR relationships are considered more inclusive because a record has several ways to qualify.

The difference between an AND combination and an OR combination is determined by the line onto which the examples are written. If examples are written on the same line, they are considered as having an AND relationship. If the examples are on different lines, they have an OR relationship.

Begin with an example of an AND relationship. List records that have cleared and are classified as deductible. Move the highlight to the CLEARED field by entering

```
[Tab]
```

Enter the example value.

        .Y.

Do the same for the DEDUCTIBLE field.

        [Tab]
        .Y.

The two examples are in an AND relationship because they are both written on the first line of the example boxes for their respective fields. Before you process the query, add the DEDUCTIBLE field to the view by entering

        [F5]

Execute the query by entering

        [F2]

The AND relationship selects only three records—the only ones having a **true** value in both the CLEARED and DEDUCTIBLE fields.

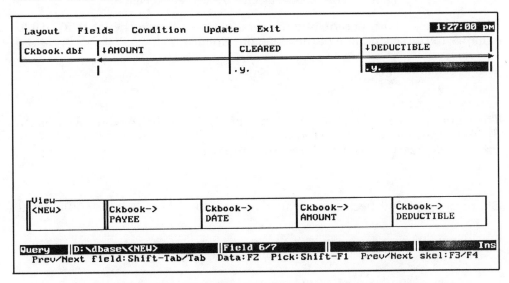

Figure 3-24. CLEARED and DEDUCTIBLE fields with an AND relationship.

Return to the Query mode by entering

        [Shift-F2]

You can change the AND relationship to an OR relationship by placing one of

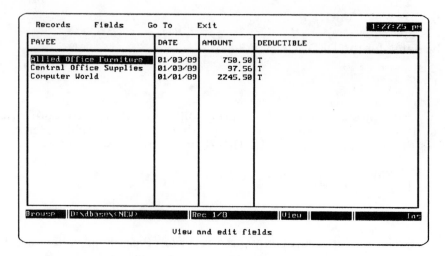

Figure 3-25. Records selected by AND combination.

the examples on a different line. In this instance, move the DEDUCTIBLE example to the second line of the skeleton. Enter

```
[Ctrl-y]
[down  arrow]
.Y.
```

The examples are now in an OR relationship because they are written on different lines of the file skeleton.
Process the query to see which records are retrieved.

```
[F2]
```

Six records qualify because a true value in *either* field is now sufficient to

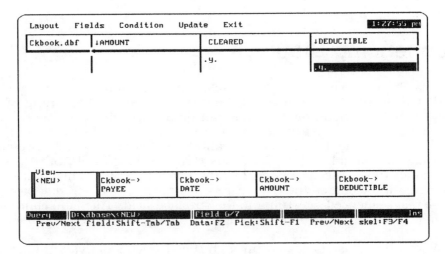

Figure 3-26. Examples written in an OR relationship.

select that record.

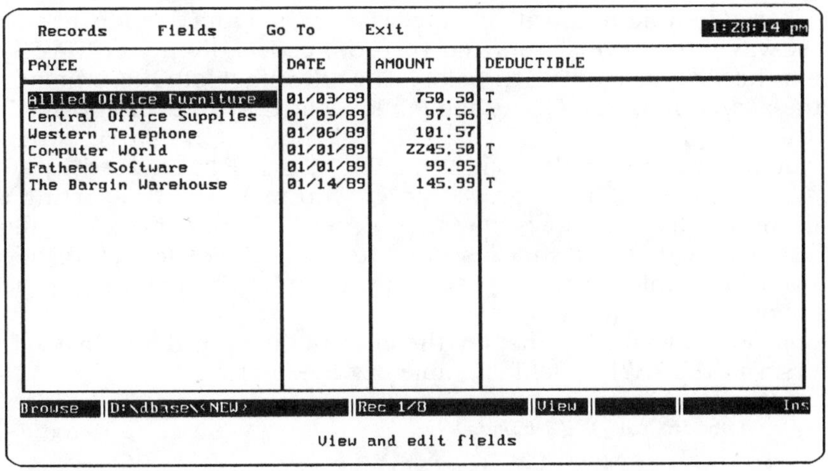

Figure 3-27. Records selected by examples with an OR relationship.

Return to the Query mode by entering

[Shift-F2]

Sequencing Displays

You may have noticed that all the displays generated from the Query mode are listed in the natural order of the database. At the beginning of this chapter you learned how indexes can be used to display records in a sequenced order, and to perform rapid searches.

The Query mode does not take advantage of indexes. Instead, it contains a sorting command listed on the Fields menu. Sorting in dBASE IV uses a different method to sequence records, than does indexing. When a database is sorted, all the data in the database is *re-written* into a new database file, where it is sequenced according to the specified field. This is in contrast to the index method where only the index key values are written into the index file.

When a database is sorted through the Query mode, you are actually generating a new copy of the database file, with its records sequenced in the specified order. This operation takes place automatically and dBASE IV assigns the new file a name, based on the time and date you executed the query. When you have finished the query, dBASE IV erases the sorted file, unless you specifically request it to be saved. The details of the process dBASE IV uses to sort queries are hidden from the user. They are significant because they reveal why the performance characteristics of a Query sort may be very poor. Since Query mode sorts ignore existing indexes, each query causes dBASE IV to sort (i.e. create a sorted copy of the entire database) each time you process the query. If the database is large, this process can take a considerable amount of time. Using the Query mode to sort is the slowest way to retrieve sequenced records, especially if you have specified fields in the database as index fields. The advantage of Query mode sorts is that the structure of the Query mode makes it easy to combine sorting with retrieval examples.

If you are working with a small database, the delay caused by sorting is negligible. As the database grows larger, you may find the sorting delay is significant. (Chapter 4 shows how the dBASE IV Command mode allows you to take advantage of field indexes to perform faster sequenced retrievals.) In the current example, sorting causes only a very slight increase in the time it takes to process the query.

Suppose you wanted to display the current query, ordered by payee. Place the cursor in the PAYEE field example box by entering

[Shift-Tab]   *(3 times)*

To enter a sorting specification you must use the Fields Sort on This Field command. Enter

[Alt-f] s

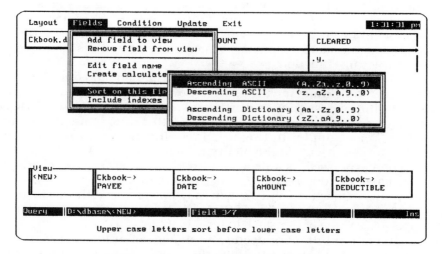

Figure 3-28. Sort on This Field menu.

The command displays a menu containing four choices. The top part of the menu allows you to select either ascending or descending ASCII sorting sequence. ASCII stands for the American Standard Code for Information Interchange (See sidebar). In this sequence, all numbers precede letters. Letters are sorted upper-case A-Z, followed by lower-case a-z. The bottom portion of the menu allows you to select *dictionary* sorting. Dictionary sorting differs from ASCII sequences in the way upper-case and lower-case letters are handled. In the dictionary sort, all words beginning with the same first letter are grouped together, with the lower-case words preceding the upper-case words.

ASCII Sort	Dictionary Sort
0	0
1	1
9	9
Apple	apple
Monkey	Apple
Zelot	monkey
apple	Monkey
monkey	zelot
zelot	Zelot

ASCII coding

The ASCII coding system is one of several coding systems used to translate computer values into characters. ASCII is used by most microcomputers. The EBCDIC (Extended Binary Coded Decimal Interchange Code) is popular on mainframe computers. Both systems serve the same function.

It is important to keep in mind all information stored in a computer is stored as numeric values. These values are binary numbers consisting of a sequence of 0's and 1's. The ASCII and EBCDIC systems assign a character, such as a letter or $, to a specific binary value. For example, in the ASCII coding system, the upper-case character **A** is assigned the binary number 01000001. This number is 65 when expressed as a decimal number. The lower-case character **a** is assigned 01100001, or 97 in decimal notation. The letter **Z** is given the value of 90 while **z** is 122. You may have noticed the decimal value of lower-case letters in the ASCII code is always 32 greater than the upper-case value of the same letter, i.e., 65(A)+32=97(a).

The actual numbers used to represent characters have an effect when you ask the computer to perform operations such as sorting or selecting ranges of values. Since any lower-case letter has a value that is greater than the corresponding upper-case value, sequencing according to ASCII values causes a word beginning with **a** to follow a word beginning with **Z**.

dBASE IV includes a dictionary sort, in which all items with the same first letter are grouped together, regardless of case. Within such a group, the lower-case characters precede the upper-case characters.

ASCII sequencing also affects logical comparisons when characters are used. Suppose you entered the example "M" into a character field. Because the specified value is an upper-case letter, items beginning with N,O,P,...Z,a,b,c,d...z, qualify. On the other hand, if the example was "m", only items beginning with n,o,p...z qualify. A...Z would be excluded.

Select the ASCII ascending sort by entering

⌐

The symbol *Asc1* is written into the example box. This means this field is the primary value for an ascending sort. You can enter additional sort keys. The purpose of the additional sort keys is to sequence the records if the primary field contains records with duplicate values. If no secondary key is specified, records with duplicate primary keys will be listed in their natural order. In this case, make the secondary key the AMOUNT field in descending order. This means if there are duplicate payees, they will be listed in descending order of the amount.

```
[Tab]
[Alt-f] s
down arrow
⏎
```

The symbol *Dsc2* is inserted, indicating this field is the secondary sort key.
Execute the query by entering

[F2]

The records now appear in order, according to the payee name.
Return to the Query mode by entering

```
 Records      Fields       Go To      Exit                        1:32:33 pm
 ┌────────────────────────┬────────┬────────┬──────────────────────────────┐
 │ PAYEE                  │ DATE   │ AMOUNT │ DEDUCTIBLE                    │
 ├────────────────────────┼────────┼────────┼──────────────────────────────┤
 │ Allied Office Furniture│01/03/89│  750.50│ T                            │
 │ Central Office Supplies│01/03/89│   97.56│ T                            │
 │ Computer World         │01/01/89│ 2245.50│ T                            │
 │ Fathead Software       │01/01/89│   99.95│                              │
 │ The Bargin Warehouse   │01/14/89│  145.99│ T                            │
 │ Western Telephone      │01/06/89│  101.57│                              │
 │                        │        │        │                              │
 └────────────────────────┴────────┴────────┴──────────────────────────────┘
 Browse   D:\dbase\NEW         Rec 1/6           View ReadOnly          Ins
                         View and edit fields
```

Figure 3-29. Records sorted by payee.

[Shift-F2]

Saving a Query

After you have created a query, you can save it as a Query file to use at a
later time. A Query file stores all the current settings required to reproduce
the query. It does not store the data (i.e. the fields and records) but only the
Query mode settings used to generate the display. This means you can use
the same query in the future. However, the results may be quite different
because of additions and changes in the content of the database. In most
situations, you will develop a number of queries that will be repeated
whenever you want to view a certain portion of the database.

   To save the query, use the Save This Query option on the Layout menu.
Enter

[Alt-L] s

```
[Alt-L] s
```

You are asked to enter a name for this query. Notice query names, since they will be used as DOS filenames, must follow the same set of restrictions as database filenames. In this case, call the query CLEARED. Enter

```
cleared ↵
```

Saving a Query as a File

The information displayed by the current display query, when you entered [F2] is temporary. When you exit the query, the sorted and selected database—which is what the query is displaying—is erased from the disk. The Query mode provides the option of saving this information as a separate database file. This is useful when you want to return to this specific group of information, without having to process the query again.

Keep in mind that *writing a query as a file* is different from *saving* a query. When you *save* a query, you are saving only the query *instructions* . These instructions can be used to produce a new query display, which will resemble, but not necessarily be the same as, the current information. This is because the data in the database may be changed or expanded. The query instructions operate on the database as it exists, when you execute the query at some time in the future. In most cases, this is what you want when you think about *saving* a query. Query files are assigned a QBE (query by example) file extension.

Writing a query as a database saves the results of the query, not the instructions. This operation is an advantage when the information is gathered from a large database that may take a considerable amount of time to process. Saving the query as a database allows you to return to this exact group of information, without having to re-sort the original database. These files are assigned DBF (database file) extensions because they are database files, just like the CKBOOK file.

To save the data as a new database file, enter

```
[Alt-L] w
```

Enter the name of the database you want to create. dBASE IV automatically inserts a database filename, matching the name you gave to this query, CLEARED.DBF. Enter

```
↵
```

Writing the query as a database takes longer than saving the query. When the operation is complete, exit the Query mode by entering

```
[Esc]
y
```

The Control Center display now shows two new files called CLEARED. One is listed in the Data column, and the other is listed in the Queries column.

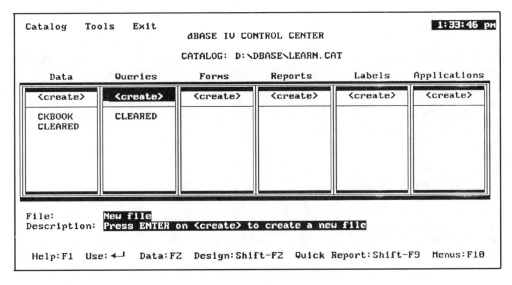

Figure 3-30. New files added to Control Center display.

Activate the query from the file by highlighting the CLEARED query file and entering ⏎.

        [down arrow]
        ⏎

dBASE IV displays a box listing three options: Use view, Modify query, or Display data. Return to the Query mode display by entering

        m

The Query mode display appears with the examples exactly as they were when you saved the query file. Exit the mode by entering

        [Esc]
        y

Loading a database created by a query is exactly like opening any database file. Move the highlight to the CLEARED database.

        [left arrow]
        [down arrow] *(2 times)*

Display the data in this file by entering

```
[F2]
```

The information is displayed, exactly as it was from the query mode. However, there is a difference. The screen you are looking at reflects not a query view of a larger database, but the contents of a unique database file. For example, this file does not have the same structure as the CKBOOK database. When data is written to a database file, the query includes only the fields that were selected to be part of the view skeleton in the query.

Display the structure of this file by entering

```
[Esc]
[Shift/F2]
[Esc]
```

The Data Design display shows this database has only four fields defined. Also note none of the fields is designated as an index field. In the original file, CKBOOK, the DATE, PAYEE, and AMOUNT fields were designated as index fields.

Return to the Control Center display by entering

```
[Esc]
y
```

Removing Files

The CLEARED.DBF file was created to illustrate a point about query operations. Since it has served its purpose, you may want to erase the file from the disk. This can be done from the Catalog menu using the *Remove Highlighted File from Catalog* command. Enter

```
[Alt-c] r
```

dBASE IV displays the message "Are you sure you want to remove this file from the catalog?". Confirm your intention to remove the file by entering

```
y
```

dBASE IV displays an error message box that says "Cannot erase open file". The highlighted database is still open for use. dBASE IV will not erase an open file. This means that you must first close the database before you can remove it. Enter

```
⏎
[Esc]
⏎ (2 times)
```

The file is now closed. Highlight the CLEARED database and carry out the Erase command.

```
down arrow  (2 times)
[Alt-c]  r
y
```

dBASE IV displays a second prompt that asks "Do you also want to delete this file from the disk?".

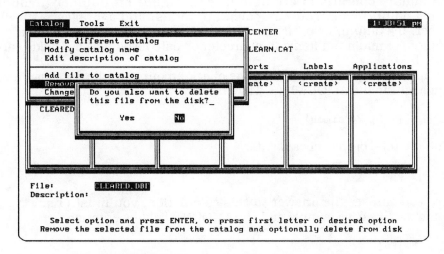

Figure 3-31. Remove file from disk message.

Enter

```
y
```

The file is erased from the disk and the Control Center display.

Summary Displays

In addition to displaying selected records and fields, the Query mode can be used to summarize the information in the database. Activate the Query mode by entering

```
[right arrow]
↵
```

The Layout menu is automatically displayed because there is no database currently open. In order to create a query, a database file must be open. To select a file, enter

```
↵
```

The program lists the database files—here, only one, CKBOOK. Select this file by entering

⏎

When a database is opened from within the Query mode, the view skeleton is empty.

Summary operations are usually carried out on number (including floating point) fields. You can calculate totals, and averages, as well as number, maximum, or minimum values. You can also count or locate the maximum or minimum items in character or date fields. Logical fields can be counted.

Suppose you wanted to total all the check amounts in the database. Place the highlight in the AMOUNT field by entering

[Tab] *(4 times)*

To find the total of the checks, enter

sum

Before you can see the answer to this calculation, you must create a view skeleton. In this case, simply add the AMOUNT field by entering

[F5]

Calculate the query by entering

[F2]

The value 4098.52 appears on the data display screen. Return to the Query mode by entering

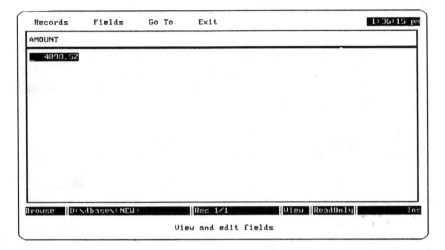

Figure 3-32. Sum of **AMOUNT** field calculated by query.

> [Shift-F2]

dBASE IV allows the following summary operators in queries:

Operator	Result
sum	totals field values
avg	calculates field average
count	counts records
max	finds largest value or last item by alphabet
min	finds smallest value or first item by alphabet

You can add calculations to any of the other fields. For example, you may want to count the number of checks by counting the check numbers. Place the highlight in the CHECK_NUM field and enter the count command in the example box.

> [Shift-Tab]   *(2 times)*
> count

Add the field to the view skeleton by entering

> [F5]

Note the CHECK_NUM view box follows the AMOUNT box. You may want to reverse their order. Try this on your own. The correct command is found at the end of the chapter under EX-4.

Execute the query by entering

[F2]

This time, there are two columns showing eight checks, totalling 4098.52. You may have noticed the display does not indicate the meaning of the value (i.e., sum, count, or average). You must recall what you specified in the various columns. Return to the Query mode by entering

[Shift-F2]

You can add examples into the field boxes to produce summaries of selected records. For instance, if you wanted to total all the DEDUCTIBLE checks,

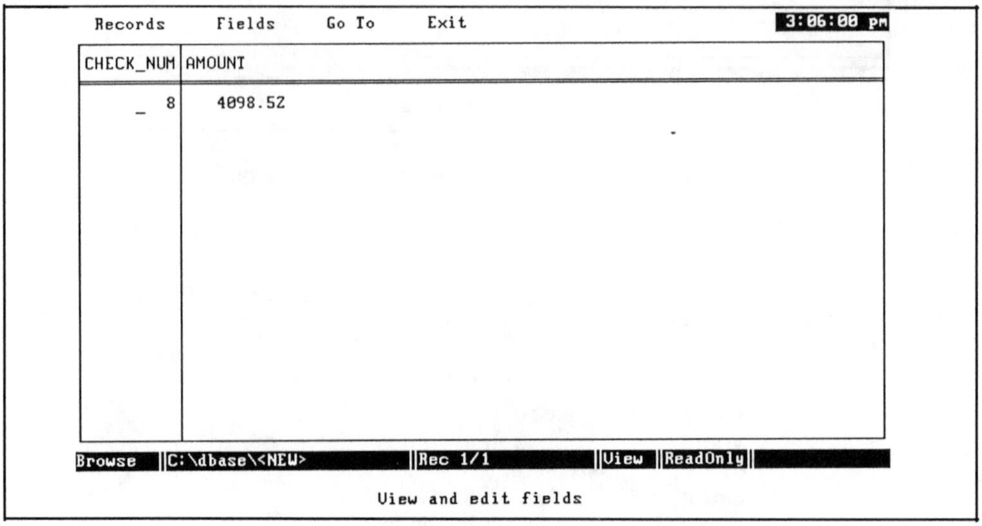

```
    Records      Fields      Go To      Exit                    3:06:00 pm

   CHECK_NUM AMOUNT

         _ 8    4098.52                                          .




   Browse  ║C:\dbase\<NEW>              ║Rec 1/1          ║View ║ReadOnly║
                             View and edit fields
```

Figure 3-33. Query calculates selected records.

you would select those records having a true value in the DEDUCTIBLE field. Add this example to the query. Try this on your own. The correct command is found at the end of the chapter under EX-5.

Display the values for this query by entering

[F2]

This time, the program calculates four records with a total value of 3239.55. Return to the Query mode by entering

[Shift-F2]

You cannot enter more than one calculation per field. For example, you may want to find the sum and average of the amounts. However, this cannot be done using both *sum* and *avg* in the same field.

Subtotal Groups

The Query mode has another method of calculation, which is also related to sorting. This feature summarizes information by groups. The Group By operator generates a summary value for each unique item in the specified field. For example, the DATE field shows that on some days more than one check was written. You can use the Group By operators to summarize each day's total.

First, remove the example from the DEDUCT field.

        [Ctrl-y]

Move to the DATE field by entering

        [Home]
        [Tab]

In the Query mode, [Home] moves to the beginning of a skeleton, and [End] moves to the end of the skeleton.

To create a summary for each day, enter

        group by

Before you execute the query, add the DATE field to the view.

        [F5]
        [F2]

The query creates a list of unique dates, summarizes the number of checks, and totals the amount for each day.

Exit the Query mode and return to the Control Center by entering

        [Esc]
        n

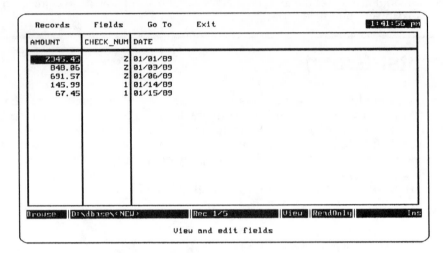

Figure 3-34. Records grouped by dates.

The Group By operator works with date, character, or number fields. It cannot be used with logical or memo fields.

Unique Lists

Another variation on the theme of grouped queries is a Unique query. A Unique query displays records having a unique value in the specified field. If two or more records have the same value, only one record with that value is displayed. Return to the Query mode by entering

⏎

Suppose you wanted to obtain a list of payees. In this case, the number of checks written to the payee does not matter. You merely want to create a list of names in which each payee appears only once.

First, clear the view skeleton of fields. This can be done by pressing [F5], while the highlight is positioned in the filename box at the beginning of the skeleton (which is the case now.)

[F5]

The Unique operator is different from other operators used thus far in the Query mode. Instead of placing the operator in a specific field, this operator is placed in the filename box at the left of the skeleton. In this example, the box reads CKBOOK.DBF, the name of the current database file. Enter

```
unique
```

The contents of the list are controlled by the selection of fields for the file skeleton. Here, create a list of unique payees by adding the PAYEE field to the view skeleton, which is currently empty.

```
[Tab]   (3 times)
[F5]
```

Execute the query by entering

```
[F2]
```

This query produces a list of payees, with duplicate payee names eliminated.

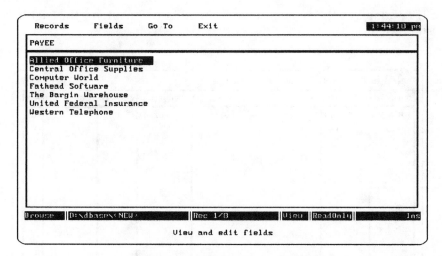

Figure 3-35. Unique records selected.

Escape from the present query and start a new query from the Control Center. Enter

```
[Esc]
```

Find

A second operator used in the filename box of the file skeleton, is the *Find* operator. Find works differently than selection operator. When the Find operator is placed into the filename box, it changes the way in which selection examples work. Instead of selecting individual records for display, all records are displayed. However, the highlight is not positioned on the first record, but on the first record matching the selection example. The Find operator functions much like the Goto Search command in the Browse mode.

Create a new query by entering

        ⏎

Enter the Find operator in the filename box.

        find

You may want to find a record with a certain date. Enter the following example in the DATE field.

        [Tab]
        {01/10/89}
        [F2]

dBASE IV displays the normal Browse mode but positions the highlight on Record 5, the first record with the date of 01/10/89.

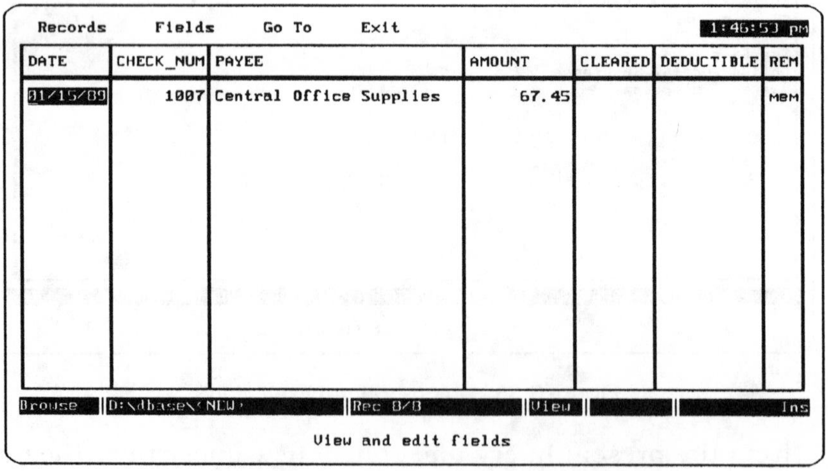

Records	Fields	Go To	Exit				1:46:53 pm

DATE	CHECK_NUM	PAYEE	AMOUNT	CLEARED	DEDUCTIBLE	REM
01/15/89	1007	Central Office Supplies	67.45			mem

Browse | D:\dbase\(NEW) | Rec 8/8 | View | | Ins

View and edit fields

Figure 3-36. Find operator positions highlight.

The Find operator does not affect the Browse mode, which operates normally from this point. Begin a new query by exiting the current mode.

        [Esc]
        n
        ⏎

Calculated Fields

Up to this point, the operations carried out in the Query mode have been based on the fields you created in the database structure. The Query mode allows you the option of creating temporary fields called *Calculated* fields. The contents of Calculated fields are determined by a formula calculating the values, based on information in existing fields. Typically, this type of field is used to generate arithmetic values calculated from the data in existing Number fields. However, dBASE IV provides special functions that perform useful operations on Date and Character fields, as well.

Clear the display skeleton.

    [F5]

Begin by creating a Calculated field based on a numeric formula. Clear the view skeleton. Try this on your own. The correct command is found at the end of the chapter under EX-6.

As an example of how a numeric calculation can be used to create a Calculated field, recall that the AMOUNT field does not show what portion of the expense is sales tax. Assuming a sales tax of 6% was charged on all the items, you can calculate what the non-taxed portion of AMOUNT originally was.

Calculated fields are created by using the Fields Create Calculated Field command.

    [Alt-f] c

This command adds a new skeleton, labeled "Calc'd Flds", to the Query mode display. This skeleton is different because the fieldname box and the example box are both empty. To create a Calculated field, you must enter a formula into the fieldname box. Enter

    amount/1.06

This field, when displayed, will show the amount of the purchase before tax.

The formula used to find the original value increased by a percentage, takes the general form, below:

    AMOUNT/(1+PERCENTAGE)

This formula calculates *x* in the question: *What number(x) increased by a certain PERCENTAGE equals the AMOUNT?*

The amount of the increase, in this case the tax amount, is then calculated.

Query Variable Names

In addition to calculating the pre-tax purchase price, it may be useful to add another field to calculate the amount of sales tax. This is an easy calculation when you already have the AMOUNT and the pre-tax price calculated. You merely need to subtract the two fields to find the amount of sales tax.

However, there is a small problem. The Calculated field you have just entered does not have an actual fieldname, as do the fields that are part of the original database structure. In order to overcome this problem, the Query mode allows you to assign a name to a field—this name is called a *variable.*

In the Query mode, an example entered into the file skeleton is assumed to refer to the contents of the field in which the example is entered. Variables provide a means by which you can refer to the contents of another field when writing an example. The first step in using variables is to place the variable name in the example area of a field you want to reference. Here, the Calculated field needs to be assigned a variable name. Variable names follow the same rules as fieldnames: 1 to 10 characters and no spaces. Enter

```
[down arrow]
purch_pr
```

Add another calculated field.

```
[Alt-f] c
```

This field calculates the amount of tax charged on each item. In the formula, you can use the variable name *purch_pr* to refer to the calculated value in that field. Enter

```
amount-purch_pr
```

The last step is to add to the view skeleton the fields you want to display. Move back to the field skeleton and add the PAYEE and AMOUNT fields.

```
[F3]
[Tab]  (3 times)
[F5]
[Tab]
[F5]
```

Next, return to the Calculated fields skeleton and add the Calculated fields to the view.

```
[F4]
[F5]
```

When you add a calculated field to the view skeleton, dBASE IV asks you to enter a fieldname for that field. This is the temporary name for the Calculated field, and appears in the data display. Enter

        sales_tax ↵

Add the other Calculated field to the view.

        [Shift-Tab]
        [F5]
        purchase ↵

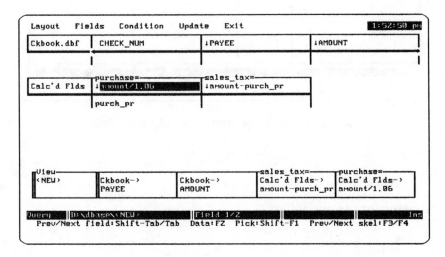

Figure 3-37. Calculated fields created in query mode.

Display the results of the query by entering

        [F2]

The display shows the amount of tax and the pre-tax purchase price for each record.

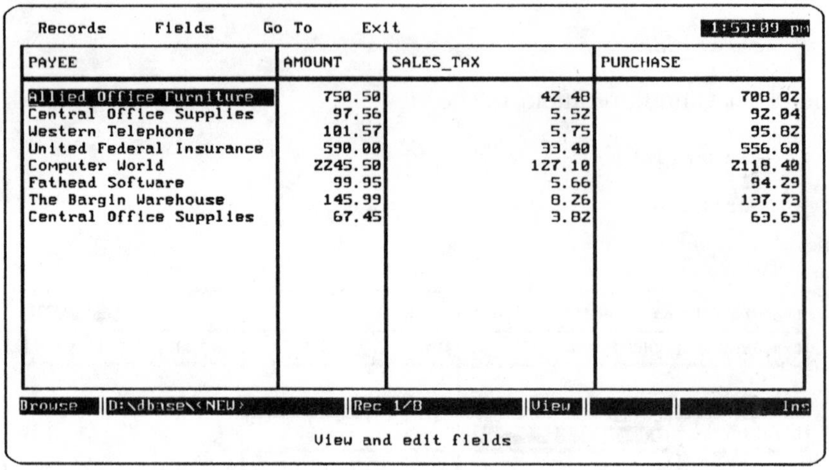

```
   Records      Fields     Go To      Exit                        1:53:09 pm
  ┌─────────────────────┬──────────┬────────────────┬─────────────────────┐
  │ PAYEE               │ AMOUNT   │ SALES_TAX      │ PURCHASE            │
  ├─────────────────────┼──────────┼────────────────┼─────────────────────┤
  │▓Allied Office Furniture  750.50           42.48                 708.02 │
  │ Central Office Supplies   97.56            5.52                  92.04  │
  │ Western Telephone        101.57            5.75                  95.82  │
  │ United Federal Insurance 590.00           33.40                 556.60  │
  │ Computer World          2245.50          127.10                2118.40  │
  │ Fathead Software          99.95            5.66                  94.29  │
  │ The Bargin Warehouse     145.99            8.26                 137.73  │
  │ Central Office Supplies   67.45            3.82                  63.63  │
  │                                                                         │
  │                                                                         │
  │                                                                         │
  │                                                                         │
  │                                                                         │
  │                                                                         │
  ├─────────────────────┴──────────┴────────────────┴─────────────────────┤
  │ Browse   D:\dbase\<NEW>           Rec 1/8          View              Ins│
  └─────────────────────────────────────────────────────────────────────────┘
                           View and edit fields
```

Figure 3-38. Values generated by calculated fields.

Save the query for use at some later time by entering

> [Ctrl-End]

Enter a name for the query file.

> y
> sales_tx ↵

A second query filename, SALES_TX, appears in the Queries column.

Date and Character Calculated Fields

While calculations based on numeric values are the most obvious use for calculated fields, dBASE IV has the ability to create calculated fields that generate data, based on the contents of Character and Date fields. Create a new query by entering

> ↵

Select the CKBOOK database for this query by entering

> ↵
> ↵

dBASE IV provides a series of date functions used to generate information from date fields. Below are some of the dBASE IV date functions:

Function	Result
DATE()	current system date
MONTH()	number value of month
DAY()	number value of day
YEAR()	number value of year
DOW()	number value day of week
CMONTH()	text, month name
CDOW()	text, day of week name

For example, by using the CDOW() function you can obtain a listing of the day of the week each check was written. Create a calculated field by entering

```
[Alt-f] c
cdow(date)
```

Create a view listing the Date and the Calculated field by entering

```
[F5]
day ↵
[F3]
[Tab]
[F5]
```

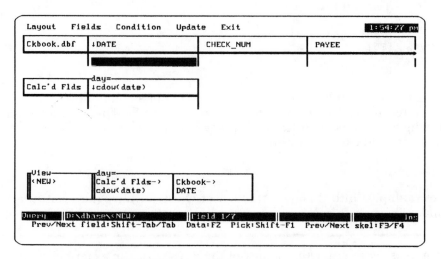

Figure 3-39. Calculated field for day of the week.

Display the results by entering

```
[F2]
```

The Calculated field lists the day of the week for each date.

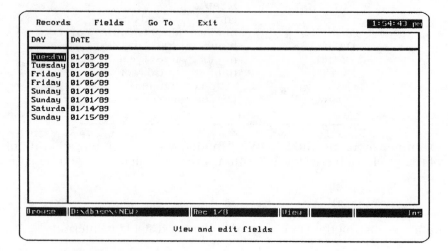

Figure 3-40. Day of the week added by a Calculated field.

Return to the Query mode by entering

    [Shift-F2]

Add the PAYEE and AMOUNT fields to the view.

    [Tab]   *(2 times)*
    [F5]
    [Tab]
    [F5]

You can select records based on the results of a calculated field. Suppose you wanted to list any checks written on weekends. This could be done by entering examples into the Calculated field example box. Move to the Calculated field skeleton by entering

    [F4]

Enter examples into this field that select weekend days (i.e. "Saturday" and "Sunday").

It is necessary to enter the names of the days with the exact characters and capitalization shown. Entering "Saturday" or "Sat." will not match the full day of the week generated by the Calculated field.

```
[down arrow]
 "Saturday"
[down arrow]
 "Sunday"
 [F2]
```

The query selects the two checks written on weekend days.

```
   Records      Fields      Go To     Exit                    1:55:45 PM
┌──────┬────────┬────────────────────────────┬──────────────────────────┐
│ DAY  │ DATE   │ PAYEE                      │ AMOUNT                   │
├──────┴────────┴────────────────────────────┴──────────────────────────┤
│ Sunday 01/01/89 Computer World               ZZ45.58                   │
│ Sunday 01/01/89 Fathead Software               99.95                   │
│ Saturd 01/14/89 The Bargin Warehouse          145.99                   │
│ Sunday 01/15/89 Central Office Supplies        67.45                   │
│                                                                        │
│                                                                        │
│                                                                        │
│                                                                        │
│                                                                        │
├────────────────────────────────────────────────────────────────────────┤
│ Browse │ D:\dbase\<NEW>        │ Rec 5/8      │ View │         │   Ins   │
├────────────────────────────────────────────────────────────────────────┤
                          View and edit fields
```

Figure 3-41. Records selected according to calculated field.

Save this query as a query file called WEEK_END by entering

```
[Ctrl-End]
y
week_end ⏎
```

Condition Boxes

The final aspect of the query process in this chapter is the Condition Box. The Condition Box is used to insert a standard dBASE IV command level expression into a query, that will operate as a filtering mechanism for records. Condition Boxes allow you to enter record selection expressions that go beyond those provided directly by the Query mode.

Using condition boxes requires an understanding of dBASE IV command-level forms and syntax. This subject is covered in detail in Chapter 4. However, some simple examples of how to use these expressions within the Query mode are useful because they point out how you can overcome some of the inherent limitations of the Query mode specifications.

Create a new query for the CKBOOK file by entering

```
⏎  (3 times)
```

The first area requiring a condition box is in the selection of records based on the contents of Memo fields. You cannot enter a character example into a Memo field skeleton example box as you would enter into a Character field example box. The special way in which Memo field data is stored requires a different method.

Suppose you wanted to select records by searching the REMARKS field, a Memo field, for the word desk.

If REMARKS were a character field, the example *Like "*desk*"* placed in the example box would work. But because REMARKS is a Memo field, you need to create a Condition Box expression. The correct form of the expression for a Memo field would be *"desk"$REMARKS.* This expression reads *"desk" is some part of the REMARKS field.*

Add a Condition Box to the query by entering

        `[Alt-c] a`

Enter an expression to the condition box.

        `"desk"$remarks`

Add fields to the view skeleton and then execute the query.

        `[F3]`
        `[Tab]` *(3 times)*
        `[F5]`
        `[End]`
        `[F5]`
        `[F2]`

The query selects Record 1. Check the contents of the Memo field by entering

        `[Tab]`
        `[F9]`

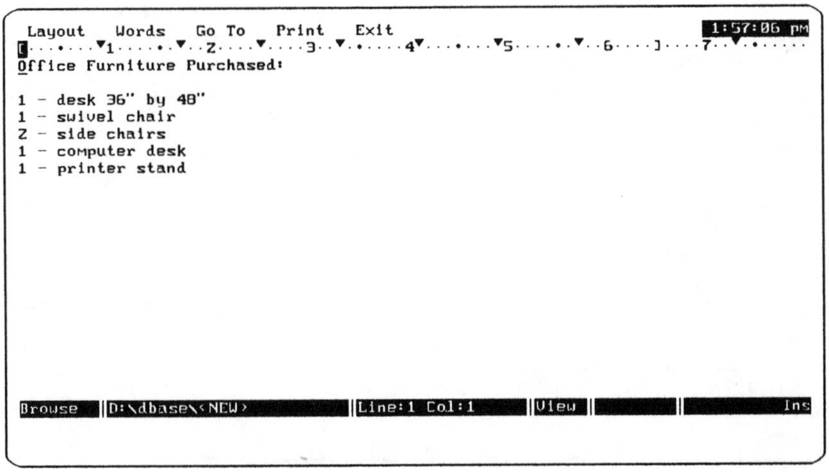

```
 Layout   Words   Go To   Print   Exit                    1:57:06 pM
[.....·..▼1·····•.▼..z·····▼·····3··▼·•·····4▼·······▼5·····•▼··6····]····7··▼·•·····
Office Furniture Purchased:

1 - desk 36" by 48"
1 - swivel chair
2 - side chairs
1 - computer desk
1 - printer stand




















 Browse  D:\dbase\<NEW>          Line:1 Col:1      View              Ins
```

Figure 3-42. Record selected by memo field contents.

Return to the Query mode by entering

```
[F9]
[Shift-F2]
```

Another operation that can be implemented in the condition box is the *case insensitive* search. The Query mode examples used with Character fields select records when the example text exactly matches the field text, including the case of the letters. The Condition Box allows you to enter specifications that use dBASE IV conversion functions to eliminate the *case sensitivity* of the selection process. One way to do this is to use the UPPER() function to convert the text to all upper-case characters. For example, the expression "WORLD"$UPPER(payee) would select payees with *world*, *World* or *WORLD* in the payee name.

Note that it is crucial that the characters within quotations are UPPER-case characters. For example the expression "world"$UPPER(payee) would *never* select any records because, by definition, the UPPER() of any text contains all upper-case characters; these would never match any of the lower-case characters in *world*. Characters entered between quotation marks are called *literals* because they are used exactly as they are entered. In dBASE IV command words, functions, filenames, fieldnames and operators, which are part of the dBASE IV command structure, are not case sensitive and can be entered in any case. Examples:

Correct:
"WORLD"$UPPER(payee)
"WORLD"$UPPER(PAYEE)
"WORLD"$upper(payee)

Incorrect:
"world"$UPPER(payee)
"world"$UPPER(PAYEE)
"world"$upper(payee)

Change the condition by entering

```
[F4]
[Home]
[Ctrl-y]
"WORLD"$UPPER(payee)
```

Execute the query by entering

```
[F2]
```

The condition expression locates the record ignoring differences in case.

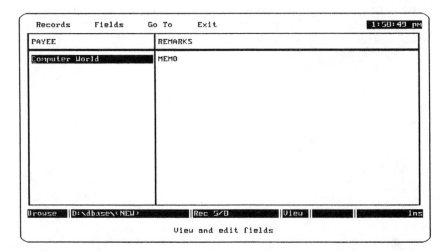

Figure 3-43. Case insensitive query created with condition box.

Close the Query mode and exit dBASE IV by entering

```
[Esc]
n
[Alt-e]  q
```

Summary

- **Indexes.** Indexes are used to sequence records in order, according to the contents of the fields. A field index can be created by entering Y in the Index column of the file structure. Indexes also provide a method by which large databases can be searched at a high rate of speed. Indexes do not change the database file. The records in the database remain stored in the order in which they were entered.

- **Query By Example.** dBASE IV provides a Query mode in which groups of records can be selected by entering examples into the Query mode skeletons.

- **Skeletons.** A skeleton is a model of some part of a database query. Each query uses a file skeleton, which lists the fields in the structure of the database. The view skeleton is used to select the fields and their order of appearance. You can also choose to use the Calculated field skeleton.

- **Examples.** The dBASE IV Query mode uses examples to select records from the database. Examples can be entered into character, number, date or logical fields. dBASE IV selects all records that match the example entered into each field.

- **Logical Operators.** Logical operators are standard mathematical inequality symbols used to indicate less than, greater than, or not equal relationships, used in selecting records.

- **Logical Combinations.** If more than one example is entered into a query, you can form them into AND or OR logical combinations of query examples. Examples entered on the same line of the example boxes are considered as AND combinations. Examples entered on different lines of the example boxes are considered as OR combinations.

- **Sorting Queries.** Sorting is performed in a query by selecting a sort order form the Fields menu. Field indexes are not used in the Query mode. When a sorted query is processed, all the selected records are re-written into a new database file. This file is erased when you are finished with the query.

- **Saving Queries.** A query file, QBE extension, saves a group of query examples for use at some later time.

- **Writing Data.** You can capture the data output by a query as a new database file. This options is useful when you have sorted a large database and wish to return to it without having to re-process the query.

- **Summary Operators.** You can calculate a summary value, sum, average, count, maximum, or minimum, by entering a Summary operator in the desired example box.

- **Group By.** The Group By operator works in conjunction with Summary operators to produce a summary sub-total for each group of unique values in the specified field.

- **File Operators.** File operators, such as Find or Unique, affect the operation of the query. Find causes the query to display all records, but positions the highlight on the record that matches the example. Unique causes the query to suppress records with duplicate values in the example field.

- **Variables.** A variable is a temporary name assigned to a field. It allows the field to be referenced in an example entered into a different field.

- **Calculated Fields.** These are fields generated by calculations on number, date, or character fields.

- **Condition Boxes.** Condition Boxes allow you to directly enter a a dBASE IV command level expression into a query. This option allows you to perform selection operations not directly supported by the Query operators.

Exercises

Ex-1
   Set the index column:

```
[PgUp]
[End]
y
[End]
y
```

Ex-2
   Activate the index:

```
[Alt-o] o
[down arrow]
⏎
```

Ex-3

Add the CLEARED field to the view:

```
[Shift/F2]
[F5]
[F2]
```

Ex-4

Change the order of the fields in the view skeleton:

```
[F4]
[F6] ⌐
[F7]
[Tab]
⌐
[F3]
```

Ex-5

Select the records for DEDUCTIBLE is true:

```
[Shift-Tab]   (4 times)
.Y.
```

Ex-6

Remove the view skeleton:

```
[F4]
[F5]   (7 times)
```

4

Command Level Operations

In the previous chapters you carried out the basic database operations of data entry and retrieval using the dBASE IV Control Center commands. However, the same operations can be carried out using the dBASE IV Command Language.

In this chapter you will learn what the dBASE IV Command Language is and how it is used, and gain an understanding of the relative advantages and disadvantages of the Command Language in contrast to Control Center operations.

To begin, load dBASE IV in the usual manner. This will place you at the main Control Center display.

What Is the Command Language?

As mentioned in Chapter 1, dBASE IV has three major levels of operation. In Chapters 2 and 3 you used the Menu system level to create a database, and then enter and retrieve data.

In this chapter you will look at how dBASE IV can be operated on the second level, that of the Command Language. The name *Command Language* provides a hint as to the major difference between it and the Control Center level. As implied by the word *language*, the commands in it are entered by writing out complete sentences. The sentences consists of actions(verbs), keywords(field names, file names, etc.), clauses(command options), literals(text or numbers) or any valid dBASE IV expression.

Each command sentence is a complete instruction that tells dBASE IV what you want to do. As in all languages, you must enter the sentence with the proper syntax, spelling, and punctuation if dBASE IV is to understand the command. This makes the command level a bit harder to work with at first, since you have to learn the correct way to write the command sentences. When you use the Control Center, the commands and options are selected from the menus, making the process easier to learn and use.

However, despite the fact that it is harder to learn, the Command Level has advantages. Once you are familiar with the commands you want to use, the Command Level allows you to work faster and more efficiently than the Control Center menus.

Another advantage of the Command Level is that you can use techniques not available from the Control Center menus. dBASE IV has so many commands that not all the commands or command sequences possible in dBASE IV can be accounted for from the Control Center menu. The Command Level offers a richer variety of operations and options than you find in the Control Center.

In most cases you will find you will use both the Control Center and the Command Level to carry out day to day operations. Every user will divide his or her work between the two modes differently, depending on personal preferences and circumstances. While it is possible to use dBASE IV totally in the Control Center or Command Level exclusively, blending the two modes into your daily work is usually preferable.

All the operations carried out through the Control Center menu can also be carried out by Command Level commands. However, the reverse is not true. There are some operations that can only be carried out at the Command Level, since there is no menu command equivalent. The Command Language provides the user with greater control over database operations than the Control Center.

The Dot Prompt Mode

The dBASE IV Command Language requires that you enter complete command sentences. The Control Center display does not provide a method by which these sentences can be entered. It is therefore necessary to exit the Control Center and activate the dBASE IV command mode. You can exit the Control Center in two ways.

[Esc]

If you enter Esc from the main Control Center display you can deactivate the Control Center by confirming the prompt that asks "Are you sure you want to abandon operation?". Note that confirming this action will not cause any loss of data. The prompt is merely the standard prompt dBASE IV displays when Esc is used to exit a dBASE IV mode.

Exit command

You can use the Exit menu to select the command Exit to dot prompt. This method avoids the "Are you sure you want to abandon operation?" message. Enter

        [Alt-e] e

This action causes dBASE IV to remove the Control Center display from the screen and replace it with the Command mode display. This display is very simple. It consists of two items. At the bottom of the screen is a highlighted bar called the *status* bar. At this moment, the left side of the bar shows the word Command indicating that the Command mode is active. The status bar is divided into five sections.

Section	Shows
1. Mode	current mode
2. File	active file name
3. Cursor/pointer	cursor or pointer location
4. Type of file	file type
5. Toggle	status of toggle keys

Above the line there is a single period next to which the cursor is flashing.

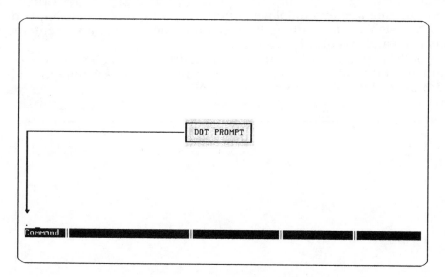

Figure 4-1. Dot prompt mode display.

The period, referred to as the *dot*, is the command entry prompt. When it is displayed with the cursor flashing, it means dBASE IV is ready to accept a command sentence. This mode is usually referred to as the *Dot Prompt* mode because the period is used as the prompt character.

Entering a Command

The most difficult part of using the Dot Prompt or Command mode is that you need to know the commands you want to enter, since there are no menus from which to choose. With a little experience, you will find that the Dot Prompt is not really so intimidating as first it appears.

It is important to understand that the logic of dBASE IV Dot Prompt operations is the same as it is in the Control Center. You still create and use files in the same way. Data entry and retrieval require the same logic. The only difference is that in the Dot Prompt mode you compose sentences, rather than pick options from a menu.

Suppose you wanted to retrieve data as you did in the previous chapter, using the query mode from the Control Center. The first step would be to open the database file from which you wanted to display data. This is accomplished with the USE command. In order to open a specific file, you must follow the USE with the name of the file you want to open. In this case you want to open the CKBOOK file. Enter

    USE ckbook ↵

What happened when you entered the command? Not very much, at least visually speaking. Following the command, dBASE IV moved the screen display up one line and displayed another Dot Prompt. This simple action has a very significant meaning. It means that the command you entered was understood and executed by dBASE IV.

If you look at status line you will also notice some small changes. The full pathname of the database file, the current record number, the total number of records, and the file type are now displayed.

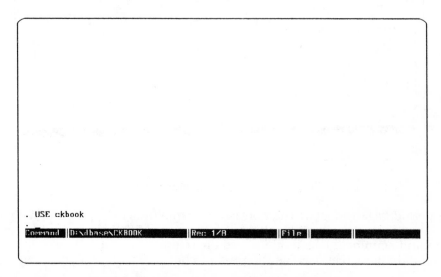

```
. USE ckbook
.
Command  D:\dbase\CKBOOK          Rec: 1/8          File
```

Figure 4-2. File opened in Dot Prompt mode.

But where is the data? Why isn't it displayed? The answer is you have not given dBASE IV a command to display it, merely one to open the file. This is an important difference between Control Center and Dot Prompt commands. Control Center commands will often execute several steps at once. For example, when you highlight a database file and press [F2], the data key, the Control Center will open the file and display the data in the Browse or *Edit* mode, whichever was used last.

However, when you enter commands at the Dot Prompt, you will find that each command performs a small part of the task. Suppose you wanted to view the data in the Browse mode. You have to enter a specific command to activate Browse. Enter

    BROWSE ⏎

dBASE IV now displays the data in the Browse mode format. To return to the Dot Prompt, enter

    [Alt-e] e

The Edit mode is accessed by entering the command EDIT.

    EDIT ⏎

dBASE IV activates the EDIT mode display.
    Return to the Dot Prompt by entering

    [Alt-e] e

Closing the database also uses a separate command, CLOSE DATABASE. Enter

    CLOSE DATABASE ⏎

Note that the information about the file is removed from the status line, indicating there is no longer an open database file.

Syntax and Structure

Before continuing it might be helpful to discuss the basic structure of commands entered in the Dot Prompt mode. All the commands have one thing in common: they begin with a command *verb*. A command verb is a word or phrase that tells dBASE IV the action you want to carry out. In the previous sequence of commands you used four command verbs: USE, BROWSE, EDIT, and CLOSE DATABASE. The entire dBASE IV Command Language contains almost 300 command verbs.

Note the terms *command* and *command verb* will often refer to the same thing. The term *command verb* is used when you want to specify the difference between the entire command sentence and the command verb that begins the sentence.

In some cases a command verb by itself is a complete command sentence. Example: CLOSE DATABASE. This command is complete because it automatically assume that the database you want to close is the one that is currently open.

On the other hand, command verbs often require the name of a file or field to complete the sentence. If you were speaking of English grammar you would call the filename or field name an object. For example, the command USE ckbook uses a verb, USE, and an object, ckbook, to form a complete command. The USE command requires an object so that dBASE IV can know which database file to open. Without the object there would be no way for the program to know what you wanted to do.

Capitalization

You may have noticed that the command sentences so far have used capitalization in a special way. The command verbs have all been entered in upper-case characters, while the objects have been entered in lower-case.

This capitalization is not necessary. dBASE IV will ignore any differences in upper- and lower-case in command sentences. dBASE IV will view all the commands listed below as the same command and perform the same action in each case.

use ckbook
USE CKBOOK
Use Ckbook
USE ckbook
use CKBOOK

But why have the commands in this book mixed upper- and lower-case letters in a special way? The answer is that a special convention is followed to make it easier for you to pick out the parts of the command that are dBASE IV command verbs or other keywords from the portions of the commands that are user-defined terms, such as file names and field names.

When you are entering commands you can use whichever case (usually the lower) that feels comfortable.

You need to keep in mind one exception to this rule. When information is enclosed in quotation marks it is called a **text literal**. Example: "Western Telephone".

Literals are used for comparison to text entered into database fields. In these cases you *must* enter the text between the quotation marks with the capitalization shown if the command is to have the proper effect.

Four Letter Abbreviations

dBASE IV allows you to take a short cut when entering command sentences. Command verbs or other keywords can be abbreviated by entering the first four letters of the command. For example, instead of entering CLOSE DATABASE you can enter CLOS DATA or close data. dBASE IV will execute the commands exactly as if you had entered the full command verbs.

Keep in mind that you can only abbreviate commands or keywords (in this book, the parts of the command sentence written in upper-case characters). You cannot abbreviate user-defined terms, such as field names. For example, the command USE ckbook cannot be abbreviated to USE ckbo because *ckbook* is the name of a file which dBASE IV must locate on the disk. If you enter ckbo, dBASE IV will look for the file CKBO.DBF, not CKBOOK.DBF.

In this book all commands will appear written with the full command word or phrase. This makes them easier to read and understand. You may feel free to abbreviate the words shown in upper-case.

File Lists

One of the advantages of the Control Center is it can be used to select files—such as database or view files—from the lists that appear on the Control Center displays. dBASE IV provides a way in which you can obtain a list of files to select from when entering commands in the Dot Prompt mode. Commands that open files, (e.g., USE) will take a special object—?. If the ? is used instead of the filename, dBASE IV displays a list of files from which you can choose. This method is an alternative to entering the exact filename. Enter

        USE ? ↵

dBASE IV displays a window that allows you to select from a list of files.

You need to keep in mind one exception to this rule. When information is enclosed in quotation marks it is called a *text literal*. Example: "Western Telephone".

Literals are used for comparison to text entered into database fields. In these cases you *must* enter the text between the quotation marks with the cap-italization shown if the command is to have the proper effect.

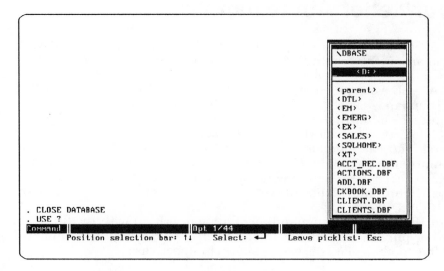

Figure 4-3. File selection window activated with ?.

You can select a file by placing the highlight on the filename and pressing ↵. You can also locate a filename, when the list is long, using the speed search method. The speed search moves the highlight to the first item that matches the letter or letters you enter.

Your instinct is probably to use the highlight to select CKBOOK.DBF. However, for the purposes of writing instructions, the speed search method eliminates problems that might be caused by differences in the file lists on different computers. (You can ignore the speed search instruction below and use the highlight method if you desire.) Enter

ckb
↵

The CKBOOK file is opened. How do you know? The status line shows the name of the database file, thus confirming the result of the command.

Adding Data

Once a database file has been opened, you can add data to it. There are three commands that allow you to enter new records.

EDIT

This command activates the Edit mode, which is the same as one used from the Control Center. To add new records, you must move past the last record in the file or use the [Alt-L] a command.

APPEND

This command is actually a form of the EDIT command. The difference is that APPEND automatically moves you to the end of the database and starts with a new, blank record.

BROWSE

This command activates the Browse mode, the same as the one from the Control Center, which has the option for appending new records, [Alt-L] a.

In this case, the most direct way to add new records is the APPEND command. Enter

> **APPEND** ↵

dBASE IV displays the editing screen display with a blank record, 9, ready to accept data. Note that the left end of the status line shows Edit, indicating that you are using the Edit mode display to enter information. Enter the following records:

> ```
> 020289
> 1008
> Sunset Variety ↵
> 25.89
> ↵
> ↵
> [F9]
> groundhog day greeting cards
> [F9]
> ↵
> 
> 020989
> 1009
> Advanced Copier Service ↵
> 175 ↵
> ```

Exit the Append mode by entering

> **[Alt-e] e**

Upon exiting, you return to the Dot Prompt mode display. Note that the status bar shows there are now a total of 10 records in the database.

The APPEND command is an example of what dBASE IV calls a *Full Screen* mode command. This type of command is in contrast to commands, such as USE or CLOSE DATABASE that execute and return immediately to the Dot Prompt. The Full Screen commands actually take over the entire screen display and continue operating until you specifically enter a command to exit. The dBASE IV Command Language contains both types of commands.

The EDIT and BROWSE commands are also full-screen commands. You can enter those modes by entering the commands at the Dot Prompt. This process is similar to selecting an operational mode from the Control Center. The main difference is that at the Dot Prompt you type the commands, while in Control Center, you select the commands from a menu. Enter

```
EDIT ↵
```

dBASE IV enters the Edit mode and displays record 10, the last entered into the database. You can switch to the Browse mode the same way that you did in the Control Center by entering

```
[F2]
```

The screen display changes to the Browse mode display. Add another record by entering

```
down arrow
y
021289
1010
Valley Power & Light ↵
101.70
```

Exit the full-screen display and return to the Dot Prompt by entering

```
[Alt-e] e
```

The status line shows there are now eleven records in the database.

Selection and Sequencing

In addition to data entry you can perform data retrieval from the Dot Prompt. When retrieving data there are two operations that you want to perform.

Selection

Selection refers to picking out specific fields and records to be displayed or edited. You can select fields, records, or some combination of both. The selection process always involves the use of a logical expression. A logical expression is a comparison that can be evaluated as being true or false.

Sequencing

Sequencing refers to the process of ordering records according to a key field or value. dBASE IV uses two methods of sequencing, sorting and indexing.

In the Control Center Query mode these operations were specified on the

Query display and executed as a unit. On the Command level you will find that each Query process requires a unique command. You will also see that there are several ways to carry out selecting and sequencing.

Fields Selection

When you use the EDIT and BROWSE commands dBASE IV will normally display all of the fields in the database structure as part of the full-screen display. You learned in the previous chapter how the view skeleton in the Query mode could be used to limit the fields displayed. You can select fields from the Dot Prompt mode by using the FIELDS clause with the EDIT or BROWSE commands. A *clause* is a keyword that can be used with certain dBASE IV command verbs to modify the way in which the verb carries out its task.

Specifically, the FIELDS clause allows you to specify which fields you want displayed in the full-screen EDIT or BROWSE. For example, suppose you wanted to browse only the PAYEE, DATE, and AMOUNT fields. Enter

        BROWSE FIELDS payee,date,amount ↵

Move to the top of the file by entering

        [Ctrl-PgUp]

The Browse display shows only the three fields specified in the command. Also note that the order in which the fields are displayed matches the order in which the field names appeared in the command. The FIELDS clause is useful in selecting and arranging the fields for a Full-Screen Display command.

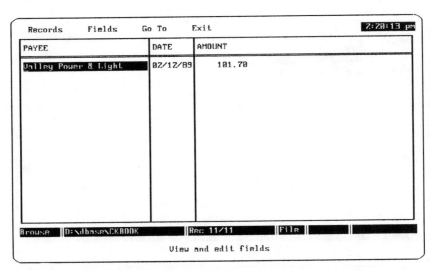

Figure 4-4. Browse mode activated for selected fields.

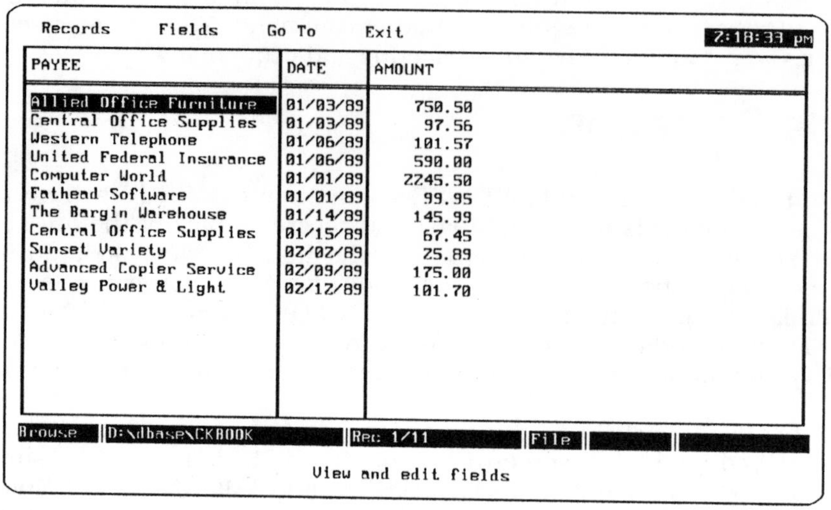

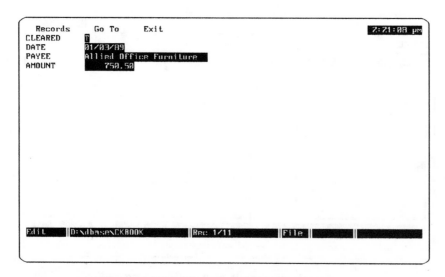

Figure 4-5. Browse with selected fields.

Return to the dot prompt by entering

```
[Alt-e] e
```

You can use the clause with the EDIT command as well. Enter

```
EDIT FIELDS cleared,date,payee,amount    ⏎
```

The full-screen edit display shows the fields you selected in the order you selected.

Figure 4-6. Fields selected for edit display.

Return to the Dot Prompt by entering

```
[Alt-e] e
```

Selecting Records

The other type of selection is the choosing of records from the database. There are two ways to select records:

Physical

Physical selection refers to selecting records according to their physical position in the database file.

Logical

Logical selection uses the stored data as the means by which records are selected. The user must specify a logical condition used to qualify the records.

The physical selection process is the simplest. The process uses special Command Language keywords called *scopes*.

RECORD n

Selects the record indicated by the value used in place of *n*.

NEXT n

Selects the next n records beginning with the current record.

ALL

Selects all records in the database from top to bottom.

REST

Selects all records in the database starting with the current record to the bottom of the database.

By default, the EDIT command assumes that you want all the records in the database included, (i.e., the default scope is ALL).

Suppose that you wanted to select just a single record, e.g., Record 7. Enter

```
EDIT RECORD 7 ↵
```

dBASE IV displays Record 7 in the Edit display. Enter

```
[PgDn]
```

The command terminates and returns to the Dot Prompt. Why? In a normal editing situation, entering [PgDn] would cause the next record in the database, (in this case Record 8) to be displayed. But because you used the scope RECORD 7 with the EDIT command, you limited its operation to the single records that you designated.

You can limit editing to a specified number of records with the NEXT scope. Enter

```
EDIT NEXT 2 ↵
```

Record 8 is displayed. Enter

```
[PgDn]
```

Record 9 appears. Enter

```
[PgDn]
```

The Dot Prompt returns. In this example the editing operation was restricted to the next two records. Keep in mind that NEXT is not directional. You could move up or down in the database. The limit is two records in one direction or the other, but not both.

You can combine a FIELDS clause with a scope to edit specific fields in specific records. Enter

```
EDIT FIELDS cleared,date,check_num   RECORD 7 ↵
```

The command causes the fields and record you specified, to be displayed for editing. You can see that the command sentences provide you with very precise control over dBASE IV operations. Return to the Dot Prompt by entering

```
[PgDn]
```

Command Shortcuts

When entering commands, you can often eliminate some of the typing by using previous commands. dBASE IV automatically remembers the last 20 commands entered at the Dot Prompt. The list of commands is called *history*. You can access any of the last 20 commands by entering the up arrow key. Enter:

```
[up arrow]
```

The command you just entered reappears. Note that the cursor is positioned at the end of the line rather than at the beginning. You can edit the command and execute the edited version. For example, you might want to use Record 5. Enter

```
[backspace]
5 ↵
[Pg Dn]
```

You can edit commands as much as necessary. For example, suppose you wanted to remove the CLEARED field from the command. Enter

```
[up arrow]
```

You can move one word at a time by using the [Ctrl-left arrow] and [Ctrl-right arrow] keys. Note that lists separated by commas with no spaces are treated as a single word. Enter

```
[Ctrl-left arrow]  (3 times)
[Del]  (8 times)
↵
[Pg Dn]
```

This time the command executed with only two fields.

Correcting Mistakes

Suppose you enter a command incorrectly. Enter

```
EDIT RECORF 7 ↵
```

dBASE IV displays a window showing you have entered a command containing an error. You have three options: 1) Cancel the command and return to the Dot Prompt, 2) Edit the command to correct your mistake, or 3) display Help. In this case choose Edit.

```
e
```

The cursor is returned to the command you have just entered. Make the correct and retry the command.

```
[backspace]  (3 times)
D 7 ↵
[Pg Dn]
```

The command is executed with the correct syntax. You can move backwards for up to 20 commands. Suppose that you wanted to execute the same command that you executed when you began this section. Enter

```
[up  arrow](5 times)
↵
  [Pg Dn]
```

Note that when browsing the list of previous commands, you can move forward by pressing the down arrow key as well as move backwards through the list. If you decide that you want to start with a clean Dot Prompt command line, you can clear the old command from the line by pressing [Esc].

Special Edit Clauses

The EDIT command also provides a clause that can be used as a shortcut to repeat the same display setup as previously used. For example, suppose you now want to edit Record 3 using the same three fields as you specified for Record 7. You don't have to add the clause *FIELDS cleared,date,check_num*. Instead, you can enter the NOINIT clause. This causes dBASE IV to use the same settings as the previous EDIT command. Enter

```
EDIT NOINIT RECORD 3 ↵
```

Record 3 is displayed with the same screen setup as used with the previous command.

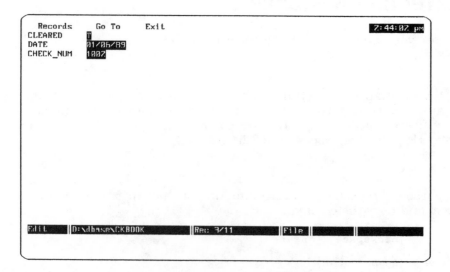

Figure 4-7. NOINIT reuses previous settings.

Return to the Dot Prompt by entering

    [PgDn]

NOINIT stands for *no initialization*. The concept is that each time the EDIT command is used, dBASE IV returns to the default settings, (i.e display all fields). By suppressing this initialization process, the command uses the set of specifications entered for that command.

You might have noticed that when you exited the Edit mode the screen cleared. It might be helpful sometimes if the data you displayed remained on the screen after you exited from the Edit mode. The data could be useful in determining what command you wanted to enter next. The NOCLEAR clause will suppress the automatic clearing that normally takes place when you exit a full-screen operation. Enter

        EDIT NOINIT NOCLEAR RECORD 9
        [PgDn]

This time the information remains on the screen after you exit the full-screen mode.

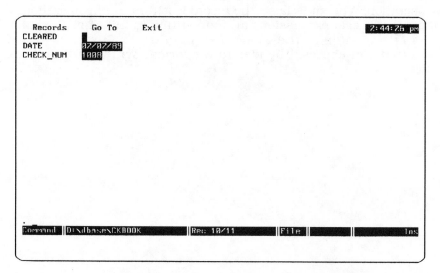

Figure 4-8. Data remains on screen after exiting.

Logical Selection

While physical selection of records is simple, it is not the most useful way of choosing the records you need to work with. Logical selection chooses records based on their contents. This is usually a more meaningful technique than selecting by record number.

One of the most important and powerful clauses in the entire dBASE IV language is the FOR clause. It provides you with the power to perform selections of almost any type in dBASE IV. The FOR clause has all the power of the Query mode—and then some—wrapped up in a single clause. You will find that most of the commands in the dBASE IV language involving records allow you to use a FOR clause as a logical selection tool.

The key to using the FOR clause is knowing how to write a logical expression. In the previous chapter, you created logical conditions by writing examples into the Query mode file skeleton. In the Dot Prompt mode you need to express those ideas in a slightly different form, called a *logical expression*. The purpose of the logical expression is to provide a test with which dBASE IV can determine which records should be included in the operation specified by the command verb.

Logical expressions always pose a true or false question, e.g., *Is the value in the CLEARED field true?* or *Is the value in the PAYEE field equal to "Western Telephone"?* If the logical expression is true, the record is included in the operation. When it is false, the record is left out of the operation.

Of course, logical expressions are not written in full English sentences, such as *Is the value in the CLEARED field true?*. Instead, dBASE IV requires that you express the idea in the formal syntax of the dBASE IV language.

Formal versus Natural Language

One popular and controversial topic in computer languages involves the concept of *natural* computer languages. dBASE IV represents a typical computer language in the sense that it expresses ideas with a sentence structure that combines some English words with mathematical notations. This is true of other popular computer languages, such as BASIC, PASCAL and C.

In English, there are many ways to express the same idea. Computer languages have traditionally sought to avoid the ambiguity of English by requiring the user to learn a formal syntax for expressing ideas in the specific computer language. dBASE IV conforms to this tradition. This places the burden for the correct translation of ideas on the user.

In recent years there has been considerable interest in creating natural computer languages that use artificial intelligence to handle ambiguities in commands. For example, most people would say that *payee is equal to "Western Telephone", payee contains "Western Telephone"* and *payee="Western Telephone"* all have the same meaning. A formal language like dBASE IV would understand only the last expression.

The Q&A program from Symantek contains a natural language interpreter that is designed to attempt to process commands entered with a variety of syntax. It is one popular example of natural language processing.

The primary drawback to natural language processing is that it puts the burden of syntax analysis on the computer and the software. The result inevitably is that since the computer has to do more work, it performs more slowly and uses more computer resources. This is always the tradeoff made when attempting to make software operations simpler for the user.

The current release of dBASE IV provides the Query mode as a method of simplifying selection. The dBASE IV language, for the most part, remains a formal computer language.

The simplest type of logical expressions are those that select records according to the data stored in logical fields. You can select a logical field in the following ways:

Expression	Result
FOR *field_name*	selects for true values
FOR .NOT.*field_name*	selects for false values

.NOT. is used to invert the logic of an expression. By using it in front of the field name CLEARED the expression will test for a false value, rather than a true one.

Suppose you want to edit all the records that have a true value in the CLEARED field. Enter

```
EDIT FOR cleared ⏎
```

dBASE IV displays the first record in the file, Record 1, that has a true value in the CLEARED field. Enter

```
[PgDn]   (3 times)
```

Note that the current record is 5, not 4. This is because Record 4 was skipped for not containing a true value in the CLEARED field. Enter

```
[PgDn]   (2 times)
```

The command terminates because you displayed the *last* record that matches the FOR clause expression. By changing the expression you can display records that contain a false value in the CLEARED field.

```
EDIT FOR .NOT.cleared ⏎
```

This time the first record displayed is 4. This makes sense because it was the first record skipped when you were looking for true values in the CLEARED field. Enter

```
[PgDn]
```

The program skips to Record 7. Once again, all records that do not qualify, based on the logical condition, are skipped during the operation. Return to the Dot Prompt by entering

```
[Alt-e] e
```

Note that you cannot access the Browse mode from the Edit mode if you use a FOR clause with the EDIT command because the dBASE IV version of BROWSE does not support a FOR clause. dBASE III users should note that this is a change from the dBASE III implementation of the BROWSE command.

Display versus Full Screen

The Query mode always displays records in the full-screen modes, Edit or Browse. The full-screen modes are handy because you can examine and change data at the same time. The Browse mode allows you the option of examining or editing a group of records at the same time. However, in order to provide this option, the information is not displayed at the highest rate of speed.

The Dot Prompt mode lets you to use access commands that display data in a format that does not allow editing. The advantage is that this works faster than the Browse or Edit mode. With a small database, such as the one used in this example, the difference in performance is small. But with larger databases the difference becomes significant. When you want to retrieve, but not edit data, you can improve the performance of dBASE IV by using the display-only commands.

dBASE IV has three primary commands that display data on the screen, but do not provide for on-screen editing.

LIST

This command displays data from all records and all fields in the database. You can select fields and records by using clauses and scopes.

DISPLAY

The DISPLAY command is a variation on LIST. The primary difference between LIST and DISPLAY is that DISPLAY has a built-in pause between each screen of information. LIST will continue to scroll vertically until all the data has been displayed.

?

This command is a variation on LIST and DISPLAY. It is used to display the data in a single field of a single record. It is the most precise and limited of the three screen output commands.

The simplest of all of the output operations is listing. Enter

```
LIST ⏎
```

dBASE IV displays all the information stored in the current database file. This type of listing is called a *file dump* because it outputs the entire database with a single command.

```
    2  01/03/89     1001 Central Office Supplies      97.56 .T.      .T.
MEMO
    3  01/06/89     1002 Western Telephone           101.57 .T.      .F.
MEMO
    4  01/06/89     1003 United Federal Insurance    590.00 .F.      .F.
MEMO
    5  01/01/89     1004 Computer World             2245.50 .T.      .T.
MEMO
    6  01/01/89     1005 Fathead Software             99.95 .T.      .F.
MEMO
    7  01/14/89     1006 The Bargin Warehouse        145.99 .F.      .T.
MEMO
    8  01/15/89     1007 Central Office Supplies      67.45 .F.      .F.
MEMO
    9  02/02/89     1008 Sunset Variety               25.89 .F.      .F.
MEMO
   10  02/09/89     1009 Advanced Copier Service     175.00 .F.      .F.
MEMO
   11  02/12/89     1010 Valley Power & Light        101.70 .F.      .F.
MEMO
.
Command ||D:\dbase\CKBOOK      ||     ||Rec: EOF/11     ||File ||   ||      ||    Ins
```

Figure 4-9. Records listed on screen.

Note that because the width of each record is wider than the screen, a second line is used for each record. In addition, because each record uses two lines, there is not enough room on the screen to show all the data at one time. The first few records scroll off the top of the screen. The DISPLAY ALL command operates exactly like LIST, with the exception that it will automatically pause when the screen has been filled. Enter

DISPLAY ALL ⏎

The command displays the first 9 records and then pauses.

```
. DISPLAY ALL
Record#  DATE    CHECK_NUM PAYEE                   AMOUNT CLEARED DEDUCTI
BLE REMARKS
    1  01/03/89    1000 Allied Office Furniture     750.50 .T.      .T.
MEMO
    2  01/03/89    1001 Central Office Supplies      97.56 .T.      .T.
MEMO
    3  01/06/89    1002 Western Telephone           101.57 .T.      .F.
MEMO
    4  01/06/89    1003 United Federal Insurance    590.00 .F.      .F.
MEMO
    5  01/01/89    1004 Computer World             2245.50 .T.      .T.
MEMO
    6  01/01/89    1005 Fathead Software             99.95 .T.      .F.
MEMO
    7  01/14/89    1006 The Bargin Warehouse        145.99 .F.      .T.
MEMO
    8  01/15/89    1007 Central Office Supplies      67.45 .F.      .F.
MEMO
    9  02/02/89    1008 Sunset Variety               25.89 .F.      .F.
MEMO
Press any key to continue... ◄────   ┌─ Display pauses after each full screen
Command ||D:\dbase\CKBOOK      ||    ||Rec: 1/
```

Figure 4-10. Display paused when screen is full.

You can tell the program to continue the displaying of records by pressing any key, except Esc. Esc cancels the command. Enter

⏎

The remaining records in the file appear on the screen.

Displaying Fields and Records

You can use language options, such as field names, scopes, or FOR clauses to control the data displayed during a listing. For example, suppose you wanted to list only the PAYEE, DATE, and AMOUNT fields. Enter

        DISPLAY ALL FIELDS payee,date,amount ⏎

The command lists the data in the selected fields from all the records in the database.

```
    MEMO
     9  02/02/89       1008 Sunset Variety                   25.89 .F.      .F.
    MEMO
Press any key to continue...
    10  02/09/89       1009 Advanced Copier Service         175.00 .F.      .F.
    MEMO
    11  02/12/89       1010 Valley Power & Light            101.70 .F.      .F.
    MEMO
. DISPLAY ALL FIELDS payee,date,amount
Record#  payee                     date       amount
      1  Allied Office Furniture   01/03/89     750.50
      2  Central Office Supplies   01/03/89      97.56
      3  Western Telephone         01/06/89     101.57
      4  United Federal Insurance  01/06/89     590.00
      5  Computer World            01/01/89    2245.50
      6  Fathead Software          01/01/89      99.95
      7  The Bargin Warehouse      01/14/89     145.99
      8  Central Office Supplies   01/15/89      67.45
      9  Sunset Variety            02/02/89      25.89
     10  Advanced Copier Service   02/09/89     175.00
     11  Valley Power & Light      02/12/89     101.70
.
Command    D:\dbase\CKBOOK          Rec: EOF/11        File               Ins
```

Figure 4-11. Selected fields listed.

You can use a FOR clause to select records. Enter the command below to display only the records that have not cleared.

        DISPLAY ALL FOR .NOT.cleared ⏎

Records 4, 7, 8, 9, 10, and 11 are listed. Try combining both a FIELDS and a FOR clause in the same command. Enter

        DISPLAY ALL FIELDS payee,date,amount FOR cleared ⏎

The result is a list of the specified fields for the records that meet the logical expression. The information forms a table of information.

```
Record#   DATE      CHECK_NUM PAYEE                          AMOUNT CLEARED DEDUCTI
BLE REMARKS
      4  01/06/89      1003 United Federal Insurance         590.00 .F.     .F.
MEMO
      7  01/14/89      1006 The Bargin Warehouse             145.99 .F.     .T.
MEMO
      8  01/15/89      1007 Central Office Supplies           67.45 .F.     .F.
MEMO
      9  02/02/89      1008 Sunset Variety                    25.89 .F.     .F.
MEMO
     10  02/09/89      1009 Advanced Copier Service          175.00 .F.     .F.
MEMO
     11  02/12/89      1010 Valley Power & Light             101.70 .F.     .F.
MEMO
. DISPLAY ALL FIELDS payee,date,amount FOR cleared
Record#   payee                 date        amount
      1  Allied Office Furniture  01/03/89    750.50
      2  Central Office Supplies  01/03/89     97.56
      3  Western Telephone        01/06/89    101.57
      5  Computer World           01/01/89   2245.50
      6  Fathead Software         01/01/89     99.95
Command   D:\dbase\CKBOOK          Rec: EOF/11     File                    Ins
```

Figure 4-12. Selected records and fields displayed.

If you are a dBASE III user you will notice that a FIELDS clause is used with the DISPLAY or LIST commands. This clause is not required and can be omitted. You can enter the commands in the same way as they were structured in dBASE III. This is an inconsistency that arises from the way commands were used in previous versions of dBASE. In dBASE IV the FIELDS can be used with DISPLAY or LIST, so that its format is consistent with EDIT.

To simplify command entry the FIELDS clause will not be used with commands like LIST and DISPLAY, where it is optional.

Selecting by Date

Selecting records by different field type requires you to write logical expressions in slightly different ways. You began by using FOR clauses because their format is simplest to use. This is one of the major advantages of using logical fields.

You now need to look at the way records can be selected by writing expressions that use the other field types available in dBASE IV. Begin with date type fields. Date fields require that you to write an expression containing a specific field name and a date value with which the contents of each field can be compared.

For example, to list all the records with the date 01/10/89, enter

```
LIST FOR date={01/10/89}  ↵
```

Records 5 and 6 are listed. Note the use of the {} to indicate that 01/10/89 is a date, rather than a number or character item. When you are writing a full expression, you can use any of the comparison operators.

Symbol	**Meaning**
>	Greater than
<	less than
>=	greater than or equal to
<=	less than or equal to
<>	not equal to
#	not equal to

List all the payees, dates, and amounts written on or after 01/15/89. Try this on your own. The correct command can be found at the end of the chapter, under EX-1. The resulting commands will list Records 8 through 11.

> **Why Display is Faster than Browse**
> One of the major points of this section is that Dot Prompt commands, such as LIST or DISPLAY, retrieve data faster than the Query mode operations, such as Browse. This is because displaying data so that they can be edited, and not just examined, is a much more complicated matter.
>   When information is output by commands such as LIST, the program can move sequentially through the database, processing each record as it is encountered. Once the data is processed and displayed on the screen, the program can forget it and turn to the next record, if any.
>   However, with a browse-type display, it is not possible to simply show the information, and move on. Editing requires that all the fields and records on the screen have memory space available for entry and updating. An array of memory is set aside for each of these potential operations. This makes processing the information in a Browse display slower and more complicated than it is for the simpler output commands, such as LIST and DISPLAY.

Using Date Functions

As discussed in Chapter 3, dBASE IV provides a number of date functions that can convert standard dates into other forms of chronological information. You can use this information to generate additional fields or to serve as a selection criteria. For example, you could use the date functions to list the date information in a different form than that in which it was entered. Recall that the CMONTH( ) function displayed the name of the month in characters, the DAY( ) function displayed the value of the day portion of the date, YEAR( ) function displayed the year value of the date and CDOW( ) function displayed the name of the week. Enter

```
LIST CDOW(date),CMONTH(date),DAY(date),YEAR(date)    ↵
```

The screen displays four columns of data generated from the dates stored in the date field.

```
Record#  DATE      CHECK_NUM PAYEE                       AMOUNT CLEARED DEDUCTI
BLE REMARKS
       5 01/10/89     1004 Computer World             2245.50 .T.    .T.
    MEMO
       6 01/10/89     1005 Fathead Software             99.95 .T.    .F.
    memo

. LIST CDOW(date),CMONTH(date),DAY(date),YEAR(date)
Record#  CDOW(date) CMONTH(date)  DAY(date) YEAR(date)
       1 Tuesday    January              3     1989
       2 Tuesday    January              3     1989
       3 Friday     January              6     1989
       4 Friday     January              6     1989
       5 Tuesday    January             10     1989
       6 Tuesday    January             10     1989
       7 Saturday   January             14     1989
       8 Sunday     January             15     1989
       9 Thursday   February             2     1989
      10 Thursday   February             9     1989
      11 Sunday     February            12     1989
.

Command  D:\dbase\CKBOOK          Rec: EOF/11      File                  Ins
```

Figure 4-13. Date functions generate data.

The information generated by the previous command illustrates another advantage of displaying data in the Dot Prompt mode. You can display the results of the calculation, such as those created by date functions, without having to create calculated fields. Since the data will not be stored, dBASE IV generates it as it move through the database, leaving only the display.

You can use a date function to select records, as well as to display data. Suppose you wanted to select records from the month of February only. If you could only select records based on the data entered into the fields, you would have to create a compound text for records greater than or equal to 01/01/89, and less than or equal to 01/31/89. But the date functions provide a much simpler formula. Instead of testing the whole dates, you can test only the month portion by using the MONTH( ) function. Enter

```
LIST date,payee,amount  FOR MONTH(date)=2  ↵
```

This command selects Records 9 through 11, the only ones with a February dates.

Selecting by Character Fields

When selecting records based on a character field, you need to keep two things in mind:

Quotation marks

When you enter text you want to use as a criterion for matching, you must remember to enclose the text in quotation marks.

Capitalization

When you are attempting to match specific groups of characters, capitalization needs to be considered.

For example, suppose you wanted to locate the record of a payee that begins with the word *Western*. Enter

        LIST FOR payee="Western" ↵

Record 3 is selected because its payee is *Western Telephone*. Find the payee that begins with *Sunset*. Try this on your own. The correct command can be found at the end of the chapter, under EX-2.

You can also use character type expressions when the result of a function is text, regardless of the type of field the function operates on. For example, when the CDOW( ) function is applied to a date field, the resulting output consists of text, (i.e. the text name of the day of the week). Imagine you wanted to list the date, payee, and amount of all records that occurred on Sundays. Enter

        LIST date,payee,amount FOR CDOW(date)="Sunday" ↵]

This command locates Records 8 and 11. The logical expression required that the expression CDOW(date) be treated as character, not date, information. The CDOW( ) function is a conversion function because it changes date information into text information and is always treated as text.

It is important to understand what is actually meant by *conversion* or *conversion function* . For example, when the CDOW( ) function is used to convert a date to the text day of the week, no change is made to the original contents of the field. The function converts the value of the field to a new value for display or evaluation purposes only. Once the value has been displayed or evaluated, it is erased from the memory of the computer. The original contents of the field, in this example a date, is unchanged. The REPLACE command will actually change the data stored in a field.

Case Insensitive Expressions

When selecting records there may be no way of knowing in advance whether or not the data has been entered in a consistent pattern of upper- and lower-case letters. Inconsistency in the use of upper- and lower-case characters is common. It can cause you to fail to select records that ought to be included because of unanticipated differences in case. dBASE IV has two functions, UPPER( ) and LOWER( ), that convert the contents of a character field to either all upper- or all lower-case characters, respectively.

The key to case insensitivity is to compare groups of characters that are all the same case. It does not really matter whether they are all upper- or lower-case, so long as they are consistent.

For example, suppose you wanted to locate records that began with the word *Central* in a case insensitive way. You could use the UPPER( ) function to convert the field text to upper-case and compare that to a text literal with all upper-case characters. Keep in mind that the text literal, (i.e. the text within the quotation) must be all upper-case characters. Enter

        LIST FOR payee="CENTRAL"   ↵

No records are found because of a difference in case between the text literal *"CENTRAL"* and the case of the characters in the PAYEE field. The next command employs the UPPER( ) function to eliminate this problem.

        LIST FOR UPPER(payee)="CENTRAL"   ↵

You can also use the UPPER( ) and LOWER( ) functions to display data as all upper- or lower-case. Enter

        LIST UPPER(payee),UPPER(CMONTH(date)),amount   ↵

```
Record#  DATE      CHECK_NUM PAYEE                    AMOUNT CLEARED DEDUCTI
BLE REMARKS
      2  01/03/89     1001 Central Office Supplies     97.56 .T.     .T.
    MEMO
      8  01/15/89     1007 Central Office Supplies     67.45 .F.     .F.
    MEMO

. LIST UPPER(payee),UPPER(CMONTH(date)),amount
Record#  UPPER(payee)            UPPER(CMONTH(date))      amount
      1  ALLIED OFFICE FURNITURE  JANUARY                 750.50
      2  CENTRAL OFFICE SUPPLIES  JANUARY                  97.56
      3  WESTERN TELEPHONE        JANUARY                 101.57
      4  UNITED FEDERAL INSURANCE JANUARY                 590.00
      5  COMPUTER WORLD           JANUARY                2245.50
      6  FATHEAD SOFTWARE         JANUARY                  99.95
      7  THE BARGIN WAREHOUSE     JANUARY                 145.99
      8  CENTRAL OFFICE SUPPLIES  JANUARY                  67.45
      9  SUNSET VARIETY           FEBRUARY                 25.89
     10  ADVANCED COPIER SERVICE  FEBRUARY                175.00
     11  VALLEY POWER & LIGHT     FEBRUARY                101.70
.
Command   D:\dbase\CKBOOK        Rec: EOF/11      File              Ins
```

Figure 4-14. UPPER( ) used to display upper case text.

In this example the UPPER( ) function is used to display text as all upper-case characters. The second item in the list is UPPER(CMONTH(date)). This expression uses two functions, UPPER( ) and CMONTH( ), to create a single effect—upper-case names of months. The CMONTH( ) is contained within the UPPER( ) function. When one function is contained within another in this manner they are said to be *nested*.

dBASE IV evaluates nested functions from the inside out. In this example it takes the inner function, CMONTH(date), and evaluates its meaning. In this case it yields a month name, January, February, etc. The text of the month name then becomes the item on which the outer function, UPPER( ), operates—converting January to JANUARY, February to FEBRUARY, and so on.

The ability to nest functions means that you can combine the effect of two or more functions to achieve a specific result. Since dBASE IV has over 125 functions, the possibilities are up to your imagination. The richness of functions and the results of nesting them is one of the advantages of working in the Dot Prompt mode.

Selecting by Number Values

Numeric selection, like character selection, requires a complete expression. For example, to locate the record with check number 1009, you would use the following command:

```
LIST FOR check_num=1009 ↵
```

Record 9 is located. One difference between the numeric and character logical expressions is that numeric value is not enclosed in quotations.

The CHECK_NUM field is unusual in terms of typical numeric fields, in that each record contains a unique value in sequence. The AMOUNT field is more typical of a numeric field, in that it contains a random assortment of values. While it is possible that you know the exact dollar and cents value of the record you are looking for, it is more likely that you have an approximate value in mind.

Imagine that you wanted to locate a record whose amount is about $100. You could simply search for that exact value. Enter

```
LIST FOR amount=100 ↵
```

No records are listed because none of the amounts are exactly $100. One way to make these searches more useful is to use dBASE IV functions to list values that are close to the value you have in mind. The ROUND( ) function is used to round numeric values to a specific number of decimal places. The function requires two items. The first is the numeric field you want to round. The second is the number of decimal places. For example, you might search for amounts in which the value, when rounded to the nearest dollar, equals 100. To round to the nearest dollar you would specify zero decimal places. Enter

```
LIST FOR ROUND(amount,0)=100 ↵
```

This time Record 6 with a value of 99.95, appears. The ROUND( ) function accepts negative numbers for the decimal place argument. A negative number implies rounding to a decimal place to the left of the decimal point. For example, rounding to -1 would round to the nearest 10. Enter

```
LIST FOR ROUND(amount,-1)=100  ↵
```

The term *argument* refers to the information placed inside a function's parentheses. Up to this point, all the functions you have used, have contained a single argument. The ROUND( ) function requires two arguments.

The result of the command is that four Records—2, 3, 6 and 11—are selected. You will note that the amount values for these records range from 97.56 to 101.70. By rounding the values to the nearest 10 all values from 95.00 to 104.49 would round to 100. You can use the ROUND( ) function as part of the display list to see the values created by the function. Enter

```
LIST amount,ROUND(amount,-1)   ↵
```

```
    3  01/06/89     1002 Western Telephone         101.57 .T.     .F.
  MEMO
    6  01/10/89     1005 Fathead Software           99.95 .T.     .F.
  MEMO
   11  02/12/89     1010 Valley Power & Light      101.70 .F.     .F.
  MEMO
. LIST amount,ROUND(amount,-1)
Record#      amount ROUND(amount,-1)
      1      750.50           750
      2       97.56           100
      3      101.57           100
      4      590.00           590
      5     2245.50          2250
      6       99.95           100
      7      145.99           150
      8       67.45            70
      9       25.89            30
     10      175.00           180
     11      101.70           100
.
Command   D:\dbase\CKBOOK         Rec: EOF/11      File                    Ins
```

Figure 4-15. Rounded values listed.

ROUND( ) is a handy way to list values that are close to, but not exactly, the same as the values you want. In most cases it will give you a better result than trying to remember the exact dollar and cents amount entered into the field.

Calculation by Expression

You can also use numeric fields to display lists of calculated values. dBASE IV recognizes the following arithmetic operators.

Operator	Calculation
+	Addition
-	Subtraction
*	Multiplication
/	Division
^	raise to power
( )	change order of calculation

You can perform arithmetic calculations using field values. In the previous chapter you used calculated fields in the Query mode to find the sales tax and pre-tax amounts. You can carry out the same arithmetic with the LIST/DISPLAY command. Note 6% sales tax is assumed to have been charged on all items. Enter

```
LIST amount,amount/1.06,amount-amount/1.06    ⏎
```

The results of the calculations are listed along with the values from the AMOUNT field.

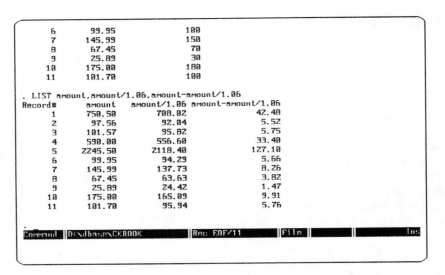

Figure 4-16. Arithmetic calculations performed.

You can even select records based on the results of a calculation, rather than the actual contents of the numeric field. The following command selects records in which the sales tax amount was greater than $10. Enter

```
LIST date,payee,amount  FOR amount-amount/1.06>10  ⏎
```

This is an example of how you can select records based on a calculated value, as opposed to merely selecting records based on the raw data entered into the fields.

Clearing the Display

When display commands are entered at the Dot Prompt, dBASE IV will simply scroll the display the required number of lines upward, to make room for the output generated by the last command. This means that the screen can contain a mixture of data that has resulted from a variety of commands.

Suppose that you wanted to begin with a blank screen. This can be done by using the CLEAR command. This command clears all data and commands off the screen, allowing the next command to start from a blank screen. Enter

```
CLEAR ⏎
```

Keep in mind CLEAR has no effect on the data stored in the database. It only removes the information from the current screen display.

Memo Fields

Another advantage of Dot Prompt mode operations is that they allow you to work with memo field data. As discussed in Chapter 2, memo field data are stored in a separate file with a different type of structure (variable length records) than the information stored in the other fields (fixed length records). When you use the Edit or Browse modes, the only data that appears for the memo field is the word *MEMO* for records with memos, and *memo* for records without memos.

You may have noticed that till now, the LIST and DISPLAY commands have operated on memo fields in the same way. However, this can be easily changed. If you specifically include the name of a memo field in the list of fields to display, the command will display the text of the memo field, instead of the word MEMO. Enter

```
DISPLAY ALL remarks ⏎
```

The text stored in the memo fields is displayed.

```
Record#   remarks
      1   Office Furniture Purchased:

          1 - desk 36" by 48"
          1 - swivel chair
          2 - side chairs
          1 - computer desk
          1 - printer stand

      2   envelopes
          manila folders
          hanging files
      3
      4   business insurance
          Policy number: 100120020ZAF
      5   286 Computer with 40 megabyte hard disk
          Invoice #75001
      6
      7   waste paper baskets
          copier paper
          computer paper
Press any key to continue...
Command  D:\dbase\CKBOOK        Rec: 1/11        File          Ins
```

Figure 4-17. Memo field text is displayed.

Complete the listing by entering

    ↵

You can combine memo text with other field information. Enter

    LIST date,remarks ↵

The dates from the DATE field are listed alongside the text of the memo field. Note that when a memo field contains more than one line of text, all the lines of the memo field are printed before the DATE of the next record begins.

Note that if blank lines are added to the end of a memo, they will print as part of the memo.

Memo Width

List the contents of the memo field along with the name of the payee.

    LIST payee,remarks ↵

The result is very hard to read because the combined width of the PAYEE and REMARKS fields is wider than the screen display.

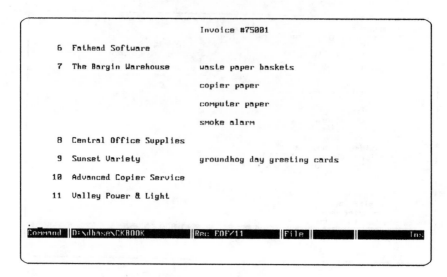

Figure 4-18. Memo listed with PAYEE field.

By default, dBASE IV will automatically list the data stored in memo fields in lines 50 characters in width. If you wanted to list the memo in a wider or narrower line width, change the default setting, the SET MEMOWIDTH TO command. For example, the previous listing would look better if the memo field was restricted to 40 characters. Enter

        SET MEMOWIDTH TO 40 ⏎

What happened? In this case there is no visible reaction by dBASE IV to the change. The only way to see the effect of the SET MEMOWIDTH TO command is to list the memo text again. Enter

        LIST payee,remarks ⏎

This time the memo field is restricted to 40 characters and fits within the width of the screen display.

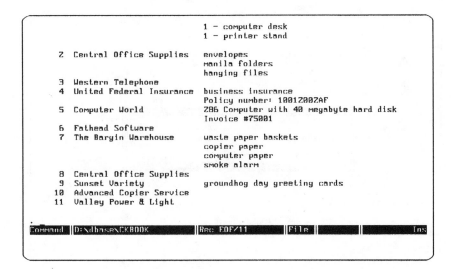

Figure 4-19. Memo width set to 40 characters.

The memo width setting will stay in force until you quit dBASE IV or issue another SET MEMOWIDTH TO command.

The Query mode does provides a means by which memo fields can be manipulated from within a query. The method involves the use of calculated fields and/or condition boxes. However, it is important to understand that calculated fields and condition boxes require you to enter dBASE IV expressions identical to those you enter at the Dot Prompt. In fact, you might think of the calculated fields and condition box options as the way the Query mode allows Dot Prompt commands to be included in a query. As you learn more about Dot Prompt commands, you will find you can apply this logic to many of the Control Center operations, including queries, screen formats, and report forms.

Selecting by Memo Fields

Selecting records based on the contents of memo fields is approached in a slightly different manner than selections made on character fields, although both fields contain character text. For example, suppose you wanted to locate the PAYEE and AMOUNT for the record that contains *smoke alarm* in the memo field. If the memo field were treated as a character field the following command would be correct: Enter

```
LIST payee,amount FOR remarks="smoke  alarm" ↵
```

When you enter this command, dBASE IV responds by displaying an error message box.

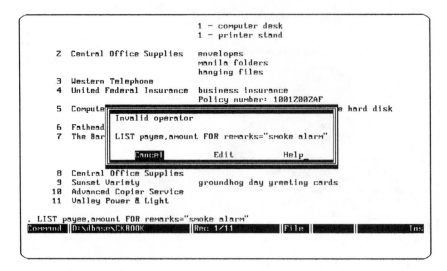

Figure 4-20.   Incorrect command for memo field selection.

Return to the Dot Prompt by entering

    ⏎

If the method above does not work how can the information stored in a memo field be used for record selection? The answer is that memo fields are searched by using the $ (sub-string) operator. This method was illustrated in the previous chapter, in which memo fields were used in the Query mode.

The $ operator takes the general form A$B. This expression can be read as "Is A any part of B?" Both A and B refer to text of some sort, either a text literal (text inside quotation marks), a character field, or a function, such as CDOW( ), that results in a text output. If A is any part of B, the expression evaluates as true; if not, false.

Using the $ method, you would enter the command to search for *smoke alarm* as follows:

        `LIST payee,amount FOR "smoke alarm"$remarks` ⏎

This time, the PAYEE and AMOUNT from Record 7 are displayed. You can combine the text of the memo field along with the other information displayed. Enter

        `LIST payee,amount,remarks FOR "smoke alarm"$remarks` ⏎

The text of the memo field is included in the display.

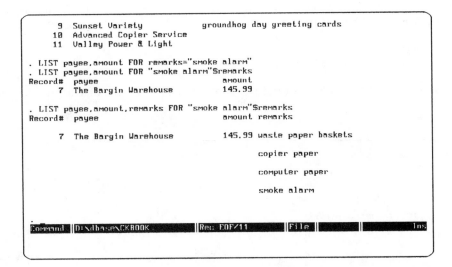

```
      9  Sunset Variety          groundhog day greeting cards
     10  Advanced Copier Service
     11  Valley Power & Light
. LIST payee,amount FOR remarks="smoke alarm"
. LIST payee,amount FOR "smoke alarm"$remarks
Record#  payee                        amount
      7  The Bargin Warehouse         145.99

. LIST payee,amount,remarks FOR "smoke alarm"$remarks
Record#  payee                        amount remarks

      7  The Bargin Warehouse         145.99 waste paper baskets

                                             copier paper

                                             computer paper

                                             smoke alarm
```

```
Command  D:\dbase\CKBOOK        Rec: EOF/11      File             Ins
```

Figure 4-21. Sub-string operator searches memo field.

You cannot use the case functions to create a case insensitive version of the same command. The command LIST FOR "SMOKE ALARM"$UPPER(remarks) is not valid because UPPER( ) will operate on a memo field directly.

Memo Field Functions

dBASE IV provides functions that operate on memo fields. These enable you to perform a number of tasks that would not otherwise be possible. The functions provided are:

Memlines( )

The function returns a numeric value equal to the number of lines of text, including blanks, contained in the specified memo. Note that the number of lines is calculated based on the current width of the memo lines, as set with the SET MEMOWIDTH TO command.

Mline( )

This function displays the text entered on a specified line of a memo field. Note that the line is determined by the current width of the memo lines, as set with the SET MEMOWIDTH TO command.

For example, you can calculate the number of lines of text in each memo with the MEMLINES( ) function. Enter

```
CLEAR ⏎
LIST MEMLINES(remarks)   ⏎
```

The command creates a list of values that tell you the size of the memo field in lines.

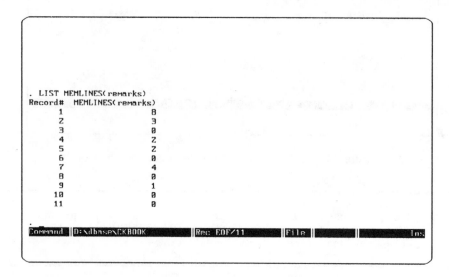

```
. LIST MEMLINES(remarks)
Record#  MEMLINES(remarks)
    1              8
    2              3
    3              0
    4              2
    5              2
    6              0
    7              4
    8              0
    9              1
   10              0
   11              0
.
Command   D:\dbase\CKBOOK          Rec: EOF/11        File              Ins
```

Figure 4-22. MEMLINES values listed.

You will note that where a memo is empty, the value for MEMLINES( ) is zero. This fact can be used to list records according to whether or not the memo fields contain text. The following command uses the logical expression MEMLINES(remarks)>0 to select records that contain memos. Enter

```
LIST date,payee,amount  FOR MEMLINES(remarks)>0
```

Records 1, 2, 4, 5, 7, and 9 are selected. The next command selects records without memo text.

```
LIST date,payee,amount  FOR MEMLINES(remarks)=0
```

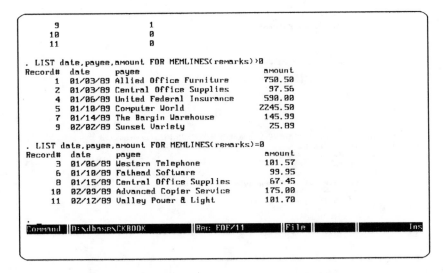

Figure 4-23. Records without memos selected.

The MLINE( ) function provides a means by which you can display a specific part of the memo field. For example, you might want to limit the memo display to a single line, e.g., the first line.

```
LIST MLINE(remarks,1)
```

The following command displays the first line of the memo, the total number of lines in the memo and uses a FOR clause to skip any records that do not contain any memos.

```
LIST MLINE(remarks,1),MEMLINES(remarks)   FOR MEMLINES(remarks)0  ⏎
```

```
     1   Office Furniture Purchased:
     2   envelopes
     3
     4   business insurance
     5   286 Computer with 40 megabyte hard disk
     6
     7   waste paper baskets
     8
     9   groundhog day greeting cards
    10
    11
. LIST MLINE(remarks,1),MEMLINES(remarks) FOR MEMLINES(remarks)>0
Record#   MLINE(remarks,1)              MEMLINES(remarks)
     1   Office Furniture Purchased:                   8
     2   envelopes                       3
     4   business insurance              2
     5   286 Computer with 40 megabyte hard disk       2
     7   waste paper baskets             4
     9   groundhog day greeting cards            1
.
Command  D:\dbase\CKBOOK         Rec: EOF/11      File              Ins
```

Figure 4-24. Memo data displayed.

You may wonder why the MEMLINES( ) values don't line up in a column. The answer is that the text drawn from the memo field by the MLINE( ) function is combining information from a variable-length file with numeric values that are listed as a fixed-length field.

When a numeric calculated field is displayed or listed, it is given a default width of 20 characters with 2 decimal places. This is the maximum width allowed in dBASE IV for numeric fields.

The MLINE( ) function inserts a line of text that contains only as many characters as are actually contained in the memo field for that record. If the line should be shorter than the current memo width setting, in this case 40 characters, dBASE IV does not pad it with blanks. The result is a list of memo lines with a ragged edge, as in a word-processor not set to justify the lines.

When a memo field's contents are listed—e.g., using the command LIST remarks—dBASE IV does pad each line with blanks so any fixed-length fields that follow are correctly aligned. The MLINE( ) function is an exception to this rule and is specifically designed to provide a means by which non-padded lines of text can be retrieved from memo fields.

You can eliminate the appearance of the ragged edge by reversing the order of the fields so that the MLINE( ) output falls at the end of the line. Enter

```
LIST MEMLINES(remarks),MLINE(remarks,1)    FOR MEMLINES(remarks)>0  ⏎
```

The list now presents an aligned appearance.

```
    10
    11

. LIST MLINE(remarks,1),MEMLINES(remarks) FOR MEMLINES(remarks)>0
Record#  MLINE(remarks,1)              MEMLINES(remarks)
     1   Office Furniture Purchased:            8
     2   envelopes                      3
     4   business insurance             2
     5   286 Computer with 40 megabyte hard disk          2
     7   waste paper baskets            4
     9   groundhog day greeting cards          1

. LIST MEMLINES(remarks),MLINE(remarks,1) FOR MEMLINES(remarks)>0
Record#  MEMLINES(remarks) MLINE(remarks,1)
     1            8 Office Furniture Purchased:
     2            3 envelopes
     4            2 business insurance
     5            2 286 Computer with 40 megabyte hard disk
     7            4 waste paper baskets
     9            1 groundhog day greeting cards
.

Command  D:\dbase\CKBOOK        Rec: EOF/11      File             Ins
```

Figure 4-25. Memo text appears aligned.

Summary Calculations

The Dot Prompt mode allows you access to commands that summarize the data stored in the database file. There are three basic summary commands:

Sum

Calculates the total of all values in a specified field.

Count

Counts the number of records in the database.

Average

Calculates the numeric average of the values in the fields.

Enter

```
CLEAR ↵
SUM ↵
```

When the SUM command is used in its most simple form, as above, it automatically calculates a database total for all the numeric fields in the database *structure.*

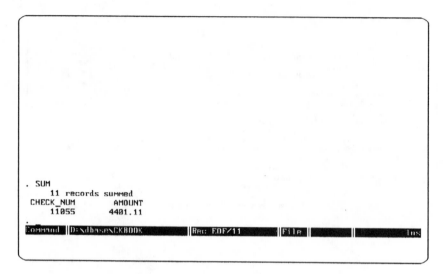

```
. SUM
     11 records summed
CHECK_NUM        AMOUNT
     11055        4401.11
.
Command  D:\dbase\CKBOOK        Rec: EOF/11        File                    Ins
```

Figure 4-26 Sum calculates total of all numeric fields.

In this example, the command calculates a total for both CHECK_NUM and AMOUNT because both are defined as numeric fields within the database structure. Note that in addition to the totals, the number of records used to calculate the totals is also displayed.

All operations that apply to numeric fields will effect both N (number) type and F (floating point) type fields. This assumption can be made throughout this book unless an exception is specifically mentioned.

You can limit the effect of the SUM command by specifying a field. Enter

SUM amount ⏎

You can also calculate averages. Enter

AVERAGE amount ⏎

You can use a FOR clause to select specific records to be included in the calculation. For example, you might wish to know the total amount of all outstanding checks. This would be very helpful when you are working with a bank statement.   The answer would require you to select only those records for which the value CLEARED was false. Enter

SUM amount FOR .NOT.cleared ⏎

The result is that there are six records with a total of $1,106.03 outstanding.

The same logic can be applied to any of the fields in the database. Suppose you wanted to know the total of all checks written in January. Enter

```
SUM amount FOR MONTH(date)=1  ⏎
```

The results are 8 records with a total of $4,098.52.

Calculations can also be performed on numeric expressions. The following command will calculate the total of all checks and the total amount of sales tax paid.

```
SUM amount,amount-amount/1.06  ⏎
```

The result shows a total of $249.12 paid in sales tax.

The COUNT command is used when you want to count the number of records that meet a specific criterion. For example, how many checks were written on Sundays?

```
COUNT FOR CDOW(date)="Sunday"  ⏎
```

The command responds by displaying *"2 records"*.

Suppose you wanted to count the records that have weekend dates. This is a convenient place to use the $ operator. Enter

```
COUNT FOR CDOW(date)$"SundaySaturday"  ⏎
```

The program shows three records that were written on weekends. Look at the fashion in which the $ operator is used in this instance. The expression CDOW(date)$"SundaySaturday" is read as *the day of the week is part of SundaySaturday*. The idea is to compare the day of the week to a larger string of characters, *SundaySaturday*. This is a simple way of writing an expression which matches any one of a list of values.

The Calculate Command

dBASE IV also contains a command called CALCULATE. This command is different from the SUM, COUNT, and AVERAGE commands in two respects.

Multiple Calculations

The CALCULATE command is capable of performing several different types of calculations at one time: it can sum, count, and average simultaneously, instead of requiring three separate commands.

Advanced Calculations

In addition to sum, average, and count, the CALCULATE command can also perform advanced mathematical calculations.

The CALCULATE command uses special options to indicate the type of calculation to carry out. The options use the same syntax as functions. Note that these are not functions because they can only be used with the CALCULATE command. dBASE IV functions can be used with any command for which you can compose a valid expression.

Option	Calculation
AVG( )	numeric average
CNT( )	record count
MAX( )	maximum value
MIN( )	minimum value
NPV( )	net present value
STD( )	standard deviation
SUM( )	sum
VAR( )	population variance

For example, the CALCULATE command can find the sum, average, and count of the AMOUNT field, in a single command. Enter

```
CLEAR ⏎
CALCULATE CNT( ),SUM(amount),AVG(amount)   ⏎
```

The command generates the three of values. You can use CALCULATE with a FOR clause to find only selected values. Enter

```
CALCULATE MAX(amount),MIN(amount),STD(amount)   FOR MONTH(date)=1 ⏎
```

The MAX( ) and MIN( ) options return the largest and smallest values respectively, from the specified fields. The SDT( ) function calculates the standard deviation of the AMOUNT field.

Keep in mind that you can calculate the same values of different fields. Enter

```
CALCULATE MAX(amount),MAX(check_num),SUM(amount)   ⏎
```

As with the DISPLAY and LIST commands, CALCULATE will operate on numeric expressions, as well as fields. Enter

```
CALCULATE SUM(amount),AVG(amount),SUM(amount-amount/1.06),AVG(amount-amount/1.06)   ⏎
```

NPV Calculation

The NPV option of the CALCULATE command performs a special financial calculation of the values in the specified fields. It calculates the *net present value* of a series of cash flows, discounted by a specific rate.

The basis of the calculation is the time adjusted value of money. For example, suppose a friend borrows $20 until next week, at which time he will pay you back. This seems fair. But what if he forgets to repay you for 6 months or a year? Is it still simply a matter of repaying the $20?

The time-adjusted value concept says no. If the $20 had been repaid on time you could have invested that money and earned interest for 6 months or a year. In order to be fair, your friend would have to add interest to his repayment. Note that according to the time-adjusted value concept, this interest is not profit. It simply brings you back to the point you would have been had the loan been repaid in a week.

You can view this same incident in another way. Suppose your friend intends to pay you back $20 in 6 months. A portion of the $20 would then be interest on what he borrowed. The amount he borrows is $20 less interest—e.g. $18 borrowed with $2 interest. The amount borrowed—$18—is the present value of the loan. The $20 repayment is the future value.

The Net Present Value calculation finds the single lump sum value, which is equal to a series of cash payments made over a period of time. The example database used in this book is not structured for this type of calculation. However, if you use a little imagination, you can perform a NPV( ) calculation on the CHECK_NUM field.

Imagine that your boss offers you a choice of salary plans: a single lump sum payment of $9000 today, or a series of 11 monthly payments corresponding to the values in the CHECK_NUM field. This means that your salary in the first month would be $1000, the check number in Record 1, $1001 in month 2, and so on. Assuming that a savings account earns 6% interest annually, the following formula calculates the net present value:

CALCULATE NPV(.06/12,check_num) ↵

Note that the annual interest rate is divided by 12 to find the monthly interest rate. The command will calculate $10,738.57. This implies you are better off to take the series of payments rather than the lump sum because the net present value of all the payments is greater.

Another way to use NPV is to evaluate an investment. Suppose the CHECK_NUM values represent yearly payments on an investment. Your initial investment is a lump sum payment of $7,000. The $7,000 represents a negative cash flow at the beginning of the investment. The following command calculates the net present value, assuming the 6% interest rate.

CALCULATE NPV(.06,check-num,-7000)

The result is $927.80. This means that the investment is marginally better than putting the money into a savings account.

Listing by Index Order

One of the principal advantages of working in the Dot Prompt mode is that you can access the indexes created automatically when Y is selected in the index column of the file structure. These indexes could not be used by the Query mode.

Before you can use the field indexes you need to know what they are. One way to find out is to check the file structure to see which fields are designated as index fields. The STRUCTURE clause can be used with DISPLAY or LIST to generate a listing of the file's structure. Enter

CLEAR ⏎
LIST STRUCTURE ⏎

```
. LIST STRUCTURE
Structure for database: D:\DBASE\CKBOOK.DBF
Number of data records:      11
Date of last update    : 05/18/89
Field  Field Name  Type       Width   Dec    Index
    1  DATE        Date           8            N
    2  CHECK_NUM   Numeric        4            N
    3  PAYEE       Character     25            Y
    4  AMOUNT      Numeric       10     2       Y
    5  CLEARED     Logical        1            N
    6  DEDUCTIBLE  Logical        1            N
    7  REMARKS     Memo          10            N
** Total **                     60
.
Command  D:\dbase\CKBOOK          Rec: 1/11          File          Ins
```

Figure 4-27. File structure listed.

This listing shows that the file is indexed on DATE, CHECK_NUM, PAYEE and AMOUNT.

The database file is currently listed in the natural order: the order in which the records were entered into the database file. In order to display the records in an index order, you must activate the index using the SET ORDER TO command. For example, to order the database by payee, enter

SET ORDER TO payee ⏎

The program responds by displaying the message Master index: PAYEE. This means that the records will not conform to the order indicated by the PAYEE field. Enter

LIST date,payee,amount ⏎

This time the records are listed not in order of their record number but alphabetically according to PAYEE.

```
   5  CLEARED      Logical      1              N
   6  DEDUCTIBLE   Logical      1              N
   7  REMARKS      Memo        10              N
** Total **                    60
. SET ORDER TO payee
Master index: PAYEE
. LIST date,payee,amount
Record#  date       payee                    amount
     10  02/09/89  Advanced Copier Service    175.00
      1  01/03/89  Allied Office Furniture    750.50
      2  01/03/89  Central Office Supplies     97.56
      8  01/15/89  Central Office Supplies     67.45
      5  01/10/89  Computer World            2245.50
      6  01/10/89  Fathead Software            99.95
      9  02/02/89  Sunset Variety              25.89
      7  01/14/89  The Bargin Warehouse       145.99
      4  01/06/89  United Federal Insurance   590.00
     11  02/12/89  Valley Power & Light       101.70
      3  01/06/89  Western Telephone          101.57
```

Figure 4-28. Records listed in PAYEE order.

Once a database has been placed into an index order, all operations will be carried out with the records listed in that order. For example, suppose you entered a command that selected checks written in the month of February. Enter

```
LIST date,payee,amount  FOR MONTH(date)=2  ↵
```

These records also appear in order by PAYEE.

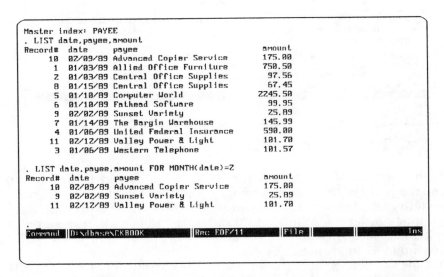

```
Master index: PAYEE
. LIST date,payee,amount
Record#  date       payee                    amount
     10  02/09/89  Advanced Copier Service    175.00
      1  01/03/89  Allied Office Furniture    750.50
      2  01/03/89  Central Office Supplies     97.56
      8  01/15/89  Central Office Supplies     67.45
      5  01/10/89  Computer World            2245.50
      6  01/10/89  Fathead Software            99.95
      9  02/02/89  Sunset Variety              25.89
      7  01/14/89  The Bargin Warehouse       145.99
      4  01/06/89  United Federal Insurance   590.00
     11  02/12/89  Valley Power & Light       101.70
      3  01/06/89  Western Telephone          101.57

. LIST date,payee,amount FOR MONTH(date)=2
Record#  date       payee                    amount
     10  02/09/89  Advanced Copier Service    175.00
      9  02/02/89  Sunset Variety              25.89
     11  02/12/89  Valley Power & Light       101.70
```

Figure 4-29. PAYEE order continues for all subsequent commands.

You can change index orders at any time in the Dot Prompt mode. Enter

```
SET ORDER TO amount ↵
LIST date,payee,amount  ↵
```

This time the records are sequenced by AMOUNT.

The Status Display

You may recall that you created a special index in which the records were sequenced by the descending value of the AMOUNT field. But what name did you give to that index order? It is not uncommon to forget. dBASE IV provides a method by which you can display the names of all the indexes related to the current database. Enter

```
DISPLAY STATUS ↵
```

The STATUS display reveals a summary of information about the current state of dBASE IV.

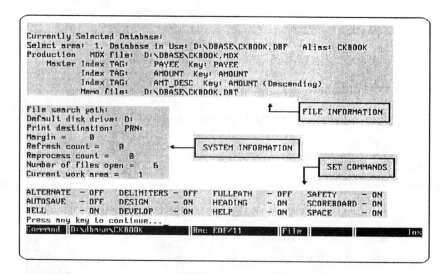

Figure 4-30. Status display.

It is the top part of the display that you are interested in. The first line tells you the name of the current database file. This matches the information on the status line. Below this all the index orders are listed. dBASE IV refers to each index order as an index tag. Index tag information is stored in a multiple-index file. These files have an MDX file extension. Each MDX file can have up to 47 index tags.

MDX files can be created in two ways. The current file, CKBOOK.MDX, was automatically created by dBASE IV when you entered Y into the Index column of one or more fields, in creating the database's structure. Had you not done so, you could have manually created an MDX file using the INDEX command. (This procedure is covered later in this book.)

There are five tags defined for the current MDX file. The listing shows the key field or expression used to create the index tag. If an index order is descending the word "(Descending)" appears next to the key. In this example all the tags have the names of fields, with the exception of the AMT_DESC tag, which you created manually in Chapter 3.

The display also lists the name of the memo field text file, CKBOOK.DBT. For now, ignore the remainder of the display.

Return to the Dot Prompt by entering

[Esc]

Strictly speaking, the DISPLAY STATUS cannot insure that all the indexes that *could* be related to this file are listed. It will display all the index orders associated with the currently opened multiple-index file or NDX index orders if used.

Now that you know the name of the manually-created index tag, place it into use with the SET ORDER TO command. Enter

CLEAR ⏎
SET ORDER TO amt_desc ⏎
LIST date,payee,amount   ⏎

```
. SET ORDER TO amt_desc
Master index: AMT_DESC
. LIST date,payee,amount
Record#  date      payee                        amount
    5    01/10/89  Computer World              2245.50
    1    01/03/89  Allied Office Furniture      750.50
    4    01/06/89  United Federal Insurance     590.00
   10    02/09/89  Advanced Copier Service      175.00
    7    01/14/89  The Bargin Warehouse         145.99
   11    02/12/89  Valley Power & Light         101.70
    3    01/06/89  Western Telephone            101.57
    6    01/10/89  Fathead Software              99.95
    2    01/03/89  Central Office Supplies       97.56
    8    01/15/89  Central Office Supplies       67.45
    9    02/02/89  Sunset Variety                25.89
.
```
```
Command  D:\dbase\CKBOOK          Rec: EOF/11       File                   Ins
```

Figure 4-31. Records listed by descending amount.

Returning to the Natural Order

If you want to return to the natural order of your database, you can do so by using the SET ORDER TO command without a tag name. Enter

```
SET ORDER TO ⏎
```

The message "Database is in natural order" is displayed, confirming the effect of the command.

Search Index Fields

As discussed earlier, one of the primary advantages of Dot Prompt operations is that you can take advantage of file indexes. This means you can use index tags to perform rapid searches. Keep in mind that in this small example database the differences in performance will not be noticeable. However, with large databases the performance improvement will be very important.

Suppose you wanted to perform a quick search for a payee. First set the index tag to the PAYEE index.

```
SET ORDER TO payee ⏎
```

The FIND command is used to search the index tag at a high rate of speed. Using FIND is simpler than searching with a FOR clause because dBASE IV assumes you are searching the field indicated by the tag. All you must do is supply the command with the text you want to locate. The FIND command is an exception to the rule that text must always be entered in commands surrounded by quotations. With FIND you simply enter the text. Enter

```
FIND Valley ⏎
```

What happened as a result of the command? If you look at the screen you will find the subtle clue. The status line shows 11/11 meaning that the active record is the eleventh record in the file. Enter

```
FIND Computer ⏎
```

The record number indicator changes to 5/11. Thus you can see how the FIND command changes the indicator to show which record contains the text that matches your search text. But how does the indicator relate to the data in that record?

The answer involves a database concept called the *pointer.* In dBASE IV the pointer always indicates one record in the database that is the *current* or *active* record. When you first open a database file, the first record in the file, Record 1 is the active record.

In the dBASE IV Command Language some commands ignore the pointer position. Other commands use the pointer position to select the record on which they will operate. For example, the LIST command is designed to begin always at the first record in the file, and process each record in sequence until it reaches the end of the file. If a FOR clause is used, LIST simply skips those records not qualifying, while still moving through the entire database. This process of examining all the records in the database when carrying out a command is called a *scan*. The LIST command normally scans the entire database file each time it is used.

However the DISPLAY command, used without the ALL scope behaves differently. DISPLAY used by itself does not automatically *scan* the database. Instead, it displays the contents of a single record. Which record will it choose? The answer is that it will display the record to which the pointer is positioned. For example, if the *status* line shows the pointer position as 5/11 that means that record 5 is the active record. If you enter DISPLAY, dBASE IV will display that record and that record only. Enter

        `DISPLAY` ↵

dBASE IV displays the data stored in the current record, Record 5. DISPLAY is a pointer dependent command because it acts on the record indicated by the pointer. LIST is pointer independent because it scans all the records in the database, no matter where the pointer is currently positioned.

Suppose you wanted to display the data with the payee *Sunset*. You have two ways to approach the problem. One way is to use the LIST command to scan the database file. Enter

        `LIST FOR payee="Sunset"` ↵

Record 9 is displayed. If you look at the record display on the status line it shows "EOF/11". *EOF* stands for *End of File*. This tells you that all the records in the database have been scanned and the pointer is now at the bottom of the file.

Now locate the same information with the FIND command. Enter

        `FIND Sunset` ↵
        `DISPLAY` ↵

The same information is displayed. However, note that the record indicator shows 9/11, not EOF/11. This means that once the record is found, the search is terminated. The program did not continue to the end of the file.

Why are there two different ways of getting the same information? The significance of these two methods lies less in the direct results, than the methods by which these results are achieved.

When a command like LIST scans a database to locate and display information, the time it takes to perform the command is directly proportional to the size of the database. The larger the database the longer it will take for the command to operate. This means when you first create a database, the LIST command works very quickly because there are only a few records in the file. But as this file grows, the LIST command becomes slower and slower. Remember scanning requires that the end of the file be reached before the command terminates.

On the other hand, the FIND/DISPLAY method implements the search differently. First, FIND does not bother to search the database file. Instead, it searches the index file for the first record in the index that matches. Recall that index files have a special tree-like structure that allows the search for a specific record to proceed along the shortest possible path, thus eliminating the need to scan all the records. When a matching record is found, FIND terminates the search. It does not bother to continue to the end of the file once a match as been found.

The result is that in a large database FIND will locate the data at a much higher rate of speed than commands like LIST. It also means that the overall size of the database will have little or no effect on the speed of a search.

Both methods have advantages and disadvantages. The LIST method is the simpler of the two because all of the necessary logic is included in a single command. LIST does not depend on other commands that have to be entered in the correct sequence. Also, LIST locates all the records that match the condition, if more than one match exists in the database. The drawback is that this method is quite slow. Note that any command used with a FOR clause will automatically perform a database scan. Put another way, using a FOR clause is actually a request to scan the entire database.

The FIND method is much more complicated. First, FIND assumes you have created an index tag for the field you want to search. Second, it also assumes you have activated the correct index tag with the SET ORDER TO command. Third, it will locates only the first matching record. Its advantage is that, given the correct pre-requisites, it will search very large databases in a small fraction of the time that LIST would require.

Of course, the third problem, finding only the first record, is not really a disadvantage. The reason is that you must keep in mind the context in which FIND is used. FIND implies that the database is indexed on the field you are searching. If there are more than one record with the same key text, they will naturally be grouped together in the index order. If you find the first record, all the others with the same information will be listed consecutively.

For example, suppose you wanted to EDIT any record or records having a payee that begins with *Central*. Enter

        FIND Central ⏎
        EDIT ⏎

Record 2 is displayed. In this situation any other records that have the same PAYEE should directly follow one another. Enter

        [PgDn]

Record 8 has the same payee. Enter

        [PgDn]

The next record is for *Computer World*. You can be sure that you have seen all the records with *Central* because they were indexed by PAYEE. Exit the edit mode by entering

        [Alt-e] e

The differences between database scans and indexed searches will appear again later in this section, and also in Part II.

Printing Lists

You can print the information displayed by the LIST and DISPLAY commands easily, using the TO PRINTER clause. The clause prompts dBASE IV to send to the printer the data on the screen. For example, you get a list of payees and amounts in payee order. Enter

```
SET ORDER TO payee ⏎
LIST payee,amount  TO PRINTER ⏎
```

The information that appears on the screen will be printed. Note that, unlike most word-processing programs, dBASE IV does not automatically issue a form feed command at the end of the printing. If you want to feed the paper to the top of the next form you must enter an explicit command to do so. The EJECT command causes dBASE IV to send a form feed command to the printer. Enter

```
EJECT ⏎
```

The remainder of the page is fed to the printer.

You can use the TO PRINTER clause in combination with other LIST command options. For example, you could print the sales tax calculations by entering

```
LIST payee,amount,amount/1.06,amount-amount/1.06    TO PRINTER ⏎
EJECT ⏎
```

You can also use selection commands. The following command prints the date, payee, and amount for all uncleared checks. Enter

```
LIST date, payee, amount FOR .NOT.CLEARED TO PRINTER ⏎
EJECT ⏎
```

Note that the printing accomplished by TO PRINTER is simply sent to the printer. This does not make any allowances for headings, page numbers, or page breaks. If your listing is longer than a single page, it will simply print right past the bottom of one page, onto the next. This is called *unformatted* printing. Unformatted printing is a quick and easy way to print information while working with dBASE IV. It is not intended to produce formal printed reports. In the next chapter you will learn how to create formatted reports using dBASE IV.

Set Commands

In this chapter you have learned how Dot Prompt commands use clauses, field lists, and expressions to create lists of specific information. It is the nature of command clauses that they only effect the specific command they are used with.

However, it is possible to select records or fields so that *all subsequent* commands affect only those records or fields. dBASE IV provides SET FIELDS TO and SET FILTER TO for this purpose.

SET FIELDS TO

This command selects specific fields from the active database. The database will then behave as if the file structure contained only those fields. The field section remains active until you use another SET FIELDS TO or close the database file. Note that commands referring to any other fields in the current selection will generate an error message. You can also generate read-only calculated fields with this command.

SET FILTER TO

This command uses a logical expression to select records. Following this command the database file will act as if it contains only those records that meet the selection criterion. This selection will remain in force until another SET FILTER TO.

SET commands are classified as *environmental* commands. This means that they determine a general characteristic of the working environment. The effect of environmental commands is not seen directly. You need to enter a command that uses that environmental factor in order to notice that anything has changed. You already encountered two environmental commands in this chapter: SET MEMOWIDTH TO and SET ORDER TO. The effect only appeared when you subsequently entered a command like LIST remarks or LIST payee.

Another attribute of environmental commands is that they stay in effect until explicitly changed or reset to the default value.

The SET FIELDS and SET FILTER commands are useful when you want to perform several operations with the same data set. These commands eliminate the need to enter the same list of fields or FOR clause for a series of commands. For example, in this chapter most of the lists have included the DATE, PAYEE, and AMOUNT fields. If you know these are the fields you want to work with, you can use a SET FIELDS command to automatically limit database operations to them. Enter

```
CLEAR ↵
SET FIELDS TO payee,date,amount  ↵
LIST ↵
```

The listing now includes only the three fields you specified in the SET FIELDS command. Notice that the order of their display is determined by the order in which the field names were entered in the command.

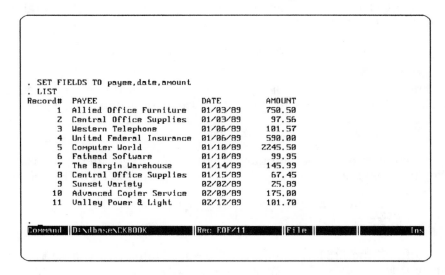

```
. SET FIELDS TO payee,date,amount
. LIST
Record#  PAYEE                    DATE       AMOUNT
      1  Allied Office Furniture  01/03/89    750.50
      2  Central Office Supplies  01/03/89     97.56
      3  Western Telephone        01/06/89    101.57
      4  United Federal Insurance 01/06/89    590.00
      5  Computer World           01/10/89   2245.50
      6  Fathead Software         01/10/89     99.95
      7  The Bargin Warehouse     01/14/89    145.99
      8  Central Office Supplies  01/15/89     67.45
      9  Sunset Variety           02/02/89     25.89
     10  Advanced Copier Service  02/09/89    175.00
     11  Valley Power & Light     02/12/89    101.70
```

```
Command   D:\dbase\CKBOOK         Rec: EOF/11      File                      Ins
```

Figure 4-32. Fields selected by SET FIELDS.

With the fields automatically selected, you now can write other LIST commands without having to bother with the field list portions. Enter

        LIST FOR MONTH(date)=2 ↵

The screen displays the three fields from the selected records. One disadvantage of the SET FIELDS procedure is that, when it is in force, you cannot refer to a field that is not part of the selection, even as part of a record selection expression. Enter

        LIST FOR .NOT.cleared ↵

This command generates a "Variable not found" error message because so long as SET FIELDS limits the fields to PAYEE, DATE, and AMOUNT, dBASE IV will behave as if other fields never existed. Return to the Dot Prompt by entering

        ↵

To return to the full field list, enter

        SET FIELDS TO ↵

The SET FILTER command establishes a selection criterion through which all subsequent data must pass. The term *filter* refers to the process by which the data retrieved will automatically be selected even when there is no explicit FOR clause. For example, you might want to limit the database to records from a particular month. Enter

```
SET FILTER TO MONTH(date)=1  ⏎
LIST ⏎
```

The database will behave as if only the records from the month of January were in the database. This will effect all subsequent commands. Enter

```
CALCULATE  SUM(amount),AVG(amount)   ⏎
```

Only the eight records from January are included in the calculations.
You can combine a SET FIELDS command with a SET FILTER. Enter

```
SET FIELDS TO check_num,date,payee,amount   ⏎
CLEAR ⏎
LIST ⏎
```

The results of the LIST command will be determined by the current environmental settings.

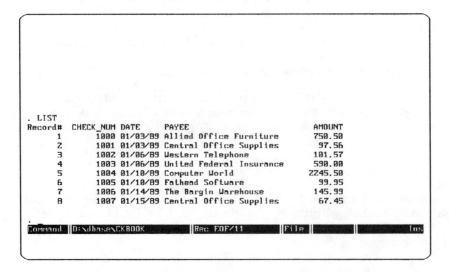

```
. LIST
Record#  CHECK_NUM DATE     PAYEE                      AMOUNT
      1      1000 01/03/89 Allied Office Furniture     750.50
      2      1001 01/03/89 Central Office Supplies      97.56
      3      1002 01/06/89 Western Telephone           101.57
      4      1003 01/06/89 United Federal Insurance    590.00
      5      1004 01/10/89 Computer World             2245.50
      6      1005 01/10/89 Fathead Software             99.95
      7      1006 01/14/89 The Bargin Warehouse        145.99
      8      1007 01/15/89 Central Office Supplies      67.45
.
Command  D:\dbase\CKBOOK        Rec: EOF/11      File              Ins
```

Figure 4-33. SET FILTER and SET FIELDS active.

Note the records are ordered by PAYEE because the PAYEE tag was the last one selected with the SET ORDER TO command. Close the database file by entering

```
CLOSE DATABASE  ⏎
```

Ending a Dot Prompt Session

You have now completed your first tour of the Dot Prompt mode. You can return to the Control Center, or exit dBASE IV directly from the Dot Prompt mode.

To return to the Control Center, you can enter the ASSIST command or use the shortcut key [F2]. Enter

    [F2]

The Control Center display appears exactly as it was when you entered the Dot Prompt mode.

Return to the Dot Prompt mode by entering

    [Alt-e] e

You can use the QUIT command to exit dBASE IV directly from the Dot Prompt mode. Enter

    QUIT ↵

Summary

In this chapter you learned how the basic database operations of data entry, editing, and retrieval can be carried out in the Dot Prompt mode, using the dBASE IV Command Language.

- **Command Language .** dBASE IV provides two basic ways to carry out operations: menu selection and Command Language. When using menus, you select the operation to be carried out from a list of choices. In the Command Language you enter command sentences that tell dBASE IV what tasks are to be carried out. The advantage of the Command Language is that you can carry out operations more directly and quickly than is possible through the menus. dBASE IV also allows a greater range of operations under the Command Language than under the Control Center menus.

- **Dot Prompt.** The Dot Prompt is used to indicate that the Command Language mode is active and ready to accept a valid command sentence. The Dot Prompt appears when you exit the Control Center display with the [Alt-e] e command. You can return to the Control Center by entering ASSIST, or using the [F2] key.

- **Files.** Database files are opened with the USE command. You must specify the filename of the database that you want to open, or enter ? to display a list of files on the disk.

- **Selection of Fields.** By default dBASE IV includes all the fields listed in the database structure when an operation is carried out. You can select specific fields using a FIELDS clause followed by a list of fields. The fields appear in the order in which they were listed in the FIELDS clause. The LIST and DISPLAY commands can accept a field list without the use of the FIELDS clause.

- **Scope.** You can direct some dBASE IV commands to operate on a specified section of the database file, using one of the scope options. They are: RECORD n, NEXT n, ALL, or REST.

- **Selection of Records.** Normally, dBASE IV will include all the records in the database when a LIST, DISPLAY ALL, EDIT, SUM, COUNT, AVERAGE, or CALCULATE command is executed. These command scan the entire database when executed. You can select records for inclusion by adding a FOR clause to the command. The FOR clause requires a logical expression used to select records from the database for processing. A logical expression is evaluated as either true or false.

- **Calculated Expressions.** You can create calculated information by adding expressions to the field lists of the LIST and DISPLAY commands. The expression can be numeric, character, or date.

- **Full Screen Modes.** The EDIT and BROWSE commands operate in a full-screen display mode. The full-screen mode allows you to display and edit all the information displayed.

- **Display Only Commands.** The LIST and DISPLAY commands are used to retrieve data for display only. If you do not intend to change or edit the data, these commands operate faster than full-screen mode commands. They also offer a wide range of options in terms of selection and calculation.

- **Functions.** A function is a special dBASE IV Command Language keyword used to perform a special calculations or manipulations in a dBASE IV expression. Functions make it possible to transform and manipulate the data stored in the fields. They generate additional information based on the field data. Functions can perform numeric, date, or character manipulations.

- **Memo Fields.** dBASE IV full screen operations will not directly display the information stored in memo fields. The display-only commands, such as LIST and DISPLAY, will display the text of memo fields if the memo field name is included in the field list. You can select records based on memo field data by using the $ operator to perform a sub-string search on the memo field text. The MEMLINES( ) function calculates the number of lines in the memo field text. The MLINE( ) function returns a specific line of text from a memo field.

- **Calculations.** Summary calculations can be performed by the SUM, AVERAGE, and COUNT commands. The CALCULATE command will carry out several different calculations at one time. The CALCULATE command recognizes special options: SUM, AVG, CNT, MAX, MIN, STD, VAR, and NPV.

- **Index Tags.** Data can be displayed in index order by activating any of the index tags available in the file's multiple-index file. An index tag is activated using the SET ORDER TO command. If no tag name is used the database is reset to the natural order.

- **Fast Searches.** When an index order is active, you can use the FIND command to perform a rapid search on the indexed field. This search takes advantage of the hierarchical tree-type structure of the index file, which significantly reduces the time required to locate an individual records.

- **Printing.** The LIST and DISPLAY command accept the TO PRINT clause that prompts dBASE IV to echo the output of the commands to the printer. This is an unformatted type of printing which does not take into account page breaks, page numbers, or form feeds. You can use the EJECT command to manually feed the remainder of the form.

- **Set Commands.** dBASE IV SET commands establish environmental parameters that effect specific types of outputs and inputs. SET FIELDS TO can be used to limit all outputs or editing operations to a specific list of fields. The SET FILTER TO command limits database operations to a specific group of records. When SET FIELDS and/or SET FILTER is in effect, the database behaves as if only the specified or selected fields and records are part of the database. Using SET FIELDS or SET FILTER without a specification returns the database to its normal contents. Closing the database automatically terminates the effect of any SET FIELDS or SET FILTER commands currently in effect.

Exercises

Ex-1
   List records on or after 01/15/89.

```
LIST payee,date,amount  FOR date>={01/15/89}  ↵
```

Ex-2
   Locate the record where payee is *Sunset.*

```
LIST FOR payee="Sunset"  ↵
```

5

Basic Column Reports

In Chapters 3 and 4 you learned how data stored in a database file can be retrieved. The operations in Chapter 3 emphasized the use of the Control Center's Query By Example mode. Chapter 4 explained how the dBASE IV Command Language can be used to query a database.

In both cases the process of data retrieval was an informal process, i.e. the data that was retrieved was not organized in a formal printed report. The information was generally formatted for screen display because it was assumed that the purpose of the query was to investigate some aspect of the data stored in the file, e.g. to answer a specific question, like *Which checks were written to Western Telephone?* In addition, you could perform summary calculations, such as field totals or averages.

A *report* deals with the same data and operations as a query. The main difference is that a report is used to organize the information into a formal output. The usual purpose of a formal report is to create a printed document based on the contents of the database file. However, reports can be displayed on the screen, usually for the purpose of previewing the final printed report, or to be stored in a text file which can then be used by another application, such as a word-processing or desktop publishing program.

The term *formal* refers to the fact that reports take into consideration such formatting problems as column widths, page numbers, page breaks, and numeric formats. These aspects of the final appearance of the report would not normally be of concern when you are simply making a database query.

In this chapter you will learn how to create formal reports with dBASE IV. You will also see how such concepts as selection, sequencing, and calculated expressions can be used within the framework of formal reports, to add power and flexibility to your reports.

To begin, load dBASE IV in the usual manner. The chapter begins with the Control Center display on the screen.

Report Forms

A dBASE IV report is created by merging the data stored in the database file with a *report form*. A report form is a special file that contains a description of the way the database should be formatted when it is printed. The report form contains information about the fields to be printed, the headings, the page numbers and other formatting specifications that produce a formal printed report.

In dBASE IV the report form is created by using the Report Form Layout screen to create a model of the final report. This screen is used to generate a *report form file*. The report form file is then used to merge the model with the current data to create the report. Storing report specifications in a file allows you to print the same report form again and again. As the database changes, the exact information on the report will change, but the basic form will stay the same.

You can enter the Report Form mode from the Control Center by highlighting the <create> symbol in the Reports column. Enter

```
[right  arrow] (3 times)
 ↵
```

dBASE IV reacts to this by displaying a message box that says "Please put a database file or view into use first". This message indicates that you must be using a database before you can create a report form. This is because the Report Form mode depends upon the database structure for data about what fields will be used in it.

In order to enter the Report From mode you must satisfy dBASE IV by opening a database file. Open the CKBOOK file by entering

```
 ↵
[left  arrow] (3 times)
[down  arrow]
 ↵  (2 times)
```

Now enter the Report Form mode.

```
[right  arrow] (3 times)
 ↵
```

This time dBASE IV activates the report form design mode. The Layout menu is automatically activated.

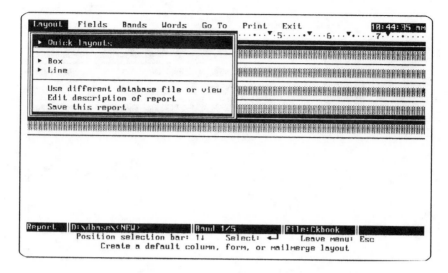

Figure 5-1. Report Form Layout display.

The first option on the menu is Quick Layout. This represents the fastest way to create a report. dBASE IV will automatically generate a standard report based on the database structure when you select this option. Before you get involved with the creation of a report, exit the menu so you can examine the basic layout screen. Enter

    [Esc]

With the menu box closed you can see the basic structure of the Report Form Layout screen. The layout consists of five sections called *bands*, drawn horizontally across the page. Each band is used to control an aspect of the formal report.

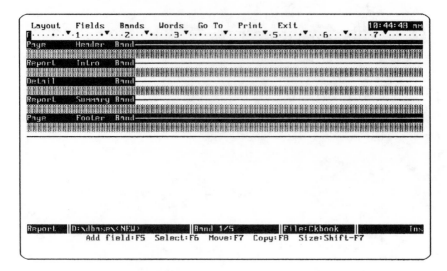

Figure 5-2. Report form bands.

The bands are:

Page Header

This band is used to specify the data that will print at the top of each page of the report. This band usually contains the page heading, column headings, the report date and the page number.

Report Intro

This band is used to print information at the beginning of the report above the data from the database file. This information is printed on the first page of the report following the Page Header text. This band is used to print any explanatory text about the report that follows. Note that this band will print only once on each report.

Detail

This band controls the information that prints for each record in the database. Typically, the contents of this band are field names or field expressions, which draw information from each record in the database. The detail band will print as many times on a page as there are records. If not all the records in the database can fit on one page, the report continues the details on subsequent pages, until the end of the file has been reached.

Report Summary

Summary information prints at the end of the report, following the printing of the last record of the Detail section. Typically, this section is used for such summary calculations as column totals or averages. This band prints only once—at the end of the report.

Page Footer

This band operates the same as the Page Header band. The only difference is that the data prints at the bottom of each page instead of the top. For example, you may prefer the page number at the bottom of the page.

The bands indicate the difference between an informal query and a formal report. In the query, data is displayed along with the field names or expressions used as column headings. A formal report has separate and specific instructions for each part of the page. For example, because the column headings (Page Header band) are controlled separately from the column contents (Detail band), you can create your own column-heading text, instead of using the field name or expression. This is very important when the report is to be read by people who know nothing about the field names or expression you would use within dBASE IV. Instead, the report can be designed to use language meaningful to the reader.

Note that the use of the bands is optional. Many reports have no need for an Intro band and some do not require any Summary band calculations. You will see that by using select bands, you can create reports that print in forms other than the typical, columnar form.

Creating a Column Report

To understand how the Report Form Layout is used to create printed reports, you will begin by creating some simple column-type reports. The fastest way to do this is to use the Layout Quick layout command to generate a report based on the structure of the database. In practice, however—unless your database has an extremely simple structure—this method will usually produce a report with too much information, since all the fields will be printed in the order they appear in the structure. You will learn later how to use the Quick Layout options effectively by controlling their operations with other dBASE IV commands.

For now you will begin by constructing a column-type report from scratch. Suppose you wanted to create a report that listed the date, payee and amount of the checks recorded in the database file. The first step would be to place the fields into the Detail band of the report form. To place an item in the Detail band you simply use the down arrow key to move the cursor to that area of the layout. Enter

```
down arrow  (5 times)
```

The cursor is now on line 0 column 0 of the Detail band. The cursor location is indicated on the status bar as Line:0 Col:0. Keep in mind that the line number shown does not refer to the actual line on the page. Instead, it simply refers to the line within the Detail band. Note that dBASE IV refers to the first line within a band as 0, not 1.

A report is generally classified by the number of lines used in the Detail band. For example, a column type report will have only a single line in it. All the items that will print in columns are distributed horizontally acroos the band.

If you use more than one line in the Detail band, you are said to be creating a *form*-type report. In this type of report each record occupies more than one line. In this case the information is not be aligned in columns that can be read straight down the page. You use this type of report when it is not possible to organize all the data entered into columns.

Finally, when the Detail band covers an entire page for each record you are said to be creating a mail-merge report. This type of report prints a complete page for each record. It is typically used to send form letters, or fill out pre-printed forms with database information.

Form and mail-merge reports are covered in a later chapter.

The difference between the report types is really one of degree, not of kind, since they are all composed of the same elements. It is the advantage of the dBASE IV Report Form Layout mode that it allows you to create reports with a variety of appearances that are composed of the same elements.

In a column-type report you will usually distribute the fields horizontally across Line 0 of the Detail band. Begin the current example with the DATE field. To add a field to a report form use the Field Add Field command, or the shortcut command keystroke [F5]. Enter

     [F5]

dBASE IV displays a window that lists information you might want to include in your report. The window consists of four columns. The left column lists the names of the fields in your database structure. Note that they are listed alphabetically, rather than in the order in which they were entered into the file structure. The next column lists any calculated fields, if any, as defined in a database query. The last two columns list such standard dBASE IV items as page date, page number (pageno), and summary calculations.

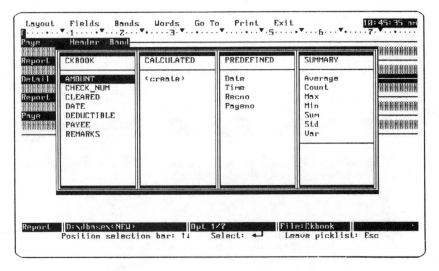

Figure 5-3. Insert field window display.

The two right columns of this display will always be the same. The two left columns may change, depending on the specific database being used.

You can select the DATE field in two ways.

Highlight

You can use the arrow keys to move the highlight to the name of the field you want to select.

Search

Enter a letter or letters for which the program will search the column. The highlight will be positioned on the first name, if any, that matches the letter or letters.

In this case type the search method. Enter

d

The highlight jumps to the first name on the list that begins with the letter D, DATE. The search method is often faster than scrolling the highlight through an entire list. To select the highlighted field, enter

⌐

Selecting the field brings up another window—the field data window. This window contains information about how the data from the DATE field will be displayed in the report.

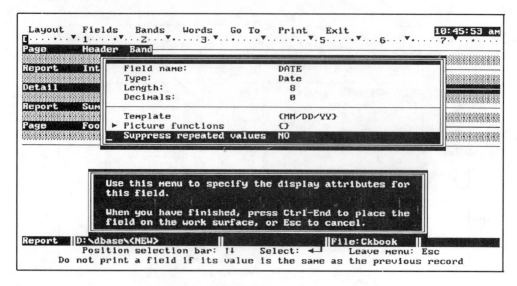

Figure 5-4. Field data window display.

The top part of the window contains information about the column. This data is picked up from the file structure. In most cases you would leave this information exactly as it is. The most common reason for changing it is to adjust the column width in cases where you prefer a different width than the one specified in the file's structure.

The bottom section of the menu contains three options that can be used to modify the appearance of the information. Note that in the case of a DATE field none of the options on this menu are available to you. In this case you can only accept the information displayed by entering

    [Ctrl-End]

You have now added a field to the Detail band. The first eight positions on the line are occupied by MM/DD/YY, indicating that the dates stored in the DATE field will print in this position. Keep in mind that the first character on the line is position 0, not position 1.

In many computer applications sequences begin with 0 as the first value, not 1.

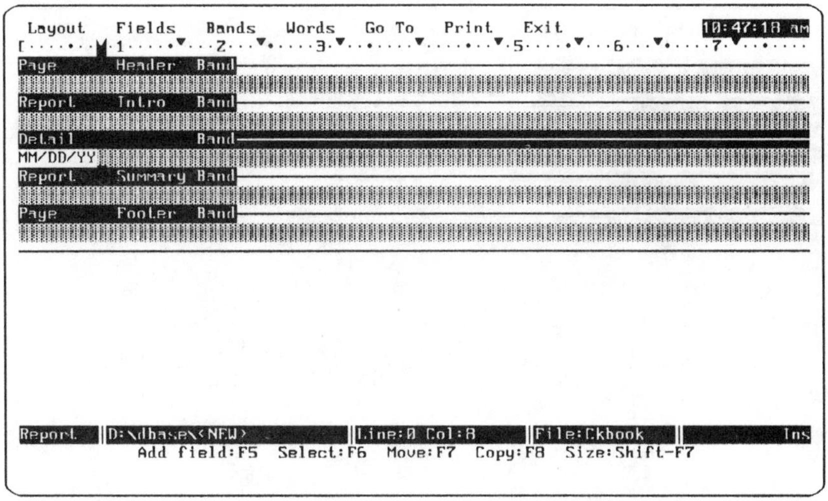

Figure 5-5. Field added to Detail band.

To add more fields to the Detail band you must move the cursor to the right so as to indicate the horizontal location of the next field. In most cases you will want to skip at least one space before inserting another field. Enter

```
[right arrow]
```

The cursor is currently positioned at column 9. Insert the PAYEE field at this position. Enter

```
[F5]
p ↵
[Ctrl/End]
```

A string of 25 X's marks the location where the PAYEE data will print. Add the third field, AMOUNT to the report. Enter

```
[right arrow]
[F5]
↵
[Ctrl/End]
```

The third field has been added to the Detail band.

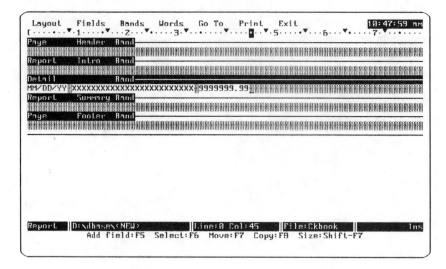

Figure 5-6. Fields added to Detail band.

You now have enough information to preview what the report will look like when it is printed. To preview the report, you can use the Print View Report on Screen command. Enter

[Alt-p] v

dBASE IV will take a few moments to generate the report form, based on your layout specifications. When this process is completed, the top of the first page of the report will be displayed on the screen.

```
01/03/89 Allied Office Furniture        750.50
01/03/89 Central Office Supplies         97.56
01/06/89 Western Telephone              101.57
01/06/89 United Federal Insurance       590.00
01/10/89 Computer World                2245.50
01/10/89 Fathead Software                99.95
01/14/89 The Bargin Warehouse          145.99
01/15/89 Central Office Supplies         67.45
02/02/89 Sunset Variety                  25.89
02/09/89 Advanced Copier Service       175.00
02/12/89 Valley Power & Light          101.70




         Cancel viewing: ESC.  Continue viewing: SPACEBAR
```

Figure 5-7. Report displayed on screen.

The current report is simply a list of the field data without any headings. This is because you have not yet filled out the bands on the report form that create them. Return to the Layout screen by entering

    [Esc]
    ⌐

Column Headings

Column headings are text printed at the top of every page that serve to identify the information printed in the columns. To add column headings to the current report you must position the cursor in the Page Header band. Enter

      [up arrow](*4 times*)

The cursor is now positioned in the band. Column headings are usually positioned directly above the data printed in the column. Move the cursor to the beginning of the line by entering

      [Home]

Column headings are *literal* text. They are printed exactly the same each time they are used in the report. This is in contrast to the fields you inserted into the Detail band, which are really symbols. For example, the DATE field is shown on the report form as MM/DD/YY. Of course, you do not expect the actual report to contain the characters *MM/DD/YY* . The program will substitute the contents of the fields into that location.

Column headings print exactly as they appear on the Report Form Layout. You can enter their text by simply typing in the characters you want at the desired horizontal position. Make sure you are working with the Text Insert mode active.

If it is active, Ins will appear on the right end of the status bar. If you do not see Ins, activate the Insert mode by entering:

  [Ins]

Enter the heading for the DATE field. It is not necessary to limit the column heading to a single line. If the field is narrow you can enter several lines for each column heading. Enter

        Date of ⌐
        Check

To enter the next column head, move the cursor to column 9 by entering

      [right arrow] *(4 times)*
      Paid To

Move the cursor to column 35. Enter

    Amount

The report form looks like this:

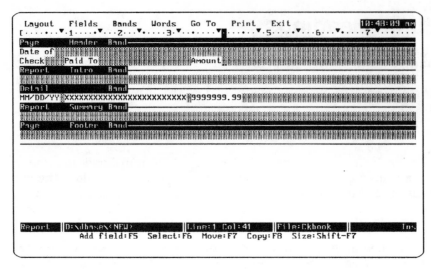

Figure 5-8. Report form with Detail and headings.

Preview the report with the column headings added by entering

    [Alt-p] **v**

```
Date of
Check    Paid To                 Amount

01/03/89 Allied Office Furniture   750.50
01/03/89 Central Office Supplies    97.56
01/06/89 Western Telephone         101.57
01/06/89 United Federal Insurance  590.00
01/10/89 Computer World           2245.50
01/10/89 Fathead Software           99.95
01/14/89 The Bargin Warehouse      145.99
01/15/89 Central Office Supplies    67.45
02/02/89 Sunset Variety             25.89
02/09/89 Advanced Copier Service   175.00
02/12/89 Valley Power & Light      101.70




-          Cancel viewing: ESC,  Continue viewing: SPACEBAR
```

Figure 5-9. Report with column headings.

Return to the report layout screen by entering

       [Esc]
       ⏎

Page Numbers and Dates

In addition to text for the column headings, it is common to include in the page header or footer bands, the current date, time, or page number. This information is inserted into a report by using the special functions listed in the Add Field window.

First, position the cursor in the Page Header band where you want to insert the date. Enter

          [Home]
       [up arrow]

 You can insert blank lines *without* changing the cursor position, with Ctrl-n. Enter

       [Ctrl-n]   *(2 times)*

Enter text that will clarify the meaning of the date.

       Report Printed On
       [space bar]

Display the Add Field window by entering

       [F5]

In this case you want to select Date from column 3, the Predefined column. Enter

       [right arrow] *(2 times)*
       ⏎
       [Ctrl-End]

The characters MM/DD/YY are inserted into the Page Header band. Keep in mind that this symbol refers to the system's date, not the DATE field of the CKBOOK database. The system's date is the real time and date maintained by the operating system.

The page number is inserted in a similar manner. Enter

       ⏎
       Page
       [space bar]
       [F5]
       [right arrow] *(2 times)*
       [PgDn]
       ⏎
       [Ctrl-End]

The symbol inserted into the Page Header band will automatically increment as each page is printed. In addition, you might want to add a title for the report that would also print at the top of the page. Enter

    ⏎ *(2 times)*
    `Checking Account Activity Report`

Templates

One advantage working with a report form has over simply listing field data is that the report form uses templates to format information. One typical use of a template is to add punctuation to numeric displays. If you look at the Details band you will see that the symbol displayed for the AMOUNT field is 9999999.99. This symbol is a template that indicates the way the values will be displayed. By default, dBASE IV automatically sets the field template to match the file structure. However, you can edit the field template to alter the way numbers are displayed.

To change a field's template you must first place the cursor on the field you want to modify. This can be done by moving the cursor to the field's location on the template. You can also use the Fields Modify Fields command to access the field without having to change cursor position. Enter

    `[Alt-f] m`

The program displays a list of all the fields in the current layout.

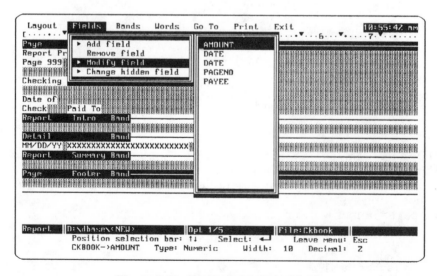

Figure 5-10. Modify fields list of fields.

Note that DATE appears twice, once for the DATE field and again for the pre-defined date function. This duplication is not of any practical significance because date-type values do not use display templates or functions.

Select the AMOUNT field by entering

⏎

The field information box is now displayed for the AMOUNT field. There are two options listed in the lower section of the box that relate to the way data is displayed on a report form: template and function.

Template

A template is a character-for-character model of the way data should be displayed. Each character in the template is a formatting option for one of the characters in the field. The size of the template controls the overall width of the printed data.

Function

Format functions are options that affect all the characters in the field.
To edit the template for the AMOUNT field, enter

⏎

Your cursor is now positioned so you can edit the template characters. The box below lists your options.

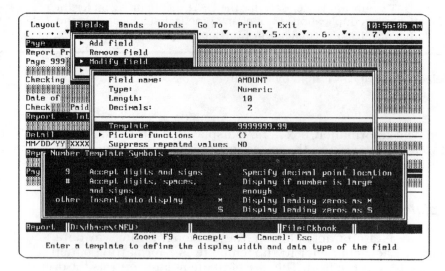

Figure 5-11. Template editing display.

You may want to insert commas to separate groups of three decimal places. This makes large numbers easier to read. For example, if you used the template 999,999.99, the value 1200.00 would be displayed as 1,200.00. Enter

```
[Home]
[Ctrl-y]
999,999.99  ↵
```

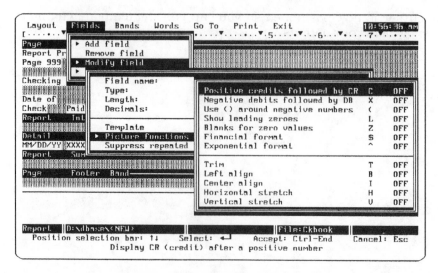

Figure 5-12. Picture functions menu.

Picture functions affect the overall display of the value. To activate a Picture function, enter

```
[down arrow]↵
```

The Picture functions options are listed on a menu.

The Picture functions menu is divided into two parts. The top part lists functions that affect the way numeric values are displayed. The first three options, C, X and), are used to display numbers in formats pertaining to the accounting profession. (CR stands for credit, DB for debit) The L option causes the full width of the column to be padded with zeros. This is useful when you want to ensure that no one alters the report by adding digits to the front of the numbers (typically used in check writing). The Z option causes 0 values to be displayed as blanks. The $ and ˆ options cause the values to be displayed in financial or scientific format.

The bottom section of the menu lists options that relate to the alignment of the data in the column.

In this case, select the Z option, to show 0 values as blanks. Note that even though the option character symbol is Z, the command letter for selection is b, because the menu option is labeled Blanks for Zero Values. Enter

```
b
[Ctrl-End]
```

Note that in this database, none of the amounts is zero. Thus this option will have no visible effect. Save the modified field settings by entering

```
[Ctrl-End]
```

Adding Summary Calculations

Suppose that you wanted your report to include a total for the AMOUNT field. To create a summary calculation, you must insert a calculation in the Summary band. Move the cursor to the band by entering

```
[down arrow] ( 9 times)
```

Before you create the calculation, you may want to draw a line across the bottom of the form, to separate the summary from the record details. Move the cursor to the beginning of the line by entering

```
[Home]
```

Single and double lines can be added to a report layout by using the Layout Line command.

The lines created with Layout Line or Layout Box use ASCII characters above 127 to form the lines and boxes. Not all printers have characters that match these codes. The exact effect of printing forms with lines or boxes included in the Report Form Layout will vary with different printers. For example, older Epson printers, MX or RX series, do not support these characters. The HP LaserJet does not, but the Series II Laserjet will.

Select Line Drawing by entering

[Alt-L] L

You can select to draw either a single line, double line, or draw a line that uses a specified character.

If your printer does not support printing of the lines or boxes, you can use the third option, Using Specified Character, to draw a line of - or =, instead of continuous-line characters.

In this case, select a double line by entering

d

The cursor shows a double line inserted into the first character on the line. You can now use the left arrow and right arrow keys to select a different starting position, or press ⏎ to start drawing the line at the current location. Begin drawing by entering

⏎

Move the cursor to column 50. As you move, the double line will be extended across the band.

When you have reached column 50, you complete the drawing processing by entering

⏎

Add another line to the Summary band by entering

⏎

Title this line Totals by entering

Totals

Move the cursor to column 35. Insert a summary command that will total the values in the AMOUNT field. Enter

[F5]

```
[right arrow] (3 times)
  s ↵
```

dBASE IV displays the summary calculation menu. This menu provides options which setup the operation of the summary calculation.

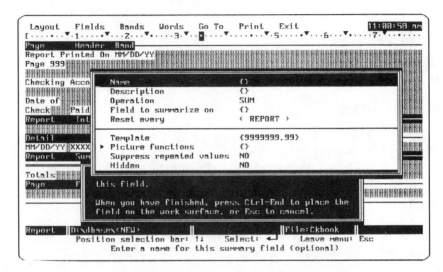

Figure 5-13. Summary calculation options.

The Name and Description settings are optional. Only one of the options on this menu is required, Field to Summarize on. This option *must* be entered or dBASE IV will not know which of the fields to calculate. It is important to keep in mind that the horizontal location of the cursor in the Summary band is not used by dBASE IV to determine which field is to be summarized.

Select the field to summarize by entering

```
f
```

A list of the fields is displayed with the numeric fields, which can be selected, shown in bold. In this case, you can select either the AMOUNT or CHECK-NUM fields. Although it may not make sense, it would be possible to summarize any numeric field at the bottom of this column. Here, select the AMOUNT field for summary by entering

```
↵
```

In addition to selecting the field to be summarized, you may want to change the template, as well. It is usually a good idea to use a same sized template for both column data and summary calculation. This ensures that the data aligns properly on the decimal places. If the column data and the summary value use different size templates, you must make sure that the decimal point in each is located in the same horizontal column.

Another factor to keep in mind is that the sum of the contents of a field is often a number that contains more digits than any of the individual values in the field. You will want to take care that the template for the summary calculation has a sufficient number of spaces to display the total. In this case, enter a template that matches that used for the AMOUNT field. Enter

```
t
[Home]
[Ctrl-y]
999,999.99  ⏎
```

Save the summary calculation by entering

```
[Ctrl-End]
```

Add another line—this time for the **average** of the AMOUNT field. Try this on your own. The correct command can be found at the end of the chapter under EX-1. Remember to select AMOUNT as the field to summarize, and change the template to match the other data in that column.

The report form will now look like this:

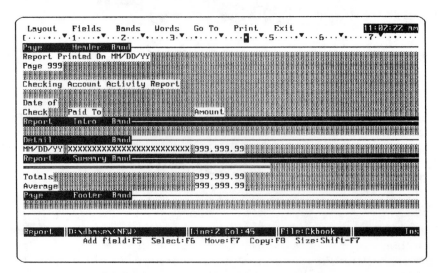

Figure 5-14. Report with summary calculations.

Preview the report by entering

```
[Alt-p]  v
```

dBASE IV takes a few moments to compile your Report Form Layout and then displays its preview.

```
Report Printed On 05/19/89
Page   1

Checking Account Activity Report

Date of
Check      Paid To                    Amount

01/03/89  Allied Office Furniture       750.50
01/03/89  Central Office Supplies        97.56
01/06/89  Western Telephone             101.57
01/06/89  United Federal Insurance      590.00
01/10/89  Computer World              2,245.50
01/10/89  Fathead Software               99.95
01/14/89  The Bargin Warehouse          145.99
01/15/89  Central Office Supplies        67.45
02/02/89  Sunset Variety                 25.89
02/09/89  Advanced Copier Service       175.00
02/12/89  Valley Power & Light          101.70
========================================
Totals                              4,401.11
Average                               400.10


_         Cancel viewing: ESC,  Continue viewing: SPACEBAR
```

Figure 5-15. Previewed report with headers and summary calculations.

Return to the Report Form Layout screen by entering

> [Esc]
> ↵

Printing a Report

Once you have created a report form and previewed the result, you will be ready to print the report. You can send the report directly to the printer without having to exit the Report Layout mode by entering

> [Alt-p]

The print menu is displayed.

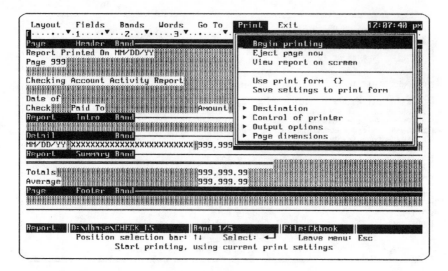

Figure 5-16. Print report menu.

The menu is divided into three sections. The first section contains the commands that actually output data to the printer or screen.

Begin Printing

Begins printing the current report with the current set of print specifications.

Eject Page Now

This option sends a form feed command to the printer. It performs the same function as the EJECT command.

View Report on Screen

This is the option you have been using so far to preview the report on the screen before you send it to the printer.
   Enter

b

The report prints.

```
Report Printed On 05/19/89
Page  1

Checking Account Activity Report

Date         Paid To                    Amount
of Check


01/03/89     Allied Office Furniture     750.50
01/03/89     Central Office Supplies      97.56
01/06/89     Western Telephone           101.57
01/06/89     United Federal Insurance    590.00
01/10/89     Computer World            2,245.50
01/10/89     Fathead Software             99.95
01/14/89     The Bargin Warehouse        145.99
01/15/89     Central Office Supplies      67.45
02/02/89     Sunset Variety               25.89
02/09/89     Advanced Copier Service     175.00
02/12/89     Valley Power & Light        101.70
-------------------------------------------------------
Totals                                 4,401.11
Average                                  400.10
```

Figure 5-17. Report printed.

When the printing is complete, you return to the Report Form Layout screen.

Saving a Report Form

Once you have created and printed your report, you can decide if you want to save it or not. Saving the report creates a file with an FRM extension that contains the specifications used to print the previous report. The advantage of saving is that you can print it again without having to compose a new report form. In most cases, it is best to save the report in case you later need to reprint it. For example, you might see a typo you hadn't noticed when you first printed the report.

You can save a report in two ways:

Save and Exit

The [Alt-e] s commands saves the current report and returns you to the main Control Center display.

Save and Continue

[Alt-L] s command saves the current report, but allows you to remain in the Report Form Layout mode to make further modifications.

It is always a good idea to save the report with [Alt-L]s, as you are developing it. This protects you from losing the specifications if a power failure or other error hangs up the computer. In this case, save the report and exit the Report Form Layout mode by entering

        [Alt-e] s

You must enter a one- to eight-character filename for the report form. Enter the name CHECK_LS (check listings).

        check_ls ↵

The specifications have been saved in a file called CHECK_LS.FRG, and you are now back at the Control Center display. Note that the name CHECK-LS appears under the Reports column.

How Reports Are Generated

You might have noticed that when you used certain commands in the Report Layout mode, such as Print View Report on Screen or Exit Save Changes and Exit, there is a significant delay before the command completes. Why does this delay exist and what does it mean?

The delay is caused by the *report generation* process. The report layout you created serves as a guide, called a template, from which dBASE IV generates a program. It is the program based on your layout that actually produces the report.

The report generation process actually requires the creation of three different types of files: 1) the Report Form Layout file, with an FRM extension, 2) the dBASE IV program text file, with an FRG extension and 3) a compiled object-code file, based on the dBASE IV program file, with an FRO extension.

When you issue a command to save, view, or print the current report, dBASE IV needs to create the program file, FRG, out of the current layout. At the bottom of the screen, is a message that reads something like "Opening file [C:\DBASE\REPORT.GEN]". The RE-PORT.GEN file is a dBASE IV Template Language file supplies the program with the basic outline used to construct a dBASE IV report program. This file is supplied with dBASE IV. (The Developers Edition contains a program that helps developers modify the Report Template form.) The program combines the general form of the report stored in the GEN file, with the specifics entered on your layout. The combined results are stored in an FRG file. The next message will read something like "Opening file [C:10104455.FRG]". Until you have save the report form and assign it a name, the program uses a temporary file name in which dBASE IV writes the actual program commands needed for the report. The filename is created from the system's clock in your computer, as a way to generate unique filenames for the temporary file. A similar method is used by some DOS commands to generate temporary filenames.

You will see the Lines value, in the center of the status bar, count from 1 to 236 in the current example. This tells you that it requires 236 dBASE IV Command Language sentences to create the report you specified in the Report Form Layout. Note that because all reports are generated from the same basic template, even the simplest report will require several hundred lines.

When the writing is completed, the message "Generation Complete, 0/0 errors/warnings produced. Template REPORT, 236 lines output", tells you that the process of conversion from report form to dBASE IV Command Language has been completed without errors.

The next step is transparent to the user. dBASE IV compiles the FRG program file into what is called an object-code file. (Part II of this book discusses object-code files.) The object-code file creates the actual report. When completed, the object-code file is executed, producing the report.

Of course, it is not necessary to understand what is happening during this process, in order to use a report. For many users, the messages that appear at the bottom of the screen won't have any significance.

The main advantage of this process is that all reports generated through the Report Form Layout are stored and used as dBASE IV Command Language programs. These programs can be modified or used as the basis of custom-designed reports or programs. In Part II of this book you can learn how to create your own dBASE IV Command Language programs. You will also be able to use these same skills to modify the programs produced by the Report Form generator.

The delay caused by the generation of the report FRG and FRO files occurs when you create or modify a report layout. Once you have saved a report, you can reprint the report as many times as you desire, without having to generate a new report. In those cases there will be no significant delay when you choose to print a report.

When you select to view the report that you are currently laying out, dBASE IV must generate a new report each time you view it. This can result in a significant delay.

This is a different process than the one used in dBASE III & III Plus. In those versions, the report form was stored in an FRM file. This was a binary coded file that could not be enhanced or modified with dBASE programming language commands. In dBASE IV, all the screens, reports, labels, and applications created in the Control Center are stored as both layout forms and programs.

Ordering Reports

The report form you just printed lists the records in the natural database order. Suppose you wanted to print the report with the records listed in order according to one of the index tags.

This can be done by using the Database Design mode to activate an index order. Enter the Design mode for the current database file.

```
[left  arrow] (3 times)
 [Shift-F2]
```

Recall that the Organize menu is displayed by default when you activate the design database mode from the Control Center. Select the Order Records by Index command.

```
o
```

Select the PAYEE index order by entering

```
P ↵
```

The PAYEE tag is activated. Any listing or reporting operation carried out from this point on, will be in the PAYEE order. Return to the main Control Center display by entering

```
[Alt-e] a
```

Highlight the CHECK_LS report form.

```
[right arrow] (3 times)
```

Select the report form by entering

```
⏎
```

You are presented with three options: Print Report, Modify Layout, or Display data. Print the report by entering

```
p
```

The Print menu is displayed over the Control Center display.

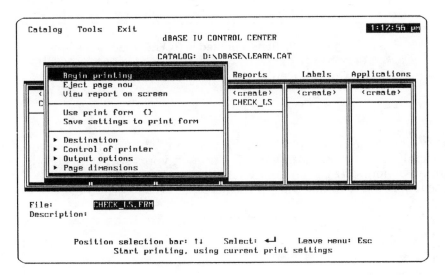

Figure 5-18. Printing a report from the Control Center display.

In this case, use the View option to display the report on the screen. Enter

```
v
```

The report is displayed exactly as it was before, with the exception that the records are listed according to the PAYEE order.

```
Report Printed On 05/19/89
Page   1

Checking Account Activity Report

Date of
Check      Paid To                    Amount

02/09/89 Advanced Copier Service      175.00
01/03/89 Allied Office Furniture      750.50
01/03/89 Central Office Supplies       97.56
01/15/89 Central Office Supplies       67.45
01/10/89 Computer World             2,245.50
01/10/89 Fathead Software              99.95
02/02/89 Sunset Variety               25.89
01/14/89 The Bargin Warehouse        145.99
01/06/89 United Federal Insurance     590.00
02/12/89 Valley Power & Light        101.70
01/06/89 Western Telephone           101.57
========================================
Totals                             4,401.11
Average                              400.10


_         Cancel viewing: ESC,  Continue viewing: SPACEBAR
```

Figure 5-19. Report printed in PAYEE order.

Return to the main Control Center display by entering

  [Esc]
  ┘

   How would you produce the same report, but with the records sequenced in descending order by AMOUNT? Try this on your own. The correct command can be found at the end of the chapter under EX-2.
   The report will look like this on the screen.

```
Report Printed On 05/19/89
Page   1

Checking Account Activity Report

Date of
Check      Paid To                    Amount

01/10/89 Computer World             2,245.50
01/03/89 Allied Office Furniture      750.50
01/06/89 United Federal Insurance     590.00
02/09/89 Advanced Copier Service      175.00
01/14/89 The Bargin Warehouse        145.99
02/12/89 Valley Power & Light        101.70
01/06/89 Western Telephone           101.57
01/10/89 Fathead Software              99.95
01/03/89 Central Office Supplies       97.56
01/15/89 Central Office Supplies       67.45
02/02/89 Sunset Variety               25.89
========================================
Totals                             4,401.11
Average                              400.10


_         Cancel viewing: ESC,  Continue viewing: SPACEBAR
```

Figure 5-20. Report displayed in descending order of amounts.

Return to the main Control Center display by entering

```
[Esc]
⅃
```

Revising a Report

You can revise an existing report any way you like, once you have seen the initial results. To make additions or changes to the CHECK_LS report, select the Modify layout option from the Select reports menu. Enter

```
    ⅃
    m
```

Inserting a Field

Suppose you realized you had omitted a field from the report form. You can easily add that field to the Detail band, in the same manner used for creating the current report form.

However, suppose you wanted to insert that field between two existing columns, instead of simply adding it to the end of the Detail band. This is a more complicated procedure because the dBASE IV Report Form Layout does not actually arrange data in columns. As you may have noted when you created the summary calculations, dBASE IV allows you to place any sort of data at any position, on any band. For example, you could have placed the sum of the CHECK_NUM field in the summary band, below the AMOUNT field. This operation would have led to a confusing report. However, dBASE IV would not have objected to that design, if that is what you decided to do.

This free-form approach to report writing has many benefits, including an ability to design non-columnar reports using the Report Form Layout mode. However, one disadvantage is that it makes the insertion of a new column require a single operation, rather than a sequence of steps. To insert a field, you must adjust the data in at least three bands.

In this case, use as an example the insertion of a check number column between the DATE and PAYEE columns. The key problem is that if you were to add a new field to the Detail band, dBASE IV does not automatically move the existing fields to the right, so as to make room for the new addition. This must be done manually before you add the new field.

Move the cursor to the Detail band by entering

```
[down arrow] (11 times)
```

You must move both the PAYEE and AMOUNT fields to the right, in order to make room for the check number. Begin by positioning the highlight on the PAYEE field.

```
[Ctrl-right arrow]
```

Highlight the data you want to move, using the [F6] command.

     [F6]

Move the cursor to the AMOUNT field by entering

     [End]
     ⏎

Enter the Moving mode using the [F7] command.

     [F7]

Move the cursor so that the beginning of the highlight is on column 20. This changes the position of the PAYEE field from column 9 to column 20. Then complete the move by entering

     ⏎

dBASE IV displays "Delete covered text and field? (Y/N)". This message is caused by your moving the field to a position that overlaps the previous position on the line. Until the move is completed, dBASE IV will act as if the fields you are moving were still positioned at the old location. Entering Y will remove the fields from their previous location, and position them to the indicated column. Enter

     y

The fields have been moved and the cursor is positioned to column 9, where you can insert the CHECK_NUM field. Enter

     [F5]
     ch ⏎
     [Ctrl-End]

The check number field is inserted into the Detail band.

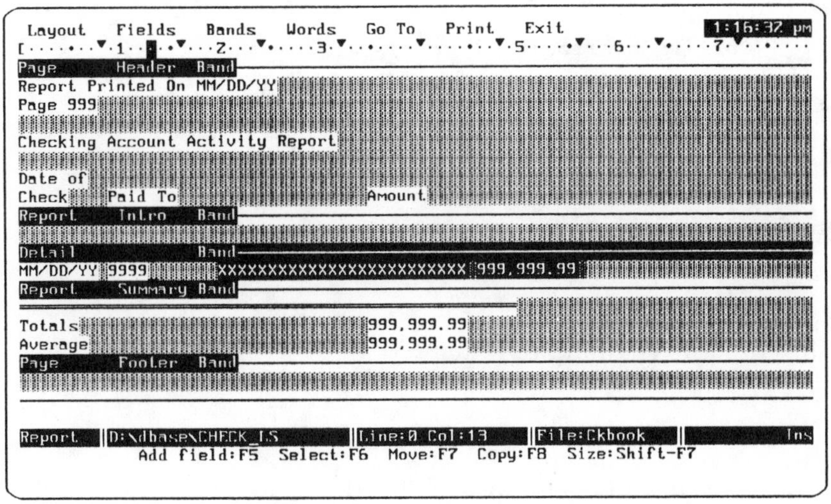

Figure 5-21. Field added to Detail band.

If you look at the other report bands, Page Header and Summary, you will notice that the insertion of a new field in the Detail band had no effect on them. The column headings and summary calculations must be moved to correctly align with the field data.

Start with the Summary band. Enter

```
[down arrow] (3 times)
[Ctrl-right arrow]
```

In this case, you want to make a vertical selection so you can move both the SUM and AVERAGE calculations. Enter

```
[F6]
[End]
[down arrow]
↵
```

Move the fields to column 46 by entering

```
[F7]
[up arrow]
[right arrow]
↵
```

The calculations are positioned beneath the correct fields.

The last modification needed is in the Page Header band. Move the cursor to the Page Header band by entering

```
[up arrow] (7 times)
```

Move to column 9 by entering

        [Ctrl-left arrow]   *(3 times)*

Highlight the headings that need to be moved.

        [F6]
        [End]

Activate the Move mode.

        [F7]

Move the cursor to column 20. Enter

        ↵
        y

Move the cursor back to column 9. Enter the heading for the CHECK_NUM field.

        Check #

The revised report form looks like this:

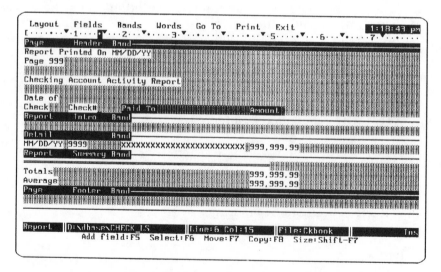

Figure 5-22. Report form after field was inserted.

Produce the report by entering

        [Alt-p] v

The revised report is displayed. Note that you forgot one small element—the line drawn between the Detail and the Summary bands has not been lengthened to account for the increased report width.

```
┌─────────────────────────────────────────────────────────────┐
│  Report Printed On 05/19/89                                  │
│  Page   1                                                    │
│                                                              │
│  Checking Account Activity Report                            │
│                                                              │
│  Date of                                                     │
│  Check     Check#     Paid To                 Amount         │
│                                                              │
│  01/10/89 1004        Computer World          2,245.50       │
│  01/03/89 1000        Allied Office Furniture   750.50       │
│  01/06/89 1003        United Federal Insurance  590.00       │
│  02/09/89 1009        Advanced Copier Service   175.00       │
│  01/14/89 1006        The Bargin Warehouse      145.99       │
│  02/12/89 1010        Valley Power & Light      101.70       │
│  01/06/89 1002        Western Telephone         101.57       │
│  01/10/89 1005        Fathead Software           99.95       │
│  01/03/89 1001        Central Office Supplies    97.56       │
│  01/15/89 1007        Central Office Supplies    67.45       │
│  02/02/89 1008        Sunset Variety             25.89       │
│  ══════════════════════════════════════════════════         │
│  Totals                                       4,401.11       │
│  Average                                        400.10       │
│                                                              │
│         Cancel viewing: ESC,  Continue viewing: SPACEBAR     │
│  _                                                           │
└─────────────────────────────────────────────────────────────┘
```

Figure 5-23. Revised report displayed.

Return to the Report Form Layout by entering

> [Esc]
> ↵

This small change illustrates the disadvantage of the free-form style used to create report forms in dBASE IV.

Memo Fields

Memo fields and their contents can be added to report forms like any other field. Return the cursor to the Detail band by entering

> [down arrow] *(4 times)*
> [End]

Add the REMARKS field to the end of the report.

> [right arrow]
> [F5]
> r ↵
> [Ctrl-End]

The memo field is inserted into the Detail band.

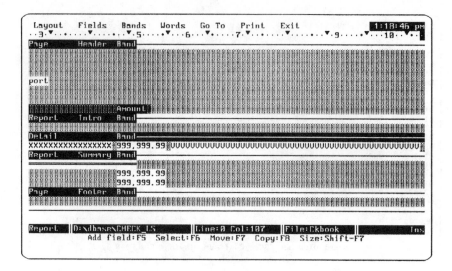

Figure 5-24. Memo field added to the report.

The memo field exhibits some interesting characteristics. First, the size of the memo field is 50 characters. This size was determined by SET MEMOWIDTH value, which has a default value 50 characters. Since the cursor was at column 57 when you inserted the field, the memo location runs from 57 to 106.

Another factor in the way this memo field was entered was the template for the field is filled with the letter *V*. This V stands for *Vertical* stretch picture function. A vertical stretch means if the contents of the field consist of more than the template width, or more than one line, the additional text will be formed into additional print lines. These will use the report template width as the line length when the report is printed. When used with a memo field, this picture function will cause the entire memo text to be written into the a column below the field template. The text will use as many lines as is needed to print the full text; the lines will wrap to fit the selected column width. Without this function, the text of the memo field would be printed with the lines retaining their original width. For example, using the V picture function the line *groundhog day greeting cards* is broken into two lines. If the picture function is omitted, the line will print at its full width. The V picture function should be used with memo fields, unless you have a specific reason for wanting the lines to stay at their original length.

Changing Field Width

The 50 character size of the memo field, added to the other fields in the Detail band, creates a report Detail line that is 106 characters wide. Many narrow carriage printers are limited to 80 or 85 character-line widths. For screen display purposes, 80 characters is the maximum line that will fit on one screen width. In this case, you may want to reduce the width of the memo field to fit the 80-character limit.

There are two ways to change the width of a field.

Modify field

You can use the Fields Modify Field command to display the field format menu. This menu contains an option to control the width of the field.

Shift-[F7]

If you want only to change the field width, and not other field characteristics, use the Shift-[F7] command shortcut key, to size the field.

To change the size of a field you must first highlight it with the cursor. Enter

        [left arrow]

With the field highlighted, activate the size mode by entering

        Shift-[F7]

In the size mode, 999.99 ⏎, the left arrow and right arrow keys will change the width of the field. To narrow the field so it will fit within an 80-column page or screen, enter

        [left arrow] *(27 times)*

The cursor is moved to column 79. Keep in mind that since the first column is 0, not 1, column 79 is the 80th column in the report.

The field sizing is completed by entering

        ⏎

Display the revised report by entering

        [Alt-p] v

The report is displayed showing the new fields, CHECK NO, and REMARKS. The V picture function causes the memo field to use as many lines as necessary to display the full text of the memo.

```
                                                2 - side chairs
                                                1 - computer desk
                                                1 - printer stand
01/06/89 1003       United Federal Insurance    590.00 business insurance
                                                       Policy number:
                                                       1001200ZAF
02/09/89 1009       Advanced Copier Service      175.00
01/14/89 1006       The Bargin Warehouse         145.99 waste paper baskets
                                                       copier paper
                                                       computer paper
                                                       smoke alarm
02/12/89 1010       Valley Power & Light         101.70
01/06/89 1002       Western Telephone            101.57
01/10/89 1005       Fathead Software              99.95
01/03/89 1001       Central Office Supplies       97.56 envelopes
                                                       manila folders
                                                       hanging files
01/15/89 1007       Central Office Supplies       67.45
02/02/89 1008       Sunset Variety                25.89 groundhog day greeting
                                                       cards
═══════════════════════════════════════════════════
Totals                                        4,401.11
Average                                         400.10
_           Cancel viewing: ESC,  Continue viewing: SPACEBAR
```

Figure 5-25. Report with memo field contents included.

The screen scrolls past the top of the report without stopping. This is caused by the use of the V picture function.

Return to the Report Form Layout display by entering

[Esc]
↵

Save the revised report by entering

[Alt-e] s

Quick Reports

The CHECK_LS report form was created from scratch using an empty Report Form Layout display. dBASE IV offers a faster way to create reports, called the Quick report method. The Quick report method automatically generates a report, based on the file structure of the database. As pointed out previously, this method, used alone, will seldom create a useful report, unless the database has a very simple structure.

However, quick reports become more important when you combine them with other dBASE IV features. One powerful combination is to use Query mode operations with the Quick report function.

You will recall that the view skeleton in the Query mode provided a quick and easy way to select and sequence fields for display in the Browse or Edit modes. The same is true of Quick reports. If you select a sequence of fields in the Query mode, then use the Quick report function to create a report, the report will conform to the current query specifications—not the overall file structure. By using the query mode to control the operation of the Quick report function, you reduce the amount of time necessary to create reports.

To see how this works, you will use the Query mode to create a report similar to the CHECK_LS report. Begin by activating the Query mode.

```
[left  arrow] (2 times)
  ↵
```

Clear all the fields from the view skeleton. This can be done by pressing [F5] in the file name box. Enter

```
[F5]
```

Add the DATE, PAYEE, and AMOUNT fields to the view skeleton.

```
[Tab]
[F5]
[Tab]  (2 times)
[F5]
[Tab]
[F5]
```

The view skeleton contains three fields. The order and contents of the view skeleton will determine the structure of the report. You can go directly to a report output by using the Shift-[F9] command. Enter

```
[Shift-F9]
```

dBASE IV will take a few moments to process the query and then display the Print report menu box.

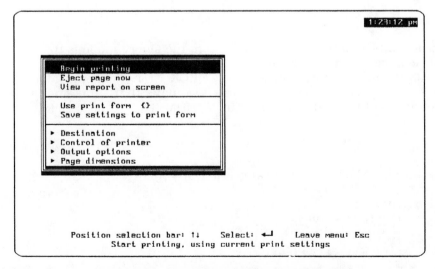

Figure 5-26. Report printed directly from query.

Display the report on the screen by entering

v

The query parameters are passed automatically to the report form generator, which directly generates the report, based on the query structure. The report is similar to the custom-designed report with the exception that the headings use the field names exactly as they were entered into the file structure.

```
Page No.   1
05/19/89

DATE        PAYEE                        AMOUNT

01/03/89    Allied Office Furniture      750.50
01/03/89    Central Office Supplies       97.56
01/06/89    Western Telephone            101.57
01/06/89    United Federal Insurance     590.00
01/10/89    Computer World              2245.50
01/10/89    Fathead Software              99.95
01/14/89    The Bargin Warehouse         145.99
01/15/89    Central Office Supplies       67.45
02/02/89    Sunset Variety                25.89
02/09/89    Advanced Copier Service      175.00
02/12/89    Valley Power & Light         101.70
                                        4401.11



 _            Cancel viewing: ESC,  Continue viewing: SPACEBAR
```

Figure 5-27. Report produced direct from Query mode.

Return to Query mode by entering

        [Esc]
        ↵

The advantage of reports generated from the Query mode is that you can quickly change the view skeleton, and in doing so, create a new report. You will recall the difficulty with which the CHECK_NUM field was added to the CHECK_LS report. Suppose you wanted to make that same change using the Query-report method. Add the CHECK_NUM field to the skeleton.

        [Shift-Tab]   *(2 times)*
        [F5]

Use the view skeleton to rearrange the field order.

        [F4]
        [Tab] *(3 times)*
        [F6] ↵
        [F7]
        [left arrow] *(3 times)*
        ↵

```
Page No.   1
05/19/89

CHECK_NUM  DATE     PAYEE                        AMOUNT

      1000  01/03/89  Allied Office Furniture       750.50
      1001  01/03/89  Central Office Supplies        97.56
      1002  01/06/89  Western Telephone             101.57
      1003  01/06/89  United Federal Insurance      590.00
      1004  01/10/89  Computer World               2245.50
      1005  01/10/89  Fathead Software               99.95
      1006  01/14/89  The Bargin Warehouse          145.99
      1007  01/15/89  Central Office Supplies        67.45
      1008  02/02/89  Sunset Variety                 25.89
      1009  02/09/89  Advanced Copier Service       175.00
      1010  02/12/89  Valley Power & Light          101.70
     11055                                          4401.11



            Cancel viewing: ESC,  Continue viewing: SPACEBAR
```

Figure 5-28. Revised report generated from Query mode.

Produce the revised report by entering

    [Shift-[F9]
    v

Note that the report form was automatically set to calculate all numeric fields with totals. In the case of the CHECK_NUM field, this creates a meaningless total at the bottom of that column.

Return to the Query mode by entering

    [Esc]
    ⌐

Customizing a Quick Report

The Query mode Quick report method is a fast way to generate reports, while retaining control over the fields included in the report, and their sequence. However, the Query mode does not provide complete control over reports. In the previous example, an unnecessary total was generated for CHECK_NUM. The Query method does not provide a means to add other calculations, such as average, to the report.

To overcome these limitations, it is necessary to modify the format of a Quick report. This is still faster and easier than creating the entire report from scratch, since most of the work can be done automatically. You need only to add or delete a few items, in order to achieve the desired customized report.

In order to use the Query setup as an initial layout for a report, save the query. Enter

```
[Alt-e] s
checks ⏎
```

This creates a Query file, CHECKS.QBE, and adds the name CHECKS to the Query column listing. Note that the Control Center display indicates that this query is still active. When a query is active, any Quick report operations automatically use the current query settings as the parameters for the report form. Activate the Report Form Layout mode.

```
[right arrow] (2 times)
     ⏎
```

The Layout menu automatically appears with the Quick layouts option highlighted. This time you will use the Quick layouts to create the report form. Enter

```
     ⏎
```

This option offers three types of reports. The Column layout creates a Detail band with a single line of fields spread horizontally. The Form layout

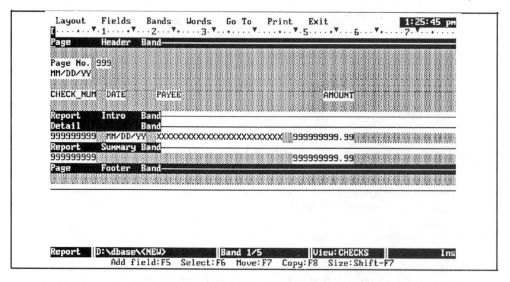

Figure 5-29. Report form generated according to query specifications.

option creates a Detail band that uses one line for each field in the database. The Mailmerge layout uses the same Detail band as the Form layout, but allocates an entire page for each record. Create a Column layout by entering

```
     ⏎
```

The Layout is automatically generated, using the view skeleton specifications to select fields and field order.

The report contains most of the elements you want to include. You only need minor changes to turn the layout into a complete report. For example, you will want to remove the Summary band total for check numbers.

Use the Fields Remove Field command to eliminate this total. Enter

```
[Alt-f]  r
```

Now select the field or calculation you want to delete. Note that the summary calculations appear as SUM(AMOUNT) and SUM(CHECK_NUM). Remove SUM(CHECK_NUM) by entering

```
[PgDn]
⌐
```

Modify the templates for the AMOUNT field and its total, using the Modify Field command. Change the template of the AMOUNT field to include commas.

```
[Alt-f]  m ⌐
⌐
[Home]
[Ctrl-y]
9,999,999.99  ⌐
[Ctrl-End]
```

Change the template of the AMOUNT sum field. This field is given the name SUM(AMOUNT) in the field selection menu. Try this on your own. The correct command can be found at the end of the chapter under EX-3.

The revised Report Form Layout will look like this:

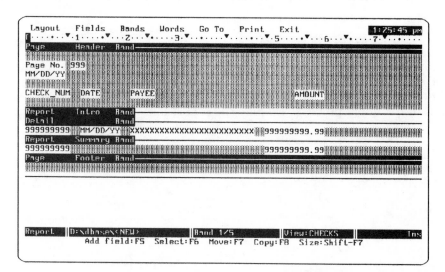

Figure 5-30. Report Form Layout created from query specifications modified manually.

Display the report by entering

```
[Alt-p] v
```

Return to the Report Form Layout mode and save the report by entering

```
[Esc]
⌐
[Alt-e] s
checks ⌐
```

Creating Reports From Query Files

You can create reports based on the specifications stored in Query files. For example, in Chapter 3 you created a Query called SALES_TX. You can use this query as the basis for generating a Quick report.

Begin by opening the SALES_TX query file.

```
[left  arrow] (2 times)
 s
 ⌐
 ⌐
```

The name SALES_TX appears above the line in the Query column, indicating that the SALES_TX query has been activated. To create a report based on this query, enter

```
[right  arrow] (2 times)
 ⌐
```

Use the Quick Layouts Columnar layout command to create a Report Form Layout.

```
 ⌐ (2 times)
```

The layout is created showing four columns of information, PAYEE, AMOUNT, SALES_TAX, and PURCHASE. The SALES_TAX and PURCHASE columns are not actual fields in the database, but calculated fields created as part of the query process. Display the report laid out by this report form.

```
[Alt-p] v
```

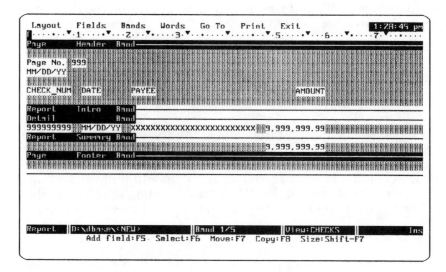

Figure 5-31. Report generated from stored query.

Return to the Report Form Layout mode by entering

        [Esc]
        ⏎

Exit the Report Form Layout mode by entering

        [Alt-e] s
        sales_tx ⏎

Calculated Columns

In the previous section you used a query that had been saved on the disk, as the basis of a report form. This query contained two fields that were created through the calculated fields facility of the Query mode. The information was generated as a result of a query. But you can create reports with calculated columns without having to create and save a query.

Create a new report form by entering

        [up arrow]
        ⏎

The current view is the SALES_TAX view. In this case, you want to activate the CKBOOK database without the SALES_TAX view. This can be done from within the Report Form Layout mode, using the Layout Use Different Database File or View command. Enter

        u

A list of database (DBF) and view (QBE) files appears on the right side of the screen. In this instance, select the CKBOOK.DBF database file. Enter

    ck ↵

Begin this report by entering the data fields in the Detail band.

    [down   arrow] *(5 times)*

This report will be different from others. All the information displayed in it will be calculated from the database fields, rather than taken directly from the database fields.

The first column will list the name of the month indicated in the DATE field. This requires the use of the CMONTH( ) function to calculate the month name. Begin the process of creating a calculated column by entering

    [F5]

To create a calculated column, place the cursor on the <create> symbol in the CALCULATED column. Enter

    [right   arrow]
     ↵

A blank box is displayed that will contain the information defining the column's contents.

```
Page No.    1
05/19/89

PAYEE                          AMOUNT      SALES_TAX      PURCHASE

Allied Office Furniture        750.50         42.48        708.02
Central Office Supplies         97.56          5.52         92.04
Western Telephone              101.57          5.75         95.82
United Federal Insurance       590.00         33.40        556.60
Computer World                2245.50        127.10       2118.40
Fathead Software                99.95          5.66         94.29
The Bargin Warehouse           145.99          8.26        137.73
Central Office Supplies         67.45          3.82         63.63
Sunset Variety                  25.89          1.47         24.42
Advanced Copier Service        175.00          9.91        165.09
Valley Power & Light           101.70          5.76         95.94
                              4401.11        249.12       4151.99




         Cancel viewing: ESC,   Continue viewing: SPACEBAR
```

Figure 5-32. Calculated column definition box.

The Name and Description items are options. The Name option provides a reference for the calculation. If no name is used, the formula used to calculate the value is displayed. If a formula is complicated, creating a name can simplify the operation. The name can be up to 10 characters in length. Enter

```
        ⏎
    month ⏎
```

Next, enter the formula that calculates the value. This is entered into the Expression line.

```
        e
    CMONTH(date)  ⏎
```

dBASE IV automatically created a template with a width of 25 characters, and inserted the Picture function, T. In both cases, these defaults must be changed.

The 25-character template is too wide for the values that will appear in this column. A 12-character template would be adequate for any month name. Change the template by entering

```
    t
    [backspace]   (13 times)
    ⏎
```

The T picture function is the Trim function. Trim causes dBASE IV to display or print as many characters as are actually contained in the text, rather than add spaces to pad the text to make the items in a column the same length. You may recall this issue arose in Chapter 4 when you used the MLINE( ) function to the display individual lines of a memo field.

In the current report, trimming the CMONTH( ) value would cause the data to the right of the column to align awkwardly. Thus, you want to remove the T function. Enter

```
    p
    t
```

While the Function menu is still displayed, you can cause the month names to appear in all upper-case letters by selecting the ! function (the command letter for this function is U). Enter

```
    u
```

Complete the calculated column by entering

```
    [Ctrl-End]
    [Ctrl-End]
```

The next column will contain the day of the week. Enter

```
[right arrow]
 [F5]
[right arrow]
  ⏎
```

Enter the name for this column.

```
  ⏎
dayofweek ⏎
```

Enter the expression for this column.

```
e
CDOW(date) ⏎
```

As with the other calculated column, dBASE IV has automatically set the Picture function to T, because the expression will yield text. The field is again set for 25 characters, which is still too wide for the contents. Change the template width to 10 characters and create all upper-case characters, at the same time. This is done by replacing the X's with !'s. Enter

```
t
[Home]
[Ctrl-y]
! (10 times)
 ⏎
```

Remove the T Picture function by entering

```
p
t
[Ctrl-End]
```

Save the calculated column by entering

```
[Ctrl-End]
```

The final date calculation lists the number of the day of the month. Create a new calculated column by entering

```
[right arrow]
 [F5]
[right arrow]
  ⏎
```

Call this column DAY.

```
  ⏎
day ⏎
```

Enter the Expression formula.

```
e
DAY(date)  ↵
```

The template is automatically set to 9999999.99. This is too wide for the day column, which never exceeds two digits. Enter

```
t
[Home]
[Ctrl-y]
99  ↵
```

Complete the column by entering

```
[Ctrl-End]
```

Numeric Calculations

The first three columns used Date functions to calculate values, based on the DATE field. You can also create calculated columns based on numeric information. In this example, enter the formula that will calculate the sales tax.

```
[right arrow]
 [F5]
[right arrow]
 ↵
```

Enter the name.

```
 ↵
sales_tax  ↵
```

Enter the formula.

```
e
amount-amount/1.06
```

In this case, the template is appropriate for the type of values you would expect in this column. Save the column by entering

```
[Ctrl-End]
```

Logical Fields

The contents of logical fields are true or false values, represented by the letters T or Y for true, and F or N for false. When you List or Browse records, you see the T or F characters that indicate the true or false values contained in the database.

However, T, F, Y, and N do not make a very clear presentation on a formal report. The purpose of a report is to provide information in a legible form, for people who have no experience with dBASE IV codes and abbreviations. Used by themselves, then, logical fields are cryptic. This is a problem, because the information in these fields can be valuable and significant.

One way to take advantage of the usefulness of logical fields is to use the IIF( ) function to convert logical values into other types of information.

IIF( ) is one of the most powerful functions in dBASE IV. It contains three arguments. The first is a logical field or expression, followed by two values or formulas. If the logical field or expression is true, the function returns the value of the first formula or value. If the logical field or expression is false, then the second value or formula is returned.

This function enables you to *convert* a logical field into a specific pair of values. Look at the following formula:

IIF(deductible,"Deductible","Not Deductible")

The function uses the field DEDUCTIBLE, as the logical argument. If the DEDUCTIBLE field is true, then the function prints *Deductible* . If the field is false, then the function prints *Not Deductible* .

The IIF( ) function allows you to create your own customized-conversion routines. You can use IIF( ) with any field or logical expression. The examples shown in this section illustrate only one of many uses for IIF( ).

Create a logical expression for the DEDUCTIBLE field. Enter

```
[right  arrow]
 [F5]
[right  arrow]
 ⌋
```

Call this column DEDUCT. Enter

```
 ⌋
deduct ⌋
```

Enter the formula.

```
e
IIF(deductible, "Deductible", "Not    Deductible")
```

You will need to change the template and the picture function. Enter

```
t
[Home]
[Ctrl-y]
X (14 times)
 ⌋
P
t
[Ctrl-End]
[Ctrl-End]
```

Memo Fields

In the CHECK_LS report you included the memo field, REMARKS. When this was done, dBASE IV automatically printed all the lines of the memo. The resulting form separated the lines of the report whenever a memo with more than one line printed.

You can control the number of memo lines that print by using a memo function in place of the memo field. For example, suppose you wanted to print the first line of the memo. A calculated column with the MLINE( ) function would do the trick. Create another calculated column.

```
[right arrow]
 [F5]
[right arrow]
 ⏎
```

Call this field MEMO. Enter

```
 ⏎
memo ⏎
```

Enter the formula that displays the first line of the memo field.

```
e
MLINE(remarks,1)  ⏎
```

Save the memo column by entering

```
[Ctrl-End]
```

The report form looks like this:

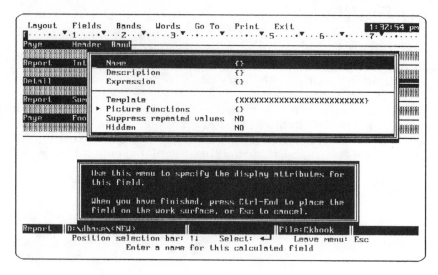

Figure 5-33. Report form with calculated columns.

To view the report you just created, enter

    [Alt-p] v

The report appears. All the data appearing on the report is the result of a calculation based on database data, but not explicitly contained within the database.

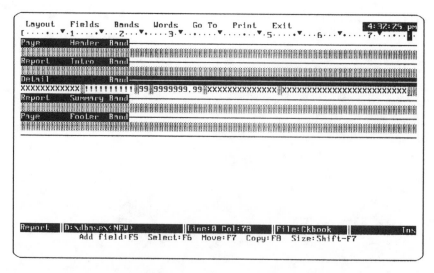

Figure 5-34. Report composed of calculated columns.

Return to the Report Form Layout mode and save this report by entering

```
[Esc]
⏎
[Alt-e] s
calccols
```

Bear in mind that a report with calculated columns usually contains standard field columns, as well. In this report, no page header data was created. You would need to do this in a formal report.

Selecting Records for a Report

All the reports you created so far, automatically print the records contained in the database file. You might want to print a report in which only selected records are included.

From the Control Center display you can create a query selection specification that controls which records appear. You can also use the Query Sort options to display the records in a specific sequence.

You will recall that when you select records using the Query mode, you cannot access the Index tags created for the database. If you wish to use the Query mode to select records, any ordering of the database records requires you to use the Query mode Sort functions.

The first step is to create a view that selects the records you want to include. Enter

```
[left  arrow] (2 times)
⏎
```

The simplest way to select records is to enter a condition by formula. This has the same effect as using the SET FILTER TO command at the Dot Prompt. Here, the filter expression is MONTH(date)=1. This expression selects only January dates for any subsequent reports. Enter

```
[Alt-c] a
MONTH(date)=1  ⏎
```

Save this query under the name TEMP, to indicate that this query is used to select records for the current operation, and is not intended for long-term storage. dBASE IV will maintain the TEMP query until you choose to delete it.

```
[Alt-e] s
temp ⏎
```

Print the CHECKS report by selecting the name CHECKS from the Reports column.

```
[right arrow] (2 times)
ch ↵
```

Select to print the report by entering

                P

dBASE IV displays an additional option box. It appears because there is a
query/view currently active, which is different from the one that was active
when you created the CHECKS report. This menu allows you to use the
current view, or load the CHECKS.QBE file from the disk. Selecting the
CHECKS.QBE option will cause the report to print the records selected by
the CHECKS view. You may recall that this view selected all records. Using
the Current view option selects records for the current filter MONTH(date)=1.

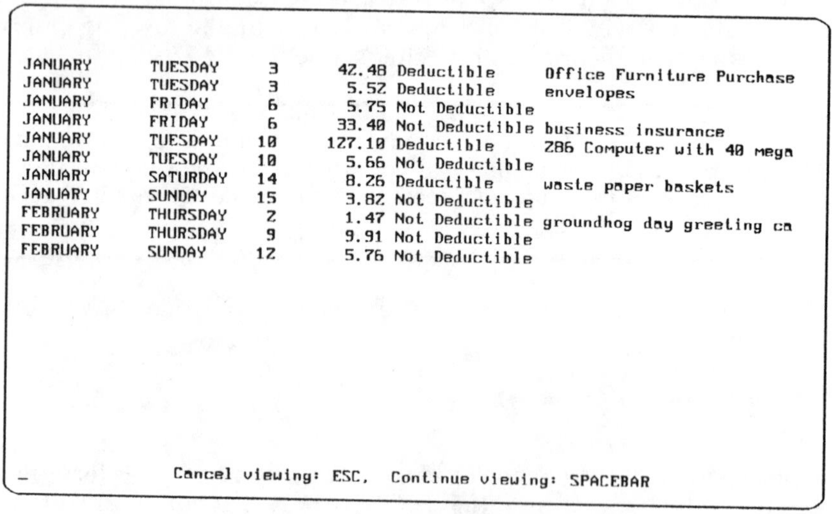

```
JANUARY      TUESDAY     3       42.48 Deductible      Office Furniture Purchase
JANUARY      TUESDAY     3        5.52 Deductible      envelopes
JANUARY      FRIDAY      6        5.75 Not Deductible
JANUARY      FRIDAY      6       33.40 Not Deductible  business insurance
JANUARY      TUESDAY    10      127.10 Deductible      286 Computer with 40 mega
JANUARY      TUESDAY    10        5.66 Not Deductible
JANUARY      SATURDAY   14        8.26 Deductible      waste paper baskets
JANUARY      SUNDAY     15        3.82 Not Deductible
FEBRUARY     THURSDAY    2        1.47 Not Deductible  groundhog day greeting ca
FEBRUARY     THURSDAY    9        9.91 Not Deductible
FEBRUARY     SUNDAY     12        5.76 Not Deductible


            Cancel viewing: ESC,  Continue viewing: SPACEBAR
```

Figure 5-35. Select current or original view.

In this example, select to use the Current view by entering

        ↵

Display the report on the screen by entering

                v

The report is now displayed. It contains only those records that meet the
current filter condition—the month of January.

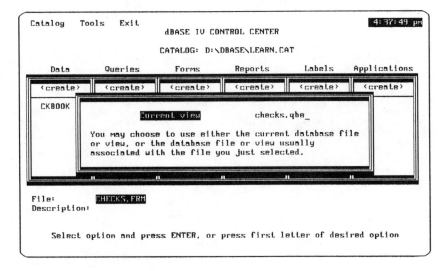

Figure 5-36. Report shows only selected records in report.

Return to the Control Center by entering

    [Esc]
    ⤶

Before you complete this chapter, you should delete the TEMP query. Keep in mind that you cannot delete a file while it is still open. The first step is to close the file. Enter

    [left arrow] *(2 times)*
    ⤶ *(2 times)*

Remove the TEMP query by entering

    t
    [Alt-c] r
    y
    y

The temporary query is removed from the query list. There are now four reports listed in the Report column.

```
Page No.    1
05/19/89

CHECK_NUM   DATE      PAYEE                        AMOUNT

    1000    01/03/89  Allied Office Furniture        750.50
    1001    01/03/89  Central Office Supplies         97.56
    1002    01/06/89  Western Telephone              101.57
    1003    01/06/89  United Federal Insurance       590.00
    1004    01/10/89  Computer World               2,245.50
    1005    01/10/89  Fathead Software                99.95
    1006    01/14/89  The Bargin Warehouse           145.99
    1007    01/15/89  Central Office Supplies         67.45
                                                   4,098.52




              Cancel viewing: ESC,  Continue viewing: SPACEBAR
```

Figure 5-37. Control Center with reports listed in Report panel.

Exit dBASE IV by entering

> [Alt-e] q

Summary

- **Reports.** A report prints or displays database information within a formal page structure. A report takes into consideration aspects of page formatting, such as page headings, page breaks, and page numbering, which are not considered when you display data in the Query mode. dBASE IV allows you to create three basic types of reports: column, form, and mailmerge. A column report places data from each record on a single line. This causes data from consecutive records to align in vertical columns. A form report places the information from each record onto two or more lines on each page. A mailmerge report is used to create form letters, or to fill in forms in which each record is printed on a separate page. All three types are generated from the Report Form Layout mode. You can enter the Report Form Layout mode from the Dot Prompt with the CREATE REPORT or MODIFY REPORT commands. If entering the Report Form Layout mode from the Dot Prompt, you need to specify the name of the report form you want to create or modify.

- **Report Forms.** A formal report is created by using the Report Form Layout mode. A report layout is a model of how dBASE IV should put together the elements of your report into a finished report. A report file consists of a list of these specifications. Once a report form has been stored, it can be printed whenever it is needed. Changes in the database information between each printing will appear when the report is re-printed. You can modify the format of a report after it has been saved.

- **Report Layouts.** Each report consists of *bands*. A band represents a type of data used to compose report pages. The report form consists of 5 bands by default. 1) The Page Header band prints at the top of each page. It is used to print page information, such as the date or page number, and the text that will serve as column headings. 2) The Intro band prints only on the first page of the report. It is used to print introductory information concerning the rest of the report. 3) The Detail band prints once for each record in the database file. Each time the Detail band prints, it will advance the file pointer to the next record, until the end of file is reached. This band usually contains field references and calculations, based on field information. 4) The summary band prints after all the records from the Detail band have been printed. The Summary band usually contains summary calculations, such as totals or averages related to the data in the columns. 5) The Page Footer band prints at the bottom of each page. This band is used to print information, such as the report title and page number, when they are not already included in the Page Header band.

- **Details.** The report details are entered into the details band of the report form. This band is typically the one in which data from the database is integrated into the report. The Detail band will print for each record in the current database view. The records will be listed in the natural order of the database, unless an Index order tag has been activated before the report is printed.

- **Fields.** Field references are added to the Detail band. When the Detail band prints for the first time, it inserts data from the first record of the database. Each subsequent printing draws data from the next record in the database, until all the records have been processed. Each field reference has a complete set of options, which control how the data will appear on the report. These options fall into two classes: templates and picture functions.

- **Templates.** Templates serve two purposes. First, the number of characters in the template determines the width of the column. Second, you can use the template characters to control what is displayed at each character position in the column. Typically, templates are used with numeric values to insert punctuation, such as commas or decimal points. In character fields you can change individual characters to upper-case.

- **Picture Functions.** Picture functions are used to control the overall formatting of the data in specific columns. A function affects the data item as a whole, as opposed to a template that controls individual characters. Picture functions can convert to upper-case, add special accounting symbols, or suppress 0 values. They can also be used to change the alignment, left, right, or center of data within a column.

- **Calculated Columns.** Data columns can be created by using a calculation—a dBASE IV formula—that calculates values based in the information in the current record. Templates and picture functions can be used with calculated columns exactly as they are with fields.

- **Printing and Viewing.** dBASE IV allows you to print the report on the line printer, or display a copy of the report on the screen. You can also direct the data to a text file for use with other operations.

- **Quick Reports.** dBASE IV will automatically generate a report, based on the current view skeleton using the Quick Report option from the main Control Center display, or the Quick Layout option from within the Report Form Layout mode. The report automatically formats the Page Header, Detail, and Summary bands. The column headings are the field names. All numeric fields are totaled in the Summary band.

- **Selecting Records.** You can select records for inclusion in a report printing by using the Query mode to create a selection condition. This condition operates as a filter to select records for the report that is to be printed.

Exercises

Ex-1
Add an average summary calculation.

```
    ⏎
    Average
```

Move the cursor to column 35.

```
    [F5]
    [right  arrow] (3 times)
    ⏎
    f ⏎
    t
    [Home]
    [Ctrl-y]
    9999
    [Ctrl-End]
```

Ex-2
Display the report in descending order of amounts.

```
[left  arrow] (3 times)
 [Shift-F2]
 o
 amt ⏎
 [Alt-e] a
[right  arrow] (3 times)
 ⏎ (2 times)
 v
```

Ex-3
Change the template of AMOUNT SUM.

```
[Alt-f] m ⏎
[PgDn]
⏎
t
[Home]
[Ctrl-y]
9,999,999.99 ⏎
[Ctrl-End]
```

6

Custom Screen Forms

The previous chapter demonstrated how to create report forms. Typically, reports are used to display information from a database file in a column form. The reports created showed a number of different ways to display information within a report form. They also showed how to modify or generate new data in a report form, through the use of calculated and standard fields.

dBASE IV provides two alternate ways of entering or displaying data: the Browse and the Edit modes. The Browse mode uses tabular layout-rows and columns—to display up to 17 records at once. The Edit mode displays information from one record at a time

In the Edit mode, fieldnames are listed in a column down the left side of the screen. Next to each fieldname is a highlighted area in which the data for that field is displayed and edited. This display, however, is a default layout. dBASE IV permits you to create custom-designed screens, which can more efficiently display the data in your files.

Custom screens have a number of benefits, some of which are obvious, while others are more subtle. The most obvious advantage is they allow you to arrange the fields in a way that is easy to read and work with. You can also label the input areas with information other than the fieldnames. This makes it easier for people who are unfamiliar with the structure of your file to know what should be entered into each field.

The input area is the highlighted portion of the screen where the data from a field is displayed. When you move the cursor to an input area, you can enter or edit the information displayed. All input areas in dBASE IV must correspond to a field or a memory variable. Memory variables can only be defined in the Dot Prompt mode. However, variables created in the Dot Prompt mode can be used from the Control Center operations. Memory variables are discussed in preceding chapters of Part I, and extensively in Part II.

Less obvious but also significant are the Edit options provided by the program. These options enable you to limit numeric entries to a certain range of values, perform validity checks on entered data, and display default values or messages at the bottom of the screen.

Custom displays can contain non-database information, such as boxes and lines. You can also add to the display text and system data, such as record numbers.

To begin, load dBASE IV in the usual manner. The Control Center should list the catalog UNTITLED or LEARN for the files created for this text.

Creating a Screen Form

Initiate the process of creating a screen display form by selecting the <create> symbol in the Forms column. Enter

```
[right arrow](2 times)
↵
```

The Screen Form Layout mode is activated, and the Layout menu is displayed. Exit the menu by entering

```
[Esc]
```

The work surface representing the screen display in this mode, is initially covered with gray characters. You create the screen by placing text, lines, boxes, and fields at the chosen locations. In this aspect, it is similar to the Report Mode work surface. However, the current screen is not divided into bands.

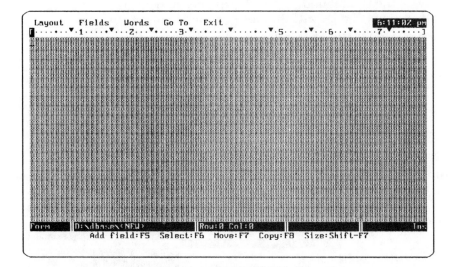

Figure 6-1. Screen Layout mode work surface.

Adding Text

Text is the simplest type of information to add to the screen layout, and can be typed anywhere on the screen surface. The text you type appears on the screen format, exactly as you enter it. Each character is treated as a text literal, meaning that it appears the same, no matter what record is being displayed.

Text information is important for two reasons.

1. Text identifies the meaning of the fields. In a custom screen layout, the fieldnames are replaced by text that identifies the fields.
2. Text can be used to make the data more easily understood. It can also contain instructions or messages for users.

In the current case, begin the screen display with some basic identification information, such as the name and address of the company.

Move the cursor to line 2. Notice the status line displays the current cursor position as Row:0 Col:0. dBASE IV assigns the upper-left corner of the screen as row 0, column 0, not row 1, column 1, as you might assume. The screen is 80 columns wide, 0 to 79, and 25 lines long, 0 to 24.

        [down arrow]*(2 times)*

Enter the name of the company.

        The LaFish Novelty Company

You can use the commands on the Words menu to position items on the left, center, or right of the layout. Suppose you wanted to center the name of the company between the edges of the screen. Display the Words menu by entering

[Alt-w]

The Position option allows you to align items to the left, center, or right of the screen. Select the Position option by entering

P

The three position options, Left, Center, or Right, are displayed in a small pop-up menu.

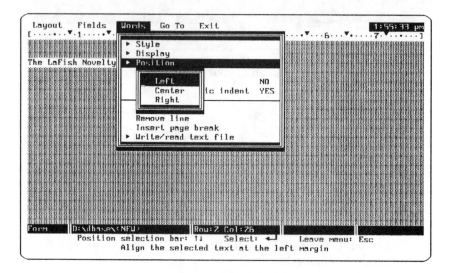

Figure 6-2. Position items options.

Select Center by entering

c

The text is positioned in the center of the screen.

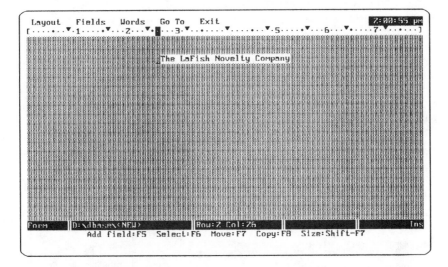

Figure 6-3. Text centered on screen layout.

Add another line of text to the layout. Enter

```
[down arrow]
  Business Checking Account
```

Center the text using the previous method.

```
[Alt-w] p c
```

Drawing a Box

You may choose to enhance the display by drawing a box around the title. The Box and Line Drawing commands are located on the Layout menu. Enter

```
[Alt-L)
```

Select Box drawing by entering

```
b
```

You can select a single or double line box. Another option allows you to use such keyboard characters as x or * to draw a box. Here, select a double line box.

```
d
```

The cursor changes to a double-line character. The first step in drawing is to place the cursor at the upper-left corner where the box is to be drawn. Keep in mind the current cursor position is not automatically considered the beginning of the box. Until you press ↵, you can move the cursor wherever you choose, in order to find the proper location for the upper-left corner of the box. In this example, the location is row 1, col 20. Move cursor to row 1, col 20.

Anchor the upper-left corner of the box at this position by entering

    ↵

Any cursor movements from this point will result in the box being drawn. Move the cursor to row 4, col 60.

    ↵

The box is drawn around the text.

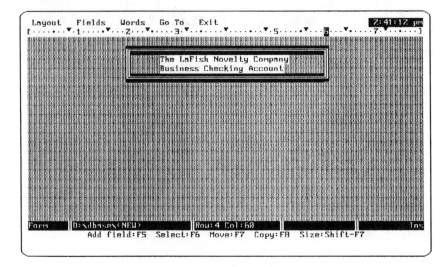

Figure 6-4. Box drawn around text.

Placing Fields

The most important items placed in the screen layout are the fields. They display the data stored in the database records. When you place a field in a screen layout, you generally also must add text to identify the field.

In this screen layout the fields will be drawn from the CKBOOK database file. You may recall that at this point there is no open database. In order to place fields, you must open the database for which the screen is being designed. The Use different Database or View operation found on the Layout menu will open the file. Enter

    [Alt-L] u

Select the CKBOOK database file.

    ck ⏎

You can now place the field input areas on the screen. The position of the first field, CHECK_NUM, is determined by the position of the cursor. If you want to move around the display faster than the left arrow and right arrow keys allow, use the following:

Key	Result
[Home]	left edge of screen
[End]	right edge of screen
[Tab]	right 1 tab (8 columns)
[Shift-Tab]	left one tab(8 columns)

Move the cursor to row 7, col 8 by entering

    [Home]
    down arrow *(4 times)*
    [Tab]

The use of these keys allows you to move more quickly than using the left arrow and right arrow keys. To insert a field, use the Add Field command on

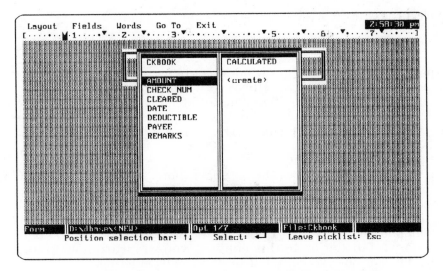

Figure 6-5. Select field for placement on screen layout.

the Fields menu, or press the shortcut key, [F5]. Enter

    [F5]

The program displays a window with a list of the fields.

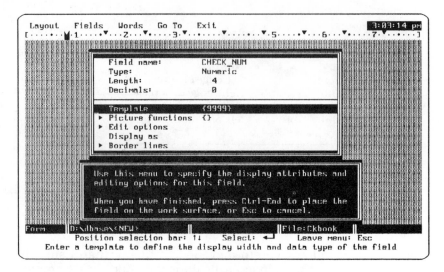

Figure 6-6. Field specifications window.

Select the CHECK_NUM field by entering

    [down arrow].⏎

The program displays another window containing a description of the field, and the options to be used with the screen layout field area.

The first two operations, Template and Picture Functions, are the same Picture and Template operations used in the Report Form generator discussed in the previous chapter. The template is set to 9999 because the field is a 4-character numeric field. No Picture Functions are selected, which is the default for numeric fields.

The next options, under Edit, are operations unique to screen displays and have no equivalent in printed reports. These operations allow you to restrict and control the editing of items within the field. The default settings for Edit options allow you to edit the fields in the custom-screen display in the same manner as editing the fields in the Edit mode (i.e. no particular restrictions). Further on in this chapter, you will learn how to use these restrictions. For now, accept the default setup by entering

    [Ctrl-End]

The field is placed onto the screen display. Note that it is simply an input area consisting of the four characters specified in the template. No text or other symbols are placed on the screen to indicate what this input area is used for. The standard dBASE IV Edit mode display always places the fieldname to the left of the field input area. In a custom-designed screen display, you can place the identifying text above, below, to the left or right, of the field. You may choose to use the fieldname, or identify the field with a word or phrase of your own selection. Because field names are limited to a single 10-character word, you can create a label for the field by entering a word or phrase describing the nature of the information. In this case, place the text above the field, instead of to the right. Move the cursor to row 6, col 8.

Enter

    Check #

The next field to be placed is the DATE field. Remember that all the fields in the Edit mode display are listed on the left side of the screen. In a custom layout, you can place the fields anywhere on the screen, to improve the appearance of the display. Place the DATE field next to the CHECK_NUM field.

```
[right arrow]
 Check Date
[down arrow]
 [Shift-Tab]   (2 times)
 [F5]
 d ↵
 [Ctrl-End]
```

You have now arranged two fields side by side, with the text above the field, giving the record's data a very different appearance.

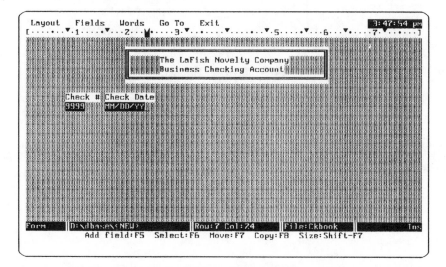

Figure 6-7. Fields arranged side by side.

Continue the process by adding the PAYEE and AMOUNT fields. Move the cursor to row 6, col 32. Place the PAYEE field at this location.

```
Payee
[down arrow]
[Shift-Tab]
[F5]
p ⏎
[Ctrl-End]
```

Add the AMOUNT field to the right of the PAYEE. Move the cursor to row 6, col 62. Enter

Amount

Move the cursor to row 7, col 58.

```
[F5]
⏎
[Ctrl-End]
```

You have now arranged the fields across the screen, rather than down, as in the normal Edit mode display.

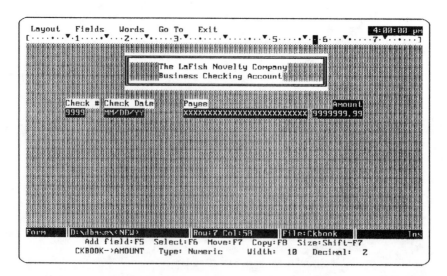

Figure 6-8. Fields placed across the screen.

The fields are arranged in such a way that the data resembles the face of a check. You might enhance this appearance by drawing a box around the fields. Move the cursor to row 5, col 5. Draw a single line box by entering

[Alt-L] b s ⏎

Move the cursor to row 9, col 75.

⌡

The box is now drawn around the fields.

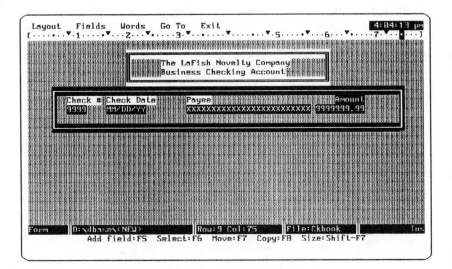

Figure 6-9. Box drawn around fields.

It is not necessary to place all the fields on every screen form. In this instance, the form inherently limits editing or entry to the four fields that are displayed.

Save the screen layout by using the Save Changes and Exit command on the Exit menu. Enter

[Alt-e] s

Enter a name for this screen layout.

check ⌡

dBASE IV takes a few moments to generate the screen format file, then returns to the Control Center display.

Generating a Screen Format File

The delay encountered in saving a screen layout is caused by the process by which dBASE IV generates the files needed to implement the screen layout.

When you create a screen layout using the design forms mode, you produce three different files. The first file, with the extension .SCR, for screen form file, contains the actual settings you entered into the screen form. The program uses the SCR file data as a guide for constructing a dBASE IV program file, based on a generalized screen layout program, FORM.GEN, which is supplied with dBASE IV. The result of this combination is a dBASE IV program file with an FMT, screen format file, extension. This file contains the dBASE IV commands needed to create an Edit mode screen display, based on the layout stored in the SCR file.

The last step is the production of the object-code file, with an FMO extension. The object code is part of the dBASE IV compiler that compiles all dBASE IV programs before they are executed. This operation checks for errors and produces a file that executes faster.

Why bother to create all three files? The SCR file allows you to edit the screen layout because it contains the layout specifications. The FMT file can be directly modified by users familiar with the dBASE IV programming language. In dBASE IV, an object-code file is required for every program that is to be executed.

The process of Screen Layout generation is similar to the process used with reports, labels, and applications. It fits in with dBASE IV's concept of an open system, where all the elements built into the Menu system are available in the programming of dBASE IV. This was not the case in dBASE III Plus, where many Menu system operations were not carried out through the dBASE language but implemented as part of the program code with equivalent programming language commands.

The form CHECK appears in the Forms column. The display indicates the CHECK form is active because it appears above the line in the Forms column. To see the effect of the form, display the data. Enter

    [F2]

The data from the first record is displayed within the screen form just created.

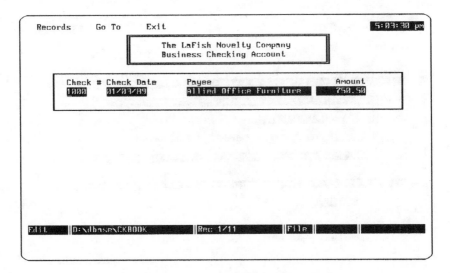

Figure 6-10. Data displayed within screen form.

You can use any of the normal Edit mode commands while the custom screen display is active. Enter

[PgDn]

Record 2 appears in the screen form. Add a new record to the database.

```
[Alt-r] a
1011
02/25/89
Dept of Trans ↵
45 ↵
```

The record is added to the database just as you would add a record in the Edit mode. Exit the Edit mode by entering

[Esc]

Adding Non-Field Information

In addition to fields, you can add other types of information to the screen form, such as record numbers or the current system's date. This information may be useful when editing or adding records.

You can modify the current screen display by entering

↵

The program displays a window with two options: Display data and Modify layout.

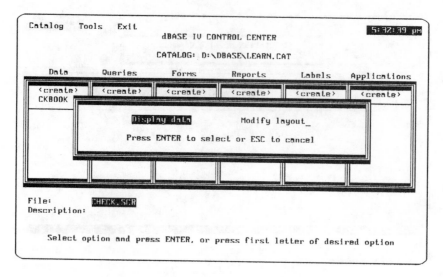

Figure 6-11. Option selection box displayed.

Select Modify layout by entering

> m

The screen layout is displayed just as stored. You can modify the layout by adding, changing, or removing items.

For example, suppose you decided the screen would look better if some space were between the two boxes. You can move one, or a group of items, to a new location on the screen. The first step is to select the items to be moved. It is important to note you must move the field and text separately from the box. Begin by moving the text and field. Move the cursor to row 6, col 8.

Now activate the Highlight mode and select the text and fields to move.

> [F6]

Move the cursor to row 7, col 67

> ⌐

Activate the move command by entering

> [F7]

The highlight jumps to row 7, col 20.

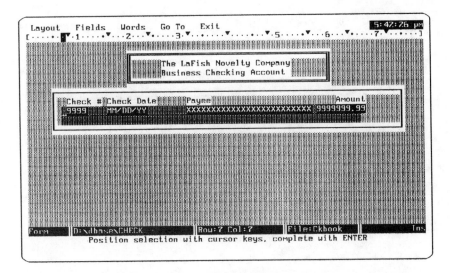

Figure 6-12. Moving text and fields.

From here, move the text and fields down one line. Position the upper-left corner to row 7, column 8, and place the text and fields at that location. Move the cursor to row 7, col 8.

⌐

The message "Delete covered text and fields?" appears at the bottom of the screen. This message appears whenever the new location overlaps part of the previous location. Enter

      y

The text and fields are moved. Now move the box. You can select a box by placing the cursor on any part of the box border. Enter

      [up arrow]*(2 times)*

Place the box in the Move mode by entering

      [F6] ⌐
      [F6]
      [F7]

Position the box one line below its previous position. Move the cursor to row 6, col 5.

⌐

The entire section, fields, text, and box, have been moved to a new location. The ability to move items around after you have placed them on the screen display is one of the main advantages of the Screen Layout mode.

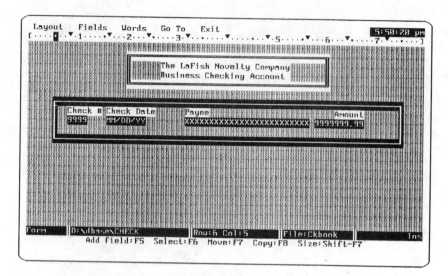

Figure 6-13. Fields, text and box moved to a new location on screen layout.

Adding a Record Number

The number of the records displayed can be ascertained from the status line. However, you may prefer your screen display to explicitly state the record number. For example, users unfamiliar with the status line's meaning may benefit from having the record number displayed as part of the entry screen.

Move the cursor to row 18, col 2. Enter the following text.

        Record #

How can you insert the actual record number into the screen display? The record number is one of the many values that can be accessed through the dBASE IV system functions. In Chapters 3 and 4 you encountered such functions as CMONTH( ), MONTH( ), or UPPER( ), that modified data stored in the database fields. dBASE IV maintains special functions that return information about the current state of its system.

Function	Returns
DATE( )	current date
DBF( )	current database name
LUPDATE( )	last update of database
RECCOUNT( )	total records in file
RECNO( )	current record number
RECSIZE( )	total size of record
TIME( )	current time

You can include any of these functions as part of the screen display. You can add these functions in the form of a calculated field. The process is similar to that of creating a report column. Begin as if you were adding a field.

> [F5]

To create a calculated field, select the <create> symbol in the CALCULATED column.

> [right arrow]⏎

Note that calculated fields do not display a line for Edit options because calculated fields are always read-only information. It would not be logical to attempt to edit a value arrived at by calculation. Instead, the fields, if any, used to calculate the value should be changed.

The fieldname and description are optional. They do not affect the final screen display, but they are useful in helping you recall the function of a calculated field. The crucial aspect of this menu is the Expression, which defines the contents of the calculated field. Enter

> e

The expression, in this instance, should be the RECNO( ) function. You can enter the function or select it from a list of functions. Here, display the list of options by entering

> [Shift-F1]

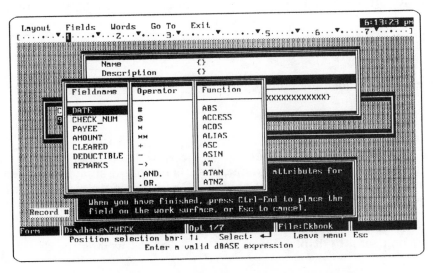

Figure 6-14. Options for calculated field listed.

Place the cursor on the Function column.

> [right arrow]*(2 times)*

You can use the cursor to select the function, or perform a speed search for the desired function. Enter

> re

The first two letters locate the READKEY function. Continue the search.

> cn ⌐
> ⌐

The RECNO( ) function is inserted into the expression line. Note that because RECNO( ) returns a numeric value, the program assumes a template with decimal places is appropriate. Change the template to an integer of a maximum of five characters. Try this on your own. The correct command is found at the end of the chapter under Ex-1.

You may want to take advantage of one of the picture functions for this field. The normal way to display a number in a numeric display area is right-aligned. In this instance, you have created a five-character area for the record number, allowing you to display numbers from 1 to 99,999. However, because there are only 12 records in the database, the calculated field would have three blank spaces before the 12. A picture function can cause the data to be left-aligned so no blanks will appear between the record number and the # sign. Display the picture functions.

> p

The B function, Left Align, causes the numbers to be aligned on the left. Enter

> b
> [Ctrl-End]

Save the calculated field by entering

> [Ctrl-End]

The LUPDATE( ) function returns the date the database file was last updated. A database is considered to have been updated whenever a record is added, edited, or removed. If a database is simply displayed or used to print a report, the file date is not changed. Note that date is written when you close the database file. The update feature is handy if you are trying to remember when you last worked with the data in the file.

Move the cursor to row 18, col 20.

It may be useful to display the day of the week, as well as the date of the last update, since knowing the day of the week may help you determine if the file requires updating. To display the day of the week, nest the LUPDATE( ) function inside the CDOW( ) function. Enter the text to identify the meaning of the calculated fields.

```
File last updated on
[right  arrow]
 [F5]
[right  arrow]⏎
```

Enter the expression that displays the day of the week of the last file update.

```
e
CDOW(LUPDATE( )) ⏎
```

The template mask for this expression is larger than it really needs to be. Change it to nine characters.

```
t
[Home] [Ctrl-y]
X (9 times)
```

Place the calculated field onto the layout by entering

```
[Ctrl-End]
```

Enter a comma and a space to separate the day of the week from the full date. Enter

```
[spacebar]
```

The next field is a calculated file that places the actual date of the last file update. The DMY( ) and MDY( ) functions provide an alternative way to display dates.

Function	Date
DMY( )	01 Jan 89
MDY( )	January 1, 89

In this instance, use the DMY( ) function to control the format of the last update indicator. Create a field displaying the LUPDATE( ) in the DMY( ) format. Try this on your own. The correct command is at the end of the chapter under Ex-2.

Creating a Graphic

The next application of a calculated field is unusual, but it serves to illustrate another way to display information. Here, the calculated field is not used to display text or numbers, but characters, to form a graphic display.

In many graphics applications, movement through a file is represented by a bar with two colors, e.g., white and gray. As you move through the file, the relative amount of each shade adjusts in order to indicate the location of the current record. For example, suppose you were positioned in the middle of the file. Instead of displaying text, such as 50%, you could indicate this by showing the bar as 50% white and 50% gray. Moving to another record would change the percentages of white and gray, so you would always have a graphic indicator of your position in the file.

How would you create such an effect in dBASE IV? The key lies in the use of the REPLICATE( ) function, which prints a specified number of characters. For example, the function REPLICATE("X",20) prints the letter X 20 times. To create the bar display mentioned previously, you must change the REPLICATE function to repeat a graphic character instead of a letter. The number of characters must, in turn, be based on the current record number.

The first problem can be solved by using the CHR( ) function to insert graphic characters into the text. CHR( ) allows you to specify a character by its ASCII value. Character 219 is a solid, white block. Character 178 is a dark, gray block. These two characters serve as the contrasting colors for the bar. Thus the expression CHR(219) displays a white block, while CHR(178) displays a gray block.

Graphics Characters

Strictly speaking, dBASE IV is not a graphics program nor is it capable of displaying graphics. The term graphics, as used in this text, refers to the special built-in characters that do not appear on your keyboard, but which are built into the screen display adapter set. These characters are used by many programs, including dBASE IV, to create special effects on the screen display. For example, the Screen Layout work surface uses these characters to create the gray background, the lines, and boxes.

The characters that can be displayed on the screen, but are not shown on your keyboard, are called the IBM extended-characters set. This set consists of 158 special characters, such as Greek letters, mathematical symbols, lines, blocks, and other special symbols.

But if these characters do not appear on the keyboard, how can they be used? The answer is that each character that can be displayed is assigned a number value. This includes the characters on your keyboard, as well as all the characters built into the computer but not placed on the keyboard. You can use these non-keyboard characters if you refer to their number. There are several ways to do this. On most IBM compatible computers, you can enter a character by holding down the [Alt] key and typing the number of that character on the numeric keypad. When you release the [Alt] key, the character appears in the text. Note that you must use the keypad, not the top row, to type the value. In dBASE IV, you can access a character using the CHR( ) function method. This function requires a numeric value that indicates which character you want to access. The value must be between 0 and 254.

The numeric portion of the calculation uses the RECNO( ) and the RECCOUNT( ) functions, which supply the record number and the total number of records, respectively. The bar is created by picking a size for the bar, e.g., 60 characters. The white section of the bar equals RECNO( )/RECCOUNT( ). If you multiply this by 60, you get the number of characters to be displayed in white: RECNO( )/RECCOUNT( )*60. The number of gray characters is the number left over from 60, once the white characters are displayed. You can calculate this value with the following expression: 60-(RECNO( )/RECCOUNT( )*60).

Each numeric expression is part of a REPLICATE( ) function, then you can produce the number of characters indicated by the calculation. For example, the following expression creates a number of white blocks, based on the value of the record number:
REPLICATE(CHR(219),RECNO(   )/RECCOUNT( )*60)
The calculation for the entire graphic would be:

```
REPLICATE(CHR(219),RECNO( )/RECCOUNT( )*60)+REPLICATE(CHR(178),60-(RECNO( )/RECCOUNT( )*60))
```

This is a very complicated expression when assembled, but each of its parts is fairly easy to understand. Typing in complicated expressions like the one above can be tedious because you must make sure all the parentheses are correctly entered. If you leave one out, or add an extra one, dBASE IV will not accept the expression. In the command below, the entry of the expression is divided into several lines to make it easier to read while you are entering it.

Move the cursor to row 19, col 10. Insert a calculated field.

```
[F5]
[right  arrow]┘
```

Enter the graphics expression.

```
e
```

Because the expression is long you can use the Zoom key, [F9], to allow you to edit on a line that runs the full width of the screen, instead of being limited to the menu width. Enter

```
[F9]
```

Enter

```
REPLICATE(
CHR(219),
RECNO( )/RECCOUNT( )*60)
+REPLICATE(
CHR(178),
60-(RECNO( )/RECCOUNT( )*60))  ┘
```

Note that in dBASE IV you are permitted to abbreviate function names by entering the first four characters only. You can save some typing effort by entering the expression using four character abbreviations. The expression would read:

```
REPL(CHR(219),RECN( )/RECC( )*60)+REPL(CHR(178),60-(RECN(    )/ RECC( )*60))  ┘
```

The template is set for the default value of a character-calculated field, 25 characters. You must expand the template to 60 characters. Enter

```
t
X (35 times)
┘
```

Save the field definition by entering

```
[Ctrl-End]
```

The layout looks like Figure 6-15.

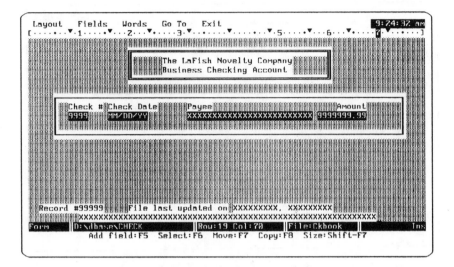

Figure 6-15. Calculated fields added to layout.

Save the modified layout by entering

    [Alt-e] s

Display the data using the new screen format by entering

    [F2]

The screen form appears with the calculated fields. Record 12, the last record added, appears in the form. The fields at the bottom of the screen show the record number and latest file update. The bar is solid because you are at the end of the file.

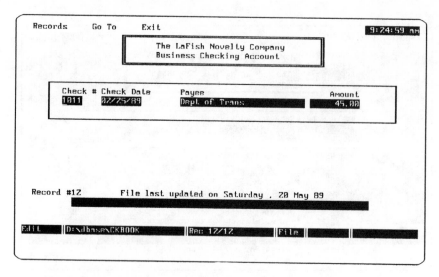

Figure 6-16. Screen form displays system information and fields.

Move to the previous record in the file.

> [Pg Up]

Record 11 appears. The right end of the bar changes to gray to indicate you are 11/12ths of the way through the database. Move to record 4 by entering

> [Alt-g] r 4 ↵

The bar is now 1/3rd white and 2/3rds gray, indicating you are 1/3rd of the way through the file.

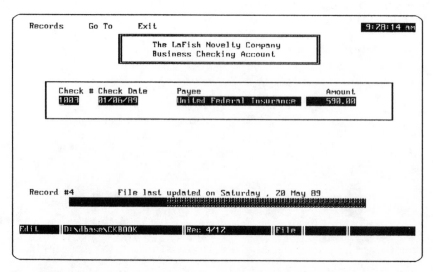

Figure 6-17. Bar changes colors in proportion to the record number.

The bar created by the calculated field updates each time a new record is displayed. The record numbers are used to calculate the relative portions of white and gray blocks, so the bar forms a visual indicator of where you are positioned in the database file.

The System functions allow you to integrate system information with database information in a number of different ways. As you can see, they can be as simple as displaying the record number, or as complicated as creating a graphic representing the same idea.

Exit the Edit mode by entering

```
[Alt-e] e
```

Copying a Screen From a File

Another advantage of custom layouts is that they do not limit you to just one layout for each database. You can create as many different layouts as you choose. You can use the layouts to view the file differently, depending upon what purpose you have in mind. For example, the CHECK screen you created may be useful for reviewing records. However, since the layout does not include all the fields in the database, you may want to create a different screen form to use for data entry purposes. One way to accomplish this is to create a new screen layout from scratch. An alternative way is to copy an existing layout and make additions, deletions, and changes. You can create a copy of an existing file by loading the file, then saving it with a separate name. This creates a copy that can be modified without disturbing the original.

Begin by opening the CHECK screen form for modifications.

```
⏎
m
```

To make a copy of this layout, use the Save This Form command found on the Layout menu. The Save This Form command differs from the Save Changes and Exit command, in two respects. First, Save This Form allows you to change or modify the current filename. Second, the Form Layout mode remains active so you can continue to work with the current form. Save the current form under the name ENTRY. Enter

```
[Alt-L] s
```

The program automatically displays the current filename as the default name. In this instance, change the name to ENTRY. Enter

```
[Home][Ctrl-y]
entry ⏎
```

The form is saved under the new filename. As soon as the saving (and generating) process is complete, the program returns to the Screen Layout mode. If you look at the status line you will see the name of the screen layout has been changed to ENTRY. Thus, any changes made to the layout affects the entry file, not the CHECK.SCR file.

Deleting Fields

The first step is to remove the calculated fields at the bottom of the display. This is done in two ways. 1) Position the cursor on the field you want to delete and press the [Del] key. 2) Use the Remove Field command found on the Field menu. It is not necessary to move the cursor to the field with this method.

Use the first method to remove the record number field. Move the cursor to row 18, col 10.

        [Del]

The field is removed from the layout. Remove the graphic bar field with the same method.

        [down arrow]
        [Del]

The Remove Field command allows you to remove a field by selecting it from a list of fields. Enter

        [Alt/f] r

The program lists all the fields currently defined in the layout.

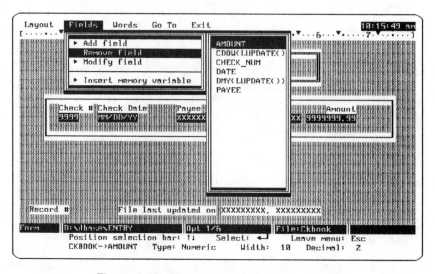

Figure 6-18. Delete fields from layout display.

Remove the update day of the week field.

```
[down arrow]⏎
```

Repeat the command to eliminate the update date field. Note that to repeat a command from the menu, you can use [F10] to return to the last menu and option used.

```
[F10] ⏎
[down arrow](3 times)
⏎
```

The text is removed by using the text editing commands. For example, to clear an entire line of text, use [Ctrl-y]. Enter

```
[up arrow]
[Home][Ctrl-y]
```

Logical Fields

Two of the three fields to be added to this layout are logical fields. Typically, these fields benefit from a custom layout because they contain only a single character, representing true or false. The data is usually an answer to a question. When you are limited to the fieldname, it is difficult to express the question you want answered with a logical true or false.

The two logical fields in the current database are CLEARED and DE-DUCTIBLE. The meaning of these fields would be more clear if you could put the full text of the question next to the field display. For example, the question "Is this expense deductible from Federal tax?" is preferable to the laconic DEDUCTIBLE.

You can easily ask this using a custom-screen display. To do so, simply enter the text of the question or statement to which the logical field relates. Move the cursor to row 12, col 5. Enter the question, then place the logical field next to it.

```
Is this expense deductible from Federal tax?
[right arrow]
[F5]
de ⏎
```

Note that the Template is set for L automatically. The L template allows Y, N, T, or F characters. Change the template to Y to allow and display only Y or N as the logical field contents. The template character must be an upper-case Y. A lower-case y is treated as the letter Y, not a template specification. Enter

```
[backspace]
Y ⏎
```

Place the field on the screen display by entering

```
[Ctrl-End]
```

Repeat the procedure for the CLEARED field. Move the cursor to row 13, col 5.

    Has this check cleared the bank?

Move the cursor to row 13, col 50.

    [F5]
    cl ↵
    t
    [backspace] Y ↵
    [Ctrl-End]

You have now placed two logical fields next to questions that elaborate on the meaning of the Y or N values displayed.

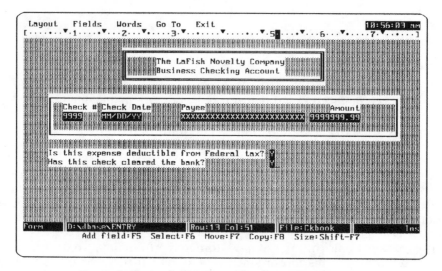

Figure 6-19. Logical fields placed onto screen layout.

Memo Fields

In the normal Edit or Browse mode displays, memo fields are displayed with the memo field markers: the word *memo* for an empty field, and *MEMO* for a field containing text.

When you create your own custom-designed screen format, you can create a window within the layout that enables you to display the contents of the memo field, instead of just the memo field marker. Begin by positioning the cursor to an empty area of the screen layout. Move the cursor to row 15, col 5. Enter

    Remarks:[right arrow]

Place the memo field, REMARKS, at this location.

```
[F5]
r ↵
```

The Field Specification menu appears. Because you have selected a memo field, the menu contains two options specific to memo fields: Display as and Border lines.

The Display as option allows you to display the memo field as a marker or as a window. The Marker option is the default value, displaying *memo* on the screen. If you select window, you can create a window where the actual text of the memo field will appear when the record is displayed. Change the value from Marker to Window by entering

```
d
```

The Border lines option allows you to select the type of border you want placed around the window. You can select a single line, double line, or a character as the border. In this example, select a double line.

```
b
d
```

Place the field onto the screen layout by entering

```
[Ctrl-End]
```

When you return to the Screen Layout work area, notice the program does not automatically display the window. Instead, you are placed into a Window Drawing mode. You can now draw a window within the screen layout and use to display the memo text. If the text is larger than can fit into the window, the program will display as much of the upper-left portion of the text as can fit.

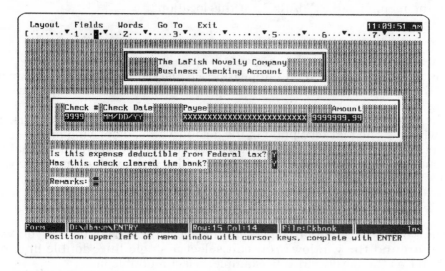

Figure 6-20. Window drawing mode activates when memo type field is selected.

Draw the window for the memo field by entering

⏎

Move the cursor to row 19, col 60.

⏎

The memo field window is placed onto the screen layout.

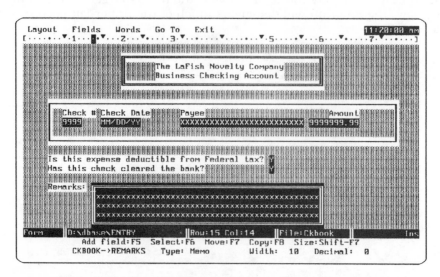

Figure 6-21. Memo field window inserted into screen layout.

Save the new screen layout by entering

    [Alt-e] s

The program should return to the Control Center display after generating the screen display files. However, current versions of dBASE IV contain a bug that causes an error when you attempt to save the revised screen layout. If you see a message box Compilation error, refer to the WORK AROUND section at the end of this chapter. There you will find instructions on how to handle this error. If you do not see the error but return to the Control Center, continue with the next section.

Working with Memo Displays

Display the database within the newly-created form by entering

    [F2]

The data appears in the new form, including the memo text that is displayed in the memo window.

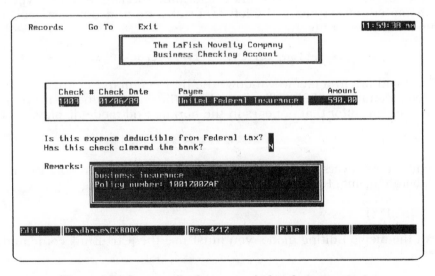

Figure 6-22.Screen display uses window for memo text.

Move to the last record in the file by entering

    [Alt-g] l

You can now fill in the three fields, DEDUCTIBLE, CLEARED, and RE-MARKS, which were missing from the screen display when you created this record. Enter

    ↵ (4 times)

Notice that the cursor moves through the fields in the order in which they appear on the screen display, not the order in which they appear in the file's structure. Enter the logical field data.

> **y**
> **n**

The cursor is now in the memo field window. Enter

> **Car**

The program beeps each time you attempt to enter a character because the memo field is not activated. Even though you can display memo text in a window, you still must use the [Ctrl-Home] or [F9] command to gain access to the memo window. Enter

> **[F9]**

The window changes from white to black, and a ruler line appears; these changes indicate that the memo field text can now be entered or edited. Note that the size of the window does not determine the length of the typed line. The memo editor scrolls to the left and right, up and down, as you move within the window. Enter

> **Car registration for the delivery truck Plate #333-X42**

Once you are in a memo window, the [F9] command changes meaning. The Zoom command, [F9], will now enlarge the editing window to the size of the full-screen editor that appears in the normal Edit mode display. Enter

> **[F9]**

The editor now covers the entire screen. This is useful when you are entering an elaborate memo. Return to the small window by entering

> **[F9]**

To exit the memo Editing mode, you must use the [Ctrl-End] command. Enter

> **[Ctrl-End]**

The window changes to white, indicating it is in the Display-only mode.

The use of memo windows provides a means by which the data stored in memo fields can be integrated into the display. Exit the Edit mode by entering

> **[Esc]**

Field Options

In addition to determining the location of input fields and placement of text, dBASE IV provides a number of editing options used to control the entry process within individual fields.

Editing Permitted

This option allows you to control whether a field should be available for editing, or limited to display-only. The standard procedure is to make all calculated fields read-only and permit editing in all database fields. You can use this option to display data on a screen format by preventing any change from being made.

Permit Edit If

This option allows editing if a specified condition is true. With it you can link the data entry into one field to the value in another field, or the fulfillment of some system condition. For example, you might restrict access to the CLEARED or DEDUCTIBLE fields to records that have a PAYEE. Conversely, you might disallow editing to any record that has a PAYEE entered. This ensures that once a check number has been entered along with a payee, it cannot be changed.

Message

This option allows you to define a message that will appear at the bottom of the screen whenever the cursor is moved to a given field.

Carry Forward

This option automatically places the value used in the previous record, into a new record. This feature has the same effect as the ditto command, except it is automatic. For example, if you tend to enter records that all have the same date, it saves time if the date is automatically forwarded to each new record.

Default Value

A default value is one that is automatically inserted into a field whenever a new record is added to the database. You can accept or edit the default. This option is useful when a field, such as a logical field, is given the same value in each new record. For example, you may want to set the DEDUCTIBLE field to Y, and the CLEARED field to N.

Smallest Allowed Value

This option restricts the entry in numeric fields to values equal to, or greater than, a specified value. For example, you may set the field to reject amounts less than $2.00, because you may never write a check for such a small amount. Entry of this small value would be a typing error and could be avoided by setting the minimum value.

Largest Allowed Value

This option limits the size of the input data to a value less than, or equal to, the specified value. This option places a maximum size on the value that can be entered into that field. Taken together with Smallest allowed value, you can limit input to a specific range of values.

Accept Value When

This option accepts a logical expression. The expression is used to perform a validity check on the data entered. For example, when you enter a date for a check, the date should always be equal to, or earlier than, the current system's date. In most cases, recording a future check date is a mistake. By entering an expression such as DATE<=DATE( ), the program automatically checks the dates as you enter them.

Unaccepted Message

This option specifies a message to be displayed if the validity check option determines that the entry is not valid. The message explains why the value is not acceptable.

Load the ENTRY screen format into the Screen Form Layout mode.

⤶ m

There are many ways to apply editing options to the fields in the screen layout. Begin by adding a message option to the memo field. It may be useful to display a message at the bottom of the screen explaining how to access the menu field for editing. You can modify a field in two ways, using the Modify Field command found on the Fields menu. If you position the cursor on a field, the Modify Field command assumes you want to change it. If you are not positioned on a field, the command lists the fields on the layout, allowing you to select from among them.

To add a message to the REMARKS field, select the field from the Modify Field list.

[Alt-f]m
r ⤶

Display the Edit Option menu.

> e

The menu lists the nine edit options. Note that only those options that can be used with memo-type fields are currently available.

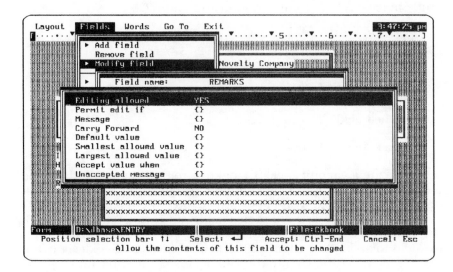

Figure 6-23. Edit options menu.

To create a message, enter

> m
> **Enter F9 to edit and Ctrl-End to save changes** ↵

Save the modified field.

> [Ctrl-End] *(2 times)*

Set default values for the logical fields: CLEARED = N and DEDUCTIBLE =Y. Begin with CLEARED.

> [F10] ↵
> cl ↵
> e
> d
> .F. ↵
> [Ctrl-End] *(2 times)*

Repeat the process to set the default for DEDUCTIBLE to true. Try this on your own. The correct command is at the end of the chapter under Ex-3.

Create a range of values for the amount. Here, limit the amounts to values between $2.00 and $15,000.00. Enter

        [F10] ↵
        ↵
        e

Select the Smallest Allowed Value option and enter 2.

        s 2 ↵

Set the largest value at 15,000.

        L 15000 ↵

Save the modified field.

        [Ctrl-End] *(2 times)*

You can create a validity check to make sure that the contents of the field meet a certain specification. One common specification is that the field not be left blank. For example, you may want to force the user to enter the name of a payee. Since PAYEE is a character field, you can determine if the field is blank by using an expression, such as PAYEE#SPACE(25). The expression tests the field to make sure that PAYEE is not equal to 25 spaces. If it is, the program rejects the entry. Create the validity check by entering

        [F10] ↵
        p ↵
        e
        a

Enter the expression that must be true if the entry is to be accepted. In this instance, it tests for a blank field.

        payee#SPACE(25)   ↵

When you create a validity check, you can also specify a message that will be displayed if the user makes an incorrect entry. In this case, the message explains the program is set to not accept a blank payee. The message can also tell the user to enter VOID if the check is voided. The Unaccepted message option displays a message when an invalid entry is made. When entering a long message, use the [F9] key to display a line the width of the screen. Enter

        u
        [F9]
        Cannot leave Payee Blank - Enter VOID if check voided ↵

Save the modified field by entering

  [Ctrl-End] *(2 times)*

Finally, create an option to prevent editing the check number, once a record has been entered. Permit Edit If lets you enter an expression, allowing editing of the field, only if that expression is true. For example, the condition payee=SPACE(25) is true if the payee field is blank. Recall that you forced the user to make an entry into the payee field, in order to fill a record. This means the expression payee=SPACE(25) is true only when you first create a record and all the fields are empty. The expression entered as the Permit Edit If makes sure the check number remains the same after it has been entered into the record. Display the edit options for the CHECK_NUM field.

   [F10] ↵
   ch ↵
   e

Enter the expression to the Permit Edit If option.

   p
   payee=SPACE(25) ↵

Save the field modifications.

  [Ctrl-End] *(2 times)*

Save the modified screen display. Note that using Edit options does not change the appearance of the screen layout. The only way to test the Edit options is to attempt to add or edit records. Return to the Control Center by entering

  [Alt-e] s

Changes made to the Edit options of existing fields should not generate a compilation error. Only changes in the number of fields or their location seem to be affected by this bug.

Display the data inside the new screen format.

  [F2]

The cursor is positioned in the DATE field because you are not allowed to edit the CHECK_NUM field after filling out the PAYEE field. Create a new record.

  [Alt-r] a

The new record appears. The cursor is positioned in the CHECK-NUM field because a new record always has a blank entry for PAYEE the field. Also note that the logical fields are automatically set for the default values.

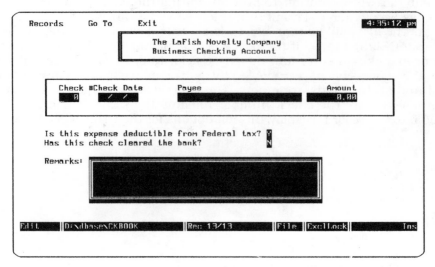

Figure 6-24. New records displayed in modified screen format.

Enter the data for the record.

```
1012
022789
```

Enter a blank payee.

⏎

The Edit option prevents a blank PAYEE Field. At the bottom of the screen the message defined for this eventuality is displayed. dBASE IV adds the (press SPACE) to the message.

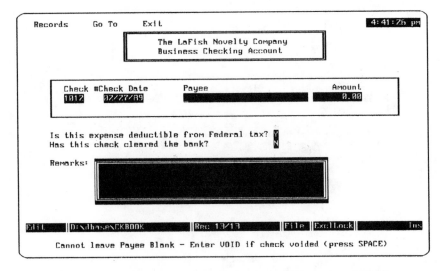

Figure 6-25. Message displayed when field entry is rejected.

Enter

>   [spacebar]
>   Western Telephone ↵

The next field is amount. Enter

>   1 ↵

This time, the program beeps and displays the message "RANGE is 2 to 15000 (press SPACE)". The message is generated by the minimum and maximum values specified as edit options. Correct your entry.

>   [spacebar]
>   175.75

Move the cursor to the memo field window.

>   [down arrow] *(2 times)*

The program displays the specified message at the bottom of the screen when the cursor is moved to the memo window field.

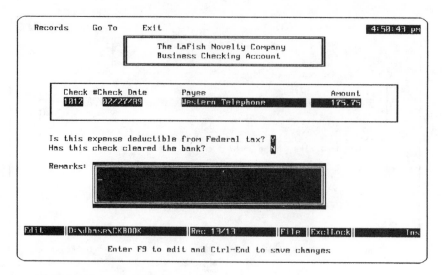

Figure 6-26. Message displayed when cursor is moved to memo window.

Enter the memo text.

```
[F9]
Includes Compuserve on-line time
[Ctrl-End]
```

Exit the Entry mode.

```
[Alt-e] e
```

Forms with Multiple Pages

dBASE IV allows you to create forms with multiple pages. In this instance, the term page is used to refer to a screen of information. Screen layouts are 25 lines long. Create a single screen layout having several screens. When the display is active, the [Pg Dn] and [Pg Up] keys can be used to move between the screens.

You can use multiple pages when you have too many fields to fit comfortably on a single page, or you want to divide the display into different sets of data. In the current example, you may choose to make a second page displaying tax information. You can use calculated fields to find the sales tax and pre-tax amounts.

Place the ENTRY screen layout into the Forms Layout mode.

```
⏎
m
```

How do you create additional pages? The program automatically divides your layout into groups of 22-line pages. All the information, text or fields, entered on lines 0 through 21 appear on the first page. Any information entered on lines 22 through 43 appear on page 2, and so on.

The screen is actually 25 lines long. However, the Edit mode reserves the top line for the menu bar and two lines at the bottom for the status and message bars, leaving 22 lines for the custom-designed screen layout. If you are writing dBASE IV programs and are working without the status and message lines, you can create 25-line screen displays.

As you move down the page, the lines scroll up so you can see more of the work surface. Move the cursor to the last line on the screen. Move the cursor to row 21, col 0.

Enter a line of text telling the user there is another page to this screen display, and how to access it. Enter

```
Page 1 of 2 -*Press PgDn for next page*-
```

Center the text using the Words menu.

```
[Alt-w] p c
```

Move to the lines that will become the second page. Note that in the layout screen the rows are numbered consecutively. dBASE IV does not indicate that line 22 will appear on the second page. You must keep track of what data is placed on what page. Move the cursor to row 28, col 0. Enter.

```
Tax Information
[F10] ↵
```

Move the cursor to row 30, col 25. Enter the amount field at this location.

```
Check Amount
```

Move the cursor to row 30, col 40.

```
[F5]
↵
```

Use the Display options to prevent editing of the amount. All the values on this page are for display purposes only.

```
e
↵
[Ctrl-End]
```

Change the template to contain commas.

```
t
[Home] [Ctrl-y]
99,999.99 ↵
```

Place the field onto the page by entering

> [Ctrl-End]

The next field is a calculated field that shows the amount of sales tax for that article. Recall the assumption of 6% sales tax on all items. Move the cursor to row 32, col 25.

> Sales Tax

Move the cursor to row 32, col 40. Enter a calculated field that uses the formula AMOUNT/1.06.

> [F5]
> [right arrow]↲
>   e
>   amount/1.06 ↲

Change the template to match the previous template.

> t
> [Home] [Ctrl-y]
> 99,999.99 ↲
> [Ctrl-End]

The last calculated field is the pre-tax amount of the check. Move the cursor to row 34, col 25. Enter the text that explains the value.

> Before tax

Move the cursor to row 34, col 40. Insert a calculated field showing the value of the check, less the amount of sales tax.

> [F5]
> [right arrow]↲
>   e
>   amount-amount/1.06 ↲

Change the template to match the other templates.

> t
> [Home] [Ctrl-y]
> 99,999.99 ↲
> [Ctrl-End]

Draw a box around the information on the second page. Move the cursor to row 27, col 15.

> [Alt-L] b s ↲

Move the cursor to row 35, col 60.

> ↲

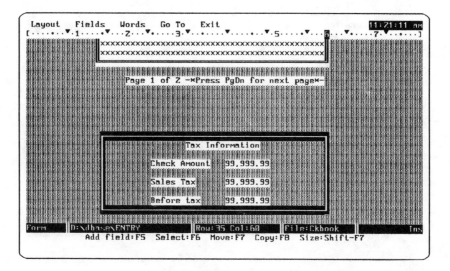

Figure 6-27. Layout of second page.

The screen will look the layout shown in Figure 6-27.

In order to ensure that the user knows how to get back to Page 1, place a message on the last line of the second page. Because each page contains 22 lines, the end of the second page is line 43. (Recall that the line counting begins with zero, making line 43 the 44th line on the screen layout.)

Move the cursor to row 43, col 0. Enter the text and center it.

```
Page 2 of 2 -* Press PgUp for previous page*-
[Alt-w] p c
```

Save the modified screen layout by entering

```
[Alt-e] s
```

When you return to the Control Center, display the data in the modified screen layout by entering

```
[F2]
```

The display appears the same as the previous version, with the exception that the text at the bottom informs the user there is a second page. To display that page, enter.

```
[Pg Dn]
```

The second page is displayed. You know the same record is still active because the status line shows the same record location, Rec 13/13, and because the value of the amount, 175.75, remains the same.

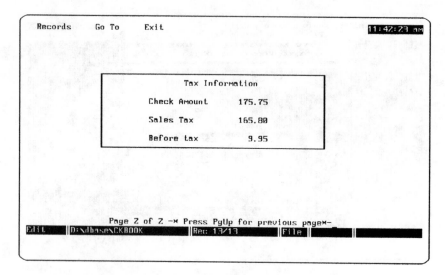

Figure 6-28. Page 2 of screen layout displayed.

Return to the first page of the layout by entering

    [PgUp]

While the record is still active, you can move between the pages as many times as you choose. Note that it is important to know the number of pages in each layout because the effect of the [PgUp] and [PgDn] keys will change when they are used on the first or last pages of the layout, respectively. The [PgUp] key used on the first page displays the first page of the previous record. The [PgDn] key used on the last page displays the first page of the next record. It is usually a good idea to label each page with a message, such as Page 2 of 4, so the user will know wether a [PgUp] or [PgDn] will move the screen to a new record, or another page of the same record.

The screen layout presents a second page for any of the records in the database file. Display the first record in the file.

    [Alt-g] t
    [Pg Dn]

The tax information for the first record is displayed.

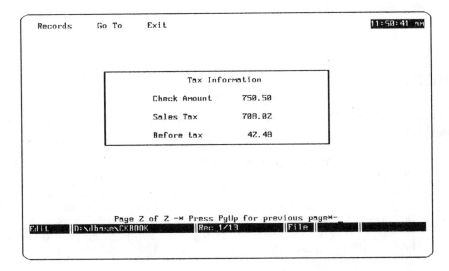

Figure 6-29. Tax information for the first record.

Exit the screen editing mode by entering

[Esc]

Returning to the Default Display

Once you have created or activated a screen format, it will be used again whenever you activate the Edit mode. But suppose you wanted to return to the default Edit mode, in which the standard dBASE IV screen display is used. There is no direct way to close all the open forms. However, when you close a database file, the forms are also closed. When the file is re-opened, the program returns the default form, unless you specifically choose another.

To return dBASE IV to the default screen display for the Edit mode, close and then re-open the CKBOOK database.

        [left arrow]*(2 times)*
        ↵ *(2 times)*

The file is now closed. Open the database again.

        [down arrow]
        ↵ *(2 times)*

Activate the Edit mode by entering

        [F2]

The screen display returns to the default style used by dBASE IV.

Exit dBASE IV to conclude this chapter's operations.

```
[Esc]
[Alt-e] q
```

Summary

This chapter showed how to create custom-designed screen displays that can be used with the Edit mode.

- **Screen Forms.** When the Edit mode is used to enter, revise, or display information, dBASE IV automatically generates a screen display. This display places the names of the fields down the left side of the screen, and the field values in input areas next to the field names. You can design one or more screen layouts to replace the default screen layout when the Edit mode is activated. Screen layouts do not affect the Browse mode, which always maintains the built-in table arrangement.

- **User-Defined Prompts.** Custom-designed screen displays allow you to enter different types of text onto the screen display, in contrast to the default layout where only field names appear. The use of text on custom-screen displays permits you to elaborate on the identity or significance of the field information. It also allows you to present other types of information and messages.

- **Field Arrangement.** The custom screen display allows you to select the placement and the order in which the fields appear. Fields can be placed at any location on the screen display. When editing, the cursor moves from left to right, then down the page, in the order in which you placed the fields. The fields do not have to be placed in the same order as they appear in the file structure. You can include any or all of the fields from the selected database in a given screen layout. You can have as many screen layouts as you choose. Note that only one layout at a time can be active. You can select display templates and picture functions for the fields included in a screen layout.

- **Memo Windows.** Custom-designed screen displays allow you to create a window used to replace the MEMO marker of memo fields. The window will display automatically as much of the memo field as possible when the record is displayed in the Edit mode. The MEMO marker does not appear when a memo window is active. Keep in mind that even though the memo text is displayed, you must still use the [F9] or [Ctrl-Home] keys to activate the memo field for entry or editing. Also recall that the [F9] key used inside a memo window does not save the memo. Instead, it opens or closes the window to full-screen size. To exit and save text in a memo window, you must use [Ctrl-End].

- **Calculated Fields.** Calculated fields can display any type of information that can be created using a dBASE IV expression. The expression can include calculations, functions, or text operations, such as conversion to upper-case. You can also use field templates and picture functions with calculated fields. When the Edit mode is activated, the values of the calculated fields are re-evaluated and displayed, based on the data in each record. Calculated fields are displayed as read-only areas. You cannot edit calculated fields.

- **Multiple Pages.** Displays exceeding the number of lines available for a single screen, are divided into pages. Each page can be accessed by using the [PgDn] or [PgUp] keys. In dBASE IV, the edit mode screen is 22 lines deep. Note that the lines to be counted begin at 0, making line 21 the last line of the display. When creating a screen display, dBASE IV does not indicate the end of each screen. You must keep track of the row numbers to place the data on the proper page.

- **Forms Layout mode.** This mode is activated when you choose to create or modify a screen layout. It allows you to design the screen layout by entering text, drawing lines and boxes, positioning fields, and positioning and defining calculated fields. When a screen layout is saved, the program generates three files, based on your activities. The first file has an SCR extension and holds the image of your layout, just as you have defined it on the Forms Layout screen. This file is used when you seek to modify the layout. The program also converts the SCR file into a dBASE IV program file with an FMT extension. Finally, the FMT file is compiled into a dBASE IV object-code file with an FMO extension. It is the FMO file that is actually used by dBASE IV to create the screen layout when you activate the Edit mode.

- **Edit Options.** Field and calculated field definitions allow you to select special Edit options. They are designed to help you control data entry. These options allow you to control the following aspects of the editing process: 1) they permit or refuse editing of a specific field, 2) they permit editing of the field based on a logical expression, 3) they can display a message at the bottom of the screen whenever the cursor is placed into the given field's input area, 4) they can carry forward the values from a previous record, 5) They can insert a default value into the current field, 6) they can limit numeric entry above a minimum value, 7) they can limit numeric entry below a maximum value, 8) they can accept data only if it meets a specified logical condition, and 9) they can display a message at the bottom of the screen when an entry is rejected.

Ex-1
Change the template.

```
t
[backspace]   (5 times) }
⏎
```

Ex-2
Create a calculated field.

```
[F5]
right arrow ⏎
e
DMY(LUPDATE( )) ⏎
t
[Home][Ctrl-y]
X (9 times)
⏎
[Ctrl-End]
```

Ex-3
Set a default value.

```
[F10] ⏎
de ⏎
e
d
.T. ⏎
[Ctrl-End]   (2 times)
```

Work Around

Format File Compilation Error

Current versions of dBASE IV sometimes encounter an error when attempting to generate a modified version of a screen layout file. The error occurs in the compiling stage of the screen format generation. dBASE IV incorrectly writes the program version (FMT extension) of the screen display file. The dBASE IV compiler finds the errors and refuses to compile the program. This generates an error message that reads "Compilation Error".

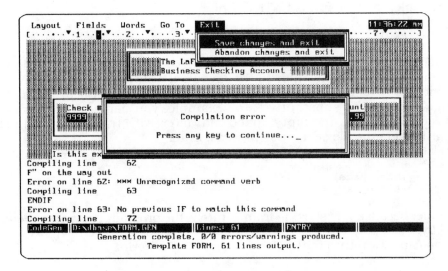

Figure 6-30. Compilation error message.

This error prevents you from using the screen format. However, you have not lost the screen layout file (SCR extension). To resolve this error, you must have dBASE IV reconstruct the FMT file generated from the SCR, Screen Layout file, from scratch. This is done by erasing the current FMT file from the disk, then editing and saving the screen layout again.

With the error message displayed, enter

     ⏎

This returns you to the Control Center display. Nothing here indicates a problem exists. However, should you try to use the screen form just created you will get the Compilation Error again. Therefore, exit the Control Center display and activate the Dot Prompt mode.

    [Alt-e] e

You must now erase the FMT file generated from the screen layout just created. This is the file that contains the errors which prevent dBASE IV from compiling the screen. The file will have the same name as the screen layout, but with an FMT extension. For example, if the screen layout is called ENTRY the file you must erase is called ENTRY.FMT. Use the ERASE command to remove the file.

    ERASE entry.fmt ⏎

The program displays the message "File has been deleted".

Activate the Screen Layout mode directly from the Dot Prompt mode using the MODIFY SCREEN command. Note that you should use the name of the screen layout corresponding to the one that encountered the error. In this example, the filename is ENTRY. Enter

```
MODIFY SCREEN entry ↵
```

In order to force the program to generate a new version of the FMT file you must make some modification to the layout. If you do not, dBASE IV will assume the screen is unchanged and skip the generation process. The change need not be substantive. For example, you can add then erase a character by typing an empty space character with the [spacebar]. The change triggers the file generation process. Enter

```
x
[backspace]
[Alt-e] s
```

This time, because it is starting from scratch, the program generates the files correctly.

You can now return to the Control Center by entering

```
[F2]
```

Be aware that the cursor location has been changed from its previous location within the Control Center display. To continue from the point at which you exited the Control Center, you move the highlight to the form with which you were working (e.g. ENTRY).

```
[right arrow](2 times)
```

7

Putting Queries, Forms and Reports to Work

The preceding three chapters have introduced the three main operations that can be carried out from the Control Center, once you have created a database file. These involve the creation of user-defined queries, report forms, and screen forms.

The purpose of this chapter is to illustrate how these functions can work together to extend the power of dBASE IV. The example file you have been working with, CKBOOK, has thus far limited itself to information about the checks you have been writing. But this represents only half the information you need to record. The other half treats the deposits made to the checking account. By recording both checks and deposits in the same database, you can obtain information about deposits, as well as checks. In addition, you can calculate the current balance in the checking account. You can also obtain information about outstanding checks and deposits to aid in the reconciliation of your bank statements.

You may think at first it is necessary to create a separate database for deposits. But in many ways, deposit information is similar to that generated by checks. For example, both have dates and amounts. You may also want to number the deposits in the same way you number the checks. A memo field, such as REMARKS, can record information about deposits just as it does about the checks.

Still, if deposits and checks are similar, how can the program tell which is which? You need to be able to tell the difference between a check and a deposit, in order to obtain a balance. The answer lies in the way that queries, reports, and screen forms are used to control how information is retrieved, displayed, and entered. For example, the first check number in the CKBOOK

317

file begins at 1000. You could use the CHECK_NUM field to keep track of deposits by defining values 0 through 999 as deposits numbers, and anything over 999 as a check. Such a distinction could be used in a query to select only checks, or only deposits. Separate screen forms would match the queries. For example, you could restrict the CHECK_NUM field to values between 1 and 999, and place the word DEPOSIT into the PAYEE field by default. You would also want to change the text identifying the transaction date to the *date* of deposit.

In addition, you could create reports that printed lists of deposits or checks only, or which calculated the current balance. By combining queries and reports, you could quickly find outstanding checks and deposits to reconcile your bank statement.

The goal of this chapter is to illustrate how queries, screens, and reports combine to get more power out of an existing database.

You might think it is better to create a separate database file for the deposits. While this is possible, it requires multiple-database operations to obtain information about checks and deposits. The same information could be obtained much more easily by creating different views of the records in a single file. In systems such as those used for financial accounting, it is usually simplest to place both cash-in and cash-out records in a common database and use fields to establish the groups in which a given record belongs.

Adding Deposits

The key to making a viable accounting system is to create a special entry form to be used whenever you want to work with deposits. The entry screen will perform the following functions:

1. It will use text and messages relating the fields to the entry of deposits. Fields that are not relevant (e.g., DEDUCTIBLE) can be omitted from the display.
2. It can use Edit options to limit data entry to certain values or automatically place values into fields. For example, it can automatically insert the word DEPOSIT as the default value of the PAYEE field. If you disallow editing in this field, a user will not be able to change the value and all deposits will be identified by the word DEPOSIT.

This form will work in conjunction with a query that selects only DEPOSIT records from the CKBOOK file. In this example, begin by creating the query in order to link the query to the screen display. By selecting the DEPOSITS screen form, you will activate the DEPOSITS query, not the entire CKBOOK database.

Create a new query.

```
[right arrow]↵
```

Select the database for the query by using the Add File to Query command.

        ⌐ ⌐

Select the fields for the query. Include all those used in the CKBOOK database, except the DEDUCTIBLE field. The simplest way to do this is to place all the fields into the display skeleton, then remove the DEDUCTIBLE field.

Since the cursor is positioned in the filename box of the skeleton, you can create a full display skeleton, (i.e. all fields included) by pressing [F5].

        [F5]

Change to the display skeleton, [F4], and remove the DEDUCTIBLE field from this skeleton.

        [F4]
        [Tab] *(5 times)*
        [F5]

Because the DEPOSIT query should activate only deposit records, you must enter into the file skeleton a query specification that selects those records. Keep in mind you have not yet decided how to distinguish the deposits from the checks. Once you decide on a method, you must apply this method consistently to all other operations. In this instance, assume all deposit-type records have the word DEPOSIT stored in the PAYEE field. Return to the file skeleton and place this specification in the PAYEE field box.

        [F4]
        [Tab] *(3 times)*
        ="DEPOSIT"

Keep in mind that the character case used in query specifications is significant. If you enter the word as lower-case *deposit* instead of upper-case *DEPOSIT* , you have to make sure that the characters entered into the PAYEE field in each deposit record match the case used in the query.

Save the query under the name DEPOSITS.

        [Alt-e] s
        deposits ⌐

Creating the Input Screen

Having created the DEPOSITS query, you can proceed to create a screen form for data enter. Activate the Screen Form Layout mode.

        [right arrow] ⌐

The Screen Form Layout mode is activated. If you look at the right side of the status line, you will see the view name DEPOSITS. This indicates that when active, this screen form will activate the DEPOSITS query, only.

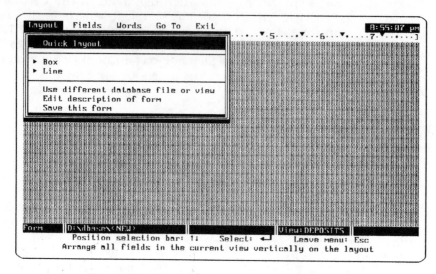

Figure 7-1. Deposits view linked to screen form.

Exit the Layout menu (which is displayed by default when you create a new screen form). Enter

    [Esc]

You have six fields to place on this screen layout. Before placing the fields, enter a text prompt to identify this screen as the deposit-entry screen. Move the cursor to row 2, col 0. Enter

    Bank Deposits
    [Alt-w] p c

The first field to be placed on the screen form will be the PAYEE field. This should be the first field because its value will be automatically generated by the screen form to read DEPOSITS. You can accomplish this by using the default and Permit Editing Edit options. Move the cursor to row 5, col 15. Enter the text for the prompt.

    Type of Transaction:
    [Tab]

Place the PAYEE field at the current position, row 5, column 40.

    [F5]
    p ↵

Display the Editing Options menu.

> e

Set the default value of this field to DEPOSITS. Because this is a character field, the default setting must be entered as a text literal (i.e. you must surround the text with quotations). The quotations distinguish the word *DEPOSIT* from the possible name of a field. Enter

> `"DEPOSIT"` ↵

Because default values entered should not be changed by the user, you can prevent accidental editing by using the Permit Editing If option, where you can enter the condition *payee#"DEPOSIT"* . What will this expression accomplish? When a new record is created, the PAYEE field is blank. According to the input area, condition editing is permitted because the PAYEE field is not equal to DEPOSIT. The default option then places the word DEPOSIT into the field. As soon as this is accomplished, the editing condition is no longer true because PAYEE is now equal to DEPOSITS. Thus the condition prevents any accidental changes to the PAYEE field and ensures that all the deposit records show DEPOSIT as the payee.

A simpler solution would be to use the turn off Editing Allowed option. However, the result of this approach is a blank entry because when the Editing Allowed option is turned off, the placement of a default value is rejected. It is necessary to use the Permit Editing If option so that when the blank record is displayed, the Permit Editing If sees it and allows the default value to be inserted. Once inserted, the condition blocks out editing from the field because the Permit Editing If condition is no longer true.

Enter

> e

Place the field onto the form layout by entering

> `[Ctrl-End]` *(2 times)*

Move the cursor to row 7 column 16 by entering the following keystrokes.

> ↵ *(2 times)*
> `[Tab]` *(2 times)*

Notice in this layout, the fields and text are aligned at the default tab stops. These are automatically placed every eight characters. The tab stops enable you to use the ↵ and [Tab] keys to quickly position the cursor and still keep the items aligned in columns.

The next field to add is the CHECK_NUM field. However, in this screen layout you will label the field *Deposit Number*. Enter

```
Deposit Number:
[Tab] (2 times)
```

Place the CHECK_NUM field at the current cursor location.

```
[F5]
c ↵
```

In this instance, you may choose to limit the deposit numbers to a range of 1 to 999 so they do not conflict with the check numbers. Enter

```
e
s 1 ↵
L 999 ↵
```

Place the field in the layout by entering

```
[Ctrl-End]  (2 times)
```

The form now has two fields laid out.

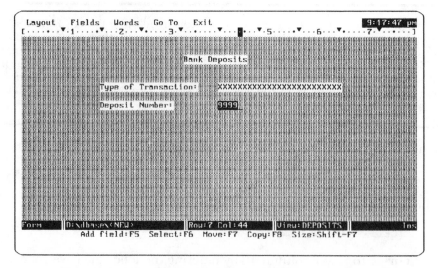

Figure 7-2. Two fields added to the DEPOSITS screen form.

The DATE and AMOUNT fields can be placed onto this screen layout without any special options. Enter

```
↵
[Tab] (2 times)
Date of Deposit:
[Tab]
[F5]
d ↵
[Ctrl-End]
↵
[Tab] (2 times)
Deposit Amount
[Tab] (2 times)
[F5]
↵
[Ctrl-End]
```

The next field is the REMARKS memo field. The most convenient way to use memos is in a memo window. Here, you place the window on the right side of the screen layout form. Move the cursor to row 6, col 55. Enter the prompt for the memo window.

```
Deposit Memo:
```

Move the cursor to row 7, col 55. Place a memo window at this location. Enter

```
[F5]
r ↵
```

Select to create a memo window and enter the Window Placement mode.

```
d
[Ctrl-End]
```

The cursor returns to the form layout work surface to allow you to draw the location for the window. Place the upper-left corner of the window at the current location by entering

```
↵
```

Draw the window by moving the cursor. Move the cursor to row 21, col 79. Enter

```
↵
```

The memo window is now placed onto the right side of the screen form. Keep in mind that row 21 is the bottom of the first page of a screen layout.

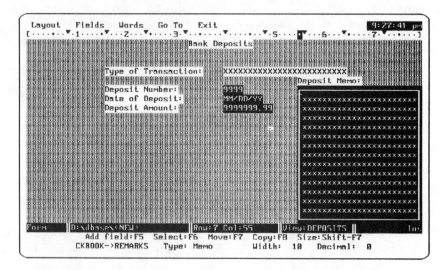

Figure 7-3. Memo window placed onto the right side of the form.

The final field to be placed is the CLEARED field. This is necessary because you must keep track of the deposits that have cleared in order to reconcile your bank statement. Move the cursor to row 12, col 16. Enter the following text as the prompt for this field.

```
Has this deposit cleared the bank?
[right arrow]
```

Place the CLEARED field at this location. Make sure the template for this field is a Y character, so the value appears as a Y or N, not a T or F. Also, set the default value for this field as false, .F. Try this on your own. The correct command is at the end of the chapter under Ex-1.

Save the screen layout as the DEPOSITS form by entering

```
[Alt-e] s
deposits ↵
```

The Control Center now shows two new files: the query file DEPOSITS and the form DEPOSITS. You can now use the query and form to enter deposit information.

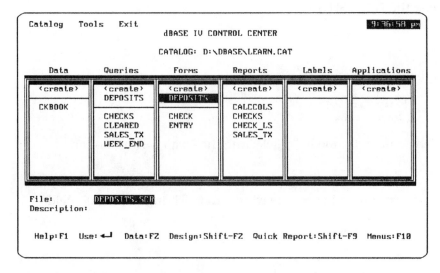

Figure 7-4. DEPOSITS query and form added to Control Center listing.

Entering the Deposits

Once the DEPOSIT query and form is created you can begin to enter data. Activate the data display by entering

        [F2]

After running for a moment or two, dBASE IV returns to the Control Center display. The data entry form for DEPOSITS did not appear. What went wrong? The current query limits the display of records to those containing DEPOSIT in the PAYEE field. However, at this point there are no records in the database that satisfy this condition. When you request the data for the DEPOSIT query, dBASE IV cannot find any records to display, thus the query terminates as soon as it begins.

   Of course, your goal is to enter the DEPOSIT records. But the nature of the Query mode requires there be at least one qualifying record to activate the Append Records mode, that would allow you to enter new records.

   In other words, you cannot get to the Append mode because there are no deposit records, while at the same time, there can be no records because you cannot get to the Append mode. The problem is solved by satisfying the program's need for a qualifying record. You can do this by closing the current query and directly accessing the database file. You can then add a record with the word DEPOSIT; when you activate the DEPOSIT query, the program will find the first record. You can edit and append deposit records from this point on. The first record serves as a *seed* for the remaining deposits.

Close the DEPOSITS query.

```
[left  arrow]
 ⏎ ⏎
```

Open the CKBOOK file.

```
[left  arrow]⏎
[down  arrow]⏎
```

Enter the data entry mode by selecting the Display Data option.

```
d
```

Add a new record and enter the word DEPOSIT in the PAYEE field.

```
[Alt-r] a
[down  arrow](2 times)
 DEPOSIT
```

Exit the entry mode.

```
[Alt-e]  e
```

With the seed record planted, activate the DEPOSIT entry screen.

```
[right  arrow](2 times)
 d ⏎
```

Choose the Display Data option.

```
d
```

dBASE IV displays another option box. The box is displayed because the view linked with the select screen is different from the current view. You are given the option of using the screen with the current view (i.e. the entire CKBOOK file) or with the DEPOSITS.QBE view.

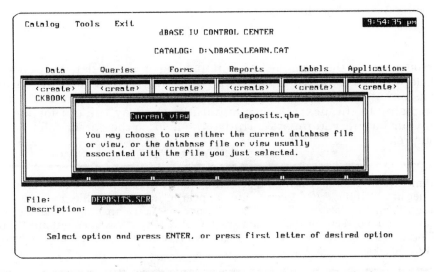

Figure 7-5. Select the view to match the screen display.

Select the DEPOSITS query. Enter

    [right arrow]↵

The DEPOSITS query and screen form are processed. Because there is already one record containing the word DEPOSIT in the PAYEE field, the program can display that record as part of the query. Now that the first deposit record has been added, you can access the DEPOSIT query directly from this point on.

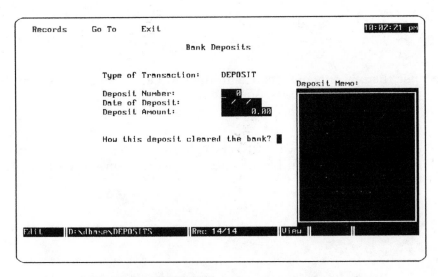

Figure 7-6. DEPOSITS screen form is displayed.

Enter the data for the deposit record.

```
1 ↵
```

The cursor moves to the memo field before moving on to the date because the memo field was placed on the same row as the CHECK_NUM field. When you create custom-screen displays, the cursor moves from left to right on the row before passing to the next. If you do not like the way the cursor moves through your layout, you must rearrange the field so the cursor follows the path you prefer.

The movement of the cursor through a screen display with input areas is determined by the order in which the @/GET commands appear in the program file. Keep in mind that screen forms are a type of dBASE IV program. You can change the cursor movement within a screen form by using the MODIFY COMMAND command to edit the FMT program file generated by the screen layout form. This technique is covered in Part II of this book.

Enter the rest of the data for this deposit.

```
[F9]
Checks:  ↵
Jacob Goren #2452 ↵
The US Navy #4252
[Ctrl-End]  ↵
```

Enter the date and amount.

```
010189
2500 ↵
```

Mark the deposit as cleared.

```
y
```

Because there is only one deposit in the CKBOOK file, the program asks if you want to add more records. Add two more deposits.

```
y
```

A new record appears. The word DEPOSIT is automatically inserted into the PAYEE field The Edit option blocks entry in this field once the DEPOSIT is placed into the field.

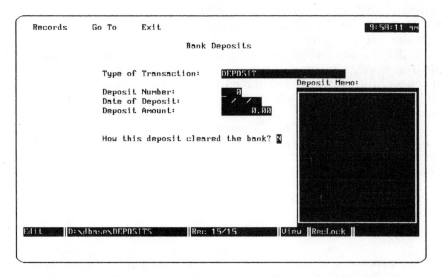

Figure 7-7. New record's PAYEE field set automatically to DEPOSIT.

Enter two more deposits.

```
2 ⌐ ⌐
013189
1200 ⌐ ⌐
3 ⌐ ⌐
021589
1900 ⌐
```

Save the deposits by entering

```
[Alt-e] e
```

Close the current query to deactivate the selection of only deposit records. This is necessary to separate the next series of files from the DEPOSIT query. Enter

```
[right arrow]
⌐ (2 times)
```

The Checks Query

Now that you established a query and a form for deposits, it is necessary to develop a query and form to use to enter and edit check records.

You already have a screen form, ENTRY, that serves this purpose. You must create a query that will use this form with the screen form.

Currently, there is a query named CHECKS, and a screen form named CHECK. You can create new queries with different names, but it makes more sense to delete the CHECKS.QBE and CHECK.SCR files, and create a new query, CHECKS, that works only with the non-deposit records in the CKBOOK database. To make things more consistent, you can change the name of the ENTRY screen form to CHECKS. This will give you two screen forms, CHECKS and DEPOSITS, linked to queries of the same name which handle the check and deposit records, respectively.

Of course, the names do not have to be the same. However, it is easier to remember how the system works when the names correspond as closely as possible to the function they carry out.

Begin by deleting the CHECKS query. A shortcut method of deleting a file from the Control Center is to highlight the filename and press the [Del] key. This is equivalent to the Remove Highlighted File from Catalog command on the Catalog menu. Enter

```
CH
[Del]
y
y
```

Repeat the process and remove the CHECK layout from the forms column. Note that in this instance, the CHECK form is deleted from the Control Center catalog, but not from the disk. Thus, at some later point, you can add the CHECK form to this, or any other catalog. Deleting the form from the Control Center keeps its name from confusing the user. You may find you want to rename the file and add it to the catalog under a different name.

If a file exists on the disk but is not part of the current catalog, you cannot create a new file that uses its name without overwriting it. In this case, the screen file CHECK.SCR will not create a disk conflict with CHECKS.SCR because of the single character difference between their names.

```
[right arrow]
c
[Del]
y
n
```

The next step is to change the name of the ENTRY screen form to CHECKS. First remove the ENTRY form from the catalog. Keep in mind you are only removing the file from the catalog, not the disk.

```
[right arrow]
e
[Del]
y
n
```

Renaming a File

The next step is to change the ENTRY.SCR file to CHECKS.SCR and add it to the catalog. The fastest way to execute a file rename operation is from the Dot Prompt. Exit the Control Center by entering

> `[Alt-e] e`

The command to rename a file is the RENAME command. It requires you to enter the old and the new name. Enter

> `RENAME entry.scr TO checks.scr ⌐`

The file's name has now been changed. Activate the Control Center display by entering

> `[F2]`

The only form listed in the Forms column is DEPOSITS. The newly named file does not appear. You must use the Add file to Catalog command on the Layout menu. Place the cursor in the Forms column. This limits the names of the files listed by the Add File to Catalog command to the files used by that column (e.g. in the Form column, only SCR, FMT, and FMO files will be listed). Enter

> `[right arrow]`*(2 times)*
> `[Alt-c] a`

Select the CHECKS.SCR file by entering

> `CHECKS ⌐`

You can enter a description of the file.

> `Check entry form ⌐`

The CHECKS form appears in the Forms column of the Control Center display.

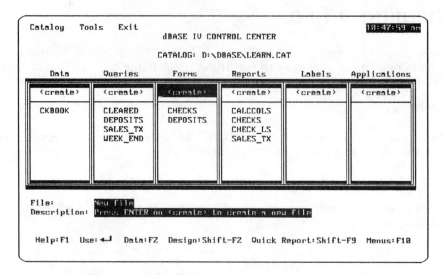

Catalog   Tools   Exit   10:47:59 am
                         dBASE IV CONTROL CENTER

                      CATALOG: D:\DBASE\LEARN.CAT

      Data   Queries   Forms   Reports   Labels   Applications

  ⟨create⟩   ⟨create⟩   ⟨create⟩   ⟨create⟩   ⟨create⟩   ⟨create⟩

  CKBOOK   CLEARED   CHECKS   CALCCOLS
                DEPOSITS   DEPOSITS   CHECKS
                SALES_TX   CHECK_LS
                WEEK_END   SALES_TX

  File: New file
  Description: Press ENTER on ⟨create⟩ to create a new file

  Help:F1   Use:◄┘   Data:F2   Design:Shift-F2   Quick Report:Shift-F9   Menus:F10

Figure 7-8. Renamed file added to Control Center catalog.

The Checks Query

The next step is to create a query that selects only checks. You can accomplish this by creating a query in which all the records *do not* have DEPOSIT as their PAYEE. Create a new query.

        [right arrow] ┘

Select the CKBOOK file as the database for the query.

        ┘ ┘

Place all the fields onto the display skeleton since you know that all the fields will be used in the CHECKS (formerly ENTRY) screen form. Enter

        [F5]

Create a query specification in the PAYEE field that selects all records having an entry not equal to "DEPOSIT". Enter

        [Tab] *(3 times)*
        <>"DEPOSIT"

---

dBASE IV allows you to use either # or <> as symbols for a *not equal to* relationship.

Save the query by entering

```
[Alt-e] s
checks ⏎
```

The next step is to link the CHECKS query, which selects the checks from CKBOOK file, with the screen form, CHECKS. Load the CHECKS form into the Screen Form Layout mode.

```
[right arrow]
[down arrow]
⏎
⏎
m
```

At the bottom of the screen display the name of the View CHECKS appears. Save the form to make the CHECKS view permanently linked to the CHECKS screen form.

```
[Alt-L] s ⏎
```

The saving process generates FMT and FMO files that link the CHECKS view to the CHECKS screen form. Return to the Control Center by entering

```
[Alt-e] s
```

Both the CHECKS query and the CHECKS form appear above the line within their respective columns, indicating that they are active at the same time. This is exactly what you intended.

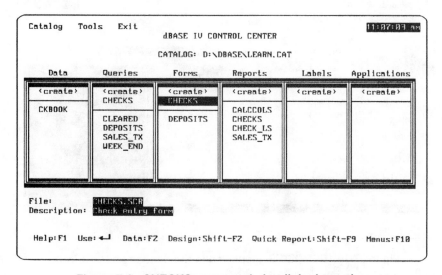

Figure 7-9. CHECKS query and view linked together.

Display the checks by entering

        [F2]

Move to the last record.

        [Alt-g] L

Note that the last record in this file is Record 13 of 16. Records 14, 15 and 16 are deposits that will not be displayed with this screen form because they do not qualify for the query.

Return to the Control Center display by entering

        [Alt-e] e

You have now created screen forms and queries that work together. By selecting the screen form, either CHECKS or DEPOSITS, you will activate both the form and the query. To display the DEPOSIT, enter

        [down arrow]
        [F2]

Select the DEPOSITS view.

        [right arrow] ⏎

The deposit records are displayed in their matching screen form.

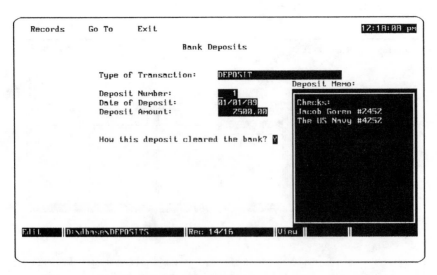

Figure 7-10. DEPOSITS displayed in the deposits screen form.

Exit the Editing mode by entering

```
[Alt-e] e
```

Creating Reports

The screen form and queries allow you to enter checks and deposits into a single file. The fields appear to have two different functions, but the records are part of a single database.

Now that you have stored both types of information, you can create reports that treat different aspects of the database. In this chapter you will create three different reports, based on checks and deposits.

1. A checking account listing with balance. This report will list all checks and deposits and calculate the current balance.
2. A checking account summary report. This report is an abbreviated version of previous reports. This report will list the monthly totals for checks and deposits and the current balance.
3. A reconciliation report. This report will list only the outstanding checks and deposits and calculate their totals. This report can be used to reconcile bank statements.

All the reports require special functions and features found in the Report Form Generator. These can be very useful in presenting information stored in database records.

Calculating the Balance

The first report you will create lists all the checks and deposits, and calculates the current balance in the checking accounts. The report requires the creation of a query. The purpose of the query is to ensure that the records are listed by date order.

Close the current view, DEPOSITS, by entering

```
[left arrow]
  ⌐ ⌐
```

Begin the creation of a new view by entering

```
  ⌐
```

This view will draw its data from the CKBOOK file. Enter

```
  ⌐ ⌐
```

The report that will use this query contains all but two fields, DE-DUCTIBLE and REMARKS. Place all the fields into the view skeleton, then remove the DEDUCTIBLE and REMARKS fields.

```
[F5]
[F4]
[Tab] (5 times)
[F5]
[Tab] (3 times)
[F5]
```

The purpose of the query is to ensure that the records are sorted into date order. Create a sort specification for the date by entering

```
[F4]
[Tab]
[Alt-f]s ↵
```

Save the query under the name BALANCE.

```
[Alt-e] s
balance ↵
```

Create the report that will calculate the checking account balance.

```
[right arrow] (2 times)
    ↵
```

The status bar shows that the BALANCE view is linked to this report. This will ensure that the report always lists the records in date order. This is important because the deposits will now appear in the correct date order, alongside the checks.

The most important part of this report is the Details band. Place the cursor at the beginning of the Details band by entering

```
[Esc]
[Tab] (5 times)
```

The first field to print will be the date field. Place the field onto the report by entering

```
[F5]
d ↵
[Ctrl-End]
```

Next to the date print the PAYEE field.

```
[right arrow]
  [F5]
  p ↵
  [Ctrl-End]
```

Next, place the CHECK_NUM field.

```
[right arrow]
 [F5]
 c ⏎
 [Ctrl-End]
```

The IIF Function

The next field to place onto the report is the AMOUNT field. But this field raises a problem. The report is intended to calculate the current balance of the checking account, but to do this, the program must be able to distinguish between amounts used for deposits and amounts used for checks. To obtain the checkbook balance, the check values must be subtracted from the deposit values.

If you were simply to place the AMOUNT field into the report as you did the previous field, dBASE IV would add all the amounts into one large total. This total would be the sum of all of the AMOUNT values, and not the difference of the deposits and the checks.

How can the program arrive at the balance? The solution to this problem is one of the most important operations in constructing a database system. It involves the use of a *conditional* operation. You have already encountered some types of conditional operations in the Edit options used with the screen form fields. Recall that these options allowed you to enter a logical expression that permitted data entry, or checked the validity of individual entries. A conditional operation is one that takes place only when a certain condition is true. If that condition is not true, the operation will not take place. The logical expression is a special form of dBASE IV calculations that evaluate as being either true or false.

This type of conditional expression, called a logical expression because it results in a true or false conclusion, is at the heart of conditional operations. For example, in the current problem you would need to create a conditional operation that would add the value if a record is a DEPOSIT, but subtract the value if the record is a check.

dBASE IV provides a function called IIF( ). It is similar to the Edit options in that it evaluates a logical expression. The IIF( ) function is a more generalized type of conditional operation than the Edit operations, however. It allows you to specify two values or expressions that correspond to two possible results of a logical expression: true or false. If the condition is true, the IIF( ) function takes on the value of the first expression. If it is false, the function is equal to the second expression.

How can this solve the problem of finding the checking account balance? To see how, you need to express the ideas being discussed in dBASE IV-type expression and syntax. First, how can the program tell if a record is a deposit or a check? You have already worked out a system for this: you will test the PAYEE field for the word DEPOSIT. In dBASE IV syntax that idea is summarized by the expression PAYEE="DEPOSIT".

When you encounter a record that is a deposit, you add the value to the total. Since adding is what dBASE IV would normally do with a numeric value, you can simply use the contents of the AMOUNT field.

Let's examine what would happen if the record were not a deposit—that is, if PAYEE="DEPOSIT" were false. In such a case, you would subtract the amount from the total. But dBASE IV is designed only to total values. The solution is to convert the AMOUNT field value into a negative number. When dBASE IV adds the negative number, the result will be the same as subtracting the positive value from the total. How do you convert a value to a negative number? You can multiply it by -1. In dBASE IV syntax AMOUNT*-1.

If you put all the elements together, you arrive at a function that has three distinct parts:

1. A logical expression that determines if the records are deposits or checks: PAYEE="DEPOSIT"
2. A value that is used if the expression is true: AMOUNT
3. A value that is used if the expression is false: AMOUNT*-1

Combining them with the function you arrive at a formula that reads: IIF(PAYEE="DEPOSIT",AMOUNT,AMOUNT*-1)

Instead of simply placing the AMOUNT field in the report, you will insert a calculated field with the result that all the deposits will be valued as positive numbers, while the checks will be negative.

Create the calculated field by entering

```
[right  arrow]
 [F5]
[right  arrow]
  e
  IIF(PAYEE="DEPOSIT",AMOUNT,AMOUNT*-1)
```

Change the template to display the values with comma separators.

```
  t
  [Home][Ctrl-y]
  999,999.99 ↵
```

You can use the Picture functions to control the format in which the positive and negative numbers are displayed. Enter

```
  P
```

The default format is to place a minus sign in front of negative numbers. Positive numbers are displayed normally. Your other options are:

Positive Credits Followed by CR

This option places the letters CR after each positive value. Example: 1,200.00CR

Negative Debits Followed by DB

This option causes the letters DB to follow negative numbers. Example: 175.00DB

Use ( ) around negative numbers. Negative numbers are enclosed in parentheses. Example: (175.00)

In this example, choose the CR/DB designations for the positive and negative values. Enter

```
p
n
[Ctrl-End]
```

When you use Picture functions, such as ( ), CR, DR, that add characters to the numeric values, keep in mind that these characters are added in addition to the template width. For example, when CR is placed into the report, it is placed in the two columns following the end of the template (e.g. 175.00CR). If you placed another field one character from the end of the template, you would find that the first character of the next field might be overwritten by the R in CR. It is important to note that the selection of these Picture functions is not reflected in the screen layout which shows only the space allocated to the template, not the combined template and Picture functions. In the current report additional space is left alongside a field that uses a Picture function that adds characters.

Place the field into the report by entering

```
[Ctrl-End]
```

The final item in the report is the CLEARED field. The contents of this field normally prints as a T or F. You can use the IIF( ) function to substitute other text or values. This example requires you to print an * if the check or deposit has cleared. Create a calculated field using an IIF( ) function to print an * if the record is marked as cleared. Enter

```
[right arrow](5 times)
 [F5]
[right arrow]↵
 e
 IIF(CLEARED, "*","") ↵
```

Change the template size from the default (25 characters) to a single character.

```
t
[Home]{Ctrl-y}
X ↵
```

Place the calculated field onto the report.

```
[Ctrl-End]
```

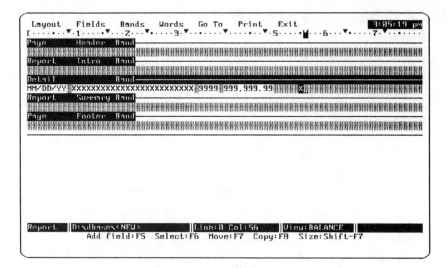

Figure 7-11. Fields entered into detail band.

The report layout should look like Figure 7-11.

Preview the report as it stands.

        [Alt-p] v

The report correctly identifies each deposit as a DB and each check as a CR.

```
01/01/89 DEPOSIT                  1   2,500.00 CR   ×
01/03/89 Central Office Supplies 1001     97.56 DB  ×
01/03/89 Allied Office Furniture 1000    750.50 DB  ×
01/06/89 Western Telephone       1002    101.57 DB  ×
01/06/89 United Federal Insurance 1003   590.00 DB
01/10/89 Computer World          1004  2,245.50 DB  ×
01/10/89 Fathead Software        1005     99.95 DB  ×
01/14/89 The Bargin Warehouse    1006    145.99 DB
01/15/89 Central Office Supplies 1007     67.45 DB
01/31/89 DEPOSIT                  2   1,200.00 CR
02/02/89 Sunset Variety          1008     25.89 DB
02/09/89 Advanced Copier Service 1009    175.00 DB
02/12/89 Valley Power & Light    1010    101.70 DB
02/15/89 DEPOSIT                  3   1,900.00 CR
02/25/89 Dept of Trans           1011     45.00 DB
02/27/89 Western Telephone       1012    175.75 DB



                Cancel viewing: ESC,  Continue viewing: SPACEBAR
```

Figure 7-12. Report lists checks as DB values and deposits as CR values.

Return to the Report Layout work surface.

```
[Esc]
 ⏎
```

The next step is to create a total in the Summary band. Enter

```
[down  arrow](2 times)
```

Move the cursor to row 0, col 52, and insert a summary calculation. Enter

```
[F5]
[right  arrow] (3 times)
 s ⏎
```

You need to select the field to summarize. Enter

```
f
```

The program displays a list of fields from which to choose.

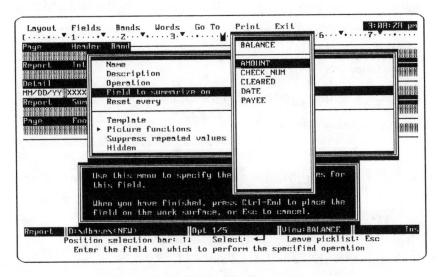

Figure 7-13. Fields listed for summary

What field should you choose? The answer is that none of the fields listed provide the correct total. This is because the list includes only the field that appears in the current query or database. The calculated fields do not appear and cannot be used to find a sum. Yet without a summary field, the purpose of this report is defeated.

However, there is a solution. You may recall that in Chapter 5 you created a report called SALES_TX that summarized the total amount of sales tax, based on a calculated field. Why were you able to do that then and not now? The answer raises a subtle but important point. In the case of the sales_tx reports, the summary fields were created not by a report calculation but by a calculated field created by a *query*. When a calculated field is created with a query, it can be selected as the summary of a report. Creating a calculation inside a report does not allow you to summarize the calculated data.

There is no inherent reason why dBASE IV does not allow you to select an expression as a summary object, since you can create just such a summary by modifying the FRG file produced from the FRM (report form) file. The dBASE IV programming language has more flexibility than is practical to build into each and every menu in the menu system.

The use of a calculated field in a query works because dBASE IV actually creates a new, temporary database to process the query specifications. The calculated fields become actual fields in the temporary database. Because query calculated fields appear in the structure of the temporary file, their names appear in the list of fields for summary calculation.

Save the current report as BALANCE and return to the BALANCE query.

```
[Esc] (2 times)
y
[Alt-e] s
balance ↵
```

Place the BALANCE query in the Query Definition mode.

```
[right arrow] (2 times)
↵
m
```

Create a calculated field in this query using the same formula as in the Detail section of report. Enter

```
[Alt-f]
c
```

Enter the formula for the calculated field.

```
IIF(PAYEE="DEPOSIT",AMOUNT,AMOUNT*-1)
```

Add that field to the display skeleton. This step is necessary in order to have the field available for use with the report form. Enter

```
[F5]
```

Enter a name for the calculated field. In this case, use the name BALANCE.

```
Balance ↵
```

Save the revised query by entering

```
[Alt-e] s
```

Return to the report form BALANCE and place it into the Modification mode.

```
[left  arrow](2 times)
  ┘
 m
```

The first step is to replace the calculation in the calculated field in the Detail section with the BALANCE field. This is necessary because you cannot access a field for a Summary function if it is not part of the Detail section. Place the cursor on the calculated field by entering

```
[down  arrow](5 times)
 [Tab]  (3 times)
```

You can delete the existing field using the [Del] key.

```
[Del]
```

Replace the field with the BALANCE field generated as part of the query.

```
[F5]
b ┘
```

Here, instead of changing the template, use the Financial Picture function to format the values with commas and dollar signs (e.g. $1,200.00)

```
p
f
[Ctrl-End]
[Ctrl-End]
```

Move to the Summary band to place the summary calculation.

```
[down  arrow](2 times)
 [Shift-Tab]  (2 times)
```

Insert the Summary field.

```
[F5]
[right  arrow] (3 times)
 s ┘
 f
```

This time the BALANCE field is available for summary.

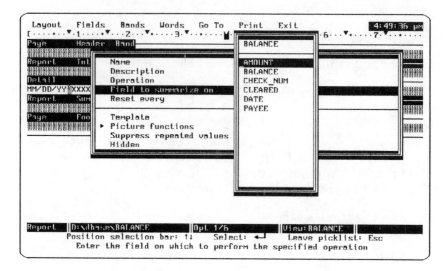

Figure 7-14. Field created by query available for use in report form.

Complete the entry by selecting the BALANCE field.

    b ↵

Select the Financial Picture function for formatting the field.

    p
    f
    [Ctrl-End]

Place SUMMARY into the report by entering

    [Ctrl-End]

Display the report on the screen.

    [Alt-p] v

The report lists all the checks as negative numbers and the deposits as positive numbers. It also shows the current account balance at the bottom of the column, $978.14.

```
01/01/89 DEPOSIT                       1    $2500.00   ×
01/03/89 Central Office Supplies    1001     $-97.56   ×
01/03/89 Allied Office Furniture    1000    $-750.50   ×
01/06/89 Western Telephone          1002    $-101.57   ×
01/06/89 United Federal Insurance   1003    $-590.00
01/10/89 Computer World             1004   $-2245.50   ×
01/10/89 Fathead Software           1005     $-99.95   ×
01/14/89 The Bargin Warehouse       1006    $-145.99
01/15/89 Central Office Supplies    1007     $-67.45
01/31/89 DEPOSIT                       2    $1200.00
02/02/89 Sunset Variety             1008     $-25.89
02/09/89 Advanced Copier Service    1009    $-175.00
02/12/89 Valley Power & Light       1010    $-101.70
02/15/89 DEPOSIT                       3    $1900.00
02/25/89 Dept of Trans              1011     $-45.00
02/27/89 Western Telephone          1012    $-175.75
                                             $978.14



        Cancel viewing: ESC.  Continue viewing: SPACEBAR
```

Figure 7-15. Report displays current account balance.

Return to the report work area by entering

[Esc] ↵

To make a complete report you might want to add column headings, page numbers, and titles. These details are covered in Chapter 5.

Save the BALANCE report by entering

[Alt-e] s

Summary Reports

The second report you will generate summarizes the checking account balance for each month. This type of report introduces the use of Group Bands. A Group Band is used to produce such group summaries as subtotals. In the checking account report you will create a Group Band that calculates the monthly balance between checks and deposits. This balance will show a rough profit or loss figure for each month, assuming you are running the business on a cash basis.

Instead of creating a report from scratch, you can simply modify the BALANCE report and save it under a new name. Place the BALANCE report into the Report Form Layout mode.

↵
m

The first step in creating a report with a Group Band is to insert a Group Band into the current layout. This is done from the Bands menu. Enter

        [Alt-b]

The Bands menu is displayed. It lists a variety of commands that affect the way bands are used. Among the options available are:

Add a Group Band

Adds a Group Band to the current report. When a Group Band is added the program inserts two bands: Group Intro band and a Group Summary band. The intro band is placed above the Detail band and the Group Summary band is placed below the Detail band. Each set of Group Bands is numbered consecutively so you can distinguish between bands.

Remove Group

This band removes a set of Group Bands from the report. The data stored on these bands is removed from the report form. Note that removing a band is not the same as *closing* a band. When a band is closed, its information is suppressed but not removed from the report form. Closed bands can be reopened.

Modify Group

This option allows you to change the specification used for grouping records.

Group Intro on Each Page

This option relates to the printing of the Group Intro band. Normally the Group Intro band prints once at the beginning of each group. If the group is large, the records may print on more than one page. In such a case, no group heading would appear at the top of the subsequent pages. If this setting is changed to ON, a Group Intro band is printed at the top of each new page that contains records from the same group.

Open All Bands

This command opens all the bands in the report that have been closed. Using this option will cause all the information defined in the report form to appear on the layout, and subsequently print on the report.

Begin Band on New Page

This option forces a new band to begin printing at the top of the next page.

Word Wrap Band

This option can be used to turn on word-wrap so that a band can contain word-processing paragraph text.

Text Pitch for Band

This option allows you to specify the type of pitch to use for the information in the current band. The options available for this feature depend upon the printer driver installed in dBASE IV.

Quality Print for Band

This option selects the print quality for the text in this band. The options available for this feature depend upon the printer driver installed in dBASE IV.

Spacing of Lines for Band

This option allows you to select single, double, or triple spacing for the data in the current band.

Page Heading in Report Intro

Use this option to suppress the printing of header information in the Report Intro band.

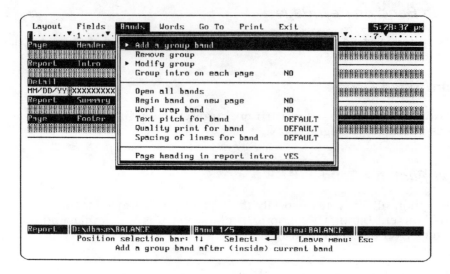

Figure 7-16. Bands menu displayed.

Add a Group Band to the current report.

⏎

When you select to add a Group Band the program displays another menu. This menu lists three ways groups can be defined.

Field Value

This option allows you to select a field from the database or query structure by which to group records. The field selected should contain data which is not unique. If the information in the field is unique then each group will contain only one record.

Expression Value

This option allows you to enter an expression that defines the record groups. With this option you can create groups on criteria other than fields. For example, if you have a date field you can use an expression such as MONTH(date) to group records by month rather than individual dates.

Record Count

This option allows you to specify the number of records which will be used as the size for each group. For example if you enter 10, then sub-total groups will occur every 10 records, regardless of their content.

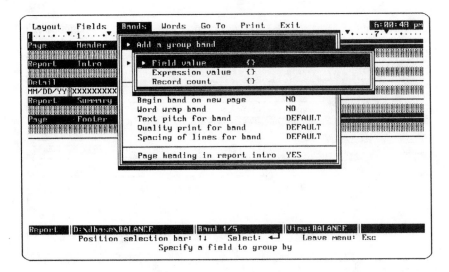

Figure 7-17. Group by menu options.

It is important to understand that grouping depends upon having the database or view indexed or sorted into an order that corresponds to the group field or expression. For example, if you wanted to group the records by month you would have to make sure that the database was sorted or indexed by date before attempting to process the report.

Groups based on fields or expressions use the processing concept called a *controlled break.* This assumes that all the records belonging to one group will be found consecutively in the file. As soon as a record with a different value in the group or *control* field is encountered, the program stops its detail processing and performs a group sub-total routine. If you process a database in which the records have not be grouped together by sorting or indexing, the breaks will occur randomly whenever a new value in the control field occurs.

In the current case, you want to use an expression that causes the break to occur whenever the month value of the date changes. Enter

```
e
MONTH(date)  ↵
```

The Group Bands are added to the screen display.

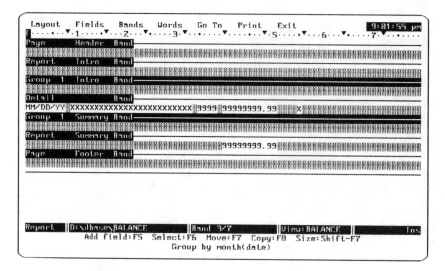

Figure 7-18. Group Bands added to the report layout.

The Group Intro band is used to display a heading or introductory information for each group. In this case, the name of the year would make a logical heading for each group. Move the cursor to the Group Intro Band and create a calculated field that will print the month and the year.

```
[down arrow]
 [F5]
[right arrow]↵
   e
```

You can use the CMONTH( ) function to obtain the name of the month, and the YEAR( ) function to find the year number. Note that the year number is a numeric value and must be converted to a character value with the STR( ) function so that both items can be entered in a single expression. Enter

```
CMONTH(date)+STR(YEAR(date),5)   ↵
```

Place the expression into the report by entering

```
[Ctrl-End]
```

Heading or Intro Bands often have more than one line. Add another line and draw a line across the screen.

```
     ↵
[Alt-L] L s
 ↵
```

Draw the line by using the left arrow or right arrow keys to move the cursor. Move the cursor to col 56. Enter:

```
     ↵
```

The Group Summary Band

The really important part of the Group Band is the Group Summary Band. It is this band that carries the calculations that create the sub-totals.

Creating a summary calculation for a Group Band is exactly like creating a summary calculation for the Report Summary Band. The difference between the two calculations is how often the value is reset. By default, summary calculations entered into the Report Summary Band are reset to zero at the beginning of each report. The value reflects all the records included on all pages of the report. The calculations entered in the Group Band will be reset to zero each time a new group begins. In this way each total that appears in the group summary will represent the values of the previous group alone.

Move the cursor to the beginning of the Group Summary Band.

```
[down  arrow](4 times)
[Home]
```

Draw a double line across the report.

```
[Alt-L]  L d
 ⏎
```

Move the cursor to col 56. Enter:

```
 ⏎
 ⏎
```

Enter the text that identifies the value.

```
Balance
[Tab]  (5 times)
```

Place a calculated field at this location that computes the value total of the BALANCE field.

```
[F5]
[right  arrow] (3 times)
 s ⏎
 f
 b ⏎
```

Set the Picture function to the Financial format.

```
p
f
[Ctrl-End]
```

Place the field into the report at the current location.

```
[Ctrl-End]
```

It is important to remember that when a report is printing the Group Summary Band is immediately followed by the Group Intro Band of the next group. It is usually a good idea to insert some blank lines at the end of the Group Summary Band so there is space left between the end of one group and the beginning of the next. Enter

⏎ *(2 times)*

The report now looks like Figure 7-19.

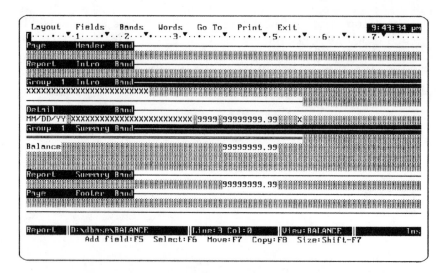

Figure 7-19. Report with Group Band.

View the report on the screen to see how the Group Band will look on the printed report.

[Alt-p] v

The first screen of the report looks like Figure 7-20.

```
┌──────────────────────────────────────────────────────────────┐
│                                                                │
│   January 1989                                                 │
│                                                                │
│   01/01/89 DEPOSIT                         1    $2500.00   ⋈   │
│   01/03/89 Central Office Supplies      1001     $-97.56   ⋈   │
│   01/03/89 Allied Office Furniture      1000    $-750.50   ⋈   │
│   01/06/89 Western Telephone            1002    $-101.57   ⋈   │
│   01/06/89 United Federal Insurance     1003    $-590.00       │
│   01/10/89 Computer World               1004   $-2245.50   ⋈   │
│   01/10/89 Fathead Software             1005     $-99.95   ⋈   │
│   01/14/89 The Bargin Warehouse         1006    $-145.99       │
│   01/15/89 Central Office Supplies      1007     $-67.45       │
│   01/31/89 DEPOSIT                         2    $1200.00       │
│   ════════════════════════════════════════════════════════    │
│   Balance                                       $-398.52       │
│                                                                │
│                                                                │
│   February 1989                                                │
│                                                                │
│   02/02/89 Sunset Variety               1008     $-25.89       │
│   02/09/89 Advanced Copier Service      1009    $-175.00       │
│   02/12/89 Valley Power & Light         1010    $-101.70       │
│   02/15/89 DEPOSIT                         3    $1900.00       │
│   _          Cancel viewing: ESC,  Continue viewing: SPACEBAR  │
└──────────────────────────────────────────────────────────────┘
```

Figure 7-20. Records grouped by month.

You can see that the balance for January was negative. Display the next page of the report by entering

> [spacebar]

This screen shows the total for February and the grand total for the entire file.

Complete the report by entering

> [Esc] ↵

Closing a Band

The report as it currently exists prints all the details, as well as the total and sub-totals. dBASE IV allows you to *close* a report band. When a band is closed, the information in that band does not print. However, the information is still part of the report form. This means that the band can be re-opened, activating the printing of that information. It also means calculations depending on the detail information will still operate correctly. This makes it possible to print a report that contains only the totals and sub-totals, while suppressing printing of the details.

Bands can be toggled between opened and closed by placing the cursor on the band marker and pressing ↵.

In the current example you will want to suppress the Detail band so that only the totals and sub-totals are printed. Place the cursor on the Detail band marker. Enter

> up arrow *(6 times)*

Close the band by entering

        ⏎

Note the band marker can still be seen on the report form but the information contained within that band is no longer visible.

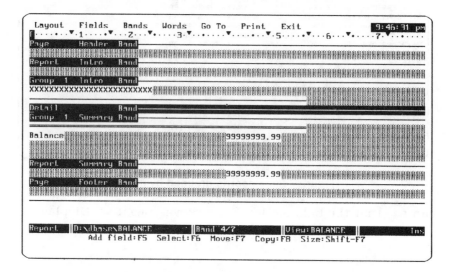

Figure 7-21. Detail band closed.

Display the report with the Detail band closed.

    [Alt-p] v

The revised reports show a succinct report on the status of the checking account. Note that the totals are exactly the same as they were when all the details were included.

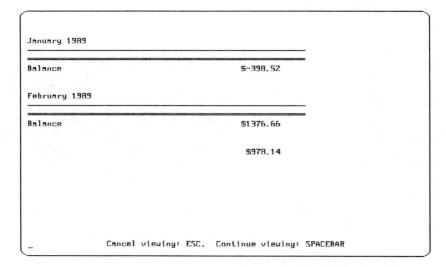

January 1989

Balance $-398.52

February 1989

Balance $1376.66

                                 $978.14

Cancel viewing: ESC. Continue viewing: SPACEBAR

Figure 7-22. Report displays only totals and sub-totals.

Complete the viewing by entering

    [Esc] ↵

Save the report under a new name, SUMMARY. Enter

    [Alt-L] s
    [Home] [Ctrl-y]
    summary ↵

Exit the report design mode by entering

    [Alt-e] s

Reconciling Bank Statements

The last of the special purpose reports in this chapter will aid you in reconciling your checkbook with the bank statement. The key to this report is the CLEARED field.

When you receive a bank statement, you must edit the database in order to mark the checks or deposits as cleared. In order to reconcile the bank statement with your checkbook balance you need to calculate the total of the outstanding checks and deposits.

This process can be automated by using an *update* query to mark the checks as cleared. You can also create special reports that will calculate the totals of the outstanding checks and deposits.

Update Queries

An update query is an alternative method of making changes in a database. Instead of editing the records, you can use an update query to make the changes. Update queries are useful when the required changes can be set up as a list of items or as a specific logical condition. When you receive a bank statement the checks that have cleared the bank are enclosed. One way to update the database is to manually display the record for each check and change the value of the CLEARED field. On the other hand, you could use an update query to make these changes. The advantage of the update query is that you could simply enter a list of the check numbers and have the program find and change the records to which they correspond.

Suppose the statement you have just received contains checks numbered 1003, 1006, 1007, 1009 and 1010. A deposit of $1200.00 is also listed as cleared on the statement.

Using the manual editing method you would have to locate and edit six records, in order to update the file. However, you can use an Update query to perform the updating automatically.

Activate the Query Design mode by entering

```
[left arrow] (2 times)
[up arrow]
⏎
```

Select the CKBOOK database as the basis for the query.

```
⏎ (2 times)
```

To create an Update query, enter an Update command (either Replace, Append, Mark, or Unmark) into the filename area of the file skeleton. This example requires you to use the Replace operation.

```
replace ⏎
```

Move to the CHECK_NUM field and enter a list of the check numbers that need to be marked as CLEARED.

```
[Tab] (2 times)
1003 [down arrow]
1006 [down arrow]
1007 [down arrow]
1009 [down arrow]
1010
```

In most cases, a bank deposit can be identified only by its amount—in this example $1,200.00. You can place this value into the AMOUNT field and the program will search for it.

The query method of updating the records used in this example assumes that the values used to locate the records are unique. In the instance of the check numbers, this ought to be the case. However, if you cannot be certain that a value (in this instance, a deposit of $1200.00) is unique, you have to use the deposit number or some other unique value, to perform the update.

Keep in mind that changes made with an Update query are permanent changes that can cause a loss of data if the wrong data is replaced. You may want to make a backup copy of the database before using a query that has not already been tested.

Move to the AMOUNT field.

> [Tab] *(2 times)*

Before entering the amount, move the highlight down one row. Doing this indicates that the value you are entering is not a combination criterion. By placing it on a different row than the last check number, it assumes an OR type relationship. Enter

> [down arrow]
> 1200

The last step specifies the replacement action to be taken when the records are located. Move to the CLEARED field. In the current example, insert a true value (.T.) in the CLEARED field of the records that match the listed values. Enter

> [Tab]
> with .t.

An Update query can be executed directly from the Query Design mode using the Perform the Update command found on the Update menu. Enter

> [Alt-u] p

When the query is completed, you will see a message that shows the replacement was made in six records, exactly the number you would have had to manually edit if you did not use the Update query.

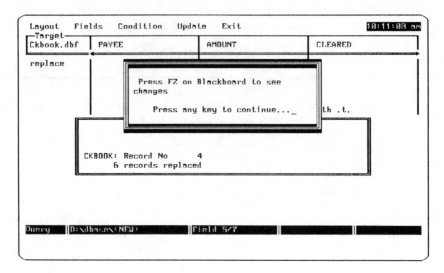

Figure 7-23. Query updates records.

The display also reminds you that you can use the Data command, [F2], to display the database so you can inspect the result of the update.

Exit the Update mode. Since the database has already been changed, there is no need to save this query. Enter

⌐
[Alt-e] a y

Totaling Deposits and Checks

The next step in the reconciliation process is to produce a report that lists outstanding checks and deposits, and calculates a total for them. This report raises an interesting problem. It requires two different totals from the same field, AMOUNT. This is slightly different than deriving the total balance of the checks and deposits, an operation that requires only one equation, which uses positive and negative numbers.

The solution is to create a query that separates checks and deposits into two different fields. For example, suppose you created a calculated field called DEPOSITS. The records that contained the word DEPOSIT in the PAYEE field would show the actual value of the AMOUNT field in the DEPOSITS field. However, records that are checks would show zero in the DEPOSITS field.

Conversely, a calculated field called CHECKS would show the AMOUNT field value for all records without DEPOSIT in the PAYEE field, and a zero value for records that are deposits. The two calculated fields, when totaled, would yield separate totals for checks and deposits. If the database were filtered so that only records which have not been marked as CLEARED were used, the totals would reflect the total for the outstanding checks and deposits.

It is not strictly necessary to create a report to display the desired totals. You could use a query to simply display the totals on the screen. The advantage of the report is it allows you to display or print the results, while a query is designed only for screen display.

Begin by producing the query that will create the two calculated fields needed for the report. Since the cursor is currently positioned on the #create# symbol in the Query column, enter

⏎

Select the CKBOOK database as the basis for the query.

⏎⏎

The report will need to contain the date, the check number, and the payee, in addition to the calculated fields CHECKS and DEPOSITS.
Add the first three fields to the display skeleton.

    `[Tab][F5]` *(3 times)*

Next are the calculated fields. These fields will use the IIF( ) function to determine if the value should be the same as the AMOUNT field or zero, based on whether the PAYEE is a deposit. Begin by creating a field that will contain only amounts for the check records.

    `[Alt-f]  c`

Both calculated fields will use the same logical expression to test the records, *payee="DEPOSIT"* . In the field that represents the values of the checks, the formula will assign a zero value to all records evaluating as true. The records evaluating as false (i.e. not deposits) will use the value stored in the AMOUNT field. The formula will read IIF(payee="DEPOSIT",0,amount). Since the formula is long, use [F9] to zoom to the full-screen Edit mode.

Enter

```
[F9]
IIF(payee="DEPOSIT",0,amount)
[F9]
```

Add this calculated field to the display skeleton and assign it the name of CHECKS.

```
[F5]
checks ⏎
```

Create a second calculated field. This one will use a formula that contains the same information as the previous formula. The only difference will be that the values *0* and *amount* are reversed. This makes sense because this field should have a zero when the CHECKS field contains an amount, and an amount when checks contain a zero. The two fields are mirror images of each other. Enter

```
[Alt-f] c
[F9]
IIF(payee="DEPOSIT",amount,0)
[F9]
```

Place this field on the display skeleton with the fieldname DEPOSITS.

```
[F5]
deposits ⏎
```

There is one more operation you need to specify to complete the query. This query should choose only those records that have not cleared. You can specify this selection by placing .F., the false value, in the CLEARED field box. Move back to the file skeleton.

```
[F3]
```

Place the highlight in the CLEARED field.

```
[Tab] (2 times)
```

Enter the false value.

```
.F.
```

You have now created a query that will select all records that have not cleared, and create two calculated fields needed to produce the report. The query display will look like Figure 7-24.

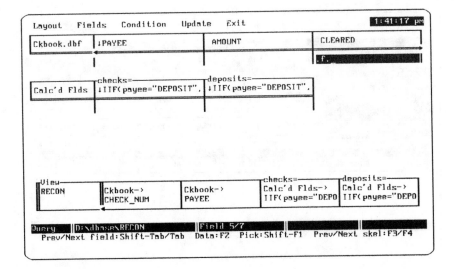

Figure 7-24. Query skeleton with checks and deposits fields defined.

Save this query as RECON by entering

```
[Alt-e] s
recon ↵
```

The Reconcile Report

The query is automatically activated when you save it. This means that you can proceed to create the report and link it with this query. Enter

```
[right arrow] (2 times)
        ↵
```

Since the RECON query is active, you can take advantage of the Quick Layout option to create the report you require. Recall that the Quick Layout option uses the fields specified in the current query. Enter

```
↵ (2 times)
```

The Quick Layout option creates a column-type report, based on the organization of the active query. In this case, it is exactly the type of report you need. The layout is shown in Figure 7-25.

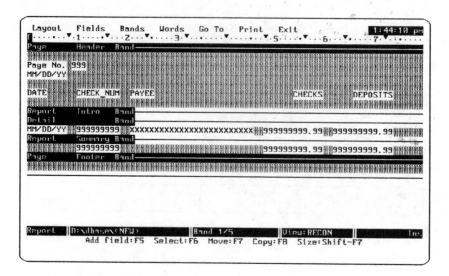

Figure 7-25. Quick layout option creates report with totals.

There are some modifications you should make to the Quick Layout report. First, because the Quick Layout method creates a total for each numeric field in the query or database, the report gives a total of the check numbers. This is not needed. Delete the total field for the check numbers.

        [Alt-f] r

The program lists all the fields and calculated fields. Delete the field that reads SUM(CHECK_NUM) by entering

        [down arrow]*(8 times)*
        ↵

Another modification is to use Picture functions to control the display of the checks and deposit values. For example, you might want to use the Financial function to format the values as dollar and cents, with commas. You might also want to use the Zero option to print a blank space when the value is zero. This eliminates the display of zeros in the checks and deposits columns.

Begin with the CHECKS field.

        [Alt-F] m ↵

Activate the Financial and Blanks for Zero Picture functions.

        p
        f
        b
        [Ctrl-End] *(2 times)*

Repeat the process and assign the same two Picture functions to the DEPOSITS field. Try this on your own. The correct command can be found at the end of the chapter under Ex-2.

Change the SUM(CHECKS) function to also display in the Financial format.

```
[Alt-F] m
[Tab] (7 times)
⏎

p
f
[Ctrl-End] (2 times)
```

Repeat the procedure for the SUM(DEPOSITS) field. Try this on your own. The correct command can be found at the end of the chapter under Ex-3.

You are now ready to display the report. Enter

```
[Alt-p] v
```

The report lists the outstanding checks and deposits and their totals, at the bottom of each column. The calculated fields have been able to distribute the values that were originally stored in a single data field, AMOUNT. This report is an example of how to logically transform the database, using the meaning of expressions and formulas, as opposed to using a physical solution, such as separate fields or databases for checks and deposits.

```
Page No.    1
05/25/89

DATE        CHECK_NUM  PAYEE                      CHECKS      DEPOSITS

02/02/89        1008   Sunset Variety             $25.89
02/25/89        1011   Dept of Trans              $45.00
02/27/89        1012   Western Telephone          $175.75
02/15/89           3   DEPOSIT                                 $1900.00
                                                  $246.64      $1900.00




              Cancel viewing: ESC,  Continue viewing: SPACEBAR
-
```

Figure 7-26. RECON report lists and sums the outstanding checks and deposits.

Keeping all the data in the same basic form but making distinctions based on the content of fields, is the best way to handle many simple financial systems. The report also illustrates how queries can transform data so that they appear on reports in very different ways than those in which they were originally entered. The ability to transform data into different forms is one of the most important concepts in database management.

Database Objects

If you have used previous versions of dBASE, you will have noticed that by using reports, forms, and queries, you have been able to create operations that in earlier versions would have required using the dBASE programming language. The key to these operations is to use the query as a background operator that supports the screen forms and reports.

Queries are significant in that they offer a different approach to database management that deviates from the traditional dBASE approach. In previous versions of dBASE, all operations were *process-oriented*. To accomplish most tasks, you needed to execute a series of operations (e.g. USE database, INDEX records, SELECT records, print REPORT). To understand dBASE, you had to think in terms of sequences of actions or procedures.

The creation of queries suggest the possibility of looking at database operations in dBASE as objects, rather than procedures. For example, in this chapter you created queries that sorted, selected, and calculated, in order to arrive at a set of data appropriate for the task. When you use a query, you do not have to think in terms of the procedures that have to be carried out—merely the set of data that is the result of the process. The set of data that is produced is a database object, just like a field or record.

It is important to note that when you create a query, you are not concerned with the sequence of operations required to arrive at the result. For example, if you create a query that selects and sorts database records, which operation is executed first? If you were working in dBASE III or III Plus, you would have to know the answer because both tasks are separate operations. The sequence would be part of knowing how to carry out the task. With a dBASE IV query, you do not know how the data gets sequenced or selected, you only know that the data is generated by the query for your use.

The change from process- or procedure-orientation, to database-object orientation is a theme that appears throughout dBASE IV. It is at the heart of the dBASE IV SQL module, which is a fully object- or set-oriented database encapsulated within dBASE IV.

Keep in mind that object oriented-commands or operations do not eliminate procedures. What they do accomplish is to hide the procedures from the user. For example, each query you create generates a dBASE IV program that contains the Program Language command sequences needed to create the database object. Hiding the procedures from the user makes thinking about databases simpler, because you can focus on the objects produced by the process, rather than the details of the process. Object- and process-orientation is discussed in more detail in Part II and Part IV.

Exit the display and save the new report as RECON.

```
[Esc] ↵
[Alt-e] s
recon ↵
```

Using the System

In this chapter you have created a number of queries, screens, and reports that helped carry out different tasks associated with the CKBOOK database. The new queries, reports, and screens create a set of tools that can be used over and over again as new data are added to the database. Before this chapter concludes, try out the various elements of this new system.

Begin by adding a new check, then a new deposit to the file. Select the CHECKS screen form.

```
[right arrow]
c ↵
↵
[right arrow]
↵
```

The check screen format displays the first check in the file. Add a new check.

```
[Alt-r] a
```

Enter the data for this check.

```
1013
030589
American Express ↵
257.89
```

Save the record and return to the Control Center by entering

```
[Alt-e] e
```

Add a deposit to the database.

```
[down arrow]
↵ (2 times)
[right arrow]
↵
```

This time, the database is presented as a deposit entry. Add a new record.

```
[Alt-r] a
4 ↵ ↵
030389
112.50
```

Return to the Control Center display.

```
[Alt-e] e
```

If the system is working correctly, the new records will be included in the reports. For example, run the SUMMARY report to get a quick checking account balance report.

```
[right arrow]
 [Pg Dn]
 ⏎ (2 times)
[right arrow]
 ⏎
  v
```

The Report shows a new account balance of $832.75. Note that there is now a sub-total for March, as well as January and February.

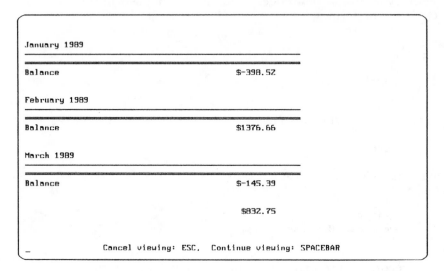

Figure 7-27. Summary report shows current balance.

Return to Control Center display by entering

        [Esc] ⏎

Exit dBASE IV by entering

        [Alt-e] q

Summary

In contrast to the six previous chapters this chapter did not explore new areas but concentrated on using concepts that were introduced earlier, in different ways. The primary purpose of this chapter has been to show how the individual parts—databases, queries, screen forms and reports—can be used together to create solutions to specific database management needs.

The examples in this chapter showed how a single database file can be used in such a way as to appear to contain two different types of data, checks and deposits. The key was to understand how both types of transactions required the same basic information. Screen displays, queries, and reports, transformed the data from its common base—the CKBOOK file—into different forms, appropriate for such operations as check entry, deposit entry, account balancing, and statement reconciliation.

- **Screen Forms.** Screen forms can be used to present the fields so that they appear to represent different items. In this chapter, separate screen layouts were used for the entry of checks and deposits, although the data for both were stored in the same database file. The Edit options available through the Screen Form Layout menus enable you to control the input of information so each screen form can have unique editing properties, even though the data is stored in a single database. One very significant use of Screen Form options is the entry of key values by default. The effect is that when the user selects the screen form, the program marks each record added with that form, as a particular type of record. The user does not have to remember to enter that key information, since it is automatically placed into the field by the screen form.

- **Queries.** In this chapter queries were used in a slightly different way than in Chapter 3, where they were used by themselves to retrieve data. In this chapter, the queries functioned mainly in the background as supporting operations for screen forms and reports. Queries provide the means of selecting and transforming database information so that it is appropriate for use with a particular form or report. Queries are able to show database information in different forms, without having to alter the information stored in the original database. Queries are also useful because they tie together a number of different types of operations such as selecting, sequencing, and calculating.

- **IIF( ) Function.** This function is important because it enables you to embed conditional logic inside dBASE IV expressions. The embedded logic allows you to perform sophisticated operations, using query processing to transform data into new values. In this chapter, the IIF( ) function was used to create calculated fields in a query that distinguished between check and deposit records, using the expression payee="DEPOSIT".

- **Reports with Group Bands.** Group Bands allow you to create reports that calculate and display information about groups of records. You can define a group in one of three ways: by field, by expression, or by record count. The field or expression methods require that the records in the database be sequenced (using Index or Sort) according the key field or expression criteria. For example, if you want to group records by date, the database must be in date order. The program assumes that a group ends, when the value in the key field or key expression changes. The Record Count method does not require a sequenced database. It creates a group every so many records.
  A Group Band consists of two bands: 1) The Group Intro band, which prints before the first record in a group. 2) The Group Summary band, which prints following the last record.

- **Closing Bands.** You can close a report band in order to suppress the printing of the information on that band. The information on the closed band is not erased, simply omitted from the printing. Closed bands can be re-opened, allowing the information to be included in the report printout.

- **Linking Queries.** Screen forms and reports can be linked to specific queries, in two ways. If a query is active when you create a report or screen form, the program automatically links the form or report to the query. You can also select a database or form with which to link a query, by using the Use different Database File or View command, found on the Layout menu.

When a screen form or report is selected, the linked query is automatically activated if no other query or database is active at the moment. If there is an active database or query when you select to execute the screen form or report, a window will appear asking you to choose the current view, or the name of the view linked to the selected form or report. Note that using the current view can produce errors when it does not match the specifications used by the form or report (e.g. the calculated field required for the report).

Exercises

Ex-1
   Place CLEARED field.

```
[F5]
cl ↵
t
[backspace]
Y ↵
e
d
.F. ↵
[Ctrl-End]
[Ctrl-End]
```

Ex-2
   Set picture function.

```
[Alt-F] m
de ↵
p
f
b
[Ctrl-End]   (2 times)
```

Ex-3
   Set picture function.

```
[Alt-F] m
{Pg Dn]
↵
p
f
[Ctrl-End]   (2 times)
```

8

Labels, Mailmerge, and Printed Forms

Although you have printed data primarily in the form of column reports, database information is the source of many types of documents. This chapter demonstrates how to create labels, form letters, and other types of printed documents from dBASE IV database information.

Begin by loading dBASE IV in the usual manner. The Control Center display should list the files you have been working with in this book.

Creating a New Catalog

In the next series of chapters you will create a new set of databases to keep track of customers, products, and sales for the LaFish Novelty Company.

You can see that the queries, reports, and screen forms created for the CKBOOK database, partially fill the columns of the Control Center display. In dBASE IV, catalogs allow you to select groups of files related to one another. The current catalog contains all the files created since CKBOOK. Each new query, screen form, or report form has automatically been added to it.

Instead of adding the new databases to the list of files related to CK-BOOK, you can create a new catalog. This will mean that only the files related to the techniques demonstrated in the next few chapters will appear in the Control Center columns.

Catalogs make the Control Center display more useful because they provide a means of controlling the files displayed. Without catalogs, the Control Center display has to list all the files, databases, report forms, screen forms, etc., stored in the current directory. Over time you may find that the lists grow so long as to be no longer convenient to select items. By dividing files into catalogs related to specific uses, you can keep the Control Center file lists to a comfortable level.

To create a new catalog use the Use a Different Catalog command located on the Catalog menu. Although the name does not imply you can create a catalog with this option, you will be able to select the <create> symbol from the top of the catalog list. Enter

[Alt-c] u ·

The <create> symbol appears at the top of the pop-up menu that lists the catalogs. Create a new catalog called ACCOUNTS by entering

⌐

accounts ⌐

The screen changes to show a blank Control Center display with the name of the new catalog, ACCOUNTS.CAT, displayed above the Control Center columns.

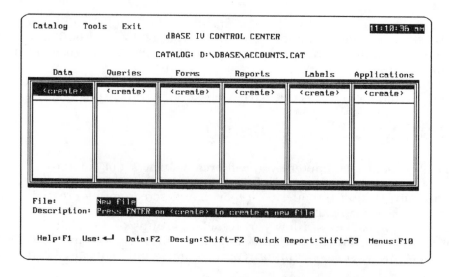

Figure 8-1. New catalog displays blank Control Center columns.

Create a new database called BUYERS. Begin by selecting the <create> symbol from the Data column. By default, this option is highlighted when you first access a catalog.

⌐

Below is the structure for the file. Enter the field specifications as listed. When you finish, the screen should look like Figure 8-2.

Num	Field Name	Field Type	Width	Dec	Index
1	COMPANY	Character	35		**Y**
2	FIRST	Character	20		N
3	LAST	Character	20		**Y**
4	STREET	Character	35		N
5	CITY	Character	20		N
6	STATE	Character	2		N
7	ZIP	Character	5		N
8	ACCOUNT_NO	Numeric	4	0	N
9	PHONE	Character	12		N
10	EXTENSION	Character	4		N

```
 Layout   Organize   Append   Go To   Exit                    11:20:19 am

                                               Bytes remaining:      3843
 ┌─────┬────────────┬────────────┬───────┬─────┬───────┐
 │ Num │ Field Name │ Field Type │ Width │ Dec │ Index │
 ├─────┼────────────┼────────────┼───────┼─────┼───────┤
 │  1  │ COMPANY    │ Character  │  35   │     │   Y   │
 │  2  │ FIRST      │ Character  │  20   │     │   N   │
 │  3  │ LAST       │ Character  │  20   │     │   Y   │
 │  4  │ STREET     │ Character  │  35   │     │   N   │
 │  5  │ CITY       │ Character  │  20   │     │   N   │
 │  6  │ STATE      │ Character  │   2   │     │   N   │
 │  7  │ ZIP        │ Character  │   5   │     │   N   │
 │  8  │ ACCOUNT_NO │ Numeric    │   4   │  0  │   N   │
 │  9  │ PHONE      │ Character  │  12   │     │   N   │
 │ 10  │ EXTENSION  │ Character  │   4   │     │   N   │
 │ 11  │            │ Character  │       │     │   N   │
 │     │            │            │       │     │       │
 └─────┴────────────┴────────────┴───────┴─────┴───────┘

 Database│ D:\dbase\<NEW>           │ Field 11/11    │     ExclLock
                Enter the field name.  Insert/Delete field:Ctrl-N/Ctrl-U
 Field names begin with a letter and may contain letters, digits and underscores
```

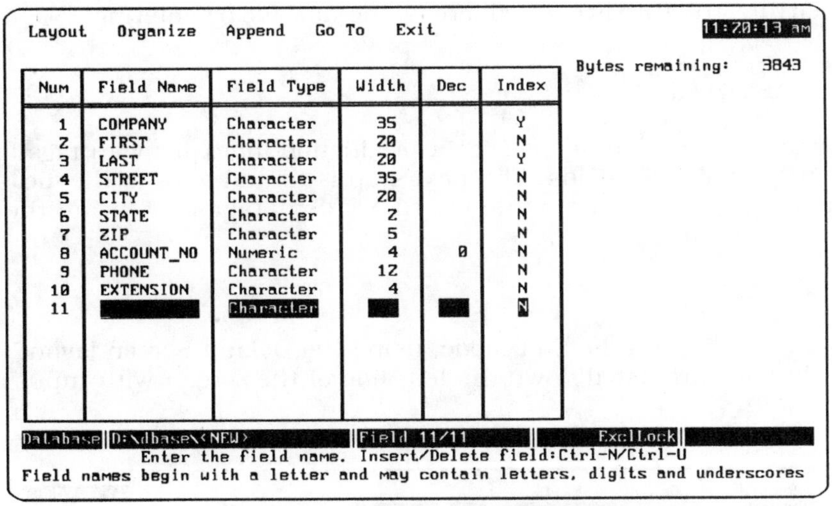

Figure 8-2. Structure of new database.

The ZIP field is entered as a character field, not as a numeric field, because in zip codes a leading zero is significant. For example, Worcester, MA has a zip code of 01610. If this number is entered into a numeric field, dBASE IV would replace the leading zero with a blank space. The zip code would print as *1610*, not *01610*. In a Character field, by contrast, the leading zero is treated like an alphabetical or numeric character, and is left in place. With this exception—i.e., the leading zero—numeric or character zip codes appear alike.

Another advantage of using a character field for the zip code is that zip codes are very often printed in combination with other items, such as the city and state. Since city and state are Character fields, it is simple to combine zip with the city and state, if zip is also a Character field. If zip were a numeric field, you would have to use the STR( ) function to convert the ZIP field to a character string, so it could be combined with other Character fields.

When the structure is entered, create the new file by entering

```
[Alt-e] s
buyers ⏎
```

The database is created, along with a production index file with tags for the COMPANY and LAST fields. The next step is to add data to the file. Here, you must enter four records into the BUYERS database. Activate the Data Entry mode by entering

```
[F2]
```

dBASE IV displays the Edit mode, using the Default Screen layout. Here, the fieldnames are listed down the left side of the screen with input areas next to each.

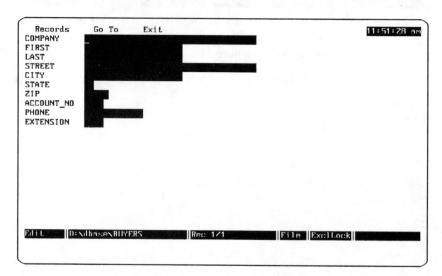

Figure 8-3. Default screen form for BUYERS database.

Enter the following records. Remember that pressing ↵ in the last field, or [Pg Dn] from any field, moves to a blank record. After you enter the last item, the cursor will be in the EXTENSION field of Record 4. Take care not press ↵ or you will display an entry screen for a fifth record. Do not bother to enter any data into this blank, should you display it.

```
Record No          1
COMPANY            House of Magic
FIRST              Janice
LAST               King
STREET             520 S. 8th St. #22
CITY               Baltimore
STATE              MD
ZIP                21202
ACCOUNT_NO         100
PHONE              301-555-3193
EXTENSION          24

Record No          2
COMPANY            Genie Light and Magic
FIRST              Thomas
LAST               Willson
STREET             1960 Lindley Ave.
CITY               Lincoln
STATE              NE
ZIP                68506
ACCOUNT_NO         101
PHONE              402-555-9980
EXTENSION

Record No          3
COMPANY            Clay's House of Fun
FIRST              Diane
LAST               Clay
STREET             14234 Riverside Dr.
CITY               Los Angeles
STATE              CA
ZIP                90044
ACCOUNT_NO         102
PHONE              213-555-9875
EXTENSION          12

Record No          4
COMPANY            Northgate Specialty Comp
FIRST              Simon
LAST               O'Keefe
STREET             303 W. Milford St.
CITY               Richmond
STATE              VA
ZIP                23229
ACCOUNT_NO         103
PHONE              804-555-8965
EXTENSION
```

Once the data has been entered, you can save the records by entering

```
[Alt-e] s
```

You are returned to the Control Center display after creating the first of the three databases you will use in the ACCOUNTS catalog.

Labels

The database just created contains names and addresses. These can be a very useful part of a business database for many reasons. One of the most common uses of an address database is to print mailing labels. dBASE IV contains a Specific Design mode that enables you to create mailing labels and print database information directly on them.

Mailing labels come in two basic types. Continuous form labels are supplied on slick backing paper perforated by sprocket holes that fit onto the printer's tractor feed. Continuous form labels can have one, two, or three labels across each row.

If you have a laser printer, you can use copier labels, which are supplied on 8.5" x 11" sheets.

A printer, such as a daisy wheel that does not have a tractor feed, is unlikely to be able to print continuous form labels successfully. The roll pressure by itself cannot hold the labels. In most cases, the slick surface of the label backing and the uneven pressure of the rollers against the platen, will cause the labels to *walk* to the left or right. The alignment will deteriorate after a dozen or so labels. If you plan to do extensive mailing label production, a tractor feed is a necessity.

To print labels you must create a Label form. Move the highlight to the <create> symbol in the label column.

```
[right arrow] (4 times)
 ⏎
```

The program activates the Label Design mode. At the top of the screen is a menu with seven items: Layout, Dimensions, Fields, Words, Go To, Print, and Exit. The label form is a small rectangle in the center of the screen, representing a single label that is 5 lines in height and 35 columns wide. By default, dBASE IV assumes you will use a label of this size.

The default mailing label form is designed to print on the most common size of mailing label—3.5" x 15/16". The 15/16" size may be confusing to the average person. The label manufacturer places the actual size of the label on the box. However, the height of the label is not as important to the computer user, as is the vertical distance between the top of one label and the top of the next. Labels that are 15/16" in height are placed 1" apart on the continuous backing. The 1/16" difference is the space between the labels.

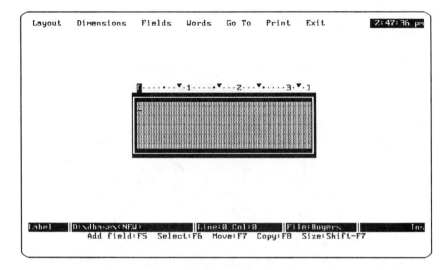

Figure 8-4. Label Design mode work surface.

dBASE IV supports nine different types of mailing labels. It also allows you to define a mailing label of your own dimensions. You can select one of the types by displaying the Dimensions menu. Enter

[Alt-d]

The program displays the Dimensions pop-up menu.

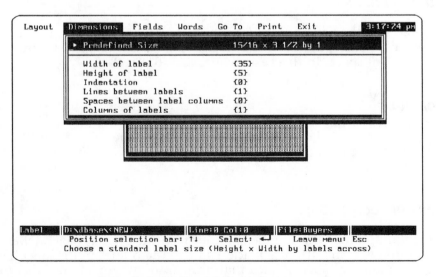

Figure 8-5. Mailing label dimensions menu.

The Dimensions menu consists of two parts. The first command is used to select one of the nine pre-set label sizes. They are:

Preset Number	Dimensions
1	15/16 x 3 1/2 by 1
2	15/16 x 3 1/2 by 2
3	15/16 x 3 1/2 by 3
4	11/12 x 3 1/2 by 3 (Cheshire)
5	1 7/16 x 5 by 1
6	3 5/8 x 6 1/2 envelope (#7)
7	4 1/8 x 9 7/8 envelope (#10)
8	Rolodex (3 x 5)
9	Rolodex (2 1/4 x 4)

The bottom half of the menu lists the specific values used to control the printing.

Width of Label

Sets the width of the label in columns. The assumption is made that you are printing at a character density of 10-pitch (characters per inch). This makes 35 columns equal to 3.5 inches of horizontal space.

Height of Label

This value sets the height of the label in lines. The assumption is made that the printer is set to print lines 1/6" high. This means every sixth line is one inch of vertical space. In this case, 5 lines is 5/6" (0.83").

Indentation

This option indents the text from the edge of the label. This is useful when you are working with pre-printed labels that have borders around their edges.

Lines Between Labels

This option specifies the number of lines to print between each label. The default value is 1 line. If you add the 1 line to the 5 lines in the label height, you get the total number of lines that print from the top of one label to the next label—in this case, a total of 6 lines, or 1" of vertical space.

Spaces Between Label Columns

This option is used when there is more than one label across the label form. You can specify the number of columns horizontally to skip, in order to reach the next label. When there are three labels across, you would leave two spaces between each column of labels. This space, added to the width of the column, gives you the horizontal location for the beginning of the label text. For example, if there are three columns of 35 column labels separated by 2 columns, the second column will print at column 37, and the third at column 73. Note that to print 3 labels across, you need to have a wide carriage printer, 14" or 132 columns.

Columns of Labels

This option sets the number of columns of labels across the label form. The default is 1, with a maximum of 6.

As far as vertical spacing is concerned, there is no difference between the height of the label and the lines between the label. For example, setting the label height to 6 lines and the lines between to 0, would print the labels exactly the same as a height of 5 with 1 line between. The difference is that lines specified as label height appear as part of the label form on the Screen layout. The lines designated as between labels do not. The default sets the label height at 5 because the sixth line would fall partly at the bottom of the label, and partly in the space between the labels. Setting the label height at 5 prevents you from accidentally trying to print data on the sixth line.

If you want to select a pre-defined label format, enter

P

The program lists the nine-label form layout included as part of dBASE IV. Select the Rolodex card size, Option 8, by entering

8

The screen layout changes to display a label form that is 50 columns wide and 14 lines long. The label form window in the center of the screen is changed, to match the dimensions of the label size you select.

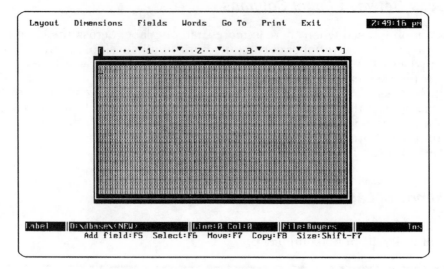

Figure 8-6. Label form layout window expended to match label size.

Return to the 3.5" by 15/16" label.

    [Alt-d]
    ⌐ ⌐

A mailing label is created by placing the fields you want to include, onto the label form. The process is similar to the creation of a report form, except that fields are placed onto the label in the location in which they will print. For example, the company name is placed on the first line, followed by the person's name on the second line, and so on.

Note that there is no Quick layout option for mailing labels. You must manually place the fields into the label form.

The [F5] command is used to place a field on the label form. Begin with the COMPANY field. Enter

    [F5]
    co ⌐
    [Ctrl-End]

The field is placed onto the first line of the label. The field is 35 characters wide—the exact width of the mailing label. Move to the beginning of the second line in the label.

    [down arrow]
    [Home]

The second line of the label form will print the name of the person—here, that means the FIRST and LAST fields. Enter

```
[F5]
f ↵
```

Before completing the placement of the field, look at the Picture function specification. The T function—the Trim Picture function—was automatically selected for this field. Trim prompts dBASE IV to truncate any trailing spaces from the field. Thus, although the template for the field is 20-characters long, when the field is printed, spaces following the last character in the field will not be printed. This is an important setting because you want the LAST field to print immediately after the FIRST name. If the T Picture function were not used, there would be a large gap of blank spaces between the first name and the last name fields. Place the field in the label form by entering

```
[Ctrl-End]
```

Move to the right one space and place the LAST field on this line. Enter

```
[right  arrow]
[F5]
L ↵
[Ctrl-End]
```

When attempting to place the field onto the label form, dBASE IV beeps and the message "Insufficient space on row, field truncated" appears at the bottom of the screen. The reason for the message is a matter of simple arithmetic. The label is 35-columns or characters wide. Both the FIRST and LAST fields are 20-characters wide with a space between the fields, for a total of 41 characters. Therefore, placing both fields on a single line exceeds the total width of the label. But the problem is more apparent than real. Recall that all the fields on the label form print with the T Picture function. The picture function truncates any trailing blanks within the field. While the FIRST field is 20-characters, the width of the printed information is limited to the actual name. For example, if the name in the FIRST field is *Steve,* the width of the printed field using the T Picture function, is only 5-characters wide. In practice, you will find most names fit comfortably onto a single line.

Test this concept by displaying the labels on the screen. Enter

```
[Alt-p] v
```

The labels print with a large gap between the first and last names. The Trim Picture function failed to truncate the trailing blanks. What happened?

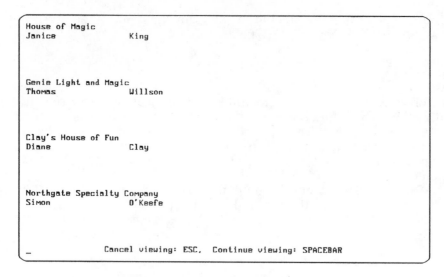

Figure 8-7. Gaps printed between FIRST and LAST fields.

Return to the Label Layout work surface.

[Esc]

When dealing with mailing-label layouts, in which fields are printed as normal text rather than data columns, the reason this happens is subtle but important. If you look carefully at the separation between the FIRST and LAST fields, you will see a gray character representing the space. This indicates the fields were separated using the right arrow key to change the cursor position.

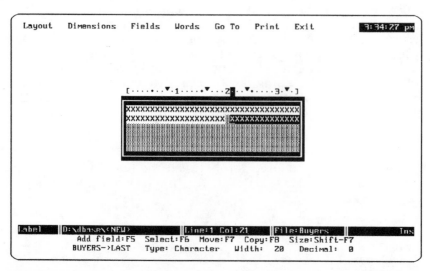

Figure 8-8. Fields not separated by [spacebar] characters are not trimmed.

In the Label Form layout, the Trim Picture function is not activated if the fields are separated by cursor movement. When cursor movement is used to place fields on the same line, the program assumes you want the fields printed at their full width, including spaces, as they would be in a columnar report.

In order to prompt the Trim function to truncate the extra spaces, you must separate the fields with an explicit character, such as the [spacebar], comma, or dash. Replace the gray character with a [spacebar] character.

```
[left arrow]
 [spacebar]
```

The area between the fields is now a solid color, matching the background color of the screen display. This small change will cause the first and last names to print properly on the label. Enter

```
[Alt-p] v
```

This time the names are separated by a single space.

```
House of Magic
Janice King



Genie Light and Magic
Thomas Willson



Clay's House of Fun
Diane Clay



Northgate Specialty Company
Simon O'Keefe



           Cancel viewing: ESC,  Continue viewing: SPACEBAR
-
```

Figure 8-9. Trailing spaces truncated from fields.

Return to the Layout work surface by entering

```
[Esc]
```

The next field, the street address, is placed on line 3 of the label form. Enter

```
[down arrow]
 [Home]
 [F5]
 srt ⏎
 [Ctrl-End]
```

The last line in the label will contain three fields: CITY, STATE and ZIP. Keep in mind you are to activate the Trim function by entering characters between the fields, not by using the cursor to move to the right. Enter the CITY field at the beginning of line 4.

```
[down arrow]
 [Home]
 [F5]
 ci ⏎
 [Ctrl-End]
```

To separate the CITY from the STATE, enter a comma and a [spacebar] character.

```
 ,
 [spacebar]
```

Insert the STATE field.

```
 [F5]
 s ⏎
 [Ctrl-End]
```

Enter a [spacebar] character to separate the ZIP from the STATE. Enter

```
 [spacebar]
```

Place the ZIP field into the label form.

```
 [F5]
 z ⏎
 [Ctrl-End]
```

The label form is now complete.

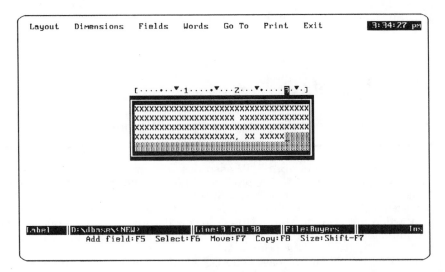

Figure 8-10. Label form completed.

Preview the labels. Enter

    [Alt-p] v

The four records from the database are displayed in the label form just designed.

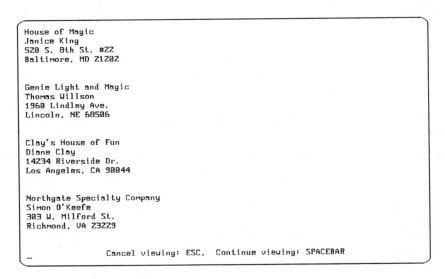

Figure 8-11. Labels form generates labels from database data.

Return to the Layout mode by entering

`[Esc]`

Printing Labels

Once you are satisfied with the label form, you can print the labels.

The label-printing portion of dBASE IV assumes you have loaded continuous-form labels into your printer. For learning purposes only, it is not necessary to use actual label forms. You can proof the labels by printing on regular continuous-form paper. However, the label program in dBASE IV is not set to feed the page to the top of the next form, when the printing stops. This is logical because the forms on label stock are individual labels. If you are printing on a full page, remember that printing labels has misaligned the paper in the printer. When you have finished printing labels and want to use the printer for full-page reports, advance the paper by using the Eject Page command from the Print menu.

Printing a report on the printer is not much different from printing the report on the screen display. However, if you are using continuous-form labels you have to properly align the first label.

Most printers require the top of the form to be aligned with the print head mechanism. However, in order to have a more compact appearance, most of the current printer designs make it difficult to clearly see the area around the print head. Normal-sized paper can be aligned by looking at the portion of the page not blocked by the print head. Labels are much more narrow than letter-sized paper; therefore, aligning the labels is very difficult to do by eye.

If you do not have mailing labels placed into your printer, you can simply print the labels on the continuous-feed paper. Remember to manually adjust the alignment of the paper following the label printing, or your next print will be out of alignment with the perforations on the paper.

In order to aid in label alignment, dBASE IV has a special command that appears only on the label Print menu, called Generate Sample Labels. This command prints a label that consists of full lines of X's. For example, the current type of label prints 35 X's for five lines.

The sample label can be used to check alignment. If the sample does not print properly, you can adjust the labels, and print again.

When you are adjusting labels not properly aligned, always attempt to correct the alignment by moving the labels forward while turning the platen. Although your instinct is to turn the labels backward to get the correct alignment, this method carries a danger. Rolling labels backward is very likely to cause the edge of a label to pull away from the paper backing and stick to a part of the printer feeding mechanism. When you then move the labels forward, a label will pull off and stick to the bottom of the roller tray. A label stuck in this position is very difficult to remove. It will often impede the printing of normal pages because it increases the friction of the paper being pulled or pushed through the printer.

By always pulling labels forward—not backward, you minimize the chances of getting a label stuck inside the printer. Doing this will waste some labels, particularly when you have finished printing and want to remove the labels from your printer. But a stuck label can ruin the printer entirely.

Generate a sample label by entering

```
[Alt-p] g
```

The program generates and prints the sample label. The program displays the prompt "Do you want more samples? (Y/N)". If the alignment of the sample label is not correct, adjust the printer and enter Y to print another label. Repeat the process until you are satisfied with the alignment of the label.

If the label is correctly aligned, entering N will prompt the program to print a full run of labels (i.e. all the labels in the current database or view). If you do not want to print labels now, terminate the printing by entering [Esc]. Enter

```
[Esc]
```

Even though you choose not to print the labels, the test labels have served their purpose. Now that the alignment has been set, your labels will print properly from this point on, unless you manually change the alignment in the printer.

Save the current label form, but do not exit the Label Form Layout mode. Enter

```
[Alt-L]  s
buyers  ↵
```

Printing Three-Across Labels

Continuous-form mailing labels can also be purchased in a three-across format. The advantage of three-across labels is that printers generally move faster, horizontally, then they do vertically. If you are printing a large number of labels and your printer shows a significant difference in printing speed between horizontal and vertical movement, printing three-across labels can save time.

You can switch between the single-column label form you have just created, and a three-column layout by making a different selection from the Dimensions menu. Enter

> [Alt-d] p 3

Display the three-across format on the screen.

> [Alt-p] v

The display of the three-across labels is not entirely accurate because the screen can display only 80-characters at once. The printed labels total 108 characters.

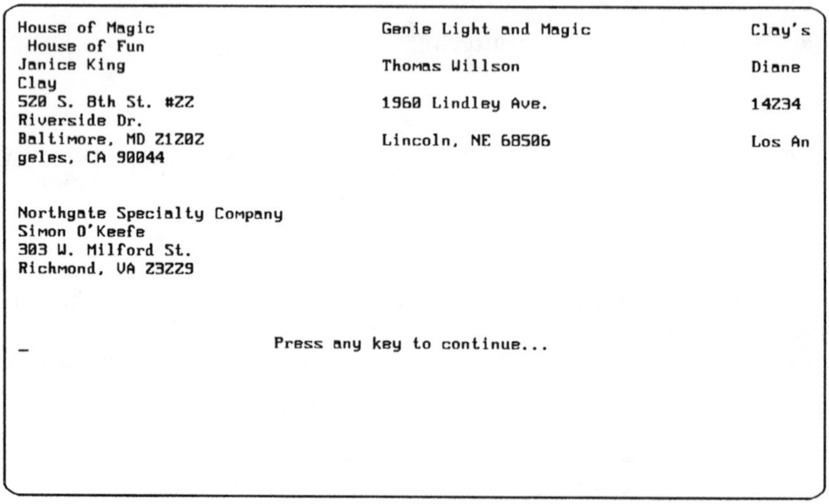

```
House of Magic              Genie Light and Magic      Clay's
  House of Fun
Janice King                 Thomas Willson             Diane
Clay
520 S. 8th St. #22          1960 Lindley Ave.          14234
Riverside Dr.
Baltimore, MD 21202         Lincoln, NE 68506          Los An
geles, CA 90044


Northgate Specialty Company
Simon O'Keefe
303 W. Milford St.
Richmond, VA 23229


_              Press any key to continue...
```

Figure 8-12. Labels printed three across.

Return to the Layout work surface. Enter

> [Esc]

Save the new label with a different name.

> [Alt-L] s
> [Backspace] *(4 times)*
> 3 ⏎

Exit the Label Design mode by entering

> [Alt-e] s

You have now created two labels: BUYERS, which is a single column label form, and BUYERS3, which is the same label form, formatted for three-column printing.

Suppressing Blank Fields

Add another record to the BUYERS database. Enter

```
[F2]
[Alt-r] a
```

Enter the name of the company.

```
Parkview Toys ⏎
```

Because you do not have the name of a person at this company, skip the FIRST and LAST field and enter the address.

```
⏎ (2 times)
2001 N. La Hunta Drive ⏎
Santa Fe ⏎
NM
76345
104 ⏎
506-777-6262
```

Save the new record by entering

```
[Alt-e] e
```

Use the BUYERS label form to display the labels on the screen. Enter

```
up arrow
⏎ (2 times)
v
```

The program generates the labels on the screen. The first four labels print exactly as they did before. Continue with the display by entering

```
[spacebar]
```

The fifth and last label is displayed using the data just added to the BUYERS database. But there is something different about the last label.

```
Parkview Toys

2001 N. La Hunta Drive
Santa Fe, NM 76345
```

Recall that you did not enter a FIRST or LAST name in this record. The result is the program prints a blank line between the company name and address. The blank line, although it would not cause the Postal Service any problems, is unsightly.

How can this problem be solved? The answer lies in the IIF( ) function, which proved so useful in Chapter 7. The IIF( ) can be used to create calculated fields in place of the simple fields used in the label form which take into account whether or not a line for the FIRST and LAST names is needed.

Exit the label display and activate the Label-design mode for the BUYERS label form.

> [Esc]
> ⏎
> **m**

Recall that the IIF( ) function allows you to create a single function that prints differently, depending upon the value of a logical expression. But how does this help you eliminate a line from the label form for some records but not others?

The answer requires the posing of another question. Suppose instead of the situation in Record 5—a record with a company name but no first and last name—the opposite is true. You have a record with a blank company field, but a first and last name to print. What sort of problem does this pose?

There would be no problem in this case. The blank company field would print a blank line above the first and last names, but the rest of the label would appear on consecutive lines. The problem only occurs when the first and last names are missing, because the company name prints on the line above the blank first and last names, making the missing data obvious.

The solution is easy to describe in non-computer terms: if the first and last names are blank, print the COMPANY field on the second line, not the first line. Is it possible to put into a dBASE IV formula the idea outlined above?

Begin with the first field in the label—the one currently highlighted. The current field always prints the text stored in the COMPANY field, which is not flexible enough to solve the problem. Delete the field from the label form.

> **[Del]**

The COMPANY field belongs on the first line when there is text of some kind in the first and last fields. The logical expression below is true when both fields are blank. The expression below is true only when the FIRST and LAST fields are blank.

> ""=TRIM(first+last)

The TRIM( ) function operates within a formula, in a manner similar to the Trim Picture function. It prompts the program to eliminate any trailing spaces from the specified character field or expression. If both FIRST and LAST are blank, once all the blanks are removed, there will be nothing remaining (i.e. a null value, "", is left).

You can use this expression to write a formula for a calculated field that prints a null if the FIRST and LAST fields are empty, or the COMPANY field if they are not. Enter

> **[F5]**
> **right arrow**
> ⏎

Enter the formula for the calculated field.

```
e
IIF(""=TRIM(first+last),"",company)    ⏎
```

The default template is 25 characters. Add ten more characters to the template, then save the field.

```
t
X (10 times)
⏎
[Ctrl-End]
```

The next step is to take on the two fields on Line 2. The logic here is similar to that used in the first line. The same logical test—are FIRST and LAST blank?—applies. Only the specified results are different.

The FIRST and LAST fields should print when they are not blank. If they are blank, the COMPANY field should print in their place.

Remove the FIRST and LAST fields from the label.

```
[down arrow]
[Del] (3 times)
```

Create a calculated field.

```
[F5]
[right arrow]
⏎
```

This time the expression is more complex. It begins with the same expression used in the previously calculated field. Enter

```
e
IIF(""=TRIM(first+last),
```

Next, comes the text that should print when the logical expression is true. Here, the COMPANY field should print if FIRST and LAST are blank. Enter

```
company,
```

Finally, comes the text that should print if the logical expression is false. In this case, that means the FIRST field should print.

```
first) ⏎
[Ctrl-End]
```

Enter

```
[spacebar]
```

Create another calculated field that prints the LAST field if it contains text, or nothing if it does not.

```
[F5]
[right arrow]
↵
e
IIF(""=TRIM(first+last),"",last)   ↵
[Ctrl-End]
```

Notice you are warned that the length of the field exceeds the label width. Because the fields are trimmed, this should not cause a problem. Save the revised label form and display the labels again.

```
[Alt-e] s
↵ (2 times)
v
```

The first four records print exactly as before. Display the fifth label by entering

```
[spacebar]
```

The fifth record now prints without the blank line. Return to the Control Center display by entering

```
[Esc]
```

If you are printing on full pages, you may need to align the paper in the printer at this point.

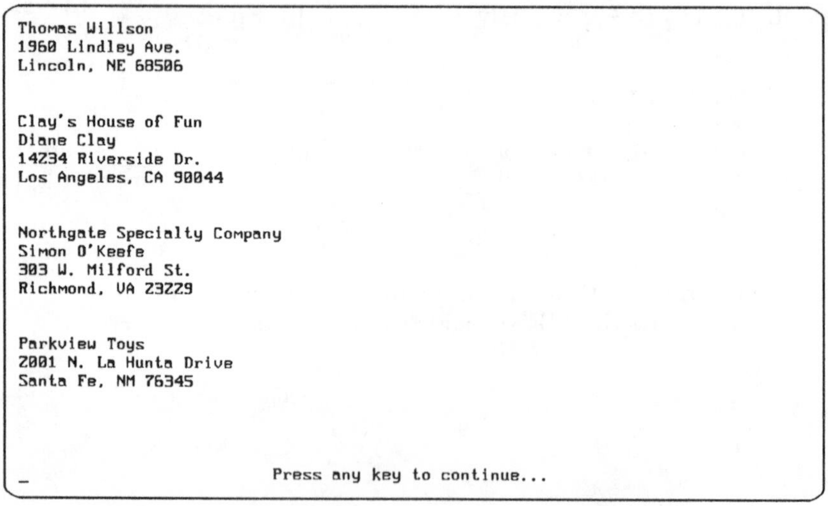

```
Thomas Willson
1960 Lindley Ave.
Lincoln, NE 68506


Clay's House of Fun
Diane Clay
14234 Riverside Dr.
Los Angeles, CA 90044


Northgate Specialty Company
Simon O'Keefe
303 W. Milford St.
Richmond, VA 23229


Parkview Toys
2001 N. La Hunta Drive
Santa Fe, NM 76345



                 Press any key to continue...
```

Figure 8-13. Blanks fields suppressed within label.

Blank Lines and Fields

The previous section explained how to eliminate blank lines occurring when not all the lines in the label are filled with data. Since this is a common problem, why doesn't dBASE IV check for blank lines automatically, when it prints the labels? Doing so would save a lot of trouble.

Interestingly enough, dBASE IV does check for blank lines, to avoid such a problem as the one that just occurred. Then why was the IIF( ) function required, here? The answer is that, technically, the blank line is not a blank line. In order for the Trim Picture function to suppress the trailing space in the FIRST field, it was necessary to place a [spacebar] character between the FIRST and LAST fields. The method used by dBASE IV to check for blanks, assumes you are printing only a single field on the line, with no literal characters, such as the space between words added to the line.

When the program checks the line, it gets fooled by the [spacebar] character followed by another field. The program thinks the line is not blank and prints the line.

In the example, it was necessary to use additional commands to make sure the blank line did not print.

Database Operations in the Dot Prompt Mode

You are now ready to create a second database for use in the ACCOUNTS catalog. This time you will perform the operations from the Dot Prompt mode. All the activities you have carried out in the Control Center are available from the Dot Prompt mode. In the next several sections of this chapter you will learn how to carry out standard operations, such as creating a database, entering data, designing and printing reports. Exit the Control Center display by entering

        [Alt-e] e

The Control Center display is removed from the screen. The Dot Prompt appears above the status line, at the bottom of the screen. Note that the status line still shows the name of the currently open database file, BUYERS. The record pointer is positioned at the End of File (EOF). When a dBASE IV operation has processed all the records in a file, the pointer is left at the end of the file. The label printing, because it included all the records in the database, has left the record pointer at the end of the BUYERS file.

Using Catalogs in the Dot Prompt Mode

The command used to create a new database from the Dot Prompt is the CREATE command. Create can be followed by the name of the file you want to create, or it can be used by itself. If you do not use the filename with

CREATE, you will be prompted to enter a filename. Unlike the file creation process initiated from the Control Center, you must assign the name to the database before you enter the Design mode, when starting from the Dot Prompt.

However, before you enter the CREATE command, there is another factor to consider. The PRODUCTS database you are about to create will be part of the ACCOUNTS catalog. When you exit the Control Center, the current catalog is automatically closed. Operations at the Dot Prompt, such as the creation of new databases, screen forms, reports, and label forms, are not automatically added to a catalog. If you create a new file now, dBASE IV will not show that file as part of the ACCOUNTS catalog when you return to the Control Center display.

When you want to include files created at the Dot Prompt in a dBASE IV catalog, you must remember to activate the catalog using two commands:

SET CATALOG TO. This command is used to select a catalog file for use.

SET CATALOG ON. In dBASE IV, selecting a catalog is one part of a two-step process. Once a catalog has been selected, it is not automatically activated. The SET CATALOG ON/OFF command must be used to activate the catalog after it has been selected. Once activated, the catalog records any new files created, or any existing files used in the catalog specified by the SET CATALOG TO command. Should you wish to carry out operations without recording the files as part of the catalog, you can deactivate the catalog by using SET CATALOG OFF.

A dBASE IV catalog is really a database file with a CAT rather than a DBF file extension. All catalog files have the following structure:

Field	Field Name	Field Type	Width	Dec	Index
1	PATH	Character	70		N
2	FILE_NAME	Character	12		N
3	ALIAS	Character	8		N
4	TYPE	Character	3		N
5	TITLE	Character	80		N
6	CODE	Numeric	3		N
7	TAG	Character	4		N

The catalog is selected with the SET CATALOG TO command or the Use a Different Catalog command, accessed from the Control Center; the catalog database is opened in Work Area 10.

A Work Area is used in dBASE IV to allow operations to be performed on more than one database file at a time. Since the catalog is a database, it needs to occupy a Work Area in order to be active while you work with other databases. You will learn more about Work Areas and how they are used, in Chapter 9.

When SET CATALOG is ON, all files used or created are recorded as records in the catalog database. If you want the file you are going to create to be added to the ACCOUNTS catalog, you must select and activate the ACCOUNTS catalog. Enter

```
SET CATALOG TO accounts ↵
SET CATALOG ON ↵
```

Nothing on the current screen display indicates that the pair of commands just entered have changed anything. This is characteristic of the Dot Prompt mode, in contrast to the Control Center, which presents information about the status of the system, as part of its normal display.

You can confirm the result of the commands you have just entered by using the DISPLAY STATUS command. Enter

```
DISPLAY STATUS ↵
```

Two items that concern the catalog appear on the DISPLAY STATUS listing. The first is the CATALOG file active in Work Area 10. Part of the screen display reads "Select area: 10, Database in Use: D:\DBASE\AC-COUNTS.CAT". Area 10 is reserved for catalogs. This line confirms that the SET CATALOG TO command opened the ACCOUNTS catalog file.

The next item is found on the second screen of the DISPLAY STATUS listing. Display the screen by entering

```
↵
```

At the top of the screen are a series of SET values, AUTOSAVE through UNIQUE. The fourth item in the first column is CATALOG. The screen shows this option is currently ON. The two pieces of information show you have selected and activated the catalog.

Complete the display by entering

```
↵
```

Creating a Database—Dot Prompt Mode

To create a new database called PRODUCTS, enter the following command:

```
CREATE products ↵
```

If you are using dBASE IV on a network, the status line will show ExclLock, on the right side of the status line. This tells you the file you are creating is protected for use by other users on the network. This function is implemented automatically, when you create a new database.

The Design mode is activated exactly as it is from the Control Center display. The only difference is, when working from the Dot Prompt mode, the database is already assigned a name.

Fill out the structure of the file as shown below.

Num	Field Name	Field Type	Width	Dec	Index
1	ID	Character	10		Y
2	ITEM	Character	30		Y
3	DESCRIPT	Character	30		N
4	VENDOR	Character	20		Y
5	COST	Numeric	10	2	N
6	PRICE	Numeric	10	2	N
7	ONHAND	Numeric	10	0	N

After you have entered the field definitions, save the new database by entering

[Alt-e] s ↵

Entering Data

The next step is to enter the data into the new database. This is always primarily a manual task in which you must enter the information, record by record. However, in some cases you can find ways to enter data indirectly. For example, suppose you intended to give products consecutive ID numbers, e.g., 100, 101, 102, etc. Instead of manually entering these numbers, you can use a dBASE IV command to automatically place the consecutive numbers in the records. Also, suppose the distributors from whom you buy inventory allow you a 38% discount off the list price of the items. Your cost can be calculated, instead of manually entered. Not only does this save time, it is also more accurate.

In looking at the structure of the new file, you can narrow down those fields that actually need manual entry, to ITEM, DESCRIPT, VENDOR, and PRICE. The ID and COST fields can be indirectly entered with dBASE IV commands. For now, you will not be filling out the ONHAND field.

Because you don't intend to fill out three of the seven fields, there is no need to display them during the data entry process. The SET FIELDS TO command allows you to select a set of fields from the current database, as the active fields. All others will be ignored, as long as the SET FIELDS TO list remains active. In this case, if you set the fields list to ITEM, DESCRIPT, VENDOR, and PRICE, when you append records to the database, the screen display will show only those four fields. The order in which the fields appear on the screen will be determined by the order in which they are listed in the SET FIELDS command. For example, if the list of fields is written VENDOR, ITEM, DESCRIPT, PRICE, the append screen display places the VENDOR field at the top of the display, followed by the three other fields, in order.

The ability to select and arrange the fields is important because most data entry tasks involve a *source document*. A source document is the written record from which you are copying the data being entered into the computer. In some rare cases, the data entered into the file comes from memory. But for the most part, there is always a document, list, rolodex card, business card, receipt, invoice, catalog, etc., from which the raw data is copied.

Since you are usually copying from a document when entering data, you can cut down on mistakes and improve your efficiency if the data field on the screen follows the same order as the data on the source documents. For example, if the source document has the vendor's name at the top of the document, it is logical to enter the VENDOR field first. The goal is to move down the list of fields, as you move down the printed document. If your file's structure does not match the source document, the SET FIELDS TO command allows you to select and rearrange the fields.

A more elaborate alternative is to create a screen form to match the source document.

Select the four fields you need to enter.

    SET FIELDS TO vendor,item,descript,price ↵

Now place the program into the Append Records mode.

    APPEND ↵

The Append mode screen display lists the selected fields in the specified order.

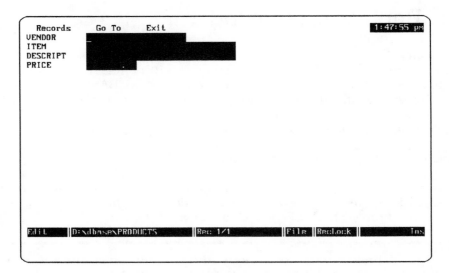

Figure 8-14. Selected fields listed in the specified order in Append mode.

You will enter four records into this database file, also. Enter the data as shown below.

```
Record No    1
VENDOR       Prestidigitation  Inc
ITEM         Cards
DESCRIPT     Cards marked for card tricks
PRICE             21.95


Record No    2
VENDOR       Prestidigitation  Inc
ITEM         Knotted scarves
DESCRIPT     Used for scarf trick
PRICE             59.95


Record No    3
VENDOR       Masquerade Supplies
ITEM         Fake blood capsules
DESCRIPT     Simulates bleeding - washabl
PRICE             12.95


Record No    4
VENDOR       Masquerade Supplies
ITEM         Groucho glasses
DESCRIPT     Glasses with nose & eyebrows
PRICE             5.95
```

When you finish entering the records, exit the Data Entry mode by entering

    [Alt-e] e

The Replace Command

The ID and COST fields were not entered because their values can be created indirectly, using the REPLACE command. The REPLACE command allows you to insert data into a field, based on the value of a dBASE IV expression. The REPLACE command can be used to change data in a single record, in all records, or in a selected group of records.

The command takes the general form of:

REPLACE *field_name* WITH *expression*

The power of the command comes from the *use of an expression.* dBASE IV expressions can produce data by calculation of numbers, dates, or text, using the full range of dBASE IV operations and functions.

When you create an update-type query, the program generates a REPLACE command, based on the information entered into the query skeletons. All actions performed by update queries can be duplicated by entering REPLACE commands at the Dot Prompt.

One of the most common uses of REPLACE is to store calculated data in numeric fields. In this example, the COST field can be calculated by discounting the PRICE field by 38%.

Remember that you have currently limited operations to the four fields specified in the SET FIELDS command. To return the program to its normal mode—all fields available—use the SET FIELDS TO command with no field names. This form of the command removes all field restrictions. Because it is not possible to REPLACE data in a non-active field, you must execute this command before you can use REPLACE. Remove the field restrictions by entering

    SET FIELDS TO ⏎

The formula for calculating a discount can be expressed mathematically as shown below. Note that the formula subtracts the discount percentage from 1, which is the same as 100%. Thus a value discounted by 38% is actually 62% (100%-38%) of the list price.

Price*(1-Discount)

You can use this formula as the expression portion of the REPLACE command. It is important to keep in mind that fieldnames used as part of a replacement expression, act as *variables*. This means that as the command moves from record to record, the value of the PRICE field will change. The value of the expression based on the PRICE field will also change. As a result, each record will have a value stored in its COST field, based on the value of its PRICE field. The ALL clause prompts the command to perform the replacement for every record in the database, starting at the top of the database and going to the last record in the file. Enter

    REPLACE ALL cost WITH price*(1-.38) ⏎

The program displays the message "4 records replaced", indicating the result of the formula was placed into four records. You can confirm the effect of the REPLACE command by listing the cost and price fields. Also list the ratio between COST and PRICE. If the command performs as expected, the ratio should be the same for all records, 62%. Enter

    LIST cost,price,cost/price ⏎

The list produces a table with the following values. The .62 values in the third column confirm the accuracy of the COST and PRICE values.

Record #	Cost	Price	Cost/Price
1	13.61	21.95	0.62
2	37.17	59.95	0.62
3	8.03	12.95	0.62
4	3.69	5.95	0.62

The next replacement task is more challenging. The goal is to place a value into each ID field that is a unique consecutive number (e.g. record 1 is 100, record 2 is 101). To do so, a value is needed that will increase with each record in the database. While there is no field in the database that meets the requirement, each record in any database file does possess a unique number—the *record* number. The RECNO( ) function is always equal to the value of the record number of the current record. By adding a fixed value, such as 99, 100, or 10000, to the record number, you can generate a sequence of consecutive numbers, because the record numbers themselves are consecutive.

There is one small technical problem. The RECNO( ) function is a numeric value, but you have defined the ID field as a character field. You can solve the problem by converting the numeric calculation to character information, or by modifying the structure of the file so the ID is a numeric value. In this case, use the STR( ) (string) function to change the numeric value to characters. Enter

```
REPLACE ALL id WITH STR(RECNO( )+99) ⏎
```

That the length of the ID field is 10 characters, is no accident. The 10 characters match the length of the value returned by the RECNO( ) function, which is always a numeric value with a width of 10.

Once again, all four records are replaced. List the results.

```
LIST id ⏎
```

The command lists the values shown below. You can see each record is automatically supplied with a unique ID number.

Record #	id
1	100
2	101
3	102
4	103

The PRODUCTS is now complete. List the contents of the entire database.

```
LIST ⏎
```

Close the database.

       CLOSE DATABASE ⏎

Activate the Control Center display by entering

       [F2]

    The Control Center display lists the new database file, PRODUCTS, along with the other files previously stored in the ACCOUNTS catalog. Using the SET CATALOG command integrated the file created at the Dot Prompt, with the other file created in the Control Center.

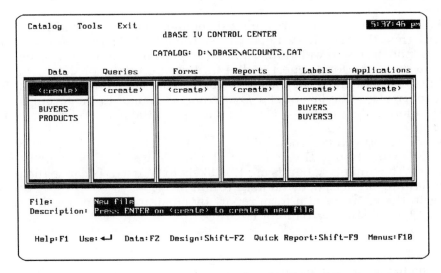

Figure 8-15. New database appears listed in Control Center catalog.

Form Reports

As with databases, report and label forms can be created in the Dot Prompt mode. Exit the Control Center display and return to the Dot Prompt mode.

       [Alt-e] e

You can create or modify a report form directly from the Dot Prompt mode by using the CREATE REPORT command. This command activates the Report Form design mode, exactly as it would from the Control Center display, except that here, you must enter the name for the report before the mode becomes active. Create a report called rolodex by entering

       CREATE REPORT rolodex ⏎

As the command begins to execute, the program displays an entry box in the center of the screen: "No database in use. Enter filename:". This occurs because both database files in the ACCOUNTS catalog are now closed. dBASE IV will not allow you to create a report without a database file being open. Enter

```
buyers ⏎
```

The report you are about to create is different from the columnar-type reports created in Chapter 5. The name ROLODEX implies you want to create an address-book type report. While it is possible to print address and phone number information in columns, this is not the format which is most typically used. Addresses are formatted in blocks, similar to those appearing on labels.

While columnar reports are the most common type of reports created with report forms, the dBASE IV Report Design mode is flexible enough to also create report forms in which information is presented differently. The basic characteristic of a form report is that its Detail section consists of at least two lines of information. The detail for each record can run from several lines to an entire page. The layout of a *form* report is similar to the layout used in a screen form. The difference is that on a report, the fields represent output areas only.

A form report can be produced by using the Detail band, exclusively. You may also want to use the Page Header or Footer bands to print page numbers. The Summary bands are less likely to be used, because the nature of the form report does not lend itself to summary.

Begin the creation of a form report by closing all unnecessary report bands. Close the Header band by entering

```
⏎
```

Close the Report Intro band by entering

```
[down arrow]
⏎
```

Close the Summary band also.

```
[down arrow] (3 times)
⏎
```

In the center of the Footer band, insert a special variable to display the page number.

```
[down arrow] (2 times)
  Move the cursor to Line 0, Col 35
```

Insert the Page Number variable. Enter

```
Page
[spacebar]
[F5]
[right  arrow] (2 times)
[Pg Dn]
⌐
[Ctrl-End]
```

The form report should look like the screen shown in Figure 8-16.

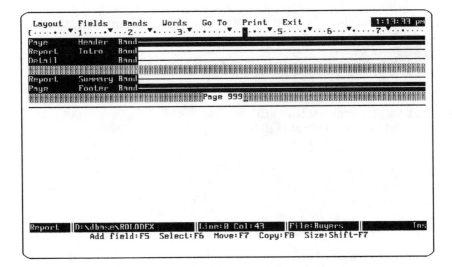

Figure 8-16. Bands setup for form type report.

The Detail Band of a Form Report

The largest and most important component in a form report is the Detail band. Its layout resembles the one used in a screen form. The main difference between the screen form and the form report is that the report offers up to a full page for each record. The screen display is limited to 25 lines.

Place the cursor in the Detail band.

```
[up  arrow] (3 times)
```

Display the record number on the first line of the report. Enter

```
Record #
[F5]
[right  arrow] (2 times)
r ⌐
```

Use the Left Align Picture function to eliminate spaces in front of the record number.

```
P
1
[Ctrl-End]
[Ctrl-End]
```

In a columnar report, you would normally work your way across the Detail band. In a form report, you can move vertically, as well as horizontally. Add three blank lines to the Detail band.

      ⏎ *(3 times)*

Place the name of the buyer on the line where the cursor is positioned. Enter

```
Name of Buyer:
[spacebar]
[F5]
f ⏎
```

Note that the T (Trim) Picture function is automatically selected. Place this field, then add the LAST name field.

```
[Ctrl-End]
[spacebar]
[F5]
L ⏎
[Ctrl-End]
```

Add three more blank lines.

      ⏎ *(3 times)*

Create a mailing address block. Begin by placing the company name.

```
[F5]
co ⏎
[Ctrl-End]
⏎
```

Place the street address on the next line.

```
[F5]
str ⏎
[Ctrl-End]
⏎
```

On the next line, place the city, state, and zip. Try this on your own. The correct command can be found at the end of the chapter under Ex-1.

When you complete the city, state, and zip, the form will look like Figure 8-17.

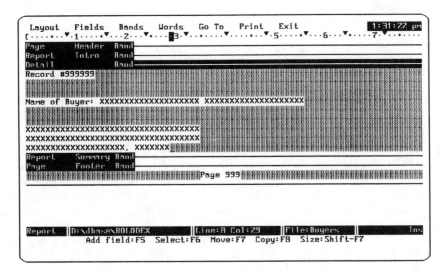

Figure 8-17. Address block placed in report design.

There are two other items to be added to this form, ACCOUNT_NO and the phone number. Skip three more lines.

        ⏎ *(3 times)*

Enter

        Account #
        [F5]
        ⏎

Select the Left Align option from the Picture function list, and place the field into the report.

        P
        l
        [Ctrl-End]
        [Ctrl-End]

Place the phone number on the same line as the beginning of the address block.

        [up arrow] *(5 times)*
        [Tab] *(2 times)*

Enter

        Phone:
        [spacebar]
        [F5]
        p ⏎
        [Ctrl-End]

Place the extension below the phone number.

```
[down arrow]
[Shift-Tab]   (2 times)
Extn:
[spacebar]   (2 times)
[F5]
e ↵
[Ctrl-End]
```

There is one last item to consider. On a form report, the program prints as many lines of data as will fit onto a single page. The exact number of records fitting on a page is determined by the number of lines that print in each Detail band. When the next record prints, the first line of its Detail section prints immediately after the last line of the previous Details section. As the report is currently designed, there is nothing to separate the end of one record from the beginning of the next. You may want to add blank lines, or some other form of marking (e.g. horizontal lines) to identify the end of each Detail section. In this case, simply add five blank lines following the Account number. Enter

```
[down arrow](4 times)
↵ (5 times)
```

The report form should now look like Figure 8-18.

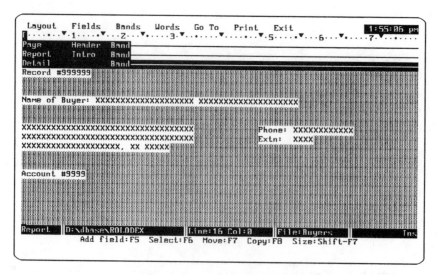

Figure 8-18. Form type report.

Display a sample of the report by entering

    [Alt-p] v

The report displays Record 1, and part of Record 2. Scroll through the report by pressing the [spacebar], until you return to the Design work surface.

Inserting Page Breaks

The form report prints the database information as a series of copies of the basic layout in the Detail section. Because each record fills only part of the page, several records are printed on one page.

Reports of this type are often more useful when each record begins a new page. Doing so here, would produce one data sheet for each buyer in the database. You can achieve this result by inserting a page break at the end of the Detail section. The page break prompts the report to skip to the beginning of the next page before it prints the next record.

The Insert Page Break command is found on the Word menu. Enter

    [Alt-w] i

A dashed line is inserted across the width of the report, indicating that a page break will be made each time the Detail section completes printing.

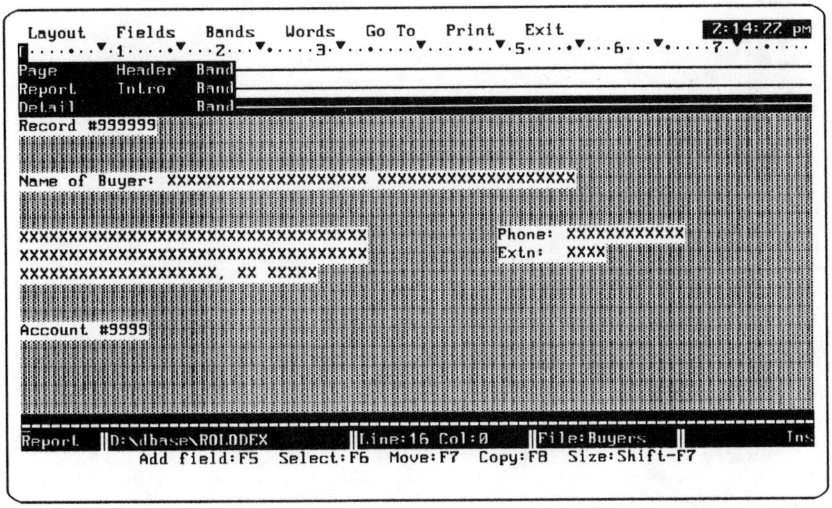

Figure 8-19. Page break marker inserted into report design.

Display the report on the screen again.

        [Alt-p] v

This time the first record is displayed alone on the first page. Each record will now appear on a separate page. Scroll through the pages of the report by pressing the [spacebar]. When you have inspected the report, save the report and return to the Dot Prompt.

        [Alt-e] s

The program generates the report form code needed to print this report and then returns to the Dot Prompt.

Printing Reports and Labels from the Dot Prompt

You can print or display reports or labels directly from the Dot Prompt mode using dBASE IV commands.

Command	Result
REPORT FORM	Prints reports
LABEL FORM	Prints labels

Suppose you wanted to print the ROLODEX report just created. Enter

        REPORT FORM rolodex ↵

The report is displayed on the screen. However, there are no pauses at the end of each screen. Instead, all the pages simply run by, automatically.

The REPORT FORM and LABEL FORM commands use the screen as the default output device. To send the report or label to the printer, you must add the TO PRINT clause. Enter the following command to send the report to the printer.

        PRINT ↵

The report is sent to the printer.

In addition to the two standard output devices, screen and printer, the REPORT FORM and LABEL FORM commands also accept a TO FILE clause. The TO FILE clause prompts the output to be sent to a text file on the disk. The file can then be used like any other text file. For example, you could load it into a word-processing program for additional enhancements. To create a text file from the rolodex report, enter:

```
REPORT FORM rolodex TO FILE rolotext
```

The command creates a file ROLOTEXT.TXT which contains ASCII text.

You can perform a similar operation with label forms. The next command displays labels using the BUYERS label form.

```
LABEL FORM buyers ⏎
```

The labels are displayed on the screen. To print the labels, simply add the TO PRINT clause.

```
LABEL FORM buyers TO PRINT ⏎
EJECT ⏎
```

This section assumes that you are printing on continuous form paper, not label stock. It would be inconvenient and unnecessary when learning new techniques to switch paper stock each time you experiment with a LABEL command. The EJECT command is used to position the paper to the top of the next page, in order to keep the paper correctly aligned in the printer.

When printing labels, you may want to generate a sample label for alignment purposes. This can be done by simply printing one label until the alignment is correct.

Note that the file shows the record pointer is at the EOF (End of File). Move it back to the top of the file by entering

```
GO TOP ⏎
```

To print a single record, use the scope NEXT 1 with the LABEL FORM command. Keep in mind that the scope NEXT 1 tells dBASE IV to use only the current record, because dBASE IV begins counting the *next* record with the current record as the first record. In dBASE IV, the term *next 1* refers to the *current* record. Enter

```
LABEL FORM buyers NEXT 1 TO PRINT ⏎
EJECT ⏎
```

You can repeat the same command as many times as necessary, until the label prints properly.

Another way to test label alignment is to use the SAMPLE clause. SAMPLE prints a label form that uses X's to demonstrate the printing area of the label. Enter

```
LABEL FORM buyers SAMPLE TO PRINT ↵
```

After the label sample has printed, you are asked "Do you want more samples?". To stop the sample printing, enter

```
n
```

As you may recall, dBASE IV allows you to access previous commands using the up arrow key. You can quickly repeat a command by entering up arrow ↵. Enter

```
up arrow ↵
```

The same label prints again. Once the labels are properly aligned, you can print the remainder by using the REST scope. Enter

```
SKIP ↵
LABEL FORM buyers REST TO PRINT ↵
EJECT ↵
```

Selecting Records for Labels and Reports

The printing so far has included all the records in the database. However, you can print or display selected records by using a FOR clause with the LABEL FORM or REPORT FORM commands. For example, suppose you wanted to print labels for buyers in California, only. Enter

```
LABEL FORM buyers FOR state="CA" ↵
```

Only the record for Clay's House of Fun is printed. You can perform a similar operation with a label report. Enter

```
REPORT FROM rolodex FOR state="CA" TO PRINT ↵
```

Setting a Filter

If you want to print or display more than one label or report using the same selection criteria, you can use the SET FILTER TO command. The SET FILTER TO command establishes a logical expression that selects records for all commands that follow. For example, suppose you want to select records in which the word Magic appeared in the company name. The expression *"Magic"$company* tests to see if the string *"Magic"* is some part of the COMPANY field. Enter

```
SET FILTER TO "Magic"$company ↵
```

Display the labels that qualify for the current filter.

>   LABEL FORM buyers ↵

Only two labels are printed because of the SET FILTER TO criterion. Because SET FILTER TO stays active until specifically released, you can enter another command and still have the same pair of records included. Enter

>   REPORT FORM rolodex TO PRINT ↵

The report prints the two records selected by the SET FILTER TO condition.

   You can remove the filter condition by entering SET FILTER TO without a condition.

>   SET FILTER TO ↵

The FOR clause performs the same selection operation as a query does when it selects records. The Dot Prompt method is much faster since it does not require the creation and generation of a query file. The clause is simply added to the REPORT FORM or LABEL FORM command.

   As you become more familiar with the processing techniques in dBASE IV, you may find you can get work done faster by directly entering the commands at the Dot Prompt, rather than navigating through the Control Center menus. Queries encompass many dBASE IV operations. If you want to perform a more specific task, such as records selection, it is simpler to use the proper clause than to create an entire query.

Indexing Reports and Labels

The labels and reports in this chapter listed the records in the order in which they were entered into the database file (i.e. the *natural* order). When an index order is active, the records will be listed on the report or label printout in the indexed order. In creating the BUYER file, you specified two fields for index order. If you do not recall what they were, you can obtain information about the index orders in two ways: 1) Use LIST STRUCTURE or 2) use DISPLAY STATUS. Enter

>   LIST STRUCTURE ↵

The program lists the structure of the database. The index column shows there are two index orders automatically created for this file: COMPANY and LAST. Enter

>   DISPLAY STATUS ↵

The top part of this display provides more detailed information about the index orders. The name of the database is shown, and below it is a list of indexes. The production index file, BUYERS.MDX, shows two tags,

COMPANY and LAST. In addition, the key expression used to create the index orders is also listed. The DISPLAY STATUS command is the best way to obtain information about indexes because it will display all the index orders, not just those included in the file's structure.

```
Select area:  1, Database  in Use: D:\DBASE\BUYERS.DBF
Production  MDX file:  D:\DBASE\BUYERS.MDX
          Index TAG:     COMPANY  Key: COMPANY
          Index TAG:     LAST Key: LAST
```

Skip the remainder of the STATUS display by entering

        [Esc]

To activate an index, use the SET ORDER TO command. For example, suppose you wanted to print labels ordered by company name. Activate the index order COMPANY by entering

        SET ORDER TO company ↵

Display the status again.

        DISPLAY STATUS ↵

This time the status display shows the word Master next to the COMPANY tag, indicating the records will be ordered according to company name.

```
  Select area:  1, Database  in Use: D:\DBASE\BUYERS.DBF
  Production  MDX file:  D:\DBASE\BUYERS.MDX
     Master Index TAG:     COMPANY  Key: COMPANY
          Index TAG:     LAST Key: LAST
```

Skip the rest of the status display by entering

        [Esc]

Using the ? Option

When you enter a REPORT FORM or LABEL FORM command from the Dot Prompt, you are expected to enter the name of the file you want to use. Most commands in dBASE IV that require the entry of a filename accept the ? option. The ?, when used in place of a filename, will prompt dBASE IV to display a pop-up menu that lists the files of the specified type that are available.

When a CATALOG is active, the lists of files displayed when the ? option is used reflects the contents of the current catalog. If SET CATALOG is OFF then the ? pop-up lists all the files of the specified type in the current directory.

Print the labels in company name order by entering

        LABEL FORM ? TO PRINT ↵

The program lists the label forms that are part of the ACCOUNTS catalog.

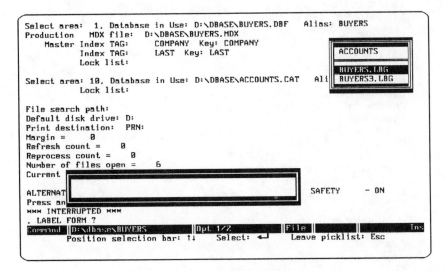

Figure 8-20. Pop-up lists label forms.

Select the BUYERS label form by entering

      ↵

The labels print in company name order.

```
Clay's House of Fun
Diane Clay
14234 Riverside Dr.
Los Angeles, CA 90044

Genie Light and Magic
Thomas Willson
1960 Lindley Ave.
Lincoln, NE 68506

House of Magic
Janice King
520 S. 8th St. #22
Baltimore, MD 21202

Northgate Specialty Company
Simon O'Keefe
303 W. Milford St.
Richmond, VA 23229

Parkview Toys
2001 N. La Hunta Drive
Santa Fe, NM 76345
```

Eject the page by entering

```
EJECT ⏎
```

How would you print the labels in order by LAST name? Try this on your own. The correct command is at the end of the chapter under Ex-2.

This time the labels print in order by last name. Why is *Parkview Toys* the first record? Recall that in this record, the LAST field is blank. The ASCII sequence order places blanks before alphabetical characters, so that records with blanks appear first in the sequence.

```
Parkview Toys
2001 N. La Hunta Drive
Santa Fe, NM 76345

Clay's House of Fun
Diane Clay
14234 Riverside Dr.
Los Angeles, CA 90044

House of Magic
Janice King
520 S. 8th St. #22
Baltimore, MD 21202

Northgate Specialty Company
Simon O'Keefe
303 W. Milford St.
Richmond, VA 23229

Genie Light and Magic
Thomas Willson
1960 Lindley Ave.
Lincoln, NE 68506
```

The use of the SET ORDER TO command is faster and simpler than creating a sorted file using the Control Center query function. Since the index orders already exist, (they were created as part of the database production index file) using the SET ORDER TO command avoids the time used by a query to sort the database. The report or label form begins to print the records immediately, because the record sequence is stored in the production index file.

Quitting from the Dot Prompt

You can exit dBASE IV directly from the Dot Prompt by using the QUIT command. Exit the program by entering

       QUIT ⏎

Note that when the QUIT command is entered, dBASE IV automatically closes all the database and catalog files.

Summary

In this chapter you learned two additional forms into which database information can be placed to produce specific types of printouts.

- **Replacing Data.** The REPLACE command can be used to perform file updates that would otherwise require the creation and execution of an Update query. The REPLACE command inserts the results of a dBASE IV expression into the specified field. If the ALL clause is used, the replacement occurs in every record.

- **Label Forms.** Label forms are used to print database information on special forms, such as continuous form labels. The Label Form Design mode displays a rectangular window, reflecting the dimensions of the label. There are nine built-in, pre-defined label forms. You can also enter size specifications manually.

  Fields are placed onto the label form to show where you want the fields placed. You can eliminate leading or trailing blanks by using the T Picture function with the fields. Note that to activate the trim effect of these fields, the space between fields must be filled with characters. If you want the fields separated, you must use a [spacebar] character. If you separate fields using the right arrow or left arrow keys, the Trim Picture function will not function properly.

  Blank lines are automatically suppressed. However, some cases where more than one blank field is used on a line, can escape the programs attention and will require special functions to suppress the blanks.

  Labels can be printed from the Dot Prompt mode using the LABEL FORM command. The default is to display the labels on the screen. When activated from the Dot Prompt mode, reports do not pause when displayed on the screen. The TO PRINT clause sends the output to the printer, as well as to the screen.

You can use the Print menu in the Label Form mode to print a test pattern for alignment. If you are working from the Dot Prompt-mode, you can use the command LABEL FORM label_name TO PRINT NEXT 1, to print a single label for alignment testing.

- **Form Reports.** A form report prints multiple lines of detail for each record, in contrast to a columnar report, which prints only one detail line for each record.

   You can cause each Detail band to print on its own page by using the Insert Page Break command to place a page break into the Detail band.

   Reports can be printed from the Dot Prompt mode by using the REPORT FORM command. The default is to display the reports on the screen. Reports do not pause when displayed from the Dot Prompt mode. The TO PRINT clause sends the report to the printer.

- **Selecting Records for Reports and Labels.** You can use a FOR clause with a REPORT FORM or LABEL FORM clause to select records for inclusion in the report or label output. The SET FILTER TO command establishes a selection criteria that affects all subsequent reports or labels. The FOR clause duplicates the records selection functions of a Control Center query.

- **Indexing Labels and Reports.** If index orders exist—typically through the production index file—you can access these orders by using the SET ORDER TO command. Once activated, the index order will cause the records printed through a report or label form, to appear in sequenced order. This method is faster than sorting records with a query.

   You can obtain a list of the index orders available by using the DISPLAY STATUS command.

Exercises

Ex-1

Place the city, state and zip code on the report form.

```
[F5]
c ↵
[Ctrl-End]
,
[spacebar]
[F5]
s ↵
,
[Ctrl-End]
[spacebar]
[F5]
z ↵
[Ctrl-End]
```

Ex-2

Print the labels in last name order.

```
SET ORDER TO last ↵
LABEL FORM buyers TO PRINT ↵
EJECT ↵
```

9

Using and Relating Multiple Databases

In this chapter you will move into a new and more complex area of dBASE IV operations. Up to this point you have used one dBASE IV database file at a time. In the previous chapter you created two databases, BUYERS and PRODUCTS. Both files contained lists of items. The BUYERS file contained a list of customers, while the PRODUCTS contained a list of products.

What happens when a business makes a sale? Assume you've sold some products and you want to use dBASE IV to record those sales. One way to do this would be to create a third database containing all the fields in the BUYERS database, all the fields in PRODUCTS, and a few extra fields for such information as the sale date.

Having created this database you could fill out one record for each item sold. However, as you filled out the fields, it would become obvious you are entering information already stored in the BUYERS and PRODUCTS database. The only new information would be the date of the sale and the quantity of the products sold. The remaining information can be drawn from the BUYERS or PRODUCTS databases, or calculated from information in those files.

By drawing information from the existing databases you derive a number of benefits.

Save Time

By drawing the information already stored, you cut down on the amount of information you need to enter.

Accuracy

Because much of the information is entered only once, you eliminate a number of potential errors that could occur if you had to enter all the information each time a sale was made.

In this chapter you will learn how multiple-database files can be used together to create a system whereby data is shared among, and linked between, more than one database.

Linking Databases

The problem posed at the beginning of this chapter was how to create a database that recorded sales, but did not require you to enter information already stored in the BUYER or the PRODUCTS database files. At the beginning of that process, it is a good idea to review exactly what information is stored in the two databases. Below are the structures of the two files in question.

The BUYERS database.

Num	Field Name	Field Type	Width	Dec	Index
1	COMPANY	Character	35		Y
2	FIRST	Character	20		N
3	LAST	Character	20		Y
4	STREET	Character	35		N
5	CITY	Character	20		N
6	STATE	Character	2		N
7	ZIP	Character	5		N
8	ACCOUNT_NO	Numeric	4	0	N
9	PHONE	Character	12		N
10	EXTENSION	Character	4		N

The PRODUCTS database.

Num	Field Name	Field Type	Width	Dec	Index
1	ID	Character	10		Y
2	ITEM	Character	30		Y
3	DESCRIPT	Character	30		N
4	VENDOR	Character	20		Y
5	COST	Numeric	10	2	N
6	PRICE	Numeric	10	2	N
7	ONHAND	Numeric	10	0	N

Altogether, there are 17 fields of information in the two files. Two other pieces of information are needed to record a sale: the date of sale and the quantity purchased. Since the PRODUCTS database contains the PRICE of the item, you can calculate the amount of the sale and the sales tax.

If you were to create a new database called SALES, it would have to contain at least two fields: DATE_SOLD and QUANTITY. But these two fields are insufficient. In order to provide a complete record of who purchased what product, you must place a key in the SALES database to indicate which buyer bought which product.

One way would be to enter the account number of the buyer, as found in the ACCOUNT_NO field in the BUYERS database. The account number can serve as a link between the information in the SALES database and the information in the BUYERS database. If you know the account number of the buyer, you can obtain all other information about the buyer by locating the record in the BUYERS database that contains the specified account number. The same sort of link can be established between the SALES database and the PRODUCTS database, using the ID field as the link.

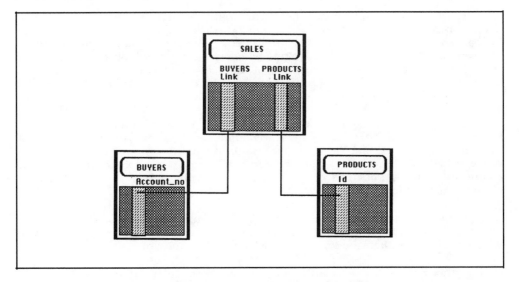

Figure 9-1. Databases linked by key fields.

When the SALES database is linked to the BUYERS and PRODUCTS databases, SALES is called the *master* or *parent* database, while BUYERS and PRODUCTS are called the *supporting* or *child* databases. The master or parent database contains the values that will be searched for in the supporting or child database.

Note that such designations as master and supporting, or parent and child, are not attributes of a specific file. Any database can, in theory, be a parent, child or both, depending on the logical relationship between the files. The terms are descriptive, and are used to express logical relationships between databases.

Linking databases using a key field allows you to have access to all related information, without having to enter or store it more than once. This remains true, even when BUYERS or PRODUCTS repeat in the SALES database. For example, suppose a buyer, account #101, makes 10 different purchases. If the databases are linked by the account number, there is no need to enter the buyer's name, address, and phone number each time. The single record in the BUYERS database will be linked to any SALES record containing account #101.

Another benefit of linking databases is that changes in the supporting databases are automatically reflected in the master database. For example, if the buyer with account #101 has a new phone number, all records linked to him will automatically reflect the change. If you were not using links, the SALES file would contain records with both the old and new phone numbers, based on when the record was filled out.

Why use the account number as a link? The answer is that, in theory, links can be made using any field in any of the databases. However, logic and human nature indicate the best choices. First, you would need a field in the supporting database that contains unique information. Linking by company name or individual's name will work, but there is always the possibility of duplicate names. By assigning account numbers, you ensure that each different buyer has a unique value. Often, social security numbers are used because they are unique.

Second, you want to make the linking field a value that can be entered with no error. Entering a company or person's name leaves an opportunity for error. For example, if the company is called The First National Bank, it could be entered as *1st National Bank* or *FNB*. Either choice might be equivalent to a person reading it, but the computer would see each as unique. In this case, the names are not identical, therefore, not the same to the program.

Using numeric account numbers should reduce the number of errors. There are only 10 numeric digits, in contrast to 52 alphabetical characters (26 upper and 26 lower). With fewer options, there are fewer chances of inputting the wrong value.

On the other hand, since arbitrarily assigned numbers mean very little on their own, one might argue that alphabetical information is easier, because its meaning is clearer. For example, the difference between account #101 and #110 is unclear just from the numbers. However, a typo such as Smith and Simth would stand out clearly.

This example uses the traditional approach, which is to assign account and product ID numbers to each unique element in the system. In Part II of this book, the programming section, you will learn how to create dBASE IV applications in which items can be selected from lists by using pop-up menus. This method is probably the most reliable way of entering data linking records in different databases.

Alias Names

It is important to understand that the term *link* refers to a logical process, not a physical connection. The link between databases is based on instructions you give the program about how to locate the corresponding records in the supporting databases. The instructions use a dBASE IV logical expression to determine which records match. For example, in order to create a link between the buyer and the sale, you would tell dBASE IV that it should look for records in which the ACCOUNT_NO field in the SALES database matches the value in the ACCOUNT_NO field in the BUYERS database (e.g. ACCOUNT_NO=ACCOUNT_NO).

However, the expression ACCOUNT_NO=ACCOUNT_NO is ambiguous because when you use the fieldname ACCOUNT_NO, there is no way of telling which database it is drawn from.

When you are working with a single database, this problem cannot occur because dBASE IV will not allow you to create two fields with the same name. But when you are using more than one database, such duplication of fieldnames is not only possible but quite likely.

If multiple database operations are to be performed, there must be some system by which fieldnames can include a reference to the database in which they occur. dBASE IV has a special notation which allows you to include a reference to the database and the field in the database. The database reference is called an alias. For example, the ACCOUNT_NO field in the sales database would be referred to as SALES->ACCOUNT_NO, while the ACCOUNT_NO field in the BUYERS database would be referred to as BUYERS->ACCOUNT_NO. The -> symbol is composed of two keyboard characters, the hyphen(-) and the greater than sign (>).

The alias name makes it possible to write an unambiguous expression about fields with the same name, in two different databases (e.g SALES->ACCOUNT_NO=BUYERS->ACCOUNT_NO).

Keep in mind that the alias name used with the fieldname is a different way of referring to a field. In the previous chapters you entered fieldnames with the alias. Since you were only working with one database at a time, the program automatically assumed the field had the alias of the open database. If you hasd wished, you could have written the alias form of the fieldname in any of the commands, and the program would have accepted it exactly as it did the fieldnames alone. Working with multiple database files, however, will sometimes require the use of alias names in order to clarify a field reference.

The alias name and the database name are automatically set by dBASE IV to be the same. However, it is possible, using the dBASE IV USE command at the dot prompt or in a program, to assign a different alias name to the database. This is useful when you keep a number of similar databases that can be interchanged for each other. For example, you might keep separate SALES databases for each year, SALES88, SALES89, etc. In normal circumstances, a link established between SALES88 and BUYERS would not work with SALES89. You can circumvent this problem by linking a generic alias name like SALES. When you use a database, the ALIAS clause will assign it the generic alias name, e.g., USE SALES88 ALIAS SALES. All references to SALES will be directed to the SALES88 database.

Create the Master Database

You are now ready to learn how dBASE IV implements multiple-database operations. Load dBASE IV in the usual manner. The ACCOUNTS catalog should be displayed in the Control Center.

The first step is to create the master or parent database, (i.e. the one that will be linked to the other databases). This database will be called SALES. Create a new database by entering

       ⏎

Enter the file structure as shown below:

Num	Field Name	Field Type	Width	Dec	Index
1	DATE_SOLD	Date	8		Y
2	QUANTITY	Numeric	10	0	N
3	ACCOUNT_NO	Numeric	0		N
4	ID	Character	10		N

Note that the ACCOUNT_NO and ID field descriptions match the ACCOUNT_NO and ID fields, exactly as they appear in the BUYERS and PRODUCTS databases, respectively.

Save the new database by entering

```
[Alt-e] s
sales ⏎
```

Activate the Append mode so you can enter records into the database.

```
[F2]
```

Enter the following seven records. Note that without referring to the other database files, you won't know who is buying what by reading the account and ID numbers. Once the files are linked, this will change.

```
Record No        1
DATE_SOLD     06/10/89
QUANTITY            2
ACCOUNT_NO    103
ID            102

Record No        2
DATE_SOLD     06/15/89
QUANTITY           10
ACCOUNT_NO    101
ID            100

Record No        3
DATE_SOLD     06/17/89
QUANTITY            5
ACCOUNT_NO    100
ID            101

Record No        4
DATE_SOLD     06/20/89
QUANTITY           10
ACCOUNT_NO    102
ID            103

Record No        5
DATE_SOLD     06/22/89
QUANTITY            4
ACCOUNT_NO    100
ID            102

Record No        6
DATE_SOLD     06/22/89
QUANTITY            1
ACCOUNT_NO    103
ID            102

Record No        7
DATE_SOLD     06/25/89
QUANTITY            5
ACCOUNT_NO    103
ID            101
```

Save the records by entering

    [Alt-e] e

Close the SALES database by entering

    ⌐ *(2 times)*

Linking Databases with a Query

The process by which two or more databases can be used together can be complex. The dBASE IV Query mode allows you to perform many operations on two or more databases, with a minimum of difficulty. Your first task will be to create a query that relates the account numbers in the SALES file to the matching records in the BUYERS file. Begin by creating a new query.

        [right arrow]⏎

In order to create a link between two files, you need to display the file skeletons of each. The Add File to Query command shown on the Layout menu allows you to select the database files for the query. Add the SALES database to the query.

        ⏎
        s ⏎

The file skeleton for the SALES database is displayed in the Query mode work surface. This display is exactly the type you have worked with previously. The next step will change this. Instead of working with the SALES file skeleton, you will add a second file skeleton to the display: that for the BUYERS database. Enter

        [Alt-L]
        a

The database files are listed in the pop-up menu on the right side of the screen. This time, select the BUYER database.

        ⏎

```
  Layout   Fields   Condition   Update   Exit                5:48:23 PM
 ┌──────────────┬──────────────┬──────────────┬──────────────────────┐
 │ Sales.dbf    │ DATE_SOLD    │ QUANTITY     │ ACCOUNT_NO           │
 ├──────────────┴──────────────┴──────────────┴──────────────────────┤
 │              │              │              │                       │
 ├──────────────┬──────────────┬──────────────┬──────────────────────┤
 │ Buyers.dbf   │ COMPANY      │ FIRST        │ LAST                 │
 ├──────────────┴──────────────┴──────────────┴──────────────────────┤
 │ ████████████ │              │              │                       │
 │                                                                    │
 │                                                                    │
 └────────────────────────────────────────────────────────────────────┘
  Query    D:\dbase\<NEW>        File 2/2
   Next field:Tab  Add/Remove all fields:F5  Zoom:F9  Prev/Next skeleton:F3/F4
```

Figure 9-2. Query displays with two database file skeletons displayed.

The Query mode display now shows file skeletons for two database files. With two skeletons, you can select fields for both databases to appear in the Edit or Browse displays. However, before you begin thinking about the fields to display, you must create a link between the two databases.

Place the highlight in the SALES database file skeleton by entering

> **[F3]**

Since the link between the files will use the ACCOUNT_NO field, place the highlight in the ACCOUNT_NO box by entering

> **[Tab]** *(3 times)*

The command that establishes a link between files is the Create Link by Pointing command, found on the Layout menu. Enter

> **[Alt-L] c**

The command inserts LINK1 into the ACCOUNT_NO box. Keep in mind that the Create Link by Pointing command is still active. To complete the command you must indicate what field in the other database skeleton is linked to the current field. At the bottom of the screen, the program displays the message "Cursor to another file & press Enter". Move the highlight to the BUYERS database skeleton.

> **[F4]**

The highlight moves to the BUYERS database skeleton. Move the highlight to the field that will serve as the linking field. In this case, the field has the same name, ACCOUNT_NO. Enter

> **[Tab]** *(8 times)*
> ↵

LINK1 is inserted into the ACCOUNT_NO box in the BUYERS database, completing the link.

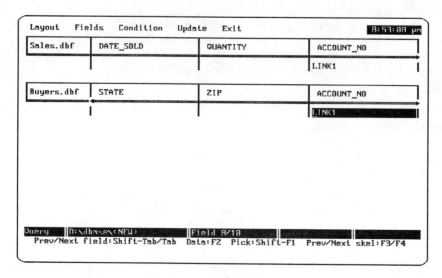

Figure 9-3. Link established between two database files.

The important factor in linking two database files is not that the fields have the same name, but that the linked fields contain the same information. The ACCOUNT_NO field in both files contain four-character numeric values. This could be done even if the fields had different names. Of course, using the same fieldname to store the same information makes it easier to think about and remember the relationship between the databases.

What does this link mean? How will it affect database operations? When a link is created between two databases, dBASE IV seeks to match records in the master database—in this example, SALES—with corresponding records in the supporting database—in this example, BUYERS. For instance, the first record in the SALES database contains the value 103 in the ACCOUNT_NO field. When this record is displayed in the Edit or Browse mode, dBASE IV automatically performs a search on the ACCOUNT_NO field in the supporting database, BUYERS. The pointer in the BUYERS file is positioned to the record that contains the same value, 103, in the linked field ACCOUNT_NO. When this occurs, a very special situation exists. Instead of having a single record pointer and a single set of fields, you have two pointers, one in SALES and one in BUYERS. The positioning of the pointers makes available all 14 field (10 from BUYERS and 4 from SALES). This means you can use some, or all, the fields in a Browse or Edit display, or eventually as part of a screen, report, or label form.

For example, suppose you wanted to list the DATE_SOLD, the ACCOUNT_NO, the COMPANY name and the PHONE number. Note that two fields come from the SALES database, but the other two fields are from the BUYERS database. In the Query mode, all you need to do to create a

combined display is to select fields from the file skeletons.
Begin with the DATE_SOLD field from the SALES database.

```
[F3]
[Shift-Tab]   (2 times)
[F5]
```

If you look closely at the view skeleton, you will see that the query uses the
alias notation, Sales->DATE_SOLD, to indicate the database source of the
field.

```
View
<NEW>  │  Sales->
       │  DATE_SOLD
```

Add the ACCOUNT_NO field to the view skeleton.

```
[Tab]  (2 times)
[F5]
```

Next, place the highlight into the BUYERS skeleton and add the COMPANY
and PHONE fields.

```
[F4]
[Shift-Tab]   (7 times)
[F5]
[Shift-Tab]   (3 times)
[F5]
```

Note that the two fields added from the BUYERS database can be identified
by the alias name Buyers->, preceding the fieldnames.

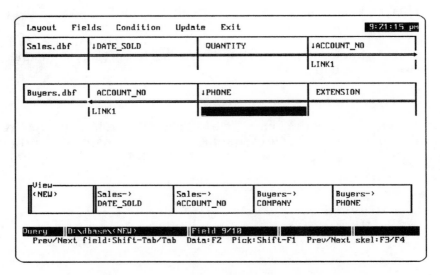

Figure 9-4. View skeleton contains fields from both databases.

To see the effect of the link, display the data by entering

[F2]

The Browse mode is activated, displaying four columns. The data in columns 1 and 2 are taken directly from the seven records in the SALES database. The information in the third and fourth column, COMPANY and PHONE, are drawn from the information stored in the BUYERS database.

```
┌──────────────────────────────────────────────────────────────────────────────┐
│    Records     Fields     Go To     Exit                      9:41:27 PM       │
│  ┌──────────┬──────────┬──────────────────────────────────┬────────────────┐  │
│  │DATE_SOLD │ACCOUNT_NO│COMPANY                           │PHONE           │  │
│  ├──────────┼──────────┼──────────────────────────────────┼────────────────┤  │
│  │06/10/89  │      103 │Northgate Specialty Company       │804-555-8965    │  │
│  │06/15/89  │      101 │Genie Light and Magic             │402-555-9980    │  │
│  │06/17/89  │      100 │House of Magic                    │301-555-3193    │  │
│  │06/20/89  │      102 │Clay's House of Fun               │213-555-9875    │  │
│  │06/22/89  │      100 │House of Magic                    │301-555-3193    │  │
│  │06/22/89  │      103 │Northgate Specialty Company       │804-555-8965    │  │
│  │06/25/89  │      103 │Northgate Specialty Company       │804-555-8965    │  │
│  │          │          │                                  │                │  │
│  │          │          │                                  │                │  │
│  │          │          │                                  │                │  │
│  └──────────┴──────────┴──────────────────────────────────┴────────────────┘  │
│  Browse    D:\dbase\<NEW>              Rec: 1/7         View  ReadOnly          │
│                          View and edit fields                                  │
└──────────────────────────────────────────────────────────────────────────────┘
```

Figure 9-5. Data combined by the file link appear in the Browse mode.

It is interesting to see that the same information from the BUYERS database is used several times. For example, three records in SALES have the ACCOUNT_NO 103. All three records match the record in the BUYERS database that contains account #103, the Northgate Specialty Company.

Change to the Edit display.

[F2]

The Edit mode displays the four specified fields. Note that both the Browse and Edit modes are ReadOnly displays. This means you can display information but you cannot use Browse or Edit to alter data or add new records.

Return to the Query mode.

        [Alt-e] t

Before you continue, save a copy of the current query.

        [Alt-L] s
        customer ↵

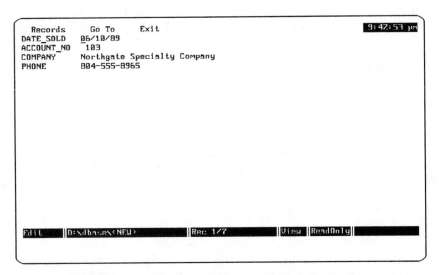

Figure 9-6. Linked data appears in Edit mode display.

Linking the Products Database

Now that you have seen an example of how two databases can be linked, try to link another pair of databases. This time, link SALES to the PRODUCTS database.

Remove the BUYERS database from the query, using the Remove File from Query command in the Layout menu.

        [Alt-L] r

Remove the LINK1 marker from the ACCOUNT_NO field.

        [Ctrl-y]

Also, remove ACCOUNT_NO from the skeleton.

> `[F5]`

Add the PRODUCTS database to the query display.

> `[Alt-L] a`
> `p ⏎`

The link between the PRODUCTS database and the SALES database will be the ID field. Place the highlight in the ID field of the SALES skeleton.

> `[F3]`
> `[Tab]`

Start the linking process by entering

> `[Alt-L] c`

The program enters LINK2. The 2 has no special significance. It is used because you previously created a LINK1. Move the highlight to the ID field in the PRODUCTS database.

> `[F4]`
> `[Tab]`
> `⏎`

The two databases are linked, using the information in the ID fields. Add the ID field from the SALES database and the ITEM and PRICE fields from the PRODUCTS database to the view skeleton. Enter

> `[F3]`
> `[F5]`
> `[F4]`
> `[Tab]`
> `[F5]`
> `[Tab]` *(4 times)*
> `[F5]`

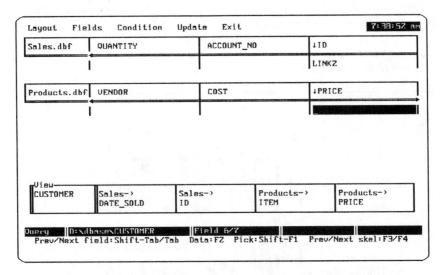

Figure 9-7. Link established between SALES and PRODUCTS.

With the link established, display the data by entering

[F2]

When the query is processed, instead of displaying the information, the program displays a message box that reads "No records selected". This means none of the values in the ID field of the SALES database, match any of the values in the ID field of the PRODUCTS database.

But this should not be the case. You know that the ID field in both databases have items in common (e.g. ID #102 appears in Record #1 of SALES and Record #3 of PRODUCTS). Why didn't the query match the records?

The answer shows a subtle but important point about the difference between character and numeric fields. If you review the structure of the files, you will see that the ID field is a character field in both the SALES and PRODUCTS databases. However, the entry of data into the fields was performed differently. You will recall that the product ID numbers were inserted into the ID field in the PRODUCTS database using a REPLACE command, REPLACE ALL id WITH STR(RECNO( )+99). On the other hand the data entered into the SALES database ID field was manually entered.

But why should this make a difference? The answer has to do with the placement of characters in the field. When you enter data from the keyboard into a character field, you are typing the characters from left to right. In ID number 102, the characters are placed in the first three places in the 10-character field. However, the expression STR(RECNO( )+99) creates a 10-character text string in which the *last* three positions are occupied with the characters 102, and the first seven characters are filled with blanks. Put another way, even though both fields contain the characters 102, the field in the SALES database has the number aligned left, while the PRODUCTS database has the characters aligned right in the field. When you are entering numbers into a character field, you need to consider the alignment factor. Numeric fields avoid this problem because dBASE IV will automatically right—align the characters.

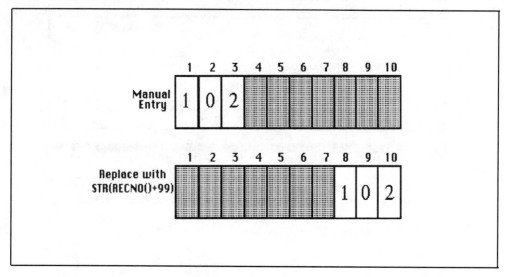

Figure 9-8. Characters aligned on left or right sides of a 10 character field.

Because the characters are in different positions within the field, the program sees the contents as different. This is what caused the problem with the link. There are several ways to solve the problem. You could change the fields to numeric, or alter the contents so both databases use the same alignment. In some cases, numbers are always entered with the same number of characters. Unused places are padded with zeros. For example in a 5-character, character-type field, you would enter numbers 00001, 00102, etc. The padding would make sure that all entries had the same alignment characteristics.

Here, you will change the fields from character to numeric. This will avoid making this error in the future. Return to the query by entering

        ⤶

Save this query so you can use it again, after you have solved the problem with the data.

```
        [Alt-L] s
        [Home]
        [Ctrl-y]
        purchases ⤶
```

Exit the Query mode.

```
[Alt-e] s
```

You need to modify the structure of the PRODUCTS and SALES databases. Highlight the SALES database.

```
[right arrow]
 s
```

Display the Design Structure mode.

```
[Shift-F2]
[Esc]
```

Change the ID field to a numeric-type field.

```
[down arrow] (3 times)
 ⌐
 n
[Ctrl-End]
 y
```

Now perform the same change on the PRODUCTS database.

```
 p
[Shift-F2]
[Esc]
 ⌐
 n
[Ctrl-End]
 y
```

Execute the PURCHASE query.

```
[right arrow]
 p
 [F2]
```

The query can now correctly match the SALES ID numbers with the ID numbers in the PRODUCTS database. The result is a ReadOnly Browse display, based on the seven records in the SALES database, Figure 9-9.

```
  Records      Fields      Go To      Exit                    10:36:42 am
 ┌──────────┬────┬──────────────────────────┬──────────────────────────┐
 │DATE_SOLD │ ID │ ITEM                     │ PRICE                    │
 ├──────────┼────┼──────────────────────────┼──────────────────────────┤
 │06/10/89  │ 102│Fake blood capsules       │       12.95              │
 │06/15/89  │ 100│Cards                     │       21.95              │
 │06/17/89  │ 101│Knotted scarves           │       59.95              │
 │06/20/89  │ 103│Groucho glasses           │        5.95              │
 │06/22/89  │ 102│Fake blood capsules       │       12.95              │
 │06/22/89  │ 102│Fake blood capsules       │       12.95              │
 │06/25/89  │ 101│Knotted scarves           │       59.95              │
 │          │    │                          │                          │
 │          │    │                          │                          │
 │          │    │                          │                          │
 │          │    │                          │                          │
 │          │    │                          │                          │
 │          │    │                          │                          │
 │          │    │                          │                          │
 └──────────┴────┴──────────────────────────┴──────────────────────────┘
 │Browse ║D:\dbase\PURCHASE      ║Rec: 1/7        ║View ║ReadOnly║
                       View and edit fields
```

Figure 9-9. Query lists data from the linked databases SALES and PRODUCTS.

Return to the Query Design mode by entering

        [Alt-e] t

Calculating Using Linked Databases

Fields in linked databases can be used for more than mere display. You can use the information in the databases to calculate values. For example, the SALES database contains the number of items sold. The PRODUCTS database contains the price of each item. By multiplying these two values, you can calculate the amount of each sale.

    Remove the DATE_SOLD and ID fields from the current view skeleton.

        [F4]
        [F5] *(2 times)*

Move the highlight to the SALES skeleton and add the QUANTITY field.

        [F4]
        [Shift-tab] *(2 times)*
        [F5]

You can use a calculated field to display the total amount of each sale. Enter

        [Alt-f] c

Enter the formula for the total amount.

        price* quantity ↵

Add the calculated field to the view skeleton.

    [F5]

Give the field the name AMOUNT.

      amount ⏎

The view should draw information from both databases, in order to create a calculated field, Figure 9-10.

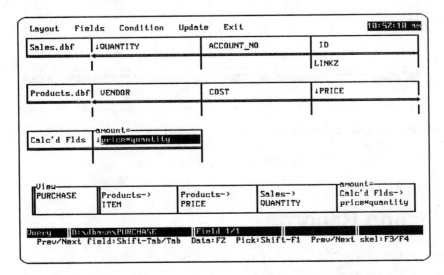

Figure 9-10. Calculated field uses data from both files.

Display the data by entering

    [F2]

The program creates the query, and displays four fields. The fourth column is the result of a calculation performed by using fields from two linked databases. In this example, the price values of some items are used more than once.

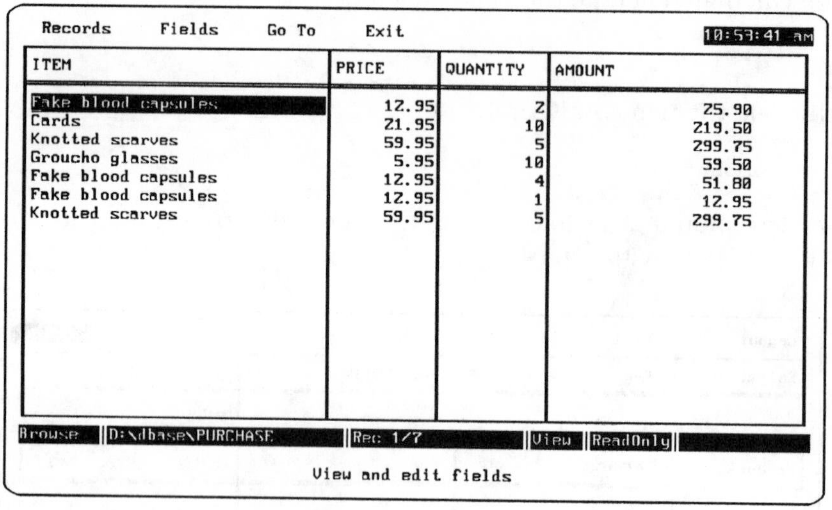

```
Records      Fields     Go To      Exit                   10:53:41 am

ITEM                            PRICE    QUANTITY   AMOUNT

Fake blood capsules             12.95        2              25.90
Cards                           21.95       10             219.50
Knotted scarves                 59.95        5             299.75
Groucho glasses                  5.95       10              59.50
Fake blood capsules             12.95        4              51.80
Fake blood capsules             12.95        1              12.95
Knotted scarves                 59.95        5             299.75




Browse    D:\dbase\PURCHASE          Rec: 1/7          View  ReadOnly
                        View and edit fields
```

Figure 9-11. Amount calculated from SALES->QUANTITY and PRODUCTS->PRICE.

Return to the Query Design mode by entering

    [Alt-e] t

Selecting Records

As with other types of queries, you can create selection criteria that select records for display. Suppose you wanted to select only those records having a total amount greater than $100. Place the expression, >100 into the calculated field box.

    [down arrow]
      >100
      [F2]

This time, only 3 records are selected. Note that they all qualify for display, because the total amount of the sale exceeded $100.

    Return to the Query Design mode by entering

    [Alt-e] t

Sorting

You can also perform sort operations to produce a sequenced display of records. First, remove the selection expression.

    [Ctrl-y]

Move the highlight to the SALES skeleton.

>   [F3] *(2 times)*

Select the DATE_SOLD field as the sort key.

>   [Shift-Tab]
>   [Alt-f] s ↵

Add this field to the view skeleton. Move the highlight to the view skeleton and move the DATE_SOLD field to the left side of the skeleton.

>   [F3]
>   [Tab] *(3 times)*
>   [F6] ↵
>   [F7]
>   [left arrow] *(4 times)*
>   ↵

Display the data.

>   [F2]

This time, the records appear in order by the DATE_SOLD.

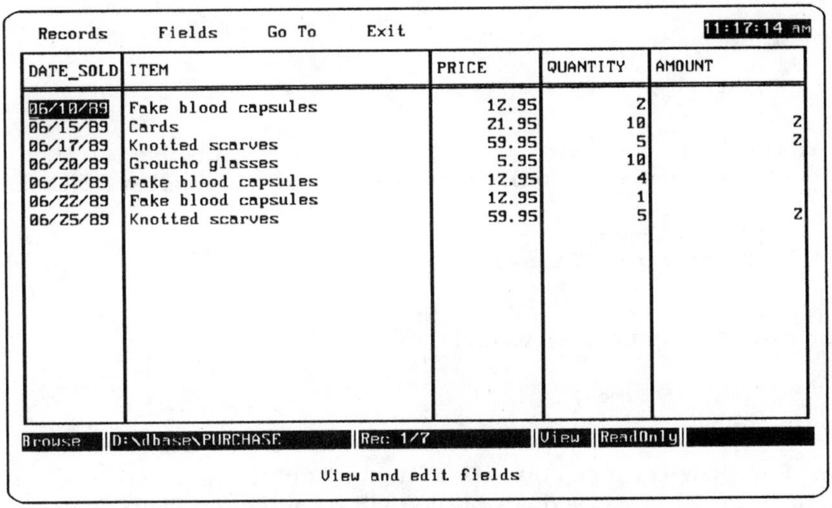

DATE_SOLD	ITEM	PRICE	QUANTITY	AMOUNT
06/10/89	Fake blood capsules	12.95	2	
06/15/89	Cards	21.95	10	2
06/17/89	Knotted scarves	59.95	5	2
06/20/89	Groucho glasses	5.95	10	
06/22/89	Fake blood capsules	12.95	4	
06/22/89	Fake blood capsules	12.95	1	
06/25/89	Knotted scarves	59.95	5	2

Records   Fields   Go To   Exit   11:17:14 AM

Browse D:\dbase\PURCHASE   Rec: 1/7   View ReadOnly

View and edit fields

Figure 9-12. Records sequenced in DATE_SOLD order.

Queries that use more than one database can perform the same operations as a single database query, but information from fields in both files can be combined to form a single display.

Return to the Query Design mode by entering

[Alt-e] t

Multiple Links

The linking process is not limited to a single-linked database. You can create any number of links between master and supporting databases. The system of ACCOUNTS requires that you link the SALES database to the PRODUCTS and BUYERS databases.

The process of creating another link is a repetition of the process used to create the initial link. First, add a skeleton to the query for the additional database.

[Alt-L] a
↵

There are now three file skeletons in the query display: SALES, PRODUCTS, BUYERS. The next step is to create the link between the SALES database and the BUYERS database, using the ACCOUNT_NO field as the link.

Place the highlight into the ACCOUNT_NO field in the SALES database.

[F3] *(2 times)*
[Tab] *(2 times)*

Create a link.

[Alt-L] c

Move the highlight to the field in the BUYERS database to which the SALES database will be linked. In this case it is the ACCOUNT_NO field.

[F4] *(2 times)*
[Shift-Tab] *(3 times)*
↵

Add the company name to view skeleton.

[Tab] *(5 times)*
[F5]

The view skeleton now consists of fields from three different databases. When the query is processed, two links will be activated from each record in the SALES file. The link to the ID field will cause the program to locate data in the PRODUCTS file that matches the ID number, and the ACCOUNT_NO link will cause the program to fetch data from the BUYERS file. The view will blend all the data into a single display, making it appear as if the data have been drawn from a single database file. Enter

[F2]

Switch to the Edit mode so you can see the entire field at one time.

[F2]

The first record combines data from all three database files, based on the linking fields ID and ACCOUNT_NO.

```
DATE_SOLD    06/10/89
ITEM         Fake blood capsules
PRICE           12.95
QUANTITY            2
AMOUNT                   25.90
COMPANY      Northgate Specialty Company
```

Note that the linking fields are not part of the display. In this case, they perform their function in the background. Display the next record.

[PgDn]

Record 2 is displayed.

Exit the Edit mode, return to the Query mode, and save the revised query.

[Alt-e] t
[Alt-e] s

The PURCHASE query provides five fields of information, based on links between the sales, products, and buyers databases.

Column Reports Using Multiple Databases

When a multiple database query is active, you can create a report using information from the fields listed in the view skeleton. You can take advantage of the Quick layout feature of the Report Form generator by first creating a query that links the databases and selects the fields you want to use.

In this case, you want to create a column report called SALES, that lists the date, company, quantity, amount, and sales tax for each sale. This requires data from all three databases, and creation of a new calculated field for sales tax.

Instead of creating a query from scratch, you can start with the PUR-CHASE query and make additions and deletions. Return to the Query Design mode by entering

[Shift-F2]

Begin by adding a calculated field to the query. This will calculate the amount of sales tax, assuming that all sales carry a 6% charge.

[Alt-f] c

Enter the formula for calculating the sales tax.

```
price*quantity*.06  ⌐
```

Add the calculated field to the view skeleton, giving it the fieldname TAX.

```
[F5]
tax ⌐
```

To complete the query, you need to setup the view skeleton to correspond to the columns in the report. This means deleting and rearranging some of the fields. Place the highlight in the view skeleton.

```
[F4]
```

Remove the item and the PRICE fields from the view skeleton.

```
[Tab] [F5] (2 times)
```

Move the COMPANY field so that it follows the DATE_SOL field.

```
[Tab] (3 times)
[F6]  ⌐
[F7]
left arrow (2 times)
⌐
```

The query view skeleton now contains the fields in the sequence necessary for the column report. Save this query under a new name so that it will not overwrite the PURCHASE query. Call it SALERPT1 (Sales Report 1).

```
[Alt-L]  s
[Home] [Ctrl-y]
salerpt1  ⌐
```

SALERPT1 is the active query. When you create the report form, it will be linked to this query automatically because it is currently active. However, it is important to realize that the current query has been designed, but not processed. In order to place into memory the fields specifications matching the current query, you *must* process the query first. Without processing, the query specifications will not affect the Quick Layout option of the Report Form generator. Enter

```
[F2]
```

The program processes the query specifications and displays a record with the fields that will be used in the column report, as shown in Figure 9-13.

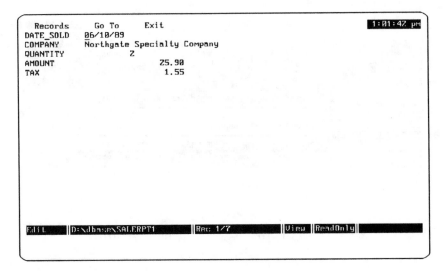

Figure 9-13. Query uses the five fields needed for the report.

Exit the Query mode by entering

    [Alt-e] e

Enter the Report Form Design mode

    [right arrow] *(2 times)*
     ⏎

Use the Quick Layout option to create a column report, based on the specifications controlled by the current query.

    ⏎ *(2 times)*

The program automatically generates the column report specifications, which include all the fields in the query, and summary totals for all the numeric fields included in the query. The Report Form layout is shown in Figure 9-14. The Quick Layout option allows you to quickly convert Query mode specifications into a formal column report.

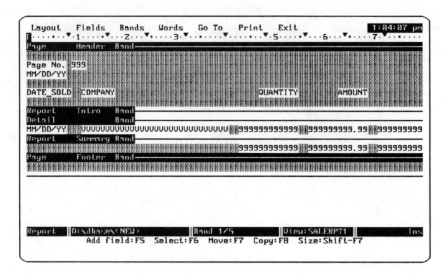

Figure 9-14. Report form automatically generated using query specifications.

Print the report.

       [Alt-p] ⏎

The report will look like this:

```
Page No.       1
06/09/89

DATE_SOLD    COMPANY                      QUANTITY   AMOUNT    TAX

06/10/89     Northgate Specialty Company      2       25.90    1.55
06/15/89     Genie Light and Magic           10      219.50   13.17
06/17/89     House of Magic                   5      299.75   17.99
06/20/89     Clay's House of Fun             10       59.50    3.57
06/22/89     House of Magic                   4       51.80    3.11
06/22/89     Northgate Specialty Company      1       12.95    0.78
06/25/89     Northgate Specialty Company      5      299.75   17.99
                                             37      969.15   58.15
```

Save the report by entering

       [Alt-e] s
       salerpt1 ⏎

Mailmerge Reports

When the data from all the databases in the ACCOUNTS catalog are linked, as they are in the queries you have just created, you have 21 fields of information available. These fields contain sufficient information to fill out a business form, such as a sales invoice.

You might want to use dBASE IV to print invoice forms for each sale recorded in the SALES database file. The dBASE IV Report Generator supports three types of reports. You have already used column and form reports. The third is a *mailmerge* report. The name mailmerge is borrowed from word-processing applications in which lists of data are merged into word-processing documents, to create forms and form letters. dBASE IV returns the compliment by including a mailmerge report in the database program.

A mailmerge report allows you to type a document similarly to the way you would create a document with a word-processing program. When you want to insert information contained in a database field, you insert a field reference into the text.

The mailmerge report form assumes that you want to create documents in which each record will print an entire page. dBASE IV will automatically insert a page break at the end of every record printed, during a mailmerge report.

In this case, you can use the mailmerge report to print an invoice for each sale in the sales database. In order to allow you to draw information from all 21 fields, you need to create a query that will link the files and make available all the fields.

Begin by creating this query.

```
[left  arrow] (2 times)
[down  arrow]
  ↵
```

Insert the first database, SALES into the query.

```
  ↵
  s ↵
```

Place all the fields from this database into the view skeleton.

```
[F5]
```

Repeat the operation for the BUYERS and PRODUCTS databases.

```
[Alt-L]  a
b ↵
[F5]
```

The program stops and displays a box that reads: "Enter field name: ACCOUNT_NO". Recall that you already placed a field called ACCOUNT_NO into the view from the SALES database. The dBASE IV Query mode requires that you enter a unique name for this second field. Enter

> [Home] [Ctrl-y]
> acct ↵

Add the fields from the PRODUCTS database to the query.

> [Alt-L] a p ↵
> [F5]

There is a conflict again, this time with the ID field. Enter a view name for this field.

> prod ↵

The next step is to link the database files. Return to the SALES file skeleton and link it to the BUYERS database on the ACCOUNT_NO field. Try this on your own. The correct command can be found at the end of the chapter under Ex-1.

Create a link between the SALES database and the PRODUCTS database in the ID field. Try this on your own. The correct command can be found at the end of the chapter under Ex-2.

When you are finished, the Query mode display should look like Figure 9-15.

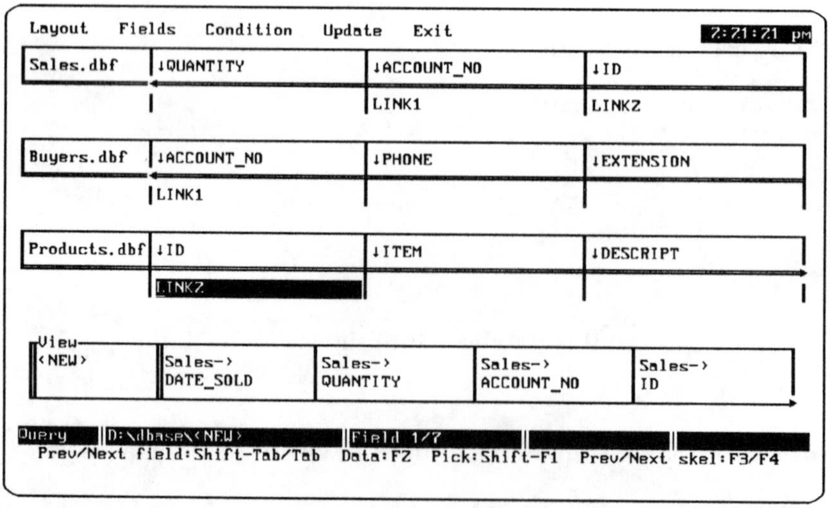

Figure 9-15. Databases linked and all fields placed into the view skeleton.

Activate the settings in this query by entering

> [F2]

The screen displays the seven records in the SALES database, along with data from all the linked fields. Keep in mind that it was necessary to activate the query by displaying the data so these fields would be available in the Design Report mode. Exit the display and save the query under the name INVOICE.

```
[Alt-e] t
[Alt-e] s
invoice ⏎
```

A Mailmerge Report Layout

The query provides the logical support for the report form. The query links the databases so that each record in the SALES database has all 21 fields of information available. You can now create a mailmerge report that places this information into an arrangement that looks like an invoice.

To create a mailmerge report, enter the Report Design mode.

```
[right  arrow](2 times)
⏎
```

Use the Quick Layout option to create a Mailmerge report.

```
⏎
m
```

The program displays a blank mailmarge report layout. It is interesting to note that when you use the Mailmerge Quick Layout option, the program does not automatically insert fields. The purpose of this option is to set the bands for a mailmerge layout. Unlike the column and form Quick Layout options, which produce ready to run reports, the Mailmerge option requires further manipulation.

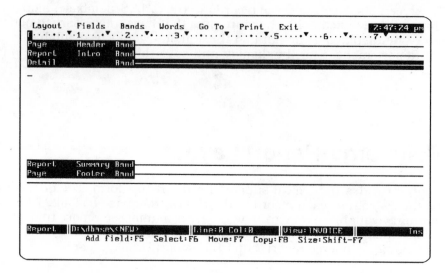

Figure 9-16. Blank mailmerge report layout screen.

A mailmerge report blends text and other types of information, and inserts them using fields or calculated fields. Begin the top of the page with the name and address of the company. Enter

```
↵ (2 times)
Invoice From: ↵
↵
The LaFish Novelty Company ↵
100 West Lake Drive ↵
Modesto, CA 94303 ↵
415-555-7878 ↵
↵ (2 times)
```

The next address block should be that of the company being invoiced.

```
To: ↵
↵
```

This requires the insertion of a field. Begin with the company field. Enter

```
[F5]
```

The field list includes all the fields contained in the three linked-database files, as shown in Figure 9-17.

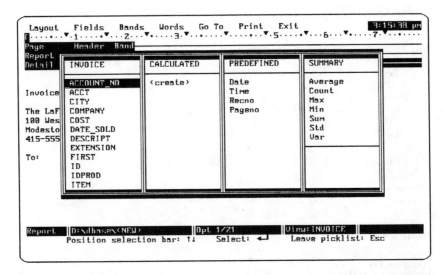

Figure 9-17. [F5] displays a list of all 21 fields from the 3 linked database files.

Select the COMPANY field.

```
co ↵
[Ctrl-End]
```

The field template appears on the work surface. Look at the bottom of the screen. The last line shows the name of the field BUYERS->COMPANY. The alias form of the name indicates from which database the data is to be drawn.

Place the street address on the next line down.

```
[down arrow]
 [F5] str ↵
 [Ctrl-End]
```

Next insert, the CITY, STATE and ZIP fields. Try this on your own. The correct commands can be found at the end of the chapter, under Ex-3.

Continue the mailmerge document by inserting the first and last name of the buyer.

```
[down arrow](5 times)
 Contact:
 [spacebar]
 [F5] f ↵
 [Ctrl-End]
[right arrow][spacebar]
 1 ↵
 [Ctrl-End]
```

With the name entered, add the phone number and extension.

```
[down arrow]
 Phone:
 [spacebar]
 [F5] p ↵
 [Ctrl-End]
[down arrow][spacebar]
 Extn: [spacebar]
 [F5] e ↵
 [Ctrl-End]
```

The report layout should look like Figure 9-18.

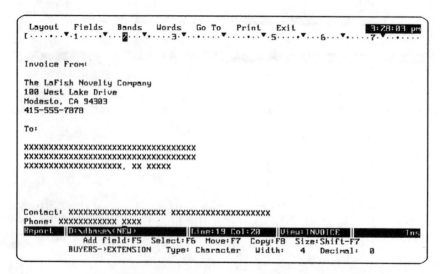

Figure 9-18. Top section of mailmerge report form.

The next section deals with information specifically related to the sale. Begin with the date. Enter

```
[down arrow](2 times)
 Date of Purchase: [spacebar]
 [F5] d ↵
 [Ctrl-End]
[right arrow] ↵
 ↵ (2 times)
```

Enter the information about the item and its description.

```
 Item: ↵
 [F5] it ↵
 [Ctrl-End]
[right arrow] ↵
 [F5] de ↵
 [Ctrl-End]
[right arrow] ↵
 ↵ (2 times)
```

The final section of the report prints the numeric information about the sale. The first two lines are the quantity and price of the item.

```
Quantity [Tab]
[F5] q ↵
```

Before you place the field, change the Picture function to remove the T (Trim) function from it. This allows the numeric data to align in a vertical column. If the T Picture function is turned on, the values align as far to the left as possible, distorting the vertical column of numbers. You need to do this with all the values, so they print in a vertical column.

```
p t [Ctrl-End]
[Ctrl-End]
[right arrow]↵
Price/item [Tab]
[F5] pr ↵
p t [Ctrl-End]
[Ctrl-End]
[right arrow]↵
```

The next three fields require the creation of calculated fields. These fields will calculate the total amount of the items, the sales tax at 6%, and the grand total.

```
Total Amount [Tab]
[F5][right arrow]↵
```

Enter the formula to calculate the total amount.

```
e
price*quantity ↵
p t [Ctrl-End]
[Ctrl-End]
[right arrow]↵
```

Next, create a field that will calculate the sales tax on the total amount. Try this on your own. The correct command can be found at the end of the chapter, under Ex-4.

Finally, insert a calculated field that will show the grand total, including the sales tax. Enter

```
Grand Total [Tab]
[F5][right arrow]↵
e
price*quantity*1.06 ↵
p t [Ctrl-End]
[Ctrl-End]
```

The Report Design work surface will look like Figure 9-19.

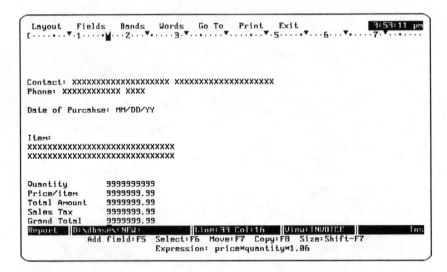

Figure 9-19. Mailmerge report with numeric and calculated fields inserted.

You can proof the report by displaying the results on the screen.

    [Alt-p] v

```
Invoice From:

The LaFish Novelty Company
100 West Lake Drive
Modesto, CA 94303
415-555-7878

To:

Northgate Specialty Company
303 W. Milford St.
Richmond, VA 23229




Contact: Simon O'Keefe
Phone: 804-555-8965

Date of Purchase: 06/10/89

_           Cancel viewing: ESC,  Continue viewing: SPACEBAR
```

Figure 9-20. Mailmerge report displayed on the screen.

Use the [spacebar] to scroll through the report one screen at a time, or press [Esc] to terminate the display. Each record in the SALES database will generate a separate invoice form.

Wraparound Text

Another feature that is characteristic of a mailmerge report is the insertion of field information in wraparound, paragraph-type text. This allows you to use the mailmarge report to create not just forms, but form letters. You can create an entire mailmerge report by entering paragraph text, with fields inserted where needed.

As an illustration of this technique, you can insert a paragraph at the bottom of the invoice form. Often, invoice forms carry special messages that you want to convey to your customers. Insert a few blank lines into the report form.

```
[End]
⏎ (2 times)
```

When you want to enter paragraph-type text, you must set the margins to create a column to wrap the text lines. The normal page margins used by a report form are usually too wide for paragraph text. You can change the margins by using the Modify Ruler command found on the Words menu. Enter

```
[Alt-w] m
```

The cursor moves to the ruler line at the top of the Report Layout display. The current left margin is represented by the [character, and the right margin—which is beyond the right edge of the screen—is represented by a] character. To change the location of a margin, move the cursor to the column where you want the margin set, and type the character [or]. Enter

```
[Tab] (2 times)
[
```

The left margin is set at column 16. Move the cursor to column 56 by entering

```
[Tab] (5 times)
]
```

You have now set left and right margins that will wrap text into lines between columns 16 and 56. Return to the work surface by entering

```
⏎
```

Enter the following text. Do not be concerned about the line endings because dBASE IV will use the margins you have set to control them. Enter

We are pleased to announce that you can now fax in your orders 24 hours a day by calling 1-800-777-1212. Please include your account number,

You can insert the correct account number into the paragraph. Enter

```
[spacebar]
[F5]
┘
[Ctrl-End]
[End]
```

The field is inserted into the paragraph. When the report is printed, the account number will be placed in this position in the paragraph. Keep in mind that if the data inserted has fewer characters than the template shows, the T Picture function will trim the blanks from the field.

Complete the rest of the paragraph by entering

```
.This will help us to process your order more quickly.
```

Save the report form by entering

```
[Alt-e] s
invoice ┘
```

The creation of this report will take longer than usual because the report program generated will contain about 500 lines of dBASE IV program code. When completed, you can use the report form to print the invoices. Enter

```
┘ (3 times)
```

Below is a sample of what the first and last pages of the invoice printout will look like.

First Page:

Invoice From:

The LaFish Novelty Company
100 West Lake Drive
Modesto, CA 94303
415-555-7878

To:

Northgate Specialty Company
303 W. Milford St.
Richmond, VA 23229

Contact: Simon O'Keefe
Phone: 804-555-8965
Date of Purchase: 06/10/89

Item:
Fake blood capsules
Simulates bleeding - washable

Quantity   2
Price/item   12.95
Total Amount   25.90
Sales Tax   1.55
Grand Total   27.45

We are pleased to announce that you can
now fax in your orders 24 hours a day by
calling 1-800-777-1212. Please include
your account number, 103. This will help
us to process your order more quickly.

Last Page:

```
Invoice From:

The LaFish Novelty Company
100 West Lake Drive
Modesto, CA 94303
415-555-7878

To:

Northgate Specialty Company
303 W. Milford St.
Richmond, VA 23229


Contact: Simon O'Keefe
Phone: 804-555-8965

Date of Purchase: 06/25/89


Item:
Knotted scarves
Used for scarf trick


Quantity                5
Price/item          59.95
Total Amount       299.75
Sales Tax           17.99
Grand Total        317.74
```

> We are pleased to announce that you can
> now fax in your orders 24 hours a day by
> calling 1-800-777-1212. Please include
> your account number, 103. This will help
> us to process your order more quickly.

The mailmerge report provides the flexibility to create reports of almost any type, that combine text with data stored in the database fields.

If you have preprinted forms, such as invoice forms, you can use the Mailmerge Document layout to simply insert the fields at the required location. Pre-printed forms designed for use with computer printers are usually supplied with a grid map, which helps you find the correct row and column location for specific data items. The row and column locations indicated on the status line of the Report Form Design mode can be used to place fields properly on the preprinted form.

dBASE IV assumes 11 inches for the page length of preprinted forms. Some preprinted forms may vary. Note that page length is set in terms of the number of lines per page. The standard line height is 1/6" per line. This means a 7" invoice would have a page length of 42 lines (6 times 7). You can save the setup for the printer in a Print form file. For more information about printing see chapter 10.

Data Entry with Multiple Databases

When you enter data into the SALES database, you do so by using the account numbers and the product ID numbers. The query display and the report forms allow you to relate data in different files, so that the links established with the SALES database can draw related information from other database files.

It might be useful to see related information as you enter data. This can be done using a screen form to display the related data, along with the raw data entered into the SALES database. Ostensibly, this seems like a fairly easy thing to accomplish. Like the report form, you could create a screen form that uses all 21 fields associated with the INVOICE query. As an example, create a screen form that is related to the current query, INVOICE.

Activate the Screen Form Design mode.

        [left arrow]⏎

In order to save time, use the Quick layout option. Enter

        ⏎

The program automatically lists all 21 fields in a column on the left of the screen display.

The Quick Layout option inserts a blank line at the top of the form. This line is left blank in order to leave room to display the menu bar. Recall that the screen forms can contain a maximum of 22 lines of information per page. This means with the first line left blank, there is just enough room—21 lines—to display all the fields on a single page.

Save the screen form.

        [Alt-e] s
        form1 ⏎

Activate the form by entering

        [F2]

All 21 fields of data are displayed for the first record in the SALES database.

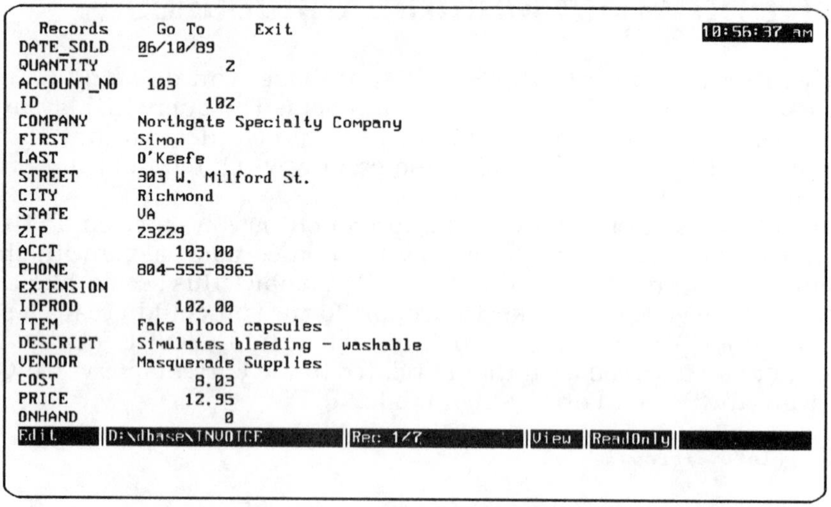

```
    Records      Go To     Exit                                    10:56:37 am
DATE_SOLD    06/10/89
QUANTITY                Z
ACCOUNT_NO   103
ID                 102
COMPANY      Northgate Specialty Company
FIRST        Simon
LAST         O'Keefe
STREET       303 W. Milford St.
CITY         Richmond
STATE        VA
ZIP          23229
ACCT             103.00
PHONE        804-555-8965
EXTENSION
IDPROD           102.00
ITEM         Fake blood capsules
DESCRIPT     Simulates bleeding - washable
VENDOR       Masquerade Supplies
COST              8.03
PRICE            12.95
ONHAND              0
Edit      | D:\dbase\INVOICE           | Rec: 1/7         | View | ReadOnly|
```

Figure 9-21. Screen form display all 21 related fields.

Display the next record in the database by entering

>   [PgDn]

There is one problem with the screen form. When dBASE IV creates a query with linked fields, the query is designated as a ReadOnly query. This means the data can be displayed or printed, but you cannot add or change records while the query is active. This limitation is not severe. You can work around it by entering data into the standard SALES entry screen, then using the ReadOnly query for display of output of the linked data. However, it is possible to create an entry screen that combines actual data entry with linked information. To create such a query and screen form you will need to operate dBASE IV from the Dot Prompt mode. The procedures are more complicated than those available in the Control Center, but they offer more power and flexibility.

Exit the current display.

>   [Alt-e] e

Exit the Control Center by entering

>   [Alt-e] e

Database Work Areas

When you are working in the Control Center, you are insulated from the dBASE IV operations that make it possible to carry out various tasks. Your goal is to create a screen form into which SALES information can be entered or edited, but which will also display information linked to records in the

BUYERS and PRODUCTS databases. You cannot accomplish this goal through the Control Center because the it automatically restricts access to multiple databases to ReadOnly operations. This automatic feature prevents you from creating a screen form that has both linked databases and data entry qualities.

In dBASE IV, the Control Center is not equipped to handle the creation of this type of screen display. But the full set of dBASE IV commands available in the Dot Prompt mode does have the power to create the screen form in question. In order to create this screen form, you need to learn the following dBASE IV Dot Prompt techniques:

1. Using database work areas.
2. Setting relations between databases.
3. Creating a query from the Dot Prompt.
4. Creating a screen form from the Dot Prompt.

The first step is to understand how dBASE IV allows you to work with more than 1 database file at a time. Begin by closing all the open database files. Enter

      `CLOSE ALL ⤶`

You learned in Chapter 4 that when you want to open a database file in the Dot Prompt mode, you use the USE command. For example to open the BUYERS database, you would enter

      `USE buyers ⤶`

When you enter this command, the status line shows the name of the database file, e.g. C:\DBASE\BUYERS. What would happen if you opened the PRODUCTS database? Enter

      `USE products ⤶`

The name of the PRODUCTS database appears on the status line, in place of the BUYERS database. When the USE command is applied in this way, the database files that you open, are opened *consecutively*. This means when you open the PRODUCTS database, any database file already open (e.g. BUYERS) is automatically closed, in order to allow the new file to be opened.

If this were the only way in which the USE command operated, then dBASE IV would not be able to work with more than one database at a time, and no links between database files could be created.

What makes multiple-database operations possible is the concept of *work areas*. A work area is space allocated in the memory of the computer for handling the input and output of information to a specific database file. When you are working in the Query mode, dBASE IV displays a *file skeleton* to represent the work area for each open database.

In the Dot Prompt mode, dBASE IV does not display visual models of what is going on. Instead of showing file skeletons, the work areas are referred to by letter or number. dBASE IV has a limit of 10 work areas, which can be referred to as 1 through 10, or A through J. By default, the first work area used is Work Area 1 or A. When you enter the command USE products, dBASE IV assumes that you mean to open the file in Work Area 1.

The trick to multiple-database operations is to use the IN clause with the USE command. The IN clause allows you to designate a work area other than the current one. When you open files in different work areas, you have access to all the fields in all the databases, because they are opened *parallel* to each other, instead of consecutively.

Suppose you wanted to open the SALES, BUYERS, and PRODUCTS databases, at the same time. You would have to use three USE commands, each one placing the database in a different work area. Enter

```
USE sales ⏎
USE buyers IN 2 ⏎
USE products IN 3 ⏎
```

In the first command, USE sales, the IN clause was omitted because the program assumes Work Area 1.

If you use the DISPLAY STATUS command, you will see that all three databases are open at the same time, in different work areas.

```
DISPLAY STATUS ⏎
```

The display lists the three databases and the index orders associated with each. The information displayed by the status listing is similar in content, but very different from the information displayed in the Query mode.

```
Currently Selected Database:
Select area: 1, Database in Use: D:\DBASE\SALES.DBF   Alias:
SALES
   Production   MDX file:  D:\DBASE\SALES.MDX
   Index TAG:    DATE_SOLD  Key: DATE_SOLD
                 Lock list:

Select area: 2, Database in Use: D:\DBASE\BUYERS.DBF   Alias:
BUYERS
   Production   MDX file:  D:\DBASE\BUYERS.MDX
        Index TAG:    COMPANY  Key: COMPANY
        Index TAG:    LAST  Key: LAST
        Index TAG:    ACCOUNT_NO  Key: ACCOUNT_NO
        Lock list:

Select area: 3, Database in Use: D:\DBASE\PRODUCTS.DBF   Alias:
PRODUCTS
   Production   MDX file:  D:\DBASE\PRODUCTS.MDX
        Index TAG:    VENDOR  Key: VENDOR
        Index TAG:    ITEM  Key: ITEM
        Index TAG:    ID Key: ID
        Lock list:
```

If you look carefully at the index tags listed under BUYERS, you will notice that a new tag has been added since you created the file in Chapter 9. When you created the file, you designated only the COMPANY and LAST fields as index fields. Now, the ACCOUNT_NO field has also been indexed.

This additional index field is the result of the links created between the BUYERS and the SALES files. As you will see, an index order for the linked field is required when two databases are linked. Since you did not initially designate this field as a index field, the query modified the file's structure in order to process the link correctly.

Another important piece of information is on the line that reads "Currently Selected Database". This line appears before the information about the database in Work Area 1. The *selected* database is the *default* database. This means if you enter a command, dBASE IV will assume that you want to operate on the selected database, rather than the database opened in other work areas. dBASE IV normally assumes that Work Area 1 contains the selected database. In this example, the SALES database is the selected database because it was opened in Work Area 1.

Exit the display listing by entering

       [Esc]

With three databases open you can display information from any one of the 21 fields contained in them. dBASE IV has a handy command that can be used to display a field, or a list of fields. The command is the ? command (sometimes called *print* because of its similarity to the Print command in the BASIC language). To display the contents of the DATE_SOLD and QUANTITY fields, enter

       ? date_sold,quantity ↵

The program displays 06/10/89 and 2, the contents of the fields. Suppose you wanted to print data stored in fields of the other open databases, such as the FIRST and LAST fields in the BUYERS database. Enter

       ? first,last ↵

dBASE IV displays an error message box. The message reads, "Variable not found". This means the program cannot locate the fields specified in the command because the fieldnames FIRST and LAST are not specific enough. As with the USE command, the program assumes any field references are made to fields that are contained in the database in Work Area 1. The FIRST and LAST fields are part of the BUYERS database open in Work Area 2. If the fields you want to use are not in the current work area, in this case Work Area 1, you must refer to the fields by their *alias* name. Exit the error box by entering

       ↵

An alias is a prefix that can be used with fields to indicate the work area in which they can be found. You can write the alias name in three ways: alias number (1-10), alias letter (A-J), or alias name. By default the alias name is the same as the database name. For example, to display the contents of the FIRST field in the BUYERS database, you would enter

> `? buyers->first` ⏎

The program returns the name Janice from the FIRST field in the BUYERS database. You can also refer to the work area by letter. For example, the BUYERS database is in Work Area B. Enter

> `? b->first` ⏎

Both commands produce the same result. The alias name has the advantage of selecting the work area by database name. However, when you know the work area for a particular database, you can reduce your typing by using the alias letter in place of the full alias name.

Like file- and fieldnames, alias names are not subject to the 4-character abbreviation rule. Alias names must be entered full-length whenever they used.

Print the values for the ACCOUNT_NO and ID fields in all the databases.

> `? account_no,id,b->account_no,c->id` ⏎

The command displays the following information:

> `103     102 100     100`

The values in the SALES database do not match the values in the BUYERS or in the PRODUCTS databases. The values printed are simply the contents of the first records in each of the open databases. While it is true that you have access to all the fields in the open databases, there is no *relationship* between the records of any one database and the others. When databases are opened, the record pointers in each database are *independent* of the others. For example, if you were to list all the records in the current database (i.e. move the record pointer through the SALES file) the other database files, BUYERS and PRODUCTS, would be unaffected. Enter

> `LIST date_sold,account_no,b->account_no,b->company` ⏎

Note that the two fields drawn from Work Area 1, DATE_SOL and ACCOUNT_NO, change for each record on the list. However the values drawn from Work Area B, ACCOUNT_NO and COMPANY, remain the same throughout the entire listing. The records in the currently selected database are processed in sequence, while the data drawn from the other databases remain the data stored in the first record.

```
Record#  date_sold   account_no   b->account_no  b->company
      1  06/10/89          103            100    House of Magic
      2  06/15/89          101            100    House of Magic
      3  06/17/89          100            100    House of Magic
      4  06/20/89          102            100    House of Magic
      5  06/22/89          100            100    House of Magic
      6  06/22/89          103            100    House of Magic
      7  06/25/89          103            100    House of Magic
```

Setting Relations

dBASE IV doesn't move the pointer in all the databases at the same time, because doing so would make very little sense. There is no reason to assume that all the databases have the same number of records. You cannot assume that all the second records belong together, nor can you assume that all the first records belong together. What is needed is a logical link between the data in each database, to link together records that logically belong together. This is what the Query mode accomplished when you linked the databases by key fields.

In the Dot Prompt mode, links between files are established using the SET RELATION TO command. This command establishes links in different databases. Once a link has been established, dBASE IV has a method by which pointer movement in one database can be related to pointer movement in another database. For example, if a relation is set on the ACCOUNT_NO fields in SALES and BUYERS, then dBASE IV will locate the record in BUYERS that contains an account number matching the account number in the current record. The data drawn from both SALES and BUYERS will create a logical unit, because the files are logically related.

There is one important prerequisite to creating a relation between two database files. The supporting database—in this example, BUYERS or PRODUCTS —*must* be indexed on the linking field. The DISPLAY STATUS listing shows that the BUYERS database contains an index tag for the ACCOUNT_NO field, and that the BUYERS database contains an index tag for the ID field.

As mentioned previously, the ACCOUNT_NO index tag in the BUYERS database was not designated in the file structure as an index field. dBASE IV automatically modified the file's structure when you created a query that linked the SALES database to that field. Had this not been the cause, you would have to create an index tag in that file using the command INDEX ON account_no TAG account_no OF buyers.

It is not sufficient that the index tags exist in the respective files. The tags must be activated so that they are the master index orders for the databases. The master index tag is the one that actually controls the sequence of the records. However, the reason the index file is so important to linking files is that dBASE IV can search the master index at a high rate of speed. In

Chapter 4 you learned that when a search is performed on an indexed database (e.g. the FIND command) the program can determine very quickly if the matching record exists, and if so, which record matches the search key. When databases are linked, the program must constantly search the supporting databases for the records that match the values in the linked fields of the master database.

You can select a master index when you open a database by using the ORDER clause. For example, to create a relation between SALES and BUYERS on the ACCOUNT_NO field, you need to open the file with the AC-COUNT_NO tag designated as the master index. Enter

```
USE buyers IN 2 ORDER account_no ⏎
```

The program displays the message "Master Index: ACCOUNT_NO" to confirm the activation of the index tag, along with the opening of the database.

The PRODUCTS database must be opened with the ID tag activated as the master index. Enter

```
USE products IN 3 ORDER id ⏎
```

Once the master indexes are activated in the supporting databases, you can use the SET RELATION TO command to link the files.

The SET RELATION command is *always* executed from the master (or parent) database. The command specifies the field in the master database that is to be linked to the supporting database. The SET RELATION command has the following general form:

SET RELATION TO *expression* INTO *alias*

In this case, you want to link the ACCOUNT_NO field to the BUYERS database. Enter

```
SET RELATION TO account_no INTO buyers ⏎
```

There is no link between the value in the ACCOUNT_NO field in the SALES database, and the record pointer in the BUYERS database. For each value in the SALES ACCOUNT_NO field, dBASE IV will search the BUYERS field for a record with the corresponding value. If you were to list fields from the SALES and BUYERS databases, you would find that the records are linked as they were in the linked query.

Enter

```
LIST account_no,buyers->account_no ⏎
```

The command lists two identical columns of values.

Record#	account_no	buyers->account_no
1	103	103
2	101	101
3	100	100
4	102	102
5	100	100
6	103	103
7	103	103

This is important because it demonstrates that the link is working correctly. For each value in the ACCOUNT_NO field of the SALES database, the program finds a corresponding record in the BUYERS database. Of course, the record in the BUYERS database is not always unique. The same record may match several sales. The command below uses the RECNO( ) function to list the numbers of the records used in each database. Enter

```
LIST recno( ),recno("buyers")  ⏎
```

Record#	recno( )	recno("buyers")
1	1	4
2	2	2
3	3	1
4	4	3
5	5	1
6	6	4
7	7	4

Notice that the alias name, "buyers" in the RECNO( ) function is used to refer to the record number of an unselected database. The listing also demonstrates how the records in the BUYERS database are matched to the ACCOUNT_NO values of the master database. The commands shown above can be used to test the validity of a relation. If you have made an error, the listings will provide a clue as to what is wrong. For example, if the supporting database is not indexed, or indexed improperly, the column will be blank.

Now that you have correctly set the relation, list the data based on that relation.

```
LIST date,b->company,b->phone  ⏎
```

The data are listed with the correct company names and phone numbers.

Linking by Expression

The Query mode display gives the impression that a database link is established between two fields. In fact, the SET RELATION command is much more flexible. The value used for the master file portion of the link can be any valid dBASE IV expression. Also note that the command does not specify the field in the supporting database to which it is linked. It only specifies the alias name of the database. This is because the link is made, not to a field, but to the key expression used for the current master index file that is active in the supporting database.

This means it is possible to link two databases on the basis of data not directly entered into the database, but calculated by some expression. For example, suppose you wanted to link two files that contained date fields. However, the supporting file contains one record for each month, rather than records matching each individual date. In this case, the master database would set the relation, not on the date field, but on the MONTH( ) or CMONTH( ) value of the date: SET RELATION TO CMONTH(date) INTO support.

The supporting database would be indexed on a similar expression: INDEX ON CMONTH(date) TAG month OF support.

The relation would function because the data in both expressions would be the names of the months. The relation would match records based on data, in this case, the month names, even though the data does not explicitly appear in either database.

To complete the setup, you must link the ID field to the PRODUCTS database. Keep in mind that you also want to maintain the link between ACCOUNT_NO and BUYERS. The SET RELATION command will overwrite any previous relations. For example, if you entered the following two commands, the second would overwrite the effect of the first, leaving only one relation between ID and PRODUCTS:

```
SET RELATION TO account_no INTO buyers ⏎
SET RELATION TO id INTO products ⏎
```

Instead, if you wanted to set multiple relations from the same master database, they must be entered in a single command with a list of relations. The order in which the relations are listed is not significant. Enter

```
SET RELATION TO account_no INTO buyers,id INTO products ⏎
```

Listing records can indicate whether the relation is working correctly; however, reading a list of values can be quite cumbersome when the database has more than a few records. In large databases, you will quickly be lost trying to read all the values. A more direct way to check if the relation is locating matching records, is to ask the program to count the number of records that find related records in the supporting databases. You can use the COUNT command to summarize the results by counting all the records in which the ACCOUNT_NO value in SALES, matches the value in the related database. Enter

       `COUNT FOR account_no=b->account_no` ↵

Perhaps a better way is to count the records, if any, that do not match. Enter

       `COUNT FOR .NOT.account_no=b->account_no` ↵

When no records are counted you can assume that all the records in the master database have found a corresponding record in the supporting database. Test the relation between ID and PRODUCTS.

       `COUNT FOR .NOT.id=b->id` ↵

Both relations have been correctly established.

Editing Fields

You have now established the same types of links between files, as those you created in the Query mode, using the Create Link command. However, there is one very important difference. When files are linked in the Query mode, any attempt to browse or edit the linked fields will create a ReadOnly display in which no editing is permitted.

    You can select to edit any group of fields from among the 21 available fields. Enter

       `EDIT FIELDS date_sold,quantity,b->company,c->item` ↵

The program displays the Edit mode with four fields. What is unusual about this display is that the fields are not part of a single database, but are drawn from three different, related databases.

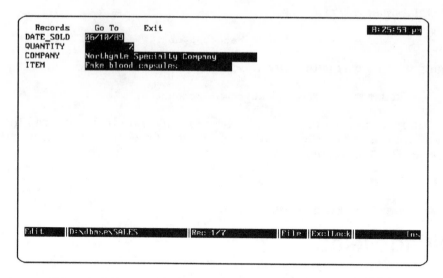

Figure 9-22. Edit display with fields from related databases.

The relations you have created in this chapter allow you to edit data, as well as display it. Change the quantity to 4. Enter

        [down arrow]4 ↵

This change will become part of the SALES database. Change the name of the item.

        [down arrow][Ctrl-y]
        Vampire Teeth

The change appears to be made to the ITEM field in Record 1. But in reality, the ITEM field belongs to another database. If you make a change in this field, the new value will be recorded in the database from which the field is drawn. The effect of this change can be more than you expect. In changing the contents of the ITEM field, you change the value for all SALES records linked to the same item. Move forward in the database to Record 5. Enter

        [PgDn] *(4 times)*

The ITEM field in this record shows Vampire Teeth. This must be the result of the change made in the ITEM field in Record 1, because prior to that, Vampire Teeth had not been entered into any of the records, in any of the databases.

If you change the ITEM field in this record, all the records linked to the same item will also change. Enter

        [down arrow] *(2 times)*
         [Ctrl-y]
         Woopie Cushion

Return to Record 1. Enter

>   [Alt-g] t

The change made in the ITEM field flows through to Record 1, because both of the SALES records are linked to the same PRODUCTS record.
Exit the Edit mode.

>   [Alt-e] e

Creating a Multiple Database Field List

When working with multiple databases, you will frequently want to work with a set of fields drawn from several related databases. In the previous Edit command, you used the Fields clause to specify which fields from the related databases you wanted to edit. The SET FIELDS command placed into memory a list of fields. This field list was automatically available to a number of dBASE IV commands that used a Fields clause, such as EDIT, LIST, CREATE SCREEN, CREATE REPORT, etc.

The SET FIELDS command is useful in single database operations, and even more so in multiple-database operations, in which you have a large number of fields in several different work areas. For example, you might create a set of key fields in the related databases you want to work with. Enter

>   SET FIELDS TO date_sold,b->company,quantity,c->item,c->price   ↵

The command establishes a set of fields that will be affected by commands, if no specific Field clause is used. Enter

>   EDIT ↵

The display contains the five fields specified in the SET FIELD list.

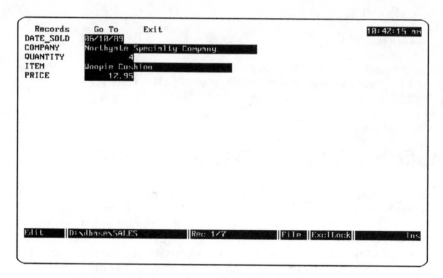

Figure 9-23. Currently field list activated by the Edit command.

Exit the display.

[Esc]

The SET FIELDS list is cumulative. This means if you enter another SET FIELDS command the fieldnames will be added to the current list. Suppose you wanted to include the PHONE and DESCRIPTION fields. Enter

SET FIELDS TO b->phone,c->descript ⏎

Display the Edit mode by entering

EDIT ⏎

Note that the description of the product no longer matches the item, because you edited the item name.

This time there are seven fields displayed with the two newest fields added to the list. Note that the new fields follow the fields designated in the previous command. Exit the display by entering

[Esc]

The SET FIELDS command has two useful options. One allows you to designate a field as Read Only by using the /R switch. The other allows you to create a Read Only field, based on a calculation. For example, suppose you wanted to prevent accidental alteration of the COST of the item. In addition, you wanted to display a field that showed the value of the sale,

PRICE * AMOUNT. You can create a calculated field by adding a full expression in the form:

calculate_field = expression

The term switch is used to refer to an option entered with a / and a letter (e.g. /R for Read Only). This option is used in dBASE IV when a command contains a list of fields. The switch allows you to designate which individual fields within the list will be affected by this option. Switches are common in programs executed from DOS. For example, the /W switch creates a wide display when used with the DOS command, DIR (e.g. DIR/W).

Using the PRICE field in another SET FIELDS command will overwrite the previous usage of the field. Enter

```
SET FIELDS TO c->cost/r,amount=c->price*quantity    ↵
```

Display the Edit mode.

```
EDIT ↵
```

The program displays the COST field in normal video, indicating it is a Read Only field. The calculated field, which is always Read Only, is also displayed. Exit the Edit mode by entering

```
[Esc]
```

The SET FIELDS command also has an ON option. When the ON option is used, you can refer to fields within the current fields list, without using the alias name. Utilizing this option makes it simpler to enter commands that use the names of fields already in the field list. Enter

```
SET FIELDS ON ↵
```

As an example of how this option works, create a field that will calculate the profit. Notice that the alias names are omitted from the commands

```
SET FIELDS TO profit=quantity*(price-cost)    ↵
EDIT ↵
```

The calculated field appears on the Edit mode display, indicating the command was able to locate the fields without the alias names because of the SET FIELDS ON command.

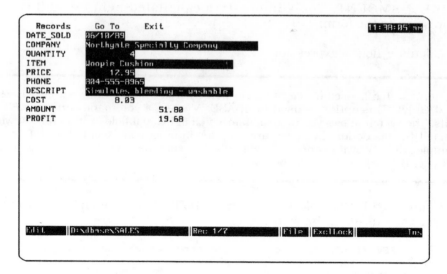

Figure 9-24. Calculated fields displayed in Edit mode.

Return to the Dot Prompt mode by entering

[Esc]

A side benefit of the SET FIELDS ON command is that the structure of the file, as displayed using DISPLAY STRUCTURE, shows active fields with a > character. Enter

    LIST STRUCTURE ⏎

Field	Field Name	Type	Width	Dec	Index
1	>DATE_SOLD	Date	8		Y
2	>QUANTITY	Numeric	10		N
3	ACCOUNT_NO	Numeric	4		N
4	ID	Numeric	10		N

To return to normal field operations, enter the SET FIELDS TO command with no list. Enter

    SET FIELDS TO ⏎

Custom Screen Forms with Multiple Databases

Editing records with fields from several databases can be a bit tricky. If you edit a field from a supporting database, you may find that you have changed values in a number of related records, not just in the records displayed on the screen. While the potential to perform such operations is interesting, in most cases you should limit editing to those fields that are part of the master or parent database. However, it would be very useful to have the fields from the linked database display information in a Read Only format.

By combining the editing of fields from the master with the display of information from the related databases, you gain the best of both worlds. A single display shows you the data to which the master records are linked, and all accidental alterations to the supporting database files are prevented.

You can use the SET FIELDS command with EDIT to achieve this type of display. Another alternative is to create a screen form using the Screen Form Design mode. You can arrange the fields in any way you like, and use Edit Options to determine which fields can be edited. The advantage of the screen form is that it gives you greater control over placement and format of fields and additional text.

You can access the Screen Form Design mode from the Dot Prompt mode by using the CREATE SCREEN command. However, when using multiple databases, you must use the SET FIELDS command to create a full list of the fields you want to use in the screen form. If you were to enter CREATE SCREEN without using SET FIELDS, you would be limited to the fields in the currently selected database. When you display the field list using [F5], dBASE IV would only list the four fields contained in the SALES database.

Using the ALL clause is a quick way to add the remaining fields. Enter

```
SET FIELDS TO ALL ↵
```

Note that the command only adds fields from the currently selected database. However, you can change the selected database using the SELECT command. Enter

```
SELECT buyers ↵
```

You have changed the active database to the BUYERS database in Work Area 2. You need to have access to the COMPANY, FIRST, and LAST fields in the screen form. Add these fields to the list. Because the SELECT command has designated the BUYERS database, it is not necessary to use alias names with the fieldnames, so long as they are in the current database.

```
SET FIELDS TO company,first,last ↵
```

Repeat the process to add the PRICE field from PRODUCTS.

```
SELECT products ↲
SET FIELDS TO price ↲
```

Reselect the SALES database. Note that you can use the alias name, letter, or number with the SELECT command.

```
SELECT a ↲
```

The fields list now contains all the fields you will use in the screen form. Enter

```
EDIT ↲
```

The program displays the fields currently in the field list. Enter

```
[PgDn]
```

Return to the Dot Prompt by entering

```
[Esc]
```

Once the field list is set properly, you can create the custom screen display. Enter

```
CREATE SCREEN salesrel ↲
```

The Screen Form Design mode is activated. This is the same design mode as the one used from the Control Center display. Begin the layout by placing the record number on the screen. Since each new sale generates a new record number, you might use this as the invoice number. Enter

```
Invoice #
[F5]
```

The program lists all the fields in the field selection box. Create a calculated field with the RECNO( ) function as its value.

```
[right arrow]↲
  e
RECNO( ) ↲
```

Remove the decimal points from the template.

```
t
[backspace]  (3 times)
↲
[Ctrl-End]
```

Using the record number as the invoice number can lead to some problems. When you sort or pack a database, the records are rearranged and their numbers are changed. If you do not pack or sort the database, the record number can serve as an identifier. In Part II of this book you will learn other methods of generating invoice numbers in dBASE IV programs.

On the next line, add the date of the sale. Enter

```
⏎ (3 times)
Date of Sale [spacebar]
[F5] d ⏎
[Ctrl-End]
```

The next section of the screen layout will contain the customer information. The only field that should be entered is the ACCOUNT_NO field. The remaining information can be obtained from the linked fields, which are Read Only. Enter

```
[Tab]
Customer Information ⏎
[Tab] (3 times)
Account # [spacebar]
[F5]
```

You need to select the account number field; but, there are two ACCOUNT_NO fields listed. Which one should you select? The two fields represent the ACCOUNT_NO fields from the SALES and the BUYERS databases. The field you want is the one from the master database, SALES. This is the field that is linked to the BUYERS database. If the relations are to function correctly, data must be entered into the SALES->ACCOUNT_NO field. How can you tell which is which? Since the field list pop-up does not indicate the database source of the fields, you have to estimate which to choose. One clue is that dBASE IV always lists the fields in alphabetical order. If there are two fields with the same name, they are listed alphabetically by alias name, even though the alias name does not appear on the display. Knowing this should lead you to guess that the second ACCOUNT_NO field belongs to SALES, while the first belongs to BUYERS. Enter

```
[down arrow]⏎
[Ctrl-End]
```

Check to see if you made the correct guess by placing the cursor in the previous field. The [F3] key moves you to the field.

```
[F3]
```

At the bottom of the screen, the field description reads:
"SALES->ACCOUNT_NO   Type: Numeric   Width: 4   Decimal: 0".
This confirms you have selected the correct field.

In practice, it is not necessary to distinguish between the fields. If there are two fields with the same name, dBASE IV selects the field from the currently selected database, unless otherwise specified. The dBASE IV report generator may show the alias name in the display, but the FMT file does not specify an alias name for the field.

Place the company name, the contact name, and the phone number, on the next few lines. These fields should be Read Only information, since they consist of data fetched from the related database. Enter

```
[right  arrow]⏎
 [Tab] (3 times)
 [F5]
 co ⏎
```

Designate this field as a nonediting field. Enter

```
r ⏎ [Ctrl-End]
```

Place the field into the screen form.

```
[Ctrl-End]
```

Place the first and last names on the next line. You can use a calculated field to combine the names in a single expression. Enter

```
[right  arrow]⏎
 [Tab] (3 times)
 [F5][right  arrow]⏎
 e
```

The expression uses the + operator to concatenate the two character fields. *Concatenate* means to combine character fields or text into a single text item—here, the FIRST and LAST name fields, and a space in between. The TRIM( ) function eliminates the trailing spaces in the FIRST field. Enter

```
TRIM(first)+SPACE(1)+last   ⏎
[Ctrl-End]
```

Next, create a section for product information, based on the ID and QUANTITY fields. Enter

```
⏎ (3 times)
[Tab] (3 times)
Product Information
⏎ (2 times)
ID [spacebar]
[F5] i ⏎
[Ctrl-End]
```

Insert a Read Only field for the PRICE.

```
        ↵
[Tab] (3 times)
Price [Tab]
[F5] pr ↵
e ↵ [Ctrl-End]
[Ctrl-End]
```

Insert the QUANTITY field as an editable field. Enter

```
        ↵
[Tab] (3 times)
Quant. [Tab]
[F5] q ↵
[Ctrl-End]
```

The remainder of the screen will contain calculated fields for the total amount, sales tax, and grand total. Enter

```
        ↵
[Tab] (3 times)
Amount [Tab]
[F5][right arrow]↵
e
price *quantity ↵
[Ctrl-End]
```

Add a calculated field for the sales tax, assuming a 6% rate.

```
        ↵
[Tab] (3 times)
Tax [Tab]
[F5][right arrow]↵
e
price *quantity*.06 ↵
[Ctrl-End]
```

Finally, add a calculated field for the grand total.

```
        ↵
[Tab] (3 times)
Due [Tab]
[F5][right arrow]↵
e
price *quantity*1.06 ↵
[Ctrl-End]
```

The screen display layout will look like Figure 9-25.

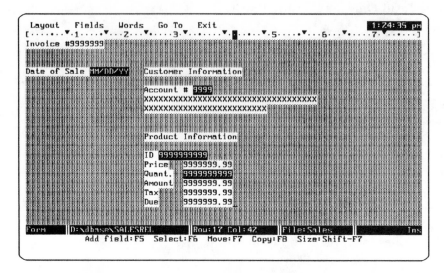

Figure 9-25. Screen layout for multiple databases.

Save the new screen form.

```
[Alt-e] s
```

Display the Edit mode.

```
EDIT ↵
```

The screen you have just created displays the data from the related databases.

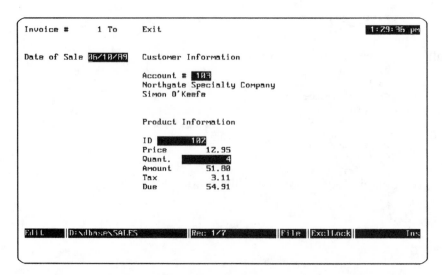

Figure 9-26. Screen displays data from related databases.

An advantage of this custom screen display is that it allows you to edit existing records, or add new records to the SALES database. Append a new record onto the file by entering

        [Alt-r] a

Placing part of the screen format on line zero of the screen layout form causes the information to hide a portion of the menu bar.

Enter the data for this new record.

            062889
            100 ⏎

dBASE IV does not automatically look up the related information. While dBASE IV is in the Editing mode (i.e. data is being entered into the field input area) the program cannot be sure you actually intend to store the new data. When you save the record by exiting or moving to a different record, dBASE IV establishes the link between the records. In order to display the data for Account 100, enter

            [Pg Up]
            [Pg Dn]

The name of the company and contact person are now displayed. Fill out the rest of the record.

            ⏎ *(2 times)*
            101 ⏎
            10
            [Pg Up]
            [Pg Dn]

The financial information is calculated automatically by the screen form field formulas, as shown in Figure 9-27.

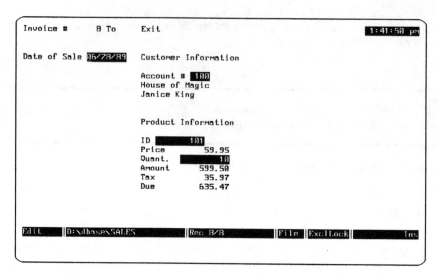

Figure 9-27. New record linked to related database information.

Exit the Edit mode by entering

    [Alt-e] e

Creating a Query from the Environment

The screen form you created depends upon setting the database files, relations, and field lists, exactly as you have them now. Quite a few commands are required to do this. A shortcut is to create a query—called a *view*—based on the currently active settings. A view stores settings similar to those stored in a query file: the names and the work areas of the database and the links between them. However, since the settings are not created with a Query mode layout, the file stores only the settings. dBASE IV distinguishes between view files (settings only) and query files (settings and query layout screen) by using VUE and QBE extensions, respectively.

---

dBASE III introduced the use of view files to the DBASE system. The Query mode and query files in dBASE IV were designed to replace the view files. The view files you create in dBASE IV are compatible with dBASE III. Of course, dBASE IV query files cannot be used by either dBASE III or III Plus. If you have a dBASE IV query that you want to convert to a dBASE III view, you must activate the query and exit the Control Center. At the Dot Prompt, use the CREATE VIEW FROM ENVIRONMENT command to create a dBASE III compatible view file that shares the query file's specifications.

The view file is created by entering the CREATE VIEW FROM ENVI-RONMENT command. A view file records the following information about the dBASE IV environment.

1. All open databases, indexes, and orders, as well as the work areas in which they are open
2. All relations set between open databases
3. The work area of the currently selected database
4. The current list of fields selected by SET FIELDS
5. The current screen form file
6. A filter condition if one has been created with SET FILTER TO.

By recording these settings, you will be able to use the SALESREL screen form, using a single command to open the view file. It will place you back into the current environment—which is necessary if you are to use the screen form properly. Creating a view file is a handy way to record an environment created in the Dot Prompt mode.

Before you create the view file, activate the ACCOUNTS catalog so this view will appear in the Control Center display. Enter

```
SET CATALOG TO accounts ⏎
SET CATALOG ON ⏎
```

Once the catalog is open, you can create the view file for this environment. Enter

```
CREATE VIEW salesrel FROM ENVIRONMENT ⏎
```

You now have a file that will appear in the Query column of the Control Center, which will duplicate the current environment.

Display the Control Center by entering

```
[F2]
```

Note that the SALESREL screen form does not appear in the Control Center display. This is because the catalog was not open when the screen form was created. You can add the screen form to the catalog using the Add file to catalog command from the Catalog menu. Place the highlight in the Forms column and display the list of screen forms. Keep in mind that the file you want to place into the catalog is a screen form, with an SCR extension.

```
[right arrow] (2 times)
[Alt-c] a
salesrel.scr ⏎
⏎
```

You can display the screen form by using the [F2] command. Enter

```
[F2]
```

The screen form is activated from the Control Center display. Exit the Edit mode by entering

```
[Esc]
```

Test the SALESREL view file by closing, then reopening it.

```
[right arrow]
⏎ (2 times)
```

Open the SALESREL view.

```
[Pg Dn]
⏎
d
```

The custom-screen format is displayed directly from the SALESREL view file. Exit the mode, and dBASE IV, by entering

```
[Esc]
[Alt-e] q
```

Summary

This chapter discussed using multiple databases from both the Control Center commands and the Dot Prompt mode.

- **Multiple Databases.** In its simplest form, dBASE IV uses one database file at a time. In many cases, data are stored and retrieved more efficiently using several database files to hold parts of the data system. Multiple-database operations save entry time because repetitive data are stored only once. Links relate the data in the different databases.

- **Work Areas.** In order to allow access to more than one file at a time, dBASE IV designates 10 different work areas. A work area is an area in the memory of the computer that is used to handle the input and output of data to a specific file. dBASE IV provides three ways to refer to a work area: by letter (A-J), number (1-10), or by the name of the open database file in a specific work area. By default Work Area 1 is the selected work area. The selected work area is used for database operations, unless you specifically select a different one.

- **Alias Names.** When a database file is opened, dBASE IV creates an alias name for that database. By default, the database is assigned the filename as the alias name. The alias name can be used in conjunction with a fieldname to specify the name of a field and the work area in which the database (of which the field is a part) is located. Example: BUYERS->COMPANY. This refers to the COMPANY field in the BUYERS database. You can also use the letter or number of the work area as the alias. If BUYERS is open in Work Area 2, then B->COMPANY is the same as BUYERS->COMPANY. The alias name of a fieldname allows you to write commands or formulas that draw data from fields in unselected databases.

- **Linking Databases.** When more than one database file is open, you can create links between the databases using the Query mode. The Query mode allows you to open file skeletons for more than one database. Each skeleton represents a file in a separate work area. The Create Link by Pointing command allows you to designate two fields in different database files that should be linked. When fields are linked, one database functions as the master, and the other functions as the supporting database. The linked field in the master contains values that can also be found in the linked field in the supporting database. When a record in the master is accessed, the program searches the values in the linked field in the supporting database, to find a record with a matching value. If found, the pointer is positioned to the matching record in the supporting database. This operation is carried out for each link in the master file, every time the record pointer is moved.

- **Index Files and Links.** The master locates coresponding records in the supporting database by using index tags. In the Query mode, if the linked field in the supporting database is not indexed, an index tag for that field is automatically created. The master does not have to be indexed.

- **Mailmerge Reports.** A mailmerge report is used to print forms and form letter output, based on the contents of a database, or series of linked multiple databases. In a mailmerge report, the data from one record appears on each page. A page break is inserted before each new record. The Report Form Design mode allows you to enter fields inserted into paragraph text, as well as place text at specific locations on the page. By default, all field data inserted into the report is trimmed, so that it will merge with the text of the form or form letter.

- **USE/IN/ORDER.** The USE command opens database files in the Dot Prompt mode. By default, USE opens the database file in Work Area 1. The IN clause allows you to open database files in any of the dBASE IV work areas. If the files contain index tags, you can select an index tag as the master index order by using the ORDER clause with the USE command.

- **SET FIELDS.** The SET FIELDS command allows you to create a list of fields that will be passed to commands, such as EDIT or LIST. If there are multiple databases open, you can include fields from any of the database files in the fields list. If the SET FIELDS

ON command is entered, it is not necessary to use alias names with unique fieldnames. When a fieldname is used, dBASE IV will search the list of fields to find the matching name, regardless of its alias. The effect of the SET FIELDS commands is cumulative. This means that the SET FIELDS commands will always add fields to the existing field list. To clear the field list from memory and return to normal dBASE IV field handling, you must enter either SET FIELDS TO with no list, or close all the databases.

- **SET RELATION.** Database files opened in different work areas can be linked using the SET RELATION command. The command is executed from the work area of the master database. When attempting to link files with the SET RELATION command, the supporting database files must have a master index that matches the expression used in the SET RELATION command. Note that relations between databases are set by matching an expression value to the key value of a supporting database's index tag. While linking fields is the most common type of relation, you can use dBASE IV expressions to create keys that are more complicated than the contents of a single field. You can include several index key specifications in a single SET RELATION command, to establish multiple links between databases. Note that a SET RELATION command overwrites any previous relations in the selected work area. To set multiple relations from one work area, you must include a list of relations in a single SET RELATION command.

- **View Files.** A view file can be created to record database, relation, fields, and screen form specifications, entered at the Dot Prompt. The view file functions like a stored query, in that it can return you to a specific setup in a single command. Unlike a query, it cannot be created or modified using Query mode skeleton displays. View files are created with the CREATE VIEW FROM ENVIRONMENT command. the command records the settings active at the time the command is issued. The file is given a VUE extension. VUE files can be added to the Control Center queries display, if added to the current catalog.

Exercises

Ex-1

Link files on ACCOUNT_NO.

```
[F3] (2 times)
[Tab] (3 times)
[Alt-L] c
[F4]
[Shift-Tab] (3 times)
⏎
```

Ex-2

Link files on ID.

```
[F3] [Tab]
[Alt-L] c
[F4] (2 times)
[[Tab] ⏎
```

Ex-3

Insert CITY, STATE and ZIP fields.

```
[down arrow]
 [F5]
c ⏎
 [Ctrl-End]
[right arrow]
 , [spacebar]
 [F5]
s ⏎
 [Ctrl-End]
[right arrow]
 [spacebar]
 [F5]
z ⏎
 [Ctrl-End]
```

Ex-4

Create a calculated field for sales tax.

```
Sales Tax [Tab]
 [F5][right arrow]⏎
e
price*quantity*.06  ⏎
 [Ctrl-End]
[right arrow]⏎
```

10

Housekeeping, Maintenance, and Configuration

This is the last chapter in Part I of this book. Part I was designed to demonstrate the fundamental concepts, operations, and techniques, of creating and designing database files, queries, and reports. It also demonstrated other items needed to arrange, control, calculate, and organize data into useful information.

The primary tools used in these operations were the commands organized in the Control Center menu. In some cases, you learned how to tap into more powerful and flexible commands, by exiting the Control Center and directly accessing parts of the dBASE IV language, through the Dot Prompt mode.

Together, the Control Center and the Dot Prompt mode provide a great degree of processing power. Part II, which begins with Chapter 11, will concentrate on the use of dBASE IV's Programming language to create customized solutions to all types of database needs.

Before going on to Part II, there are a number of commands and procedures to learn. These procedures fall under the categories of housekeeping, maintenance, and system configuration, and involve such tasks as copying, renaming and backing-up files, deleting, exporting or importing data, and customizing the basic configuration of the dBASE IV system. As with many of the procedures in Part I, these housekeeping, maintenance, and system configuration tasks can be executed from the Control Center menus, or accessed directly through the Dot Prompt mode. The Control Center commands have the advantage of being menu-selected options. On the other hand, the Dot Prompt commands offer faster execution and direct access to specific commands.

This chapter also demonstrates a non-programming method of automating procedures in dBASE IV, by recording keystroke macro commands.

Do not confuse keystroke macros, a new feature in dBASE IV, with macro substitution, a feature appearing in dBASE II through IV. Macro substitution is covered in Part II of this book, as an aspect of the Programming language of dBASE IV. Keystroke macros do not require the creation of programs and can be created directly from the Control Center display.

Begin this chapter by loading dBASE IV in the usual manner. The Control Center will be displayed with the ACCOUNTS catalog files listed in the columns.

dBASE IV Files and File Operations

Databases hold important information. While the information you enter may not seem earthshaking to everyone, it is probably very important to you. File operations, such as backing up copies of your files, are operations whose value you do not appreciate until something goes wrong. dBASE IV has three ways of carrying out file operations:

1. The DOS Utilities option on the Tools menu. As part of the Control Center system, dBASE IV provides a menu-driven system for implementing most standard file operations, such as Copy, Rename, and Delete. Filenames and attributes are listed in a pop-up menu, from which they can be selected for specified file operations, one at a time, or in groups.
2. dBASE IV language commands from the Dot Prompt mode. The dBASE IV language supports all the basic file operations, such as File Copy, Delete, and Rename.
3. Accessing DOS commands through dBASE IV. If you have sufficient memory, you can access the DOS command interpreter through dBASE IV and execute DOS commands without leaving dBASE IV. You can access DOS from the Control Center, or from the Dot Prompt mode.

Memory and dBASE IV

How much memory is sufficient to operate dBASE IV? The specifications for dBASE IV require 640K of internal RAM memory. (See Chapter 2 for a discussion of disk versus RAM memory) However, this figure can be misleading. When you execute a program, the crucial factor is not how much memory is installed in the computer, but how much is available to the program at the time you are attempting to execute it. The memory available for program use is called the *Transient Program Area* or *TPA*.

Why would the TPA vary even though the amount of memory installed in the computer is the same each time (e.g. 640K)? The answer is that when you execute dBASE IV, it is possible there are additional programs already using memory space that remain resident when dBASE IV is loaded. The most obvious example is the operating system, DOS. The amount of memory used by DOS varies with each new version, and typically, increases with each new version. If you are operating on a network, the network software takes up additional space in the memory. Some network NETBIOS software uses too much memory to permit the use of dBASE IV, or limits some of its operations. Other sources of memory usage are utilities, such as SideKick, which remain in memory until you re-boot the computer.

You can obtain the size of the TPA by running the CHKDSK program. Remember, the value you are looking for is the last value listed, bytes free. If you have at least 500,000 bytes free, you should be able to carry out all the operations in PART I of this book. Less memory than this may interrupt some operations.

Note that if you have expanded memory installed in your computer, version 1.0 of dBASE IV *cannot* take advantage of this memory. This is also true of extended memory. For example, if you have a 1-megabyte AT computer, only 640K is usable (conventional) memory. The additional 384K is extended memory, which is ignored by DOS and dBASE IV.

File operations are those operations affecting the entire file as a unit, in contrast to database operations, which deal with fields and records within a database. There are three basic file operations you must perform from time to time: copying a file, deleting a file, and renaming a file.

All these activities can be performed outside of dBASE IV, using DOS commands or DOS shell programs, such as the Norton Commander.

For information about the Norton Commander see the Brady publication *Inside the Norton Utilities* by Rob Krumm.

When performing file operations on dBASE IV files, it is important to understand that many dBASE IV activities require the use of several related files. These files are often created automatically, based on the specifications you enter into the structure of a database file. There are three types of files that can be generated when a file is created. All the files have the same name (i.e. the name specified when you create the database) but different file extensions. They are:

1. **DBF file.** A file with a DBF extension is the main database file. This file contains the file structure, plus all the data entered into all the records, with the exception of memo-field information. The file's structure, along with other information, such as the current number of records and the date of the last file update, are stored at the beginning of the file. This area is called the file *header*. The size of the header is 35-bytes plus 32 for each field. The maximum size is about 8000 bytes.

2. **DBT file.** The DBT extension stands for *database text*. This file contains the text entered into memo fields, specified in the DBF file's structure. If there are no memo fields defined for a particular database, no DBT file is created for that file.

3. **MDX file.** If you enter Y in the index column of any of the fields in the file's structure, dBASE IV automatically creates a multiple index file (MDX extension) to hold the index information required to implement the indexes specified in the files structure. If none of the fields are set as index fields, no MDX file is created. The MDX file created because of the Index column in the file structure, is called the *production* index. The production index is special because it is automatically opened whenever you open the associated DBF file. When a production index is created, dBASE IV modifies the file header, so the program knows a production index exists for this database file.

In addition, each of the operations shown in the Control Center produces files with a unique extension.

QBE

This file contains the query screen layout and the query commands. When you copy this file, you can modify the query using the Query Design mode. If this file is deleted, the query is deleted.

QBO

This extension is used with object-code files, compiled from QBE files. If you erase this file, dBASE IV creates a new copy based on the matching QBE file.

SCR

Files with this extension contain a screen-layout design. This file must be present to modify a screen layout. However, if you erase this file you can use, but not modify, the screen, as long as the FMT version of this layout exists.

FMT

Files with this extension contain the dBASE IV language commands needed to implement the screen form design, SCR extension. If you delete this file, you can use the SCR file to generate another copy of the FMT file. Note, in order to prompt dBASE IV to generate a new copy, you must make some change, no matter how inconsequential, to the layout. The change triggers the generation of a new copy of the FMT file.

FMO

Files with this extension contain the object-code version of the FMT file. If this file is erased, it is automatically created when you use the screen form.

FRM

Files with this extension contain the report-form-design layout. This file is required to modify a report form.

FRG

Files with this extension contain the dBASE IV Programming language commands needed to implement the report-form layout stored in the FRM file. If this file is erased, it can be generated again by making any type of modification to the FRM file.

FRO

Files with this extension contain the object-code version of the FRG file. If this file is erased, it is automatically created when you use the report form.

LBL

Files with this extension contain the label-form-design layout. This file is required to modify a label form.

LBG

Files with this extension contain the dBASE IV Programming language commands needed to implement the label-form layout stored in the LBL file. If this file is erased, it can be generated again by making any modification to the LBL file.

LBO

Files with this extension contain the object-code version of the LBG file. If this file is erased, it is automatically created when you use the label form.

---

dBASE IV automatically generates temporary files when performing tasks, such as processing queries or previewing report forms. These temporary files have $VM or $ED file extensions. The filenames are unique numeric sequences generated from the system's clock.

dBASE IV automatically places these temporary files in the current disk directory. You may find it is more advantageous to place these temporary files into a different drive and/or directory. By doing so, you can isolate the temporary files physically, from valid dBASE IV files stored in the \DBASE directory. If you have a limited amount of space on the current disk, you may also want to direct the temporary files to a particular disk drive where space needed for these files does not pose a problem.

You can change the location for these files by performing a DOS operation *before* you run dBASE IV. Use the DOS SET command to define a SET called TMP. The TMP set will be the path of the directory into which most of these temporary files should be written. Example: SET TMP D:\JUNK\

This command, when issued before you run dBASE IV, places the temporary files into the JUNK directory in the D drive. Note the \ must be entered at the end of the directory name. You can include the SET command in a batch file that runs dBASE IV, then erase any temporary files after you quit. Example:

```
TMP=D:\JUNK\
DBASE
DEL D:\JUNK\*.$*
```

Note that even with this setting, some commands (such as those modifying a macro) still write the temporary files in the dBASE IV default directory.

File Operations from the Control Center

File operations are performed in the Control Center by using the Tools menu. Enter

```
[Alt-t]
```

The Tools menu lists six options: Macros, Import, Export, DOS utilities, Protect data, and Settings. File operations are performed from the DOS Utilities option. Enter

```
d
```

When the DOS Utilities option is selected, dBASE IV displays the DOS

Operations mode. In this mode, a large pop-up menu is displayed in the center of the screen. The pop-up window lists five pieces of information about each file.

Name/Extension

This column shows the full DOS filename and extension of the files in the current directory. If the directory is not the root directory of the current disk, the symbol <parent> appears. This option moves you up one level to the parent directory of the current directory. If the current directory contains sub-directories, they will be listed at the top of the file list.

Size

This is the size of the file in bytes. If the item is a directory, the symbol <DIR> appears in place of the file size.

Date & Time

This column shows the time and date the file was created, or last updated. The time and date are taken from the operating system.

Attrs

The information in this column consists of letters, representing the file attributes of the selected file: a = Archive, s= System, h= Hidden, and r = Read Only. Note, many dBASE IV files are marked as Read Only. New files are automatically assigned the *a* attribute until they are backed up with DOS backup or XCOPY commands.

Space used

This column lists the amount of disk space occupied by the file.

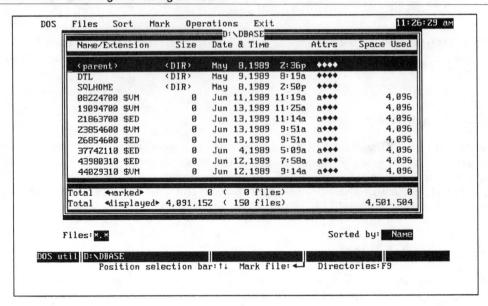

| DOS | Files | Sort | Mark | Operations | Exit | 11:26:29 am |

```
              ═════════════D:\DBASE═════════════
   Name/Extension    Size    Date & Time        Attrs    Space Used

  <parent>         <DIR>    May  8,1989  2:36p  ♦♦♦♦
  DTL              <DIR>    May  9,1989  8:19a  ♦♦♦♦
  SQLHOME          <DIR>    May  8,1989  2:50p  ♦♦♦♦
  08224700 $VM         0    Jun 11,1989 11:19a  a♦♦♦      4,096
  19094700 $VM         0    Jun 13,1989 11:25a  a♦♦♦      4,096
  21863700 $ED         0    Jun 13,1989 11:14a  a♦♦♦      4,096
  23854600 $VM         0    Jun 13,1989  9:51a  a♦♦♦      4,096
  26854600 $ED         0    Jun 13,1989  9:51a  a♦♦♦      4,096
  37742110 $ED         0    Jun  4,1989  5:09a  a♦♦♦      4,096
  43980310 $ED         0    Jun 12,1989  7:58a  a♦♦♦      4,096
  44029310 $VM         0    Jun 12,1989  9:14a  a♦♦♦      4,096
 ─────────────────────────────────────────────────────────────
 Total   ◄marked►          0  (     0 files)                  0
 Total   ◄displayed► 4,091,152  ( 150 files)          4,501,504


     Files: ▓.▓                            Sorted by: ▓Name▓

 ▓DOS util▓▓D:\DBASE▓
            Position selection bar:↑↓  Mark file:↵  Directories:F9
```

Figure 10-1. DOS utilities mode display.

Size versus Space used

The dBASE IV DOS Utilities file display shows two values for the files listed. One is the size of the file and the other is the space used by the file. If you are not familiar with how data is stored on disks, the two values may be confusing.

When a disk—hard or floppy—is formatted, it is divided into a series of data storage units called sectors. Typically, MSDOS computers use sectors that are 512 bytes. A byte is the amount of space needed to stored a single character. In addition to the sector, the formatting process also establishes a minimum unit of storage allocated when a file is written. This minimum unit is called a cluster. A typical hard disk has a cluster size of 4,096 bytes, a 360K floppy of 1,025 bytes, and a 1.2 floppy of 512 bytes.

When a file is written to a disk, DOS allocates space in blocks, based on the cluster size for that disk. For example, suppose you have a file containing 450 bytes. On a hard disk, that file would be stored in a single cluster of 4,096 bytes. In this instance, there are 3646 bytes allocated to the file, but not used. This space represents a wasted area because it cannot be used by any other file. Note, if you copy the file to a 1.2 floppy disk, the slack space is reduced to 62 bytes.

You may wonder why the cluster size is set so large for a hard disk. It is because the cluster size seeks to strike a balance between two contradictory goals. A small cluster size cuts down wasted space, making storage on the disk more efficient. However, this increases the number of individual data units on the disk, causing the operating system to take longer to locate, read, and write data. On the other hand, a larger cluster size would improve the speed of disk read and write operations.

DOS version 2 created 8,192 byte clusters, which were found to be inefficient for PC operations where users are likely to create many small files, as opposed to a few large files. DOS version 3 reduced the standard cluster size for a hard disk to 4,096 to make more efficient use of the disk space for typical PC applications.

The allocation system makes it possible for a file to show 0 as its size, but actually occupy several thousand bytes of disk space. This happens when files are opened, but never actually closed. dBASE IV writes these types of temporary files when processing certain operations. The result is a file whose actual size is never written to the disk. However, the name of the file being written in the disk directory causes DOS to allocate one cluster to that file. Thus the file shows 0 for its size, but when it is erased, it frees a full cluster on a hard disk that is 4,096 bytes.

You can move the highlight through the listing, one filename at a time, using the up arrow and down arrow keys, or one screen at a time, using [Pg Up] or [Pg Dn]. The bottom of the file-list window shows statistics for the directory in the form of the total number of files, their size, and the amount of space they occupy on the disk. At the top of the screen is a menu bar with six options: DOS, Files, Sort, Mark, Operations, and Exit.

Below the file window are two boxes labeled *Files* and *Sorted By.* These boxes show which files have been selected for display, as well as the sort order used to display the filenames. The default values are *.* for all files, and in alpha numeric order, by name.

The term *wildcard* refers to the symbols used by DOS to represent filenames. The * allows any name or extension to qualify, while a ? is a wildcard for a specific character. The wildcard *.* means all files. If you use characters in combination with *, you can select groups. For example, *.DBF means all files with a DBF extension. SALES*.* would list all files beginning with SALES. dBASE IV recognizes the DOS wildcards.

The Files menu allows you to change the directory and file specification wildcard. For example, suppose you wanted to list only the MDX index files. Enter

    [Alt-f] d

Enter the file specification wildcard.

    *.mdx ⏎

The window is redisplayed, with only the MDX files in the current directory listed.

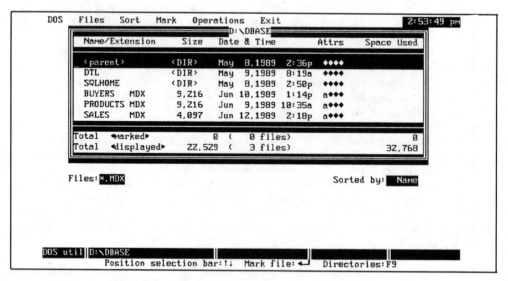

Figure 10-2. Display restricted to MDX files only.

Return the list to all the files by entering

```
[Alt-f]  d [Ctrl-y]
*.* ⌐
```

You can change the sorting sequence of the files, using the Sort command. Enter

```
[Alt-s]
```

You can select one of four sort orders: Name, Extension, Date & Time, Size. Select to sequence the files by extension. This is often useful because it groups the files by type.

```
e
```

The files are now sorted by group. Note, you may not be able to see the difference because of the temporary files at the top of the display.

In addition to the file-list display, you can switch to a directory-tree display. Enter

```
[F9]
```

The directory tree shows each directory on the disk as part of a diagram, depicting the relationship between directories. You can change the directory by moving the highlight with the up arrow and down arrow keys, and pressing ⌐ when you have highlighted the correct directory.

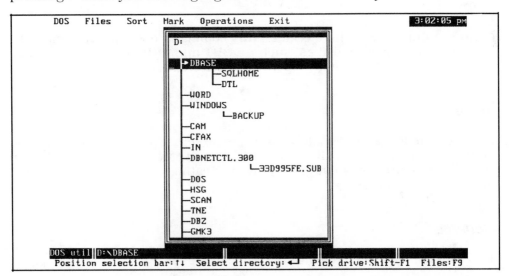

Figure 10-3. Directory tree displayed.

Return to the file display by entering

`[F9]`

Deleting Files

The Operations menu lists the file operations you can perform in this mode. Enter

`[Alt-o]`

The menu lists the operations that can be performed on files:

Delete

Erases the file from the disk. Once erased, files cannot be recovered by ordinary means.

Erased files can sometimes be recovered by special programs, such as the Norton Utilities programs. Note, recovery of erased files with such programs depends on certain specific conditions, making it impossible to assure recovery of erased files, in all cases.

Copy

Creates a duplicate of the file. Note, this command does not automatically copy logically-associated files, such as DBT and DBF files with the same name. It copies only those files specifically selected.

Move

Changes the location of a file to another directory or drive. You can also change the name of the file when it is moved. Moving is different from copying, in that the original file is erased, creating only a single copy of the file in its new location.

Rename

This option allows you to change the name of the file.

View

Displays the file. This option makes sense only for ASCII-text type files. Using this option with other file coding information in binary values, produces incomprehensible results. If you view a file, and the display is blank or filled with what seems to be an arbitrary selection of graphics and characters, you have opened a binary-type file.

Edit

This option loads the selected file into the dBASE IV editor. As with view, this option should be used only with ASCII text files, such as PRG program files, or TXT text files. (Files created with word-processing programs, such as WordPerfect or Word, cannot be edited with the dBASE IV editor, unless they have been saved as text files, rather than normal WordPerfect or Word document files.)
　　Enter

　　　　　⏎

The operations marked with the triangle, such as Delete, can be performed on the currently highlighted files, a selected group of marked files, or all the files currently displayed in the file window. Note, the display option refers to all files included in the current display, as well as those that are visible when you scroll the display.
　　Operations Menu Map:

```
Operations

Delete        Single File
              Marked Files
              Displayed Files

Copy          Single File
              Marked Files
              Displayed Files

Move          Single File
              Marked Files
              Displayed Files

Rename        Single File
              Marked Files
              Displayed Files

View
Edit
```

Cancel the menus by pressing

```
[Esc] (2 times)
```

Suppose you wanted to remove all the temporary files in the current directory. You could erase one file at a time, mark a group of files to be erased, or use the display option to select a group of files for this, and delete all the files. Begin by deleting a single file. Use the down arrow key to position the highlight on the first file in the listing with a $ED, or $VM extension. Note, because the names of these files are generated automatically, the names appearing on your computer will differ from those in the illustrations, except the extensions will be similar.

> [down arrow] *(until a temporary file is highlighted)*

To erase this file, enter

> **[Alt-o] d** ↵

The program displays a window, showing the full pathname of the file, drive, directory, name, and extension, and asks you to Proceed—i.e. delete the file—or Cancel the command. Enter

> ↵

The file is removed from the list, meaning it is erased from the disk. You can delete a group of marked files with a single command. A file is marked by moving the highlight to that file, then pressing the ↵ key. The triangle character appears next to each file you mark. The marking system is most useful when you have a group of files not sharing a common name structure, e.g., SAMPLE.DBF and TEXT.TXT. Marking the files allows you to operate on them as a group.

> [down arrow] *(until a temporary file is highlighted)*
> ↵

Skip a file and mark the next file down.

> [down arrow] *(2 times)*
> ↵

When you mark a file with ↵, the highlight does not automatically advance. To move to the next file in the list you must enter the down arrow or up arrow key.

You now have two files marked. Delete the file by entering

> **[Alt-o]** ↵

Select to delete all the marked files by choosing the Marked Files option from the menu.

> **m** ↵

Both files are removed from the disk. If the files share a common name structure, such as the same filename or extension, the Display option is the simplest and fastest way to treat all the files as a group. You can control which files are displayed by using the Files menu. In this case, select all the files whose extensions begin with $. This indicates they are temporary files that need to be deleted. Enter

```
[Alt-f] d
[Ctrl-y]
*.$* ⌐
```

The files window displays only those files matching the wildcard. Scroll to the bottom of the display window by entering

```
[End]
```

Only the temporary files are displayed. Delete all the files using the Displayed Files option on the Delete menu. Enter

```
[Alt-o] d d ⌐
```

The program flashes the names of the files as they are removed. When the task is completed, the display does not show any filenames because all the qualified names are erased.

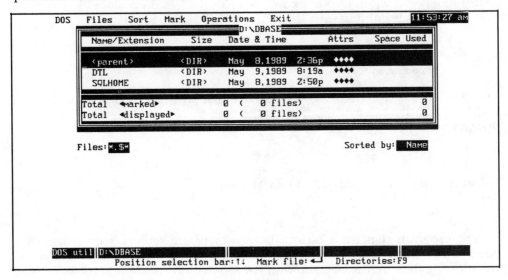

Figure 10-4. All temporary files erased from the disk.

Return the display to show all the files.

```
[Alt-f] d
[Ctrl-y]
*.* ⌐
```

The remaining files are listed in the window.

Copy and Backup Files

The most common—and probably important—file operation is making copies of files. Copies are needed for two reasons. The first reason is security. In order to ensure against a loss of data caused by equipment failure, you need to make backup copies of your files. In addition, you may want to guard against data loss caused by user error. The difference between a backup for protection against equipment failure, and a backup against user error, is that in order to protect against a hardware problem, the files must be copied to a removable media, such as a floppy disk. If you are protecting yourself against user error, you can place the backup on the hard disk with a different name, or in a different directory. Backup files are your only real insurance against a variety of problems that can disrupt your system.

When you make a copy of a database file, you must consider there may be more than just the DBF file to copy. The dBASE IV system provides for the automatic creation of three physical files—DBF, DBT and MDX—for each new database you define. The best way to backup these files is to use a file section wildcard, employing the filename and an * for the extension, so all the files that may be part of the same database setup, are backed up as a unit.

In order to perform the backup operation, you need a formatted floppy disk with enough room to hold the database files you created.

Suppose you wanted to backup the PRODUCTS database. First, select only those files beginning with the name PRODUCTS. Enter

```
[Alt-f] d
[Ctrl-y]
products.* ↵
```

The file list shows the PRODUCTS.DBF file and the production index, PRODUCTS.MDX. Copy these files to the disk in drive A. Begin with the copy operation.

```
[Alt-o] c
```

Select the Displayed Files option by entering

```
d
```

The program displays a box in the center of the screen. This box allows you to enter the drive and directory, which is the destination for the copies of the files. By default, the box shows the last location entered. If you are using this option for the first time this session, the name of the drive and directory will be the current drive and directory.

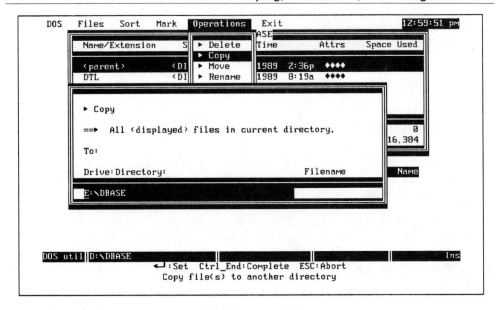

Figure 10-5. Copy destination entry box.

To copy the files onto the floppy disk in drive A, enter

```
[Ctrl-y]
a:
[Ctrl-End]
```

The program copies the name of each of the files, as it is copied to drive A. To confirm the files have actually been copied, change the display to show drive A.

```
[Alt-f] c
[Ctrl-y]
a: ↵
```

The files are listed on drive A, confirming the copying process was a success. Return to the hard drive by entering

```
[Alt-f] c
[Ctrl-y]
c:\dbase ↵
```

The assumption is made that the hard disk you are working on is C, and dBASE IV is in a directory called DBASE, on this disk. If you are working on D, E, F, etc., simply substitute that drive letter in the command.

Return the display to list all files.

```
[Alt-f] d
[Ctrl-y]
*.* ↵
```

Repeating Operations with Macros

Operations that are repeated periodically can be automated by creating a keystroke macro. The term *keystroke macro* refers to a process whereby strokes you enter are recorded by the program. Each recording is assigned to a specific key combination. When you press this combination, the program replays the keystroke sequence. The net result is that each time the keystrokes are replayed, the same operation is carried out. Keystroke macros provide a very simple, yet quite powerful way of programming dBASE IV to carry out specific tasks, without having to make all the menu selections manually.

The backup procedure just carried out is a good example of a task that ought to be done on a regular basis. Typically, you should backup important files each time they are changed, once a day or once a week, depending on how often you update a file. The macro system allows you to execute the backup with a single keystroke, rather than having to navigate through all the menus each time you want to backup the file.

Keep in mind that when you replay a macro, the program needs to be in the state it was in when you first began the recording. If this is not the case, you may find that the keystrokes in the macro do not match up correctly with menus and options. In order to avoid this, it is best to choose a starting point that is easily duplicated.

Thus, the first step in recording a macro is to decide where you want to begin. With the backup macro you may begin at the DOS Utilities display, or back at the Control Center display. In this case, start at the Control Center. The idea is to start the macro at the location that saves you the most time. The Control Center is a good choice here, because it is where you are most likely to be, once you have made additions or changes to your databases.

Return to the Control Center display by entering

```
[Alt-e] ↵
```

After reaching the starting point for recording the macro, begin the creation process by turning on the recording mode. The [Shift-F10] key combination allows you to turn on macro recording. Enter

```
[Shift-F10]
```

dBASE IV displays a small box in the center of the screen, which carries the title "dBASE IV Macro Processing".

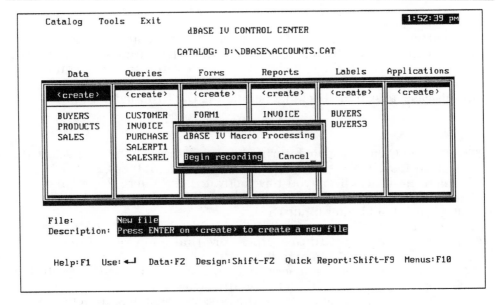

Figure 10-6. Start macro recording box displayed.

The Begin Recording allows you to activate the Keystroke Recording mode. Enter

◡

When you select to begin recording, the program displays another box. This reads: "Press the key that will call this macro". dBASE IV allows you to assign macros to two types of keys.

Alt-Function

You can select a function key, F1-F9, as the macro command key. When you want to replay the macro, combine [Alt] with the function key, e.g., [Alt-F1], to start the replay. The advantage of the function key combinations are they can be used in any Control Center menu, since they do not conflict with the Control Center Alt-letter combination menu commands. The combination of [Alt-F10] cannot be defined by the user for a macro command because it is used as part of the letter-key macro system.

Letter Keys

In addition to the 10 function key combinations, you can assign a macro to letters **a-z.** These letter macros are accessed through the use of the [Alt-F10] key. For example, a macro assigned to the letter A is replayed by entering [Alt-F10] a. Preceding the letter with the [Alt-F10] key avoids conflict with the [Alt-letter] combinations used to activate Control Center menus.

The system provides 35 macro assignments. The 9-function key macros can be executed with a single keystroke. The 26-letter macros require two keystrokes to execute.

In this case, assign the backup operation to the F1 function key. Enter

```
[F1]
```

The Control Center display returns. However, there is one change. At the bottom of the display is the message "Recording Macro; Press Shift-F10 E to end". This message confirms you have activated the Macro Record mode. It also tells you that when you reach a point where you want to stop the recording, you should enter [Shift-F10].

The next objective is to perform the task the macro is to repeat. In this example, this is a DOS Utilities procedure that copies the PRODUCTS database and associated files, to a disk in drive A.

When you are recording a macro, it is best to enter the letter keystrokes for menu operations, rather than to use the arrow keys. The reason for this is that using arrow keys depends on the physical relationship between the items and the menus. This means you must always have the highlight in the same place when you start. In addition, you may have noticed the highlight in a menu remains at the last option used when it is activated. This throws off a macro that assumes the highlight is at the top of the menu. By using the letter keystroke you avoid problems caused by differences in location within the menus.

Activate the DOS Utilities display.

```
[Alt-t]  d
```

Select the PRODUCT files.

```
[Alt-f]  d
[Ctrl-y]
products.*  ↵
```

Copy the files to drive A.

```
[Alt-o]  c d
[Ctrl-y]
A:
[Ctrl-End]
```

The program pauses and asks if you want to overwrite the last backup. This happens each time you backup another copy of the same file onto the backup disk. Enter

```
↵ (2 times)
```

The last step is to return the file selection to *.*, and return to the Control Center display.

```
[Alt-f]  d
[Cyrl-y]
*.*  ⌐
[Alt-e]  e
```

You have arrived at the Control Center. You can stop the macro recording. Enter

```
[Shift-F10]
```

Now the box is larger, and contains three options:

End Recording

This command stops the recording and stores the macro. After using this option you can replay the macro. Note that the storage of the macro is temporary for the current session of dBASE IV.

Insert User-input Break

This option creates a user break within the macro. The break pauses the macro and allows you to enter information into dBASE IV. Following the pause, the macro continues to replay. These pauses allow you to create macros that run in sections. Each section pauses for the user to enter some information needed to complete the processing. This information, which may typically include the name of a database or report, may change each time the macro is executed. The result is a macro that can be used with a variety of different files. You will learn how to use pauses further on in this chapter.

Continue Recording

This option simply continues the recording without inserting a pause.

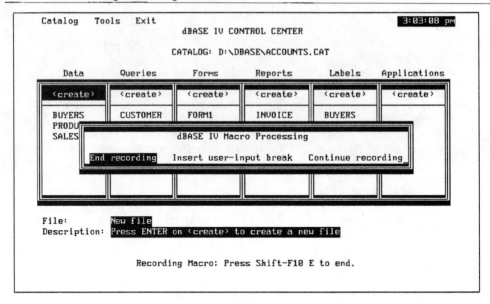

Figure 10-7. The program display the stop macro recording box.

Complete the macro by selecting the End Recording option.

    e

You have now recorded a macro. Once it has been recorded, you can replay the macro as often as you desire by entering the key combination—here, [Alt-F1]. Enter

    [Alt-F1]

The program replays the keystroke you entered. The menus respond to the recorded keystrokes as if you were entering the commands from the keyboard, again. One difference is when a macro is replayed, it is replayed as fast as the program can process the keystrokes. This makes macro processing faster, as well as simpler than manually repeating the procedure.

Macros with Pauses

The macro you created carries out the same operation (i.e. backup the PRODUCTS files) each time it is executed. But suppose you wanted to backup the BUYERS, SALES, or CKBOOK databases and associated files. One way to do this is to create a more *generalized* macro. Generalized macros are created by inserting pauses within the macro at one or more points. The points are the places in the process where you specify the exact data you want to use. In this case, the key point in the macro is the entry of the filename, which is then used to select the records to copy. Instead of recording the actual name—e.g. PRODUCTS—you could insert a macro pause. Each time the macro reaches this point, it pauses to allow the user to enter the part of the macro that changes each time. When this is done, the

macro is resumed by pressing [Shift-F10].
Create just such a generalized macro. Enter

```
[Shift-F10]  ⏎
[F2]
```

Enter the same keystrokes as the previous macro.

```
[Alt-t] d
[Alt-f] d
[Ctrl-y]
```

It is here you will enter the filename that is used to select the files. For example, the possible wildcards might be BUYERS.*, SALES.*, or CKBOOK.*. You may want to backup all the DBF files with *.DBF, or the report forms with *.FR?.

Report form file extensions are FRM, FRG and FRO.

Insert a pause into the macro.

```
[Shift-F10]
```

This time, select Insert User-input Break by entering

```
i
```

dBASE IV returns to the file filter entry blank. When the macro is played back, it pauses for a user input, right after the [Ctrl-y] keystroke is played back.

Users then have the option of entering as many keystrokes as they like. Note that when they enter a ⏎ character, it is taken as a signal that they want to terminate the Insert User-Input Break and allow the rest of the macro to continue playback.

Your goal is to create a macro allowing users to enter the wildcard of choice. All other keys remain the same. There is a problem, however. How can you complete the recording unless you enter a valid wildcard? If you attempt to perform a copying operation with no files selected, dBASE IV displays an error message. The error message is not the problem—the fact that you need to respond to the error message is. For example, if you must press a key to respond to the error message, this key is recorded as part of the macro. However, when you replay the macro and the user enters a valid wildcard, that exact keystroke is replayed even though it is not needed.

In this instance, you are caught in the middle. If you complete the macro by entering a valid command, in effect have created a macro just like the first macro, which copies specific files. If you skip the wildcard, the macro runs into an error, making your recording inaccurate.

One solution is to create two macros: one to get to the point where the wildcard is entered, and a second to use after the wildcard is entered. Another method is to continue recording the current macro and use the Macro Modify command to remove the wildcard.

Continue entering keystrokes. Enter a valid wildcard.

```
sales.*
```

From this point on, the keystrokes are recorded without a pause. Enter

```
 ↵
[Alt-o] c d
[Ctrl-y]
a:
[Ctrl-End]
[Alt-f] d
[Ctrl-y]
*.* ↵
[Alt-e] e
```

Terminate the recording by entering

```
[Shift-F10] e
```

Modifying a Macro

The macro just recorded is almost the same as the first macro. The only exception is the insertion of a pause instruction. Unfortunately, the pause is followed by the wildcard *sales.**, which should not to be part of this macro if it is to function as a general backup command. In order to change the macro once it has been recorded, use the Macro Modify command found on the Macros menu. You can gain access to the Macros menu from the Tools menu. Enter

```
[Alt-t] m
```

The Macro menu is displayed. The menu had three sections. The top section contains the same commands as are displayed in the macro recording boxes.

Begin Recording

Initiates macro recording.

End Recording

Terminates the macro recording.

Append to Macro

Allows you to record more keystrokes to be added to an existing macro.

Insert User-Input Break

Inserts a user pause into a macro.
   The center section of the menu contains operations that can only be performed from the Macro menu.

Modify

This option displays the keystroke macro as a series of keystroke keywords. You can delete, move, and insert keystroke keywords. When the macro is replayed, it executes the keystrokes based on your edited version.

Name

This permits you to store a descriptive name to help you remember the function of a particular macro. This is purely descriptive and has no effect on the actual contents of the macro.

Delete

Removes a macro from the list of macros.

Copy

Creates a duplicate of a selected macro and assigns the duplicate a different macro key.

Play

This option allows you to execute a macro by selecting it from a list of macros. The advantage of this options is any descriptive names used for macros are listed along with the macro keys.

Talk

When ON, this function causes the macro keywords to appear in the status lines, as the macro executes. It is used to help you track down problems occuring in macros.

The macro TALK option is not the same function as the SET TALK option.

The bottom section of the menu has two commands related to the storing of macros in disk files. Macros are stored in memory until you exit dBASE IV. If you wish to use the macros again during another session, you *must* save the macros using the Save Library command on the Macros menu. If not, the macros will be lost when you exit dBASE IV.

Load Library

This command is used to load a macro library file from the disk. Each file can contain a set of up to 35 macros. Macro files are assigned the KEY file extension. If you load a macro file from the disk, the macros loaded from the file are combined with any existing macro as long as the macros are assigned to different keys. If there is a conflict (i.e. one of the macros being loaded has the same key assignment as an existing macro) the macro being loaded replaces the existing macro.

Save Library

This command transfers the macros as currently defined in the memory of the computer, to a file on the disk. The file is given a .KEY file extension by default.

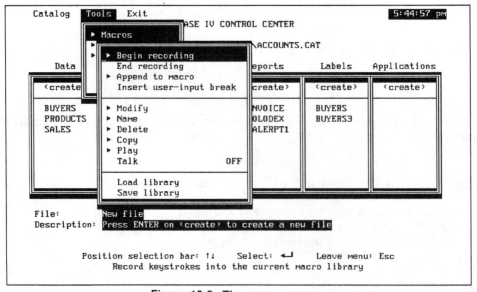

Figure 10-8. The macro menu.

In this instance, you need to modify the keystroke in a macro. Enter

    m

dBASE IV displays a table listing the macros currently defined. The names of the macros appear next to the keys. By default, the macros are assigned the name of the key, until you use the Macro Name command to enter a different name. Across from the name is a value. This value is the number of keystrokes included in the macro.

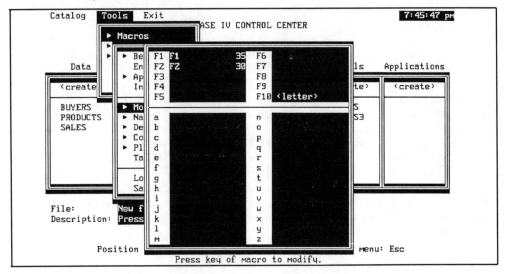

Figure 10-9. Macro table display.

You can select a macro to modify, by pressing the key associated with the macro.

You cannot create a macro from scratch using the Modify command. The macro must first be created by recording, before you can modify it.

    [F2]

dBASE IV displays the dBASE IV Editor used for entering data into a memo field. Instead of a memo, the text in the editor is a text representation of the keystrokes entered during the recording of the macro.

```
{Alt-t}d{Alt-f}d{Ctrl-y}{InpBreak}sales.*{Enter}
{Alt-o}cd{Ctrl-y}a:{Ctrl-End}{Alt-f}d{Ctrl-y}*.*{Enter}
{Alt-e}e
```

The text of the macro consists of two elements.

Macro keywords

Macro keywords are text symbols used to represent special keys and key combinations recorded as part of the macro. These keywords are enclosed in curly brackets, {}, to indicate they are not ordinary characters, but special keys. In addition to the keywords, dBASE IV uses the special symbol {InpBreak} to represent the place in the macro where a break for user input should occur.

Text characters

All the characters, including any spaces not enclosed in {}, are literal text characters. They are inserted into the macro exactly as they appear in the macro listing.

The macro is divided into three lines. There is no particular significance to this division. The macro is always interpreted as a continuous string of keystrokes, unless an {InpBreak} is encountered. The division into three lines is an arbitrary division to help make the macro easier to read. You may feel free to redivide the macro into fewer or more lines, if that makes it easier to understand.

In this case, remove the sales.* following the {InpBreak}. To make this change, all you need do is delete characters. You can use the Goto Forward search command to position the cursor, instead of pressing the right arrow key. Enter

```
[Alt-g] f
sales ↵
```

Delete the characters.

```
[Del] (7 times)
```

The macro now allows user input made during the break, to be the wildcard filter for the copying. Save the revised macro. Enter

```
[Ctrl-End]
```

You can replay the revised macro.

```
[Alt-F2]
```

The macro runs automatically until it reaches the pause. The program displays the message "Macro playback suspended, press Shift-F10 to resume macro playback", below the filter input area. Enter a file filter wildcard. This time, make it the CKBOOK files.

```
ckbook.*
```

To resume the macro playback, enter

> `[Shift-F10]`

The macro completes the copying process, then returns to the Control Center.

Saving Macros

As mentioned previously, dBASE IV stores macro information in memory during the current dBASE IV session. In order to use a macro again in another session, you must save, then reload a macro library file. Suppose you wanted to save the macros just created. Enter

> `[Alt-t]  m`

The Save Library command creates a macro library file for the current macro set in memory. Enter

> `s`

You need to enter a filename for the macro library. dBASE IV assigns the KEY extension to the file. Enter

> `backup ⏎`

When dBASE IV is loaded, it will not automatically load the macro library file. In order to gain access to the macros, you must use the Library Load command from the Macros menu. You can also use the Restore Macro command if you are working from the Dot Prompt.

Exit the menus by entering

> `[Esc]` *(2 times)*

File Operations from the Dot Prompt

The basic file operations, such as copy, delete, and rename can be performed at the Dot Prompt. The Dot Prompt provides two methods of carrying out these operations:

dBASE IV Commands

The dBASE IV Command language contains commands that can erase, copy, and rename files. There is no single command to move a file. Moving is accomplished by copying a file, then deleting the original.

RUN Access to DOS

You can use the dBASE IV command, RUN. RUN provides you with access to DOS commands, such as COPY, XCOPY (DOS 3 and higher), REPLACE, DEL, and RENAME.

You can also access DOS through the Control Center menus by using the Tools DOS Utilities DOS command ([Alt-t] d [Alt-d]). There are two options: Perform DOS command and Goto DOS. The Perform DOS command executes one DOS command, then returns to the Control Center. The Goto DOS activates a DOS session within dBASE IV. You can enter as many DOS commands as you desire. The DOS command EXIT returns you to the Control Center. The syntax of DOS commands remains the same no matter how DOS is accessed.

Exit the Control Center and activate the Dot Prompt mode by entering

```
[Alt-e] e
```

The dBASE IV language commands that can be used for file operations are:

Command	Functions
COPY	copy DBF files only
COPY FILE	copies any type of file
DELETE FILE	same function as ERASE
DIR	lists directory of files
ERASE	erases a file from the disk
LIST FILES LIKE	lists files with wildcard
RENAME	changes the name of a disk file
TYPE	displays the contents of a text file

The DOS commands commonly used for file operations are:

Command	Functions
COPY	copies files
DEL	erases a file from the disk
DIR	list a directory of files
ERASE	same as DEL
RENAME	changes the name of a disk file

There are special forms of copying available on later versions of DOS 3.0 and higher. The XCOPY commands can be used in place of COPY. The advantage of XCOPY is it uses more of the available memory to copy files, resulting in improved speed. REPLACE is a special form of copying, whereby files are copied only when they match the names of existing destination files. You may want to investigate these commands to improve the way you make copies and backups.

The primary difference between dBASE IV file commands and DOS file commands is dBASE IV commands do not accept wildcards, while DOS commands do (with the exception of those commands that list files, only.)

However, the dBASE IV commands ERASE and COPY allow you to use the ? option, giving you the ability to select a filename from a pop-up list of files. The dBASE IV commands are best used when working on one specific file. The DOS commands work best when you want to affect a group of files that can be covered with a wildcard.

Keep in mind that in order to use the RUN command to access DOS commands through dBASE IV, you must have sufficient memory available to allow dBASE IV to load a copy of the COMMAND.COM command interpreter into memory. If this memory is not available, the dBASE IV commands can be used to erase, copy, and rename files, one at a time.

The fastest way to duplicate the wildcard backups or deletions of files performed in the Control Center, is to use the RUN command to access DOS. For example, to copy all the CKBOOK files to drive A, enter

    RUN copy ckbook.* a: ↵

The exclamation point (!) can be used as an abbreviation for the RUN command. Example:

    ! copy ckbook.* a: ↵

The program accesses DOS and executes the DOS COPY command. You can perform the same type of action with the DEL command. Here, erase the CKBOOK files from the disk in drive A.

    RUN del a:ckbook.* ↵

To perform similar actions with dBASE IV commands you must enter the specific filenames you want to use. For example, to copy the CKBOOK.DBF file to A, enter

    COPY FILE ckbook.dbf TO a:ckbook.dbf ↵

To delete this file, enter

    ERASE a:ckbook.dbf ↵

The ERASE command in dBASE IV accepts the ? option, which lists files.

       `ERASE ? ⏎`

The program displays a pop-up menu on the right side of the screen, listing all files of all types. You can delete a file by highlighting, then selecting the filename you want to delete. Return to the Dot Prompt without deleting any files, by entering

       `[Esc]`

If you want access to DOS in order to enter a series of commands, you can do so by executing the COMMAND program. Enter

       `RUN command ⏎`

The DOS prompt appears as it would if you exited dBASE IV. You can enter a series of DOS commands without returning to dBASE IV each time.

The COMMAND program is the DOS command interpreter stored in the file COMMAND.COM. When you use COMMAND as the DOS command to run, you start a full DOS session that continues until you specifically terminate the session with the DOS command EXIT.

When you want to exit DOS and return to dBASE IV, use the DOS command EXIT.

       `exit ⏎`

Clear the screen display by entering

       `CLEAR ⏎`

Listing Directories

In dBASE IV you can list files in the same two ways you execute file operations. The dBASE IV command DIR is set by default to list only DBF files. Enter

       `DIR ⏎`

The program lists the DBF files in a special display, showing the filename, number of records, last update, and size of the file.

```
Database Files      # Records  Last Update    Size
BUYERS.DBF                  5  06/11/89       1144
PRODUCTS.DBF               4  06/12/89        742
SALES.DBF                  8  06/12/89        426
CKBOOK.DBF                16  05/25/89       1218
```

If you want to list files other than DBF files, follow the DIR command with a wildcard. For example, to list all the files in the directory, enter

    DIR *.* ↵

This time the program lists all the files in the directory. Note, only the filenames are listed without information about the date and size of the files.

The LIST FILES and LIST FILES LIKE commands duplicate the DIR command. They are maintained in dBASE IV for compatibility with earlier versions.

The DOS DIR command displays a full list of the files, including the date and size characteristics.

    RUN dir ↵

Both dBASE IV DIR and DOS DIR recognize standard DOS wildcard and pathnames. For example, to list all the files on drive A: you could use either of the following commands.

    DIR a:*.*. ↵
    RUN dir a: ↵

The main difference lies in the format used to display the file directory. Clear the screen of data by entering

    CLEAR ↵

As in DOS, you can change the default disk so file operations execute on the specified disk. The command in dBASE IV to change disks is SET DEFAULT TO, followed by the drive name. For example, to make drive A the default drive, enter

    SET DEFAULT TO a: ↵

List all of the files.

    DIR *.* ↵

The program lists all the files on drive A.

It is important to understand DOS does not recognize the change in drives made within dBASE IV. If you were to run the DOS DIRECTORY command, you would find it still shows the same directory as before. Enter

    RUN dir ↵

The hard disk directory—not the floppy disk directory—is displayed. To change the DOS drive, you must enter a DOS command, RUN a: ↵, which changes the DOS directory. When dBASE IV first loads, the two directories are the same, but it is possible to create a situation where the DOS and dBASE IV file commands operate on different parts of your system. Change the default disk back to the original drive (assumed to be C) by entering

>   SET DEFAULT TO c: ⏎

Clear the display by entering

>   CLEAR ⏎

Duplicate Databases

The file operations performed so far are operations that have acted on the files, without considering their content. The next group of topics deals with operations that create files used on the contents of databases.

The first task involves making duplicate databases. In dBASE IV, DBF files do not always stand alone. The memo field text files, DBT extensions and the production index file, MDX extension, often work together for a working database. When making a duplicate of an existing database you must consider the DBT and MDX files that might be associated with the DBF file, in order to create a working duplicate.

A good example of what is involved in making a duplicate file is the CKBOOK file. This database has both a memo field and a production index file. What would happen if you simply use the DOS COPY or dBASE IV COPY FILE commands to make a duplicate of the DBF file? Enter

>   COPY FILE ckbook.dbf TO book.dbf ⏎

The COPY FILE duplicates the information in the file and stores this duplicate information in a file called BOOK.DBF. Is BOOK.DBF a useable database? Place the file in use.

>   USE book ⏎

When dBASE IV attempts to open the file, it encounters a problem because there is no BOOK.DBT file to correspond to memo field in the structure of BOOK.DBF. The message in the box reads "Memo file not found. Ok to create empty memo file".

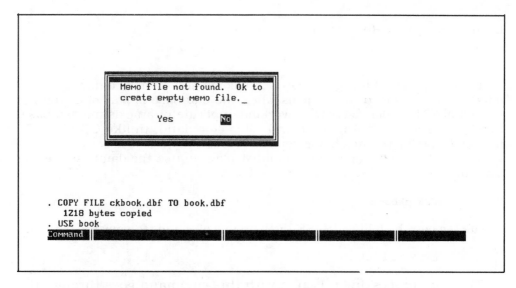

Figure 10-10. Memo field text file cannot be found for duplicate.

If you answer Yes to this prompt, a new DBT file is created for this file. However, all the memo field data is lost because the new file is empty. Enter

n

The program then realizes there is no production index file, BOOK.MDX. The message reads "Production MDX file not found". The program does not offer you the option to create the MDX file. You can select to cancel the USE command or open the database without the production index (Proceed).

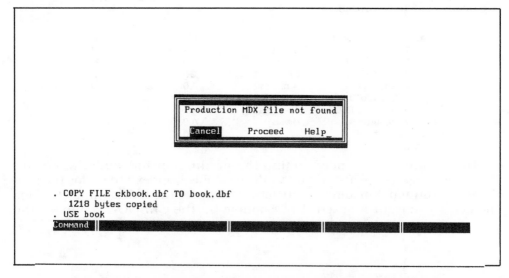

Figure 10-11. Production index missing from copied database file.

In this case, choose to cancel the command.

⌐

Using the COPY FILE or a DOS COPY command to make a duplicate of a database file can lead to problems when the database is part of a group of related files. In order to create a working duplicate of an existing database, use the dBASE IV COPY command. This command, unlike COPY FILE, interprets the information being copied.

To use the COPY command you must place in use the database file you want to duplicate.

USE ckbook ⌐

Create the copy by telling dBASE IV the name of the file to copy the data to.

COPY TO book ⌐

The copy processing initiated with this command goes through the database file, record by record, and creates a new DBF and DBT file containing the same records and fields as the current database, including the memo fields.

USE book ⌐

The file opens with an error. What about the production index file? Enter

LIST STRUCTURE ⌐

The COPY command changes the structure of the new file so the index fields are always set to N values.

Field	Field Name	Type	Width	Dec	Index
1	DATE	Date	8		N
2	CHECK_NUM	Numeric	4		N
3	PAYEE	Character	25		N
4	AMOUNT	Numeric	10	2	N
5	CLEARED	Logical	1		N
6	DEDUCTIBLE	Logical	1		N
7	REMARKS	Memo	10		N
** Total **			60		

This eliminates the need to find the production index file, when the BOOK database is opened. If you want to establish index orders for the new database you must modify the structure, and set the index values to Y for the fields you want indexed. For example, in the CKBOOK database the

PAYEE field is set for an index order. To duplicate this order in this file, enter

```
MODIFY STRUCTURE ↵
[down  arrow](2 times)
 [End]
 y [Ctrl-End]
 y
```

The production index for the BOOK database is established.

Dividing a File

The COPY command can be used for more than just creating an exact duplicate of a file. You can use the COPY command to copy only selected records from a file. This technique can be used to divide a large database into several smaller files. For example, suppose you determine it would be better to work with individual files for each of the months, instead of having one file containing all checks for all months. You can use the COPY command with a FOR clause. The FOR clause uses a logical expression to select which records are copied, just as a FOR clause used with the LIST command (Chapter 4) selected records to be listed. The BOOK file has records with dates from both January and February. The expression MONTH(date)=1 selects those records having a January date. If you attach this to a COPY command you create a file having only January records.

```
COPY TO book_jan FOR +MONTH(date)=1  ↵
```

The program displays the message "10 records copied", indicating 10 of the 16 records were selected for copying because they had January dates. Following the same concept, create a file, BOOK_FEB, for February records. Try this on your own. The correct command is at the end of the chapter under Ex-1.

The program lists six records copied for the BOOK_FEB file, accounting for all 16 records. You can open and use either of the monthly databases.

```
USE book_feb ↵
LIST ↵
```

All the records in this file contain February dates. The COPY FOR command can be used to separate records into individual files.

You can also divide files based on their physical location in the file, using scopes. For example you can copy the next 100 records to a new file by entering *COPY TO newfile NEXT 100*. Recall the NEXT clause includes the current record as the first record of the next 100.

Combining Files

In addition to dividing files into smaller files, you can go the other direction and combine files to make a larger file. Suppose you wanted to combine monthly files into a single file, for two or more months. The APPEND FROM command allows you to add records stored in one database, into another database. Keep in mind for this operation to take place the two databases must share at least one field in common. dBASE IV can add data only when there are common fields.

Suppose you wanted to combine the records in the BOOK_JAN database and the BOOK_FEB database. You must decide where to place the combined records. For example you may simply want to combine BOOK_JAN with the currently open database, BOOK_FEB, or the other way around. In this case, combine the records from BOOK_JAN with BOOK_FEB. Enter

```
APPEND FROM book_feb ↵
```

The program adds copies of the 10 records in BOOK_JAN to the current database, resulting in a database with all 16 original records. Is BOOK_FEB a duplicate of BOOK? Not exactly. Because of the order in which the records were added to the BOOK_FEB database, the record numbers are different from the original file BOOK. Other than that, all the data is the same.

Summary Files

A variation on the idea of dividing and combining databases is the creation of summary files. A summary file is a database containing summary information about records in a given database. You already know how to display summary information about a database using queries, reports, and commands, such as SUM and CALCULATE. However, all this information is for display, only.

Suppose you wanted to sum this information in a database. You can create a database in which summary information is stored, by using the TOTAL command. The TOTAL command compresses a database into a series of subtotal records. Like the groups in a subtotal report, the command focuses on a key field. All the records having the same value in the key field, will be compiled into a single record that can contain subtotals of numeric fields, if desired..

Assume you want to create from the SALES database, a database that stores the number of units of each product sold. Open the SALES database.

```
USE sales ↵
```

In order to produce the summary database, you must make sure the records in the current database are sequenced in order by the key field. Here, the key field is the ID field, which contains the ID number for each product. You can sequence records by sorting or indexing. If you select to index, you can create a standard or a production index file. The production index is best if you anticipate performing this operation again, at a later time. A production index is created by changing the Index option in the file's structure to Y. Enter

```
MODIFY STRUCTURE ⌐
[down  arrow] (2 times)
 [End]
 y [Ctrl-End]
 y
```

The database is now sequenced in order, by product ID number. Confirm this by entering

```
LIST id ⌐
```

The ID numbers appear in order. Once the file sequenced properly, you can create a summary file. The TOTAL command has the following general form:

TOTAL ON *key_field* TO *new_database* FIELDS *field_list*

The items in the field list are the numeric fields you want totaled. When the command is executed, only one record is written in the new database for each unique ID numbers. The data in the TOTAL database is taken from the first record in each ID number group. The exceptions are the numeric fields listed in the field list; they contain the total of all the records with the same ID number. Enter

```
TOTAL ON id TO num_sold FIELDS quantity ⌐
```

The program displays two messages: "8 records totaled and 4 records generated". This means eight records in the SALES database were totaled during the process. Four new records were generated in the new database, one for each unique ID number.

To see the results of the TOTAL, open the new database and list the contents.

```
USE num_sold ⌐
LIST id, quantity ⌐
```

Record#	id	quantity
1	100	10
2	101	20
3	102	9
4	103	10

The listing shows the units sold for each item. This procedure produced a database containing values that can only be calculated through a query, using the GROUP BY operator, or through a report with group subtotals. The advantage of this method is the data is stored in a database, which can be directly accessed without having to run a report or query.

Note, the nature of the totaled database can cause some confusion. List all the fields.

```
LIST ↵
```

The TOTAL command creates a database with the same structure as the source database. In this instance, the information stored in the DATE_SOLD and ACCOUNT_NO fields is not meaningful. It is simply the data that was in the corresponding fields in the first record in the source database for each ID group. If you did not know what you were looking for, you could easily assume the dates had some meaning in connection with the other field data.

```
Record#  DATE_SOLD    QUANTITY  ACCOUNT_NO       ID
      1  06/15/89          10         101       100
      2  06/17/89          20         100       101
      3  06/10/89           9         103       102
      4  06/20/89          10         102       103
```

You may want to modify this file so it contains only the two meaningful fields. One way to do this is to modify the structure and delete the unwanted fields. Another method involves the COPY command. COPY accepts a FIELDS clause that specifies which fields in the structure you want to copy. For example, to copy only the ID and QUANTITY fields into a new database, enter

```
COPY TO quansold FIELDS id,quantity  ↵
USE quansold  ↵
LIST ↵
```

The QUANSOLD database contains only the data that should logically be grouped together.

```
Record#                 ID    QUANTITY
      1                100          10
      2                101          20
      3                102           9
      4                103          10
```

Deleting Records

Removing records from a database file in dBASE IV is a two-step process.

Marking Records

Marking a record for deletion does not actually remove information from the database. In fact, the records marked for deletion function in exactly the same way as those not marked for deletion, unless special commands or clauses are used to select undeleted records. Each record contains an extra character of information, over and above the total of all the characters in all the fields. This special character is normally a blank. When a record is marked for deletion, this character is changed to an asterisk (*).

Packing the file

Deleting a record simply places a mark in the record. To actually remove deleted records from the database, you must perform a PACK. A PACK is an operation whereby the entire database file is re-written. Only the records not marked as deleted are included in the new copy. All the records marked as deleted are erased from the file and cannot be recovered. Since the file is rewritten, record numbers change, because some records move up to fill the slots formerly occupied by deleted records.

As mentioned in Chapter 9, the change in record numbers taking place when a database is packed, makes reliance on the record number of a database as a reference number, risky. In Chapter 9, the record numbers in the SALES database were used as invoice numbers. If records were deleted and packed from the SALES file, some records would have their invoice numbers changed. You should use the record number as a reference, only if you do not intend to pack the database.

The two steps, marking for deletion and packing, are not closely related in time. You may leave records marked for deletion for months or years, before you pack, if at all. dBASE IV can be set to ignore deleted records without having to physically remove them from the database. Maintaining deleted records in the database may seem an odd idea. Perhaps it is best to think of deleted records as simply inactive. This allows you to process the undeleted records, the deleted records, or all the records, at different times, regardless of their deletion status. A packed database cannot gain access to deleted records because they have been physically removed from the file.

There are five important commands related to deleted records.

Command	Function
DELETE	marks records as deleted
RECALL	removes the deletion mark from records
SET DELETED ON/OFF	when set on, the program ignores deleted records
PACK	physically removes deleted records from a database
ZAP	wipes out all records with one command

Open the BOOK database.

        USE book ⏎

You can mark records for deletion in two ways.

The DELETE command

The DELETE command can be used to delete one or more records. You can delete records based on their physical position by using a scope, e.g., DELETE NEXT 10. You can use logical criterion in the form of a FOR clause, e.g., DELETE FOR MONTH(date)=1.

[Ctrl-u] in full screen modes

When records are displayed in full-screen editing modes, such as Browse or Edit, entering [Ctrl-u] toggles the deletion mark for the current record. The term toggle means that [Ctrl-u] changes the deletion status to deleted, if the record is currently undeleted, or to undeleted if it is currently deleted.

Suppose you wanted to delete all the cleared records. Enter

        DELETE FOR cleared ⏎

The program displays the message "6 records deleted". List the DATE, PAYEE, and AMOUNT fields.

        LIST date,payee,amount, cleared ⏎

The listing shows the six records marked for deletion. The * following the record number, are also the 6 records marked as cleared.

Record# cleared	date	payee	amount	
1	*01/03/89	Allied Office Furniture	750.50	.T.
2	*01/03/89	Central Office Supplies	97.56	.T.
3	*01/06/89	Western Telephone	101.57	.T.
4	01/06/89	United Federal Insurance	590.00	.F.
5	*01/10/89	Computer World	2245.50	.T.
6	*01/10/89	Fathead Software	99.95	.T.
7	01/14/89	The Bargain Warehouse	145.99	.F.
8	01/15/89	Central Office Supplies	67.45	.F.
9	02/02/89	Sunset Variety	25.89	.F.
10	02/09/89	Advanced Copier Service	175.00	.F.
11	02/12/89	Valley Power & Light	101.70	.F.
12	02/25/89	Dept of Trans	45.00	.F.
13	02/27/89	Western Telephone	175.75	.F.
14	*01/01/89	DEPOSIT	2500.00	.T.
15	01/31/89	DEPOSIT	1200.00	.F.
16	02/15/89	DEPOSIT	1900.00	.F.

You can add more deleted records by entering more DELETE commands. Suppose Record 10 is simply a mistake. Delete this record by entering

        DELETE RECORD 10 ↵

If you delete a record that is already marked for deletion, the record remains marked for deletion.

You can remove a deletion mark by using the RECALL command. RECALL operates like delete, except that it replaces the * with a space. If the record is already undeleted, RECALL has no effect. Suppose you decide not to delete Record 1. Recall this record by entering

        RECALL RECORD 1 ↵

List the database again.

        LIST date,payee,amount, cleared ↵

The two changes, 1 recalled and 10 deleted, are reflected in the listing.

Record# cleared	date	payee	amount	
1	01/03/89	Allied Office Furniture	750.50	.T.
2	*01/03/89	Central Office Supplies	97.56	.T.
3	*01/06/89	Western Telephone	101.57	.T.
4	01/06/89	United Federal Insurance	590.00	.F.
5	*01/10/89	Computer World	2245.50	.T.
6	*01/10/89	Fathead Software	99.95	.T.
7	01/14/89	The Bargain Warehouse	145.99	.F.
8	01/15/89	Central Office Supplies	67.45	.F.
9	02/02/89	Sunset Variety	25.89	.F.
10	*02/09/89	Advanced Copier Service	175.00	.F.
11	02/12/89	Valley Power & Light	101.70	.F.
12	02/25/89	Dept of Trans	45.00	.F.
13	02/27/89	Western Telephone	175.75	.F.
14	*01/01/89	DEPOSIT	2500.00	.T.
15	01/31/89	DEPOSIT	1200.00	.F.
16	02/15/89	DEPOSIT	1900.00	.F.

You can delete all the records with DELETE ALL. RECALL ALL undeletes all records.

You can set dBASE IV to ignore the deleted records by using the SET DELETED ON command. Enter

    SET DELETED ON ⏎

Repeat the LIST command.

    LIST date,payee,amount, cleared ⏎

Only the undeleted records appear. Any processing performed from this point on, utilizes only the unselected records. To gain access to all the records, enter

    SET DELETED OFF ⏎
    LIST date,payee,amount, cleared ⏎

All the records in the database are now listed.

The final step that removes deleted records, is PACK. The PACK command is a form of the COPY command. It copies all the undeleted records to a new database, deletes the old database, then renames the new database with the original name. All this takes place automatically, once you enter a PACK command. Enter

    PACK ⏎

If you are working on a network, you must have exclusive use of the database in order to perform a PACK. To gain exclusive access, enter SET EXCLUSIVE ON, then re-open the database, USE book. You will then be able to perform the PACK. For more information about network operations in dBASE IV, see Part III of this book.

The packing process displays the message "10 records copied", indicating the packing process is a form of copying. In addition, dBASE IV automatically rebuilds the production index, so it is accurate for the revised database.

Special Memo Operations

As you have learned in this book, memo fields are different from other field types, in several respects. Memo fields are used to hold blocks of text that are too large to store in simple character fields. In order to make memo fields more useful, dBASE IV provides special commands, allowing you to insert text prepared with text-editing or word-processing programs in dBASE IV memo fields, into a text file that can be read by most word-processing programs.

The two commands involved with special memo operations are variations on the COPY TO and APPEND FROM commands.

COPY MEMO

This command copies the text of a memo field into a DOS ASCII text file. The ADDITIVE clause allows the text of the memo to be added onto an existing text file, if desired.

APPEND MEMO

This command copies a text file prepared with a text-editor, word-processor, or other application that generates an ASCII text file, into a specified memo field. Text appended into a memo with this command, is added to the end of the memo. The OVERWRITE clause allows you to replace the existing memo, if any, with the imported text.

Most of the popular word processing programs allow you to save a document as ASCII text format. In WordPerfect 4.2 and 5.0, the command [Ctrl-F5] allows you to save the document as a text file. In Microsoft Word 4.0, use [Esc] T L and select No for the Formatted option. In Word 5.0, use [Esc] T L, and select Text Only for the format.

Keep in mind when you create a text file, it is preferable that ⏎ characters be inserted at the end of each paragraph, rather than at the end of each line. This is because the dBASE IV editor attempts to wrap the lines according to the current memo width. If the text file has ⏎ characters at the end of each line, the wraparound creates too many lines. For example, the typical word-processor file converted to a text file with a ⏎ at the end of each line, is 65 characters in length. The default dBASE IV memo width is 50. When the text is displayed, the first line is 50 characters, the second 15 (65-50) the third 50, the fourth 15, and so on. If the text file contained only paragraph end ⏎ characters, the lines in a paragraph could be re-wrapped to fit any memo width setting.

These two commands make it possible to store and retrieve all types of text as memo fields in a database. For example, you could store the text of business letters prepared with a word-processing program, as part of a database, instead of storing the text in separate files on the disk.

The ADDITIVE clause makes it possible to create a text file containing the contents of several memo fields.

---

dBASE IV programs are text files. You can store entire programs as memo fields within a database. The memo's can be copied out to file form when needed, but stored as part of a large database when not in use.

The current record contains a memo in the REMARKS field. Enter

```
? remarks ↵
```

The memo field displays several lines of text. Copy this text to a separate disk file by entering

```
COPY MEMO remarks TO text1 ↵
```

The command creates a text file, TEXT1.TXT, containing the text of the memo field.

You can add the text of the second record's REMARKS field to the text file by entering

```
2 ↵
COPY MEMO remarks TO text1 ADDITIVE ↵
```

You can display the text of the file inside the editor.

```
MODIFY FILE text1.txt ↵
```

The text shows the memo text from both Record 1 and Record 2. Exit the editor by entering

```
[Alt-e] a
```

You can import any text file into a memo field. Move to Record 4, which has a blank memo field.

```
4
```

Recall you can use the TO FILE clause with commands, such as LIST, REPORT and LABEL, to create text files from the output of those commands, instead of sending the data to the printer. For example, you can use the TO FILE clause with the LIST STRUCTURE command, to create a text file out of the structure listing. Enter

```
LIST STRUCTURE TO FILE filestru ↵
```

You can import the text file just created onto the REMARKS memo field. Enter

```
APPEND MEMO remarks FROM filestru.txt ↵
? remarks ↵
```

The memo field lists the data contained in the file structure listing.

Exchanging Data

In addition to the import and export of memo text, dBASE IV has a number of ways in which data can be imported from other applications, and ways in which data can be exported to other applications.

Copy To/Export

The COPY TO recognizes a TYPE clause that converts dBASE IV data in different types of files compatible with different applications. Some of the file types are generic-text formats recognized by many programs. Others are specific to popular applications. The EXPORT command is specifically designed for PFS file databases.

Import

The IMPORT command converts a non-dBASE IV database into a dBASE IV database.

Append From

This command adds data from non-dBASE IV files to existing dBASE IV database files. All non-dBASE IV format files rely on the sequence of the data, to determine which fields the data will be inserted into. The first data item in the source file is placed into the first field of the importing database, the second in field 2, and so on. If the data being imported uses a sequence that differs from the sequence used in the structure of the importing database, the results may be unusable.

The file types supported by dBASE IV are:

DBASEII

Data stored in a dBASE II format file.

DELIMITED

Appends data from a delimited text file. A delimited file is a text file with a specific format. Each record is a string of characters, ending with carriage return/line feed characters. Each field is separated by a comma, and text fields are surrounded with ". Number fields are not surrounded by ". Example:

```
19890103,1000,"Allied  Office Furniture",750.50,Y,Y
19890106,1003,"United  Federal Insurance",590.00,F,F
```

Note that dates in text-delimited files must be entered as YYYYMMDD number sequences, for dBASE IV to recognize the data as date-type data. Example: 01/03/89 should be written as 19890103. Logical fields appear as non-delimited letters T, Y, F or N.

DELIMITED WITH char

This format allows you to select a character, other than " to mark off text fields. The following file uses a / to delimit text fields. Each record is a string of characters ending with carriage return/line characters. Example:

```
19890103,1000,/Allied  Office Furniture/,750.50,Y,Y
19890106,1003,/United  Federal Insurance/,590.00,F,F
```

DELIMITED WITH BLANK

This file format uses a single blank space to separate data items, and is usually used when all the data is numeric. Each record is a string of characters ending with carriage return/line characters. Example:

```
19890103 1000 Allied  750.50 Y Y
19890106 1003 Federal 590.00 F F
```

DIF

The DIF (Data Interchange Format) was developed for transferring information stored in VisiCalc spreadsheets. Spreadsheet rows are treated as records, and the columns are treated as fields.

FW2

Imports database information created with Framework II. The file must be either a Framework database or spreadsheet.

RPD

Appends records from a RapidFile, RPD file.

SDF

SDF stands for Standard Data Format. This is a text file that does not use a character to mark the ends of fields. Instead, each field contains a specific number of characters. This type of file is called a fixed-length field format, and is the method used by dBASE IV to store data. Importing of data from this type of file assumes the total number of characters, including blank spaces in each field of the SDF file, matches the length of the fields in the dBASE IV file structure. Each record is a string of characters, ending with carriage return/line characters. A TXT file extension is assumed. Example:

```
United Federal Insurance      590.00FF
The Bargain Warehouse         145.99FT
```

SYLK

The SYLK (Symbolic Link) format was developed by Microsoft for interchanging data with their spreadsheet applications, Multiplan and Excel. Spreadsheets should be saved row major format.

WKS

Appends data stored in a Lotus 1-2-3 Release 1A, file format.

The export file types in addition to the others are:

DBMEMO3

While dBASE IV can access dBASE III files, the files are automatically converted to dBASE IV files, a modification affecting the ability of dBASE III to read these files. If you wish these file to be readable by dBASE III, you must export the data using COPY to the DBMEMO3 type file. Specialized field types are not compatible with all file types. With the exception of DBMEMO3, memo fields are ignored.

PFS

PFS File format dBASE IV. The PFS database cannot have more that 255 fields, and not more than 254 characters in any one field. Note that because PFS database files rely on screen location to determine fieldname, dBASE IV creates a screen format file with the same name, but an FMT extension to match, as closely as possible, the PFS layout. Also. since PFS does not uses fieldnames, but relies on text of an indefinite length as field labels, the fieldnames are truncated in many cases.

Exit dBASE IV from the Dot Prompt by entering

    quit ↵

Summary

This chapter discussed operations needed to copy and delete files and records.

- **Macros.** You can create keystroke macros by recording in dBASE IV. Macros allow you to replay a sequence of keystrokes, as many times as needed. Macros help automate repetitive operations, such as file backups. Macro recording is controlled by the [Shift-F10].

- **DOS Utilities.** Operations, such as file copying, deleting, moving, and renaming, can be carried out through the Control Center using the DOS Utilities option found on the Tools menu. This option displays a window listing files and directories. You can use the display to select one, or a group of marked files. You can also use a wildcard option to list only the files meeting a certain specification. The selected file or files can be deleted, copied, or moved. You can also view or edit a text file.

- **DOS Access.** You can directly access DOS and execute DOS commands when leaving dBASE IV. This can be done in the Control Center by using the DOS option in the DOS Utilities display, or by using the RUN command in the Dot Prompt mode. You must have a sufficient amount of free memory available to load the COMMAND.COM file, usually about 25K of memory.

- **dBASE IV commands.** dBASE IV commands can be used to copy, erase, and rename files. The dBASE IV versions of these commands require you to enter exact filenames and can only operate on one file at a time. These commands do not accept wildcards, but they can work with the ? option, which displays a pop-up menu with a list of files to select from.

- **Related Files.** dBASE IV database files, DBF extension, can have two other supporting files, DBT for memo fields and MDX for the production index file, which are required to operate the database. When DOS COPY or COPY FILE is used to duplicate a DBF file, no attention is paid to the related DBT or MDX files. If the copied DBF file requires corresponding DBT and/or MDX files, an error occurs when the copied file is put into use. Use COPY TO to duplicate dBASE IV database DBF files.

- **Dividing Files.** The COPY TO command can create duplicate databases. If the source database contains memo fields, a copy of the DBT file is also generated. References in the file's structure to a production index are removed from the structure of the new database. The FOR and FIELDS clauses can be used to select records and/or fields from the original database so that the duplicate contains only part of the original file's data. This technique allows you to divide a database into a series of smaller databases.

- **Combining Files.** The APPEND FROM command allows you to combine the information stored in separate databases. When data is appended into a database from another file, only the data stored in matching fields is transferred, if the files have different structures. If the files have the same structure, all the fields are transferred.

- **Summary Files.** The TOTAL command is a special form of the COPY TO command. TOTAL uses the value in a specified key field to create a new database with one record for each unique value in the key field. You can select one or more numeric fields to be totaled. The totals for each group of records with the same value in the key field appears in the records of the new database. The new database has the same structure as the original. Use this command to capture subtotal information, or to eliminate duplicate records.

- **Exchanging Data.** The COPY TO and APPEND FROM commands use the TYPE clause to write or read data stored in non-dBASE IV formats. APPEND FROM TYPE adds the imported data to an existing dBASE IV database. The IMPORT command creates a new database from the imported information. The EXPORT command handles the exporting of data in the PFS file format.

Exercises

Ex-1

Copy February records.

```
COPY TO book_feb FOR MONTH(date)=2  ↵
```

Part II

Programming

11

Automating Tasks with Program Files

This chapter begins PART II where you will learn how to use the Programming language built into dBASE IV. Learning *programming* is viewed with trepidation by many people, but this fear is unfounded. Working with any software program requires you to understand the structure and internal logic of the application. Part I was designed to help you learn the broad concepts dBASE IV uses to handle database operations. In addition, it taught you the techniques needed to operate the dBASE IV program. These concepts can easily be transferred from the interactive operations as performed in the Control Center or Dot Prompt modes, to the creation of programs based on many of the same commands and techniques. If you understand Part I you can easily learn how to write programs.

There are many reasons that users construct programs, but the most important one is programs allow you to customize the dBASE IV system into one that closely reflects your own work environment. The ability to customize a program has been a characteristic of the most popular computer applications, like Lotus 1-2-3 and the earlier versions of dBASE. By their very nature, major applications—dBASE IV, for instance—are designed to use generic terms such as databases, files, fields, records, indexes, queries, links, and reports, to describe the elements and operations that can be carried out. However, in a given business environment the abstract concepts of database management must be related to the concrete tasks the business must perform.

For example, in order to obtain the current checking account balance would you open a database, ask a query, or process a report? Part I demonstrated that all three activities, as well as other options within those general categories, were needed to obtain the balance. Learning dBASE IV is about how you can relate its operations to your own daily tasks.

Other people in your business will probably want access to the same information. One way to allow access is to provide them with a copy of this book and let them learn everything you learned about dBASE IV and database management. While this is a perfectly fine idea, it takes effort, time, and motivation. A more efficient approach is to change the look and feel of dBASE IV, so its menus and options correspond to the terms and procedures your co-workers already understand. Instead of the Control Center display, you might design your own set of menus that read Add Checks, Display Current Balance, etc. Individuals looking at these options would not need to know how to relate dBASE IV terminology to the task—they could simply select the option, based on what they already understand about the business.

But how can you create these menus and how can they take the place of the many keystrokes and selections you have had to make to get to this point? The answer lies in the dBASE IV Programming language. You have already gotten an idea of how programming works when you created the macros in Chapter 10 of Part I. A macro records the keystrokes needed to perform a specified task. The keystroke can then be played back as many times as needed to carry out the same task. A dBASE IV program allows you to write down, in the form of a text-file, a series of commands that need to be executed. You can then tell dBASE IV to execute that list of commands. The program carries out the commands in a similar manner to the way a macro plays back keystrokes that were previously recorded.

The Programming language allows you to perform all the operations in the Control Center and the Dot Prompt mode, and more. Writing dBASE IV programs ranges from simple procedures to entire program systems that shape dBASE IV into complete applications.

In this chapter you will begin to write a simple, but surprisingly powerful program.

One difference between a macro and a program is a macro records the keys you press. A program consists of actual lists of commands. Programs are easier to read and understand because they state the commands and operations being carried out. Macros are lists of keystrokes. For example, in the Control Center the keys [Alt-c] r y y delete a file. Note, since the specific file is the result of the position of the highlight when the sequence is entered, you cannot tell from the macro exactly what happens. On the other hand, the dBASE IV command ERASE sales.dbf indicates exactly what will happen when the command is executed.

If You Have Written dBASE III Programs

If you have had experience writing programs in dBASE III & III Plus, you will find the dBASE IV language offers a number of new ways to approach the construction of programs. The dBASE IV language is compatible with all dBASE III & III Plus programs. However, you may find many of the new features in the dBASE IV language will enable you to find better ways to structure your applications, particularly through the use of the special menu, pop-up, and window commands. This book will concentrate on the latest techniques available in dBASE IV to write applications.

Deferred Execution

The most obvious characteristic of a program is that it *defers* the execution of commands. When you are working in the Control Center or Dot Prompt modes, dBASE IV carries out the commands you select or enter, as you enter them. This is the *immediate* execution mode. In an immediate execution mode there is no delay between the entry of the command and the time the computer carries out the task.

Immediate execution has some obvious disadvantages. First, you must wait until the current task is complete before you enter the next selection. For example, printing several reports may require a sequence of several steps, such as activating a database or a query, then selecting and printing the report. If you are printing more than one report, you will have to repeat some of the steps. In the immediate execution mode, you must wait during the query processing and the report printing before you can go on to the next task. Second, there is no record of how you carried out the tasks. If you want to repeat them, you must correctly go through all the steps a second, third, or fourth time.

As shown in Chapter 10, keystroke macros, a form of programming, can help you record and playback keystroke sequences.

In contrast, when a program is created the execution of the commands is *deferred.* This means when a program is written, dBASE IV ignores the commands. In fact, programs are written as text files. dBASE IV pays no attention to the content of the file until you are ready to execute the program. At that point, dBASE IV begins to read the program files and execute the commands listed in it. The deferred mode of execution has several advantages. First, since the commands are written down, dBASE IV can execute the entire sequence without further input from the user. Once started, a program can print a series of reports without requiring the user to wait while each step is carried out. dBASE IV reads and carries out the next command in the program, as soon as the last command is completed. One program can generate hours or days worth of work by dBASE IV.

Second, you can easily repeat the actions of a program by telling dBASE IV to read the same list of commands, again. Programs can be run over and over again because they are stored on the disk, just like database information. Your dBASE IV program becomes a database of procedures used to carry out tasks associated with the database information also stored on the disk.

There are other more subtle, but important benefits of deferred execution. Programs can be structured. This means a list of commands can contain instructions about how the program should be carried out in addition to the instructions that manipulate the database information. The program can be structured to stop and ask for certain key pieces of information, carrying on a pre-programmed dialog with the user.

Program structure also enables you to create applications with alternative procedures. The program will automatically choose one of the alternatives, based on some logical condition. The IIF( ) function, introduced in Chapter 5, showed how a single command could contain alternative formulas. Programs use structures allowing the existence of alternate commands or command sequences selected by the value of logical expressions.

Programs, Routines, and Subroutines

The simplest type of program is a list of commands the computer carries out by reading down a list. This type of program is called a *linear* program because the logic moves in a straight line down the list of commands, just as you would read a list from top to bottom. Linear programs are similar in usage to keystroke macros.

The concept of deferred execution provides an opportunity to think about dBASE IV operations in a wider purview. Instead of thinking from command to command, as you do when you are working in the Control Center, you can think in terms of sequences of commands carrying out entire tasks. When you write a program, you can create applications that carry out tasks requiring dozens, hundreds or thousands of keystrokes.

Any reasonably complicated task can be divided into a series of separate steps. For example, getting ready to go to work in the morning may consist of 1) Morning exercise, 2) Shower 3) Dress for work and 4) Breakfast. Each part would be called, in programming terms, a *routine*. As with any task analysis, you can quickly see each routine consists of smaller steps. For example, the Morning Exercise routine might consist of 1) Get out of bed, 2) Get dressed for running 3) Go running. These smaller routines are called *subroutines*. Even subroutines can be broken into smaller parts, i.e., subroutines of subroutines. In programming terminology, when a routine is contained within a larger routine it is said to be *nested* inside the routine.

Interestingly, when thinking about routines you can often see the same task performed as part of different routines. For example, both the Morning exercise and Dress for work routines require you to put on clothing. You might use a single subroutine nested within both routines.

You can see the key to creating complex and powerful programs is the ability to perform a logical *task* analysis. When you are learning to program, it makes sense to start with simple routines, each of which carries out a small task. You can then assemble, mix, and match these smaller routines into larger routines. A complete system contains many small routines assembled together.

This approach to learning programming is called a *modular* approach. To return to the morning analogy, you could treat getting dressed for exercise and getting dressed for work as two separate, unrelated routines. This would be the linear approach. The modular approach would be to create a single routine for dressing, constructed in such a way that you would simply substitute the type of clothing into the routine related to either exercise or work attire.

In this book the creation of modular programs, ones that can be easily adapted from one situation to another, will be stressed. The program that follows begins with simple routines and demonstrates how they can be built into a full database application.

---

dBASE IV includes the use of one and two dimensional arrays. This makes it possible to create more modular programs than was possible in dBASE III & III Plus, which lacked this feature.

The dBASE IV Compiler System

When you create a dBASE IV program you do so by creating a text document. The document is similar to text entered in a memo field or a document created with a word-processing program. dBASE IV uses the same editor for entering programs, as it does for entering memo text.

In fact, dBASE IV programs can be prepared with any program that writes the text in ASCII text files. dBASE IV does not care how you create text.

However, before dBASE IV can carry out the commands stored in the program text file, it must *compile* the program. The compiling process is one in which the program reads the entire program file. It searches the program for any commands it cannot understand, such as those with typographical errors or incorrect syntax. If all the commands are OK, the compiler creates a new copy of the program, which can be directly executed by dBASE IV.

The original text-file is called the *source* file—the file you create when you write a dBASE IV program. The file created by the *compiler* is called the *object* file. dBASE IV can only execute object files. dBASE IV source-code files have a PRG (program) file extension. The object-code files produced by the compiler have a DBO (data-base object) file extension.

The PRG extension for programs is the default dBASE IV extension. You can use other extensions if you desire, so long as you specify the full filename and extension in the commands that refer to the source-code file. However, once compiled, all object-code files are given the required DBO extension.

The compiling process has several benefits. First, the compiler checks for errors in the program. The compiler will not create an object-code file if the source file contains errors. In this way the compiler eliminates error that would otherwise stop your program when it executes. In addition, the object-code file is compressed so it will execute faster.

In order to make this system as simple as possible, dBASE IV automatically compiles your programs as you execute them. This means you do not have to actually run the compiler. dBASE IV creates the needed object-code files automatically. This is prompted by the dBASE IV *development* system. By default, the system is active. You can turn off the system by using the SET DEVELOPMENT OFF command.

The term *compiler* as used in dBASE IV is used in a slightly different sense than it is in general microcomputer terminology. A compiler is usually taken to mean a program that translates a text-file written in a computer language into a binary file directly understood by the computer. For example, a PASCAL compiler creates a program that can be run on any machine supporting the machine language of the compiler. No other special software is needed.

The dBASE IV compiler creates a compressed version of the text-file. It is not a machine language program. The dBASE IV compiled program can only be executed on a computer having a copy of dBASE IV. In this sense, the dBASE IV compiler is not a true compiler. References in this text to compiling refer only to the meaning of the process within dBASE IV, not to the more general concept of compilers.

---

dBASE IV provides two ways to create programs.

Manual Entry

The manual entry process involves the writing of program source code files in a text-editing or word-processing program. You can use the dBASE IV editor or an editing program of your own choice to create these files.

The Applications Generator

dBASE IV is supplied with a special program to generate source code files for programs automatically, based on your specifications. The concept of the applications generator is that many programs use similar structures with only minor differences. For example, if you are creating a menu, the basic structure of the menu is usually the same, but the specific choices change from menu to menu. With the applications generator program, you fill in the specifications and the program writes the source code file automatically.

While the applications generator is very helpful, it is more easily used when you already know the basics about program writing. Put another way, it is very hard to generate a program if you don't know how programs are constructed and organized.

In this book you will learn to use the applications generator as a supplement to writing applications from scratch.

Your First Program

You have reached the point where you will begin to write dBASE IV programs. Load the dBASE IV program in the usual manner. The AC-COUNTS catalog should be displayed in the Control Center.

Exit the Control Center and activate the Dot Prompt mode by entering

```
[Alt-e]  e
```

Linear Programs

The purpose of programming is to accomplish tasks requiring more than a single command to complete. In dBASE IV, most tasks require some combination of commands: files must be opened and closed, index orders must be selected, records must be selected, and so on.

One of the tasks related to the CKBOOK file was that information, such as the total amount of checks or the current account balance, had to be calculated. In the Control Center you were able to get this information by using a combination of a query and a report. Even though this process worked, it was more than necessary. The query and the report combined, have more power than is required to find the account balance. While there is no harm in using their power, the time it takes to process a query and a report is greater than necessary, when all you need do is find the account balance, or the sum of the checks. However, if you wanted to take advantage of the organization of the Control Center, this was the only way to accomplish the task.

Suppose you want to calculate the total amount of the checks. You could use the Dot Prompt command to attack the problem more quickly. First open the CKBOOK file. Enter

```
USE ckbook  ↵
```

Next, select only the records marked as checks. Here, you would test the PAYEE field to eliminate records containing DEPOSIT in this field.

```
SET FILTER TO payee#"DEPOSIT"  ↵
```

Calculate the total of the AMOUNT field.

```
SUM amount  ↵
```

The program displays the total, $4,621.86.

To complete the operation, close the database. This returns the program to the state it was in before you began.

```
CLOSE DATABASE  ↵
```

Which is more convenient—the Control Center query and report or the Dot Prompt commands? The Dot Prompt commands clearly operate faster as individual commands to perform each part of the task. But it takes more time to enter the sequence of commands than it does to select and run a query and a report from the Control Center.

However, you can avoid the necessity of entering individual commands each time, by writing a dBASE IV program with the same four commands.

You can review the commands to be included in the program by listing the history.

> **LIST HISTORY** ⏎

Each command accomplishes one part of the overall task. The job is now to create a dBASE IV program that performs the same four actions.

To create a program, begin with the MODIFY COMMAND command. This command is oddly named because it seems to imply more than it really means. The MODIFY COMMAND command simply activates the dBASE IV editor. The program you create is merely a text file, with the commands you want to execute listed as lines in the document. Enter

> **MODIFY COMMAND chkstats** ⏎

The editor display looks like the display used to edit memo fields. The display has the same five menus: Layout, Words, Go To, Print, and Exit. The primary difference is the Layout and Exit menus have more options.

Modify Command Menus:

Layout
    Modify a different program
    Edit description of program
    Save this program

Words
    Style
    Display
    Position
    Modify ruler
    Hide ruler
    Enable automatic indent
    Add line
    Remove line
    Insert page break
    Write/read text file

Go To
    Go to line number
    Forward search
    Backward search
    Replace
    Match capitalization

Print
    Begin printing
    Eject page now
    Line numbers
    Use print form
    Save settings to print form
    Destination
    Control of printer
    Output options
    Page dimensions

Exit
    Save changes and exit
    Abandon changes and exit
    Run program
    Debug program

The program is created by entering the commands. Enter the commands shown below. Note a ↵ should be entered at the end of each line. Enter

```
USE ckbook
SET FILTER TO payee#"DEPOSIT"
SUM amount
CLOSE DATABASE
```

The commands in the program are the same as those you entered manually at the Dot Prompt. Save the program by entering

```
[Alt-e] s
```

dBASE IV returns to the Dot Prompt. Note that none of the commands you entered has any effect on the status of the program. The commands are only text, until the program file is compiled and executed.

The compiling process, by default, automatically occurs when the file is executed. The compiling process is performed the *first* time a program is executed. Once the object-code file, in this case CHKSTATS.DBO, has been created, dBASE IV executes this file each time CHKSTATS is requested. The command that executes a program file is the DO command. DO is followed by the name of the program you want to execute. Enter

```
DO chkstats ↵
```

When the program begins to run, the screen displays a message reading "Compiling line". The number of the lines runs from 1 to 4—exactly the number of lines in your program. The message indicates that the compiler is checking and compiling the program. When the compiling is complete, the compiler writes the object file, DBO extension, to the disk, then immediately executes the program. The result is the amount of the checks is displayed on the screen, exactly as it was when you entered the commands manually.

Execute the program again. Enter

```
DO chkstats ↵
```

This time the program executes, but is not compiled because dBASE IV can now use the object file already stored on the disk to carry out the program's commands.

Controlling the Screen Display

The program you created simplifies the task of calculating the total amount for the checks in the CKBOOK file. However, the results of the program, as seen on the screen display, are far from clear. In order to understand what the program accomplished, you must know what the commands in the program did. Only then is it clear what 4621.86 means.

You can improve the program by adding commands that explain clearly to the user what the meaning of the number is.

One improvement is to clear the screen of all information before displaying the value. This can be accomplished with the CLEAR command.

Another useful addition is to display a message that tells the user what the number means. The ? command can be used to place messages in your program. Recall that ? displays a list of items on the screen. In this case, the item is a text literal, i.e., a message surrounded by quotations.

To make changes to a program, load the program into the editor using the same command as was used to create the program.

```
MODIFY COMMAND chkstats ↵
```

Insert the CLEAR command at the beginning of the program. Make sure the Insert mode is active. If the mode is active, Ins appears on the right side of the status line. If you are not in the Insert mode, activate it by pressing

[Ins]. In addition to the CLEAR command, add a ? command, which will be followed by a message explaining the numbers value. Remember to press ↵ at the end of each line. Enter

```
CLEAR
```

Move the cursor to Line 4. Enter

```
? "The Total of all checks is:"
```

Use the shortcut key, [Ctrl-End], to save the program.

```
[Ctrl-End]
```

Run the modified program by entering

```
DO chkstats ↵
```

The program is compiled again because changes were made to the original source-code file. Whenever you run an application, dBASE IV compares the time and date of the PRG file, with the time and date of the corresponding DBO file. If the PRG file has more recent data, the program assumes changes have been made and the program needs to be recompiled.

When the program is compiled and executed, results of the new program are displayed. The screen now provides a clear picture of what the data is about.

```
The Total of all checks:

    13 records  summed
       amount
       4621.86
```

This is an improvement, but much of the display was automatically generated by dBASE IV. For example, the last three lines of the display were automatically written to the screen by the SUM command. Many—but not all—dBASE IV commands place information on the screen automatically. This automatic information is called *talk*. Commands generating talk do so to provide a visual feedback to the user. In order to create useful programs, you should have complete control of the screen display. You can turn off the display of talk using the SET TALK command. Load the program into the editor.

You can save some typing by using the dBASE IV history buffer. For example, the command shown below, MODIFY COMMAND chkstats, was entered just two commands ago. You can avoid retyping the command by entering up arrow twice. This places the command on the edit line. Pressing ↵ reexecutes the command. In this book, for the sake of clarity, all commands are written out explicitly. However, feel free to use the history buffer to avoid extra typing, whenever you can. Even when there are slight changes, you can edit commands in the history buffer just by displaying those that are close in syntax to the command you want to enter. Editing commands can also save a lot of typing.

```
MODIFY COMMAND chkstats ↵
```

Insert SET TALK at the beginning of the program. Remember to press ↵ at the end of each command.

```
SET TALK OFF
```

It is important to remember changing settings, such as TALK, during the execution of a program, carries over into the dBASE IV environment, after the program is completed. If you SET the TALK OFF in a program, it is usually a good idea to SET the TALK ON again, at the end of the program. Like closing databases, setting options back to their default settings is considered good programming form. Move the cursor to the end of the program. The shortcut key combination [Ctrl-PgDn] will accomplish this.

```
[Ctrl-Pg Dn]
```

Enter

```
SET TALK ON
```

Another aspect of good programming form is to always end the program with the RETURN command. The RETURN command tells dBASE IV your program is finished, and control should be passed back to the Dot Prompt. You may have noticed, even without the RETURN command in the program, dBASE IV returns control to the Dot Prompt following the last command in the file. In effect, dBASE IV assumes a RETURN command should follow the last command in the program. In a simple program such as this, dBASE IV compensates for the lack of a RETURN. However, it is a good habit to place the RETURN command at the end, even in the simplest program.

```
RETURN
```

Save and execute the program.

```
[Ctrl-End]
DO chkstats ↵
```

What happened? The SET TALK command did exactly what it was supposed to do; it suppressed the display of the talk. But you may not have realized that, in suppressing the talk, you also suppressed the value you wanted to display.

Is there a way to display only the value without the rest of the talk? The answer brings you to one of the most important topics related to writing dBASE IV programs.

Memory Variables

The solution to this problem, and to many others encountered in programming, lies in the use of *memory variables*. A memory variable is an alternative way to store information during a dBASE IV session. Like a field, the memory variable has a name (1 to 10 characters) and stores information in one of the basic data types—character, numeric, date, logical, or floating decimal point.

You cannot store the contents of a memo field in a memory variable.

However, unlike fields, memory variables are *not* stored in disk files. Instead, memory variables are stored in the internal memory of the computer, meaning the values are temporary. All memory variables are erased when you quit dBASE IV. Memory variables created by a program have an even shorter life. dBASE IV automatically erases all memory variables created by a specific program, as soon as the program is finished.

Although memory variables are temporary, they have one advantage over fields. Because they are stored in memory, not in files, they can be accessed at any time. To access field data, you must open the proper database and position the pointer to the correct record, in order to obtain the value. Memory variables, on the other hand, each have a unique name. You can reference a memory variable, regardless of what databases are or are not open.

Memory variables have three basic functions:

Statistical Values

Memory variables are particularly useful in holding statistical values derived from database information. For example, the total sum of all the checks is a statistical summary of the values stored in a number of records. Since the value is about the entire database, it does not make sense to place this value into any one field within the database itself. Because memory variables are held apart from the database information, they are a perfect place to put totals, counts, averages, and other statistical information.

Passing Values

Variables are also used to pass a value from one part of a program to another. For example, suppose you wanted to copy a value from one database field and place it into a field in another database. One way to do this is to copy the information from the first database, into a memory variable. You can then activate another database and place the value in the memory variable, into the field of the new database.

Control Program Flow

Variables are also used to control program operations. Programs often need to keep track of special values used to control the flow of a program. For example, suppose a program is to repeat an operation ten times. A variable can be used to store the value of the number of repetitions. When the variable reaches ten, the program stops.

---

dBASE IV is set by default to allow the definition of 500 different memory variables. However, there must be sufficient memory in the computer to hold all 500. By default, dBASE IV uses memory in blocks of 28K. Each 28K block can hold 50 variables.

Once a variable is defined, it can be treated in much the same way as a field. It can be displayed on the screen, or used as part of dBASE IV expressions and formulas.

You will learn how to use variables in a wide variety of ways. In this particular case, you want to capture the value generated by the SUM command. Once captured, you can display the value with the ? command.

Once again, load the CHKSTATS program into the editor.

```
MODIFY COMMAND chkstats ⏎
```

The command to change is the SUM command. As written, the SUM command generates only talk. With the talk turned off, the SUM command displays nothing. However, the SUM command accepts a TO clause. The TO clause causes the command to place the value it calculates into a memory variable. For example, by adding TO total_amt to the command, you cause the value to be place into a variable called TOTAL_AMT.

```
Move the cursor to line 6
```

Change the command to use the memory variable.

```
[End]
TO total_amt ⏎
```

The command now reads: SUM amount TO total_amt. Your task is not complete, however. Placing information into a memory variable does not place information on the screen. This requires a specific command, such as ?. Use ? to display the value of the TOTAL_AMT variable. Enter

> `? total_amt`

Before you save the program, there is another change to make. The two ? commands are separated by the SUM command. Another good programming habit is to place all the output commands, when possible, in a group. This makes it easier to locate the part of the program that sends data to the screen, or the printer. If you get into the habit of scattering the output commands throughout the program, it can be difficult to adjust the output because you have to search around to find the output commands. In a small program like this, it really doesn't matter where the commands are placed. But as you write longer programs, keeping groups of related commands together make it easier to read and revise a program.

However, you have already entered the commands separately. How can you change the sequence? The dBASE IV editor (unlike the dBASE III and III Plus editor) has commands allowing you to copy and move blocks of text. In this case, use the move command to rearrange the commands.

Here, move the SUM command up so the two ? commands are grouped together. The first step is to highlight the block of text you want to move.

> `[up arrow]`
>   `[Home]`

The cursor is now at the beginning of Line 6, the line containing the SUM command. To begin the highlighting process, enter

> `[F6]`

The S is highlighted. To extend the amount of text in the highlight, use any of the directional movement keys. Enter

> `[right arrow]`

The highlight is extended 1 character, to include the U. A quick way to include the entire line is to use the [End] key, which moves the cursor, and in so doing stretches the highlight to the end of the line. Enter

> `[End]`

With the entire line highlighted, complete the selection process by entering

>   ⏎

Once the text has been highlighted, activate the Move mode. Enter

> `[F7]`

Move the cursor to the location where you want the highlighted text placed. In this case, that is one line up. Enter

```
[up arrow]
```

Move the highlighted text by entering

```
[F7]
```

The program moves the text, and in so doing, rearranges the commands into the desired order.

To see the results of the change, save and execute the program. The Exit menu provides a shortcut. The Run command saves the program and runs the application in a single step. Enter

```
[Alt-e] r
```

The program now produces two lines of information.

```
The Total of all checks:
        4621.86
```

This information is displayed because you have two ? commands inside the program. All the other activity generated by the program is hidden from the user. This simple program demonstrates the essence of all programs. The processing required to carry out the task is hidden from the user. Only the information you need to see is displayed. In a sense, programs are visual illusions. The user thinks in terms of the data displayed on the screen. You are not aware of the structure and objects being manipulated in the background. Since the user only knows what is presented on the screen, the quality and clarity of that display is crucial to the success of the program. As you will see, much of the effort expended in programming is directed towards controlling and selecting what information is displayed on the screen.

Formatting Displayed Items

When the CHKSTATS program displays the memory variable TOTAL_AMT, the number is displayed without punctuation (such as a comma between the thousands place and the hundreds place). Recall in Report and Screen forms, the field definition menu box included an option for a *template* and a *picture function*. These options allowed you to control certain aspects of the way information in the fields was displayed.

The template was a model of the way the field should be formatted, when displayed. For example, a numeric field would be formatted with a template like 999,999.99. The character *9* represents any digit from 0-9. The comma shows where a comma should be inserted, if the value has a sufficient number of digits. Templates determine format on a character-by-character basis. For example, if the 999,999.99 is used, and the value to be displayed has more than 6 digits to the left of the decimal place (e.g. 1,000,000) the template overflows. Thus, instead of displaying the actual numbers in the template format, dBASE IV displays an * (e.g. ***,***.**). You should always allow sufficient room in the template for the largest number you are likely to display.

A Picture function is a single character added to a template, along with an @ symbol. Picture functions work on values to be displayed as a whole. For example, the $ function places a $ before the first digit of the number.

A template is attached to a ? command using the PICTURE clause. Example: PICTURE "999,999.99"

Before you add these formatting commands to your program, you can experiment with the effect of different types of templates and Picture functions by creating a memory variable you can use as an example in the Dot Prompt mode.

Memory variables can be created using the STORE command, which has two forms. For example, the two commands below create a memory variable called TEST_VAL, and assign the value of 1555 to the memory variable.

```
STORE 1555 TO test_val
test_val=1555
```

The second command is the shorthand version of STORE, which is used when you are storing a value to a single variable.

The long form of STORE is used when you want to assign one value to a list of memory variables, e.g., STORE 10 TO test1,test2,test3,test4.

Create the TEST_VAL variable and assign it a value of 1555 by entering

```
test_val=1555 ↵
```

You can print the value of variable with the ? command. Enter

```
? test_val ↵
```

The 1555 is displayed. Display the value again, this time using a PICTURE clause, to format the value according to a template. Enter

```
? test_val PICTURE "999,999.99" ↵
```

Now, the value is displayed according to the format shown in the template, *1,555.00.* If you add a $ to the template, dBASE IV fills any of the unused digits with $ characters. Enter

```
? test_val PICTURE "$999,999.99" ↵
```

The value is displayed with $$$ in front. Instead of the $ template character, you could use the $ Picture function. A function affects the overall format of the template. The $ Picture function displays a single $ character before the first digit of the value. Picture functions are always the first characters in the template. They are preceded by an @ symbol, and separated from the rest of the template by a space. To use the $ picture function, enter

```
? test_val PICTURE "@$ 999,999.99" ↵
```

The value is displayed as $1,555.00. The screen shows the last four commands and the result of those commands.

```
. Test_val= 1555
   1555
. ? test_val
   1555
. ? test_val PICTURE "999,999.99"
 1,555.00
. ? test_val PICTURE "$999,999.99"
$$$1,555.00
. ? test_val PICTURE "@$ 999,999.99"
$1,555.00
```

Horizontal Location

In addition to controlling the format of the displayed values, you can also control the horizontal position of the information, using an AT clause. The AT clause, when attached to a ? command, allows you to designate the column on the screen where the first character should be displayed. dBASE IV divides the screen into 80 columns. Remember, dBASE IV begins with column zero, not column 1. That means the last column on the right of the screen (the 80th column) is column 79.

By default, the ? command displays the data beginning in column zero. You can use the AT clause to select a different horizontal location. Enter

```
? test_val AT 30 ↵
? test_val AT 60 ↵
```

The values are displayed beginning at column 30, and column 60, respectively.

If you paid close attention to the values displayed on the screen, you may have noticed the values seem to print further to the right than the AT function seems to specify. The command using AT 30 ought to have started the value in the left half of the screen. Instead, it appears the value is printed just about center screen, close to what would be column 40. Why is this true?

What would happen if you printed the value at column 0? Enter

```
? test_val AT 0 ↵
```

The 1555 appears to print to the right of column. The value is offset when it prints, because when you create a numeric memory variable, it is automatically assigned a length of 10 characters. Unlike fields, you do not have an opportunity to set the length of the memory variables when you create them. The reason the value appears to print farther to the right than it should, is because the value acts as if it were a 10-character numeric field. When you print the value, the first 6 characters are blank spaces. When the value is printed at column 0, the first digit actually appears at column 6.

You can eliminate these extra spaces by using the T picture function. The T function, meaning TRIM, eliminates any leading or trailing blanks. You can use both the AT and PICTURE clause at the same time. Enter

> `? test_val AT 0 PICTURE "@T" ⏎`

This time, the first digit appears in column 0. You can combine all the PICTURE and AT elements into a single command. Enter

> `? test_val AT 30 PICTURE "@T$ 999,999.99" ⏎`

The formatted value prints at the exact location specified by the AT command. You can add these options to the ? command in your program. Enter

> `MODIFY COMMAND chkstats ⏎`

Move the cursor to Line 5.

Add an AT clause to command so it prints at column 25. Change the command to read:

> `? "The Total of all checks:" AT 25`

Move the cursor to Line 7. Add both an AT and a PICTURE clause to this command. Change the command to read:

> `? total_amt AT 25 PICTURE "@T$ 999,999.99"`

The entire program now reads:

```
SET TALK OFF
CLEAR
USE ckbook
SET FILTER TO payee#"DEPOSIT"
SUM amount TO total_amt
? "The Total of all checks is:" AT 25
? total_amt AT 25 PICTURE "@T$ 999,999.99"
CLOSE DATABASE
SET TALK ON
RETURN
```

Save and execute the revised program.

> `[Alt-e] r`

The program now displays the information aligned at column 25, rather than on the left side of the screen, and the value is formatted as dollars and cents.

```
The Total of all checks:
$4,621.86
```

Adding More Information

The program currently finds the total amount of all the checks. There are probably other kinds of information about the checking account status you would like to know, as part of a general report. You can enlarge the report to include this information. Load the program into the dBASE IV editor.

```
MODIFY COMMAND chkstats ⏎
```

In addition to calculating the total amount of the checks, you may want to know the number of Checks written. Instead of using the SUM command, you might replace it with a CALCULATE command. The CALCULATE command (discussed in Chapter 4) can perform several types of calculations. In this case, it can calculate both the number of checks and the total amount.

Move the cursor to Line 5. Remove the SUM command by entering

```
[Ctrl-y]
```

The CALCULATE command uses special options to signify which calculations are to be performed. In order to sum and count records with a single command, you will use the SUM( ) and CNT( ) options.

SUM( ) and CNT( ) are options for the CALCULATE command, not dBASE IV functions. These options have meaning only when used with the CALCULATE command. dBASE IV functions can be used in any dBASE IV expression.

Because you will be calculating two values, you need two variable names to hold the values. The values are assigned to the memory variables, based on the order in which the options and variable names appear. This means the first calculation option is assigned to the first memory variable, and so on. Note, when you use the TO clause with a calculate command, the number of calculation options must match the number of memory variable names, or the command will be rejected by the compiler as having invalid syntax.

Enter the CALCULATE command. Remember to enter ⏎ at the end of each new command line.

```
CALCULATE SUM(amount),CNT( ) TO total_amt,num_checks
```

In addition to the number and amount of the checks, you may want to calculate the number and amount of the deposits.

In order to work with the deposit, you can change the filter setting to select deposit records, instead of check records. Enter a new SET FILTER command to change the way the records are being selected. In this case, change the command to select records that have DEPOSIT in the payee field.

```
SET FILTER TO payee="DEPOSIT"
```

Following the change in database filters, you can perform a new set of calculations. The operations will be the same—i.e., the SUM(amount) and CNT( ) options will be used to calculate the amount of the deposits and their number. However, the values will be stored in different variables. Add another CALCULATE command.

```
CALCULATE SUM(amount),CNT( ) TO total_dep,num_dep
```

The program now has 4 values stored in variables:
TOTAL_AMT, NUM_CHECKS, TOTAL_DEP, NUM_DEP.

However, merely calculating the values is half of the job. You must also include commands to display the values. Only the TOTAL_AMT variable is currently displayed on the screen. You must add commands to display the other three variables.

Printing On The Same Line

The TOTAL_AMT information was printed on two separate lines. You may want to combine information so several items print on one line. There are three basic ways to approach this task, each one having certain advantages.

The simplest method is to print items as a list—a series of items separated by commas. For example, to print information about the number of checks, you can write a text message and the value as items in a list.

Move the cursor to line 10. Add the command shown below, in which two items are printed as a list. Note, the first command is positioned at column 25 with an AT clause, but the second item has no AT position designated. In this case, dBASE IV assumes the second item should be placed onto the same line at the next available location, to the right of the first item. The location of the second item is *relative* to the location of the first item. The first item is given an *explicit* location, e.g., column 25.

```
? num_checks AT 25 PICTURE "@T","checks written."
```

A second method of combining information on a single line is to create an expression consisting of all the elements. Writing an expression is simplest when all the items on the line are text fields, literals, or variables. When you want to display items combining character information with numeric, date, or logical values, it is necessary to convert the non-character items to characters.

The most common conversion is that of a numeric value into a character value. The TRANSFORM( ) function is designed to convert a numeric value to characters, and at the same time, format the number using picture templates and Picture functions. The TRANSFORM( ) function has the following general form:

TRANSFORM(*numeric_exp,picture_template*)

The *numeric_exp* can be any valid dBASE IV numeric expression, including fields, memory variables, or formulas. The *picture_template* is the same type of template, including the Picture function you have been using with the PICTURE clause. Add the command below.

```
? "The Total of all Deposits is: "+;
TRANSFORM(total_dep,"@T$   999,999.99" AT 25
```

The third approach to the task of printing more than one item on a line, is to use a separate command for each item. The trick is there are two forms of the ? command: ? and ??. The standard command, ?, always inserts a ↵ *before* it displays the item or items listed with the command. This means each ? begins a new line. The ?? form of the command prints its data at whatever line or column follows the last item printed. The ?? does not insert a ↵. The result is ?? commands will continue printing on the same line, assuming there is sufficient room to fit the data on the screen.

The ?? allows you to list several commands, with only a single line appearing on the screen. The next item to be displayed is the number of deposits. Begin with a command to print the number of deposits, at column 25.

```
? num_dep AT 25 PICTURE  "@T"
```

The next command uses ?? to place text on the same line. Note, the text begins with a blank space. This is necessary because the program places the next item in the next column on the line. If you did not begin the text with a space, the text and the number would run together.

```
?? " deposits made."
```

What about the account balance? It is not necessary to look into the database to find this value. You have already captured the check and deposit totals in memory variables. All you need do to determine the account balance is subtract the memory variables. Add two more commands to the program to display the balance. Note, the first command begins with ?, meaning it will begin on a new line. It is followed by ??, which places the value on the same line as the text. The text of the first command ends with a blank space to separate the value from the end of the text.

```
? "The current account balance is: " AT 25
?? total_dep-total_amt  PICTURE "@T$ 999,999.99"
```

The entire program now looks like this:

```
SET TALK OFF
CLEAR
USE ckbook
SET FILTER TO payee#"DEPOSIT"
CALCULATE SUM(amount),CNT( ) TO total_amt,num_checks
SET FILTER TO payee="DEPOSIT"
CALCULATE SUM(amount),CNT( ) TO total_dep,num_dep
? "The Total of all checks is:" AT 25
? total_amt AT 25 PICTURE "@T$ 999,999.99"
? num_checks AT 25 PICTURE "@T","checks written."
? "The Total of all Deposits is: ";
    +TRANSFORM(total_dep,"@T$  999,999.99"
? num_dep AT 25 PICTURE "@T"
?? "deposits made."
? "The current account balance is: " AT 25
?? total_dep-total_amt  PICTURE "@T$ 999,999.99") AT 25
CLOSE DATABASE
SET TALK ON
RETURN
```

Save and execute the program.

```
[Alt-e] r
```

Compiling Errors

As dBASE IV compiles your program, something unexpected happens. Instead of running the program just written, dBASE IV encounters an incorrectly written command within the program. The line number, 11, and the text of the command, are displayed on the screen. The compiler writes the type of error—Syntax error—below the line. When the compiling is complete, dBASE IV displays a message box on the screen telling you there has been a Compilation error. Keep in mind while the message is telling you there is an error in Line 11, it is also telling you all the rest of the lines in the program are correct. Only Line 11 needs attention.

```
Compiling line       11
? "The Total of all Deposits is: "+TRANSFORM(total_dep,"@T$ 999,999.99"
Error on line 11: Syntax error
Compiling line       18




                        Compilation error
                   Press any key to continue..._
```

Figure 11-1. Error message displayed during compiling.

Finding syntax errors with the dBASE IV compiler has a number of advantages over the interpreter system used in dBASE III & III Plus. One advantage of the compiler is it displays all the lines with errors at one time. This is because it continues to scan the program, even though it has encountered an error. In dBASE III & III Plus, the error is discovered only when you run the program; in this case, the program stops when the first error is found. If there is another error later in the program, you do not learn about it until you correct the first error, then try to run the program a second time. In dBASE IV, all the errors appear when the compiler checks the file, so if only one error shows up, you can infer all the rest of the commands are correct.

When an error occurs during the compiling process, the program cannot be executed because the compiler will not create an object-code file (DBO extension) for a file with errors. You must correct the error before running the program. Acknowledge the message by entering

     ⏎

The error causes the program to return to the Dot Prompt mode. In order to correct the error, you must return to the Edit mode. Enter (Remember, you can use the up arrow to access commands in the history buffer to save time.)

     MODIFY COMMAND chkstats ⏎

You know from the error messages that Line 11 contains the problem. You can use the GO TO menu to move the cursor to a specific line number. Enter

     [Alt-g] g 11 ⏎

In this instance, you encounter a common mistake in dBASE IV syntax. The closing parentheses at the end of the TRANSFORM function has not been plced. This is an easy error to make because a template used with a PICTURE clause does not require parentheses. But this template is used as part of a TRANSFORM function, which does require parentheses. Add the missing character by entering

```
[End]
)
```

While you are editing, you may notice you did not use an AT function with this command. Unlike the others, it will begin display at column zero. Correct this by adding an AT clause to the line, so the rest of the information will begin at column 25.

```
[spacebar]
AT 25
```

Save and execute the corrected program.

```
[Alt-e]  r
```

This time, all 18 lines of the program compile correctly and the program is executed. It displays the information about the CKBOOK records, as designed by the commands within the program.

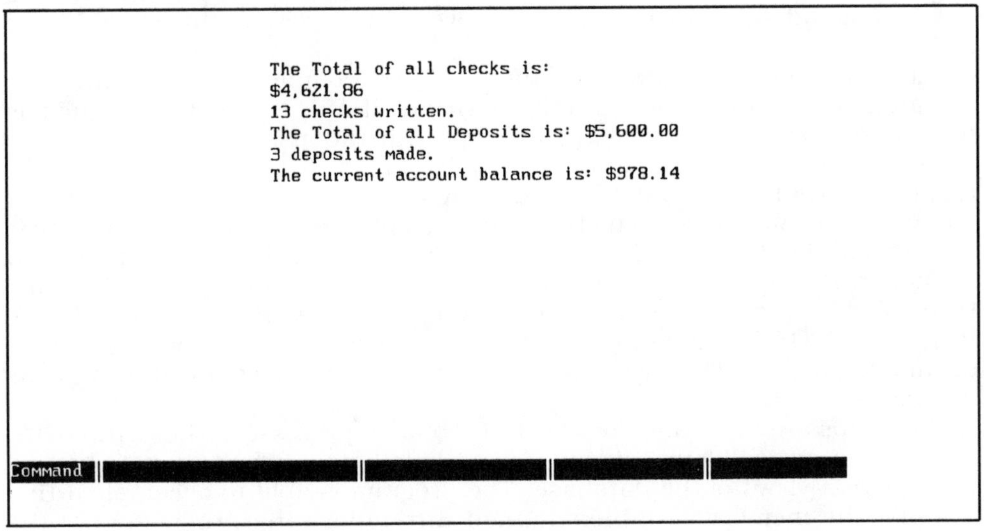

```
                    The Total of all checks is:
                    $4,621.86
                    13 checks written.
                    The Total of all Deposits is: $5,600.00
                    3 deposits made.
                    The current account balance is: $978.14




Command
```

Figure 11-2. Error message displayed during compiling.

Syntax and Logical Errors

In any Programming language, there are two general categories of errors: syntax (or usage) errors and logical errors. A syntax error is made when you enter a command with the wrong command word, clause, or punctuation. Syntax errors are similar to spelling or grammar errors in writing. Omitting the closing parentheses is a punctuation error that can be detected by matching the opening and closing parentheses.

A logical error is one that occurs when the commands are executed. Logical errors involve the meaning of the command. It is quite possible to write a grammatically correct command that cannot be carried out, because its logic does not fit the situation. For example, the command ? total is a valid command because it is written in the correct form. Whether it is logically correct can only be determined by its context within the program. If the command is executed and there is no field or memory variable with the name *total* available, the command is logically incorrect and generates a *runtime* error. A runtime error is the result of the context in which a command is executed, not the grammar of the command.

The dBASE IV compiler does not attempt to resolve potential logical errors. There is one exception. When you execute an SQL program, the compiling process includes a detailed analysis of the SQL query used in the program. If references are made to SQL tables or columns that do not exist—what would be logical errors in dBASE IV—the compiler flags those errors and rejects compiling of the SQL application. SQL commands and programming are covered in Part IV of this book.

The program you created, although not very complex, demonstrates the advantage of programming over other forms of dBASE IV operations, such as the Control Center query, screen, and report operations.

In the Control Center operations detailed in Part I, you created query and related reports that operated on CKBOOK as a check database or a deposit database. This was done using the Query mode to select one group of records from within the database. But a query cannot be two things at one time. You cannot create a query to sum all the checks and all the deposits at the same time. The query can select records based on PAYEE="DEPOSIT" or PAYEE#"DEPOSIT, but not both. This is because queries are basically static database objects. They represent a particular view of the database or databases.

Programs are not static objects, but dynamic processes. The CHKSTATS program uses two different filter commands to obtain information, based on two different views of the database. The program is able to accomplish this because the memory variables defined throughout the program hold the results of operations, for use later in the program. For example, the program begins by selecting only the checks and calculating their total. By storing that value into a memory variable, the program can go on and perform different database operations, and still retain the value it calculated.

The CHKSTATS program illustrates a program that is different from a query, screen layout, or report, in that a program can be constantly changing the way data is being manipulated, as it executes. In a program, the sequence in which the commands are issued is every bit as important as the commands and specifications, themselves. In order to find the total amount of the checks, you *must* issue the CALCULATE command in the proper sequence, i.e., after the first SET FILTER, but before the second SET FILTER command. When you create a query, it does not really matter in what order the query specifications are entered, since the result is a single view of the database.

As your programs begin to get more complex, the importance of the sequence of the commands becomes even greater.

Vertical Spacing

The CHKSTATS program displays all the lines of information consecutively on the screen. It may improve the readability of the display if the items could be separated vertically. You can create vertical spacing between print items by printing blank lines. The ? command used without an item or list of items, still generates a ⏎ on the screen, having the effect of displaying a blank line. For each ? you enter there will be one blank line.

```
MODIFY COMMAND chkstats ⏎
```

Move the cursor to Line 8. If you were to insert a blank line before the first line of information, all the subsequent lines would be positioned further down the page. Add two blank lines.

```
?
?
```

Move the cursor to Line 13. Insert two blanks at this point, to separate the check information from the deposit information.

```
?
?
```

Move the cursor to Line 18 and insert two more blanks.

```
?
?
```

The blank lines space out the information vertically. Save and run the program by entering

```
[Alt-e] r
```

The screen display shows the data separated by blank space, into three different sections. While the separation does not add any concrete data to the display, it does make the data easier to read.

This time, all 18 lines of the program compile correctly and the program is executed. It displays the information about the CKBOOK records, as designed by the commands within the program.

```
                    The Total of all checks is:
                    $4,621.86
                    13 checks written.


                    The Total of all Deposits is: $5,600.00
                    3 deposits made.


                    The current account balance is: $978.14




Command
```

Figure 11-3. Blank lines used for vertical spacing.

Replicating a Character

Another enhancement you can make to the screen display is to draw
horizontal lines. One way to do this is to use the REPLICATE( ) and CHR( )
functions (as seen in Chapter 6) to repeat a character a sufficient number of
times to create a line. MSDOS computers have special characters appearing
on the screen display, but are not found on the keyboard. These characters
are used by programs to draw lines and boxes on the screen. You can access
these characters within a dBASE IV program by using the CHR( ) function.
The CHR( ) function allows you to use a character by entering its decimal
ASCII values. The characters and values used for drawing horizontal lines
are shown in the table below.

Character	Value
	176
	177
	178
	196
	205
	219

You can display any one of the characters by using the CHR( ) function in
a ? command. Enter

        ? CHR(205) ↵

The XX character appears on the screen in column 0. You can use the AT clause to place the character at any horizontal location.

> `? CHR(205) AT 39` ⏎

The character is now displayed in the center of the screen.

The REPLICATE( ) function repeats a specific character a specified number of times. Enter

> `? REPLICATE(CHR(205),80)` ⏎

This command draws a double line across the page.

You can add lines created by the replication of these characters to your program, to further enhance the display.

> `MODIFY COMMAND chkstats` ⏎

Move the cursor to Line 9. Add the REPLICATE( ) and CHR( ) functions to draw a double line across the screen.

> `[End] [spacebar]`
> `REPLICATE(CHR(205),80)`

Move the cursor to Line 14. Place the cursor at the beginning of the line.

> `[Home]`

This time, insert a new line that will draw a single line across the screen. Inserting a new line causes the two sections to be separated by three lines, with the single line drawn between the two blanks.

> `? REPLICATE(CHR(196),80)`

You can place the same command following the deposit information. Instead of entering the line from scratch, you can create a duplicate of the line with the copy procedure. Begin by highlighting the command just entered.

> `[down arrow]`
> `[F6]`
> `[End]`
> ⏎

Enter the COPY command.

> `[F8]`

Move the cursor to Line 20, where you will place the copy. Enter

    [F8]

Make another copy and place it at Line 24.

    [F8]
 [down arrow] *(4 times)*
   [F8]

Save and execute the program.

    [Alt-e] r

This time, the program displays lines drawn across the screen, separating sections of the display.

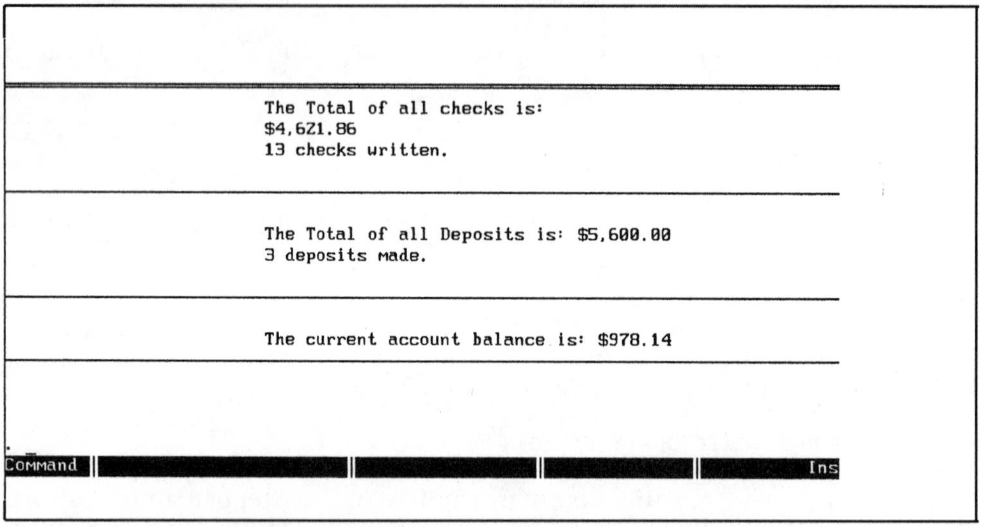

```
The Total of all checks is:
$4,6Z1.86
13 checks written.




The Total of all Deposits is: $5,600.00
3 deposits made.




The current account balance is: $978.14
```

Command   Ins

Figure 11-4. Blank lines used for vertical spacing.

Centering Items

AT clauses used with the ? and ?? commands, utilized actual values, such as 25, to place the information at specific columns. However, the value used with the AT clause does not have to be a literal number. It can be a formula calculating a location value.

One reason for using a formula with the AT command is to center information horizontally on the screen. dBASE IV does not have a command or function to directly center items. You can, however, calculate what the horizontal location should be, in order to center an item.

Suppose you wanted to center the text Checkbook Statisticsn the screen. To experiment with the problem, create a memory variable containing this text. Enter

```
title="Checkbook  Statistics"  ⏎
```

Since the screen is 80-characters wide, you should place the text so there is the same amount of space on the left and right sides. To do this you must know how many characters are in the text you want to center. dBASE IV has a function-LEN( )-to calculate the number of characters in a character field, variable, or expression. Enter

```
? LEN(title)  ⏎
```

The command displays the value 20, indicating the number of characters in the text item. If there are 20 characters in the text, and 80 overall across the screen, that leaves you with 80-20 = 60 columns of blank space. If you divide this between the left and right sides of the screen, you find there will be 30 columns on either side of the text. In this case, printing the text at column 30 will display the title centered horizontally. Enter

```
? title AT 30  ⏎
```

In order to arrive at the value of 30, you must perform some simple arithmetic. There is no reason why dBASE IV can't perform the same calculation. Enter

```
? title AT (80-LEN(title))/2  ⏎
```

The expression (80-LEN(title))/2 is a generalized formula to find the correct location for any text item. If you change the text stored in TITLE, the command automatically calculates the correct location. Enter

```
title="Summary  of the CKBOOK database"  ⏎
? title AT (80-LEN(title))/2  ⏎
```

The new phrase is centered correctly. It is important to understand the formula will work only if the text is stored in a memory variable before you use the ? command to display it. When the text is stored in a variable, you can refer to it in your command.

Add a title to the CHKSTATS program.

```
MODIFY COMMAND chkstats  ⏎
```

Move the cursor to Line 8. Define a variable called TITLE, with the text for the screen title.

```
title="Checkbook  Statistics  Summary Screen"
```

Add a ? command that uses the formula discussed above, to center the text.

```
? title AT (80-LEN(title))/2  ⏎
```

Save and execute the program by entering

        [Alt-] r

The title text appears centered above the rest of the display.

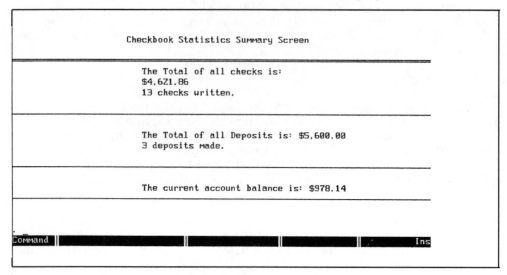

```
                    Checkbook Statistics Summary Screen

                    The Total of all checks is:
                    $4,621.86
                    13 checks written.



                    The Total of all Deposits is:  $5,600.00
                    3 deposits made.



                    The current account balance is:  $978.14




Command                                                                    Ins
```

Figure 11-5. Title text centered horizontally.

Programs That Carry on a Dialog

In the first part of this chapter you learned the basics of program creation with dBASE IV. This section explores programs that carry on a *dialog* with the user. Dialog refers to programs that pause and allow the user to respond to queries, before continuing to execute the next sequence of commands.

Pausing a program for user input has many implications for the look, feel, and function of applications. In its simplest form, a pause suspends the execution of commands until the user presses a key. Taken a step further, the key or keys entered by the user can be used as data elements in the program. The user can enter some information—a value, text, or date—that affects the rest of the commands in the program. This means that the output of the program will change, depending upon what the user enters as the program is running.

Full Screen Formatting

The two programs you created so far in this chapter, have used the ? command. ? falls into the category of *streaming*-output commands. Streaming-output commands always place output in a sequence of lines. The vertical position of each new item is on the next line below the previous item.

When you reach the bottom of the screen, new lines would cause the data at the top of the screen to begin to scroll off the display. Streaming-output commands correspond to the way data is placed onto the printed page. When data is printed, it is placed onto the paper in a strict sequence, beginning in the upper-left corner of the page, and moving left to right on each line, from top to bottom on each page. The very nature of the way printing takes place requires the output to move in a continuous stream or scroll.

But the screen display is not so limited. As demonstrated in the Control Center menu system, information can be displayed in various locations on the screen, in a variety of orders. It is possible to display data at the bottom of the screen, then to open a pop-up menu at the top of the screen. Commands taking advantage of the screen display in this way are called Full Screen formatting commands. The term *full screen* refers to commands that view the screen display not as a scroll, but as a two-dimensional grid. The screen is really divided into a series of cells arranged in rows and col-umns. Each cell is large enough to contain a single character. The rows are numbered from 0 to 24 (25 rows) and the columns from 0 to 79 (80 columns). Row zero is the top line of the screen display, while column zero is the left-most column on the screen.

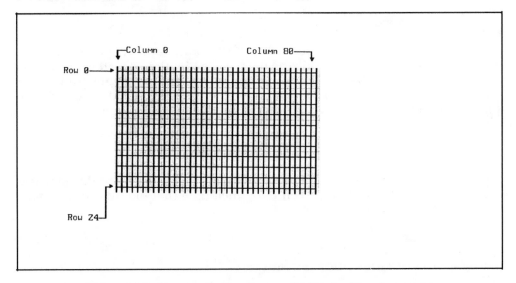

Figure 11-6. Screen display view as 25 line by 80 column grid.

The Full Screen formatting commands address locations on the screen by their row and column location. The most powerful of the Full Screen commands is the @/SAY command. @/SAY takes the following general form:

@ ROW_NUMBER, *column_number* SAY *expression*

The @/SAY command allows you to designate both the horizontal and vertical location of the text. Because the command contains expli-cit instructions as to the row and column location, you can display information on any part of the screen display, in any order. If there is already information at the location you select, the old information will be overwritten and the new data placed on top of it.

You can use @/SAY to place information, as defined by any valid dBASE IV expression, at any location on the screen. Enter

```
@ 10,10 SAY "T = " ⏎
```

The data appears starting at the specified location on the screen. You can enter another @/SAY command and place data on the screen above the previous item.

The coordinates used in the @/SAY or other Full Screen commands, *must* fall within the limits of the screen display, in this example 0-24 vertically and 0 to 80 horizontally. Values exceeding those parameters will generate an error when the program attempts to execute the commands. The compiler will not catch this type of error. It will only become evident after the program is executed, and the command with the error is executed.

```
@ 5,60 SAY "example" ⏎
```

Note, when you enter the second @/SAY command, the screen display does not *scroll* upward. Instead, the data placed by the second command is added to the current display. Each subsequent @/SAY command adds more information to the screen. You can place information, based on dBASE IV variables and functions, as well as literal text. The DATE( ) function displays the current date. Enter

```
@ 0,0 SAY DATE ( ) ⏎
```

The current date appears on the upper-left corner of the screen display. The CLEAR command erases all screen data, including that placed on the screen with @/SAY commands. Enter

```
CLEAR ⏎
```

Create a variable with a numeric value.

```
value=111999 ⏎
```

The @/SAY command recognizes the same type of PICTURE clause as the ? used. For example, to display the value formatted with a template, you would enter

```
@ 15,10 SAY value PICTURE "999,999.99" ⏎
```

The @/SAY command also recognizes a COLOR clause, which makes it simpler to apply color changes locally on the screen. When COLOR is used, it changes the color of the data output by the individual @/SAY command. The clause has the same effect as the COLOR=*color_code* commands used with the ? command. The following command displays the value in black on white characters.

```
@ 5,50 SAY value PICTURE "999,999" COLOR N/W ⏎
```

Note, the color affects only the output of the specific @/SAY. Enter another command.

```
@ 12,40 SAY value/2 PICTURE "999,999" ⏎
```

The information is printed in normal video, indicating the COLOR clause is localized to one command at a time.

The @/SAY command can be used to overwrite information currently on the screen. Repeat the command just entered, but do not divide the value by 2. Enter

```
@ 12,40 SAY value PICTURE "999,999" ⏎
```

The value prints over the previous number. This may seem like a small point, but imagine what this would look like if it were executed from within a program. It would appear the value at that location had changed from one value to another. You can create interesting effects by overwriting data. For example, enter the same command, but change the color to bold (bright white) characters.

```
@ 12,40 SAY value PICTURE "999,999"COLOR W+/N ⏎
```

The effect gives the illusion that you changed the color of the text. You can even make the text blink using an * with a color code.

```
@ 12,40 SAY value PICTURE "999,999"COLOR W*/N ⏎
```

What happens when you mix full screen with streaming-output? Enter

```
? value ⏎
```

The Streaming-Output command ?, causes the screen display to scroll up, including the items placed on the screen by the @/SAY commands. When you enter a Streaming command, dBASE IV treats the information currently on the screen, regardless of how it got there, as if the information were printed on paper. When the next line is added to the screen, the rest of the information is moved up like paper in a printer. This also means the row and column locations of all the items has changed.

In most cases, you want to avoid mixing streaming-output with full-screen output because of the distortion it creates.

The Status and Scoreboard Displays

When you begin to work with full-screen output, there are two important aspects of the screen display to consider: the status line and the scoreboard display.

The status line is the bar appearing across the bottom portion, Line 22, of the screen display. The status line is used to display information about mode, active databases, the records pointer, and the status of keys, such as [Ins] or [caps Lock].

dBASE IV attempts to make the status line a permanent part of the screen display. All streaming-output data is placed onto the screen on lines 0 through 21. But the @/SAY command can direct data to lines 22, 23 and 24, as well as the first 22 lines (0 through 21) of the screen display. Enter

```
@ 22,10 SAY value ⏎
```

What happened? The value flashed on the screen, but was almost immediately overwritten by the status line display. Enter

```
@ 24,10 SAY value ⏎
```

As with the attempt to display information on Line 22, the value placed on Line 24 is overwritten as soon as it is written on that line.

Although you can address all 24 lines of the screen display with the @/SAY command, in practice, the status display limits operations to Lines 0 through 21.

You can turn off the status line display using the SET STATUS command. When STATUS is off, the line does not appear on the screen and you can address all 25 screen lines. Enter

```
SET STATUS OFF ⏎
```

The status line is removed from the screen display. The Dot Prompt and cursor move down to Line 24 on the screen display. Note, a change in the status setting causes dBASE IV to clear the screen. Remember that SET STATUS causes the screen display to clear. Enter

```
@ 22,10 SAY value ⏎
```

This time, the value is printed on Line 22 and remains in Line 22.

The scoreboard is a part of the screen display that becomes active only when the status line is set off. The scoreboard is an area on the top line, Line 0, of the screen used to display the status of [Ins], [Caps Lock], and [Num Lock]. Press

```
[Caps Lock]
```

If you look at the top line, you see Caps displayed. Press

```
Press [Caps Lock]
```

The Caps display is removed. What would happen if you used an @/SAY command to place data at the location on the screen where Caps had been displayed? Enter

```
@ 0,50 SAY value ⏎
```

The value flashes on the screen, then disappears. As with the status line, dBASE IV maintains this area of the screen display for scoreboard information. This is true even when the scoreboard shows no data at this location.

If you want to use Line 0 for @/SAY commands, you can turn off the scoreboard display by using the command SET SCOREBOARD. When SET STATUS and SET SCOREBOARD are both OFF there is no screen feedback on the status of the [Ins], [Caps Lock], and [Num Lock] keys. Enter

```
SET SCOREBOARD OFF ⏎
```

The screen display is once again cleared. Only the Dot Prompt and the cursor are visible.

Input Area with Get

To create a program that carries on a dialog you must have a way of pausing the program for input. The streaming-output system uses INPUT, ACCEPT, and WAIT. The full-screen system uses a clause with the @ command. The GET clause creates an input area for the specified value at the specified location on the screen.

For example, the following command displays the VALUE variable at row 5 column 10 on the screen display, in an input area. Enter

```
@ 5,10 GET value ⏎
```

The GET clause displays the current value of the variable at the location, but does so in reverse video, e.g., black on white, or some special color combination on color screens. However, the cursor is still positioned next to the Dot Prompt.

The input area is larger than the value to be displayed. This is because numeric memory variables are always stored with a width of 10 characters.

How do you get the cursor in position to enter or edit information? The answer is the READ command. The READ command is used following one or more @/GET commands. When issued, it causes the cursor to be positioned in the first input area on the screen. You can enter or edit the information displayed in the input area. Any values or changes entered will be stored as the revised value for the memory variable or field displayed at that position. Enter

   READ ⏎

The cursor is now positioned at the beginning of the input area. You can enter a new value for the VALUE variable. Enter

   1200 ⏎

Not only is the screen display changed, but the value of the VALUE variable has been changed. Enter

   @ 10,10 SAY value ⏎

 The variable is now equal to the new number entered into the input area. The use of @/GET for input has several advantages. First, you gain explicit control of the location of the input area. Second, the input area is clearly marked as to its full size by the reverse video. Third, the current value of the variable is displayed in the input area. The user has the option to accept the current value by pressing ⏎, entering a new value, or using the editing keys to modify the value.

The editing keys used in a @/GET input area are the same as those used in the data entry screens displayed in the Control Center, Edit and Browse modes.

Initialization of Variables

@/GET INPUT areas can be used for input of any type of data, numeric, characters, date, or logical. The INPUT command, which could also accept all four types of data, requires you to enter the information in the correct expression form, in order to indicate what type of data is being entered. For example, to enter character information, you enclose the text in quotation marks. Date information is enclosed in curly brackets, {}.

 The @/GET command uses a different approach. Suppose you wanted to use an @/GET area for the entry of a date into a variable called TODAY. Clear the screen display.

   CLEAR ⏎

Create an input area for the TODAY date variable.

   @ 10,30 GET TODAY ⏎

When you enter this command, the program responds with an error message box that says "Variable not found". Why?

The answer points up one of the fundamental differences between INPUT, ACCEPT, and WAIT, and the @/GET command. INPUT, ACCEPT, and WAIT automatically create the memory variable needed to store the input. The @/GET command does not create the memory variable. The reason is, @/GET can display an input area for either a field or a memory variable, while the other commands work only with memory variables. For example, when you read the command INPUT TO example you know *example* must be a memory variable. However, the command @ 10,0 GET example could refer to a memory variable or a field in an open database. You cannot tell without knowing the context, what the command refers to.

Exit the error box by entering

⏎

dBASE IV requires that a memory variable or field referenced with an @/GET command, be defined as a field or memory variable *before* the @/GET is issued. Assigning an *initial* value to a memory variable is called *initialization* of the variable. The error currently displayed on the screen is caused by a reference in an @/GET command to a memory variable, today, that was not initialized.

But what about the type of the data? When you initialize a variable, the type of data used to give the variable its initial value determines its type. For example, if you want to initialize a variable as a date variable, you must set the variable equal to a date. To create a blank date you set the variable equal to {00/00/00}. Enter

```
today={00/00/00}  ⏎
@ 10,30 GET Today  ⏎
```

The input area appears in the center of the screen, formatted as a date. But is this really a date-entry area? Enter a value that is not a valid date.

```
READ  ⏎
130189  ⏎
```

Because the input area is defined as a date-type variable, the program checks the validity of the date, just as it does when you enter information into a date field.

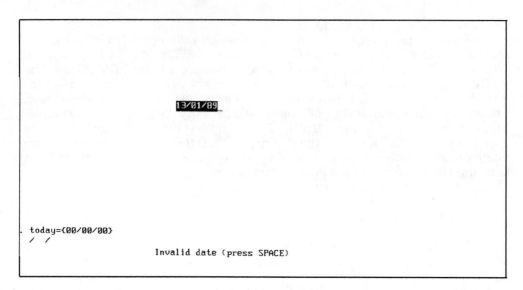

```
.  today={00/00/00}
    /  /
                        Invalid date (press SPACE)
```

Figure 11-7. @/GET input area checks date entry for validity.

Correct the entry by entering a valid date.

```
[spacebar]
12 ↵
```

Display the TODAY variable.

```
? today ↵
```

The date, 12/01/89, which you entered into the input area, is now the value of the TODAY variable.

Character Input Areas

When you want to enter character data into an input area, you must initialize the variable before you call it, with an @/GET command. However, unlike date (8 characters) and numeric (10 characters) variables, the width of a character variable is not pre-set. The width can vary from 1 to 254 characters, based on the length of the text string used to initialize the variable. For example, the command *title="Summary"* creates a 7-character text variable. This means when displayed with @/GET, you can change any of the seven characters, but you cannot lengthen the entry. It is important to remember when you initialize a character-type memory variable, you are setting the maximum entry size in the same way you select a width for a field when you are creating a database.

A handy way to define a character-type variable is with the SPACE( ) function. For example, the command *title=SPACE(15)* creates a 15-character text variable filled with fifteen blank spaces. Enter

```
title=SPACE(15)  ↵
@ 10,10 GET title ↵
READ ↵
```

Enter the text into the input area.

```
Sales Summary ↵
```

Display the current contents of the memory.

```
DISPLAY MEMORY ↵
```

The display lists three memory variables: one character, one date and one numeric.

```
TITLE        pub  C   "Sales Summary"
TODAY        pub  D   12/01/89
VALUE        pub  N        1200  (1200.000000000000000)
```

Exit the memory display by entering

```
[Esc]
```

Multiple Input Areas

When you created the calculation program, the input commands executed one after the other. When the first prompt was displayed, you had no way of knowing what other information you would be asked to enter. The @/SAY and @/GET commands allow you to display up to 1023 input areas on one screen before you issue the READ command. This means you can see all the prompts and the input area before you begin entering information.

Since most input areas require a label or some type of identification, dBASE IV allows you to combine the @/SAY and the @/GET commands into a single form: @/SAT/GET. Begin by clearing the display.

```
CLEAR ↵
```

The @/SAY/GET combination makes is simple to place a prompt and an input area on the screen. Enter

```
@ 7,20 SAY "Enter the Title" GET title ↵
```

The program displays the text *Enter the Title*, a blank space, then the input area for the TITLE variable. The last value entered into that variable is displayed. This is another difference between @/GET and the input commands. INPUT, ACCEPT, and WAIT, overwrite any information previously entered into the memory variable. @/GET displays the last entry, if any, in the input area.

The blank space between text and the input area is automatically inserted by dBASE IV. If you desire to place the input area next to the text without leaving a blank space, you have to issue separate @/SAY and @/GET commands. Example:

```
@ 7,20 SAY "Enter the Title"
@ ROW( ),COL( ) GET title
```

Note, this solution works properly only as part of a program. It does not function correctly at the Dot Prompt.

Instead of activating the input area with the READ command, place another input area on the screen.

```
        @ 9,20 SAY "Enter the date" GET today ⏎
```

There are now two input areas on the screen. Add the third variable to the same screen.

```
        @ 11,20 SAY "Enter Amount" GET value ⏎
```

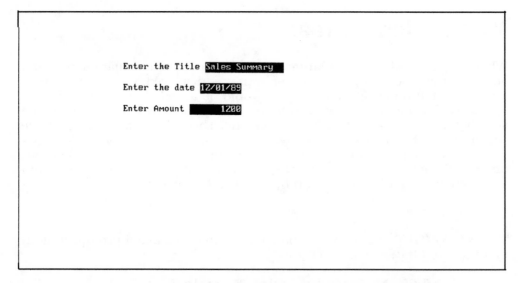

Figure 11-8. Multiple @/GET input areas on the same screen display.

You can activate all three areas with a single READ command. Enter

      `READ` ⏎

The cursor moves to the first input area. You can move from area to area, just as you would move between fields in the Edit mode display. Enter

      `down arrow`

The cursor is now positioned in the TODAY date field. Enter

      `up arrow`

    The cursor moves back to TITLE input area. This is another advantage of the @/GET input areas. Unlike, INPUT or ACCEPT, you can move back and make changes in previous areas. All the areas stay active until you have exited the last input area, or used [Ctrl-End] to exit.

      `[Ctrl-End]`

The cursor leaves the input area and return to the Dot Prompt.

Cursor Movement

As you have seen, when you display more than one @/GET input area on the screen, you can move the cursor from one input area to another, just as you would in the Edit mode display. But in what order will the cursor move from input area to input area?

    The cursor moves in the order in which the @/GET commands were issued. This order may or may not conform to the locations of the input areas on the screen. When you look at a screen display, such as the one currently on the screen, your logical assumption is the cursor moves from top to bottom through the input areas. But this is not always the case. Enter

```
        CLEAR ⏎
        @ 10,10 SAY "Title" GET title ⏎
        @ 6,10 SAY "Date" GET today ⏎
        READ ⏎
```

The cursor moves to the TITLE input area, not the TODAY input area, because the @/GET commands for TITLE was executed first. Enter

      `[down arrow]`

    Even though you pressed the down arrow key, the cursor appeared to move upward on the screen to the TODAY input area. The order in which the @/GET commands were issued is what counts, not the location of the GET areas on the screen. It is quite easy to create a very confusing screen display if you issue the @/GET commands in random order. Make sure there is a logical relationship between the locations of the @/GET's and the order in which they are executed.

On the other hand, you can control the way the cursor moves through the fields by changing the sequence of the @/GET commands. This is very important when you are placing more than one GET area on the same line. In the dBASE IV Screen Layout program, the cursor always travels from left to right on the same line before moving to the INPUT areas on the next line. However, you can create the @/GET's in such a way that the cursor travels down one column from top to bottom, before it moves to the next column on the page.

Exit the current screen input areas by entering

```
[Ctrl-End]
```

You have probably surmised that the @/SAY/GET structure is the same structure dBASE IV uses when it presents you with its Full-Screen Editing modes. When you create a screen form in the Control Center, the screen layout form (SCR) is translated by dBASE IV into a program that contains @/SAY and @/GET commands, corresponding to the layout created. Later in this chapter you will learn how to create your own screen forms from scratch, using the @/SAY/GET command structure.

A Full-Screen Calculation Program

You now know enough about the @/SAY/GET commands to create a calculation program using Full-Screen commands to display the text, the input areas, and the results. As an example, create a new program that calculates information, such as the monthly payment on a loan.

Open a new program file called PAY.

```
MODIFY COMMAND pay ↵
```

The program begins with the commands setting the environment. In this case, set off the TALK, STATUS, and SCOREBOARD, so you can work with the entire screen display/

```
SET TALK OFF
SET STATUS OFF
SET SCOREBOARD OFF
CLEAR
```

The next section of the program initializes the variables used to hold the user's input. There will be three numeric values, PRIN, RATE and YEARS. Since all three will be initialized with the value of zero, use the STORE/TO command to define all three values with a single command. You will also create a text variable for the title.

```
* initialize variables
STORE 0 TO prin,rate,years
title="Loan Analysis"
```

If you want to center an item on the screen, use the formula *(80-LEN(title))/2* as the column value in the @/SAY command. The COLOR clause is used to display the text in bold. The rest of the commands place text on Lines 7 through 15, aligned on column 10.

```
@  5,(80-LEN(title))/2  SAY title COLOR W+/N
@  7,10  SAY "Amount of the Loan"
@  9,10  SAY "Rate of Interest"
@ 11,10  SAY "Number of Years"
@ 13,10  SAY "Monthly Payment"
@ 15,10  SAY "Total Finance Charge"
```

Once the text prompts have been placed on the screen, the @/GET commands will be used to display the input areas. The @/GET commands use the line values corresponding to text of the prompts, but use column 40 as the horizontal position. The READ command activates the input areas.

```
@  7,40  GET prin
@  9,40  GET rate
@ 11,40  GET years
READ
```

When the user has filled out the input values, you can calculate the results. In the first command below, the variable MONTHLY is defined, using the PAYMENT( ) function. The PAYMENT( ) function returns the monthly payment for a loan, when supplied with the loan amount, the rate of interest charged, and the number of payment periods.

PAYMENT(*loan_amount,rate,periods)*

If you are calculating a loan that is paid in monthly installments, you have to divide the annual interest rate by 12 and multiply the number of years by 12. The expression rate/100/12 converts an interest rate entered as a whole number annual interest rate, in the decimal value for the monthly interest rate. For example, if you enter 12 as the rate, the expression divides it by 100, 12/100 = .12 and then divide that by 12, .12/12 =.01, arriving at a 1% monthly interest rate.

```
monthly=PAYMENT(prin,rate/100/12,years*12)
```

In addition to the monthly payment, you can compute the total amount of interest that will be paid, i.e., the total finance charged, over the life of the loan. You can calculate this value by finding the total amount paid (monthly payment times the total number of payments) and subtracting the original amount of the loan.

```
fincharge=monthly*years*12-prin
```

Once the values have been calculated, you can display them so the user can see the results. The @/SAY commands use the COLOR clause to display the results in black on white video, to match the black on white video used by the @/GET input areas.

```
@ 13,40 SAY monthly PICTURE "999,999.99" COLOR N/W
@ 15,40 SAY fincharge PICTURE "999,999.99" COLOR N/W
WAIT
```

Why is the WAIT command included? The answer is when you set the STATUS ON at the end of the program, dBASE IV clears the screen display, automatically. The result is the user would not have time to read the results on the screen. The WAIT command is a simple way to pause the screen display before the program terminates. Complete the program by resetting the environment.

```
SET STATUS ON
SET SCOREBOARD ON
SET TALK ON
RETURN
```

Save and execute the program.

```
[Alt-e] r
```

Enter values into the input areas. In this case a loan, such as a car loan, $12,000 for 3 years at 10%.

```
12000 ↵
10 ↵
3 ↵
```

The program calculates the monthly payment and the total amount of interest charged over the length of the loan. The @/SAY and @/GET commands create a more sophisticated and readable screen dialog. These tools create a program easier to understand, that has a more comfortable feel to it.

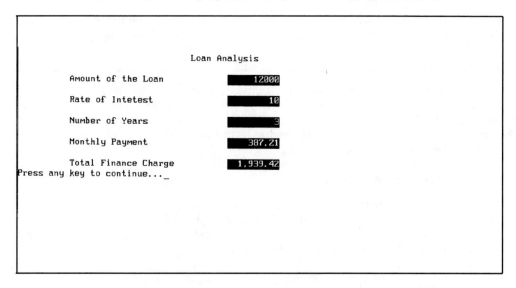

Figure 11-9. @/**SAY** and @/**GET** commands create program dialog.

Return to the Dot Prompt by entering

⏎

Input Area Options

The @/GET command has a number of clauses and functions allowing you to control the way information is input into the input areas displayed with the command. You have already seen that the type of information input into an @/GET area is determined by the type of the value used to initialize the variable.

@/GET PERMITS you to exercise other types of controls over what is input. One way to control the entry of numeric values is to use a RANGE clause. The RANGE clause allows you to establish numeric maximum and minimum values, which can be input into the area. The RANGE clause has the following general form:

RANGE *minimum_value,maximum value*

For example, if the input area is supposed to contain only percentages, you would want to restrict the entry to values from 1 to 100. Enter

```
@ 10,10 GET value RANGE 1,100 ⏎
READ ⏎
⏎
```

The VALUE variable is still active because variables defined at the Dot Prompt remain in memory until you quit dBASE IV, or you specifically clear them from memory. The CLEAR MEMORY command erases all memory variables.

The RANGE clause will not permit you to reenter the value 1200, because the input area is restricted to values from 1 to 100. The program displays the message "RANGE is 1 to 100 (press SPACE)" appears at the bottom of the screen to inform the user why the value is not accepted.

Exit the input area by entering

```
[spacebar] [Esc]
```

You can set a minimum or maximum, by entering only one value. Suppose you wanted to set only an upper limit of 99, for the entry. Note, when setting a maximum value only, you must still enter a comma before the number, to function as a placeholder. Enter

```
@ 10,10 GET value RANGE ,99 ↵
READ ↵
  ↵
```

Once again, the value 1200 causes an error. The message reads "RANGE is None to 99 (press SPACE)". This time, make a valid entry.

```
[spacebar] 10 ↵
```

Since 10 satisfies the RANGE limit, it is accepted as a valid entry. The error message generated by the RANGE clause picks ups its values from the RANGE clause. While accurate, the message deals more with the programming concept than with terms that related to the subject matter of the display.

Another method of controlling entry into an @/GET area is to use the VALID clause. The VALID clause allows you to establish a broader type of validity check than RANGE. With the VALID clause, you can enter any dBASE IV logical expression. If the value entered into the @/GET area causes the expression to evaluate as true, the entry is accepted. Otherwise, it is rejected. By default, the VALID clause displays the message "Editing condition not satisfied (press SPACE)". This message is even more cryptic than the one displayed by the RANGE clause. However, the VALID clause has the benefit of working with the ERROR clause. The ERROR clause allows you to define a message that will be displayed when you enter an invalid entry.

The VALID clause supersedes the RANGE clause because you can use it to create a validity check for all types of variables. The VALID clause allows the use of all operators. You can use a validity check expression using values other than the one you are entering as a criterion. The following command uses the VALID clause to restrict entry.

The values used with the RANGE clause are inclusive, i.e. RANGE 0 means VALUE>=0, which would allow entry of 0. The VALID clause allows you to use expressions that are not inclusive by using the > and < operators. For example, VALUE>0 would not allow zero but still allow decimal values greater than zero.

The ERROR clause allows you to enter a character expression that will be displayed when an invalid entry is made. Enter the following command. The command is quite long so that it is printed on more than one line. You should enter the command as a single line only, pressing ↲ where indicated.

```
@ 10,10 GET value VALID value>0.AND.value<100  ERROR "Enter a percentage 1 to 99" ↲
READ ↲
120 ↲
```

The message appearing at the bottom of the screen is the message specified in your @/GET command. Enter a valid value.

```
[spacebar] 10 ↲
```

You may want to display a message for the user before she makes an error. The MESSAGE clause allows you to specify a message appearing at the bottom of the screen, when the cursor is positioned in the @/GET area. Enter

```
@ 10,10 GET value MESSAGE "Enter a whole number 1-99" ↲
READ ↲
```

The message appears at the bottom of the screen, as soon as the cursor is positioned in the input area. You can combine the MESSAGE, VALID, and ERROR clauses, to make a small system of operations that help control the input in each @/GET area. You can apply these clauses to as many @/GET areas as you believe necessary within the limits imposed by memory. Exit the entry area by entering

```
↲
```

Decimal Places

Suppose you wanted to enter a value, such as 8.5, for the rate of interest. Would there be any problem? Enter

```
@ 10,10 GET value ↲
READ ↲
8.5
```

As you attempted to enter the decimal point, the program beeped and exited the input area, leaving only the whole-number portion of the value. Because the value was initialized as a whole number—no decimal portion—dBASE IV rejected the entry of a decimal value. You can resolve this problem by using a PICTURE clause with a @/GET command. Previously, you used the PICTURE clause with @/SAY and ? to format the output of values. In this case, use it to setup the input area for the entry of a specific number of decimal places. The template "99999999.9" creates an input area accepting a decimal value. Enter

```
@ 10,10 GET value PICTURE "99999999.9"  ↵
READ ↵
8.5 ↵
```

The value is accepted because the PICTURE clause prepared the way for a value with a decimal portion. The PICTURE clause works with both the @/SAY and @/GET commands, but the reason for its use is slightly different.

Another way to make use of the picture with a @/GET is to add a special character that identifies the type of entry. For example, the template "9999999.9%" displays a % sign on the right side of the input area. The % has no numeric significance or value, but serves to reinforce the idea that this entry area should contain a percent. Enter

```
@ 10,10 GET value PICTURE "9999999.9%"  ↵
READ ↵
11.5 ↵
```

The input area displays the % sign. However, the cursor simply skips the character when you make an entry.

You can now apply these new tools to the PAY program. Load the program into the editor.

```
MODIFY COMMAND pay ↵
```

Move the cursor to Line 15. Add a message clause to the @/GET command. Delete the current command.

```
[Ctrl-y]
```

Insert a new command using the VALID, ERROR, MESSAGE, and PICTURE clauses. Because the command is so long, the semicolon (;) is used to divide it into two parts.

```
@ 9,40  GET rate VALID rate>0.AND.rate<100   ERROR "Value must be 1 to 99";
PICTURE "9999999.99%" MESSAGE "Enter an annual percentage rate"
```

Save and execute the revised program.

```
[Alt-e] r
10000 ↵
```

The area shows room for one decimal place and the message appears at the bottom of the screen.

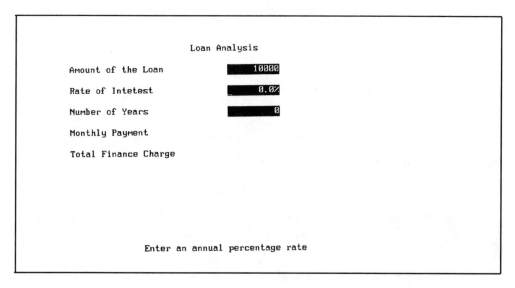

Figure 11-10. @/GET clauses used to control input into @/GET area.

If you intend to use messages in your program, avoid writing data to Line 24 with @/SAY/GET commands.

Complete the entry using

```
9.5
5 ↵
```

The program uses the 9.5% value to calculate the payment and finance charge. Complete the program by entering

```
↵
```

Lines And Boxes

In addition to the use of colors to highlight or differentiate parts of the screen, the use of lines and boxes can also enhance the display of a program. Previously, you learned you could create lines across the screen by using the REPLICATE command to repeat a line character. A full-screen command, @/TO, allows you to draw lines or boxes between two points on the screen display. The command requires two sets of coordinates: one for the upper-left corner and the second for the lower-right corner. Enter

```
@ 5,10 TO 10,70 ↵
```

The program draws a box between the specified points. If the coordinates have the same column or row value, the effect is to draw a straight line. Enter

        @ 17,5 TO 17,75 ↵

You can draw double lines by adding the DOUBLE clause to the @/GET command. Enter

        @ 6,20 TO 9,60 DOUBLE

The PANEL clause draws a solid border.

        @ 2,10 TO 4,40 PANEL ↵

You can also specify a color combination to use with the @/TO command. For example, if you wanted to draw the box with a bold white line, you would enter

        @ 11,5 TO 15,30 COLOR W+/N ↵

The boxes can be combined with @/SAY and @/GET commands. You can estimate the location for the coordinates by looking at the location of the box. For instance, suppose you wanted to place the TITLE variable in the center of box you just created at 11,5.

The vertical location would be midway between 11 and 15, Line 13. The horizontal position would be a bit more complex. You would have to use a modified form of the centering formula. In this case, the box is 25 columns wide. However, the box starts at column 5. The formula (25-LEN(title))/2+5 centers the text within the box. Enter

        @ 12, (25-LEN(title))/2+5   SAY title ↵

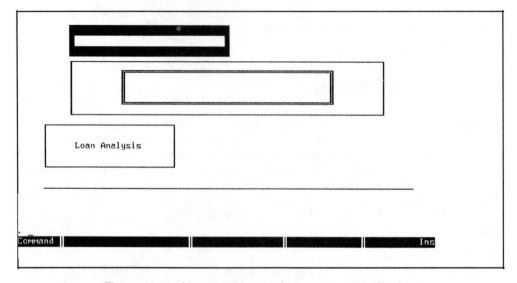

Figure 11-11. Lines and boxes drawn on screen display.

Clear the screen by entering

```
CLEAR ↵
```

If you want to combine lines and boxes, you have to make some manual adjustments for the locations where the lines meet. Draw a box, then a line that divides the box.

```
@ 5,20 TO 10,40 ↵
@ 7,20 TO 7,40 ↵
```

Note, where the box and the line meet, the line character overwrites the box character. In order to have a smooth connection between the line and the side of the box, you must place characters combining horizontal and vertical lines, at the ends of the line. These characters are part of the extended character set built into the computer.

Character	Value
┤	180
┴	193
	194
┬	195

Enter

```
@ 7,20 SAY CHR(195) ↵
@ 7,40 SAY CHR(180) ↵
```

The line across the box is now properly connected.

In addition to drawing lines and boxes on the screen, you can use variations on the @ command to change the color of information already placed on the screen, or erase specific blocks of characters. Place some text inside the top half of the box.

```
@ 6 25 SAY title ↵
```

The @/FILL/COLOR command changes the color, but not the characters within a specific area of the screen. Enter

```
@ 5,20 FILL TO 7,40 COLOR W+ ↵
```

Without changing the characters, the color of the characters is changed to bold. Return the characters to normal white by entering

```
@ 5,20 FILL TO 7,40 COLOR W ↵
```

If you do not specify a color, the area is cleared of all characters.

```
@ 6,21 FILL TO 6,39 ⌐
```

The text is removed from the screen display. Note, in dBASE IV the command @/CLEAR TO performs the same function as @/FILL TO when no color is used. The commands @ 6,21 FILL TO 6,39 and @ 6,21 CLEAR TO 6,39 have the same meaning.

The @/TO, @/FILL TO and @/CLEAR TO commands combined with @/SAY/GET provide the power to create a wide variety of interesting effects. These effects do not change the substance of your program, but increase the visual interest your program has for the person looking at the screen display. To get a feel for what can be done with these commands, modify the PAY program.

```
MODIFY COMMAND pay ⌐
```

Move the cursor to Line 7. Insert the following commands to draw a box around the information, and a line separating the input data from the results. @/SAY commands are used to place the characters that smooth out the points where the line and box meet.

```
@ 4,8 TO 16,52
@ 12,8 TO 12,52
@ 12,8 SAY CHR(195)
@ 12,52 SAY CHR(180)
```

Move the cursor to Line 22.

Use the @/FILL TO command to paint the text in the top half of the box, bold. The addition of color draws attention to the top half of the box. The @/FILL TO is simpler than adding COLOR clauses to each of the @/SAY commands.

```
@ 7,10 FILL TO 11,39 COLOR W+
```

Move the cursor to the beginning of Line 24, the line immediately following the READ command. At this point, insert two @/FILL TO commands to change the color of the text in the top and bottom half of the screens. The top returns to normal white and the bottom is set to bold. This helps draw attention to the bottom half of the display.

```
@ 7,10 FILL TO 11,39 COLOR W
@ 13,10 FILL TO 15,39 COLOR W+
```

The last change replaces the WAIT command with a full-screen command that better fits the visual format of the program.

Move the cursor to Line 30. Delete the WAIT command.

```
[Ctrl-y]
```

Create a one-character variable called PAUSE.

```
pause=SPACE(1)
```

Use an @/SAY/GET command to display the "Press Any Key" message. The GET area for the PAUSE variable pauses the program until any key is pressed.

The color combination N/N, black on black, creates an invisible input. Any character entered will be black on the black background. Also note the insertion of a comma before the N/N. This is because when COLOR is used with a @/SAY/GET command, you can specify two sets of colors. The first is for the normal color used by the @/SAY portion of the command. The second set of colors is the enhanced color settings used by the GET portion of the command. It is the GET portion that you want to blank out.

```
@ 24,34 SAY "Press Any Key" GET pause COLOR ,N/N
READ
```

Save and execute the program.

```
[Alt-e] r
10000 ↵
8.5
5 ↵
```

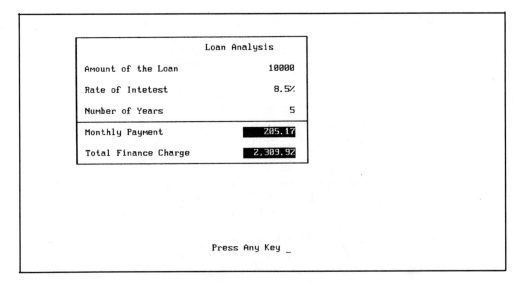

Figure 11-12. Boxes, lines and colors used to enhance screen display.

The modifications made to the program do not actually change the substance of the calculation. They do, however, change the visual appearance of the program so it presents a more interesting visual display.

Summary

This chapter explained how to write programs displaying statistical information about data stored in single or multiple databases. These programs are able to present data faster, and in more flexible screen styles, than can be achieved by the Control Center queries or Dot Prompt commands. They can also be executed as many times as needed, once they have been created.

- **Writing Programs.** In dBASE IV, programs are text files created with the dBASE IV editor, or any other program that can produce ASCII text files. Program files are assigned the PRG file extension. The commands in the program do not execute, until the entire program has been stored as a disk file and run though the dBASE IV compiler.

- **Compiling.** When a program is compiled, the text commands in the PRG file (the source code) are converted into a compressed format (object code), which can be understood and executed by dBASE IV. During the compiling process, commands are checked for correct syntax. If errors exist, the compiler will not create the object-code file, meaning the program cannot be executed until all the syntax errors are eliminated.

- **Linear Program.** In a linear program, the commands are executed as a list, from top to bottom, with no pauses. The commands used in a linear program can be used at the Dot Prompt, enabling you to test commands and clauses before integrating them into a program.

- **Statistical Programs.** The programs display summary information about the database or databases. Unlike queries, a single statistical program can view the file's data in as many different ways as needed. The program can display information from all the views (SET FILTER) used in the program.

- **Variables.** A memory variable is a value stored temporarily in the memory of the computer. A variable created at the Dot Prompt remains in memory until you quit dBASE IV, or specifically erase the value. A variable created during the execution of a program remains in memory until the program is terminated. Memory variables can be numeric, character, date, or logical type information. Variables cannot be memo-type information.

- **Environmental Sets.** dBASE IV uses SET commands to control the way information is displayed. SET TALK controls the display of information generated by some commands as feedback. SET PRINT controls the echo of data displayed on the screen to the printer. SET CONSOLE turns the screen display on and off. It is used to suppress screen display during printing.

- **?/??.** These commands place data on the screen display or on the printed page, when SET PRINT is ON. The ? is always preceded by a ⏎. ?? prints following the last printed item. The AT clause specifies a horizontal location for the display. The PICTURE clause allows you to specify a template and template functions to use on the displayed data. The STYLE clause selects special effects, such as bold display or print.

- **Video Attributes.** The SET COLOR command allows you to change the color, foreground, and background of the screen display. The colors change for any data displayed following SET COLOR. Previous information's colors remain as they were originally displayed. This allows you to use SET COLOR to mix different colors on a single screen. The colors used on the screen have no effect on the printed text.

- **@/SAY/GET.** The @/SAY, @/GET and @/SAY/GET commands allow you to place data onto any part of the screen display, in any order. The @/GET commands establish input areas displaying the values of variables or fields. You can display up to 255 GET input areas on one screen display. The GET input areas are activated with the READ command. Once activated, the cursor moves through the GET areas in the order in which they were placed on the screen, not their physical location. The @/GET command accepts a number of clauses to help control what information is input into the GET areas.

- **RANGE.** The RANGE clause is used with @/GET to limit the entry into a numeric field or variable to a specified range of values. You can specify a maximum value, a minimum value, or both. The range is inclusive, i.e., it includes the values used to specify the range. An invalid entry causes a beep and a message at the bottom of the screen.

- **VALID.** This clause allows you to enter a dBASE IV logical expression as a validity check. When the data is entered, the expression specified with the VALID clause must evaluate as true, or the entry is rejected. The clause beeps and displays a message at the bottom of the screen.

- **ERROR.** The ERROR clause is used in conjunction with the VALID clause. ERROR accepts a dBASE IV character expression used as the message, when an invalid entry is made. The clause allows you to define a message of your own design to be displayed when invalid entries are made.

- **MESSAGE.** This clause allows you to specify a dBASE IV character expression to be displayed whenever the cursor is positioned in the GET input area.

- **@/TO.** This command draws a box or line between the specified screen coordinates. You can draw a double line by using the DOUBLE clause, or a solid border using the PANEL clause.

- **@/FILL TO COLOR.** This command can be used to change the color of a rectangular area of the screen. The command does not overwrite the characters, so long as a COLOR is specified. If no color is specified, it erases the characters.

- **@/CLEAR TO.** This command erases the characters in a specified rectangle of the screen display.

- **READ.** This command is used following one or more @/GET commands. It activates the GETS and places the cursor in the first GET area on the current screen display. Only one READ is necessary to active up to 255 GET areas.

- **Initialize Variables.** The Streaming-Input commands initialize the specified variables, each time the command is executed. The Full-Screen commands require the variables referenced by the commands be initialized before they are called by @/SAY or @/GET. Variables are initialized using a form of the STORE command. If fieldnames are used, the database must be open.

Program Listing

The PAY.PRG program.

```
SET TALK OFF
SET STATUS OFF
SET SCOREBOARD OFF
CLEAR
* initialize variables
STORE 0 TO prin,rate,years
@ 4,8 TO 16,52
@ 12,8 TO 12,52
@ 12,8 SAY CHR(195)
@ 12,52 SAY CHR(180)
title="Loan Analysis"
@ 5,(80-LEN(title))/2  SAY title COLOR W+/N
@ 7,10  SAY "Amount of the Loan"
@ 9,10  SAY "Rate of Interest"
@ 11,10  SAY "Number of Years"
@ 13,10  SAY "Monthly Payment"
@ 15,10  SAY "Total Finance Charge"
@ 7,40  GET prin
@ 9,40  GET rate VALID rate>0.AND.rate<100  ERROR "Value must be 1 to 99";
PICTURE "9999999.9%" MESSAGE "Enter an annual percentage rate"
@ 11,40  GET years
@ 7,10 FILL TO 11,39 COLOR W+
READ
@ 7,10 FILL TO 11,49 COLOR W
@ 13,10 FILL TO 15,49 COLOR W+
monthly=PAYMENT(prin,rate/100/12,years*12)
fincharge=monthly*years*12-prin
@ 13,40 SAY monthly PICTURE "999,999.99" COLOR N/W
@ 15,40 SAY fincharge PICTURE "999,999.99" COLOR N/W
pause=SPACE(1)
@ 24,34 SAY "Press Any Key" GET pause COLOR ,N/N
READ
SET STATUS ON
SET SCOREBOARD ON
SET TALK ON
RETURN
```

12

Structures in Programs

In the previous chapter you learned how dBASE IV programs are written. The programs demonstrated how dBASE IV can be used to create custom-designed programs that transform dBASE IV into a tool to carry out specific tasks. By controlling the information displayed on the screen, asking the user to input information, and performing behind-the-scenes operations, dBASE IV can be shaped into a tool that addresses specific needs. Users with little or no understanding of dBASE IV, can use the customized programs because of the way the program dialogue is carried out. This is the great advantage of a customized environment. Instead of having to teach each user the entire dBASE IV system, you can create programs that limit or direct the user along specific usage paths.

In this chapter you will learn how to use some of the very powerful programming tools that allow you to build screen displays, with the same sophistication found in the dBASE IV Control Center, including menus, menu bars, and pop-up menus.

Pop-up Menus

Some of the most powerful tools provided by the dBASE IV Programming language reside in the pop-up menu commands. In the dBASE IV Control Center, you used pop-up menus to select commands and options. Figure 12-1 shows the Catalog pop-up menu displayed as part of the Control Center.

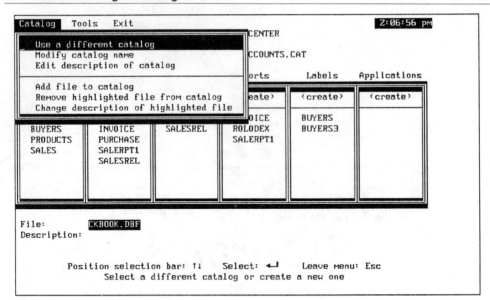

Figure 12-1. Typical pop-up menu displayed as part of the Control Center.

Pop-up menus consist of a box displayed on the screen. The interior of the box contains a list of commands or options. The highlight moves up and down in the box, from command to command. When you have located the command or option you want, you press ↵ to make that selection. When you make a selection, dBASE IV reacts by carrying out the task or option related to the particular item selected.

The pop-up menus that appear as part of the Control Center display have been defined at the factory for your use. However, by using the dBASE IV Programming language, you can create pop-up menus of your design that will display your own set of commands or options. You can also use the dBASE IV Command Language to specify what action should take place when a selection is made. As an example, you will create a simple pop-up menu program that allows a user to choose to browse either checks or deposits from a pop-up menu.

Begin by loading dBASE IV in the usual manner and activating the Dot Prompt mode.

The Pop-up Menu Toolbox

In order to create a custom-designed pop-up menu, dBASE IV provides commands that allow you to define the options of the pop-up menu. The pop-up menu commands operate a bit differently than such Screen Dialog commands as ? and @/SAY/GET, which you encountered in Chapter 11. Those commands gave you the ability to place information on the screen at specific locations, but you were required to specify each and every aspect of the screen. Recall that when two rectangles overlapped, you had to manually place the correct characters at the line intersections.

The pop-up menu commands are different, in that the structure of the pop-up menu is built into dBASE IV in a general way. dBASE IV will automatically create the box for the pop-up menu, list the bars vertically in the menu, create the highlight, allow you to move the highlight up and down in the menu, and recognize ↵ as a signal you have made a selection. All you need to tell dBASE IV is how many bars you want to display and what the text of the menu bars should be. The pop-up menu commands take care of all other details needed to create and display the pop-up.

The set of commands you use to create the pop-up menu can be thought of as your toolbox. All pop-up menus use the same set of tools, only the specifics about the actual bars changes from menu to menu. The pop-up menu commands are:

DEFINE POP-UP

This command defines the pop-up menu by assigning it a name and specifying row and column locations of the upper-left corner of the pop-up menu box. You also have the option of specifying the lower-right corner of the menu. If you do not include the lower-right location, dBASE IV automatically calculates the minimum size required to display all the bars.

DEFINE BAR

For each bar in the pop-up menu you must use one DEFINE BAR command. The main purpose of this command is to specify what text should be displayed on each bar of the menu. You also have the option of specifying a message that will appear at the bottom of the screen when the bar is highlighted.

ON SELECTION POP-UP

This command specifies an action that dBASE IV will take when you make a menu selection.

ACTIVATE POP-UP

This command activates a pop-up menu. When the menu is active, it is displayed on the screen. Control of the program passes to the pop-up menu. This means you must use the up arrow, down arrow, and ↵ keys to make a selection from the menu. Note that you cannot activate a menu unless you have already defined the menu.

DEACTIVATE POP-UP

This command removes the menu from the screen and allows control to pass to the next command in the program. Keep in mind a pop-up can be reactivated by using ACTIVATE POP-UP.

RELEASE POP-UP

This command is used to erase the pop-up menu definition from memory. Like SET commands, menus defined as part of a program remain stored in the memory until you quit dBASE IV, or specifically remove it from memory.

BAR( )

The BAR( ) function returns a numeric value equal to the bar highlighted when the pop-up menu selection was made. The BAR( ) function is used to evaluate which bar from the menu was selected.

The stated goal is to make a menu allowing the user to browse either the checks or the deposits stored in the CKBOOK file. The program you create will actually have two distinct parts. The first part will define and activate the pop-up menu. When completed, the user will make selection. The second part of the program must contain the dBASE IV commands that will carry out the task selected by the user. You will call this program POP1 (pop-up menu example 1). Begin by entering

```
MODIFY COMMAND pop1 ⏎
```

Begin the program by using the SET commands that permit you to use the entire screen display.

```
SET TALK OFF
SET SCOREBOARD OFF
SET STATUS OFF
```

Since all the operations in this program will involve the CKBOOK database, open this file.

```
USE CKBOOK
```

The next command defines the name and the location of the pop-up menu box. In this case, the name of the pop-up menu will be CHECKS. The name is needed because a program contains as many pop-up menus as there is room in the memory to store.

The DEFINE POP-UP command includes the optional clause *TO 12,50*. This option sets the lower-right corner of the menu at a specific location. If not used, dBASE IV calculates the length and width of the menu, based on the number of bars and the width of the longest text bar.

When using the TO clause, be careful to estimate that you have left sufficient room to display the items. Here, rows 8 to 12 are used to display three bars. If you do not leave room for all the bars, the menu will scroll vertically. If the menu is not wide enough for all the text, the right edge of some options many be truncated.

```
* define pop-up menu
DEFINE POP-UP checks FROM 8,30 TO 12,50
```

With the menu defined, you need to define the individual bars. Each DEFINE BAR command consists of two parts:

1. **BAR _n._** _n_ is the number of the bar and defines the bar's position in the menu. If the bar numbers are not consecutive, the program displays blank spaces to fill in those missing. The highlight skips over the blanks.
2. **PROMPT _character_expression._** You can use any valid character expression with a menu bar. The program displays the text of that bar in the pop-up menu.

The MESSAGE clause is optional. It causes a message to be displayed at the bottom of the screen when you position the highlight on the menu bar. Typically, the message is used to elaborate on the meaning or use of the menu-bar option.

```
DEFINE BAR 1 OF checks PROMPT "Browse Checks"
DEFINE BAR 2 OF checks PROMPT "Browse Deposits"
```

The third bar is the EXIT bar. When a pop-up menu is used by itself (not as part of a menu system, such as the Control Center) you should always make the last option in the menu an Exit option. Note that the MESSAGE clause is used with this bar.

```
DEFINE BAR 3 OF checks PROMPT "Exit Program";
    MESSAGE "Return to the dot prompt."
```

Pop-up Selection and Procedures

The last part of the menu-definition process is the ON SELECTION POP-UP command. This command creates a trigger that is activated when a selection is made in the pop-up menu (i.e. the user enters ↵). You can specify any valid dBASE IV command to be activated when a selection is made.

However, you can only specify a _single_ command to be triggered by the selection. Many dBASE IV operations require a sequence of commands to carry out a task. The solution lies in the use of the DO command to execute a _procedure._ You will recall that DO is used in the Dot Prompt mode to execute a program. When DO is issued _inside_ a program, it executes the specified program or procedure.

What is a procedure? For all intents and purposes, a procedure is a dBASE IV program. The only difference is instead of being placed in its own program file, the procedure is stored in the same file as the current program. When the DO command is encountered, dBASE IV searches the current file to find a PROCEDURE command that matches the name. If it finds the procedure it executes the commands listed under that procedure name. The procedure stops when a RETURN command is encountered.

Procedures allow you to break a program into a series of smaller parts called modules or subroutines. In this case, using the ON SELECTION POP-UP command to run a procedure allows you to get around the one-command limit. The command DO show_data executes the show_data procedure that can contain as many commands as needed to perform the task related to the menu-bar option.

```
* select action
ON SELECTION POP-UP checks DO show_data
```

Following the definition of the pop-up menu, the ACTIVATE MENU command can be used to display the pop-up menu, as well as activate the selection process. In this instance, the screen is cleared so the pop-up menu is the only item displayed on the screen.

```
* show menu to user
CLEAR
ACTIVATE POP-UP checks
```

Once activated, the pop-up menu will remain in control of the program until a DEACTIVATE POP-UP command is issued. In this program, this deactivation option will be associated with the Exit option.

Following the DEACTIVATE, this program terminates. Note that the RELEASE pop-up command is used to remove the pop-up menu from the memory of the computer. If RELEASE is not used, the menu definition stays in memory, even after the program concludes.

```
RELEASE POP-UP checks
SET TALK ON
SET SCOREBOARD ON
SET STATUS ON
RETURN
```

Writing a Procedure

The main section of this program creates and displays the pop-up menu. But this section alone does not produce a finished program. You need to create a procedure that will carry out one or more related tasks.

A procedure is a program within a program. In traditional programming terms, it is called a *subroutine*. The concept of procedures and subroutines is that it is usually easier and more efficient to break a program into modular portions. Here, the procedure is used to carry out the specific tasks indicated by the pop-up menu.

Procedures can be placed into a dBASE IV program following the RETURN command at the end of the main program. The main program is the one that starts at the beginning of the PRG file. A procedure is marked by the PROCEDURE command and is followed by the name of the procedure.

Procedure names can be up to 10 characters, while program names are limited to 8 characters, due to the current limitation of DOS to 8-character filenames.

```
PROCEDURE show_data
```

Once a procedure is started, you can enter commands just as you would in a program. Remember, each procedure that began with a PROCEDURE command must end with a RETURN command.

The DO CASE Structure

The pop-up menu creates a significant problem in writing a program that will carry out different tasks, based on the value of the bar selected. In order to handle this and similar problems, Programming languages allow for the creation of *conditional structures*. A conditional structure is one in which commands can be placed so they will be executed only when a specific condition or set of conditions occurs. Conditional structures use logical expressions to evaluate conditions. When a specific expression is true, a matching set of commands are executed.

The term *structure* implies that conditional structures are not simply individual commands like USE or SET TALK ON. Instead, the structures consist of several commands that mark off sections of the program. For example, the PROCEDURE and RETURN commands form a structure that creates a subroutine within a program. Both commands work together to create the structure. Even though they may be separated physically by many other commands, they function as a single logical structure.

dBASE IV provides two basic conditional structures:

IF/ELSE/ENDIF

This structure is used when you want to chose between two alternative tasks.

DO CASE/ENDCASE

This structure allows you to create a list of two or more tasks that can be selected, based on specific conditions.

In this instance, you have three bars. You will use a DO CASE structure to create alternative operations, depending upon which of the three bars is selected.

The first command in a DO CASE structure is simply DO CASE. The command marks the beginning of a DO CASE structure and does not require additional information.

```
DO CASE
```

Following the DO CASE command you can specify the specific cases you want to account for. Each case begins with a CASE command. The CASE command is always followed by a logical expression. It is the value of the expression that determines if the commands that follow are executed. If the expression is true, the commands following CASE are executed. If the expression is false, the commands are skipped. The program looks further down the program to find another CASE, if any, and determines if the expression associated with that CASE is true.

In this program each CASE will use a BAR( ) function to determine if the bar number was selected in the menu. For example, the expression BAR( )=1 would be true if the user selected the first bar in the pop-up menu.

Note that the CASE command is indented from the left margin. Indenting is used to make the logic of a program easier to recognize. Commands are indented to show that their execution is conditional on a previous command, or that the command is part of a specific structure. Indenting has no actual effect on the execution of the program, and in fact, all indents are stripped when the program is compiled into the object file. However, indenting is needed if you are to write programs that can be easily understood by yourself or others who might want to read them.

```
CASE BAR( )=1
```

Following the CASE command you should enter the processing commands you want to execute as part of the selection. In this case, bar 1 activates check editing. A filter is established to select only the checks from the CKBOOK file. The BROWSE command, with the NOMENU and NOAPPEND clauses, is used to display the selected data.

```
SET FILTER TO payee#"DEPOSIT"
GO TOP
BROWSE NOAPPEND NOMENU
```

The GO TOP command is used following the setting of a filter, to ensure the display begins at the top of the selected records, when the Browse mode is activated.

The next part of the structure is another CASE. This time, the case will execute if bar 2 is selected. The filter used for this option selects all the deposits for display.

```
CASE BAR( )=2
SET FILTER TO payee="DEPOSIT"
GO TOP
BROWSE NOAPPEND NOMENU
```

The third CASE is associated with the Exit option. It is this CASE that includes the command to DEACTIVATE the pop-up menu.

```
CASE BAR( )=3
     DEACTIVATE POP-UP
     CLOSE DATABASE
```

After you have constructed the operations for each CASE, end the DO CASE structure with the ENDCASE command. In programs, there must be a matching ENDCASE command for every DO CASE command.

```
ENDCASE
```

It is possible to construct a DO CASE structure so that more than one of the CASES can be true at the same time. The DO CASE structure will always select the *first* true CASE encountered. All the other cases, even if they too are true, are ignored.

The ENDCASE command is the last command in the procedure. The end of the procedure is marked by a RETURN command.

```
RETURN
```

Save and execute the program by entering

```
[Alt-e] r
```

When the program is compiled and executed, it displays the 3-bar menu in the center of the screen, as shown in Figure 12-2.

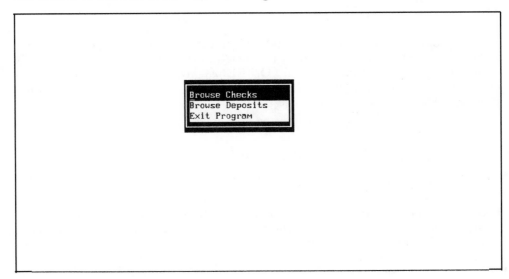

Figure 12-2. Pop-up menu displays program's options.

Select to Browse the deposits by entering

> **down arrow** ⏎

The program displays the Browse mode with the deposit records displayed, as seen in Figure 12-3.

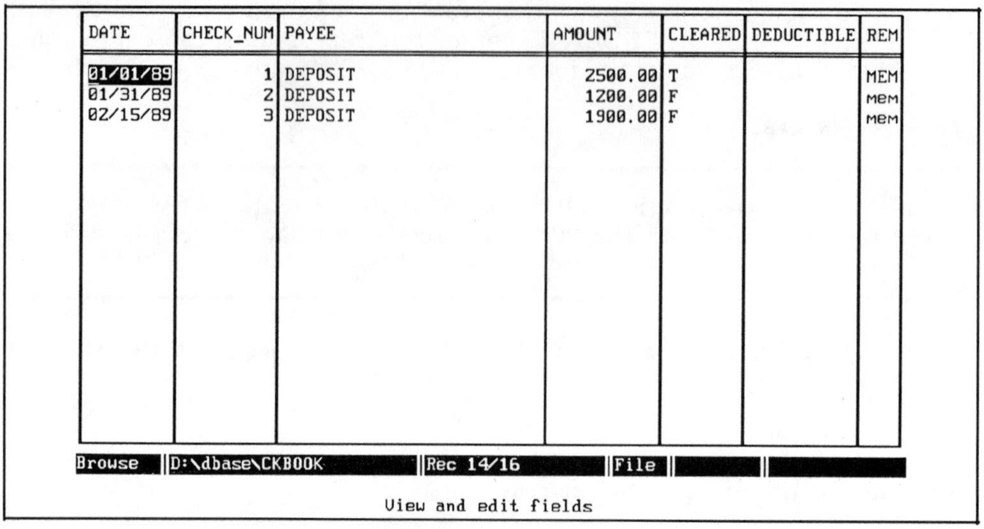

DATE	CHECK_NUM	PAYEE	AMOUNT	CLEARED	DEDUCTIBLE	REM
01/01/89	1	DEPOSIT	2500.00	T		MEM
01/31/89	2	DEPOSIT	1200.00	F		mem
02/15/89	3	DEPOSIT	1900.00	F		mem

```
Browse   D:\dbase\CKBOOK        Rec 14/16      File
```
View and edit fields

Figure 12-3. Browse mode activated from pop-up menu selection.

Exit the Browse mode by entering

> **[Ctrl-End]**

The program redisplays the menu. Why? Remember that once activated, the pop-up menu retains control of the program until the menu is specifically deactivated. This means when the ON SELECTION POP-UP procedure is completed, the pop-up menu redisplays itself and allows the user to continue making selections. Select to Browse the checks.

> **[up arrow]** ⏎

This time the check records are displayed. Return to the menu by entering

> **[Ctrl-End]**

If the first character in the text of the menu bar is unique, you can use that character to select the bar. Here, the third bar is the one that begins with the letter E. You can exit by entering

> **e**

The program terminates and you return to the Dot Prompt.

Special Pop-up Menu Features

The pop-up menu just created displays the text used in the DEFINE BAR commands. This type of menu requires you to define each bar individually. dBASE IV has special options in which the text of the bars is automatically defined by using information already stored in one form or another. The options are used with the DEFINE POP-UP command and eliminates the need to use the DEFINE BAR commands. The special options are:

POP-UP FIELD

This option allows dBASE IV to use the contents of a field as the pop-up menu bars. Each record displays the contents of the specified field as one bar. If there are more bars (i.e. records) than can be displayed at one time, the pop-up menu scrolls to allow all records to be displayed.

POP-UP STRUCTURE

This options lists the names of the fields from the structure of the current database, as bars in the pop-up menu. This option provides an easy way for users to select fieldnames from a menu.

POP-UP FILES

This option uses the filename in the current directory as the menu bars. You can use a LIKE clause with a DOS wilcard to select groups of files for display. For example, POP-UP FILE LIKE *.DBF limits the bars to DBF files only.

PROMPT( )

The PROMPT( ) function works in conjunction with a pop-up menu, similarly to the BAR( ) function. PROMPT( ) returns the text of the menu-bar item selected. When you are working with the options that automatically define the text of the menu bars, you cannot know in advance what text will appear on which number bar. The BAR( ) function that returns the number of the bar, would not be useful in evaluating the item selected. The PROMPT( ) function that returns the text of the selected bar, provides you with a method by which the text of the selected bar can be used with other commands.

Keep in mind that PROMPT( ) always returns a character-type string, even if the displayed bars represent the contents of a numeric or date field. To evaluate the PROMPT( ) function as a number, you would have to use the VAL( ) function to convert the characters to a numeric value, or the CTOD( ) function to convert characters to a date-type value.

As an example of how these special options can be used, you will create a program, POP2.PRG, that will allow you to edit a record by selecting the payee name from a pop-up menu.

```
MODIFY COMMAND pop2 ↵
```

In this instance, you will go directly to the heart of the program. The program begins with opening the CKBOOK file and using a filter to select only the check records.

```
USE ckbook ORDER payee
SET FILTER TO payee#"DEPOSIT"
```

The next command defines a pop-up menu, PAYEE, as a FIELD pop-up. In this case, only the upper-left corner is specified. The length and width will be automatically calculated by dBASE IV. Note that a message is included with the DEFINE POP-UP command. The message will appear at the bottom of the screen at all times, when the pop-up is displayed. Since the bars are defined automatically, you will not be able to assign individual messages to each pop-up. The message tells the user she must press the [Esc] key to exit the pop-up menu. Automatic pop-ups do not allow you to create an Exit bar. You can exit a pop-up by entering right arrow, left arrow, or [Esc]. The up arrow and down arrow keys are used to move the highlight up or down.

```
DEFINE POP-UP payee FROM 2,30 PROMPT FIELD payee;
    MESSAGE "Press Esc to Exit"
```

As in the previous program, the ON SELECTION POP-UP command is set to execute a procedure—here, called SHOW_CHK.

```
ON SELECTION POP-UP payee DO show_chk
```

After the menu has been defined, it can be activated.

```
ACTIVATE POP-UP payee
```

When you exit the menu, it is released from memory and the program ends. When a pop-up is released, it is also automatically deactivated.

```
RELEASE POP-UP payee
RETURN
```

The procedure SHOW_CHK uses the selection made from the pop-up menu, as the key to which records to display. In this case, since the

CKBOOK is indexed on the PAYEE field, you can use the PROMPT( ) function to locate the record containing a payee that matches the text of the menu bar.

```
PROCEDURE show_chk
SEEK PROMPT( )
```

Once the record is located, you can use the CHECKS screen form created in Chapter 6 to display information from the record. The SET FORMAT TO command activates the stored screen form, CHECKS.FMT, similarly to the way it is activated from the Control Center. The difference is that here, its display is integrated into the flow of the program. Screen layouts created in the Control Center can be integrated into custom programs with the SET FORMAT TO command. The READ command activates the input areas for editing.

```
SET FORMAT TO checks
READ
CLEAR
RETURN
```

Save and execute the program by entering

```
[Alt-e]  r
```

The pop-up menu lists all the payees in the CKBOOK file.

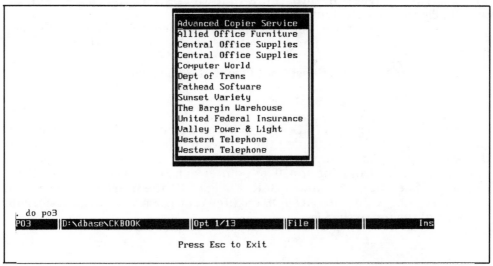

Figure 12-4. Payee names listed in pop-up menu.

You can display any of the records by selecting a bar. dBASE IV automatically implements the *speed search* option if you enter a character instead of an arrow key. Enter

        f

The highlight jumps to the first bar that begins with the letter F. Select that record by entering

         ⏎

The program displays the record using the CHECKS screen layout. Return to pop-up menu by entering

        [Ctrl-End]

The menu is still active. This means you can select more records for display, until you decide to exit. In this case, exit by entering

        [Esc]

There is one flaw in the logic of the program. It is related to records that have the same information in the fields used to define the pop-up menu. The command SEEK PROMPT( ) will always locate the *first* record in the database index that matches the text. But if there is more than one record with the same payee, the program will always select the first matching record, regardless of the bar you select.

To resolve this problem, you need to change the way the bar is selected; thus, if you choose the second of two identical payees, that record is displayed and not the contents of the first.

Load the program into the editor to make the changes.

        MODIFY COMMAND pop2 ⏎

Below is a revised version of SHOW_CHK procedure. The change uses the value of the BAR( ) by positioning the pointer to the record corresponding to the selected bar. For example, if you select bar 4, you can move the pointer to the 4th record from the top. The pointer can be moved with the SKIP command. The numeric value of BAR( ) tells SKIP the number of records to move. Preceding SKIP with GO TOP ensures that the program always begins counting at the top of the file.

```
PROCEDURE show_chk
GO TOP
SKIP BAR( )
SET FORMAT TO checks
READ
CLEAR
RETURN
```

Save and execute this modified version of the program.

```
[Alt-e]  r
```

Select the first record for Central Office Supplies by entering

```
[down  arrow] (2 times)
 ↵
```

The amount for this check is 67.45. Return to the menu and select the second record for Central Office Supplies. Enter

```
[Ctrl-End]
[down  arrow] (3 times)
 ↵
```

This record is different because it has an amount of 2245.50. The modification works correctly. Exit the program by entering

```
[Esc]  (2 times)
```

Scanning and Loops

Another powerful tool in programming lies in the use of loops. Loops enable a program to repeat a portion of the program code. The repetition is related to some logical condition whose veracity will determine the number of times the loop repeats.

Like the conditional commands, loops are structures. This means a loop is defined by a set of commands that mark locations within a program, as being controlled by the program structure—in this case, a repeating loop.

dBASE IV provides two types of loops:

DO WHILE/ENDDO

The DO WHILE loop is a general purpose programming structure. The DO WHILE command specifies a logical expression. If the expression is true at the time the DO WHILE command is encountered, control of the program passes to the loop. The effect of this control is that the commands following DO WHILE, until the ENDDO command, form a closed loop. These commands repeat until the expression controlled by the loop becomes false. Keep in mind that the logical expression that controls the loop is tested only at the end of each loop when the ENDDO is encountered. If the expression value changes in the middle of a loop, the program will not know this until it reaches the next ENDDO command.

It is possible to create a DO WHILE loop that never stops because the expression used to control the loop is never false. When using a DO WHILE loop, take care to plan carefully the circumstances under which the loop will be terminated, or your program will loop forever.

SCAN/ENDSCAN

A SCAN loop is a special purpose loop. Its repetitions are linked to the movement of the pointer through a database file. When a SCAN command is encountered, the pointer is positioned at the beginning of the current database files. The commands following SCAN are executed until an ENDSCAN is reached. The ENDSCAN automatically moves the pointer to the next record and repeats the loop. If the pointer is at the end of the file, ENDSCAN terminates the loop.

EXIT

The EXIT command is used to force the end of a loop, regardless of the value of the expression or the position of the record pointer. If EXIT is executed, the program skips the rest of the commands in the loop and begins executing the next commands, following the ENDDO or ENDSCAN command.

As an example of how loops are used, you will create a program called LOOP, which will be used to calculate statistics about the CKBOOK database records. The program will allow you to calculate values for a particular month, or all months. Begin by entering

```
MODIFY COMMAND loop ↵
```

The program begins with the SET TALK OFF command. After clearing the screen, two windows are defined. The DEFINE WINDOW command creates a window on the screen display. The windows can be activated and deactivated like pop-up menus. Unlike pop-ups, the windows have no special contents. They simply help you place information into separate areas of the screen display. Windows have one special quality. Any information covered by a window when it is activated, will be redisplayed when the window is deactivated.

As with menus, defining a window displays nothing on the screen. It merely allocates memory for use with the window definition. The ACTIVATE command actually displays the window. When activated, the cursor and all outputs from the program to the screen, remain inside the window until it is deactivated or released.

```
SET TALK OFF
CLEAR
DEFINE WINDOW pick_month FROM 6,10 To 8,70 DOUBLE
DEFINE WINDOW results FROM 10,25 TO 19,65
```

A variable called pick_month is defined as a string of 15 blank spaces. This will be the variable into which the user can enter the name of the month for which she wants to gather statistics. The CKBOOK file is opened.

```
pick_month=SPACE(15)
USE ckbook
```

The basic elements of the program have been defined and opened. You are ready to begin the first loop. The program will allow the user to make as many selections as desired. In order to do this, the part of the program in which the user enters selections must be part of a loop.

In this instance, a shortcut method of creating a loop will be used. This type of loop is called an *automatic* loop because it uses the logical true value, .T. as the expression. Recall that a DO WHILE loop requires a logical expression so that the program will know what conditions require the loop to repeat, and what conditions require the loop to terminate. A shortcut commonly used is to simply force a loop to be true by inserting a true logical value, .T., in place of an expression. Since by definition .T. is always true, the loop will automatically repeat.

Of course, at some point you want to stop the repetition. dBASE IV makes this possible by including the EXIT command in the programming language. EXIT will force a loop to stop, regardless of the logical expression. The combination of DO WHILE .T. and EXIT, provide a shortcut way of handling a loop. This type of shortcut is often used when the determining factor in the loop is the user's request to quit, which is the case in this example program.

```
DO WHILE .T.
```

The first command executed inside the loop is the ACTIVATE window command which displays the small window PICK_MONTH.,

```
ACTIVATE WINDOW pick_month
```

Inside the window, use @/SAY/GET to display a prompt and an input area for the user's selection for the month. In this case, the entry will be made with the aid of the M picture function. The M function allows you to create a list of options that will be automatically inserted into the GET input area, each time the user presses the [spacebar]. This function is useful when available user options are limited to a specific set of choices. In this instance, the choices are the months of the year, plus options for all months, and quitting the program.

The options are entered as a list, following the @M picture function. As the [spacebar] is pressed, they appear in the input area in the order in which they were entered. The function also allows the user to select an option from the list by typing the first letter of an item. For example, if the user enters an A, April will appear. A second A moves to the next matching item, August. The list then recycles in a loop.

The READ command is needed to activate the input area.

```
::@ 0,0 SAY "Select Month To Summarize " GET;
pick_month PICTURE "@M January,February;
,March,April,May,June,July,August,September;
,October,November,December,All   Months,Quit"
READ
```

Following the user's selection, a DO CASE structure is used to determine what should happen next. The first case is linked to the selection of the Quit option by the user. If that is true, the CASE will execute the EXIT command. Exit will automatically terminate the loop. The program will then look for the first command following the ENDDO command and continue the program from this point.

```
        DO CASE
            CASE pick_month="Quit"
                EXIT
```

The second CASE is used when the user selects All months. The SET FILTER TO command removes any restrictions currently set on the database records.

```
            CASE pick_month="All"
                SET FILTER TO
```

The last option is not listed under a CASE, but under a special CASE called OTHERWISE. The OTHERWISE case is used to create a *default* option. If none of the other cases is true, OTHERWISE is automatically selected as true. In this instance, OTHERWISE filters the database for records that match the user's month selection. Note that it is necessary to TRIM( ) the variable because the length of the month names vary and you don't want to include trailing blanks in the match criterion.

```
            OTHERWISE
                SET FILTER TO CMONTH(date)=TRIM(pick_month)
        ENDCASE
```

Following the DO CASE structure the program executes a procedure called
SHOW_DATA.

```
        DO show_data
```

Following the end of the procedure, the ENDDO command is used to mark the end of the loop. The ENDDO command establishes a mark that shows dBASE IV the set of commands controlled by the previous DO WHILE command. In this program, the ENDDO will cause the selection process to repeat until the user selects Quit, which activates the Exit command, terminating the loop.

```
    ENDDO
```

Following the loop, the LOOP program ends by resetting dBASE IV to the state it was in before the program began.

```
CLOSE DATABASE
RELEASE WINDOWS pick_month,results
SET TALK ON
RETURN
```

The next part of the program is the SHOW_DATA procedure.

```
PROCEDURE show_data
```

This procedure will analyze the CKBOOK database to find the number of checks and deposits, their total amount, the amount of cleared checks, and the amount of deductible expenses for the specified month, or all months.

One way to arrive at these values is to use commands, such as COUNT and SUM. However, since you need to count records in several different ways, you would have to issue several COUNT and SUM commands, each using a different criteria to select records.

The main drawback of this method is that each SUM or COUNT could require the program to scan all the records in the database. In a small file such as the CKBOOK file, this is not significant. But in larger databases, this approach would be quite slow.

As an alternative you can create a custom-designed scan, using the SCAN/ENDSCAN command. This command allows you to perform as many calculations as you need, while making only one pass through the database file.

The first step is to initialize a series of memory variables to hold the totals you will accumulate while moving through the database.

```
STORE 0 TO nchecks,checks,ndeposits,deposits,clr,ded
```

The SCAN command begins a full pass through the database. Recall that records that do not fit the SET FILTER expression are automatically skipped. You do not have to enter a GO TOP command because SCAN automatically begins at the top of the database.

```
SCAN
```

Counters and Accumulators

Gathering statistics while scanning a database, requires a special use of memory variables. In many cases, memory variables are simply assigned a value, e.g. name="Smith" or check=100. Assigning a value in this way wipes out any previous value assigned to that variable. For example, entering *name="La Fish"* overwrites any previous value for the variable NAME.

However, when you are gathering statistics, you do not want to simply capture the amounts from different records. You want to accumulate a total of all the values of the records selected. Look at the two commands below. Command (A) simply copies the value of the AMOUNT field into the variable

CHECKS. But command (B) does something very different. It adds together the current value of CHECKS and the current value in the AMOUNT field, and stores that total back into the CHECKS memory variable. Each time command (B) is executed, the value of CHECKS accumulates. If this command is executed each time a new record is selected, the value of CHECKS at the end will be the total of all the AMOUNT fields.

(A) *checks=amount*
(B) *checks=checks+amount*

This special form of writing a variable definition is called an *accumulator*. Of course, the command itself accumulates nothing. It must be used inside a loop in the correct way, in order to obtain the desired value.

A variation on the accumulator is a *counter*. A counter adds a fixed value, usually 1, to the memory variable each time.

nchecks=nchecks+1

If this command is executed once for each selected record, it will end up with a count of the number of records selected.

Counter and Accumulator memory variables inside a loop make it possible to gather many different values in a single pass through the database.

The final element is the use of IF/ELSE/ENDIF structures. The structure makes it possible to allow a specific counter or accumulator to execute only under specific conditions. The next section of the program uses an IF/ELSE/ENDIF structure to distinguish between checks and deposits. If the record evaluates as a deposit, the DEPOSITS and NDEPOSITS variables are changed. If not, CHECKS and NCHECKS are used.

```
IF payee="DEPOSIT"
    deposits=deposits+amount
    ndeposits=ndeposits+1
ELSE
    checks=checks+amount
    nchecks=nchecks+1
ENDIF
```

As the loop moves to each record, the values are stored in the appropriate variables, based on the restrictions imposed by the IF/ELSE/ENDIF structure.

IF/ENDIF structures are used below to accumulate totals for cleared and deductible records.

```
IF cleared
    clr=clr+amount
ENDIF
IF deductible
    ded=ded+amount
ENDIF
```

The ENDSCAN command repeats the loop, until all the records have been processed.

```
ENDSCAN
```

The test of the procedure displays the values that have been accumulated in the RESULTS window.

```
ACTIVATE WINDOW results
@ 0, 1 SAY "No. Checks"
@ 1, 1 SAY "Amt. Checks"
@ 2, 1 SAY "No. Deposits"
@ 3, 1 SAY "Amt. Deposits"
@ 4, 1 SAY "Balance"
@ 5, 1 SAY "Deductible"
@ 6, 1 SAY "Cleared"
@ 0,20 SAY nchecks PICTURE "999,999"
@ 1,20 SAY checks PICTURE "999,999.99"
@ 2,20 SAY ndeposits PICTURE "999,999"
@ 3,20 SAY deposits PICTURE "999,999.99"
@ 4,20 SAY deposits-checks PICTURE "999,999.99"
@ 5,20 SAY ded PICTURE "999,999.99"
@ 6,20 SAY clr PICTURE "999,999.99"
```

The commands below show a special use of a DO WHILE loop to pause a program. The INKEY( ) function returns a numeric value when any key on the keyboard is pressed. When no key is pressed, the function returns 0. This means so long as the user does not press a key, the DO WHILE loop using the expression INKEY( )=0, will cycle endlessly. When any key is pressed, the program continues.

```
@ 7,1 SAY "Press Any Key"
DO WHILE INKEY( )=0
ENDDO
```

When the user has finished with the statistics, the window is deactivated and the procedure terminates. The program moves back to the PICK-_MONTH window for another selection.

```
DEACTIVATE WINDOW results
RETURN
```

Save and execute the program by entering

```
[Alt-e] r
```

The window appears with the first item on the list, January, placed inside the input area.

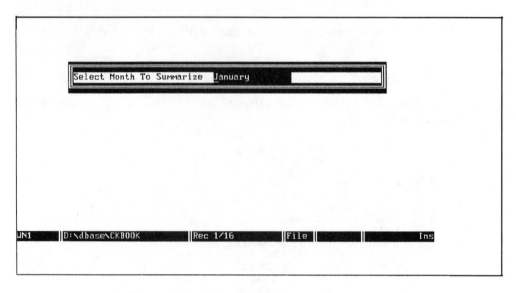

Figure 12-5. Input area shows first item on list.

Enter

    [spacebar]

The entry changes to February. Calculate the statistics for that month by
entering

    ↵

The information concerning the account activity in February is displayed.
The program is paused, due to the DO WHILE INKEY( )=0 loop, until you
decide to press a key.

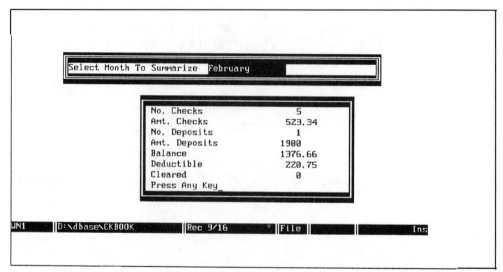

Figure 12-6. Statistics for February displayed.

Return to PICK_MONTH window, by entering

    ↵

Calculate the totals for all months. Enter

    a *(3 times)*
    ↵

Exit the program by entering

    ↵
    q ↵

User-Defined Functions

A user-defined function is a special type of procedure. It is useful when you need to execute a short procedure to obtain a specific value, and to create functions of your own design. The function can be used within a program to carry out calculations or conversions, or at the Dot Prompt when the procedure file has been opened.

For example, dBASE IV contains many string functions, such as UPPER( ) and LOWER( ), which can be used to convert text to all upper- or all lower-case characters. However, there is no function that converts text so that the first letter of each word is in upper-case, while the rest are in power cases, e.g. *Walter Lafish.* this type of text is often called the *proper* format because it is the style typically used with proper nouns.

You could use the user-defined function techniques to create a function called Proper( ), which would convert strings into this format.

A user-defined function is used like a standard dBASE IV function within a command line. For example, suppose you create a user-defined function called Proper. You would use it in a command just as you would an ordinary function.

    LIST *Proper(last)*

User-defined functions can be used in two ways. They can be used as procedures within a program file, or in the Dot Prompt and Control Center modes.

In order to use the function in the Dot Prompt or Control Center modes, the program file that contains the user-defined function is opened with the SET PROCEDURE TO command. This command loads the procedures into memory in the same way that macros or memory variables are loaded. They will remain in memory until you quit dBASE IV, or close the procedure file with CLOSE PROCEDURE or CLOSE ALL.

While in memory, you can use the user-defined function just as you would one of the built-in dBASE IV functions. This is true even if you activate the Control Center. So long as the procedure file is open, dBASE IV will know how to carry out the user-defined functions.

If you use these functions on a regular basis by including them in a report or query, you must remember to open the procedure file before you attempt to use the query or report.

Structure of a User-Defined Function

A user-defined function is written like a procedure. It begins with a FUNCTION command followed by the name of the user-defined function. The function names follow the same rules as procedure or program names.

Immediately following the FUNCTION command, must be a PARA-METERS command. The PARAMETERS command is used to assign the values enclosed as arguments in the user-defined function to memory variables, for processing by the function. For example, suppose you used a user-defined function in a program that read: *Proper("JOHN")*. The first two lines of the function would read:

```
FUNCTION proper
PARAMETERS oldtext
```

The PARAMETERS command assigns the text *JOHN* to the variable named oldtext.

At the end of each function is a special form of the RETURN command. RETURN also includes the name of the variable whose value will be returned as the value of the user-defined function, e.g. RETURN(new text).

Below is a user-defined function called Proper, that will convert a word into first letter upper- and the remainder lower-case letters. Begin by creating the program file.

```
MODIFY COMMAND userfunc ↵
```

Enter the commands for the user-defined function.

Below is a procedure file that contains a pair of user-defined functions. The Mkprop function can be used by itself to convert a single word to the proper *format*. The second function uses Mkprop to create a function called Proper, which will convert a string that contains more than one word into the *proper* format.

The Mkprop function starts with a word stored in a variable called *oldword*, and returns a converted string called *newword*. The function divides the word into two parts, converting the first character to upper-case, and the rest to lower-case.

The Proper function begins with a string called *oldtext* and returns a converted string called *newtext*. This function uses the Mkprop function to convert a series of words in a single character string. Proper consists of a loop that sends one word at a time to the Mkprop function.

```
FUNCTION mkprop
PARAMETERS oldword
first_char=UPPER(LEFT(oldword,1))
other_char=LOWER(RIGHT(oldword,LEN(oldword)-1))
newword=first_char+other_char
RETURN(newword)


FUNCTION proper
PARAMETERS oldtext
SET STATUS OFF
SET TALK OFF
IF .NOT.SPACE(1)$oldtext
    newtext=Mkprop(oldtext)
ELSE
    newtext=""

    DO WHILE SPACE(1)$oldtext
        word=SUBSTR(oldtext,1,AT(SPACE(1),oldtext))
        oldtext=SUBSTR(oldtext,AT(SPACE(1),oldtext)+1)
        newtext=newtext+Mkprop(word)
    ENDDO
    newtext=newtext+Mkprop(oldtext)
ENDIF
SET TALK ON
RETURN(newtext)
```

Save, but do not execute, the program.

```
[Alt-e] s
```

Activate the procedure file by entering

```
SET PROCEDURE TO userfunc ⏎
```

You can now use the Proper( ) function as if it were part of the dBASE IV language. Enter

```
? Proper("MORGAN  REBECCA  KRUMM") ⏎
```

The program uses the instructions in the user-defined functions to return *Morgan Rebecca Krumm*.

Close the procedure file by entering

```
CLOSE PROCEDURE ⏎
```

Summary

This chapter discussed the use of structures in dBASE IV programs.

- **Pop-up Menus.** dBASE IV has a built-in group of commands that can create user-defined pop-up menus, similar in structure and usage to the Control Center pop-up menus. You can define the individual bars to use options that automatically generate bars, based on field contents, file structure, or filenames in a directory. You can specify a command to execute when a selection is made from a pop-up menu. The PROMPT( ) and BAR( ) functions allows you to evaluate selections made by the user.

- **Conditional Structures.** A conditional structure uses a logical expression to decide if a set of commands should or should not be executed. The IF/ENDIF structure allows you to select between two alternative sets of commands. the DO CASE structure permits two or more alternative sets of commands.

- **Loops.** A loop is a structure that repeats a set of commands, until a logical expression evaluates as false, or the loop is forced to terminate with an EXIT command. The DO WHILE command sets up a general purpose loop. The SCAN command creates a loop that automatically increments the record pointer, each time the loop recycles.

- **User-Defined Functions.** A user defined function is a special type of program designed to be called from a program, or from the Dot Prompt mode. The SET PROCEDURE command can be used to load user-defined functions into the active dBASE IV session.

Program Listings

Program POP1.PRG

```
SET TALK OFF
SET SCOREBOARD OFF
SET STATUS OFF
USE CKBOOK
* define pop-up menu
DEFINE POP-UP checks FROM 8,30 TO 12,50
DEFINE BAR 1 OF checks PROMPT "Browse Checks"
DEFINE BAR 2 OF checks PROMPT "Browse Deposits"
DEFINE BAR 3 OF checks PROMPT "Exit Program";
    MESSAGE "Return to the dot prompt."
* select action
ON SELECTION POP-UP checks DO show_data
* show menu to user
CLEAR
ACTIVATE POP-UP checks
RELEASE POP-UP checks
SET TALK ON
SET SCOREBOARD ON
SET STATUS ON
RETURN

PROCEDURE show_data
DO CASE
    CASE BAR( )=1
        SET FILTER TO payee#"DEPOSIT"
        GO TOP
        BROWSE NOAPPEND NOMENU
    CASE BAR( )=2
        SET FILTER TO payee="DEPOSIT"
        GO TOP
        BROWSE NOAPPEND NOMENU
    CASE BAR( )=3
        DEACTIVATE POP-UP
        CLOSE DATABASE
ENDCASE
RETURN
```

Program POP2.PRG

```
USE ckbook ORDER payee
SET FILTER TO payee#"DEPOSIT"
DEFINE POP-UP payee FROM 2,30 PROMPT FIELD payee;
   MESSAGE "Press Esc to Exit"
ON SELECTION POP-UP payee DO show_chk
ACTIVATE POP-UP payee
RELEASE POP-UP payee
RETURN

PROCEDURE show_chk
SEEK PROMPT( )
SET FORMAT TO checks
READ
CLEAR
RETURN
```

Program LOOP.PRG

```
SET TALK OFF
CLEAR
DEFINE WINDOW pick_month FROM 6,10 To 8,70 DOUBLE
DEFINE WINDOW results FROM 10,25 TO 19,65
pick_month=SPACE(15)
USE ckbook
DO WHILE .T.
   ACTIVATE WINDOW pick_month
   @ 0,0 SAY "Select Month To Summarize " GET;
   pick_month PICTURE "@M January,February;
   ,March,April,May,June,July,August,September;
   ,October,November,December,All   Months,Quit"
   READ
   DO CASE
     CASE pick_month="Quit"
          EXIT
        CASE pick_month="All"
            SET FILTER TO
        OTHERWISE
            SET FILTER TO CMONTH(date)=TRIM(pick_month)
   ENDCASE
   DO show_data
ENDDO
CLOSE DATABASE
RELEASE WINDOWS pick_month,results
SET TALK ON
RETURN

PROCEDURE show_data
STORE 0.00 TO nchecks,checks,ndeposits,deposits,clr,ded
SCAN
    IF payee="DEPOSIT"
```

```
            deposits=deposits+amount
            ndeposits=ndeposits+1
        ELSE
            checks=checks+amount
            nchecks=nchecks+1
        ENDIF
        IF cleared
            clr=clr+amount
        ENDIF
        IF deductible
            ded=ded+amount
        ENDIF
    ENDSCAN
ACTIVATE WINDOW results
@ 0, 1 SAY "No. Checks"
@ 1, 1 SAY "Amt. Checks"
@ 2, 1 SAY "No. Deposits"
@ 3, 1 SAY "Amt. Deposits"
@ 4, 1 SAY "Balance"
@ 5, 1 SAY "Deductible"
@ 6, 1 SAY "Cleared"
@ 0,20 SAY nchecks PICTURE "999,999"
@ 1,20 SAY checks PICTURE "999,999.99"
@ 2,20 SAY ndeposits PICTURE "999,999"
@ 3,20 SAY deposits PICTURE "999,999.99"
@ 4,20 SAY deposits-checks PICTURE "999,999.99"
@ 5,20 SAY ded PICTURE "999,999.99"
@ 6,20 SAY clr PICTURE "999,999.99"
@ 7,1 SAY "Press Any Key"
DO WHILE INKEY( )=0
ENDDO
DEACTIVATE WINDOW results
RETURN
```

Part III

Networking

13

Using dBASE IV on a Network

Operating dBASE IV on a network is, to a large degree, the same as operating dBASE IV on a single-user computer. All the commands and procedures discussed in the first two parts of this book also apply to dBASE IV when it is running on a network. However, when you are using dBASE IV on a network, some of the commands behave differently than they do when you are working on a single-user system. In addition, dBASE IV supplies a number of options, commands, and functions, specific to the types of operations and problems encountered when the program is used on a network.

This chapter demonstrates the basic concepts and problems associated with using dBASE IV on a network. It also presents the built-in facilities available to network dBASE IV users, and how networks affect the basic procedures used in dBASE IV.

In Chapter 14, you will learn to write programs allowing you to create your own custom-designed network operations, using the concepts learned in this chapter.

About Networks and Databases

It is important to understand the vast majority of microcomputer systems existing today were originally designed to operate as stand-alone computer systems. The key software component of any computer system is the operating system software. The MSDOS (Microsoft Disk Operating System) software used in most PC, PC-XT, PC-AT, and PS/2 or compatible computers assumes all operations take place on a single-user system. The operating system assumes only the person using the keyboard on the current computer, can gain access to the data stored on the disks in that computer.

However, it is common today to link together stand-alone computers into configurations called *Local Area Networks*, LAN's for short. LAN's provide a means by which computers can gain access to the devices attached to other computers in the system.

The most common type of network is one where one or more computers is designated as a *server* computer. This computer makes its *resources* available to other computers on the network. The *resources* most commonly used are disks for data storage, and printers. It is also possible to use other types of devices, such as modems, across a network.

The computer having access to the server's resources is called a *user.* The user has access to all the devices attached to its own computer, plus the resources available on the network's server computer (or computers).

Some networks, TOPS for example, do not distinguish between server and user computers. In such networks all computers have the same potential access to all other computers. These are called *peer-to-peer* networks.

The actual network consists of hardware and software components.

Hardware

Networks require a physical link to be established between computers, so they can communicate. This is done by placing a communications board in each computer and linking the boards together with cables. The board and cable are the physical path along which network communications travel.

Software

Establishing the physical link between computers does not, in and of itself, create the network. In order to function as network computers, each computer must load a program extending DOS operations to include network operations. This software is referred to as the NOS (Network Operating System.) The network operating system determines how you refer to network operations and which network commands will operate on that system. The network systems from Novell and 3Com are two of the most popular systems.

The most important benefit of networks for database users is many users can share the same database files. The data in these files can be information covering the work of several users, an entire work group, or company. All the users on the network can access the same common database files, allowing dBASE IV to serve as a common source of information.

However, when files are being accessed by multiple users, there are some special considerations arising that are not of concern in stand-alone systems.

Security

Because a network permits users access to data stored by other users, it is often desirable or necessary to control which users have access to which database files. A security system creates password protection for dBASE IV and the files used by it. Files used by a dBASE IV system that has security activated are encrypted, thus the data in the file can only be accessed with the proper password. Keep in mind, files protected in this way cannot be accessed through DOS commands.

Security can be an issue when computers are configured as stand-alone systems, but employed at different times by multiple users. This is often the case when a single computer is kept in an office where many persons have access. You can use the dBASE IV security system on a stand-alone computer, in a similar manner to how it is used on networked computers. Since the dBASE IV security system is not linked to the network operating system, it makes no difference to dBASE IV if there is a network when the security system is used. Security is viewed as a network operation mainly because it has traditionally not been addressed in applications designed for stand-alone computers.

Exclusive Use

Operations, such as modification of the structure, or creation of an index file or tag, require the database to remain unchanged for the duration of the time it takes to complete the operation. These commands also change the data in the database in such a way that a view of the file displayed prior to the change, may be inaccurate. In order to avoid conflicts between users, file access must be limited to single users when changes like MODIFY STRUCTURE, INDEX ON, and other commands are executed. Other users cannot view or modify the file until it is released from the exclusive use of those making changes.

File Locking

Certain dBASE IV operations, such as REPLACE, can change the data in one or more records within a database. Operations like REPLACE (when acting on more than one record) should not be performed on a database being used by more than one user. File locking limits file access to the user who is performing the REPLACE, DELETE, or other similar operations. Note, a locked file can be opened and displayed by other users. The restriction applies only to editing of data.

Record Locking

Updates made to individual records require that no other users make changes to a specific record at the same time. Record locks limit the access of individual records from updates, to one user at a time. Another user can edit records, other than the locked record.

File and record locks are temporary restrictions imposed to protect the integrity of the database files. They are not related to the security system operations restricting access, based on user name and password.

dBASE IV's built-in system of file and record locking is automatically instituted whenever dBASE IV is run on a network, i.e., on a computer booted onto a networked operating system. In this chapter, you will examine the dBASE IV security system and the automatic files and record locking features.

Security

Unlike most of the information in this book, this section on the security system should not be used as a step-by-step lesson, until you have read through the section at least one time. This is because the creation of a security system on your copy of dBASE IV is a change permanently affecting the program and your data files. Once implemented, the password protection features become a permanent part of your dBASE IV system and cannot be removed, short of erasing all the program and database files protected with the system. This means a *total reinstallation of* dBASE IV is required.

For this reason, it is best you read through this section to decide if you want, or need, to implement the dBASE IV protection system, before actually creating it on your copy of dBASE IV. In order to make it easier to imagine what your screen would look like during the various operations, this section will include many screen images.

The key command in the dBASE IV security system is the PROTECT command. The PROTECT command can be executed in two ways.

Control Center

The Protect data command found on the Tools menu executes the dBASE IV Protection system. You are asked to confirm this selection because it makes permanent changes to the dBASE IV system.

Dot Prompt

The command PROTECT activates the protection system when entered from the Dot Prompt, or inserted into a program.

Both methods activate the same protection system routines. The operation of the command is determined by the current state of the dBASE IV system.

System Not Protected

By default, dBASE IV is installed on your computer in an unprotected state. This means all users can have access to any of the database files. If you execute the PROTECT command when the database is not already protected, you establish a password protection system active from that time onward. During this process, you will establish at least one user password. Once created, you must use the password, or you will not be able to gain access to dBASE IV.

Protected System

In a protected system, the PROTECT command is used to modify the current protection setup.

The security system allows you to protect dBASE IV on three levels.

User Access

User access refers to the ability of an individual to log into the dBASE IV program. When the protection system has been created, loading dBASE IV, e.g., entering *dbase* ⏎, prompts the protection system password entry screen to appear. Unless you can enter a valid password log-on, you will not be allowed access to dBASE IV.

File Access

You can restrict the use of certain database files. Access is permitted in terms of four types of operations: READ—view the contents of the file; UPDATE—modify the records in the database; EXTEND—add new records to the database; DELETE—delete records from the database. The system allows you to fine tune which users are allowed to perform what types of operations on the database files.

Field Access

You can specify individual field attributes for different users. There are three types of field access: FULL—the user can view and change data in this field; READ ONLY—the user can view but not change the data in this field; NONE—the field cannot be viewed or modified by the user.

Each of the file or field access types is called a *privilege*. The ability to add records to a database is called the *extend privilege*.

The system of program, file, and field access is organized on the basis of access level codes. The codes are numeric values from 1 to 8. Each user in the system is assigned an access level number. The lower the value of the number the greater the access. For example, the most important users, i.e., those who should have access to all files, are given the access code of 1. The users with the least access privileges are given an access code of 8.

File and field access is then restricted in terms of the access level codes needed to access the file or field. For example, if a file is assigned the access code of 4 for File UPDATE, users with an access level of 1 through 4 could edit the records, while users with access codes 5 through 8 could not.

Users are defined by two names: the user name and the group name. Each user must belong to a group. You must have at least one group name. The group names correspond to work groups or departments within a company. In a small company, a single group name, e.g., the company name, could be used for all users. In order to access dBASE IV, you must enter the group name, the user name, and the password.

All file and record protection is based on group name, so it makes sense to organize user groups along the lines of who needs access to which group of database files.

Establishing a Protection System

Suppose you installed dBASE IV and created the files used throughout Part I-CKBOOK, SALES, BUYERS and PRODUCTS. How would you setup a protection system for these files?

The first step is to run the protection system from the Control Center, [Alt-t] p, or from the Dot Prompt, PROTECT. In this example, the assumption is you are starting from the dot-prompt mode. Enter

    PROTECT ↵

The program displays the screen shown in Figure 13-1. You are asked to enter a password, which will become the master password for the database administrator. The administrator is the individual who creates, modifies, or deletes user names, passwords, and privileges. The administrator password is needed only when you run the PROTECT command. Passwords assigned to users do not allow access to the PROTECT command—only the master administration password permits this access.

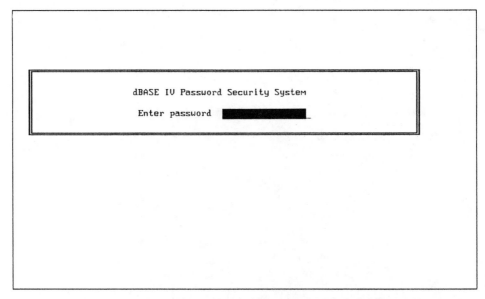

dBASE IV Password Security System

Enter password

Figure 13-1. Screen display shown when creating a protection system.

Passwords can be up to 16 characters in length and can consist of any sequence of alphanumeric characters. Selecting the actual passwords takes some care and imagination. You want to choose something that is easy or logical to remember, but not so obvious that it can be easily guessed by an unauthorized person seeking to gain access to the system. The passwords used in these examples are selected so you can easily follow the references in this chapter. It is probably better for security reasons to avoid having all passwords follow a specific pattern, as they do in this chapter.

Passwords *can contain blank spaces.* For example, the password *lafish walter* is valid.

To create the master password, you would enter something like

```
lafish ⏎
```

When you enter the password, dBASE IV asks you to confirm the password just entered, as seen in Figure 13-2. You must reenter the same password or the protect command is terminated. Reentering the same password ensures you know the spelling of the password entered.

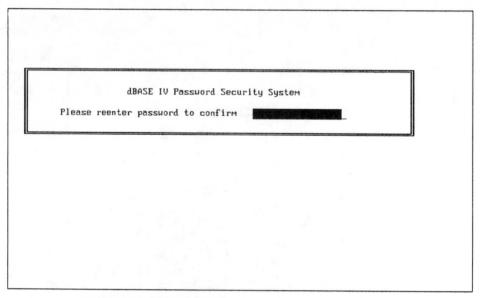

Figure 13-2. Asked to confirm entry of master password.

Enter your password a second time.

```
lafish ⏎
```

The program displays the Protect mode screen and menus, as in Figure 13-3. The mode displays 4 menus: Users, Files, Reports, and Exit.

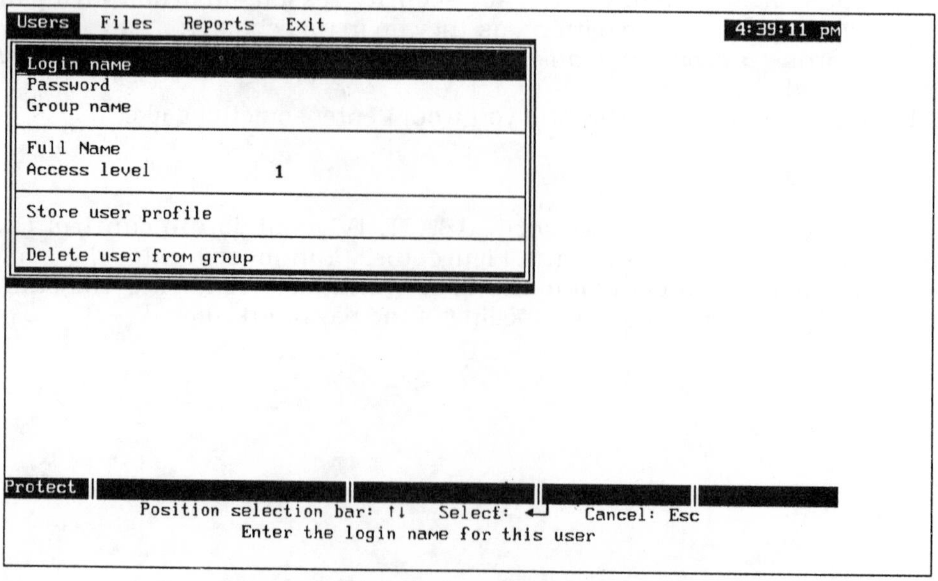

Figure 13-3. Protect mode screen display.

The users menu is automatically displayed and is used for creating user-access specifications. Suppose you have four individuals, including yourself, who should have access to the dBASE IV program: Carolyn, Kerri, and Mike. You must create a profile for each of these users, but in order to do so you must also know the name or names of the group to which these users belong. Here, the group will be called BOOKS, i.e., users who have access to the *books*—financial data—of the business.

The first profile is for Carolyn.

The process of creating a user profile begins with the Login name option on the Users menu. The login name is name the user employs to login to the dBASE IV system. Usually this is the name of a user, or an abbreviation of this name. The LOGIN name is limited to 8 characters. Enter

    ⌐
    carolyn ⌐

The login name is automatically converted to upper-case characters. The highlight moves to the Password option. Enter the password for this user.

    ⌐
    user 1 ⌐

In the Protect-mode display, the passwords of individual users are displayed. In a security situation, be sure when working in this mode, unauthorized individuals cannot observe your screen display.

This password is not a good example of a secure password and is used only to allow you to follow the logic of the instructions easily.

The highlight advances to the group name, where you will enter the name of the group to which this user belongs. Group names are also limited to 8 characters.

    books ⌐

The highlight moves to the Full Name, which is optional. It is not used as part of the security system and is not needed to log onto dBASE IV, or protect files and fields. The name is used as an alternative user name, when operating in a multi-user environment, and when you are using the LKSYS( ) function on a converted database. (The LKSYS( ) function and database conversion are covered in Chapter 14.) If this option is not used, the LOGIN name is used for identification of the user. The full name allows you to enter a 24-character name.

Enter a full name. In this case, the phone extension is added to the full-name display.

    ⌐
    Carolyn Santa Extn 45 ⌐

The access level option sets the access level for the user, controlling the privileges available to this user. The access level code is a whole number from 1 to 8. The default value, 1, is the supreme access level code, and a user with this code can access all databases and fields. Assigning a higher number restricts users from viewing some files or fields.

Since file and field protection is optional, you may wish to simply use the dBASE IV protection system as a login system. In such a case, all users would be assigned the access code of 1 because they would all have equal access to the database files.

The display now shows the setting for granting the user, CAROLYN, access privileges to all the files and fields, as seen in Figure 13-4.

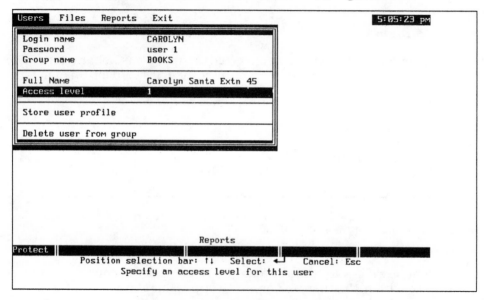

Figure 13-4. **User profile for CAROLYN.**

When you complete a user's profile, save it as part of the protection system by using the Store user profile command. Enter

    s

The profile is stored and a new blank profile screen is displayed. Create a second profile file for the user Kerri. Enter

    ↵
    kerri ↵
    ↵
    user 2 ↵
    ↵
    books ↵
    ↵
    Kerri Flynn Extn 67 ↵

Here, you may want to assign Kerri a lower access code than Carolyn, enabling you to restrict Kerri's access to certain files or fields. If you do not use the File menu to develop profiles of specific files, the access code designations will not have any meaning because all files will be available, as soon as the user logs onto dBASE IV.

In this instance, make Kerri a 4. Enter

⏎
4

The profile for Kerri is shown in Figure 13-5.

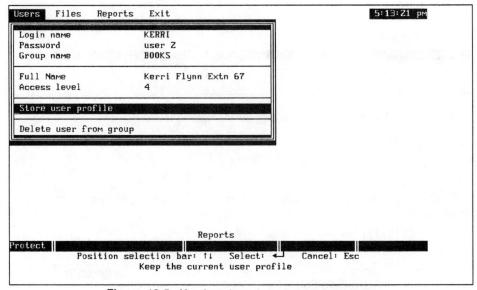

Figure 13-5. Kerri assigned access code level 4.

Save this user profile by executing the Store user profile command.

s

Finally, create a user profile for Mike. Enter

⏎
mike⏎
⏎
user 3 ⏎
⏎
books ⏎

In this case, skip the optional Full Name but enter an access level of 8. Mike is a part-time employee who should have access to only the least secure information, as seen in Figure 13-6. Enter

a
8

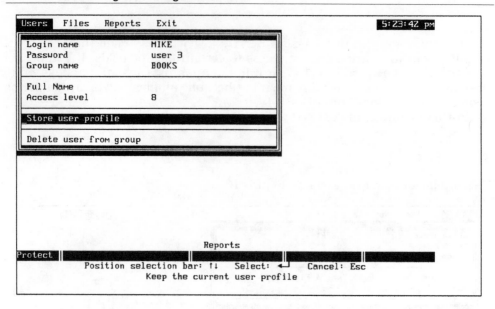

Figure 13-6. Mike assigned the lowest level of access.

Save this profile by entering

s

You can review or print a list of the current users by using the Report menu. Enter

[Alt-r]

The menu consists of two parts: user information and file information.

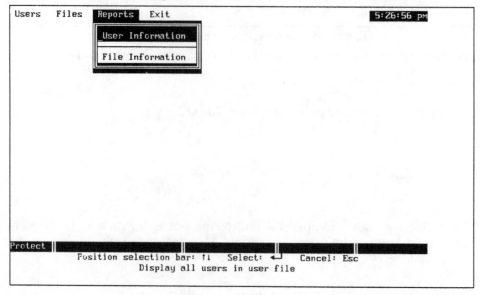

Figure 13-7. Reports menu.

Select User information by entering

u

You have the option of printing this data or displaying it on the screen. Select to display the data on the screen by entering

n

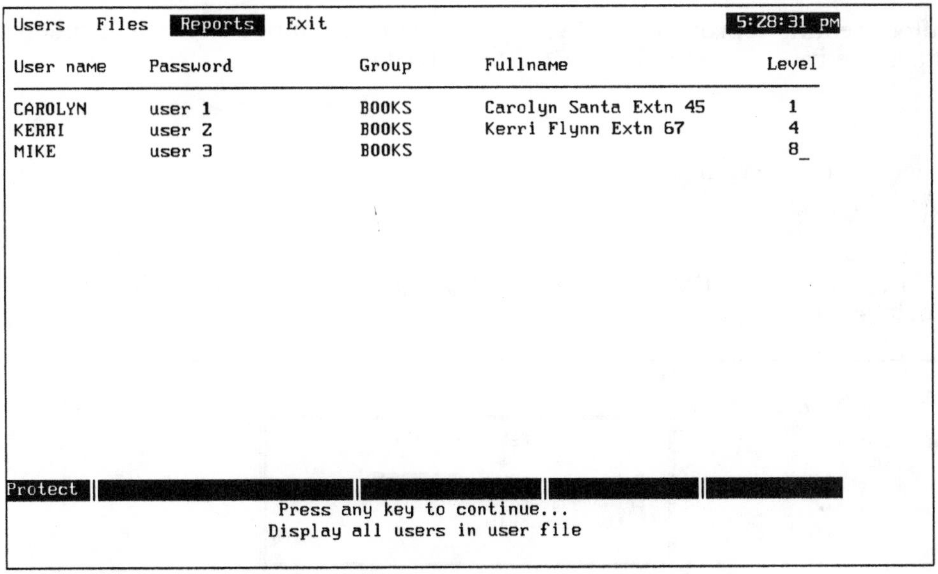

```
 Users    Files   Reports   Exit                          5:28:31 PM

 User name    Password         Group     Fullname              Level

 CAROLYN      user 1           BOOKS     Carolyn Santa Extn 45    1
 KERRI        user 2           BOOKS     Kerri Flynn Extn 67      4
 MIKE         user 3           BOOKS                             8_








 Protect
                        Press any key to continue...
                        Display all users in user file
```

Figure 13-8. User information listed.

Figure 13-8 demonstrates a list of users.

The user report listing displays all the passwords on the screen. If you had printed the report, the passwords would appear on the printout. Take care that this display is not seen by unauthorized persons. Also take care to dispose of printed copies of the report in a secure manner. Return to the menu by entering

⌡

Creating user profiles is all you need do to establish a login security system. *Login* refers to the requirement that the user enter a valid user name, group, and password, in order to gain access to the dBASE IV system. If this is the only security you wish to implement, you have completed the tasks required in the Protect mode. In this example, assume you have established the protection you desire, for the time being.

Keep in mind, none of the specifications you entered are a permanent part of dBASE IV, yet. They become so if you use the Exit menu to save the data. Enter

[Alt-e] s

The data is written to the disk. Exit the mode.

        e

The system is now password protected.

Logins

After creating a protected dBASE IV system, you must login each time you start the program. Quit dBASE IV by entering

        quit ⏎

Restart the program.

        dbase ⏎

Instead of the dBASE IV logo, the program now displays the dBASE IV Login screen, Figure 13-9.

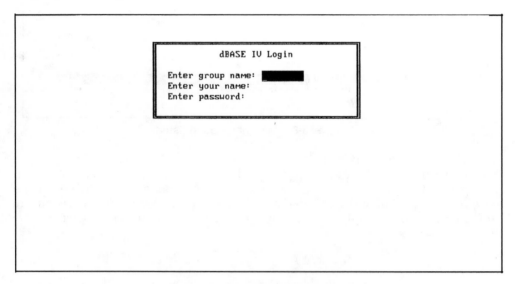

Figure 13-9. dBASE IV login in screen.

In order to gain access to the program, you must enter a valid group name, user name, and password. Enter

        books ⏎
        carolyn ⏎
        user 1 ⏎

The protection system then releases dBASE IV to run normally. The program will not function exactly as it did before you created the protection system.

Forced Logins

The user login is made only once during each dBASE IV session. However, if you desire to login again without quitting dBASE IV, you can force the login procedure to activate by entering the LOGOUT command at the Dot Prompt mode.

If the Control Center is active, exit it by entering

    [Alt-e] e

To force another login, enter

    LOGOUT ⌐

The program displays the same login screen it displayed when you first loaded the program.

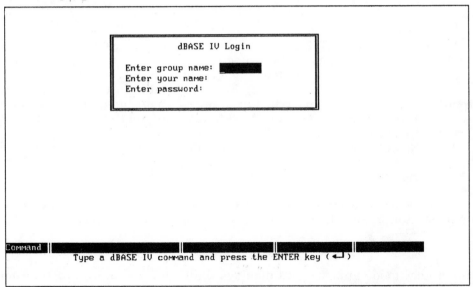

Figure 13-10. Log screen forced to activate with LOGOUT command.

You can login to a different user than the one you initially logged to when the program was loaded. This time, login as Mike.

        books ⌐
        mike ⌐
        user 3 ⌐

File and Field Protection

The protection established so far controls logins to dBASE IV. If you desire, you can extend the protection system to control access to specific files, and even fields within those files. File and field protection, function only if you have users whose access code levels are other than the default value 1. If all the users have access levels of 1, file and field access codes have no function because the highest value assigned is 1.

Here, you have three users with different access code levels:

User	Level
Carolyn	1
Kerri	4
Mike	8

You can use the PROTECT command to set the access level of various databases and fields from access by users, such as Kerri and Mike. Carolyn, with a 1 access code, is unaffected by the file and field protection.

For example, suppose you want Kerri to be able to view and edit the records in the CKBOOK database, but to prevent her from adding or deleting records in this database. On the other hand, you don't want Mike to have access to this file, at all.

To place protection on a file, activate the Protect mode. Enter:

```
PROTECT ⏎
```

In order to gain access to the protection mode, you must enter the master administrator password. This example uses LAFISH as the password. Enter

```
lafish ⏎
```

The Protect mode appears and displays the Users menu. To protect a file, activate the Files menu.

```
[Alt-f]
```

The File menu is displayed, as shown Figure 13-11.

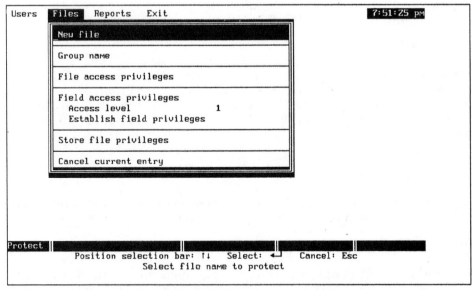

Figure 13-11. File menu in protection mode display.

The first option on the menu, New File, is used to select a database file for protection. Enter

⌐┘

The program displays a pop-up menu listing all the database files, as shown Figure 13-12.

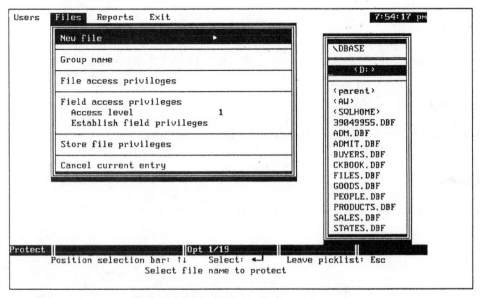

Figure 13-12. Files listed for selection.

This example uses the CKBOOK file. Enter

  ckbook ⏎

The next item is Group name. This is the name of the group of users who have access to the file. Each file can belong to *only* one group of users. Here, the user group is called BOOKS. If you want to allow users in the BOOKS group to have access to this file, you must enter this name as the group name.

  g
  books ⏎

The next option on the menu is File access privileges. This option allows you to establish which user levels can have access to this file. Enter

  f

When you select this option, a box is displayed on the right side of the screen, as in Figure 13-13, listing the four areas where access may be restricted for a file.

Read

If the user qualifies for this option, she can display the data in the database file. If she does not qualify for this option, she is restricted from using the file.

Update

This option allows the user to make changes to existing records.

Extend

This option allows the user to add records to the database.

Delete

This option allows the user to delete and recall records.

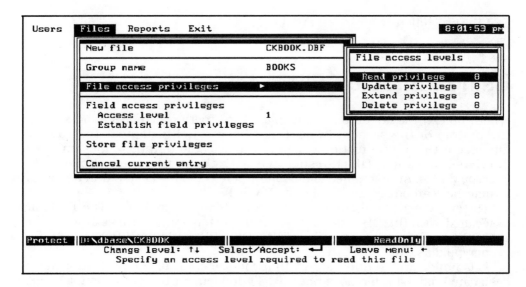

Figure 13-13. File privileges listings.

The default value for all options is 8, and allows all users to Read, Update, Extend, and Delete records in this database. To activate restrictions, you must change one or more levels. The goal was to allow Kerri to read and update, but not add or delete, records. In addition, Mike was not to have access to the file at all. Therefore, in order to prevent Mike—access level 8—from accessing this file, the Read Access has to be at least 7. Enter

```
r
7
```

Since level 8 users cannot access the file for display, they are effectively prevented from using the database at all. However, Kerri, level 4, is not to be permitted to add or delete records. This means Extend and Delete should be at least level 3 functions. Enter

```
e
3
d
3
```

The privileges are set accordingly to implement the restrictions. Save the settings and return to the Dot Prompt.

down arrow

The Store file privileges command stores the settings for this file. Enter

```
s
```

Exit the protection mode by entering

```
[Alt-e] e
```

Using Protected Files

When you exit the file protection display, the program displays a message at the bottom of the screen, indicating files are being copied. In order to implement the file protection scheme, the selected database files and any database text files (DBT) associated with those files, are copied into encrypted files. An *encrypted* file is one where the data is stored in a special format that can be accessed only by dBASE IV.

The encrypted database file is given a CRP file extension. The DBT file associated with the DBF file is given a CPT extension. In this example, the CKBOOK.DBF file is encrypted as CKBOOK.CRP and the CKBOOK.DBT file is encrypted as CKBOOK.CPT.

It is important to understand that the selection of file protection for a designated database file does not actually implement the protection scheme. Instead, encrypted versions of the normal dBASE IV files are created. They exist side-by-side, with the original files on the disk. If you take no further action, dBASE IV continues to use the original database files and ignores the encrypted files. The protection scheme you select will have no effect on database operations.

In order to actually implement the protect scheme, you must replace the normal database files with the encrypted versions. It is a good idea to copy the original database files onto a backup disk or directory.

Assuming you have a backup disk in drive A, enter

```
! copy ckbook.d* a: ↵
```

Delete the files from the present directory.

```
! del ckbook.d* ↵
```

Rename the CRP and CPT files to DBF and DBT extensions, respectively.

```
RENAME ckbook.crp To ckbook.dbf ↵
RENAME ckbook.cpt To ckbook.dbt ↵
```

You have now implemented the protection scheme. Change the user to Kerri. Enter

```
LOGOUT ↵
books ↵
kerri ↵
user 2 ↵
```

Open the CKBOOK file.

```
USE ckbook ↵
```

List the data.

LIST ⏎

The program lists the information in the file. This makes sense because Kerri has the correct access level for viewing data, but not for adding records. Enter

APPEND ⏎

The program does not activate the Append mode. Instead, because the access code level of the user is not sufficient for appending, an error message is displayed, as shown in Figure 13-14, which reads "Unauthorized access level".

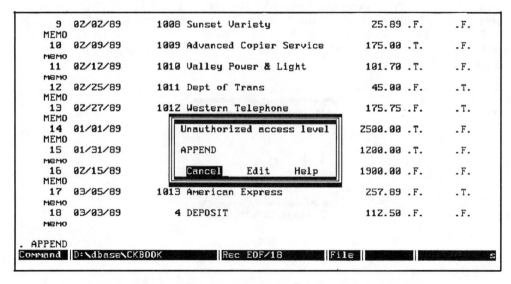

```
    9  02/02/89    1008 Sunset Variety            25.89 .F.      .F.
  MEMO
   10  02/09/89    1009 Advanced Copier Service  175.00 .T.      .F.
  MEMO
   11  02/12/89    1010 Valley Power & Light     101.70 .T.      .F.
  MEMO
   12  02/25/89    1011 Dept of Trans             45.00 .F.      .T.
  MEMO
   13  02/27/89    1012 Western Telephone        175.75 .F.      .T.
  MEMO
   14  01/01/89    ┌────────────────────────┐  2500.00 .T.      .F.
  MEMO             │ Unauthorized access level │
   15  01/31/89    │                        │  1200.00 .T.      .F.
  MEMO             │ APPEND                 │
   16  02/15/89    │ ┌──────┐               │  1900.00 .F.      .F.
  MEMO             │ │Cancel│  Edit   Help  │
   17  03/05/89    └─┴──────┴───────────────┘   257.89 .F.      .T.
  MEMO             1013 American Express
   18  03/03/89       4 DEPOSIT               112.50 .F.      .F.
  MEMO
. APPEND
Command ║D:\dbase\CKBOOK        ║Rec EOF/18    ║File ║              ║   s
```

Figure 13-14. Access denied because of access code level.

Cancel the command.

⏎

If you change the user to Carolyn she will be able enter the Append mode because she possesses a sufficiently high access code level. Note, as a 1-level user, Carolyn will always have access to all files.

LOGOUT ⏎
books ⏎
carolyn ⏎
user 1 ⏎
USE ckbook ⏎
APPEND ⏎

The mode is activated because of the user-access code assigned to the current user. Exit the Append mode.

```
[Alt-e] e
```

Change to Mike.

```
LOGOUT ↵
books ↵
mike ↵
user 3 ↵
USE ckbook ↵
LIST ↵
```

This time, the message reads "No fields to process". The reason for the message is that Mike does not have READ access to the file. The message is a reflection of how dBASE IV implements this restriction: It limits the SET FIELDS to those fields permitted by the protection settings. In this case, when the READ access level is insufficient, no fields are listed, as seen in Figure 13-15.

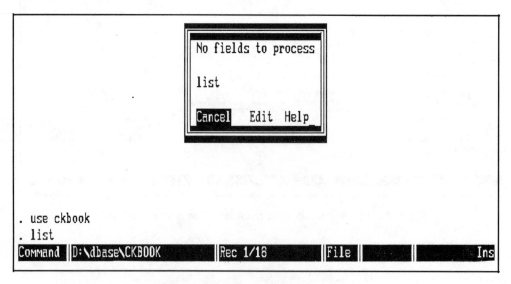

Figure 13-15. Display access denied.

Exit the error box.

```
↵
```

Modifying a Protected Database

When you create an encrypted database file, you cannot make changes, such as MODIFY STRUCTURE, to the encrypted file. In addition, if you are using an encrypted database as discussed in the previous section, you cannot change the protection attributes of encrypted files. dBASE IV does not allow you to directly modify a file's protection settings. The only way to change the file is to create a new set of file protection attributes for the database, replacing the existing set of protection attributes.

These changes must be made from an unencrypted version of the database file. Thus, you must go through a special procedure to create a normal—i.e. unencrypted—version of the database, modify that copy, then reprotect the modified database.

Before you can make these changes to a database, a user with the correct access level—typically, a user with level 1 access—will have to login. In this example, CAROLYN has access level 1. Enter

```
LOGOUT ↵
books ↵
carolyn ↵
user 1 ↵
```

Begin by placing the CKBOOK database in use.

```
USE ckbook ↵
```

The SET ENCRYPTION command controls whether or not copies made of database files will be encrypted. When the Protection system is active, the SET ENCRYPTION setting is ON by default. In this case, you want to make a copy of the CKBOOK file that is not encrypted. Turn off the encryption setting for copies by entering

```
SET ENCRYPTION OFF ↵
```

Create a copy of the current database using the COPY command. Using COPY FILE or RUN COPY will not remove the encryption, because those commands make duplicates of files without examining the contents. COPY looks at and analyzes the contents of the file being copied. Enter

```
COPY TO ckbook1 ↵
```

Place the unprotected version of the database in use.

```
USE ckbook1 ↵
```

You can now use the CKBOOK1 database to overwrite the encrypted files stored as CKBOOK.

```
COPY TO ckbook ↵
```

Select to overwrite the existing files.

```
o
```

You can now make changes to the file's structure if you desire. In addition, you can make changes to the file's protection settings. Close the files and set the encryption on again. The CKBOOK file is now an unencrypted file containing all the data that was in the encrypted version of the file.

```
CLOSE ALL ↵
SET ENCRYPTION ON ↵
```

Field Protection

In addition to the use of protection for a file, you can also protect specific fields within a file. By default, all fields in a protect file gives the user FULL access. This means if a user is allowed UPDATE access to the file, she can edit and view any of the fields. You can change the field status of individual fields to:

R/O

This designation makes the field a Read Only field that cannot be edited.

None

None suppresses the display of the field.

Setting field attributes is similar to setting file protection attributes. Begin by entering the Protection mode.

```
PROTECT ↵
lafish ↵
```

Select the Files menu.

```
[Alt-f]
```

In order to change the protection settings for a file, you must enter the name and the group of the file you want to protect.

```
n
ckbook ↵
g
books ↵
```

In this instance, set the protection values based on fields, rather than entire files. For example, level 4 users, like Kerri, can have access to all fields, but the amount and date fields is Read Only. Level 8 users, like Mike, can have access to all fields, but date is Read Only and the amount field does not appear at all.

For example, to establish the privileges for access code level 4, set the access code number in the Access level setting under the Fields access privileges heading to 4.

> a
> 4

You can then display a list of the individual fields by using the Establish field privileges option.

> e

The program displays a pop-up menu where all the files are listed. Next to each File is FULL. This is the default setting for the field attributes, allowing edit and viewing access to all fields.

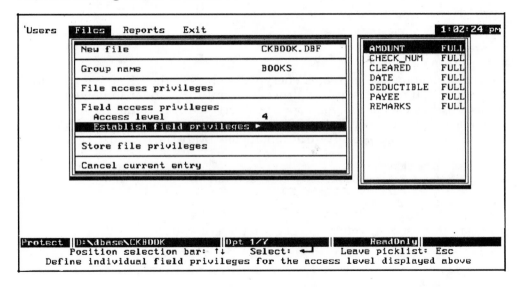

Figure 13-16. File protection attributes listed.

Here, the AMOUNT and DATE fields should be set to R/O, Read Only.

You can change the attribute of an individual field by moving the highlight to this field and entering ↵. Each ↵ toggles the attribute to the next option.

For example, to change the currently highlighted field, AMOUNT, to R/O, enter

> ↵ *(2 times)*

Move the highlight to DATE. Enter

> ↵ *(2 times)*

To save these settings and move on to another access level, enter

> [left arrow]

Change to level 8 by entering

```
a
8
e
```

The same list of fields appears. In this instance, change AMOUNT to NONE and DATE to R/O.

```
⏎
down arrow (3 times)
⏎ (2 times)
left arrow
```

Save the new protection scheme.

```
s
[Alt-e]  e
```

The protection mode creates encrypted copies of the CKBOOK DBF and DBT files. You must follow the procedure outlined under Implementing a Protection System, where you copy the encrypted files to the DBF and DBT filenames. The commands below accomplish this task. Note, SET SAFETY OFF is used to tell dBASE IV to automatically overwrite the existing files.

```
SET SAFETY OFF ⏎
COPY FILE ckbook.crp TO ckbook.dbf  ⏎
COPY FILE ckbook.cpt TO ckbook.dbt  ⏎
SET SAFETY ON ⏎
```

You can now use the protect file. Login for a level-8 user.

```
LOGOUT ⏎
books ⏎
mike ⏎
user 3 ⏎
USE ckbook ⏎
EDIT ⏎
```

The Edit mode displays the fields according to the protection settings assigned to the access level—here, level 8. The AMOUNT field does not appear at all because for a level-8 user, this field has the NONE attribute. The DATE field appears, but is a Read Only field that cannot be changed because the field protection attribute is R/O.

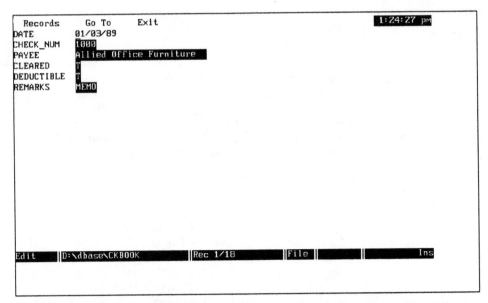

Figure 13-17. Fields displayed according to access level field specifications.

The field attributes allow you to fine-tune the protection schemes, down to the individual user levels to match individual field qualities.

Exit the file by entering

```
[Alt-e]  e
CLOSE ALL ↵
```

You can use combinations of file and field protection. Keep in mind, file protection attributes take precedence over all field attributes. For example, if a file is set to level 7 for update, a level-8 user will find all fields Read Only, even though their field settings are shown as FULL. The only use of the field attribute, in this case, would be to select NONE for the fields that should not be displayed.

File Operations on a Multi-User System

The primary benefit of using dBASE IV on a multi-user system is that information can be shared by several users at the same time. When a database is being accessed by more than one user, it is said to be operating in a Shared mode.

dBASE IV automatically implements a system of file and record locking, ensuring the accuracy and the integrity of the database files used in a *shared* mode. There are two primary concerns involved with multi-user databases.

Updates

When more than one user is making changes, additions, or deletions to the records in a database file, it is possible two or more users will attempt to change the same record at the same time. If unprotected the database file could be corrupted by simultaneous changes made by different users. dBASE IV automatically locks a record to give sole control of data entry to the first user who edits a record. All other users must wait until the first user has completed her entry and moved onto another record.

Accuracy

Changes made by one user will affect the accuracy of the data seen by other users working on the same file. Suppose for example, two users—Carolyn and Kerri—are working with the same database file. Kerri is making changes to the data in the records, while Carolyn is performing statistical operations on the records in the databases. Even though only Kerri is making changes to the database file, Carolyn is affected by them because they could change the value of the statistical summaries she is making. dBASE IV automatically prevents Carolyn from calculating the SUM of a field while Kerri is making changes to one of the records. The SUM command will be released only once Kerri has completed the change in the record.

dBASE IV goes about the task of protecting the accuracy and the integrity of the data in three ways.

Exclusive Access

Some dBASE IV commands require only a single user to have access to a database file if the specified operation is to be carried out with accuracy and data integrity. When a file is used exclusively, no other user can gain access to the file with a USE command.

The most common commands affected by this requirement are MODIFY STRUCTURE and INDEX ON. Since MODIFY STRUCTURE affects all the records in the database, it would be impossible to ensure the accuracy of changes made by other users when the file structure is being changed. The INDEX ON command needs to read key expressions from all the records. Changes made while an index is being generated could render the index inaccurate. Exclusive use is automatically set in the Control Center when you execute a command requiring exclusive use of the database. At the dot-prompt mode you must enter the SET EXCLUSIVE ON command *before* opening the database you want to perform the operation on.

Files opened in the exclusive mode cannot be shared by other users. Once opened in an exclusive mode, the database remains unavailable to other users until it is specifically released from this mode. Exclusive use can only be terminated by closing the database. Also note if a database is already in shared use, a user cannot obtain exclusive use until all the other users exit the file.

Commands that require exclusive access:

CONVERT
INDEX ON
INSERT
MODIFY/CREATE   APPLICATION
MODIFY/CREATE   LABEL
MODIFY/CREATE   QUERY
MODIFY/CREATE   REPORT
MODIFY/CREATE   SCREEN
MODIFY/CREATE   STRUCTURE
PACK
REINDEX
RESET
ZAP

File Locking

File locking differs from exclusive use in that the locked database is still shared by other users. A locked file's data can be read by more than one user at a time. dBASE IV locks a file when one of the users is performing an operation affecting more than a single record, but does not require exclusive use. When locked, a file accepts updates from only the user who has established the file lock. All other users are restricted to viewing data, until the lock is removed.

For example, the CALCULATE command locks the file on which it is performing a calculation. This ensures the totals arrived at reflect the state of the database when the command began to execute. dBASE IV automatically locks and unlocks the file for the duration of the execution of the command. This means as soon as the command (e.g. CALCULATE) is complete, other users can gain access to records in order to make changes.

Commands that cause automatic file locking:

APPEND FROM
AVERAGE
CALCULATE
COPY
COPY STRUCTURE
COUNT
DELETE scope, DELETE FOR, DELETE WHILE
INDEX
JOIN
LABEL FORM
PROTECT
RECALL scope, RECALL FOR, RECALL WHILE
REPLACE scope, REPLACE FOR, REPLACE WHILE
REPORT

Commands that cause automatic file locking (continued):

SORT
SUM
TOTAL
UPDATE

Record Locking

Record locking takes place when a record in a shared database is edited. The first user to gain access to the record is given editing privileges. Other users can read the record or edit any other record, other than the locked record. Record locks are automatically removed when the record is saved, i.e., when the user making the changes moves to another record.

Commands that cause automatic record locking

APPEND
DELETE
RECALL
REPLACE
EDIT*
BROWSE*

* These commands allow access to more than one record. Record locking will take place in the Edit or Browse modes, when the user attempts to edit any field in the current record.

If a file is opened in the Exclusive mode, record and file locking are unnecessary because these files cannot be accessed by other users.

In the following sections, details about typical operations in a multi-user environment are presented. The examples are given within the context of a specific example. The example uses the databases found in Part I: CKBOOK, SALES, BUYERS and PRODUCTS.

The examples shown assume there are two users with full access to all databases, i.e., no protection is involved, or both users have access level 1.

The users in this example are MORGAN and CAROLYN. The assumption is users are working off a file server with the drive destination of E:, and the dBASE IV program is stored in E:\DBASE. As with the previous section, read through this section first, before attempting to enter the commands or similar commands appropriate to your network configuration.

It is important to understand that dBASE IV will automatically perform file and record locks, as illustrated in the following pages, even when there is only one user logged into a given file, or on the network system. dBASE IV's network operations are triggered by the presence of the LAN operating system in the memory of the computer. Thus, even though you may be the only user on the network, your dBASE IV will display record locking messages and require exclusive access for certain operations. The only way to avoid these requirements is to boot the computer with DOS, perhaps from a floppy disk that does not contain the network operating system. This may not possible in all situations.

Listing Users

When you load dBASE IV in a multi-user environment, you can get a list of the users with the command LIST USERS. The current user is indicated with a >. For example, if Morgan enters

        LIST USERS ⏎

The screen will display:

        Computer name

        Carolyn
    >   MORGAN

If Carolyn enters:

        LIST USERS ⏎

The screen will show:

        Computer name

    >   CAROLYN
        MORGAN

The list shows the users in alphabetical order. The list is the same for all computers, with the exception of the location of the >.

The user names shown with the LIST USERS commands are the network names of the work stations, logged onto the network. This is not necessarily the same as the user names employed with the protection system. The ACCESS( ) and USER( ) functions are oriented toward the dBASE IV protection system. LIST USERS does not use the protection system user name.

When databases are opened in a shared mode, both users have access to all database records. If one of the users begins to edit a record, dBASE IV automatically implements a record lock on that file. When this happens, other users are not allowed to edit this record, until the user with the record lock completes the editing and moves to another record.

To demonstrate in detail how this operation takes place, the following commands show two users, Morgan and Carolyn, editing the CKBOOK database. The example uses Dot Prompt commands, but the record locking operations are the same when commands are executed from the Control Center.

Morgan enters the following commands to begin editing the database.

```
USE ckbook ↵
EDIT ↵
```

Carolyn enters the following commands to gain access to the CKBOOK file. The only difference is, Carolyn selects to use the Browse mode.

```
USE ckbook ↵
BROWSE ↵
```

It is important to remember when record locking is implemented, it is the user who first makes a change in a record that gets the record lock. It does not matter which user was first to access the database or move to the specified record.

At this point, both users are positioned on record 1. Morgan's screen shows:

```
DATE            01/03/89
CHECK_NO        1000
PAYEE           Allied Office Furniture
CLEARED         T
DEDUCTIBLE      T
REMARKS         MEMO
```

Morgan decides to change the check number from 1000 to 2000 by entering down arrow

```
2
```

As soon as Morgan enters the first new character, the number 2, the program reacts by beeping. In addition to the beep, there are two changes on the screen.

1. At the bottom of the screen a message reading "(press SPACE)" appears.
2. On the right side of the status line "RecLock" appears.

These changes are the result of the automatic record locking system of dBASE IV. When Morgan attempted to place a new character in the record, dBASE IV locked the record. In order to inform the user of the changed status, a beep sounded and the new information was displayed. Note, the keystroke setting off the record lock was *not* passed onto the database record. Therefore, you must reenter the character you typed, in this case, 2.

First, enter the [spacebar] to acknowledge you are alerted to the record lock.

    [spacebar]

Now enter the data into the field.

    2000

Other users with access to the same file—in this example, Carolyn—will still see the record as it was prior to the change. The record will remain the same until Morgan completes entry and moves to another record. Carolyn's screen shows:

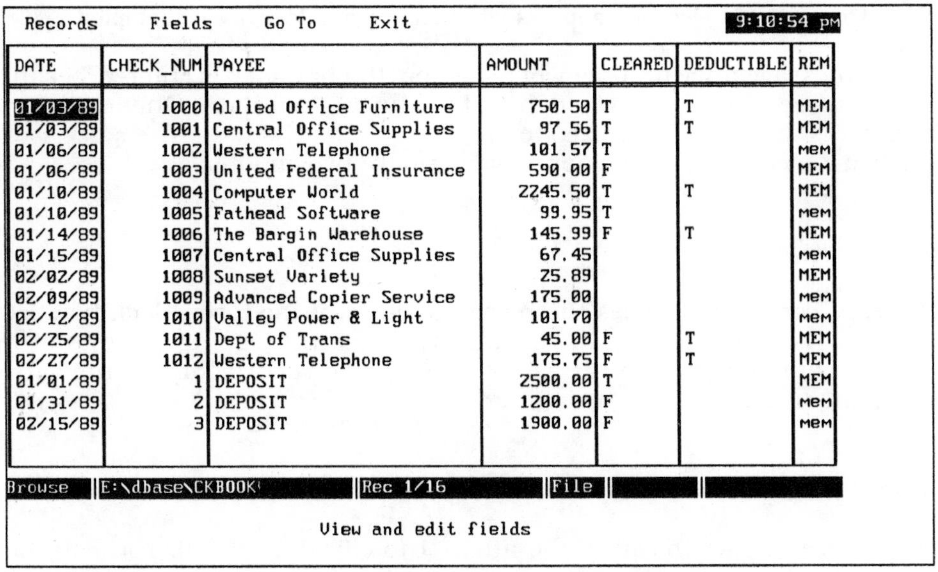

Records	Fields	Go To	Exit				9:10:54 PM

DATE	CHECK_NUM	PAYEE	AMOUNT	CLEARED	DEDUCTIBLE	REM
01/03/89	1000	Allied Office Furniture	750.50	T	T	MEM
01/03/89	1001	Central Office Supplies	97.56	T	T	MEM
01/06/89	1002	Western Telephone	101.57	T		mem
01/06/89	1003	United Federal Insurance	590.00	F		MEM
01/10/89	1004	Computer World	2245.50	T	T	MEM
01/10/89	1005	Fathead Software	99.95	T		mem
01/14/89	1006	The Bargin Warehouse	145.99	F	T	MEM
01/15/89	1007	Central Office Supplies	67.45			mem
02/02/89	1008	Sunset Variety	25.89			MEM
02/09/89	1009	Advanced Copier Service	175.00			mem
02/12/89	1010	Valley Power & Light	101.70			mem
02/25/89	1011	Dept of Trans	45.00	F	T	MEM
02/27/89	1012	Western Telephone	175.75	F	T	MEM
01/01/89	1	DEPOSIT	2500.00	T		MEM
01/31/89	2	DEPOSIT	1200.00	F		mem
02/15/89	3	DEPOSIT	1900.00	F		mem

Browse	E:\dbase\CKBOOK	Rec 1/16	File		

View and edit fields

Figure 13-18. Other user's screen will not update while record is locked.

If Carolyn attempts to edit any field of the record, dBASE IV will prevent the editing because the record is locked for use by Morgan. If Carolyn attempts to change the date of Record 1 by entering,

    0105

A message appears in the center of the screen saying the record is already being edited by another user.

```
  Records      Fields      Go To      Exit                    9:14:26 PM

 DATE      CHECK_NUM PAYEE                     AMOUNT   CLEARED DEDUCTIBLE REM

 01/03/89       1000 Allied Office Furniture    750.50 T       T          MEM
 01/03/89       1001 Central Office Supplies     97.56 T       T          MEM
 01/06/89       1002                                                      mem
 01/06/89       1003                                                      MEM
 01/10/89       1004   Record in use by another                T         MEM
 01/10/89       1005   Retrying lock, Press ESC to cancel.               mem
 01/14/89       1006                                           T         MEM
 01/15/89       1007                                                     mem
 02/02/89       1008                                                     MEM
 02/09/89       1009 Advanced Copier Service    175.00                   mem
 02/12/89       1010 Valley Power & Light       101.70                   MEM
 02/25/89       1011 Dept of Trans               45.00 F       T         MEM
 02/27/89       1012 Western Telephone          175.75 F       T         MEM
 01/01/89          1 DEPOSIT                    2500.00 T                 MEM
 01/31/89          2 DEPOSIT                    1200.00 F                 mem
 02/15/89          3 DEPOSIT                    1900.00 F                 mem


 Browse    E:\dbase\CKBOOK         Rec 1/16        File

                        View and edit fields
```

Figure 13-19. Message appears when editing of a lock file is attempted.

This message appears only when the fourth character is entered because the first three characters are identical to the original data. Only the fourth character is different, 3 changed to 5.

When a message like this appears, you have two options:

Wait for release

dBASE IV constantly retries the record to check if the record lock has been removed. As soon as Morgan releases the record by going on to another record or closing the file, dBASE IV locks the record for the next user attempting to gain access.

Cancel Edit

You can press [Esc] to cancel the attempt to edit this record. You can then go on and perform other operations until the record lock is removed.

As an example, suppose Morgan releases the record lock by moving to the next record in the database. Morgan enters

    [Pg Dn]

Carolyn's screen changes immediately in three ways:

1. **Record Update.** The data entered by Morgan now appears on the screen display of Carolyn's computer.
2. **Record Lock.** The record is now locked for Carolyn's use.

3. **Press SPACE Message.** The press SPACE message appears at the bottom of the screen.

As with the previous record lock, the keystroke triggering the automatic locking procedure—here, the character 5—is not passed through to the database. Instead, 5 must be reentered to be part of the changes being maked to the database. Carolyn enters:

```
[spacebar]
0105
```

Record 1 is now locked for Carolyn's use and is accepting her changes alone, until the entry is complete.

File versus Record Locks

When a user has a record lock on a record of the database file, other users can perform operations on other records within the same database, without encountering the record locking system, as long as the command is affecting only one record at a time. In the current example, Carolyn has locked Record 1 in the CKBOOK database. However, other users, Morgan for instance, can edit other records in the same database, or append new records. Morgan enters

```
[Alt-r] a
```

The Edit mode is changed to the Append mode and a new blank record is displayed. dBASE IV automatically applies a record lock to the newly appended record and Morgan is the only user who can append records to the file. When you add a new record to the file, dBASE IV does not permit another user to also add records, even though it appears the two new records are separate entries.

For example, if Carolyn attempts to enter the Append mode, the record lock applied to Morgan's new entry prevents Carolyn from gaining access. Below, Carolyn enters the Append command from her workstation.

```
[Alt-r] a
```

dBASE IV responds with a record lock message, as shown in Figure 13-20.

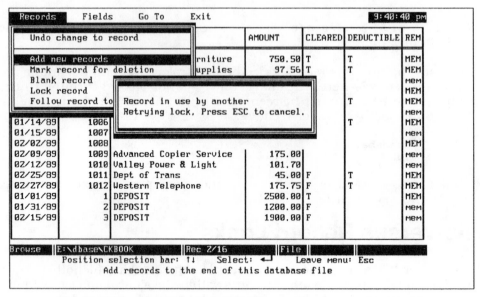

Figure 13-20. Record lock system allows only one user to append.

However, the record lock does allow Carolyn to edit or change any other record in the file, as long as she does not attempt to append while Morgan is appending. Suppose, while locked out of the Append mode, Carolyn decides to delete Record 1. Carolyn enters

       [Esc]

to cancel the attempt to append records. To delete Record 1, Carolyn enters

        1 ⌐
        DELETE ⌐

Record 1 is marked for deletion. Suppose she also decides to delete all the deposits recorded in the file. Carolyn enters

        DELETE FOR payee="DEPOSIT" ⌐'

This command generates a file lock message box as shown in Figure 13-21.

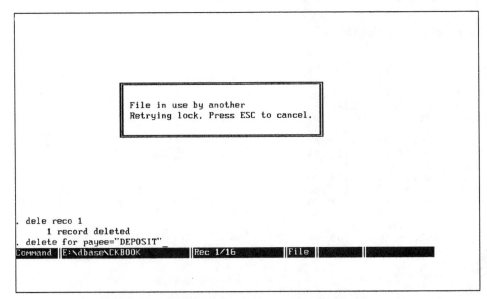

```
                    ┌──────────────────────────────────┐
                    │ File in use by another           │
                    │ Retrying lock, Press ESC to cancel.│
                    │                                  │
                    └──────────────────────────────────┘




. dele reco 1
      1 record deleted
. delete for payee="DEPOSIT"_
 Command  E:\dbase\CKBOOK         Rec 1/16         File
```

Figure 13-21. DELETE FOR generates file lock message.

Why did this delete command generate an error message while the previous command did not? The answer is the DELETE RECORD 1 command affects only a single record in the database. When a FOR clause is used, the command has the potential to effect any number of records. dBASE IV only executes commands having the potential to modify more than one record, if the file can be locked. dBASE IV cannot apply a file lock while another user already has a record or file lock on the same database. Thus, the attempt to DELETE FOR is not permitted, because Morgan still has a record lock on the Append mode.

If Morgan releases the record lock by exiting the Append mode, Carolyn's command will execute. Morgan exits the Append mode by entering

```
[Esc]
```

As soon as Morgan enters [Esc], dBASE IV executes the suspended DELETE FOR command. The program applies a file lock for Carolyn, for the duration of the DELETE FOR command. The lock is released as soon as the DELETE FOR command is completed.

If either user were to list the records in the CKBOOK database, they would see the four deleted records. Morgan enters the following:

```
LIST date,amount ↵
```

The listing will look like:

```
 1    *01/05/89     750.50
 2     01/03/89      97.56
 3     01/06/89     101.57
 4     01/06/89     590.00
 5     01/10/89    2245.50
 6     01/10/89      99.95
 7     01/14/89     145.99
 8     01/15/89      67.45
 9     02/02/89      25.89
10     02/09/89     175.00
11     02/12/89     101.70
12     02/25/89      45.00
13     02/27/89     175.75
14    *01/01/89    2500.00
15    *01/31/89    1200.00
16    *02/15/89    1900.00
```

Set Lock

As you have seen, commands effecting more than one record at a time, such as a DELETE FOR, cannot execute unless dBASE IV can lock the file. File locks cannot be applied while other users have applied a file or record lock to the same database.

However, some commands requiring a file lock do so for the purposes of accuracy, rather than data integrity. Commands such as CALCULATE or COPY, lock files to ensure the records are not changed while the command is being carried out. In many cases, the need for a file lock may not be crucial because the potential changes in the records will not have a significant effect on the usefulness of the operation.

You can set dBASE IV to perform certain non-writing commands, i.e., commands that do not not actually modify the information in the source database, but either calculate or copy the data, so they can be performed without having to lock the database. This allows you to perform operations, such as CALCULATE or COPY, while a record or file lock is active for another user.

The command used is SET LOCK. When SET LOCK is OFF, the following commands do not require a file lock to operate.

Commands affected by SET LOCK:

    AVERAGE
    CALCULATE
Commands affected by SET LOCK (continued):

    COPY
    COPY STRUCTURE
    COUNT
    INDEX ON (NDX indexing only)
    JOIN
    LABEL FORM
    REPORT FORM

Commands affected by SET LOCK (continued):

    COPY
    COPY STRUCTURE
    COUNT
    INDEX ON (NDX indexing only)
    JOIN
    LABEL FORM
    REPORT FORM
    SORT
    SUM
    TOTAL

By default, SET LOCK is ON, which requires a file lock for the above commands.

Suppose Carolyn begins to edit the CKBOOK records. In this case, she will be replacing the original data into CKBOOK's first record. Carolyn enters

        EDIT ⌐
        0103

This activates the record lock message. Enter

        [spacebar]
        0103 ⌐
        1000

At the same time, Morgan wants to sum the AMOUNT field. Morgan enters

        SUM amount ⌐

Because of Carolyn's file lock, the command does not execute. dBASE IV cannot lock the database for Morgan and the "File in use by another" message is displayed. Morgan can change the SET LOCK default mode to curcumvent the record lock. Morgan cancels the attempted SUM command.

        [Esc]

Morgan then uses SET LOCK to turn off the file locking for commands like SUM.

        SET LOCK OFF ⌐

Morgan executes the command again.

        SUM amount ⌐

This time, the command ignores the record lock and calculates the total of field. The total is 14,084. When Carolyn releases Record 1, the change in the check number field becomes available to all users. Carolyn enters

        [Alt-e] e

Morgan executes the SUM command again.

        SUM ⏎

This time, the same command returns a different value.

```
. Sum
   16 records summed
CHECK_NUM              AMOUNT
      14084            10221.86
. Sum
   16 records summed
CHECK_NUM              AMOUNT
      13084            10221.86
```

Viewing Morgan's screen alone, there is no apparent reason for the altered value. Of course, the reason is Carolyn released a record with a changed value.

Using SET LOCK can lead to potential inaccuracies in the way operations are carried out. However, in many cases the difference is not significant. Afterall, if Carolyn had edited the record in the time between the two SUM commands, the result would have been the same with the LOCK set ON as it was with the LOCK set OFF. Because the effect of multi-user changes is time-related, you have to judge if these changes are significant enough to require file locking.

Place the database back to its original condition by recalling all the deleted records.

        RECALL ALL ⏎

Exclusive Access

Certain dBASE IV commands require the exclusive use of a database. The exclusive use of a database means no other user can have access to the same file for viewing or editing. Operations such as REINDEX, PACK, or MODIFY STRUCTURE, require exclusive use.

There are two ways to get exclusive use of a database.

SET EXCLUSIVE ON

Once executed, any following USE command opens the database files for use by the current user, only.

USE EXCLUSIVE

The EXCLUSIVE clause used with the USE command allows you to open the specified database in the Exclusive mode. The Exclusive mode applies only to this command. Normally, USE commands without the EXCLUSIVE clause opens databases in a shared-access mode.

Suppose Morgan wants to reindex the production index file of the CKBOOK file. If Morgan enters

      REINDEX ↵

The command is rejected because it requires the user to have exclusive access to the file.

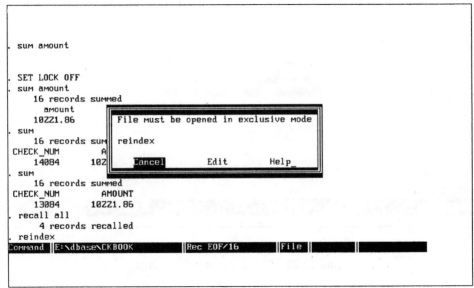

Figure 13-22. REINDEX cannot be executed by a file shared with other users.

Morgan must change the command by entering

      ↵

The exclusive access needed to perform REINDEX cannot be achieved, as long as another user has access to the database. Carolyn must first release the database by closing it from her workstation. Carolyn enters

      CLOSE ALL ↵

Morgan can open the database in the Exclusive mode. Enter

      USE EXCLUSIVE ckbook ↵

The status line shows "ExclLock", meaning this file cannot be accessed by another user until it is released by the current user.

Morgan can now execute the REINDEX command.

        REINDEX ↵

While a file is in exclusive use by one user, any attempts to open that file by other users generates an error. For example, if Carolyn tries to open CKBOOK again, by entering USE ckbook ↵, The program would display the error message "File in use by another", as shown in Figure 13-23.

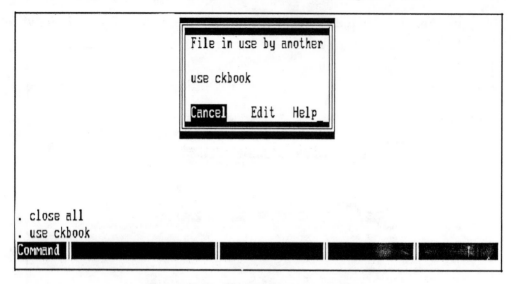

Figure 13-23. File in use error message.

Figure 13-23. File in use error message.

Notice this message is an error message, not a file lock message. The difference is this message will not disappear if the other user unlocks the file. When an error message is displayed, dBASE IV will not automatically retry the locked file. You must reenter the command manually, in order to retry access.

Return to the Dot Prompt by entering

        ↵

Morgan can release the file from exclusive use by closing the database. Morgan enters

        CLOSE DATABASE ↵

The SET EXCLUSIVE ON command is useful when you want to open a series of files in the Exclusive mode, without having to use the clause with each command.

Summary

- **Protection.** dBASE IV allows you to create a password protect version of dBASE IV, which can only be accessed by users with the correct passwords. The system is organized around the use of the PROTECT command, which establishes the users and the passwords they can use. Protection can be applied to single or multi-user systems.

- **Administrator.** The Administrator is the person or persons who have knowledge of the master password used to gain access to the Protection system. The master password is established the first time the PROTECT command is issued. From then on, only users who know the password can add, change, or modify the users and passwords on the system.

- **User.** A user is someone who is given a password so that they can log onto a protected dBASE IV system. The user is also assigned a user name and a group name. Each user is also assigned an access level code from 1 to 8. These codes are used by file and field protection schemes to restrict access to certain users.

- **File Protection.** The user passwords protect the dBASE IV program. You can protect the data stored in the DBF files by protecting the DBF file itself. When a file is protected, an encrypted copy of the file is made. The file is assigned access code values for reading data, changing data, deleting records, and adding records. The encrypted file can only be accessed by users who have correctly logged onto dBASE IV and have an access code that permits them to carry out the operation they want to perform.

- **Field Protection.** Protection can be applied to individual fields inside a database. You can restrict access to a field, or allow Read Only access. These restrictions can be applied to any of the database fields. A set of field restrictions can be filled out for each of the 8 potential access levels. Should field and file protection be applied to the same database field, protection takes precedence over field protection.

- **Sharing Databases.** When opened on a Local Area Network, database files can be operated in a shared-access mode. In this mode, multiple users can have *read* access to the data in a given database file. dBASE IV will automatically prevent data corruption by locking records and files, based on the operations requested by each user.

- **Record Locking.** When a user attempts to change the data in a record, that record is locked for their use so that no other users can make changes to that record until the first user has completed editing. Users attempting to edit a locked record will receive a message indicating that the record is locked.

- **File Locking.** When a command requires data from more than one record, dBASE IV attempts to lock the entire file for the duration of the operations. Other users can read, but not edit, the database file while it is locked. File locks cannot be applied when the file or one record in that file is already locked by another user.

- **Exclusive Locking.** Commands that affect or rely on the overall structure and contents of the database, require that the database be in Exclusive mode in order to carry out the operation. The Exclusive mode prevents other users from opening the database. Other users cannot gain even Read Only access of a database opened in the Exclusive mode. The SET EXCLUSIVE or USE EXCLUSIVE commands, activate files in the Exclusive mode.

- **Set Lock.** When SET LOCK is OFF, commands that read but do not change more than one record in the database, will execute, even when dBASE IV cannot apply a file lock to the database. The results of commands executed under SET LOCK OFF may contain inaccuracies, since the latest changes made in certain records might not be included in the operation.

14

Programming on a Network

Chapter 13 illustrated how dBASE IV automatically handles file operations on a multi-user system. In many situations, the built-in automatic file and record locking commands are adequate, and no further programming is necessary. Note that the programs shown in Part II of this book run on a network using the built-in network file and recording locking features, without additional modifications.

Programs that create indexes or pack databases may require the addition of SET EXCLUSIVE ON in order to run on a network.

This chapter presents concepts related to user-designed file and record-locking routines. These routines can be designed to replace the automatic file and record-locking features discussed in Chapter 13 with your own routines.

In creating these routines you will still rely on dBASE IV to create and implement the file and record locks. The difference is you can control the messages and the alternative actions carried out when a file or record lock is encountered.

dBASE IV refers to this type of file and record locking as *explicit* locking, in contrast to the *automatic* system of locks described in Chapter 16.

You can create programs that can handle multi-user conflicts, based on EXCLUSIVE use, file, and record locks. In these programs, you can define your own method of handling record and file locks. This means you can define your own messages and routines that execute when record or file locks are involved.

The chapter begins with dBASE IV loaded in a multi-user network

The chapter begins with dBASE IV loaded in a multi-user network environment. All users have logged on and the Dot Prompt mode is active.

Editing on a Network

In Chapter 13, you saw that dBASE IV automatically places a record lock on a record, when editing is initiated by any user. That record will then be protected from entry for all users except the user that has locked the record. When another user attempts to get access to this record, a message is displayed saying the record is currently locked. The message stays on the screen until the record is released by the current user, or the current user presses [Esc] to cancel the command.

Record locks typically affect programs that attempt to edit and/or append records to a database. dBASE IV will not permit more than one user to edit the same record, or more than one user to append records to a file. The network system displays the same record lock message for both circumstances.

A reason for creating a network program is to gain greater control over the way record lock situations are handled. dBASE IV provides commands and functions that allow you to establish your own system for handling record-editing conflicts.

To begin understanding how programs can be adapted to run on networks, look at the program listed below. This program is designed for a single-user system. The program asks the user to enter the check number of the record to be edited, then searches for a record with that number. The IF/ELSE/ENDIF structure activates the EDIT mode if the record is located, or displays a window with a message if no matching record is located.

```
SET TALK OFF
SET STATUS OFF
SET SCOREBOARD OFF
CLEAR
USE ckbook
DEFINE WINDOW notfound FROM 8,20 TO 11,60 DOUBLE
DO WHILE .T.
   * enter check to edit
   key=0
   @ 10,10 SAY "Enter Check Number" GET key PICTURE "9999"
   READ
   * if check number = 0 exit program
   IF key=0
      EXIT
   ENDIF
   * find check
   LOCATE FOR check_num=key
   IF FOUND( )
      EDIT NEXT 1 NOMENU NOAPPEND
ELSE
      ACTIVATE WINDOW notfound
      ? "Check number "+LTRIM(STR(key))+"  not found."
      WAIT
      DEACTIVATE WINDOW notfound
   ENDIF
ENDDO
RELEASE WINDOW notfound
SET TALK ON
SET STATUS ON
SET SCOREBOARD ON
RETURN
```

If you were to run this program on a multi-user system, what modifications would you have to make? If you wanted to use the built-in locking routines you could simply run the program exactly as written. dBASE IV will automatically lock the records being edited. However, you might want to create a routine that handles record locking in a different manner than the automatic method built into dBASE IV.

For example, dBASE IV locks a record as soon as you begin to change information in it. It does so by beeping and asking the user to press the [spacebar]. While useful, this method has some points that can be addressed in other ways.

First, the user will not be able to tell if she can edit the record until she tries. Since dBASE IV permits the user to display the record even if another user has locked it, the user must attempt to edit the record in order to determine if it is locked. It might be better to determine if the record is able to be edited before it is displayed.

Second, checking the accessibility of the record before it is displayed eliminates the need to perform the sometimes awkward beep/[spacebar] routine. This makes editing smoother for the user.

Third, checking the lock status of the record before the record is displayed in the full-screen editing mode, enables you to present the user with a number of alternative actions she might want to select, if the requested record cannot be locked for her use.

These and other features can be built into a program by using the explicit record locking commands and functions provided in dBASE IV. Before you modify the program shown above, you need to get some background information about the tools used in dBASE IV for record locking.

Explicit Record Locking

In order to create your own record locking routine, you need to be familiar with the SET REPROCESS command and the RLOCK( ) function. These two items are the basis upon which user-defined record locking routines are built.

SET REPROCESS

SET REPROCESS controls how dBASE IV reacts to a file-lock situation. The term *reprocess* refers to the program's attempts to gain access to a record that is locked by another user. By default, the SET REPROCESS value is set to 0. If this is the case, when dBASE IV encounters a locked record it will attempt an infinite number of retries to gain access to that record. The program displays a message box and continues to try to gain access until the record is released by the other user, or the current user enters [Esc] to cancel the command.

If REPROCESS is set to a value between 1 and 32,000, the program will make the specified number of attempts to lock the record, then go on to the next command. The key benefit of setting the reprocess to 1 or higher is that dBASE IV will no longer simply stop and wait, when a record lock is encountered. This enables a program to execute commands following the location of a record lock. If the REPROCESS is set for 0, the program would pause at the record lock and wait for the user to cancel the command, based on the default message.

Setting the reprocess to a value greater than 0 allows you to control the response to a locked record, rather than having the program automatically paused.

SET REFRESH TO

This command is related to the use of EDIT and BROWSE on a multi-user system. The information displayed on the EDIT or BROWSE modes display is not updated with changes made by other users until dBASE IV is forced to re-evaluate the display. For example, if a user is looking at a record being edited by another user, the changes will not appear on the screen until the current user performs a task, such as attempting to edit, or moving back and forth in the database. The SET REFRESH command can be used to set a time period from 1 to 3600 seconds, at the end of which the program automatically rewrites the screen display, including changes from other users, without the current user having to enter any keystrokes. For example, SET REFRESH TO 10 means the screen will be updated every ten seconds without further user input. The default value for REFRESH is 0, which means no automatic update of the screen.

RLOCK( )

The RLOCK( ) function operates in a different manner from most of the functions in dBASE IV. For the most part, functions return values based on current conditions. Functions generally do not change a condition, but merely report on its status. However, many of the dBASE IV network functions have a dual character. Like other functions, RLOCK( ) returns a value, specifically a logical value, based on the lock status of a specific record. In addition, the RLOCK( ) function will also carry out an operation. When RLOCK( ) is evaluated, it attempts to place a record lock on the specified record.

---

dBASE IV will recognize the LOCK( ) function as identical to RLOCK( ). LOCK( ) maintains compatibility with dBASE III and III Plus. In this book, RLOCK( ) is used in order to clearly distinguish record from file locks (FLOCK( )).

This type of operation generated by a function is counter to the way most dBASE IV functions work, and makes RLOCK( ) hard to understand at first. To get a better understanding of how this function works, you can experiment with the function at the Dot Prompt level.

Place a database in use. As an example, use the CKBOOK file.

```
USE ckbook ⏎
```

Assuming no one else on the network is working with this file, you can make the additional assumption that all the records are available for record locking.

Suppose you want to work with Record 3. In order to have the option of editing the record, you have to *explicitly* lock the record so another user cannot prevent you from editing it, should you decide to do so.

Move the record pointer to the record you want to lock.

```
3 ⏎
```

To place a lock on this record you must use the RLOCK( ) function. If you recall, functions cannot be directly entered into dBASE IV. They must be used as part of an expression, and expressions are used as part of dBASE IV commands.

The situation is odd because your goal, to lock the record, seems more appropriate for a command than a for a function. For example, the command ? RLOCK( ) appears to tell you whether or not the current record is locked.

However, the command ? RLOCK( ) does more than simply tell you the current status of the record. It actually changes the status by locking the experiment, all the records in CKBOOK are unlocked because you have just opened the database. If the function RLOCK( ) tells you the current status of the record, it should return a false value, .F., because the current record is not locked. Enter

? RLOCK( ) ↵

What happened? First, the function displayed a true value, .T., indicating that the record is *locked*. How can that be if all of the records were in an unlocked state when you entered the command?

The answer is that RLOCK( ) does not simply report on the current status, but actually attempts to change that status. When RLOCK( ) is used, it changes the status of an unlocked record to locked. If you look at the status line you will see it shows "RecLock," indicating that Record 3 is locked by the current user.

```
USE ckbook
3
CKBOOK: Record No     3
? RLOCK ( )
.T.
.
Command E:\dbase\CKBOOK        Rec 3/16        File RecLock
```

One way to think about how the RLOCK( ) function works is to imagine that the function does not ask the question "Is this record locked?," but rather "Can this record be locked?"

When the RLOCK( ) function is used with a record that is currently *unlocked*, it returns a value of .T. because an unlocked record can be locked. The function goes a bit further and actually places the lock on the record, making the potential lock an actual event.

As you will see when you use RLOCK( ) in a program, the function performs the same operation, regardless of the command used with it. For example, DISPLAY RLOCK( ), IF RLOCK( ), CASE RLOCK( ), all have the same effect on the records lock status.

When explicit record locks are used, dBASE IV keeps a list of locked records and can display that list as part of the STATUS display. Enter

DISPLAY STATUS ↵

Under the database information section of the display, you will see that Record 3 is listed as locked.

```
Currently Selected Database:
Select area: 1, Database in Use: E:\DBASE\CKBOOK.DBF    Alias: CKBOOK
Production  MDX file:  E:\DBASE\CKBOOK.MDX
      Index TAG:    PAYEE Key: PAYEE
      Memo file:  E:\DBASE\CKBOOK.DBT
      Lock list:    3 locked
```

Return to the Dot Prompt by entering

[Esc]

Suppose that while you are working with CKBOOK, another user tries to access the same record in the CKBOOK file. As in the previous chapter, assume that you have two users, Morgan and Carolyn. It is Morgan who has just placed the explicit lock on Record 3.

Carolyn attempts to enter the same commands that Morgan just entered.

```
USE ckbook ↵
3 ↵
? RLOCK( ) ↵
```

Because Morgan has locked the record, dBASE IV displays the message "Record in use by another," as shown in Figure 14-1.

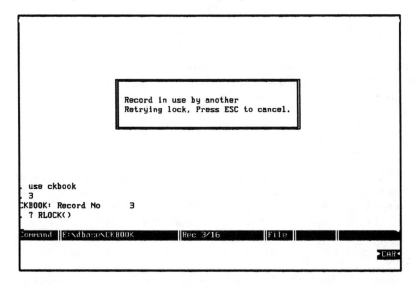

Figure 14-1. Record locking message activated by RLOCK( ) function.

In this case, the record lock message is generated without having to actually edit the record with the Edit or Browse modes. The RLOCK( ) function allows you to deal with record locking independently of the operation you want to perform on the record. For example, the purpose of the lock might be to delete, recall, or replace data within the record.

Cancel the command by entering

```
[Esc]
```

When you cancel the command, dBASE IV then displays the value of the function, .F. Keep in mind the meaning of the .F. value, in this case—it does not mean the record is *not locked*. Rather, it means the record cannot be locked for the current user, in this case Carolyn, because it is already locked by Morgan.

Turning off the Lock Message/pause

When Carolyn entered the RLOCK( ) function, dBASE IV automatically displayed the standard message and paused the program until the user specifically canceled the attempt to lock the file. But suppose you simply wanted to test the status of the record, without having the message displayed and the program paused.

You can turn off the automatic lock message/pause by changing the REPROCESS setting. If REPROCESS is set to a value greater than zero, the program will attempt only the specified reprocess attempts and then stop. In addition, once the reprocess value is 1 or greater, the program will no longer display the message about record locking. Carolyn enters

```
SET REPROCESS TO 1 ↵
? RLOCK( )
```

This time, the RLOCK( ) function checks the status of the record and returns the value, here .F., without pausing or displaying the message.

You can set the reprocess to make more attempts to access the record by increasing the SET REPROCESS value. Enter

```
SET REPROCESS TO 100 ↵
? RLOCK( )
```

This time, there is a delay of about 5 seconds while the program tries 100 times to lock the record. If Morgan had released the record anytime during the 100 retries, dBASE IV would have established the lock on the record for Carolyn and discontinued the retries. If all the retries fail, the function returns the .F. value.

The number of reprocessing attempts should be set based on the length of time you want to delay the attempt to lock and record, and the completion of the command. Setting REPROCESS to 1 returns the function in the shortest amount of time.

Unlocking a Record

Once you have established an explicit record lock, the lock stays in place until it is explicitly removed. For example, suppose Morgan, who has currently locked Record 3, moves the record pointer to another record. Morgan enters

```
1 ↵
```

What has happened to the record lock? Carolyn tries to lock Record 3 again by entering

```
? RLOCK( ) ↵
```

The program will still return the value .F. for Carolyn. Why? The answer is that the lock set by Morgan on Record 3 will stay in place until it is removed with the UNLOCK command. The UNLOCK command removes the record lock from all records in the selected database. Morgan enters

```
UNLOCK ↵
```

Carolyn then enters

```
? RLOCK( ) ↵
```

Carolyn now establishes a lock on Record 3, because Morgan has released the lock from that record.

Note that the logic here may seem a bit inconsistent. Records are locked with a function, RLOCK( ), but unlocked with a command UNLOCK. However, once you get used to the implementation it seems to work quite well. The locking operation of the function actually saves a step in programming, since you can test and lock in a single step, IF RLOCK( ), rather than testing and locking in two steps.

Program with Explicit Record Locking

You can now apply SET REPROCESS, RLOCK( ), and UNLOCK to the editing program shown previously. Create the program called LOCKREC by entering

```
MODIFY COMMAND lockrec ↵
```

The program begins with the usual SET commands:

```
SET TALK OFF
SET STATUS OFF
SET SCOREBOARD OFF
```

In addition to the SET commands that control the screen display, you also must set the REPROCESS value so that the record lock handling will be defined by the program, instead of by the automatic dBASE IV method.

```
* turns off automatic record lock message
SET REPROCESS TO 1
```

The program then opens the database file.

```
CLEAR
USE ckbook
```

The program also defines a message window used to display appropriate messages, such as when a matching record cannot be found.

```
DEFINE WINDOW notfound FROM 8,20 TO 13,60 DOUBLE
```

The next section of the program is a DO WHILE loop, in which the user is asked to enter the number of the check to edit. The program then uses a LOCATE command to find a record, if any, that contains that check number.

```
DO WHILE .T.
key=0
@ 9,5 TO 11,50
@ 10,10 SAY "Enter Check Number" GET key PICTURE "9999"
READ
IF key=0
   EXIT
ENDIF
LOCATE FOR check_num=key
```

The FOUND( ) function is used to determine if a matching record can be located.

```
    IF FOUND ( )
       * test for existing record lock
```

If a record is found that matches the check number, the record must be locked so the user can have the option to enter data. In this program, the record will only be displayed if it can be locked. The RLOCK( ) function is used with an IF command to implement the lock.

The command IF RLOCK( ) will evaluate as true if the selected record is not currently locked by another user. In that instance, the RLOCK( ) function will serve two purposes: 1) it will place a record lock on the selected record, and 2) it will cause the IF command to evaluate as true, therefore executing the commands following the IF.

In this case, the command that will execute is an EDIT command that allows editing of the current record. When the EDIT is complete, the UNLOCK command releases the record lock so other users can access the record.

```
        IF RLOCK ( )
           EDIT NEXT 1 NOMENU NOAPPEND
           UNLOCK
```

The ELSE command associated with IF RLOCK( ) is used to display a message box that tells the user the record she was searching for has been located, but it is already locked by another user.

```
        ELSE
           ACTIVATE WINDOW notfound
           ? "Check number "+LTRIM(STR(key))+"  found -"
           ? "Record in use by another user."
           WAIT
           DEACTIVATE WINDOW notfound
        ENDIF
```

The final part of the program includes an ELSE section, matched to the IF FOUND( ) command. In this case, the window is displayed with a message that tells the user no record with the specified record number is found. The program then ends the DO WHILE loop and resets the environment.

```
ELSE
   ACTIVATE WINDOW notfound
   @ 1,5 SAY "Check number "+LTRIM(STR(key))+"  not found."
   WAIT
   DEACTIVATE WINDOW notfound
 ENDIF
ENDDO
CLOSE DATABASE
RELEASE WINDOW notfound
SET REPROCESS TO 0
SET TALK ON
SET STATUS ON
SET SCOREBOARD ON
RETURN
```

Save the program by entering

```
        [Alt-e]  s
```

Compile the program.

```
        COMPILE lockrec ↵
```

You can execute this program on all workstations. For example, both users, Morgan and Carolyn, execute this program by entering

```
        DO lockrec ↵
```

The program displays the check number entry box, as shown in Figure 14-2.

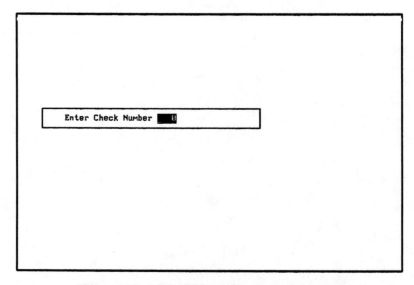

Figure 14-2. LOCKREC program opening screen.

The same screen appears on all workstations. Suppose Carolyn searches for check number 1002. Carolyn enters

    1002

The program locates the record. Because no other users have locked this record, the program displays the record in the Edit mode.

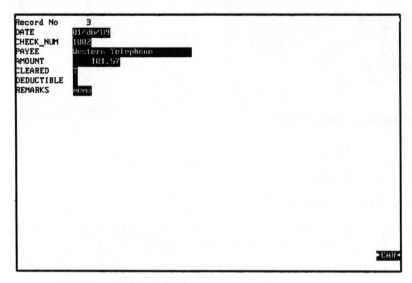

Figure 14-3. Unlocked record is accessed for editing.

If a second user attempts to access the same record, the program will display a window that contains a message. Morgan enters

    1002

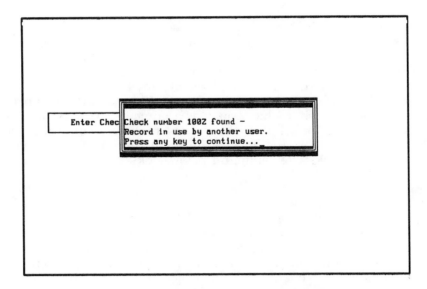

Figure 14-4. Message displayed when record already locked.

Morgan continues by entering

⏎

In the meantime, Carolyn completes her use of the record by entering

    [Ctrl-End]

Morgan reenters the check number.

    1002

Morgan is now able to lock and edit the record. The program shows how explicit record locking can be used in a program that permits multiple users edit access to records. The same program and record locking technique applies to the use of the APPEND, DELETE, RECALL and REPLACE commands, as long as the commands are not used with a scope or FOR clause affecting more than one record.

Exit the programs. Morgan would enter

    [Ctrl-End] *(2 times)*

Carolyn would enter

    [Ctrl-End]

Locking Multiple Records

In some circumstances, you may want to place record locks on more than one record in a database file. The advantage of locking more than one record is you can know in advance that records you have not yet selected with the record pointer, have already been locked for your use. The RLOCK( ) function can lock more than one record if you place into the function two character strings as arguments: 1) a character string which consists of a list of the record numbers to be locked, 2) a character string with the alias name of the database in which to perform the lock. The command below locks records 4, 7, and 10 in CKBOOK.

? RLOCK("4,7,10","ckbook")

For example, suppose in the check book file you wanted to lock in advance, all the deposit records. You can use a program like the one below, to scan the database for the record numbers of the deposits. The program creates a character string called LOCKLIST that contains the record numbers. This character string is inserted by way of macro substitution into the RLOCK( ) function.

```
SET TALK OFF
USE ckbook
locklist=""
SCAN FOR PAYEE="DEPOSIT"
    IF ""=locklist
        locklist=LTRIM(STR(RECNO(   )))
    ELSE
        locklist=locklist+","+LTRIM(STR(RECNO(    )))
    ENDIF
ENDSCAN
? RLOCK("&locklist","ckbook")
RETURN
```

Note that this type of operation is limited by the maximum size of a text string and the maximum size of a character string, which is 254 characters.

Alternative Actions

The LOCKREC program demonstrated how you can use explicit record locking to create a program that locks records before they are displayed. In contrast to the automatic record locking built into dBASE IV, the LOCKREC program assures users they would have editing privileges on records that are displayed. This is done by applying the record lock before the record is displayed for editing. The lock is removed only after the Edit mode is exited.

Another reason for writing programs with explicit record locking is to create your own custom-designed options for dealing with locked records. In the LOCKREC program, if a locked record is encountered, a message is displayed telling the user the record is in use by another user. Following the message, the user is returned to the check number entry display to make another selection.

One improvement you can make is to display a menu of alternatives from which the user can select. For example, when a locked record is encountered, you could offer the user the choice of searching for a different check number, displaying the information in the record in a Read Only (no editing) display, or retrying the record lock a specified number of times.

Create a new program called LOCKREC1. Since much of the code in LOCKREC1 will be similar to LOCKREC, you can begin by creating a copy of LOCKREC. Enter

```
COPY FILE lockrec.prg TO lockrec1.prg ↵
MODIFY COMMAND lockrec1 ↵
```

The beginning of this program is identical to the LOCKREC program

```
SET TALK OFF
SET STATUS OFF
SET SCOREBOARD OFF
* turns off automatic record lock message
SET REPROCESS TO 1
CLEAR
USE ckbook
DEFINE WINDOW notfound FROM 8,20 TO 13,60 DOUBLE
```

The next section is added to the program in order to define a popup menu with three options: Retry Access to Record, Display Record Only, and Search for a Different Record.

The popup menu will be displayed when the user encounters a record locked by another user. The ON SELECTION POPUP command sets the command DEACTIVATE POPUP to execute when a selection is made from the popup. This causes the program to execute the next command in the program when a selection is made.

```
DEFINE WINDOW times FROM 9,50 TO 13,75
DEFINE POPUP locked FROM 7,45
DEFINE BAR 1 OF locked PROMPT "Retry Access to Record"
DEFINE BAR 2 OF locked PROMPT "Display Record Only"
DEFINE BAR 3 OF locked PROMPT "Search for a different record"
ON SELECTION POPUP locked DEACTIVATE POPUP
```

The next section of the program is identical to the LOCKREC program.

```
DO WHILE .T.
key=0
@ 9,5 TO 11,40
@ 10,10 SAY "Enter Check Number" GET key PICTURE "9999"
READ
IF key=0
   EXIT
ENDIF
LOCATE FOR check_num=key
IF FOUND( )
   * test for existing record lock
   IF RLOCK( )
      EDIT NEXT 1 NOMENU NOAPPEND
      UNLOCK
```

The major modification in the program is the action that will take place should the program encounter a record lock when attempting to access a record. In this case, the DO command is used to execute a procedure called LOCKED.

```
   ELSE
   DO locked
```

The remainder of the main section of the program is identical to LOCKREC.

```
   ENDIF
ELSE
   ACTIVATE WINDOW notfound
   @ 1,5 SAY "Check number "+LTRIM(STR(key))+"  not found."
   WAIT
   DEACTIVATE WINDOW notfound
ENDIF
ENDDO
CLOSE DATABASE
RELEASE WINDOW notfound,times
RELEASE POPUP locked
SET REPROCESS TO 0
SET TALK ON
SET STATUS ON
SET SCOREBOARD ON
RETURN
```

Following the main section of the program, procedures are defined. The first procedure is the LOCKED procedure and is executed when a record lock is encountered. The procedure begins with the activation of the LOCKED popup menu. Recall that the menu was defined at the beginning of the main routine to display three choices for the user to select when a locked record is encountered.

```
PROCEDURE locked
ACTIVATE POPUP locked
```

Once the user makes the selection from the popup, the program must evaluate the selection and perform commands corresponding to it. A DO CASE structure is used to carry out commands based on the BAR( ) value selected from the popup menu.

The first bar in the popup allows the user to retry access to the locked record. This option is implemented by a separate procedure called RETRY.

```
DO CASE
 CASE BAR( )=1
   DO retry
```

If bar 2 is selected, the record is displayed in a Read Only mode. In this case the NOEDIT clause used with the EDIT command displays all fields as Read Only. This allows the user to view the record but not edit the data.

Also note the SET REFRESH command is used to update the Read Only screen every 5 seconds, with the changes made by the user who has locked the record.

```
  CASE BAR( )=2
    SET REFRESH TO 5
    EDIT NEXT 1 NOMENU NOAPPEND NOEDIT
    SET REFRESH TO 0
```

The procedure is completed with the ENDCASE. Note that option 3 on the popup requires no special commands, since the main program loop is designed to return the user to another search screen automatically.

```
ENDCASE
RETURN
```

The final part of this program is the RETRY procedure. This procedure allows the user to enter a value for the number of attempts to place a lock on the selected record. The procedure uses a window into which the user can enter a value up to 9,999 for the number of tries.

```
PROCEDURE retry
ACTIVATE WINDOW times
times=0
@ 0,0 SAY "How many retrys?" GET times PICTURE "9999"
@ 1,0 SAY "Attempt: "
READ
```

Once the user has entered a selection, a loop is executed that counts from 0 to the specified number. Each cycle of the loop uses an IF RLOCK( ) command to test whether the record has been released by the user who had established a lock on the record. If so, the record is locked for the use of the current user, and the EDIT command is executed.

```
done=0
DO WHILE done<=times
 @ 1,10 SAY LTRIM(STR(done))
 IF RLOCK( )
    DEACTIVATE WINDOW times
    EDIT NEXT 1 NOMENU NOAPPEND
```

Once access to the record has been achieved, there is no reason to continue the loop. The EXIT command terminates the loop and RETURN concludes the procedure.

```
    EXIT
 ENDIF
 done=done+1
ENDDO
DEACTIVATE WINDOW times
RETURN
```

Save and compile the program by entering

```
        [Alt-e] s
        COMPILE lockrec1 ⏎
```

The LOCKREC1 program illustrates how a program can be constructed so that when a user encounters a locked record, a popup menu of options is automatically displayed. In this case, the options cover the three main methods of handling a locked record: 1) retry access to the record, 2) access the record in a Read Only mode, or 3) move to a different record.

As an example, suppose the two users, Morgan and Carolyn, run the LOCKREC1 on their respective workstations.

```
        DO lockrec1 ⏎
```

Carolyn begins the session by searching for the record that contains 1002. Because she is the first user to access the database, she will be able to lock the record she selects. Carolyn enters

```
        1002
```

The record is displayed for Carolyn to edit. While Carolyn is using that record, Morgan attempts to access it. Morgan enters

```
        1002
```

The program encounters a record lock and displays the popup menu with the user's options for dealing with a locked record, as seen in Figure 14-5.

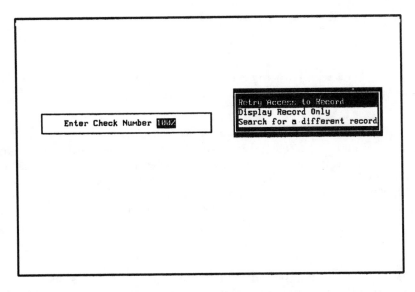

Figure 14-5. Pop-up menu appears when locked record is encountered.

The first option is to retry the record lock to see if it has been released by the previous user. Morgan enters

⌐

When the Retry Access to Record option is selected, the program displays a window into which the number of retry attempts can be entered. The PICTURE function limits the value to 9,999, although there is no limit to the number of times this loop could retry the record.

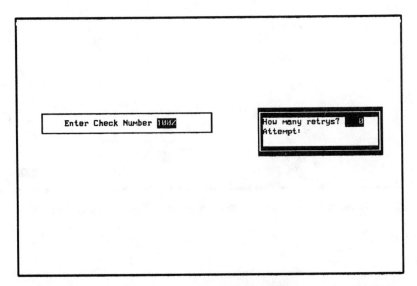

Figure 14-6. Window allows user to enter number of retry attempts.

In this case, Morgan enters 200.

        200 ⏎

The program displays a running count of the number of retries made. During this process, Carolyn leaves the record by entering

        [Ctrl-End]

Carolyn's action releases the lock on the record. Morgan's workstation is now able to place a lock on that record. This changes the value of the expression IF RLOCK( ) to .T., which stops the retry loop so the record can be edited. Morgan now has access to the record.

Now that Morgan has locked the record, Carolyn decides to search for the same check number again. Carolyn enters

        1002

The popup menu is activated for Carolyn this time. She selects to display the record with Read Only access. Carolyn enters

        d

Carolyn's screens show the information from the record in a Read Only format, as seen in Figure 14-7.

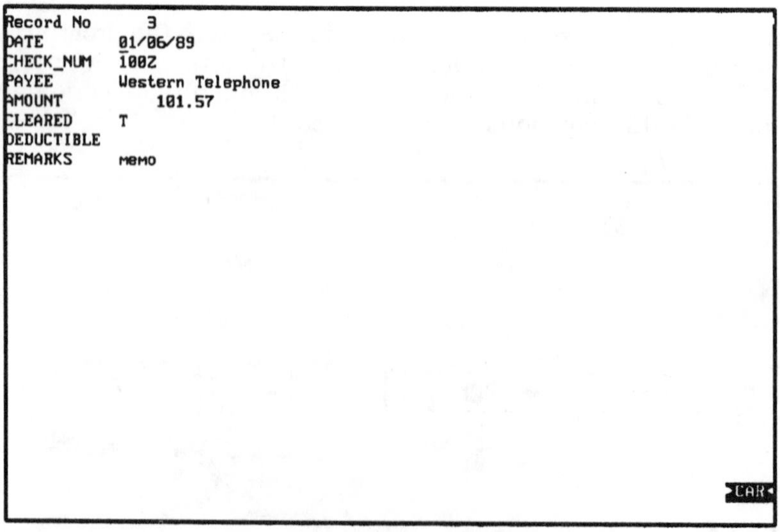

```
Record No       3
DATE        01/06/89
CHECK_NUM   1002
PAYEE       Western Telephone
AMOUNT          101.57
CLEARED     T
DEDUCTIBLE
REMARKS     memo




                                                         ►CAR◄
```

Figure 14-7. Read Only display selected for locked record.

Both users exit the program. Carolyn enters

[Ctrl-End]   *(2 times)*

Morgan enters

[Ctrl-End]

File Locks

The previous program dealt with conflicts between users caused by record locking. In addition to record locks, dBASE IV can lock files in two ways.

FLOCK( )

The FLOCK( ) function works in a similar manner to RLOCK( ), except that it locks an entire file against changes in any of the records. This type of file lock allows users Read Only access to all the file records, but prevents updates or additions to the file. File locks are used with commands that affect more than one record in a database, such as INDEX, REPLACE ALL, or SUM. Note that Read Only commands, such as SUM, can execute on a locked file but the latest changes entered into the database may not be reflected in the calculation.

Like RLOCK( ), FLOCK( ) returns a logical value, while at the same time attempting to lock the database file. The logic of using FLOCK( ) is basically the same as RLOCK( ). The only difference is FLOCK( ) is used when you want to SUM a field or DELETE more than one record in a database. RLOCK( ) is used when you are operating on one record at a time.

Note that you cannot apply a file lock if any of the records in the database is locked for use with another user. FLOCK( ) will be false if it encounters a file or record lock for another user.

Exclusive Use

Commands that affect the entire database, such as MODIFY STRUCTURE, require that the database be placed into exclusive use with the SET EXCLUSIVE ON or USE EXCLUSIVE commands. When another user attempts to use a file that is open for the exclusive use of a previous user, an error is encountered. In order to handle this conflict, you must create your own error handling routine and replace the standard dBASE IV error handler using the ON ERROR command.

The program below is a calculation program that finds the balance of the checks and deposits entered into the CKBOOK file. The program needs to have access to the CKBOOK file and preferably lock the file from modifications while the calculation is being made.

The program must take into account that the requested file might be in exclusive use by a previous user, or that a file lock is not possible because a previous user has locked the file or a record within that file.

Create a new program called FILELOCK by entering

      MODIFY COMMAND filelock ⏎

The program begins with the usual SET commands.

```
SET TALK OFF
SET STATUS OFF
SET SCOREBOARD OFF
CLEAR
```

The REPROCESS value is set to 1, to control the automatic file and record locking messages.

```
SET REPROCESS TO 1
```

A window called CONFLICT is defined. This window will be used to display messages and options to the user when a conflict involving another user is encountered. If the program does not encounter any conflict, this window will not be used.

```
DEFINE WINDOW conflict FROM 10,10 TO 17,70 DOUBLE
```

The next command is an ON ERROR command. If a file conflict occurs because a database is open for the exclusive use of another, the result is not a file lock but an error. If you want to build in a routine that will handle this type of error you must specify that routine in the ON ERROR command. The command below sets dBASE IV to execute the CONFLICT procedure when an error occurs.

```
* on error used to trap exclusive use errors
ON ERROR DO conflict
```

The next command is one of the most common commands in dBASE IV. However, when you are operating in a multi-user environment, the effect of this command can be quite different than it is in a single-user environment. If the file has already been opened for the exclusive use of another user, this command will produce an error. It is at this point in the program that the ON ERROR command activates the error handling routine, CONFLICT. The CONFLICT procedure will appear at the end of this program.

```
USE ckbook
```

The next section of the program allows the user to input a month value to select records for a specific month, or accept zero to calculate all the records in the file.

```
month=0
title="Calculate  Account  Balance"
@ 5,(80-LEN(title))/2  SAY title
prompt="Enter  Month or 0 for all months"
@ 11,(78-LEN(title))/2   SAY title GET month PICTURE "9"
READ
```

An IF/ELSE/ENDIF structure is used to select a record filter if necessary.

```
IF month>0
  SET FILTER  TO MONTH(date)=month
  GO TOP
  result="Balance  for the month of "+CMONTH(date)+":"
ELSE
  result="Overall  Account  Balance:"
ENDIF
```

At this point in the program you must consider whether another user has established a file or record lock. Keep in mind if the file was opened for the exclusive use of another, you would have encountered a problem when you issued the USE command. Once you've arrived at this point in the program, you can assume you can open the CKBOOK database file for some degree of shared operation. You need to determine whether or not you can lock the database for the calculation you want to make.

In this case, use the FLOCK( ) function with a DO WHILE command. The DO WHILE .NOT.FLOCK( ) starts a loop if the database cannot be locked.

```
DO WHILE .NOT.FLOCK( )
```

If the loop is activated it means another user has established a record or file lock on the database. The first option covered inside the loop is to perform the calculation without locking the database. This means changes entered by the user with the current lock on will not be incorporated into the total. The next section of the program allows the user to select to perform the calculation on the unlocked database.

```
use_locked=.T.
ACTIVATE WINDOW conflict
@ 1,0 SAY "File or Record in use by another  user."
@ 2,0 SAY "Balance may not reflect  latest  changes."
@ 3,0 SAY "Calculate  anyway?" GET use_locked PICTURE "Y"
READ
```

If the user enters Y to indicate she wants to perform the calculation on the unlocked database, the program uses the SET LOCK OFF command to allow the calculation to be performed. The actual calculation is carried out in the FIND_BAL procedure.

```
IF use_locked
    DEACTIVATE WINDOW conflict
    SET LOCK OFF
    DO find_bal
    SET LOCK ON
    EXIT
```

If the user selects not to calculate an unlocked database, the program asks if the user wants to repeat the attempt to lock the database.

```
ELSE
  @ 2,0 CLEAR
  @ 2,0 SAY "Retry Access to file?" GET use_locked PICTURE "Y"
  READ
```

If the user enters N, the assumption is made she wants to exit the application.

```
IF .NOT. use_locked
    EXIT
ENDIF
```

If she enters Y, the loop concludes, sending the program back to the DO WHILE .NOT.FLOCK( ) at the top of the loop. In effect, executing DO WHILE .NOT.FLOCK( ) repeats the attempt to lock the file for the current user. This loop can continue for as many file locking attempts as desired.

```
 ENDIF
 DEACTIVATE WINDOW conflict
ENDDO
```

Following the loop are instructions that perform the calculation through the FIND_BAL routine. This section of code will execute if the file lock can be placed on the database, IF FLOCK( ). Note that the file must be explicitly unlocked following the file lock.

```
IF FLOCK( )
  DO find_bal
  UNLOCK
ENDIF
```

In this program the ending commands, SET TALK ON, etc., are placed into a procedure called END because the program has to have three end points. Placing the ending commands in a procedure saves the trouble of entering them in three different places.

```
DO end
RETURN
```

The first procedure is FIND_BAL. It uses the IIF( ) function with the

SUM command to calculate the account balance. A pause in the program is created with the DO WHILE INKEY( )=0/ENDDO combination.

```
PROCEDURE find_bal
SUM IIF(payee="DEPOSIT",amount,amount*-1)    TO balance
@ 18,(70-LEN(result))/2  SAY result
@ ROW( ),COL( )+1 SAY balance PICTURE "@$T 999,999.99"
@ 24,30 SAY "Press any key"
DO WHILE INKEY( )=0
ENDDO
RETURN
```

Error Handling

The next procedure is more complicated and is designed to handle an error that might occur during the execution of the program. In this case, you wish to divide the errors into two classes. Recall that all dBASE IV errors have an error number. This value is captured in the ERROR( ) function when an error occurs.

Errors 108 or 372 will occur when an attempt is made to access a database that is already opened for exclusive use of another. The program tests the value of the ERROR( ) function to determine if the error was caused by an exclusive-type file lock.

```
PROCEDURE conflict
* error cause by file set exclusive by other user
ACTIVATE WINDOW conflict
IF ERROR( )=372.OR.ERROR( )=108
```

If this is the source of the error, the program gives the user the choice of attempting to retry the access to the file.

```
  do_again=.T.
  @ 0,0 SAY "File already in use."
  @ 1,0 SAY "Retry access?" GET do_again PICTURE "Y"
  READ
```

If the user enters Y, indicating that she wants to retry access to the database, the RETRY command is used. RETRY is a command employed primarily in user-defined error routines. The command returns the program to the command that was executed when the error occurred. The command is executed again.

In this program, the USE ckbook command generates the error. The RETRY command causes the USE command to be executed again. If, during the time between the first and second executions of the USE command, the previous user has relinquished control of the database, the current user can gain shared access to the file, enabling her to continue with the program.

```
IF do_again
   DEACTIVATE WINDOW conflict
   RETRY
```

If the user does not want to retry access to the database, the program should be terminated.

```
ELSE
   DO end
   CANCEL
ENDIF
```

If the error is caused by something other than an EXCLUSIVE file lock, the assumption is made that the program should be terminated. Before the program is terminated, the CONFLICT window is used to display the error message—MESSAGE( ) function, and the error number—ERROR( ) function, as a point of reference in attempting to understand the error.

```
ELSE
   @ 0,0 SAY "Error occurred during execution"
   @ 1,0 SAY "dBASE reports "+MESSAGE( )
   @ 2,0 SAY "Error #"+LTRIM(STR(ERROR( )))
   @ 3,0 SAY "Press any Key"
   DO WHILE INKEY( )=0
   ENDDO
   DO end
   CANCEL
ENDIF
RETURN
```

The final procedure, the END procedure, consists of commands that return dBASE IV to its default configuration at the termination of the program. In this program there are several exit points because a user-defined error handling routine is used. Placing the end commands in a procedure makes it easy to carry out all the housekeeping chores, without having to repeat the commands several times in the program.

```
PROCEDURE end
RELEASE WINDOW conflict
CLEAR
CLOSE DATABASE
SET TALK ON
SET STATUS ON
SET SCOREBOARD ON
SET REPROCESS TO 0
ON ERROR
RETURN
```

Save and compile this application.

```
[Alt-e] s
COMPILE filelock ⏎
```

To illustrate how this program operates, you will go through a sample session with two users, Morgan and Carolyn. Carolyn begins by loading the LOCKREC1 program and editing the record with check number 1001.

Carolyn enters

```
DO lockrec1 ⏎
1001
```

Morgan attempts to run the FILELOCK program selecting to calculate the balance of all the records.

```
DO filelock ⏎
⏎
```

The FILELOCK program encounters the record lock placed on the CKBOOK file by the LOCKREC1 program. The result is that the FILELOCK command locks the CKBOOK file. It displays the message box telling Morgan that another user has locked the file.

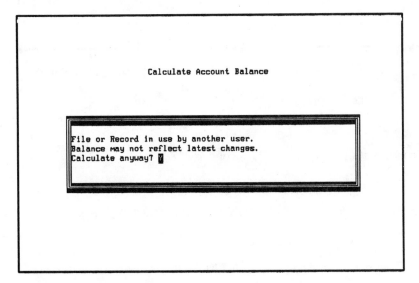

Figure 14-8. Program encounters record lock from another program.

Note that the CKBOOK file is being used by two different programs at the same time.

Morgan decides to perform the calculation without the assurance of the file lock, by entering

```
⏎
```

The program uses the SET LOCK command to allow the SUM command to calculate the balance, even though the file has not been locked by the program.

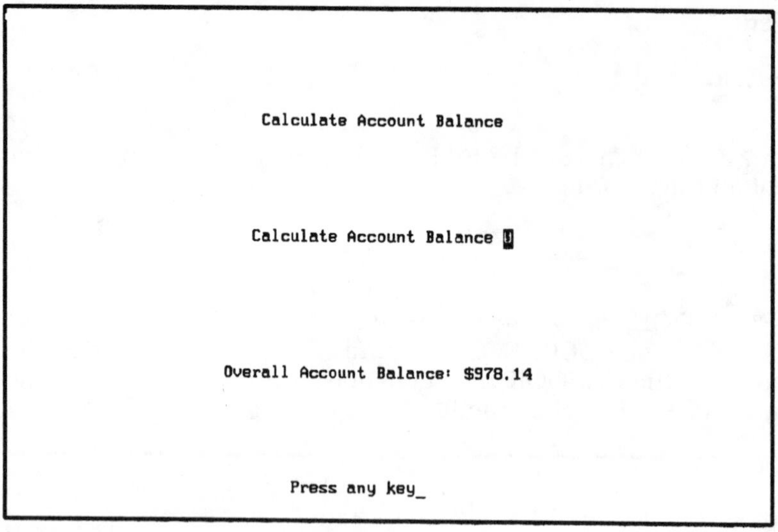

```
                          Calculate Account Balance




                          Calculate Account Balance █




                       Overall Account Balance: $978.14




                             Press any key_
```

Figure 14-9. Program uses SET LOCK OFF to calculate balance.

Morgan exits the program.

⏎

Carolyn exits the LOCKREC1 program.

[Ctrl-End] *(2 times)*

Morgan now places the CKBOOK file in EXCLUSIVE use by entering

USE EXCLUSIVE ckbook ⏎

Carolyn now wants to execute the FILELOCK program by entering

DO filelock ⏎

When the program attempts to execute the USE CKBOOK command, it generates an error because Morgan has exclusive access to the CKBOOK file, as seen in Figure 14-10. The error handling routine, CONFLICT, displays a message box telling the user that the file is in use by another user. The option to retry access is given.

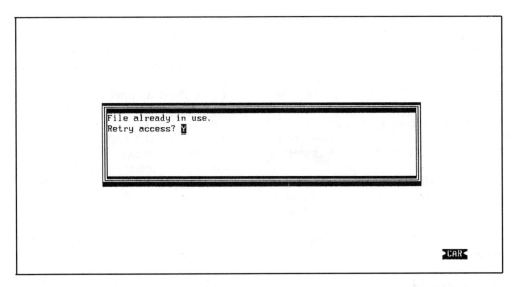

Figure 14-10. Program encounters a file open for exclusive use by another user.

Carolyn attempts to access the file again by entering

⏎

Since Morgan still has exclusive use of the file, the error box appears again. However, Morgan releases the file by entering

CLOSE ALL ⏎

The changes are not automatically reflected on Carolyn's screen. A file error will not be retried, as file and record locks are automatically retried a number of times. Each error requires a specific response. Carolyn enters

⏎ *(2 times)*

The program completes its calculation.

The FILELOCK program illustrates how normal file locks and file lock errors caused by the EXCLUSIVE use of a file, can be handled with dBASE IV programs.

Lock Function System

The information presented by dBASE IV about locks placed on files by other users has, so far, been limited to the existence of those locks. dBASE IV provides an optional enhancement that will allow you to obtain more information about the file or record lock. The lock system can be used to determine at what time and date a record lock was applied, the name of the user who applied the lock, and if a record has been changed by another user since it was originally accessed.

However, this information can be accessed only if the database in use has been converted to a *network lock system* database. The conversion is accomplished with the CONVERT command. When a database is converted, dBASE IV adds a new field to the file structure called _DBASELOCK. This field is called a *hidden* field because it cannot be used as part of the normal field data listed for a database. While it appears in the file structure listing, it cannot be referenced in a command or expression as a fieldname. The use of the _DBASELOCK field is reserved for the dBASE IV network system that will write data into this field as network operations take place.

The information in the _DBASELOCK field can be accessed indirectly by the use of the CHANGE( ) and LKSYS( ) functions. These functions have meaning only when the open database is a converted database. These functions permit you to obtain information about the changes or the locking of individual records. In the following paragraphs, you will learn how converted files can be used with the special functions in dBASE IV programs.

Converting Files

The first step in using the dBASE IV lock system functions is to open a *converted* database. A converted database is one that has been changed with the CONVERT command to contain a special hidden field called _DBASELOCK. You can convert any dBASE IV database to a converted-type database using the CONVERT command.

There is one circumstance in which a conversion is not possible. If you have used or defined all the possible fields in the database structure, CONVERT will not be able to add a new field for the hidden field.

Suppose you want to convert the CKBOOK file to a converted database. The first step is to open the file in the exclusive USE mode. Since the CONVERT command changes the structure of the database, you cannot use the command with a database unless you have established exclusive access to the file. Enter

```
USE EXCLUSIVE ckbook ↵
```

With the database opened for exclusive use, you can enter the CONVERT command. When CONVERT is entered, dBASE IV copies the current database to a file with the same name, but with a CVT extension. For example, the CKBOOK.DBF file is copied to CKBOOK.CVT. The database file is then altered to contain a 16-character field called _DBASELOCK. This hidden field makes it possible for dBASE IV to keep track of the time, date, and the name of the user who applied a lock to a record. You can also determine when another user makes a change to the record on which the current user's record pointer is positioned.

The CONVERT command has one optional clause, the TO clause. The TO clause, in this case, does not represent a file or memory variable destination. The TO clause allows you to vary the size of the _DBASELOCK field from 8 to 24 characters. The default size is 16. Using a value smaller than 16 limits the amount of information that can be recorded about a lock. For example, using the TO 8 clause would limit the information in the _DBASELOCK field so that dBASE IV could not determine the date, time, or user name for a record lock. You can, however, determine if the record is being modified by another user. A value of 16, the default returns an 8-character user I.D. name.

On the other hand, using a value of more than 16 with the CONVERT command, displays user I.D. names longer than 8 characters. The length of the user I.D.'s used on the network, determine whether or not you desire to use this option.

Convert the current database by entering

       CONVERT ↲

dBASE IV displays the message that 16 records have been copied. List the structure of this file.

       LIST STRUCTURE ↲

The list shows the addition of the lock system field, _DBASELOCK.

```
Structure for database:      E:\DBASE\CKBOOK.DBF
Number of data records:           16
Date of last update   :      07/06/89
```

Field	Field Name	Type	Width	Dec	Index
1	DATE	Date	8		N
2	CHECK_NUM	Numeric	4		N
3	PAYEE	Character	25		Y
4	AMOUNT	Numeric	10	2	N
5	CLEARED	Logical	1		N
6	DEDUCTIBLE	Logical	1		N
7	REMARKS	Memo	10		N
8	_DBASELOCK	Character	16		N
** Total **			76		

Once the database is converted, you can use the lock system functions, LKSYS( ) and CHANGE( ), to get information about what other users are doing to the database you are using in a shared mode.

Release the CKBOOK file from EXCLUSIVE use by entering

       CLOSE ALL ↲

User ID Messages

Once a database has been converted to a lock system database, dBASE IV will automatically include the name of the user in the messages it displays when locks are encountered. No special functions are needed for this addition. dBASE IV senses that a lock system database is in use and adds the user name to the message.

As an example, suppose Carolyn is running the LOCKREC1 program. Carolyn enters

```
DO lockrec1 ↵
1000
```

Carolyn has now locked the first record in the CKBOOK database for her use.

Suppose now Morgan attempts to access the same record. Morgan enters

```
USE ckbook ↵
? rlock( ) ↵
```

Since the record is already locked by Carolyn, dBASE IV automatically activates its built-in record lock message. But this time, because the open database is a converted file, the name of the user who has placed the lock on the file appears in the message, as shown in Figure 14-11.

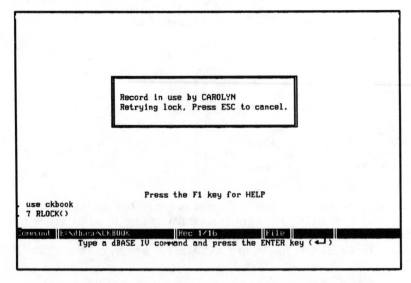

Figure 14-11. User's name appears in record lock message.

The name of the user will also appear in the automatic message for file locks, as well. Morgan can exit the display by entering

```
[Esc]
CLOSE ALL ⌐
```

Carolyn exits her program by entering

```
[Ctrl-End]  (2 times)
```

When files are locked for exclusive use, the text of the error message generated by dBASE IV will contain the name of the user who has set the exclusive lock. This means that the MESSAGE( ) function used as part of user-defined error routines will also display the name of the user.

You could modify the FILELOCK program to include this function in the locked file display.

```
MODIFY COMMAND filelock ⌐
```

Move the cursor to Line 66 of the program, the 6th line in the CONFLICT procedure. It currently reads:

```
@ 0,0 SAY "File already in use."
```

Change this line to display the text of the MESSAGE( ) function.

```
@ 0,0 SAY MESSAGE( )
```

Save the program.

```
[Alt-e]  s
```

Suppose Carolyn has locked the CKBOOK file for her EXCLUSIVE use. Carolyn enters

```
USE EXCLUSIVE ckbook ⌐
```

Morgan attempts to run the modified copy of the FILELOCK program.

```
DO filelock ⌐
```

The message displayed specifically shows the name of the user, in this example Carolyn, who has placed the lock on the file.

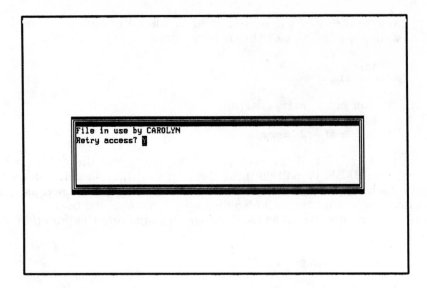

```
File in use by CAROLYN
Retry access? ▊
```

Figure 14-12. File locked error message includes user name.

Morgan exits the program by entering.

      n

Carolyn releases the database by entering

      CLOSE ALL ↵

Lksys( )

The LKSYS( ) function is designed to read information stored in the hidden field _DBASELOCK. LKSYS( ) can be used in three ways:

LKSYS(0). Returns a text value equal to the time that the last lock was set. The time is an 8-character string in the form of hh:mm:ss, in 24 hour format.

LKSYS(1). Returns an 8-character string in the date format mm/dd/yy of the last lock encountered.

LKSYS(2). Returns a character string that contains the name of the user who established the last lock.

Note that all values returned by the LKSYS( ) function are character values, including LKSYS(1), which returns the date of the lock. This makes it easy to add LKSYS( ) data to character expressions.

The values for the LKSYS( ) function are set when a user encounters a lock established by another user. The lock can be a record, file, or exclusive lock. The value of the LKSYS( ) function remains set to that value until another lock is encountered. Keep in mind the LKSYS( ) function does not register that a lock exists until an attempt has been made by the current user to lock a record or file with a RLOCK( ) or FLOCK( ) function. If the locking function returns a true value, i.e., the record or file was unlocked and the current user was able to establish a lock, the LKSYS( ) function returns a null value for all three value types.

As an example, suppose Carolyn runs the LOCKREC1 program by entering

```
DO lockrec1 ↵
1000
```

The program displays the record that contains the check number 1000. Because the LOCKREC1 program is using the converted database file CKBOOK, the date, time, and user ID are stored in the _DBASELOCK field of that record. If another user attempts access to this record, the information will be available for display with the LKSYS( ) function.

Morgan opens the CKBOOK file and attempts to place a record lock.

```
USE ckbook ↵
? RLOCK( ) ↵
```

Because Carolyn already has locked this record, Morgan sees the built-in lock message showing this record is locked. Morgan enters

```
[Esc]
```

In addition to displaying the message, dBASE IV has placed into memory the information stored in the _DBASELOCK field of the locked record. You can display that information by using LKSYS( ). Morgan enters

```
? LKSYS(0),LKSYS(1),LKSYS(2)   ↵
```

The command causes the program to display the time, date, and user name related to the lock. Morgan's screen looks like this:

```
. USE ckbook
. ? RLOCK( )
.F.
. ? LKSYS(0),LKSYS(1),LKSYS(2)
20:46:17 07/06/89 CAROLYN
```

The information provided by LKSYS( ) can be used in programs to elaborate the data displayed when a lock is encountered. For example, you might want to modify the LOCKREC1 program to include information about the lock provided by the LKSYS function.

Create a copy of the LOCKREC1 program called LOCKREC2.PRG by entering

```
COPY FILE lockrec1.prg TO lockrec2.prg ↵
MODIFY COMMAND lockrec2 ↵
```

There are two areas of change in the new version of this program. The changes will add three bars to the popup menu. These will be display-only bars that list the LKSYS information. The SKIP option creates bars that display popup information, but are not highlighted as options.

The popup menu definition portion of the program currently reads:

```
DEFINE POPUP locked FROM 7,45
DEFINE BAR 1 OF locked PROMPT "Retry Access to Record"
DEFINE BAR 2 OF locked PROMPT "Display Record Only"
DEFINE BAR 3 OF locked PROMPT "Search for a different record"
ON SELECTION POPUP locked DEACTIVATE POPUP
```

The idea is to add three new bars to the menu that will display the lock system information. The original three bars will be defined as bars 4 through 6. The new section will read as shown below. The changes are displayed in **bold**. You will notice that bars 1 and 2 are not defined. This is because these bars will display information based on the user, if any, who has locked the record. Such information cannot be defined at the beginning of the program because the record locking operations have yet to take place. The first two bars can only be defined at a point in the program when the file or record lock operation has already taken place.

```
DEFINE POPUP locked FROM 7,45
DEFINE BAR 3 OF locked PROMPT REPLICATE(CHR(196),30)    SKIP
DEFINE BAR 4 OF locked PROMPT "Retry Access to Record"
DEFINE BAR 5 OF locked PROMPT "Display Record Only"
DEFINE BAR 6 OF locked PROMPT "Search for a different record"
ON SELECTION POPUP locked DEACTIVATE POPUP
```

The first and second bars will be defined at the beginning of the LOCKED procedure. This ensures that the values for the LKSYS( ) function will be those that relate to the record lock just attempted. In addition, you must change the bar numbers in the LOCKED procedure from bars 1 and 2 to 4 and 5. The revised section of the LOCKED procedure will look like this:

```
PROCEDURE locked
DEFINE BAR 1 OF locked PROMPT "Record Locked by "+LKSYS(2)  SKIP
DEFINE BAR 2 OF locked PROMPT "At "+LKSYS(0)+" on "+LKSYS(1) SKIP
DO CASE
   CASE BAR( )=4
      DO retry
   CASE BAR( )=5
      SET REFRESH TO 5
      EDIT NEXT 1 NOMENU NOAPPEND NOEDIT
      SET REFRESH TO 0
ENDCASE
RETURN
```

Save and execute the program by entering

```
[Alt-e] r
1000
```

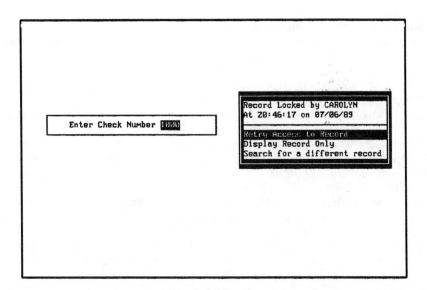

Figure 14-13. Popup menu shows LKSYS( ) information about record lock.

Recall that in this example, Carolyn's workstation still has a lock on the same record. This will cause the revised popup menu to appear as shown in Figure 14-13.

The LKSYS( ) functions used as prompts in the top of the menu, inform the user about the date, time, and user name associated with the record lock.

Morgan exits the program by entering

```
s
[Ctrl-End]
```

Carolyn exits the program she is running by entering

```
[Ctrl-End]   (2 times)
```

Protection System Functions

If you are using file protection, you can obtain information about the current login name and access code by using the USER( ) and ACCESS( ) function.

USER( ) returns the name of the user who has logged into dBASE IV. Note that this name may not be the same name that appears for the user in the LIST USERS or LKSYS(2) functions. These commands use the user ID as passed from the network operating system. The User name used in the dBASE IV protection system is defined separately within dBASE IV and may vary from the workstation name assigned by the LAN operating system.

The ACCESS( ) function returns a numeric value equal to the access code level as defined in the user profile in the protection system. You can use these codes from within a program to control access to certain parts of the program. Note that the level of security provided by using the ACCESS( ) function is limited, since the program code stored in the PRG file is not encrypted by the protection system. If you remove the PRG source code files and leave only the DBO files, users will not be able to change programs to circumvent security options.

Change( )

The CHANGE( ) function provides the programmer with the ability to update displays when changes are made in records by other users.

The SET REFRESH command performs this function automatically, for information displayed with the EDIT or BROWSE modes. If you are using @/SAY/GET commands to display information, the SET REFRESH command will not affect that display.

You can use the CHANGE( ) function within a program to implement a routine that will react whenever another user makes a change to the current record.

The CHANGE( ) function is related to the dBASE IV lock system field, _DBASELOCK, which appears in converted databases. When the user positions the pointer to a record, dBASE IV reads the current values in the _DBASELOCK field into memory.

Each time the CHANGE( ) function is used, the program re-reads the values in the _DBASELOCK field. If the program finds that the data in the _DBASELOCK field is identical to the information about that record stored in memory, the value returned for the function is .F., i.e., no change has been made in the record. If the values are different, the function returns a true value, .T., indicating another user has made a change to the data in that record.

The CHANGE( ) function is typically used to trigger a message that tells the user a change has taken place, and/or a procedure that re-writes the screen to show the latest changes have been activated. This effect is automatic when SET REFRESH is used to EDIT or BROWSE, but needs to be specifically programmed when using @/SAY/GET screen displays.

The CHANGE( ) function is potentially more efficient than the SET

REFRESH system because CHANGE will be triggered only when a change has been made. SET REFRESH, on the other hand, re-writes the screen every so many seconds, whether or not any user has made any changes to the record.

Keep in mind that a change will not register with SET REFRESH or with CHANGE( ) until the user has saved the record to which she is making changes. Since editing changes in dBASE IV are not permanent until a record is saved, changes in data will not flow through until that point is reached.

As an example, you can modify the LOCKREC2 program. Recall that in the LOCKREC2, one of the options on the popup menu is a Read Only Edit display.

In order to see how the CHANGE( ) function operates, you can create a new version of the program that uses @/SAY commands to display the information, and a CHANGE( ) function to ensure that changes made by other users appear on the screen as they are saved.

Begin by making a copy of the LOCKREC2 program.

```
COPY FILE lockrec2.prg TO lockrec3.prg ↵
```

Open the LOCKREC3 program for editing.

```
MODIFY COMMAND lockrec3 ↵
```

The first change is in the DO CASE section in the LOCKED procedure that should begin on line 54. The current section reads as follows:

```
DO CASE
   CASE BAR( )=4
      DO retry
   CASE BAR( )=5
      SET REFRESH TO 5
      EDIT NEXT 1 NOMENU NOAPPEND NOEDIT
      SET REFRESH TO 0
ENDCASE
```

Remove the commands shown above in **bold**, and replace them with the DO command shown in **bold**, below.

```
DO CASE
   CASE BAR( )=4
      DO retry
   CASE BAR( )=5
      DO readonly
ENDCASE
```

The next step is to move to the end of the file and add a procedure called READONLY. Enter

```
[Ctrl-Pg Dn]
```

The procedure begins with the name of the procedure and a command to clear the screen.

```
PROCEDURE readonly
CLEAR
```

The procedure continues by placing the record number at the top of the screen.

```
@ 1,0 SAY "Record #"
@ ROW( ),COL( ) SAY RECNO( ) PICTURE "@T"
```

The next section uses a DO WHILE loop in conjunction with the FIELD( ) function, to display the fieldnames and contents for this record. The field information is displayed in **bold**, while the fieldnames are in normal video.

```
fnum=1
DO WHILE fnum<=7
    fname=FIELD(fnum)
    @ ROW( )+1,0 SAY STR(fnum,2)+".  "+FIELD(fnum)
    @ ROW( ),15 SAY &fname COLOR W+
    fnum=fnum+1
ENDDO
```

When the loop is completed, you must pause the program to allow the user to read the displayed information. The pause can be created with a simple WAIT command. However, when the program is paused with a wait or @/SAY/READ combination, no other commands can be processed by the program.

A better solution is a DO WHILE loop set for INKEY( ) = 0. This will create a loop that cycles until a key is pressed. The program will appear paused, but commands can be executed inside the loop.

```
@ 24,0 SAY "Press Any Key"
DO WHILE INKEY( )=0
```

Here, you can test continuously for a change in the data, made by the user who has locked the record. The IF CHANGE( ) command creates a structure that executes if dBASE IV determines the user who has locked the record actually uses the lock to change the data.

```
    IF CHANGE( )
```

If CHANGE( ) evaluates as true, a change has been made by the other user. In this instance, the program displays a message at the bottom of the screen telling you a change has been made. The LKSYS( ) function can be used to include the name of the user in the message. Note that the color W* is a blinking white background.

```
    @ 20,0 SAY LKSYS(2)+" has made changes to record." COLOR N/W*
```

In addition to displaying the message, the program will re-display all the fields, so that the new information will appear on the display. However, before the information is displayed, you must reset the information about the contents of the _DBASELOCK field in the memory, just as you are about to display the latest information entered into the record. Recall that the CHANGE information is reset each time the pointer is positioned to a record. The command GOTO RECNO( ), moves the pointer to the current record. While this command does not seem to accomplish a lot, it does cause the CHANGE system to update the record lock information to the current values.

```
GOTO RECNO( )
@ 1,0 SAY "Record #"
@ ROW( ),COL( ) SAY RECNO( ) PICTURE "@T"
fnum=1
DO WHILE fnum<=7
  fname=FIELD(fnum)
  @ ROW( )+1,0 SAY STR(fnum,2)+".  "+FIELD(fnum)
  @ ROW( ),15 SAY &fname COLOR W+
  fnum=fnum+1
ENDDO
```

Following the display, the structure, loop, and procedure can be terminated.

```
   ENDIF
ENDDO
CLEAR
RETURN
```

Note that the IF structure inside the loop will cycle, as long as the user does not press a key. This is true even if the IF CHANGE( ) structure displays a revised record. The program is still awaiting a user key-press.

Save the program.

```
[Alt-e] s
```

To see how the CHANGE( ) function operates, go through an example session with the users MORGAN and CAROLYN.

Carolyn begins by running the program and accessing the record with check number 1002. She enters

```
DO lockrec3 ⏎
1002
```

Morgan runs the program and attempts to access the same record.

```
DO lockrec3 ⏎
1002
```

The program displays the popup menu with information about when the file lock was placed. Morgan selects to display the data in Read Only format by entering

```
d
```

```
Record #3
 1. DATE        01/06/89
 2. CHECK_NUM   1002
 3. PAYEE       Western Telephone
 4. AMOUNT          101.57
 5. CLEARED     T
 6. DEDUCTIBLE  F
 7. REMARKS     memo




Press Any Key_
```

Figure 14-14. Data displayed by @/SAY commands.

The program displays the data on the screen with @/SAY commands.

Carolyn changes the date in the record she is currently editing by entering

010789

Carolyn then saves the record by entering

[Ctrl-End]

Morgan's screen changes as soon as Carolyn saves her change. Morgan sees the flashing message and the new date appears in the DATE field.

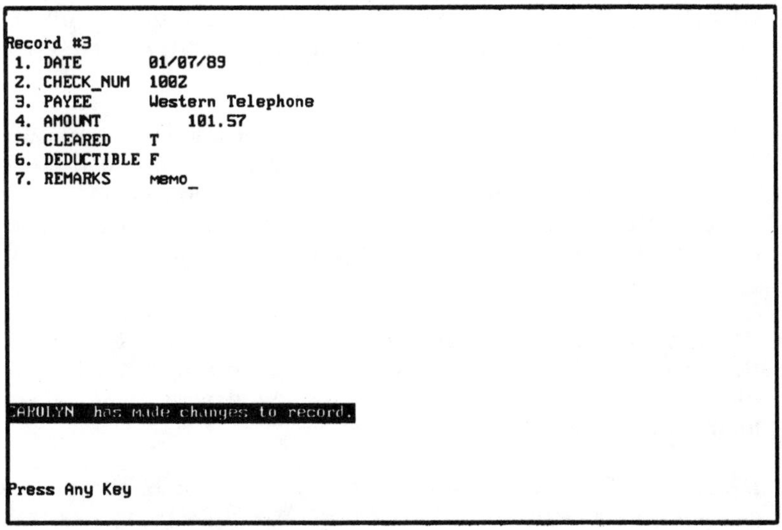

```
Record #3
1. DATE       01/07/89
2. CHECK_NUM  1002
3. PAYEE      Western Telephone
4. AMOUNT         101.57
5. CLEARED    T
6. DEDUCTIBLE F
7. REMARKS    memo_




CAROLYN  has made changes to record.


Press Any Key
```

Figure 14-15. Record updated when a change is made by another user.

Exit the programs. Morgan enters

⏎ *(2 times)*

Carolyn enters

⏎

Summary

This chapter covered the basic techniques needed to write dBASE IV programs that will run on networks.

- **Explicit Locks.** In addition to the dBASE IV automatic system of record, file, and EXCLUSIVE locks, you can also design user-defined programs that handle conflicts occuring when operating databases on a network. The dBASE IV programming language contains special commands and functions that work in conjunction with the standard dBASE IV language, to provide complete networking capabilities. When you program your own record and file locking routines, you use explicit file locks. This means you specifically place a lock on a record or file, rather than having dBASE IV place a lock when a conflict occurs. dBASE IV automatic file or record locks are implemented at exactly the point where a usage conflict occurs. User-defined explicit file or record locks can implement locks at any point in a program.

- **UNLOCK.** When files or records are locked with explicit locking operations, they remain locked until explicitly released with the UNLOCK command.

- **RLOCK( ).** This function is used to lock records. When this function is used with a command, it tests to see if the current record is locked. If the record is locked by another user, it returns a false value. If the record is not locked, it locks the record for the current user and returns a value of true. The value remains true until the record is unlocked.

- **FLOCK( ).** This function operates the same as RLOCK( ), except that it locks all the records in the file. Note, an attempt to place a file lock will be rejected if another user already has a file or record lock established.

- **EXCLUSIVE Use.** When files are locked for exclusive use, they cannot be accessed by other users. Attempts to access the file will result in an error message. If the locked database is a converted database, the error message will contain the name of the user who has placed the EXCLUSIVE lock.

- **Converting Files.** dBASE IV can convert a standard dBASE IV database file for use with special network functions. The conversion process adds a hidden field called _DBASELOCK to the database structure. This field is used to record information about locks.

- **LKSYS( ).** This function is used to display the time, date, and user name, related to a specific record or file lock. LKSYS( ) can be used only if the open database has been converted with the CONVERT command.

- **CHANGE( ).** This function works with a converted database and can be used to determine if the current record is being changed by other users. This function allows you to integrate updates into programs where information is displayed, without using the EDIT and BROWSE commands. EDIT and BROWSE can be automatically updated by the SET REFRESH command. @/SAY/GET screen displays are not affected by SET REFRESH.

Program Listing

Program: LOCKREC.PRG

```
SET TALK OFF
SET STATUS OFF
SET SCOREBOARD OFF
* turns off automatic record lock message
SET REPROCESS TO 1
CLEAR
USE ckbook
DEFINE WINDOW notfound FROM 8,20 TO 13,60 DOUBLE
DO WHILE .T.
    key=0
    @ 9,5 TO 11,50
    @ 10,10 SAY "Enter Check Number" GET key PICTURE "9999"
    READ
    IF key=0
        EXIT
    ENDIF
    LOCATE FOR check_num=key
    IF FOUND( )
        * test for existing record lock
        IF RLOCK( )
            EDIT NEXT 1 NOMENU NOAPPEND
            UNLOCK
        ELSE
            ACTIVATE WINDOW notfound
            ? "Check number "+LTRIM(STR(key))+"  found -"
            ? "Record in use by another user."
            WAIT
            DEACTIVATE WINDOW notfound
        ENDIF
    ELSE
        ACTIVATE WINDOW notfound
        @ 1,5 SAY "Check number "+LTRIM(STR(key))+"  not found."
        WAIT
        DEACTIVATE WINDOW notfound
    ENDIF
ENDDO
CLOSE DATABASE
RELEASE WINDOW notfound
SET REPROCESS TO 0
SET TALK ON
SET STATUS ON
SET SCOREBOARD ON
RETURN
```

Program LOCKREC1.PRG

```
SET TALK OFF
SET STATUS OFF
SET SCOREBOARD OFF
* turns off automatic record lock message
SET REPROCESS TO 1
CLEAR
USE ckbook
DEFINE WINDOW notfound FROM 8,20 TO 13,60 DOUBLE
```

```
DEFINE WINDOW times FROM 9,50 TO 13,75
DEFINE POPUP locked FROM 7,45
DEFINE BAR 1 OF locked PROMPT "Retry Access to Record"
DEFINE BAR 2 OF locked PROMPT "Display Record Only"
DEFINE BAR 3 OF locked PROMPT "Search for a different record"
ON SELECTION POPUP locked DEACTIVATE POPUP
DO WHILE .T.
    key=0
    @ 9,5 TO 11,40
    @ 10,10 SAY "Enter Check Number" GET key PICTURE "9999"
    READ
    IF key=0
        EXIT
    ENDIF
    LOCATE FOR check_num=key
    IF FOUND( )
        * test for existing record lock
        IF RLOCK( )
            EDIT NEXT 1 NOMENU NOAPPEND
            UNLOCK
        ELSE
            DO locked
        ENDIF
    ELSE
        ACTIVATE WINDOW notfound
        @ 1,5 SAY "Check number "+LTRIM(STR(key))+"  not found."
        WAIT
        DEACTIVATE WINDOW notfound
    ENDIF
ENDDO
CLOSE DATABASE
RELEASE WINDOW notfound,times
RELEASE POPUP locked
SET REPROCESS TO 0
SET TALK ON
SET STATUS ON
SET SCOREBOARD ON
RETURN


PROCEDURE locked
ACTIVATE POPUP locked
DO CASE
    CASE BAR( )=1
        DO retry
    CASE BAR( )=2
        SET REFRESH TO 5
        EDIT NEXT 1 NOMENU NOAPPEND NOEDIT
        SET REFRESH TO 0
ENDCASE
RETURN

PROCEDURE retry
ACTIVATE WINDOW times
times=0
@ 0,0 SAY "How many retrys?" GET times PICTURE "9999"
@ 1,0 SAY "Attempt: "
READ
done=0
DO WHILE done<=times
```

```
      @ 1,10 SAY LTRIM(STR(done))
      IF RLOCK( )
          DEACTIVATE  WINDOW times
          EDIT NEXT 1 NOMENU NOAPPEND
          EXIT
      ENDIF
      done=done+1
ENDDO
DEACTIVATE  WINDOW times
RETURN
```

Program LOCKREC2.PRG

```
SET TALK OFF
SET STATUS OFF
SET SCOREBOARD OFF
* turns off automatic record lock message
SET REPROCESS TO 1
CLEAR
USE ckbook
DEFINE WINDOW notfound FROM 8,20 TO 13,60 DOUBLE
DEFINE WINDOW times FROM 9,50 TO 13,75
DEFINE POPUP locked FROM 7,45
DEFINE BAR 3 OF locked PROMPT REPLICATE(CHR(196),30)   SKIP
DEFINE BAR 4 OF locked PROMPT `Retry Access to Record"
DEFINE BAR 5 OF locked PROMPT "Display Record Only"
DEFINE BAR 6 OF locked PROMPT "Search for a different  record"
ON SELECTION POPUP locked DEACTIVATE POPUP
DO WHILE .T.
    key=0
    @ 9,5 TO 11,40
    @ 10,10 SAY "Enter Check Number" GET key PICTURE  "9999"
    READ
    IF key=0
        EXIT
    ENDIF
    LOCATE FOR check_num=key
    IF FOUND( )
        * test for existing record lock
        IF RLOCK( )
            EDIT NEXT 1 NOMENU NOAPPEND
            UNLOCK
        ELSE
            DO locked
        ENDIF
    ELSE
        ACTIVATE WINDOW notfound
        @ 1,5 SAY "Check number "+LTRIM(STR(key))+"  not found."
        WAIT
        DEACTIVATE  WINDOW notfound
    ENDIF
ENDDO
CLOSE DATABASE
RELEASE WINDOW notfound,times
RELEASE POPUP locked
SET REPROCESS TO 0
SET TALK ON
SET STATUS ON
SET SCOREBOARD ON
RETURN
```

```
PROCEDURE locked
DEFINE BAR 1 OF locked PROMPT "Record Locked by "+LKSYS(2)  SKIP
DEFINE BAR 2 OF locked PROMPT "At "+LKSYS(0)+" on "+LKSYS(1)  SKIP
ACTIVATE POPUP locked
DO CASE
    CASE BAR( )=4
        DO retry
    CASE BAR( )=5
        SET REFRESH TO 5
        EDIT NEXT 1 NOMENU NOAPPEND NOEDIT
        SET REFRESH TO 0
ENDCASE
RETURN


PROCEDURE retry
ACTIVATE WINDOW times
times=0
@ 0,0 SAY "How many retrys?" GET times PICTURE "9999"
@ 1,0 SAY "Attempt: "
READ
done=0
DO WHILE done<=times
    @ 1,10 SAY LTRIM(STR(done))
    IF RLOCK( )
        DEACTIVATE WINDOW times
        EDIT NEXT 1 NOMENU NOAPPEND
        EXIT
    ENDIF
    done=done+1
ENDDO
DEACTIVATE WINDOW times
RETURN
```

Program LOCKREC3.PRG

```
SET TALK OFF
SET STATUS OFF
SET SCOREBOARD OFF
* turns off automatic record lock message
SET REPROCESS TO 1
CLEAR
USE ckbook
DEFINE WINDOW notfound FROM 8,20 TO 13,60 DOUBLE
DEFINE WINDOW times FROM 9,50 TO 13,75
DEFINE POPUP locked FROM 7,45
DEFINE BAR 3 OF locked PROMPT REPLICATE(CHR(196),30)   SKIP
DEFINE BAR 4 OF locked PROMPT "Retry Access to Record"
DEFINE BAR 5 OF locked PROMPT "Display Record Only"
DEFINE BAR 6 OF locked PROMPT "Search for a different record"
ON SELECTION POPUP locked DEACTIVATE POPUP
DO WHILE .T.
    key=0
    @ 9,5 TO 11,40
    @ 10,10 SAY "Enter Check Number" GET key PICTURE "9999"
    READ
    IF key=0
        EXIT
    ENDIF
```

```
        LOCATE FOR check_num=key
        IF FOUND( )
            * test for existing record lock
            IF RLOCK( )
                EDIT NEXT 1 NOMENU NOAPPEND
                UNLOCK
            ELSE
                DO locked
            ENDIF
        ELSE
            ACTIVATE WINDOW notfound
            @ 1,5 SAY "Check number "+LTRIM(STR(key))+"  not found."
            WAIT
            DEACTIVATE WINDOW notfound
        ENDIF
    ENDDO
    CLOSE DATABASE
    RELEASE WINDOW notfound,times
    RELEASE POPUP locked
    SET REPROCESS TO 0
    SET TALK ON
    SET STATUS ON
    SET SCOREBOARD ON
    RETURN


    PROCEDURE locked
    DEFINE BAR 1 OF locked PROMPT "Record Locked by "+LKSYS(2)  SKIP
    DEFINE BAR 2 OF locked PROMPT "At "+LKSYS(0)+" on "+LKSYS(1)  SKIP
    ACTIVATE POPUP locked
    DO CASE
        CASE BAR( )=4
            DO retry
        CASE BAR( )=5
            DO readonly
    ENDCASE
    RETURN

    PROCEDURE retry
    ACTIVATE WINDOW times
    times=0
    @ 0,0 SAY "How many retrys?" GET times PICTURE "9999"
    @ 1,0 SAY "Attempt: "
    READ
    done=0
    DO WHILE done<=times
        @ 1,10 SAY LTRIM(STR(done))
        IF RLOCK( )
            DEACTIVATE WINDOW times
            EDIT NEXT 1 NOMENU NOAPPEND
            EXIT
        ENDIF
        done=done+1
    ENDDO
    DEACTIVATE WINDOW times
    RETURN

    PROCEDURE readonly
    CLEAR
    @ 1,0 SAY "Record #"
```

```
@ ROW( ),COL( ) SAY RECNO( ) PICTURE "@T"
fnum=1
DO WHILE fnum<=7
    fname=FIELD(fnum)
    @ ROW( )+1,0 SAY STR(fnum,2)+".  "+FIELD(fnum)
    @ ROW( ),15 SAY &fname COLOR W+
    fnum=fnum+1
ENDDO
@ 24,0 SAY "Press Any Key"
DO WHILE INKEY( )=0
    IF CHANGE( )
        GOTO RECNO( )
        @ 20,0 SAY LKSYS(2)+"  has made changes to record." COLOR N/W*
        @ 1,0 SAY "Record #"
        @ ROW( ),COL( ) SAY RECNO( ) PICTURE "@T"
        fnum=1
        DO WHILE fnum<=7
            fname=FIELD(fnum)
            @ ROW( )+1,0 SAY STR(fnum,2)+".  "+FIELD(fnum)
            @ ROW( ),15 SAY &fname COLOR W+
            fnum=fnum+1
        ENDDO
    ENDIF
ENDDO
CLEAR
RETURN
```

Program FILELOCK.PRG

```
SET TALK OFF
SET STATUS OFF
SET SCOREBOARD OFF
SET REPROCESS TO 1
DEFINE WINDOW conflict FROM 10,10 TO 17,70 DOUBLE
* on error used to trap exclusive use errors
ON ERROR DO conflict
USE ckbook
month=0
title="Calculate  Account Balance"
@ 5,(80-LEN(title))/2  SAY title
prompt="Enter  Month or 0 for all months"
@ 11,(78-LEN(title))/2  SAY title GET month PICTURE "9"
READ
IF month>0
    SET FILTER TO MONTH(date)=month
    GO TOP
    result="Balance  for the month of "+CMONTH(date)+":"
ELSE
    result="Overall  Account Balance:"
ENDIF
DO WHILE .NOT.FLOCK( )
    use_locked=.T.
    ACTIVATE WINDOW conflict
    @ 1,0 SAY "File or Record in use by another user."
    @ 2,0 SAY "Balance may not reflect latest changes."
    @ 3,0 SAY "Calculate anyway?" GET use_locked PICTURE "Y"
    READ
    IF use_locked
        DEACTIVATE WINDOW conflict
        SET LOCK OFF
```

```
        DO find_bal
        SET LOCK ON
        EXIT
    ELSE
        @ 2,0 CLEAR
        @ 2,0 SAY "Retry Access to file?" GET use_locked PICTURE "Y"
        READ
        IF .NOT. use_locked
            EXIT
        ENDIF
    ENDIF
    DEACTIVATE WINDOW conflict
ENDDO
IF FLOCK( )
    DO find_bal
    UNLOCK
ENDIF
DO end
RETURN

PROCEDURE find_bal
SUM IIF(payee="DEPOSIT",amount,amount*-1)    TO balance
@ 18,(70-LEN(result))/2  SAY result
@ ROW( ),COL( )+1 SAY balance PICTURE "@$T 999,999.99"
@ 24,30 SAY "Press any key"
DO WHILE INKEY( )=0
ENDDO
RETURN

PROCEDURE conflict
* error cause by file set exclusive by other user
ACTIVATE WINDOW conflict
IF ERROR( )=372.OR.ERROR( )=108
    do_again=.T.
    @ 0,0 SAY MESSAGE( )
    @ 1,0 SAY "Retry access?" GET do_again PICTURE "Y"
    READ
    IF do_again
        DEACTIVATE WINDOW conflict
        RETRY
    ELSE
        DO end
        CANCEL
    ENDIF
ELSE
    @ 0,0 SAY "Error occurred during execution"
    @ 1,0 SAY "dBASE reports "+MESSAGE( )
    @ 2,0 SAY "Error #"+LTRIM(STR(ERROR( )))
    @ 3,0 SAY "Press any Key"
    DO WHILE INKEY( )=0
    ENDDO
    DO end
    CANCEL
ENDIF
RETURN

PROCEDURE end
RELEASE WINDOW conflict
CLEAR
CLOSE DATABASE
```

```
SET TALK ON
SET STATUS ON
SET SCOREBOARD ON
SET REPROCESS TO 0
ON ERROR
RETURN
```

Part IV

SQL

15

Using SQL

This chapter begins Part IV of this book. The purpose of this chapter is to teach you what dBASE IV SQL is and how it is used. Since SQL represents a distinct part of dBASE IV, it would be useful to begin with a general orientation to the topic of SQL.

What SQL Is

dBASE IV is a powerful and complicated program. If you have read and worked through the first three parts of this book that statement comes as no surprise. But as of the writing of this book, dBASE IV only operates on MSDOS-type microcomputers. Other microcomputers or larger mini and mainframe computers have their own databases.

Suppose you were in a situation, a change in employment perhaps, where you were forced to work on a different type of computer, (i.e. one on which dBASE IV was not available). The skills you developed working with dBASE IV databases could not directly be applied to the new computer's database. You would have to learn a new system that might or might not resemble the familiar dBASE IV system.

Suppose that instead of each computer system or database software being unique, all programs operated on a common set of commands. Once you learned that command set, you could move to any computer database system and begin working immediately. In this scenario your skills in working with computer databases can be moved from one computer system to another—they are *transportable*.

This is the basic goal behind SQL. The letters SQL stand for Structured Query Language. SQL was originally developed on main frame computers to provide a common core of database commands that could be used across a wide range of computers, operating systems, and database software. The goal of SQL is to provide a device-independent set of basic database-query tools.

Device independence means that SQL will look and feel pretty much the same to a user, regardless of what computer, operating system, or software is running.

The commands and structures used in SQL form a core of operations designed to perform a wide range of database queries. It is important to note that SQL is not a complete database system or a complete programming language. SQL cannot stand alone because it has only limited data entry and report formatting capabilities. SQL will always appear within a larger database system, such as dBASE IV, which already has these features. The program that supports SQL is often referred to as the front-end application.

SQL is chiefly concerned with the topic of queries (i.e. request for retrieval of information from the database). dBASE IV has two methods of query—the query by example mode, and the Dot Prompt commands. SQL provides a third method of retrieving data. SQL is an attempt to create a standard method by which users can retrieve data from a database, without having to know details about the structure of the application.

Like most computer standards, SQL will show slight variations, depending upon the environment in which you are operating. dBASE IV SQL supports most of the commands and operations used by the various implementations of SQL.

Why Use SQL?

There are two reason for using SQL. First, if you are familiar with SQL commands you can apply this knowledge to dBASE IV databases by using dBASE IV SQL. While you will still need to know some information about dBASE IV, you can perform data retrieval operations using the SQL commands and syntax with which you are already familiar.

Second, SQL offers an alternative method of carrying out complicated queries. SQL is considered very strong in the area of dBASE IV's *multiple database* operations, where query operations are the most complex.

If you use dBASE IV on a microcomputer exclusively, you may find that SQL is not necessary for your work. However, learning about SQL and SQL operations may be used in and of themselves, since SQL is based on a different approach to database management than is dBASE IV.

The SQL Approach

SQL differs from dBASE IV in a fundamental way. dBASE IV is oriented towards the *operations* required to obtain a set of information. In dBASE IV you are concerned about opening files, selecting index tags, moving the record pointer, setting filters, etc. In order to obtain a specific set of information (i.e. the answer to a definitive question such as the total amount of sales for account number 101) you need to know what operations to execute and in what order. Only after performing the correct sequence of operations can the desired data be obtained. dBASE IV is a *process*-oriented program.

SQL approaches database operations from an *object* orientation. The set of data you want to obtain is the object of the query. The query is a description of the database object, not the operations needed to obtain it. In SQL the mechanism, techniques, and operations needed to obtain information are hidden from the user. The user does not tell SQL how to find the information. Instead, the user tells the program what the information should look like. SQL, using whatever methods it decides, retrieves the desired data.

The SQL approach has several advantages. The SQL command set is much smaller than dBASE IV's. This in part reflects the fact that dBASE IV commands refer to procedures that are all different, and SQL refers to database objects that all have the same basic structure. This should make SQL much simpler to learn and faster to use, because the user does not need to know or enter commands concerning how the query should be carried out.

Because the *how* portion of the query is hidden from the user, SQL can be adapted to use all types of applications as the basis of the query. In dBASE IV, the SQL commands are implemented through dBASE IV. This means when an SQL command is issued, dBASE IV retrieves the data by using such commands as OPEN, SET FILTER, SET FIELDS, etc. The difference is that you, as the user, are not aware of how the information is retrieved. The ultimate goal would be to carry out database retrieval operations using the same commands, across a range of micro, mini, and main frame computers.

Keep in mind that while developments in microcomputer technology have made this goal possible, only parts of this integrated system are available today. dBASE IV SQL represents an initial step in the direction of the development of standard database retrieval by combining the dominant microcomputer database system, dBASE, with the dominant database retrieval system on mini and main frame computers: SQL.

Projected Future of SQL and dBASE IV

Ashton-Tate, makers of dBASE IV, and Microsoft are combining to produce a new network oriented application called SQL Server, which will allow a file server to process SQL queries issued by such programs as dBASE IV, Lotus 1-2-3, or Microsoft's Excel. SQL server will run under the OS/2 LAN manager software being developed by Microsoft.

The concept of an SQL server is that SQL queries will be processed by the network file server, and only the results of the query will be returned to the network workstation. This approach will have two major benefits. First, the performance of programs using SQL on a network will improve greatly. In the current dBASE IV implementation of SQL, the workstation running dBASE IV must handle all phases of the query processing. This means each workstation must manipulate the entire SQL database in order to process a request for data. For example, suppose you entered a query that selected 1 name out of a database with 10,000 rows of data. In order for the workstation to process the query, the server would have to feed the entire database through the network to the workstation so that the proper row or rows could be selected. If more than one workstation is making a request for data from the same database, the amount of traffic on the network increases geometrically, slowing all operations.

With the SQL server in place, the workstation sends the SQL query to the server. The server then processes the request and sends back only the requested data. The workstation computer is required to handle only the SQL query and the retrieved data. This greatly reduces the information passed through the network. For example, if an SQL query addressed to a database with 10,000 rows returns only one row, the server will pass back only the one row to the workstation, not the entire database. The network communicates only the data needed based on the SQL query.

A second benefit of the SQL server approach is that almost any program can be adapted to perform SQL queries. Since the implementation of the queries will be handled by the SQL server, the application running on the workstation needs only to pass the SQL command to the server.

The current version of SQL in dBASE IV running under DOS does not work this way. dBASE IV itself must process the SQL query by converting it into dBASE IV commands and procedures. Each workstation running dBASE IV must have sufficient memory to process the entire query. This also means the network server must feed back to the workstation the entire table or database to process the query, thus degrading the network performance.

The bright spot is that programs or procedures designed with the current version of dBASE IV SQL should be entirely compatible with SQL server operations. The commands will be exactly the same. The only difference is they will work faster because of the performance advantages of the SQL Server. SQL operations under DOS represent a new area where many of the key elements have yet to be firmly established.

What SQL Does and Does Not Do

SQL is heavily weighted in the direction of creating database objects. These objects are sets of information retrieved from a database according to the description entered in the SQL command. In dBASE IV you learned that in addition to retrieval, you must have data entry, screen forms, report forms, and mailing labels in order to have a complete database application. SQL does not provide such facilities as an EDIT mode for data entry, or a label-form generator for printing mailing labels. SQL concentrates on retrieving data, not on data entry or output.

In dBASE IV you need to rely on its modes and operations to handle most aspects of data input and output. In SQL the concern is with the database process that involves the selection and retrieval of stored data.

dBASE IV SQL allows you to use data in both standard dBASE IV operations and in SQL operations. You must understand the relationship between SQL and dBASE IV in order to effectively use dBASE IV SQL.

SQL Terminology

Because SQL was created outside the dBASE IV environment, many of the terms used in SQL are the same as those found in dBASE IV, but with a different meaning.

This book uses the term *standard* dBASE IV to refer to the dBASE IV program without SQL. *SQL* in this book refers specifically to the implementation of SQL found in dBASE IV.

Below are some terms used in SQL, with a discussion of how they are related to standard dBASE IV terms.

Database

In standard dBASE IV the word *database* refers to a physical object (i.e. a database file with a DBF extension). In SQL the term database refers to a logical entity that can encompass the information stored in a large number of files. An SQL database is similar to a standard dBASE IV *catalog*, since a catalog groups many different physical files together. An SQL database may contain any number of DBF files.

Table

In SQL, the term table refers to a standard dBASE IV database file, DBF. An SQL database can contain one or more tables. A table is organized in columns and rows in the same way a standard dBASE IV is organized in fields and records.

Column

A column in SQL is the same as a field in standard dBASE IV.

Row

A row in SQL is the same as a record in standard dBASE IV.

Cursor

An SQL cursor does not refer to the line that indicates the typing location. In SQL the term cursor refers to a special procedure that enables you to isolate an individual table row. SQL cursors function a bit like the record pointer in a standard dBASE IV database.

You are now ready to begin working with SQL. Load dBASE IV in the usual manner. Exit the Control Center and activate the Dot Prompt mode by entering

        [Alt-e] e

Starting SQL

You can activate an SQL session from within dBASE IV by entering the command SET SQL ON at the Dot Prompt. Enter

        SET SQL ON ⏎

The prompt changes from the Dot Prompt to the SQL prompt, which consists of the letters SQL and a period. When the SQL prompt is active you can enter both SQL and dBASE IV commands. Keep in mind that not all dBASE IV commands can be used in SQL. Standard dBASE IV commands that refer to such database file operations as USE, EDIT, BROWSE, INDEX, SET FILTER, SET FIELDS, SUM, CALCULATE, MODIFY STRUCTURE, REPLACE, etc. cannot be used in the SQL mode.

You can exit SQL and return to standard dBASE IV by entering

        SET SQL OFF ⏎

You can exit both SQL and standard dBASE IV by entering the QUIT command in the SQL mode. Note that dBASE IV will always load the standard dBASE IV mode. If you want to start dBASE IV in the SQL mode you must make a change in the CONFIG.DB file by adding the command SQL=ON to the startup keywords list. See Chapter 16 for information about CONFIG.DB.

Activate SQL again by entering

```
SET SQL ON
```

Creating an SQL Database

The first step in working with SQL is to select or create a database. In this case, begin by creating a database called ACCOUNTS, that will contain roughly the same information you used in the accounts catalog in standard dBASE IV. The SQL command CREATE DATABASE is used to create a new SQL database. Note that this command is terminated with a semicolon (;) character. All SQL commands end with semicolons. If you forget to include this mark, dBASE IV will not execute the SQL command. Enter

```
CREATE DATABASE accounts; ↵
```

SQL responds with the message "Database ACCOUNTS created," meaning a subdirectory has been created with the name ACCOUNTS on the hard disk. Assuming dBASE IV is stored in the DBASE directory, this would make the new database directory \DBASE\ACCOUNTS.

It is in this new directory that all the files related to the SQL database ACCOUNTS will be stored. As part of the creation process, SQL automatically creates 13 files, and places them in the new SQL database directory: SYSTABLS.DBF, SYSCOLS.DBF, SYSIDXS.DBF, SYSKEYS.DBF, SYS-VIEWS.DBF, SYSVDEPS.DBF, SYSSYNS.DBF, SYSAUTH.DBF, SYSCO-LAU.DBF, SYSTIMES.DBF, SYSTIME.MEM. These files are called the *system tables*. The tables are used by SQL to record information about the data entered into the SQL database. Later in this chapter you will learn how to use the SQL system tables.

You can list the SQL databases by using the SHOW DATABASE command. Enter

```
SHOW DATABASE; ↵
```

SQL displays a list of the SQL databases, including the directory path in which the SQL database files are stored.

NAME	CREATOR	CREATED	PATH
ACCOUNTS		07/09/89	D:\DBASE\ACCOUNTS

The CREATOR column is used when SQL is operated on a password protected system. The user who issues the CREATE DATABASE has his or her name placed into the SQL system tables as the CREATOR, e.g. ACCOUNTS CAROLYN 07/09/89 E:\DBASE\ACCOUNTS. See Chapter 13 for information about the protection system.

SQL Tables

The heart of SQL operations is the *Table*, consisting of columns. (An SQL table is the same as a standard dBASE IV database.) Each column is assigned a name and a data type. SQL columns support the following types of data:

Char

Creates a character column from 1 to 254 characters in width. This is the same as a standard dBASE IV character field.

Date

Creates an 8-character date in the mm/dd/yy format, the same as a standard dBASE IV date field.

Decimal

Creates a numeric column with a fixed number of decimal places. This is similar to a standard dBASE IV numeric field, except that the decimal point is not counted as a character. A standard dBASE IV numeric field of 6 with 2 decimal places, would be the same as a NUMERIC column 5 with 2 decimal places.

Float

Creates a numeric column using the same floating-point decimal method employed by the standard dBASE IV field type FLOAT.

Integer

Creates a column for whole numbers with 11 character, 10 if a negative sign is used.

Logical

Creates a column that operates in the same manner as a standard dBASE IV logical field.

Numeric

Creates a column that operates in the same manner as a standard dBASE IV numeric field.

Smallint

Creates a column that accepts whole numbers from -99,999 to 999,999.

SQL tables do not support memo-type columns. An SQL table is limited by the same parameters as a standard dBASE IV database: 255 columns not to exceed a total of 4000 characters. Table and column names follow the same conventions and limitations as standard dBASE IV database file names (8 characters) and field names (10 characters).

There are two SQL commands that affect table structure.

CREATE TABLE. Creates a new table in the current database with the designed columns.

ALTER TABLE. Adds columns to an existing table. Similar to MODIFY STRUCTURE.

Suppose you wanted to create an SQL table that would hold the same information as the CKBOOK database created in Part I of this book. You would need to enter a CREATE TABLE command. The command has the following general form:

CREATE TABLE *table_name* (*column_list*);

The column list consists of the specifications for the table's columns. For example, to create a numeric field called amount, you would enter AMOUNT NUMERIC(10,2). Each column description is separated by a comma. The command you will enter will create a table called CHECKS with the columns DATE, CHECK_NUM, PAYEE and AMOUNT.

Entering SQL Commands

SQL and standard dBASE IV also differ as to the way commands are entered. In standard dBASE IV most procedures are the result of a series of short commands or the activation of entry modes, such as the MODIFY STRUCTURE mode. In SQL complex operations are most often the result of a single command. SQL does not use entry modes. These factors combine to create SQL commands that are long and complicated to enter. In order to make it easier to enter and read long SQL commands, you can enter the commands in two ways:

At SQL prompt. You can enter SQL commands like standard dBASE IV commands, as a single line of up to 1,024 characters. If you enter a command wider then 80 characters, the display will scroll to the right to make room for the commands.

Full Screen Editing. If you enter [Ctrl-Home] at the SQL prompt, the program displays the dBASE IV editor. You can enter the SQL command in the editor by breaking it into a number of different lines. The ↵ character will be ignored by SQL because the end of the command is marked with a semicolon. The editor makes it easier to enter SQL commands because you can place each part of the commands on a separate line. You can also use the editing options to correct any mistakes before you enter the command with [Ctrl-End].

Also keep in mind that the four character abbreviation rule that allows you to abbreviate dBASE IV commands and command words, *does not apply to SQL commands*. For example, the SQL command CREATE DATABASE accounts; *cannot* be abbreviated as CREA DATA accounts;. You must enter all SQL commands and command keywords (shown in UPPER-CASE characters) as they are shown in their full length.

In this case, use the Full Screen Editing method. Enter

```
[Ctrl-Home]
```

Enter the following command to create the CHECKS table.

```
CREATE TABLE checks  ↵
(ck_date DATE,  ↵
check_num SMALLINT,  ↵
payee CHAR(25),  ↵
amount NUMERIC(10,2));
```

You always have the option to switch to the Full-Screen mode, even if you have begun to enter the command at the SQL prompt. For example, if you enter CREATE TABLE, then decide you want to use the Full-Screen editor, you can enter [Ctrl-Home] at any time and display the commands you entered up to that point, in the editor.

You can use the history buffer in SQL as you can in standard dBASE IV by pressing the up arrow and down arrow keys to display the twenty previous commands. When you locate a command in the history buffer, it can be placed into the Full-Screen editor by entering [Ctrl-Home]. Keep in mind that in the history buffer all commands appear as single lines. If the command was written originally on several lines in the editor using [Ctrl-Home] will re-display the command in multi-line format.

To execute the command, enter

```
[Ctrl-End]
```

The window is closed and the SQL command is converted into a single-line command automatically. The command is executed, creating the new table CHECKS. SQL confirms the results of the command with the message "Table CHECKS created."

In this text all SQL commands will be written in a multi-line format. You have the option of entering the command as a single line or in a multi-line format. If you are entering the command as a single line, keep in mind that you will need to insert spaces to separate command words. For example, the CREATE TABLE command shown above in multi-line format would read as follows in a single line format:

```
CREATE TABLE checks (ck_date DATE,check_num SMALLINT,payee CHAR(25),amount
NUMERIC(10,2));
```

Note that spaces are not needed when items are written in a list separated by commas.

The ALTER TABLE command allows you to add new columns to an existing table. You might want to add a column that corresponds to the DEDUCTIBLE field in the CKBOOK database file.

To add a column to a table, use the ALTER TABLE command. The ALTER TABLE command uses the same structure as CREATE TABLE, except the keyword ADD is used to indicate the column is being added to an existing table. The SQL command language is designed to read so the meaning of the commands comes across in relatively plain English. As you will see, such commands tend to be a bit wordy as compared to programming languages that use more compact, but less descriptive syntax. Enter the command below to add a column to the table.

The multi-line format assumes that you enter [Ctrl-End] following the semicolon, if the command is entered in multi-line format, or ↵ if entered on a single line.

```
ALTER TABLE checks
ADD (deductible LOGICAL);
```

The program responds with the message "Column DEDUCTIBLE added to table CHECKS," indicating you have achieved your goal. Note that the ALTER TABLE command *always* adds the new column at the end column or rightmost position in the table. You cannot insert a new column between or to the left of existing columns.

Data Entry

When you have created a table, you will want to place data into that table. Each set of data added to the table is called a *row*. An SQL row is the same as a standard dBASE IV record.

Data entry with SQL is quite different than in standard dBASE IV. In standard dBASE IV, data is typically entered in a Full-Screen editing mode like the Edit or Browse modes, in which data is entered into input areas displayed on the screen. SQL is not designed to support specific methods of Full-Screen editing. There are three ways that information can be placed into an existing SQL table:

Insert

The INSERT command allows you to add a new row of data to an exiting table. Unlike the Edit or Browse modes in dBASE IV, INSERT is not a Full-Screen editing mode. Instead, INSERT requires that the data be written into the INSERT command as a list. The list of data items *must* conform to the order in which the column names are listed in the table structure. The INSERT command adds rows (i.e. it functions like the APPEND command in standard dBASE IV).

Update

The UPDATE command is used to add or replace existing data in a column of an existing row. The UPDATE command performs a function similar to the REPLACE ALL command in standard dBASE IV. Placing a specific value into a specific record is much more complicated in SQL. Since SQL does not maintain a record pointer, you must enter a command that contains a logical expression so the program can locate the row on which you want to make the replacement.

Load Data

The LOAD DATA command is usually the most practical SQL data entry command. This commands loads information already stored in files into an SQL table. In reality, this is the method SQL assumes will be used to enter data. The LOAD DATA command allows you to enter data in a number of different formats using dBASE IV or other common microcomputer applications. LOAD DATA operates the same as the standard dBASE IV APPEND FROM (Chapter 10).

File types that can be imported with LOAD DATA:

dBASE II, III and IV DBF files
RapidFile RPD files
Framework II FW2 files (database and spreadsheet frames)
Lotus 1-2-3 Ver 1A WKS files
Multiplan or Excel SYLK format files
Visicalc DIF files
ASCII text files delimited with commas or blanks

If you are using dBASE format files, data is placed into the columns on the basis of matching column names to field names. If the field name in the dBASE file does not match a column name, the data is ignored. If you are using non-dBASE files, the data is placed into the columns based on sequence. This means the order of the data in the file, and the order of the columns in the table must match exactly. Also, keep in mind that dates should be stored as text in the mm/dd/yy format in order to be converted to dBASE IV dates.

It is important to understand that SQL is concerned with the implementation of a standard method of formulating database queries. The creation of the databases (i.e data entry) is left open. The raw material for SQL can be created in any number of ways. For example, in dBASE IV SQL the source files of raw data are dBASE IV DBF files. Other implementations of SQL read different types of files, typically standard ASCII text files. When using SQL for retrieval, the user is not supposed to know what sort of files the data is actually stored in. For these reasons, SQL does not dictate how data entry is carried out. This may be a source of confusion to those used to a program with all necessary modules supplied as part of the application. In larger computer systems, data entry and retrieval are historically done by different departments. Because the same individual rarely enters and retrieves, the use of different techniques for data entry and retrieval would not cause any confusion. In the world of microcomputers, data entry and retrieval are often done by the same individual or group of individuals. The fact that SQL does not provide a data entry standard may appear as a weakness.

The INSERT command is impractical for all but the simplest data entry. However, it is probably a good idea to see at least one example of how it would be used. The command below adds one row to the CHECKS table. The data items are entered as a list of literal items. The date items are marked by {}, and the text items by "". The Numeric data does not require delimiters.

When you enter data, you have two options:

All Columns

When you have a data item for each column, you can simply enter the list of items so long as there is one item for each column, and the items are entered in the order in which the columns in the table were created.

Selected Columns

You can enter data into a selected group of columns by specifying two lists: one of column names and one with corresponding data items.

The command below avoids the need for a column list by assigning a data item for each column in the table. Enter

```
INSERT INTO checks
VALUES
({03/03/89},
1013,
"Acme Products",
550.5,
.T.);
```

The program displays the message "1 row(s) inserted," to confirm the entry of the row.

The next command inserts only three items into three of the five columns. In this case, it is necessary to specify the columns into which the items will be placed.

```
INSERT INTO checks
(payee,ck_date,amount)
VALUES
("Walnut Creek Supply",
{03/15/89},
275);
```

Suppose you wanted to fill in the check number in the row you just inserted. Unlike standard dBASE IV, where you could use the record number to select a specific record for updating, SQL requires you to use a logical expression to locate the row. The UPDATE command requires the use of a WHERE clause to choose the row or rows to be updated. The WHERE clause in SQL is similar to the FOR clause in standard dBASE IV. The WHERE clause requires a logical expression. Logical expressions follow the same rules in SQL as in standard dBASE IV. In this example, you want to place a check number in the row in which the PAYEE column contains *Walnut*. The UPDATE command has three parts:

UPDATE *table name*
SET *column = value*
WHERE *logical expression;*

If you leave out the WHERE clause, the command updates all the rows with the new value (the equivalent of REPLACE ALL). Enter

```
UPDATE checks
SET check_num=1014
WHERE payee="Walnut";
```

The program displays the message "1 row(s) updated," indicating that the value was placed into only one row of the table.

Displaying Data

In the previous section you inserted and updated the rows in a table. But how can you be sure of this? You need to be able to retrieve the data to confirm what you have done. The command that retrieves data in SQL is the SELECT command. Probably 90% of the operations in SQL involve some form of this command.

Do not confuse the standard dBASE IV SELECT command with the SQL SELECT command. In standard dBASE IV the SELECT command activates a work area. SQL does not use work areas. SELECT in SQL retrieves data.

The simplest form of SELECT lists columns from a specified table, as shown below.

SELECT *column name list*
FROM *table name;*

For example, to list all the check numbers from the CHECKS table, enter

```
SELECT check_num
FROM checks;
```

SQL displays the check numbers in the two rows of the table stored in the CHECK_NUM column.

```
CHECK_NUM
    1013
    1014
```

The * can be used as a symbol meaning *all columns* in the column selection area of the command. The following command lists all the columns in the table:

```
SELECT *
FROM checks;
```

The program displays all the data entered into the table, so far.

CK_DATE	CHECK_NUM	PAYEE	AMOUNT	DEDUCTIBLE
03/03/89	1013	Acme Products	550.50	.T.
03/15/89	1014	Walnut Creek Supply	275.00	.F.

If the data table produced by the selection command contains more rows than can be displayed on the screen at one time, the program will scroll the information on the display. You can freeze the scrolling by entering [Ctrl-s]. Entering [Ctrl-s] a second time resumes the scrolling. Another solution is to use the SET PAUSE ON command. This command will automatically pause the table display after each screen and wait until a key is pressed before scrolling the next screen of data.

Loading Data from a File

As you can see, inserting and updating data with SQL commands alone is a tedious and difficult business. In most cases it is simpler to enter data using the standard dBASE IV Full-Screen editing mode as provided by the Edit and Browse commands. When you enter the data into a dBASE IV DBF, file you can use the LOAD DATA command to copy the information into the SQL table.

For example, the CKBOOK file created in Part I of this book contains check information for the months of January and February. You might want to load this data into the present CHECKS table.

In loading data from a file you must take into consideration the structure of the data, as compared to the structure of the SQL table. If the file you are working with is a dBASE IV DBF file, data will be inserted into the SQL table only when the column name matches the field name exactly. If the names are not matched, the data will be ignored.

In the current table, the columns names match four of the fields in the CKBOOK DBF file (CHECK_NUM, PAYEE, AMOUNT AND DEDUCTIBLE). The only problem is the CK_DATE column does not match the DATE field. You can resolve this problem by making a copy of the CKBOOK database, in which the name of the DATE field is changed to CK_DATE.

Activate standard dBASE IV by entering

        SET SQL OFF ⏎

Keep in mind that the SQL database is still open. You have only left the SQL command mode. When you return, you can continue working with the ACCOUNTS database.

Make a copy of the CKBOOK database.

        USE ckbook ⏎
        COPY TO checks ⏎

Activate the CHECKS database and modify the structure. (Use USE EXCLUSIVE if you are working on a network.)

        USE checks ⏎
        MODIFY STRUCTURE ⏎

Change the name of the first field from DATE to CK_DATE by entering

        [Ctrl-y]
        CK_DATE
        [Ctrl-End]
        y *(2 times)*

Close the database and return to SQL.

        CLOSE ALL ⏎
        SET SQL ON ⏎

When you return to SQL, the status line shows the DB (database) ACCOUNTS is still active. You can now use the LOAD DATA command to copy the information in the CHECKS DBF file into the CHECKS table. The LOAD DATA command requires the name of the file from which the data is to be loaded, and the name of the table into which it is to be placed.

One interesting factor is the use of directories. Recall that dBASE IV SQL uses a directory, e.g. \DBASE\ACCOUNTS, to hold its files. The CKBOOK and CHECKS DBF files are stored in the default directory, e.g. \DBASE. In the LOAD DATA command the directory name is used to indicate the exact location of the file from which you want to load the data. Enter

```
LOAD DATA FROM \dbase\checks
INTO TABLE checks;
```

To confirm the addition of the data, use the SELECT command to list the contents of the table.

```
SELECT *
FROM checks;
```

SQL displays a table that contains all the information added to the CHECKS table.

CK_DATE	CHECK_NUM	PAYEE	AMOUNT	DEDUCTIBLE
03/03/89	1013	Acme Products	550.50	.T.
03/15/89	1014	Walnut Creek Supply	275.00	.F.
01/03/89	1000	Allied Office Furniture	750.50	.T.
01/03/89	1001	Central Office Supplies	97.56	.T.
01/06/89	1002	Western Telephone	101.57	.F.
01/06/89	1003	United Federal Insurance	590.00	.F.
01/10/89	1004	Computer World	2245.50	.T.
01/10/89	1005	Fathead Software	99.95	.F.
01/14/89	1006	The Bargain Warehouse	145.99	.T.
01/15/89	1007	Central Office Supplies	67.45	.F.
02/02/89	1008	Sunset Variety	25.89	.F.
02/09/89	1009	Advanced Copier Service	175.00	.F.
02/12/89	1010	Valley Power & Light	101.70	.F.
02/25/89	1011	Dept of Trans	45.00	.T.
02/27/89	1012	Western Telephone	175.75	.T.
01/01/89	1	DEPOSIT	2500.00	.F.
01/31/89	2	DEPOSIT	1200.00	.F.
02/15/89	3	DEPOSIT	1900.00	.F.

Using dBASE IV for SQL Data

The lack of an Edit or Browse mode in SQL would be a major limitation unless you understand the relationship between SQL and dBASE IV. The individual SQL tables are actually dBASE IV DBF files, modified slightly to use with SQL. The CHECKS table is stored in a file called CHECKS.DBF in the SQL directory (\DBASE\ACCOUNTS).

---

dBASE IV uses the first byte in the header of a DBF file to indicate information about the database file. Bits 4,5,6 are used to indicate the database is part of the SQL system. dBASE IV allows you to edit these databases but such commands as MODIFY STRUCTURE will not operate on files tagged as SQL databases. Structure modifications must be done through SQL.

---

dBASE IV permits you to access SQL DBF files for editing or appending, using the standard dBASE IV Edit, Browse and Append modes. For example, suppose you wanted to add a row to the CHECKS table using the Append mode.

The first step is to exit the SQL mode and return to the Dot Prompt.

```
SET SQL OFF⏎
```

You can open an SQL database file exactly as you would any DBF file, with the exception that you need to specify the directory in which the file is stored: \DBASE\ACCOUNTS. Enter

```
USE \dbase\accounts\checks.dbf ⏎
APPEND ⏎
```

Enter a deposit record.

```
031289
4 ⏎
DEPOSIT ⏎
1100
[Ctrl-End]
```

Close the database and return to SQL.

```
CLOSE ALL ⏎
SET SQL ON ⏎
```

You can check to see if the new record actually appears in the SQL table. Enter

```
SELECT *
FROM checks;
```

The new record appears as if it had been directly entered into the SQL table. Although SQL does not provide a very useful method of direct data entry, dBASE IV allows you to take advantage of its entry modes through LOAD DATA, or by directly editing an SQL database.

CK_DATE	CHECK_NUM	PAYEE	AMOUNT	DEDUCTIBLE
03/03/89	1013	Acme Products	550.50	.T.
03/15/89	1014	Walnut Creek Supply	275.00	.F.
01/03/89	1000	Allied Office Furniture	750.50	.T.
01/03/89	1001	Central Office Supplies	97.56	.T.
01/06/89	1002	Western Telephone	101.57	.F.
01/06/89	1003	United Federal Insurance	590.00	.F.
01/10/89	1004	Computer World	2245.50	.T.
01/10/89	1005	Fathead Software	99.95	.F.
01/14/89	1006	The Bargain Warehouse	145.99	.T.
01/15/89	1007	Central Office Supplies	67.45	.F.
02/02/89	1008	Sunset Variety	25.89	.F.
02/09/89	1009	Advanced Copier Service	175.00	.F.
02/12/89	1010	Valley Power & Light	101.70	.F.
02/25/89	1011	Dept of Trans	45.00	.T.
02/27/89	1012	Western Telephone	175.75	.T.
01/01/89	1	DEPOSIT	2500.00	.F.
01/31/89	2	DEPOSIT	1200.00	.F.
02/15/89	3	DEPOSIT	1900.00	.F.
03/12/89	4	DEPOSIT	1100.00	.F.

Importing Databases

SQL also provides a means by which you can load an entire dBASE IV DBF file into SQL as a table in the current database. This process is different from LOAD DATA in that it creates that table at the same time the data is imported. For example, there are three databases used in the ACCOUNTS system—BUYERS, PRODUCTS, and SALES—that could be integrated into the ACCOUNTS SQL database using the DBDEFINE command.

This command converts dBASE IV DBF files into dBASE IV SQL tables. The DBDEFINE command requires that you place a copy of the DBF files, and any production index files associated with them, into the SQL database directory. In this example that means you could copy the three specified DBF files and the MDX production index files associated with them into the \DBASE\ACCOUNTS directory.

Begin with the SALES file. Enter

```
! copy \dbase\sales.*  \dbase\accounts  ⏎
```

The SALES.DBF and SALES.MDX are copied. (The SALES.SCR file is copied along with them. You can simply ignore this file since it is not used in SQL.) Repeat the process for the BUYERS and PRODUCTS databases.

```
! copy \dbase\buyers.*  \dbase\accounts  ⏎
! copy \dbase\products.*  \dbase\accounts  ⏎
```

You have placed all the files needed into the SQL database directory. You can now use the DBDEFINE command to convert the copied files into SQL tables.

DBDEFINE can be used in two ways. You can convert a specific DBF file by using the name with DBDEFINE. If no names are used with DBDEFINE, the program searches the directory for DBF files and converts all non-SQL DBF files to tables in the current SQL database.

Version 1.0 of dBASE IV will exhibit bugs when DBDEFINE; is used without a specific file name.

Add the BUYER.DBF file to the database by entering

```
DBDEFINE buyers;
```

The program responds with the message:

```
Table(s) DBDEFINED:
BUYERS

DBDEFINE successful
```

This confirms the addition of the BUYERS DBF file to the SQL database.

Repeat the process for PRODUCTS and SALES.

```
DBDEFINE products;
```

Enter the command to add the SALES file.

```
DEDEFINE sales;
```

You now have four tables entered into the ACCOUNTS SQL database.

Selecting Data from Tables

Once you have inserted, loaded, or imported the tables and data into the SQL database, you have arrived at the place where SQL was designed to function. SQL uses essentially a single command, SELECT, to retrieve all types of data. This is in contrast to standard dBASE IV, in which the commands you need vary depending on the type of retrieval operation you need to carry out.

In SQL the SELECT command is the basis of all retrieval. Clause and options used with SELECT allow it to perform a wide variety of operations. In its simplest form, SELECT uses the FROM clause to specify the table from which the data should be displayed. For example, to list the data from the SALES table, enter

```
FROM sales;
```

The data from the table is listed. You will recognize the data as the contents of the SALES DBF file.

DATE_SOLD	QUANTITY	ACCOUNT_NO	ID
06/10/89	4	103	102
06/15/89	10	101	100
06/17/89	5	100	101
06/20/89	10	102	103
06/22/89	4	100	102
06/22/89	1	103	102
06/25/89	5	103	101
06/28/89	10	100	101

You will notice that in this display the column width is set by the width of the column names. To produce a more compact display, turn off the column headings by entering

```
SET HEADING OFF ⏎
```

Repeat the selection.

```
SELECT *
FROM sales;
```

This time the column width is changed to fit the exact width of the columns.

Since the ACCOUNT_NO column is narrower than the others, the display is a bit narrower overall.

```
06/10/89            4    103   102
06/15/89           10    101   100
06/17/89            5    100   101
06/20/89           10    102   103
06/22/89            4    100   102
06/22/89            1    103   102
06/25/89            5    103   101
06/28/89           10    100   101
```

Reactivate the headings by entering

        SET HEADING ON ⏎

Column List

The SELECT command allows you the option of selecting specific columns from a table to list. Suppose that you wanted to retrieve the last and first name columns from the BUYERS table. Enter

        SELECT last,first
        FROM buyers;

SQL retrieves a table that consists of the last and first columns from the BUYERS table.

Expressions in Column List

SQL permits you to include dBASE IV expressions as column specifications. This means that it is possible to retrieve columns similar to the result you can obtain with calculated fields in standard dBASE IV. For example, suppose you wanted to list the cost, price, and amount of profit on the items in the PRODUCTS table. Enter

        SELECT cost,price,price-cost
        FROM products;

SQL produces a table in which the third column is the result of a calculation carried on between the first two columns.

```
SQL. select cost,price,price-cost  from products;
        COST       PRICE       EXP1
        13.61      21.95        8.34
        37.17      59.95       22.78
         8.03      12.95        4.92
         3.69       5.95        2.26
```

You can display the results of most dBASE IV numeric, character or date expressions as SQL calculated columns. For example you could list the days of the week for the DATE_SOLD column using the CDOW( ) function.

```
SELECT CDOW(date_sold)
FROM sales;

CDOW(DATE_SOLD)
Saturday
Thursday
Saturday
Tuesday
Thursday
Thursday
Sunday
Wednesday
```

The Where Clause

The WHERE clause is used with the SELECT and other SQL commands to create a logical criterion by which rows are selected as part of an SQL query. The WHERE clause can accept any valid dBASE IV logical expression. In SQL expressions, column names take the place of field names.

Suppose you wanted to select all the checks with a date in the month of February. You would use an expression like MONTH(ck_date)=2. Note that you can use most dBASE IV functions and operators in SQL logical expressions. Enter

```
SELECT *
FROM checks
WHERE MONTH(ck_date)=2;
```

The program displays the records that qualify for the selection.

CK_DATE	CHECK_NUM	PAYEE	AMOUNT	DEDUCTIBLE
02/02/89	1008	Sunset Variety	25.89	.F.
02/09/89	1009	Advanced Copier Service	175.00	.F.
02/12/89	1010	Valley Power & Light	101.70	.F.
02/25/89	1011	Dept of Trans	45.00	.T.
02/27/89	1012	Western Telephone	175.75	.T.
02/15/89	3	DEPOSIT	1900.00	.F.

SQL also keeps track of the number of rows selected. The system variable sqlcnt (SQL count) is updated after each SELECT command to contain a value equal to the number of rows selected. You can use the variable like any memory variable. Keep in mind that the value will change automatically after each selection. To display the number of rows selected by the last SELECT command, enter

```
? sqlcnt ⏎
```

The program displays the number 6, the number of rows selected by the last command.

Logical Operators

SQL uses the same logical operators as dBASE IV, but the syntax is slightly different.

dBASE IV	SQL
.NOT.	NOT
.OR.	OR
.AND.	AND

Logical operators serve the same purpose in SQL. They are used to create compound expressions. The NOT operator is used to invert the value of an expression. For example, suppose that you wanted to list all the checks *not* deductible. Enter

```
SELECT*
FROM checks
WHERE NOT deductible;
```

The program lists all the checks that have a .F. value in the DEDUCTIBLE column.

CK_DATE	CHECK_NUM	PAYEE	AMOUNT	DEDUCTIBLE
03/15/89	1014	Walnut Creek Supply	275.00	.F.
01/06/89	1002	Western Telephone	101.57	.F.
01/06/89	1003	United Federal Insurance	590.00	.F.
01/10/89	1005	Fathead Software	99.95	.F.
01/15/89	1007	Central Office Supplies	67.45	.F.
02/02/89	1008	Sunset Variety	25.89	.F.
02/09/89	1009	Advanced Copier Service	175.00	.F.
02/12/89	1010	Valley Power & Light	101.70	.F.
01/01/89	1	DEPOSIT	2500.00	.F.
01/31/89	2	DEPOSIT	1200.00	.F.
02/15/89	3	DEPOSIT	1900.00	.F.
03/12/89	4	DEPOSIT	1100.00	.F.

The AND and OR operators allow you to create compound predicates that are exclusive (AND) or inclusive (OR). Suppose you wanted to retrieve all the deposits made in January. This requires two conditions, selecting for January and selecting for DEPOSIT in the PAYEE column. The AND operator is used to join the two expressions.

```
SELECT *
FROM checks
WHERE MONTH(ck_date)=2
AND payee="DEPOSIT";
```

The program selects a table that consists of two deposits made in January. Suppose you now wanted to list the checks only from January. This would require the addition of the NOT operator.

```
SELECT *
FROM checks
WHERE MONTH(ck_date)=2
AND NOT payee="DEPOSIT";
```

SQL also contains three other logical predicates. They are:

BETWEEN

This predicate is a shortcut way to express a restriction in terms of a numerical range. In dBASE IV if you want to select amounts between 100 and 200, you must use an expression like:
amount>=100.AND.amount<=200
The BETWEEN predicate simplifies the expression to *amount BETWEEN 100 AND 200.*

LIKE

The LIKE predicate allows you to use a wildcard expression for matching data. An underscore character (_) will match any single character and a % matches any group of characters. (The _ and % work in a manner similar to the ? and * wildcards in DOS.)

---

dBASE IV has a function called LIKE( ), which allows you to implement wildcard-like matches similar to the effect of the LIKE predicate in SQL. Note that the dBASE IV LIKE( ) function uses the character ? and * for wildcard representations.

IN

The IN predicate allows you to match a column with one of a list of items. IN is a shorthand version of a series of expressions using the same column name linked by OR operators. For example, you could select rows for the Virginia/Maryland area with the expression WHERE state IN ("VA","MD").

The $ operator can be used in a similar manner to the IN predicate. The state example would be written as *state$"VA MD"* .

Suppose that you wanted to select the rows from the CHECKS tables with values between 500 and 1000. Enter the following SQL command.

```
SELECT *
FROM checks
WHERE amount BETWEEN 500 AND 1000;
```

The program returns a table with three checks that fall into that range.

```
CK DATE      CHECK_NUM PAYEE                      AMOUNT DEDUCTIBLE
03/03/89         1013 Acme Products              550.50 .T.
01/03/89         1000 Allied Office Furniture    750.50 .T.
01/06/89         1003 United Federal Insurance   590.00 .F.
```

The LIKE predicate is used on character columns when you want to select rows with a partial match. In many cases the effect of the LIKE predicate can be duplicated by standard dBASE IV expressions. One type of match not easily duplicated in dBASE IV is a right end match. For example, suppose you wanted to select rows from the CHECKS table in which the payee name ended with the word *Insurance*. In a LIKE predicate the wild-card string "%Insurance" would select those rows. Enter

```
SELECT *
FROM checks
WHERE payee LIKE "%Insurance";
```

The selection returns a single row.

```
SQL. select * from checks where payee like "%Insurance";
CK DATE      CHECK_NUM PAYEE                      AMOUNT DEDUCTIBLE
01/06/89         1003 United Federal Insurance   590.00 .F.
```

The IN predicate is used when you want to select records based on a match of one value from a list of possible values. This type of selection is useful when a group consists of items not numerically or alphabetically similar. For example, a sales territory could logically combine Virginia and Maryland, although the spelling of the names gives no clue as to their proximity. Enter

```
SELECT city,state
FROM buyers
WHERE state IN ("VA","MD");
```

The command retrieves two rows from the BUYERS table.

```
CITY            STATE
Baltimore       MD
Richmond        VA
```

You can also use IN to select from a list of dates or numeric values. In the example below, all rows in the SALES table that match account numbers 100 or 102 are selected.

```
SELECT*
FROM sales
WHERE account_no IN(100,102);
```

DATE_SOLD	QUANTITY	ACCOUNT_NO	ID
06/20/89	10	102	103
06/22/89	4	100	102
06/28/89	10	100	101

The SQL predicates provide flexibility in the writing of SQL expressions in a language that is structured like English sentences and less mathematical than standard dBASE IV. Of course, English-like commands are always more wordy, therefore more time consuming to type. If you are used to short dBASE IV commands, you will find SQL commands a great deal longer to enter, since each command operates as a complete set of retrieval instructions. In standard dBASE IV, the work is divided between several commands, such as USE, to select the database, and LIST, to display the data. The SELECT command contains the table, column, and criterion information in a single command.

Getting Database Information

In standard dBASE IV, there are a number of ways to obtain information about the database files with which you are working. The LIST STRUCTURE and LIST STATUS commands display a wide range of information. The STATUS line also displays information about the current database.

In SQL this information is not as readily available. For example, suppose you wanted to display the names of the columns of a specific table. SQL does not recognize the LIST STRUCTURE command. Instead, SQL stores information about the SQL database in special files called *systems tables*. These tables are:

Table Name

SYSAUTH	contains information about table protection
SYSCOLAU	contains information about column protection
SYSCOLS	contains information about all columns in all tables
SYSIDXS	contains information about indexes
SYSKEYS	contains index key expressions for columns
SYSSYNS	contains information about SQL synonyms
SYSTABLS	contains information about tables and Views
SYSTIMES	contains time stamp information for network operations
SYSVDEPS	contains information about SQL Views
SYSVIEWS	contains details about SQL Views

The SYSCOLS table would be the one to work with in order to obtain information about the structure of a table. The SYSCOLS table contains the following columns:

Column Name	Data
COLNAME	column name
TBNAME	table name
TBCREATOR	user id (protection system)
COLNO	column number
COLTYPE	column data type
COLLEN	column width
COLSCALE	decimal places
NULLS	not used
COLCARD	number of unique values, indexed column
UPDATES	Y/N accept updates

For example, to display the column names from the CHECKS table, enter

```
SELECT colname,coltype,collen
FROM syscols
WHERE tbname="CHECKS";
```

All column and table names are stored in upper-case characters in the system tables. Make sure that you use upper-case characters when trying to match column or table names.

The information returned is equivalent to the LIST STRUCTURE information available in standard dBASE IV.

COLNAME	COLTYPE	COLLEN
CK_DATE	D	8
CHECK_NUM	N	6
PAYEE	C	25
AMOUNT	N	10
DEDUCTIBLE	L	1

Sequencing Selections

In standard dBASE IV, the sequence in which records appear is controlled by the index tags, when they exist, selected as the master index at the time when a retrieval command is issued. Note once again that in standard dBASE IV, it is the order in which the commands are processed that determines the outcome.

In SQL the order of the records is determined by the use of the ORDER BY clause with the SELECT command. You can select ascending (ASC) or descending (DESC) order. If no specification is made, ascending order is assumed.

It is important to remember that the column or columns used for sequencing the rows *must appear* in the column list following the SELECT command. For example, if you want to order the rows by zip code, the ZIP column must be included in the column list.

If you are operating on a network, it is necessary to place the program into EXCLUSIVE use when you are using an ORDER BY clause. This is because dBASE IV requires that databases be opened in the EXCLUSIVE mode if indexing or sorting is to be performed. Network users enter

```
SET EXCLUSIVE ON ⏎
```

Retrieve a listing of the city, state, and zip codes from the BUYERS table, in ZIP code order. Enter

```
SELECT city,state,zip
FROM buyers
ORDER BY zip;
```

The program retrieves that data in ZIP code order—ascending order by default.

```
CITY          STATE    ZIP
Baltimore     MD       21202
Richmond      VA       23229
Lincoln       NE       68506
Santa Fe      NM       76345
Los Angeles   CA       90044
```

You can reverse the sequence of the rows with the DESC option. Enter

```
SELECT city,state,zip
FROM buyers
ORDER BY zip DESC;
```

```
SQL. SELECT city,state,zip  FROM buyers ORDER BY zip
CITY          STATE   ZIP
Los Angeles   CA      90044
Santa Fe      NM      76345
Lincoln       NE      68506
Richmond      VA      23229
Baltimore     MD      21202
```

You can combine a WHERE and ORDER BY clause. Fr example, suppose that you wanted to retrieve the checks in payee order. Note that the WHERE clause precedes the ORDER.

```
SELECT *
FROM checks
WHERE NOT payee="DEPOSIT"
ORDER BY payee;
```

CK DATE	CHECK NUM	PAYEE	AMOUNT	DEDUCTIBLE
03/03/89	1013	Acme Products	550.50	.T.
02/09/89	1009	Advanced Copier Service	175.00	.F.
01/03/89	1000	Allied Office Furniture	750.50	.T.
01/03/89	1001	Central Office Supplies	97.56	.T.
01/15/89	1007	Central Office Supplies	67.45	.F.
01/10/89	1004	Computer World	2245.50	.T.
02/25/89	1011	Dept of Trans	45.00	.T.
01/10/89	1005	Fathead Software	99.95	.F.
02/02/89	1008	Sunset Variety	25.89	.F.
01/14/89	1006	The Bargain Warehouse	145.99	.T.
01/06/89	1003	United Federal Insurance	590.00	.F.
02/12/89	1010	Valley Power & Light	101.70	.F.
03/15/89	1014	Walnut Creek Supply	275.00	.F.
01/06/89	1002	Western Telephone	101.57	.F.
02/27/89	1012	Western Telephone	175.75	.T.

Indexes in SQL

In Part I of this book the difference between sorting and indexing database files was discussed in detail. When you use an ORDER BY clause with an SQL command, it is not apparent how SQL is creating the order, since SQL hides the processing of the rows from the user.

Since dBASE IV SQL is based on standard dBASE IV operations, the difference between indexing and sorting is significant in terms of performance. Sorting is the slower method because the table must be sorted each time a query is made. If an index exists for a specific column, SQL uses the index order that is immediately available because it is stored in an index file. The use of indexes with SQL speeds up the processing of selections ordered by those columns for which an index is established.

If you find you are using a particular column for ordering, you will benefit by creating an index for that column.

Unlike standard dBASE IV, indexes can be created only for actual columns in SQL. In standard dBASE IV, indexes can be built using expressions instead of actual field data.

You can obtain a list of the indexes currently stored as part of the SQL database by selecting information from the SYSIDXS table. Enter

```
SELECT tbname,ixname
FROM sysidxs;
```

SELECT lists all the indexes available for all the tables in the SQL database.

```
TBNAME       IXNAME
BUYERS       COMPANY
BUYERS       LAST
BUYERS       ACCOUNT_NO
PRODUCTS     VENDOR
PRODUCTS     ITEM
PRODUCTS     ID
SALES        DATE_SOLD
```

Suppose that the ZIP code order used in the previous section was commonly used to retrieve data. To speed up processing of a query based on that order, enter

```
CREATE INDEX zip
ON buyers
(zip);
```

The program responds with the message "Index ZIP created." You might want to make a record index for the ZIP column for a descending order. Note that in the following command the name of the index is different from the column name. Enter

```
CREATE INDEX zip_desc
ON buyers
(zip DESC);
```

The program responds with the message "Index ZIP_DESC created." You can create the command to list the names of the indexes to see if SQL has actually added the new orders to the database index list.

```
SELECT tbname,ixname
FROM sysidxs;
```

The new index orders are added to the list of index orders available to SQL. Keep in mind that SQL will not show any signs that you have established indexes for columns. SQL will automatically use the index orders when required to implement a query. The only difference between having and not having an index for a column is the overall speed at which the query can be processed. With small tables, such as those used in this book, there is little perceptible difference in performance. However, on large tables the performance advantage is significant.

```
TBNAME       IXNAME
BUYERS       COMPANY
BUYERS       LAST
BUYERS       ACCOUNT_NO
PRODUCTS     VENDOR
PRODUCTS     ITEM
PRODUCTS     ID
SALES        DATE_SOLD
BUYERS       ZIP
BUYERS       ZIP_DESC
```

ORDER BY clauses that refer to indexed columns do not require the SET EXCLUSIVE ON setting when running in a network environment. This is because index orders are maintained as data is added or changed in the database tables, and a complete sort is not needed to sequence the rows at the time of retrieval.

Unique Indexes

Both standard dBASE IV and SQL use UNIQUE indexes. The meaning of a UNIQUE index, however, is different in SQL than it is in standard dBASE IV.

In standard dBASE IV, a UNIQUE index ignores records that have duplicate values for the index key expression. The effect is to process the records in the database, skipping those with duplicate key values.

In SQL, a UNIQUE index is created to *prevent* the entry of rows with values in the index column, which match a value in any of the existing rows. For example, unique identification numbers, such as social security numbers, account numbers, or product numbers, ought to be unique (i.e. no two rows having the same value in that column). If you create a UNIQUE-type SQL index, SQL will check each row being added or updated, and rejects an entry if one of the rows contains a duplicate value in that column.

In the ACCOUNTS database the ID column in the PRODUCTS table or the ACCOUNT_NO column in the BUYERS table are typical examples of columns that should logically contain unique values.

There is already an index for this column. dBASE IV SQL will not create a new index with the same name (i.e. overwrite the old index) as will standard dBASE IV. In order to create a new index, you must first Drop (delete) the old index. To drop an index you need enter only the index name.

This implies that index names in SQL must be unique. If two tables have the same column name you must create a unique index name for one of the columns if you intend to have indexes for both columns.

In this case, create a new index for the ACCOUNT_NO column in the BUYERS table. Drop the existing index by entering

```
DROP INDEX account_no;
```

The program confirms the deletion with the message "Index ACCOUNT_NO dropped." Next, create a new index for that column using the UNIQUE option.

```
CREATE UNIQUE INDEX account
ON buyers
(account_no);
```

It is necessary to use an abbreviated name for the ACCOUNT_NO index because SQL only allows 8-character index names. When indexes are imported as part of a DBDEFINE operation, SQL permits the existence of 10-character index names. The 8-character limit is enforced, however, when creating an index from SQL.

The program confirms the creation of the index with the message "Index ACCOUNT created." The UNIQUE index will prevent you from entering a row in the BUYERS table with a duplicate account number. You can test this by inserting a row into the BUYERS table with a duplicate account number. Enter

```
INSERT INTO buyer
(Company,city,account_no)
VALUES
("Jan's World of the Unusual","San  Francisco",100);
```

The program rejects the command because the account number, 100, is a duplicate of an existing number. Cancel the command

```
⌐
```

Change the command to read

```
INSERT INTO buyer
(Company,city,account_no)
VALUES
("Jan's World of the Unusual","San  Francisco",105);
```

This time the row is accepted because the account number is not a duplicate.

Unlike normal indexes, UNIQUE indexes have a tendency to slow down SQL processing when you are using INSERT and UPDATE commands. This is because the program must check all the rows in the table to make sure that the new or revised row does not contain duplicate information. Use UNIQUE indexes only when necessary to avoid performance degradation.

Distinct Selections

A variation on the idea of a unique index would be to select only those rows that have a unique value in a particular column. This form of SELECT is equivalent to a UNIQUE index in standard dBASE IV in which duplicate records are skipped in an index listing.

For example, suppose you wanted to list each product number that appears in the SALES table once. This selection would provide a list of products that have been sold at least one time. Enter

```
SELECT DISTINCT id
FROM sales;
```

The program retrieves the four unique values found in that column.

```
ID
100
101
102
103
```

Keep in mind that the DISTINCT clause defines a unique value, based on the columns listed in the command. For example, if you had listed the columns ID and ACCOUNT_NO, a duplicate row would have to have the same ID and ACCOUNT_NO combination as another row that would be skipped as a duplicate. The DISTINCT clause cannot be applied to just one of the columns.

The SELECT DISTINCT command uses a standard dBASE IV INDEX ON/UNIQUE command to create a temporary index for the selection. The SQL command must conform to the standard dBASE IV index key limitation of 100 characters. Therefore, the columns listed with SELECT DISTINCT must have a total width of 100 characters or less.

Summary Queries

SQL selections can be used to calculate specific values. SQL uses five *aggregate* functions that can be used in place of the column list with the SELECT command. These *aggregate* functions are:

Function	Calculation
AVG( )	calculates the numeric average
COUNT( )	number of rows selected same as SQLCNT value
SUM( )	total of a numeric column
MIN( )	lowest value in column, character, numeric or date
MAX( )	highest value in column, character, numeric or date

For example, to calculate the total amount of the AMOUNT column in the CHECKS table, enter

```
SELECT SUM(amount)
FROM checks;
```

The program calculates the value and displays it under the heading SUM1.

```
        SUM1
       12147.36
```

You can combine the aggregate functions with the WHERE clause to calculate selectively. Suppose that you wanted to total only the checks in the CHECKS table. Enter

```
SELECT SUM(amount)
FROM checks
WHERE NOT payee="DEPOSIT";
```

The program calculates the total of the checks only.

```
        SUM1
       5447.36
```

Change the command to calculate the value of the DEPOSITS by removing the NOT operator. Enter

```
SELECT SUM(amount)
FROM checks
WHERE payee="DEPOSIT";
```

The total of the deposits is displayed.

```
        SUM1
        6700
```

Another way to summarize the data in a table is by subtotal groups. This type of summary is produced in standard dBASE IV by a report with subtotal groups, or the TOTAL command. For example, suppose you wanted to calculate the total number of units of each product sold based on the data stored in the SALES table.

The SELECT command would list a column or columns to identify the rows as well as an aggregate function to perform a calculation on each group. Enter

```
SELECT id, SUM(quantity)
FROM sales
GROUP BY id;
```

The program returns a list of unique ID numbers with the total quantity sold, calculated for each ID. Note the G_ that appears before ID indicates that ID is a group column.

```
    G_ID   SUM1
    100     10
    101     20
    102      9
    103     10
```

The HAVING clause allows you to select groups by virtue of the group value. The HAVING clause is interesting because it operates on the results of the aggregate function, rather than the row data itself. The WHERE clause selects rows, directly based on their column contents.

Suppose you wanted to list only those product ID numbers that have sold more than ten units. You would use a HAVING clause rather than a WHERE clause, because the selection is based on the result of a GROUP BY aggregate function, not directly on the contents of the QUANTITY column.

The expression used by the HAVING clause will include an aggregate function. The expression *SUM(quantity)>10* would select aggregate totals that exceed ten. Enter

```
SELECT id, SUM(quantity)
FROM sales
GROUP BY id
HAVING SUM(quantity)>10;
```

The HAVING clause selects the one group whose sales exceed ten units.

G_ID	SUM1
101	20

Indirect Totals

One disadvantage of the SQL processing is that the GROUP BY clause can form groups based solely on the basis of column data. This is often a handicap when you want to group rows according to month. If the column contains the full date, it cannot be used to group according to month. The solution is to create a new column and fill it with the month value of the dates based on the date stored in another column.

Suppose you wanted to total the checks by month. The first step would be to create a new column for the month. You would use the ALTER TABLE command. Enter

```
ALTER TABLE checks
ADD (ck_month CHAR(15));
```

The program confirms the creation of the column with the message "Column CK_MONTH added to table CHECKS." Next, use the UPDATE command to fill the new column with the name of the month. The key to this procedure is you can use dBASE IV character, numeric, and date expressions with the UPDATE command. In this case, use the CMONTH( ) function to place the name of the month into the CK_MONTH columns. Enter

```
UPDATE checks
SET ck_month=CMONTH(ck_date);
```

Because no WHERE clause was used with the UPDATE command, SQL displays a message warning you you will change all the rows in the table. Enter

⏎

All 19 rows are updated. The next command will use the CK_MONTH column to total the checks for each month. Note that a WHERE clause is used to eliminate the DEPOSIT rows from the operation.

```
SELECT ck_month,SUM(amount)
FROM checks
WHERE NOT payee="DEPOSIT"
GROUP BY ck_month;
```

The program displays totals for the three months for which there are checks in the CHECKS table.

```
G_CK_MONTH                SUM1
February                523.34
January                4098.52
March                  825.50
```

Multiple Table Selections

Up to this point, all the selections you have been making draw data from a single table. One of the most powerful features of SQL is its ability to draw data stored in several tables with a single selection.

In standard dBASE IV, drawing related sets of data from more than one database file requires a series of commands that include commands to open files in different work areas and create relations among the various database files. In SQL, all the data tables are part of a single database. SQL does not require that you open specific files in specific work areas, or that you designate relations between tables.

All the procedures needed to retrieve the data are automatically generated by SQL. All you need enter is a SELECT command that specifies which data set you want to retrieve.

For example, suppose you wanted to retrieve a list of companies with the date of the sales made to those companies. That list requires data from both the SALES table and the BUYERS table. The company names drawn from the BUYERS table are matched to sales dates by the column both tables have in common, ACCOUNT_NO.

In terms of SQL notation, you need to use a SELECT command with a FROM and WHERE clause. The SELECT command is followed by the list of columns to be displayed. As long as the column name is unique, you do not have to indicate the table from which it is drawn. This makes selecting columns simpler than selecting fields in standard dBASE IV, which requires an alias name for each field in a non-selected database.

The FROM clause lists the tables being used for the selection. The tables can be listed in any order.

The WHERE clause plays an important part in a multiple table selection. The WHERE clause must contain an expression that indicates how the information in the tables is to be related. SQL refers to this relation as a *join*.

The *join* condition is a logical expression typically relating two columns, one from each table, which contain matching values. In the case of SALES and BUYERS tables, the matching columns are the ACCOUNT_NO columns. When two tables contain columns with the same name, SQL allows you to differentiate between the two by adding the table name as a prefix to the column name. A period character is used as punctuation.

This means that if you want to refer to the ACCOUNT_NO column in the BUYERS table, you would use BUYERS.ACCOUNT_NO. The ACCOUNT_NO column in the SALES table would be SALES.ACCOUNT_NO.

When all three elements are placed into a single selection command, they provide SQL with a description of how to retrieve the desired data. Enter

```
SELECT company,date_sold
FROM buyers,sales
WHERE sales.account_no=buyers.account_no;
```

The SQL command generates the dBASE IV operations necessary to create a relation between the two tables, and thereby retrieve the related data. Note that in SQL you do not have to know what is going on behind the scenes. The results of the previous command appear as a two-column table.

BUYERS->COMPANY	SALES->DATE_SOLD
Northgate Specialty Company	06/10/89
Genie Light and Magic	06/15/89
House of Magic	06/17/89
Clay's House of Fun	06/20/89
House of Magic	06/22/89
Northgate Specialty Company	06/22/89
Northgate Specialty Company	06/25/89
House of Magic	06/28/89

The display shows that SQL performs the join in a manner similar to the way standard dBASE IV handles relations. In this case, the program looked up the company name that matched the account numbers found in the SALES table. The same name repeats each time the account number repeats in the SALES table. You do not have to include the join columns in the selected table. The join columns function in the background to determine which rows in the tables will be matched together.

The headings on the columns use the standard dBASE IV alias notation *alias_name->field_name*. This is a clue that dBASE IV SQL uses the commands and operations detailed in Part I of this book, to create multiple database relations.

You can use an ORDER BY clause to sequence the rows by one of the columns specified in the SELECT command. The following command retrieves the same table ordered by company name.

```
SELECT company,date_sold
FROM buyers,sales
WHERE sales.account_no=buyers.account_no
ORDER BY company;
```

```
BUYERS->COMPANY                      SALES->DATE_SOLD
Clay's House of Fun                  06/20/89
Genie Light and Magic                06/15/89
House of Magic                       06/17/89
House of Magic                       06/22/89
House of Magic                       06/28/89
Northgate Specialty Company          06/10/89
Northgate Specialty Company          06/22/89
Northgate Specialty Company          06/25/89
```

Multiple table selections can also use calculated columns. Suppose you wanted to use SQL to retrieve a table that showed the date, quantity, unit price, and the total amount of the sale. The data requires a Join between the SALES and PRODUCTS tables, based on the ID column. In addition, the total amount of the sales, is a calculation between the QUANTITY column of the SALES table and the PRICE column of the PRODUCTS table.

Despite the complexity of the request, it can be handled with a single SQL selection command. Enter

```
SELECT date_sold,quantity,price,price*quantity
FROM sales,products
WHERE sales.id=products.id;
```

The program retrieves the data from the requested columns and also calculates the values for the expression. The calculated column is labeled EXP1.

SALES->DATE_SOLD	SALES->QUANTITY	PRODUCTS->PRICE	EXP1
06/10/89	4	12.95	51.80
06/15/89	10	21.95	219.50
06/17/89	5	59.95	299.75
06/20/89	10	5.95	59.50
06/22/89	4	12.9	551.80
06/22/89	1	12.95	12.95
06/25/89	5	59.95	299.75
06/28/89	10	59.95	599.50

Suppose instead of the date of the sale, you wanted to list the company name along with the quantity, price, and total. This table would require the use of *three* tables: SALES, PRODUCTS and BUYERS.

The SQL command needed to retrieve this data follows the same pattern as the previous multiple table commands. The only difference is that you need to enter two Join expressions. One specifies the Join between SALES and PRODUCTS, while the other specifies the Join between SALES and BUYERS. The two Join criteria are merged with an AND operator. The two Join expressions are placed on individual lines in the command below. This has no effect on the meaning of the command. It is done to make the logic of the selection command easier to read. When writing SQL commands you can take advantage of the multi-line format to write the specifications in small chunks. This often makes it easier to compose a complicated command. Enter

```
SELECT company,quantity,price,price*quantity
FROM sales,products,buyers
WHERE
sales.id=products.id
AND
sales.account_no=buyers.account_no;
```

The program retrieves a table of data, which relates the information stored in all three tables. Because the company column is 35-characters wide, each row of the table is 82-characters wide. This causes the lines to wrap the last two characters onto the next line.

Since the SELECT column list can include calculated columns, you can use dBASE IV expressions to control the way values are displayed. For example, to limit the width of a particular character column, you can use the LEFT( ) function to select part of the column for display. In numeric columns you can use the TRANSFORM( ) function to create formatted numeric displays such as those created by the picture templates used in standard dBASE IV. The command below uses dBASE IV functions to truncate the COMPANY column to 30 characters, allowing each row to fit on a single line of screen display.

```
SELECT LEFT(company,30),quantity,price,price*quantity
FROM sales,products,buyers
WHERE
sales.id=products.id
AND
sales.account_no=buyers.account_no;
```

The table displayed is much easier to read because you have cut down the row length to fit on the 80-column display.

LEFT(BUYERS->COMPANY,30)	SALES->QUANTITY	PRODUCTS->PRICE	EXP1
Northgate Specialty Company	4	12.95	51.80
Genie Light and Magic	10	21.95	219.50
House of Magic	5	59.95	299.75
Clay's House of Fun	10	5.95	59.50
House of Magic	4	12.9	551.80
Northgate Specialty Company	1	12.95	12.95
Northgate Specialty Company	5	59.95	299.75
House of Magic	10	59.95	599.50

Adding an ORDER BY clause can sequence the table in a specific order. Note that the ORDER BY clause must use one of the column names used in the SELECT column list. The command below displays the company name and the total amount of the sale in order by company name. Enter

```
SELECT company,price*quantity
FROM sales,products,buyers
WHERE sales.id=products.id
AND
sales.account_no=buyers.account_no
ORDER BY company;
```

The command produces a two-column table ordered by the company name.

```
BUYERS->COMPANY                        EXP1
Clay's House of Fun                   59.50
House of Magic                       219.50
House of Magic                       299.75
House of Magic                        51.80
Genie Light and Magic                599.50
Northgate Specialty Company           51.80
Northgate Specialty Company           12.95
Northgate Specialty Company          299.75
```

Summaries with Multiple Tables

Suppose you wanted to use a multiple table query to calculate summary information, using aggregate functions such as SUM( ) or AVG( ), or the GROUP BY clause to calculate sub-totals for groups.

Assume you want to calculate the total amount of all sales. The way the tables are structured, this requires the sum of the product of the QUANTITY column from the SALES table, multiplied by the PRICE column from the PRODUCTS table. The summary calculation can be made by using the expression *quantity*price* as the argument for the SUM( ) aggregate function, e.g. *SUM(quantity*price)*.

In order to match the prices with the quantities, the tables will be joined in the product ID column. Enter

```
SELECT SUM(price*quantity)
FROM sales,products
WHERE sales.id=products.id;
```

The command causes the program to relate the rows in the joined tables and arrive at the total value of all sales.

```
                 SUM1
                 1594
                 .55
```

Once the Join criteria are set, you can perform several calculations. The command below calculates the total cost and profit for all the sales.

```
SELECT SUM(price*quantity),SUM(cost*quantity),
SUM(price*quantity-cost*quantity)
FROM sales,products
WHERE sales.id=products.id;
```

The results of the three calculations are displayed.

```
   SUM1         SUM2          SUM3
 1594.55       988.67        605.88
```

Another type of summary table is one that uses the GROUP BY clause along with a specific calculation to arrive at group subtotals. If you wanted to list the total sales for each of the products sold, you would have to group the rows by the ITEM column in the PRODUCTS table. In order to calculate the total amount of each product you must join the PRODUCTS table with the SALES table on the product ID column. The command below calculates the total sales grouped by ITEM.

```
SELECT item,SUM(price*quantity)
FROM sales,products
WHERE sales.id=products.id
GROUP BY item;
```

The table that results shows the totals for each of the inventory items sold.

```
G_ITEM                      SUM1
Cards                     219.50
Groucho glasses            59.50
Knotted scarves              1199
Woopie Cushion            116.55
```

You can perform a similar calculation, finding the totals for each *company* by linking all three tables, again. In this case, the displayed columns will draw data from all three tables. Each pair of tables is related by part of a compound Join expression. Enter

```
SELECT company,SUM(price*quantity)
FROM sales,products,buyers
WHERE
sales.id=products.id
AND
sales.account_no=buyers.account_no
GROUP BY company;
```

The table that results shows group totals for each of the companies that have purchased items.

```
G_COMPANY                   SUM1
Clay's House of Fun        59.50
Genie Light and Magic     219.50
House of Magic            951.05
Northgate Specialty       364.50
Company
```

SQL multiple table operations do not require the user to specify the exact mechanisms by which the data in the joined tables is related. By specifying the Join criteria, the user then allows SQL to use its own methods of arriving at the resulting table. In standard dBASE IV, the user must open files and create relations, in order to obtain similar results. In SQL all the tables in the database can be used with any SELECT command, without having to open or relate files.

Views

As you work with a particular SQL database, you will find there are specific selection commands you will perform repeatedly. In some cases, the command you repeat will use largely the same information with small variations, such as WHERE clauses to narrow the number of rows selected.

SQL Views provide a means of storing a complex selection command as a single View. You can then select information based on the View name instead of the column and tables, which comprise the View. The advantage of a View is you can eliminate the entry of a complicated or wordy selection command you tend to use often.

For example, if you refer to the table structure from time to time, you might want to create Views that simplify the selection of data from the system tables. The command that selects the structure information about the BUYERS table would be:

```
SELECT colname,coltype,collen
FROM syscols
WHERE tbname="BUYERS";
```

The CREATE VIEW command uses the AS clause to define a View name as an entire selection command. In CREATE VIEW the text of the selection is the View specification. The command that follows creates an SQL View called ST_BUY (structure BUYERS). Enter

```
CREATE VIEW st_buy
AS
SELECT colname,coltype,collen
FROM syscols
WHERE tbname="BUYERS";
```

The result of the command is not a table listing, but the creation of a View confirmed with the message "View ST_BUY created." The View can then be used in a selection command as if it were a table. For example, to display the structure of the BUYER table. Enter

```
SELECT *
FROM st_buy;
```

The View carries out the original selection stored under that View name, listing the data from the SYSCOLs tables about the structure of the BUYERS table.

```
COLNAME          COLTYPE    COLLEN
COMPANY          C              35
FIRST            C              20
LAST             C              20
STREET           C              35
CITY             C              20
STATE            C               2
ZIP              C               5
ACCOUNT_NO       N               4
PHONE            C              12
EXTENSION        C               4
```

The advantage of the View is that you have simplified what you must enter and remember, in order to obtain the information.

Views can contain any valid SQL selection. Suppose you wanted to display customers, dates of purchase, and items purchased. This query would require a three-table joined selection.

```
SELECT company,date_sold,item
FROM buyers,sales,products
WHERE
sales.id=products.id
AND
sales.account_no=buyers.account_no;
```

Because this is a table you might want to produce on a regular basis, you could simplify the selection by creating a View. The command below creates a View called ACTIVITY, which contains the three-table Join selection, shown above. Enter

```
CREATE VIEW activity
AS
SELECT company,date_sold,item
FROM buyers,sales,products
WHERE
sales.id=products.id
AND
sales.account_no=buyers.account_no;
```

You can now use that View to display all or part of the information selected by that View. To display the entire table, enter

```
SELECT *
FROM activity;
```

By using the View name you reduce significantly the size of the command you need to enter. Further, you can treat the View as if it were a table. For example, you could display the item and company by item order with the following command, using the ACTIVITY View as if it were a defined table.

```
SELECT item,company
FROM activity
ORDER BY item;
```

```
ITEM                  COMPANY
Cards                 Genie Light and Magic
Groucho glasses       Clay's House of Fun
Knotted scarves       House of Magic
Knotted scarves       Northgate Specialty Company
Knotted scarves       House of Magic
Woopie Cushion        Northgate Specialty Company
Woopie Cushion        House of Magic
Woopie Cushion        Northgate Specialty Company
```

Views allow you to create subsets of data that can in turn be treated as sets, or subdivided into smaller sets. Also, you can reduce the complexity of a given query by storing commonly used base selections as Views.

New Tables

Another useful tool lies in the ability to create a new table out of data selected from existing tables. Tables created in this manner are usually temporary tables, which will be dropped automatically from the database when it is stopped, or dBASE IV is terminated. You can select to make a table a permanent part of an SQL database if desired.

The purpose of the new tables is to allow you to manipulate data in ways that may not be possible, as they are stored in the current database tables. Temporary tables allow you to make changes to a column or columns using the UPDATE command, without losing the original data.

For example, suppose you wanted to calculate the balance of the checking account. This is more difficult in SQL than in standard dBASE IV because SQL will not perform aggregate operations such as SUM( ) on the results of an expression using an IIF( ) function. The IIF( ), as used in Part I, created a formula that added deposits and subtracted checks. One way to obtain this kind of balance using SQL is to create a temporary table that will allow you to manipulate the sign of the amounts without changing the data in the CHECKS table.

New tables are created by using the SAVE TO TEMP clause with a SELECT command. This clause directs the output of a SELECT command into a new table with the specified name. For example, copy the PAYEE and AMOUNT columns into a new table called BALANCE.

```
SELECT payee,amount
FROM checks
SAVE TO TEMP balance;
```

Instead of displaying the selected data, the program creates a new table. Display the data by entering

```
SELECT *
FROM balance;
```

The data in the two columns of the temporary table BALANCE are displayed, confirming the action of the previous command.

```
PAYEE                      AMOUNT
Acme Products              550.50
Walnut Creek Supply        275.00
Allied Office Furniture    750.50
Central Office Supplies     97.56
Western Telephone          101.57
United Federal Insurance   590.00
Computer World            2245.50
Fathead Software            99.95
The Bargain Warehouse      145.99
Central Office Supplies     67.45
Sunset Variety              25.89
Advanced Copier Service    175.00
Valley Power & Light       101.70
Dept of Trans               45.00
Western Telephone          175.75
DEPOSIT                   2500.00
DEPOSIT                   1200.00
DEPOSIT                   1900.00
DEPOSIT                   1100.00
```

You can use an UPDATE command to change all the check amounts to negative values.

```
UPDATE balance
SET amount=amount*-1
WHERE NOT payee="DEPOSIT";
```

With the rows updated (i.e. divided into positive and negative values) you can find the balance.

```
SELECT SUM(amount)
FROM balance;
```

The program returns the balance.

```
     SUM1
  1252.64
```

You can create a permanent new table with the SAVE TO TEMP clause by using the KEEP keyword. The KEEP option creates a dBASE IV DBF file with the contents of the table. Example:

```
SELECT payee,amount
FROM checks
SAVE TO TEMP balance KEEP;
```

Note that this DBF file is not automatically integrated into the current SQL database. To add it you must use the DBDEFINE command.

Deleting Rows

You can delete rows from a table by using the DELETE command. Keep in mind that in SQL, deleted rows are physically removed. This is different from standard dBASE IV in which delete operations only mark records for deletion. In SQL, once records are deleted they cannot be restored.

As an example, the following command deletes the DEPOSIT rows from the BALANCE table. The BALANCE table is used as an example because it consists of temporary data. Enter

```
DELETE FROM balance
WHERE payee="DEPOSIT";
```

The message "4 row(s) deleted" confirms the removal of the data. Remember, these rows are not recoverable because the DELETE command in SQL is permanent, unlike DELETE in standard dBASE IV.

Dropping Tables

You can remove a table from the database with the DROP TABLE command. The table can be a permanent table or a temporary table that is no longer needed. When you DROP a table, all the data is erased from the disk and cannot be recovered. In this case, DROP the remainder of the BALANCE table from the database.

```
DROP TABLE balance;
```

The program confirms the erasure with the message "Table BALANCE dropped."

Programs Using SQL Databases

SQL is not a complete database management system. It is a core application that contains a set of commands specifically designed to help the user retrieve tables of information from the SQL database.

SQL operations can be integrated into programs and executed as dBASE IV applications. The application can use the SQL commands to retrieve data. The SQL command can be embedded into the flow of standard dBASE IV programming commands and structures. As you have seen, SQL makes it simpler to write requests for data stored in multiple databases. You might want to use the SQL procedures to simplify program writing.

The main problem with SQL database operations is that the information retrieved by an SQL query is simply dumped on the screen. Often this makes reading the information awkward or difficult, because you cannot control the way the data appears.

In standard dBASE IV you can use the database pointer system to select one record at a time for processing. In SQL all the data is retrieved as a block. That data block is difficult to display or print.

SQL provides a means of handling the data retrieved with an SQL query, one row at a time. The method involves the use of an SQL cursor. Using the SQL cursor involves a method by which data selection retrieved with an SQL query can be broken up into separate rows and processed in a row-by-row manner. This is similar to the way records can be processed in standard dBASE IV. SQL cursors can only be implemented in a programming mode. While a full discussion of SQL programming is beyond the scope of this book, it might be instructive to look at two sample programs that illustrate how SQL data can be managed.

The first program will display SQL data using dBASE IV @/SAY commands to create a Full-Screen layout. The second program will show how an SQL table can be printed with page breaks.

All SQL programs are entered into files with a PRS, not a PRG extension. The extension prompts the dBASE IV compiler that the program is going to use SQL database commands instead of standard dBASE IV file operations. Keep in mind that the SQL program can contain all dBASE IV commands, functions, and structures, with the exception of standard dBASE IV file operations. This means when SQL operations are used, such commands as USE, COPY, and MODIFY STRUCTURE cannot be used.

In order to create a program that handles data row-by-row, you will need to use the following special SQL commands:

DECLARE CURSOR

This command is used to define the data selection that will be processed, row-by-row. The DECLARE CURSOR command will contain a SELECT command that defines the rows and columns to be processed.

OPEN

The OPEN command activates the CURSOR. This means the selection specified in the DECLARE CURSOR command is actually executed. Following the OPEN command, the total number of rows selected is stored in the SQLCNT variable. The data is ready for row-by-row processing.

FETCH

This command performs two functions. First, it transfers the information in the current row of the selection to dBASE IV memory variables. Second, it selects the next row in the selection for processing. By repeating a series of FETCH commands you can move through a selection in a manner similar to the way the standard dBASE IV record pointer moves through a DBF file.

CLOSE

This command terminates the CURSOR operation.

Sqlcode

Sqlcode is a special system variable—like SQLCNT—that is set by SQL following a FETCH command. The value of the variable is always 0, except in two cases. The value is set to -1 if an error occurs during the FETCH command, or to 100 if the cursor was positioned on the last row of the selection when the FETCH command was executed.

Create an SQL program named SQL_CUR by entering

```
MODIFY COMMAND sql_cur ⏎
```

The program begins with three commands that control the screen display mode.

```
SET TALK OFF
SET STATUS OFF
SET SCOREBOARD OFF
```

The next section of the program initializes the variables. In this case, the DECLARE command is used to create a nine element array—MV (memory variable)—to hold the nine columns of information that will be selected from the SQL database. The ROW_NUM variable will be used to keep track of the row being processed, since SQL does not generate row numbers like standard dBASE IV generates record numbers.

```
* create memory variables
DECLARE mv[9]
row_num=1
```

Do not confuse the dBASE IV command DECLARE, which creates an array of memory variables, with the SQL DECLARE CURSOR command. This program uses both commands.

Before the SQL operations transpire, a blinking message is placed on the screen to inform the user that something is going on. The SQL operations may take a few moments. The screen will remain blank while the processing is taking place. It is always a good idea to post a message to the user saying the program is working on an operation.

```
@ 10,22 SAY "Selecting Data" COLOR W*
```

The first step in the SQL processing is to START the ACCOUNTS database. The command ends with a semicolon because it is an SQL command *embedded* in a dBASE IV program.

```
START DATABASE accounts;
```

The next step is to define the cursor with the SQL DECLARE CURSOR command, to set the specifications for data retrieval. The DECLARE CURSOR command contains a complete SELECT command. This select command is not executed when the DECLARE CURSOR is executed. Instead, it is stored until an OPEN command for the cursor is executed. It is the open command that actually processes the rows related to the query. The cursor is given the name CUSTOMER.

```
* define cursor selection
DECLARE customer CURSOR FOR
SELECT company,first,last,phone,city,date_sold,quantity,price,item
FROM sales,buyers,products
WHERE sales.id=products.id
AND sales.account_no=buyers.account_no;
```

Once declared, you can open the cursor. Opening the cursor actually causes the program to draw the data out of the tables in the SQL database.
* select data

```
OPEN customer;
```

With the SQL cursor now open, you can clear the screen because you are ready to begin displaying the data one row at a time.

```
CLEAR
```

Following the OPEN command for the CUSTOMER cursor, the SQLCNT variable contains a value equal to the total number of rows selected. It is important to transfer this value to a standard memory variable if you want to use it in the program. Further SQL commands will alter the value of this variable. In this case, the variable TOTAL_ROWS will contain the total number of rows in the cursor.

```
total_rows=sqlcnt
```

While you know in advance that there will be rows selected for the cursor in general, it is a good idea to protect your program from cursors that do not have any rows selected. The section below tests the SQLCNT and terminates the program if 0 rows are selected.

```
IF sqlcnt=0
    @ 10,10 SAY "Database Empty"
    WAIT
ELSE
```

If there are rows in the cursor you can then proceed to display the data, row-by-row. This can be done inside a DO loop.

```
DO WHILE .T.
```

The first command in the loop is a FETCH command. FETCH is the link between dBASE IV and SQL operations. The FETCH command transfers the data from the column of the current row of the SQL cursor into a series of memory variables. Keep in mind that the number of memory variables *must* match exactly the number of columns specified for the selection in the DECLARE CURSOR command. If they do not match, an error will be generated.

Also, recall that the data is placed into the memory variables in the same sequence as the column names appear in the DECLARE CURSOR command.

FETCH also automatically increments the row so the next FETCH command will draw from the second row of the selection, and so on, each time until all rows are processed.

Executing an OPEN command causes the cursor to be recycled back to the first row in the selection. Unlike the dBASE IV record pointer, the cursor moves only one row at a time, in a forward direction. No other types of movement are possible.

```
FETCH customer INTO
mv[1],mv[2],mv[3],mv[4],mv[5],mv[6],mv[7],mv[8],mv[9];
```

Following the FETCH command, it is standard to evaluate whether a new row of data was actually returned, or if it encountered the end of the selection. The system variable SQLCODE is set at 100 when a FETCH command reaches the end of the selection. Here, the commands below terminate the program when the cursor has all its rows processed.

```
IF sqlcode=100
    EXIT
ENDIF
```

If the FETCH command returns valid data, the SHOW_ROW procedure is executed to display the information on the screen.

```
DO show_row
```

The ROW_NUM variable is incremented after each row is displayed.

```
row_num=row_num+1
```

The last section closes the loop and contains the commands to re-set the environment when the program is over.

```
    ENDDO
ENDIF
CLOSE customer;
STOP DATABASE;
SET TALK ON
SET STATUS ON
SET SCOREBOARD ON
RETURN
```

The SHOW_ROW procedure is used to display the information transferred into the memory variables by the FETCH command.

```
PROCEDURE show_row
```

The first command uses the variables ROW_NUM and TOTAL_ROWS to display a message "Record 1 of 8" (or one similar) at the top of each screen. This helps the user know where he or she is in the selection.

```
@ 1,5 SAY "Record #"+LTRIM(STR(row_num))+"  of
"+LTRIM(STR(total_rows))
```

The rest of the commands simply display the data in the memory variables, taking advantage of the screen display functions available with the @/SAY command.

```
@ 4,8 TO 10,70
@ 5,10 SAY "Customer:"  COLOR N/W
@ 6,15 SAY mv[1]
@ 7,15 SAY TRIM(mv[2])+"  "+mv[3]
@ 8,15 SAY mv[4]
@ 9,15 SAY mv[5]
@ 14,8 TO 19,70
@ 15,10 SAY "Purchase:"  COLOR N/W
@ 16,15 SAY mv[6]
@ 17,15 SAY mv[9]
@ 18,15 SAY mv[7]*mv[8]  PICTURE "@T$ 999,999.99"
@ 24,30 SAY "Press any Key"
```

The end of this procedure uses a DO WHILE INKEY( ) type pause.

```
DO WHILE INKEY( )=0
ENDDO
RETURN
```

The advantage of this program is that it can be created or modified by someone who is familiar with Screen Layout in dBASE IV, but not comfortable with multiple database processing. The SQL commands are much simpler to learn when retrieving data from multiple database files, or in SQL terminology tables. The combination of screen layout programming and SQL database operations makes this a much simpler program to write than using standard dBASE IV alone.

Save and execute the program by entering

```
[Alt-e]  r
```

When a PRS-type program is compiled, dBASE IV performs a more vigorous check of the SQL commands than it applies to standard dBASE IV program commands. The SQL commands are checked for both syntax and logic. If the tables, columns, etc., referred to in the embedded SQL commands do not match the existing values in the SQL database, the program will not compile. The advantage of this is the SQL programs that compile will almost always execute correctly. However, this also means it is not possible to write and compile SQL programs without having a set of matched SQL tables, etc., present on the computer. In contrast, it is quite possible, but not recommended, to write and compile a standard dBASE IV application without ever having the DBF files specified in the program on your computer.

When the program has compiled, the flashing message is displayed while the SQL cursor is created and opened. Figure 15-1 shows what the screen looks like when SQL data is displayed by the program.

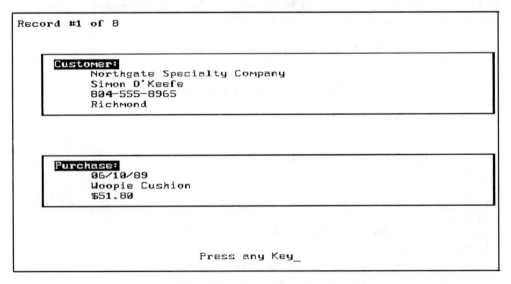

Figure 15-1. SQL data displayed by program.

Enter

⏎

The next record appears. Each ⏎ displays the next row in the SQL cursor. Enter

⏎ *(7 times)*

The full code of the program appears at the end of the chapter.

Printing SQL Information on Pages

Below is a program called SQL_PRT. It is a modified version of the SQL_CUR program shown above. It uses the same SQL cursor setup as the previous program, but replaces the SHOW_ROW procedure with procedures PRT_ROW, PAGE_TOP, and PAGE_END, that print the information as rows on a report. The program echos the printed information on the screen because the SET CONSOLE OFF command is not used to suppress the screen display.

```
SET TALK OFF
SET STATUS OFF
* create memory variables
DECLARE mv[6]
row_num=1
page_num=1
@ 10,12 SAY "Selecting Data" COLOR W*
START DATABASE accounts;
* define cursor selection
DECLARE customer CURSOR FOR
SELECT company,city,date_sold,quantity,price,item
FROM sales,buyers,products
WHERE sales.id=products.id
AND sales.account_no=buyers.account_no;
* select data
OPEN customer;
CLEAR
total_rows=sqlcnt
IF sqlcnt=0
    @ 10,10 SAY "Database Empty"
    WAIT
ELSE
    DO page_top
    DO WHILE .T.
        FETCH customer INTO
        mv[1],mv[2],mv[3],mv[4],mv[5],mv[6];
        IF sqlcode=100
            EXIT
        ENDIF
        DO prt_row
        row_num=row_num+1
    ENDDO
    DO page_end
ENDIF
CLOSE customer;
STOP DATABASE;
SET TALK ON
SET STATUS ON
RETURN

PROCEDURE prt_row
SET PRINT ON
? LTRIM(STR(row_num,3))+","
?? mv[1]
?? mv[2]
?? mv[3]
?? mv[6]
```

```
?? mv[4] PICTURE "999"
?? mv[4]*mv[5] PICTURE "999,999.99"
IF PROW( )>58
 DO page_end
    DO page_top
ENDIF
SET PRINT OFF
RETURN

PROCEDURE page_top
SET PRINT ON
?
?
? "Customer Report"
?
?
? "Company","City"  AT 36,"Date" AT 45,"Qty" AT 49,"Total" AT 60
?
SET PRINT OFF
RETURN

PROCEDURE page_end
SET PRINT ON
?
?
? page_num AT 39
SET PRINT OFF
EJECT
page_num=page_num+1
RETURN
```

Summary

This chapter discussed the use of SQL-type databases in dBASE IV.

- **SQL.** SQL stands for Structured Query Language. SQL represents an object oriented approach to processing database information. SQL is designed to hide the methods and procedures used to retrieve data from a database, from the user. The users select data by writing a structured description of the data they want to retrieve. SQL then generates the activities needed to retrieve the data. SQL is a standard used on main frame and mini computer systems, where most databases are custom designed. SQL allows users with this experience to perform database tasks on a microcomputer, using commands they are familiar with. SQL also offers an alternative to standard dBASE IV data retrieval operations.

- **SQL Databases.** A database in SQL is a collection of files that contain information organized into row and column tables. A single database can have a large number of data tables. You can access any of the tables at any time through the SQL database.

- **SQL Tables.** The heart of the SQL database system is data tables. The tables are organized in columns and rows. The columns designate the type of information to be stored. Each column has a unique name. The rows represent individual sets of data.

- **Data Entry.** SQL allows data to be added to database tables in four ways: 1) INSERT adds new rows to a database table, 2) UPDATE modifies data in existing rows, 3) LOAD DATA loads information from dBASE, spreadsheet or text files into SQL tables, and 4) DBDEFINE converts a dBASE IV database file into an SQL table. You can also open an SQL table using dBASE IV Edit and Browse mode operations.

- **Queries.** The main operation in SQL is a query. The SELECT command processes a query—a request for data—through the SQL database. You can request data from specific columns. The WHERE clause is used to select rows based on a logical criterion. dBASE IV expressions can be used as part of the column list. The ORDER BY clause will sequence the retrieved data in specific orders, either ascending or descending.

- **Summaries.** SQL recognizes aggregate functions that calculate such statistics as sums, averages and counts of column data. The GROUP BY clause will generate sub-total summaries, based on the values in a specified column. The HAVING clause can be used to select sub-total rows based on a logical criterion.

- **Multiple Tables Queries.** SQL requires no special commands to perform relational queries using multiple tables. The WHERE clause contains a Join specification, indicating columns that contain data that relates (links) the rows of different tables. SQL implements the query without requiring the user to issue processing instructions, as must be done in standard dBASE IV.

- **Programming with SQL database.** dBASE IV programs can contain embedded SQL database operations in program files that use the PRS extension. However, you cannot mix standard dBASE IV file operations with SQL database operations. All other dBASE IV commands, such as function, screen handling commands, and program structure commands, can be used with SQL database operations.

- **SQL Cursors.** SQL cursors are used in SQL programs to allow the program to process one row of data at a time from a retrieved database table. The FETCH command is used to transfer one row of data at a time into dBASE IV memory variables. By using FETCH with SQL cursors you can write programs that duplicate the type of program written in standard dBASE IV, only the SQL programs take advantage of SQL's simplified data retrieval facilities.

Program Listings

Program: SQL_CUR.PRS

```
SET TALK OFF
SET STATUS OFF
* create memory variables
DECLARE mv[9]
row_num=1
@ 10,12 SAY "Selecting Data" COLOR W*
START DATABASE accounts;
* define cursor selection
DECLARE customer CURSOR FOR
SELECT company,first,last,phone,city,date_sold,quantity,price,item
FROM sales,buyers,products
WHERE sales.id=products.id
AND sales.account_no=buyers.account_no;
* select data
OPEN customer;
CLEAR
total_rows=sqlcnt
IF sqlcnt=0
    @ 10,10 SAY "Database Empty"
    WAIT
ELSE
    DO WHILE .T.
        FETCH customer INTO
        mv[1],mv[2],mv[3],mv[4],mv[5],mv[6],mv[7],mv[8],mv[9];
        IF sqlcode=100
            EXIT
        ENDIF
        DO show_row
        row_num=row_num+1
    ENDDO
ENDIF
CLOSE customer;
STOP DATABASE;
SET TALK ON
SET STATUS ON
RETURN

PROCEDURE show_row
@ 1,5 SAY "Record #"+LTRIM(STR(row_num))+"   of
"+LTRIM(STR(total_rows))
@ 4,8 TO 10,70
@ 5,10 SAY "Customer:"  COLOR N/W
@ 6,15 SAY mv[1]
@ 7,15 SAY TRIM(mv[2])+"  "+mv[3]
@ 8,15 SAY mv[4]
@ 9,15 SAY mv[5]
@ 14,8 TO 19,70
@ 15,10 SAY "Purchase:"  COLOR N/W
@ 16,15 SAY mv[6]
@ 17,15 SAY mv[9]
@ 18,15 SAY mv[7]*mv[8]  PICTURE  "@T$ 999,999.99"
@ 24,30 SAY "Press any Key"
DO WHILE INKEY( )=0
ENDDO
RETURN
```

Part V

Configuration

16

System Configuration and Customization

The complexity and power of dBASE IV is reflected in the wide number of settings and default parameters it uses. The default values and options are set at the factory, based on how the program is commonly used. In a program as broadly based as dBASE IV, many users will want to make changes in the settings to suit their particular circumstances.

dBASE IV allows you to modify the settings and default values on two levels:

Temporary Settings. You can change settings for the current dBASE IV session. These settings will be forgotten when you exit dBASE IV. The next time you load the program, dBASE IV reverts to the default settings.

Permanent Settings. You can make permanent default changes in dBASE IV that will be activated each time you load the program.

This chapter provides information about how the dBASE IV settings can be changed and what the available options are.

Temporary Changes

Temporary changes are those changes made to the system after its been loaded. These changes stay in effect for the current session only. The next time dBASE IV is loaded, the default settings return.

There are four ways to change the settings:

Tools Settings. From the Control Center the Settings option on the Tools menu (Figure 16-1) allows you access to 16 dBASE IV settings, plus the display options that set screen colors. In addition, printing a report or label form allows you access to the Print menu, which contains settings specific to printing.

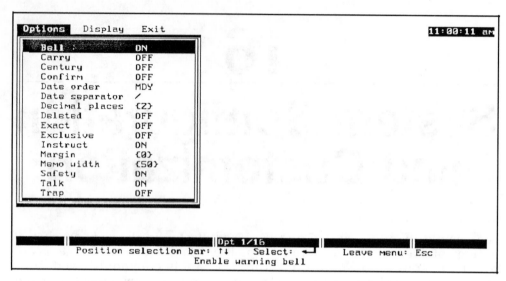

Figure 16-1. Settings display activated from the Tools menu.

Set. The SET command issued at the Dot Prompt mode provides access to a menu of 42 optional settings (Figure 16-2). In addition, you have access to the display options for screen colors, the keys option for defining programmable function keys, disk specifications for selecting DOS drives, and directories and files, which select special purpose files.

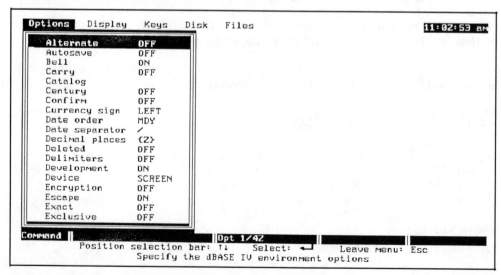

Figure 16-2. Settings displays when SET command issued from Dot Prompt mode.

SET/TO commands. You can issue individual SET/TO commands from the Dot Prompt mode. The dBASE IV Command Language contains 80 SET commands that affect a wide variety of system settings.

Programs. You can establish customized environments by writing programs that include specific combinations of SET commands. Note that SET commands issued in dBASE IV programs remain active following the program, unless you specifically issue commands that reset dBASE IV to its original state.

All four methods have the ability to make temporary changes in the settings. Settings entered with any of these methods are forgotten by the program after it is quit. The program will revert to the original default settings when it is reloaded.

Set Commands

The most powerful approach to setting dBASE IV options is to use the SET commands from the Dot Prompt mode. The menu versions displayed by SET ⌐ or the Control Center Tools menus, display a subset of the full-command structure. The menus provide ease of use. In the Dot Prompt mode you must compose the commands correctly in order to select an option.

A list of all the temporary settings available in dBASE IV follows. The purpose of this section is to group related settings together. The dBASE IV documentation contains more detail about the SET commands, but the information is organized in strict alphabetical order.

Control Center

SET DESIGN. This option affects only the Control Center operations. When ON, the Exit menus offer options to switch to the Design mode. Setting this option off eliminates this option from the menu. The default setting is ON.

Data Entry

The commands in this section affect the way data is entered in the Edit and Browse modes, and through custom screen layouts.

SET AUTOSAVE. When ON, dBASE IV saves each record as it is entered or edited. When OFF, dBASE IV waits until a specific amount of data has been entered before actually writing the changes to the disk. The default if OFF. Set ON if you are concerned about power failures.

SET BELL. Controls the beeps issued by dBASE IV. When OFF, the program is mute. The default is ON. SET BELL TO allows you to define the tone of the beep by entering values for the frequency and duration of the bell tone.

SET BLOCKSIZE. Controls the size of the text block manipulated by memo field operations. The default value is 1. If you are working with many large memo entries, you can improve performance by increasing the block size. Expanding the blocksize, up to 32K, allows dBASE IV to read more text from each memo in each disk access.

SET CARRY. When ON, all the information is automatically copied from a previous record into a new record. The default is OFF.

SET CONFIRM. When ON, this option requires the entry of a ↵ in order to advance to the next field. The default is OFF.

SET DELIMITER. Controls the character and display of field delimiters. It was originally used in dBASE II to mark field locations on the screen. dBASE IV uses reverse colors to mark field locations.

SET ENCRYPTION. Applies to the protection system only. It determines if copies of existing data files will be encrypted or normal. The default is ON, which means copies are encrypted. Turn off to make unencrypted copies.

Data Retrieval

SET DECIMALS. Sets the default number of decimal places for values produced by calculations or functions. The default is 2.

SET DELETED. Determines if records marked as deleted should be processed. The default is OFF, which means deleted records are processed.

SET EXACT. When ON, requires character string match for content and length, when a logical expression is evaluated. The default is OFF, allowing partial matches to be evaluated as true.

SET FIELDS. This command is used to control which fields can be displayed or accessed. The default is to display all fields in all open databases.

SET FILTER. This command controls which records can be processed. The command uses a logical expression to select records. The default setting is to select all records in the database.

SET HEADING. When ON, dBASE IV displays the field or expression as a column heading in LIST, DISPLAY, SUM, and AVERAGE commands. OFF suppresses this display. The default is ON.

SET INDEX. This command is used to open or select an index file or tag, which is used to sequence the output of dBASE IV commands in a specific order. This command cannot create new index orders.

SET MEMOWIDTH. Sets the width in characters for the maximum line size, for the display of memo text. The default is 50 characters.

SET NEAR. Affects the location of the record pointer following a SEEK or FIND assuming that no match is found (the FOUND( ) function is false.) If SET NEAR is ON, the pointer is placed at the record that follows the record which most nearly matches the search key. The default is OFF, and the pointer is placed at the end of the file if a match cannot be found.

SET ORDER. Selects a master index order when more than one index order is available to a database.

SET RELATION. Establishes a link between database files that have common information.

SET SKIP. When active, it moves the pointers of more than one linked database each time the pointer moves in any of them.

SET SQL. Activates/deactivates the SQL mode of database processing.

SET UNIQUE. When ON, it causes records with unique key values only to be included in index files that are created. Has no effect on existing index files.

Files

SET CATALOG. Activates a catalog file for recording files being used in a dBASE IV session. It is automatic in the Control Center, but defaults to OFF at the Dot Prompt mode.

SET DEFAULT. Used to change the active disk.

SET PATH. Used to change the active disk directory.

SET SAFETY. Determines if a warning message is issued when a file is overwritten. The default is ON. OFF causes files to automatically be overwritten with no warning.

Networks

SET EXCLUSIVE. When ON, places an exclusive lock on all files opened. The default is OFF.

SET LOCK. When OFF, this allows commands that read but do not write data to perform operations on a database that has a record or file lock placed on it. The default setting, ON, requires a file lock before such commands as SUM or COPY can be used.

SET REFRESH. This command is used to automatically update the screen display of the Edit or Browse modes, displaying any changes made by other users. The time is set in seconds. The default is 0 (i.e. no automatic updates once the record is displayed).

SET REPROCESS. Determines the number of times the program attempts to access a record or file locked by another user. The default is 0, meaning dBASE IV will make an infinite number of retries.

Output Devices

SET ALTERNATE. This command is used to create, activate, and deactivate output to a text file. When selected and ON, all information placed on the screen with streaming-output commands, such as ?, ??, LIST, and DISPLAY is copied into a text file. Use this command with programs to create text files with custom formats.

SET DEVICE. Selects the device, screen, printer, or file where @/SAY output should be directed. The default is the screen.

Printing

SET MARGIN. Sets the left margin. The default is 0.

SET PRINTER ON/OFF. When ON, all streaming output (?, LIST, DISPLAY) is echoed to the printer. The default is OFF.

SET PRINTER TO. Allows you to specify a port, such as LPT2, or a file to which streaming output is directed. Used to override the default printer setup.

Programming

SET DEBUG. Works with SET ECHO. When ON, it prints the commands as they execute. The default is OFF.

SET DEVELOPMENT. When ON, causes dBASE IV to automatically compile an application if the object file date is earlier than the source code file date. Ensures the latest version of a program is the one that executes. The default is ON.

SET ECHO. When ON, displays commands on screen as they are executed. The default is OFF.

SET ESCAPE. When ON, the [Esc] key terminates a program or command. When OFF, [Esc] is ignored. The default is ON.

SET FUNCTION. Use this to program function keys.

SET HISTORY. Determines the storage size of the history buffer. The default is 20 commands.

SET PROCEDURE. Opens and activates a procedure file.

SET STEP. When ON, dBASE IV pauses for a ⏎ after each program command executes. The default is OFF.

SET TITLE. Works with SET CATALOG. When ON, the program asks you to enter a description when a new file is added to a catalog. The default is OFF.

SET TRAP. When ON, activates the DEBUG mode when a program error occurs. The default is OFF.

SET TYPEAHEAD. Sets the size of the typeahead buffer. The default is 16 characters.

SET VIEW. Activates a QBE or dBASE III VUE file.

Screen Display

SET BORDER. Use this command to define the default style of borders used on menus and windows. The default is single lines.

SET CURRENCY. Determines the character and position of the currency symbol displayed when a currency format function is used. The default is $ to the left of the value.

SET COLOR. Controls the colors displayed on the screen.

SET CONSOLE. When OFF, no information appears on the screen. Used to suppress screen data when printing with streaming-output commands. The default is ON.

SET DATE. Use to determine types of date format. The default is mm/dd/yy.

SET DISPLAY. Selects the screen driver MONO, EGA, etc.

SET FORMAT. Use this command to establish a custom-designed format file to be used for the layout of records in the Edit or Append Command-Display modes.

SET HELP. When ON, dBASE IV prompts you for help display when errors are encountered. The default is ON.

SET INSTRUCT. When ON, dBASE IV displays messages at the bottom of the screen when selections are made from menus in the Control Center, or Full-Screen modes. The default is ON.

SET INTENSITY. When ON, input areas appear in a contrasting color combination. The default is ON.

SET MESSAGE. This command can be used to display a character string as a message at the bottom of the screen, below the status line.

SET ODOMETER. Use this command to change the numbering increment of commands that display counts of records being processed. The default is 1.

SET PAUSE. When ON, this command causes screen displays to automatically pause after a screen is filled. The default is OFF.

SET POINT. Sets the character to be displayed for the decimal point. The default is a period.

SET PRECISION. Use this to change the precision of numbers stored as a result of calculations. The default is 16 decimal places.

SET SCOREBOARD. When OFF, allows @/SAY commands to write on line zero of the screen display. The default is ON.

SET SEPARATOR. Sets the character used as a separator between numbers. The default character is a comma.

SET SPACE. When ON, dBASE IV inserts a space between items specified in a list with the ?, ??, LIST, and DISPLAY commands. The default is ON.

SET STATUS. When ON, dBASE IV displays the status line on line 22 of the screen display. Turn OFF to write @/SAY data on lines 22 through 24. The default is ON.

SET TALK. Turn OFF to suppress feedback generated by dBASE IV commands. The default is ON.

SET WINDOW. This command is used to define an editing window for memo field entry. Works in conjunction with DEFINE WINDOW.

Time and Date

SET CENTURY. When ON, displays a 4-character year value for dates. The default is OFF.

SET CLOCK. This command controls the display and location of the clock on the screen. The clock is automatically displayed in the Control Center, but is OFF by default in the Dot Prompt mode.

SET DATE. Selects the type of date format used for the display and entry of dates. The default is American, mm/dd/yy.

SET HOURS. Selects 12-hour or 24-hour time display. The default is 12 hour time.

SET MARK. Controls the character used to separate values in a date. The default character is /.

Permanent Changes

If you want to make changes that will become part of the dBASE IV setup each time you load the program, you need to alter the CONFIG.DB file. The CONFIG.DB file is used to store user-defined default settings. Each time the dBASE IV program is loaded, it scans the directory for the CONFIG.DB file and reads this file to determine what settings the user selected for dBASE IV. If there is nothing in the CONFIG.DB file about a specific feature, dBASE IV sets that feature to the factory default settings.

The CONFIG.DB file can be altered in two ways:

DBSETUP. As part of the dBASE IV system, you are supplied with a program called DBSETUP. This is the program used by dBASE IV when you install dBASE IV on your computer. You can also use the program following installation to enter new selections into the CONFIG.DB file.

Editing. The CONFIG.DB file is a text file similar in structure to a dBASE IV program file. You can change this file using the MODIFY FILE command to place the file in the dBASE IV editor, or by using any text editor.

Keep in mind that any changes made using the DBSETUP program are written as text commands into the CONFIG.DB file. This means you can make changes to the CONFIG.DB file using either method, depending on whether you want the help of the menu system in DBSETUP or not.

The SET( ) Function

dBASE IV provides a special function that returns the current setting of SET commands that use ON/OFF or numeric values. For example, suppose you wanted to know if the SET SAFETY command was currently on or off.

The SET( ) function requires the name of the setting you want to check. The name is a single word such as "bell" for SET BELL, or "memowidth" for SET MEMOWIDTH. Enter the following command:

```
? SET("safety")  ↵
```

dBASE IV displays ON or OFF, depending on the current setting. If the setting uses a numeric value, this value is returned. Enter

```
? SET("memowidth")   ⏎
```

The program returns the value of 50, or whatever the current memowidth setting happens to be.

You can apply the four-letter rule to the string used for the SET function. This means SET("memo") is equal to SET("memowidth").

The SET( ) function also allows you to have additional flexibility in programming. In the programs shown in Part II and III, the SET commands are placed at the beginning and the end of the program. The assumption is made that all the settings are currently at the default values. For example, the assumption is made that the TALK and STATUS settings are always on at the beginning of a program. The programs always begin with set OFF commands and end by turning the set back ON.

Below is a model of a program that begins by changing the TALK and MEMOWIDTH sets and ends by resetting the values to the default values.

```
SET TALK OFF
SET MEMOWIDTH TO 20
...commands...
SET TALK ON
SET MEMOWIDTH TO 50
```

But suppose the user has changed default settings to something other than the standard defaults. When the program is complete, you may end up turning on TALK or MEMOWIDTH to a standard default, which will not match this system's defaults. The SET( ) function makes it possible to store the settings in memory variables, then use those values to reset the actual default according to the current version of dBASE IV, rather than assuming the system uses the standard defaults.

The program model below shows the SET function is used to transfer the current settings to memory variables. At the end of the program the variables are used to reset the system to its condition prior to the execution of the program.

```
set_talk=SET("talk")
set_mw=SET("memowidth")
SET TALK OFF
SET MEMOWIDTH TO 20
...commands...
SET TALK &set_talk
SET MEMOWIDTH TO set_mw
```

Note that in order to change an ON/OFF setting you must use the & to macro substitute the text string stored under the variable name into the command that accepts a literal not a variable.

It is very important to remember that in version 1.0 of dBASE IV, the SET( ) function will not operate on functions using text arguments other than ON/OFF. For example, the SET DEVICE command uses arguments SCREEN, PRINT, and FILE. The command ? SET("device") generates an error because it can only return ON/OFF, or a numeric value.

DBSETUP

The DBSETUP program is a separate application from dBASE IV, and is run from DOS. The file DBSETUP.EXE is copied into the \DBASE directory as part of the dBASE IV installation process.

To use DBSETUP, select the \DBASE directory and enter the following at the DOS prompt:

    dbsetup ⏎

When the copyright notice appears, enter

    ⏎

The screen displays the main DBSETUP menu, as seen in Figure 16-3. There are five items on the menu:

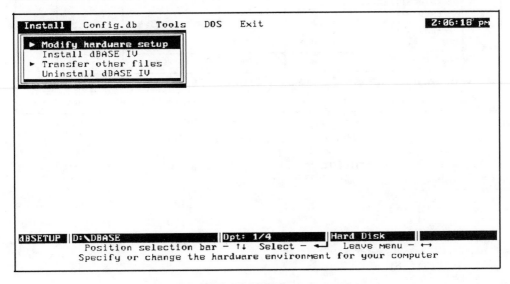

Figure 16-3. DBSETUP main menu.

Install. This option allows you to change the hardware specifications used for dBASE IV, copy other modules such as the dBASE IV samples file or tutorial files, or Uninstall dBASE IV from the current hard disk system. The most important option on this menu is the hardware option, since that is where printer specifications can be set. The *Config.db* option is the most important one because it allows you to modify the default system settings. You can create a new CONFIG.DB file or modify the existing CONFIG.DB.

Tools. The tools menus provide three special operations that provide useful information about your computer. 1) Display Disk Usage displays information about the organization and usage of the current disk (figure 16-4); 2) Test Disk Performance runs a test to determine the speed of the disk operations; 3) Review System Configuration displays information about the hardware in the computer system.

```
Install   Config.db   Tools   DOS   Exit                    2:17:13 PM

   info for disk ...........   D:
   sector size in bytes .... 1,024   cluster size in bytes ...  4,096
   number of surfaces ......     6   number of tracks ........    400
   sectors per track .......    17   oem name ..............NOSYSTEM
   Not a standard DOS file allocation scheme.city in files ..    512

   usage                          sectors       bytes       clusters

   DOS system area
     DOS boot area
     file allocation table
     root directory
   space in use        ( 80%)      32,908     33,697,792      8,227
   locked out          (   %)
   available           ( 20%)       7,832      8,019,968      1,958

   total              (100%)       40,740     41,717,760     10,185

dBSETUP   D:\DBASE           Opt: 1/3         Hard Disk
                     Press any key to continue. _
  Show disk usage, allocation scheme, and format information for current drive
```

Figure 16-4. Disk usage summary.

DOS. This menu provides access to DOS so you can execute DOS commands while in the DBSETUP program.

Exit. Exits DBSETUP.

To modify the current CONFIG.DB, you would enter

    [Alt-c] m ↵

The program then displays a new menu, as shown in Figure 16-5.

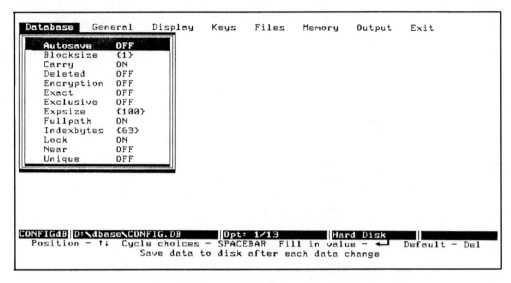

Figure 16-5. CONFIG.DB setting menu in DBSETUP program.

The settings are divided into seven areas. The menus show the settings and the current default settings that will be used by dBASE IV when the program is loaded. The menus break down as follows:

The Database menu

Autosave	OFF
Blocksize	{1}
Carry	ON
Deleted	OFF
Encryption	OFF
Exact	OFF
Exclusive	OFF
Expsize	{100}
Fullpath	ON
Indexbytes	{63}
Lock	ON
Near	OFF
Unique	OFF

The General menu

Bell	
Century	OFF
Clock	
Command	{}
Confirm	OFF
Currency	
Date	AMERICAN
Debug	OFF
Delimiters	
Design	ON
Development	ON
Do	{20}
Escape	ON
Help	ON
History	{20}
Hours	12
Instruct	ON
Memowidth	{50}

The Display menu

Display mode	EGA25
Standard - All	{}
Normal text	{}
Messages	{}
Titles	{}
Enhanced - All	{}
Highlight	{}
Boxes	{}
Information	{}
Fields	{}

The Keys menu

F1	
F2	assist;
F3	list;
F4	dir;
F5	display structure;
F6	display status;
F7	display memory;
F8	display;
F9	append;
F10	edit;
Ctrl-F1	
Ctrl-F2	
Ctrl-F3	
Ctrl-F4	
Ctrl-F5	
Ctrl-F6	
Ctrl-F7	
Ctrl-F8	

The Files menu

Alternate	{}
Catalog	{}
Default	{}
Files	{99}
Path	{}
Safety	ON
SQLdatabase	{}
SQLhome	{d:\DBASE\SQLHOME}
View	{}

The Memory menu

Bucket	{2}
Ctmaxsyms	{500}
Gets	{128}
Mvblksize	{50}
Mvmaxblks	{5}
Refresh	{0}
Reprocess	{0}
Rtblksize	{50}
Rtmaxblks	{10}

The Output menu

Console	ON
Decimals	{2}
Device	SCREEN
Echo	OFF
Fastcrt	OFF
Headings	ON
Intensity	ON
Margin	{0}
Noclock	OFF
Odometer	{1}
Pause	OFF
Printer	
Scoreboard	ON
Space	ON
Tabs	{}

The menu system allows you to change ON/OFF settings by pressing ↵ to toggle the value. Other items that have fixed options use the [spacebar] to toggle them. When a value, string, or file name is needed, DBSETUP will display an entry box when you press ↵.

The primary advantage of working through the DBSETUP menus is you are sure that the resulting CONFIG.DB file will not contain syntax errors or incompatible options. When you manually edit the CONFIG.DB file, no syntax checks are performed.

Another advantage is that the DBSETUP shows the default values for all the settings in dBASE IV.

Editing the CONFIG.DB File

You can also make changes to the CONFIG.DB file by directly editing it with the dBASE IV editor, or any other text editor.

You can load the CONFIG.DB file into the editor by entering

```
MODIFY COMMAND config.db  ↵
```

A typical CONFIG.DB is shown in Figure 16-6. Each setting in the file consists of a single line. The line begins with a keyword which represents the setting, e.g., DISPLAY for SET DISPLAY, STATUS for SET STATUS. The keyword is followed by an =, and a setting value such as ON, OFF, a numeric value, or a filename or path.

```
 Layout    Words    Go To    Print    Exit                        4:04:03 PM
[ · · · · · ·▼1· · · · ·▼· ·2· · · ·▼· · ·3· ·▼· · · ·4▼· · · · ·▼5· · · · ·▼· ·6· · · ·▼· · · ·7· ·▼· · · · · ·
 ⁻
 ×
 ×        dBASE IV Configuration File
 ×        Wednesday July 12, 1989
 ×

 DISPLAY               = EGA25
 ENCRYPTION            = OFF
 MVMAXBLKS             = 5
 PDRIVER               = ASCII.PR2
 SQL                   = ON
 SQLHOME               = d:\DBASE\SQLHOME
 STATUS                = ON




 ┌──────────┬─────────────────────┬──────────────────┬──────────────┬────────────┐
 │ Program  │ D:\dbase\CONFIG     │     │Line:1 Col:1  │     │         │          Ins│
```

Figure 16-6. CONFIG.DB file loaded into the dBASE IV editor.

As in program files, blank lines or lines that begin with an * are ignored. The * lines serve as note or comment lines. When the file is written by the DBSETUP program, space is left after the keyword so all the = and values will align in a column. Although not necessary, this makes the file easier to read. You can write a valid command with no additional space, e.g., *DISPLAY = MONO*. It is not necessary to delimit strings when you are entering file or directory names.

After you have made the modifications, you can save the new configuration by entering

    [Alt-e] s

Remember that when you change the CONFIG.DB file from within dBASE IV, the changes will have *no effect* until you quit, then reload dBASE IV. This is because dBASE IV reads the CONFIG.DB file as it begins to load, and does not look at the file until the program is loaded again.

If you erase the CONFIG.DB entirely or change its name, dBASE IV will load with the standard default values set for every option. Note that means black and white displays on color screens, and the program defaults to the Dot Prompt mode instead of the Control Center. It is important to understand that the apparent default colors and the use of the Control Center as the Default Operating mode result from the CONFIG.DB file created during the installation process. The real standard default for color is black and white, and the operating mode default is actually the Dot Prompt mode.

CONFIG.DB Only Settings

The CONFIG.DB file can use keywords to set all the settings controlled within dBASE IV by the SET commands. In addition, there are special settings that can *only* be set in the CONFIG.DB file. These settings generally deal with allocation of memory space, which must be set prior to the loading and executing of the dBASE IV program. Once the program is loaded, you must quit dBASE IV and reload to change these settings. Some of significant settings are described below:

Custom Screen Memory. dBASE IV uses memory to store information entered into GET areas, and to allocate GET areas on the screen. The BUCKET setting controls the amount of memory used to hold input into GET areas. The GET setting controls the number of input areas that can be active at one time. Defaults:

    BUCKET=2 (kilobytes)
    GETS=128

Command Execution. The COMMAND keyword is followed by a dBASE IV command that should be executed as soon as the program is loaded. This command is typically used to start the Control Center, COMMAND=ASSIST, or to execute a program COMMAND = DO *filename*.

Prompt. You can change the prompt from a dot to some other character or string of characters. For example, entering *PROMPT= Command?* causes dBASE IV to display *Command?* in place of the dot in the Dot Prompt mode.

SQL. If you set dBASE IV to load and operate like an SQL dBASE IV program, you can use three keywords in the CONFIG.DB file.

```
* turns SQL mode on
SQL = ON
* sets the location of the master SQL files
SQLHOME = \DBASE\SQLHOME
* name the SQL database to start
SQLDATABASE = accounts
```

Editing. You can substitute a text editor or word processing program of your own for the dBASE IV text editor. When you execute a command or operation that requires text editing, the designated editor or word processor is activated instead of the dBASE IV editor. The editor must be able to read and write ASCII text files. Keep in mind that this feature is subject to memory limitations. When editing, there must be room to load the word processing program along with dBASE IV. With version 1.0, memory requirements are such that most full powered word processing programs will not run in memory along with dBASE IV. The WP keyword sets the program called when memo fields are edited. The TEDIT keyword sets the program called when MODIFY COMMAND is used. They do not have to call the same program.

The Norton Editor from Peter Norton Computing is a small but powerful editor that works well with dBASE IV. It will fit into the memory on most systems. The editor features split window editing of two files, as well as mouse support. To load the editor you would place these lines in the CONFIG.DB.

```
WP=ne
TEDIT=ne
```

Printer Driver and Fonts. dBASE IV supports printer drivers and allows you to set printer drivers and fonts. You can load up to 4 drivers at one time. You can also define fonts by entering the commands needed to select fonts on your printer. dBASE IV uses three keywords, PRINTER, PRINTER FONT, and PDRIVER. dBASE IV printer driver files are supplied on System Disk #2. All driver files end with a PR2 extension.

PRINTER establishes a printer driver to be part of the dBASE IV system. The command below sets PRINTER 1 as a Citizen printer using the GENERIC printer driver.

```
PRINTER 1 = GENERIC.PR2 NAME "Citizen 120 D" DEVICE LPT1
```

The text name of the printer appears in the print menu when you display the destination option, Figure 16-7.

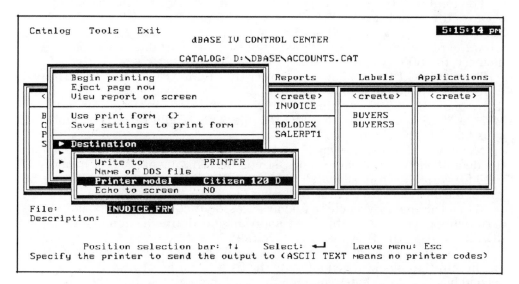

Figure 16-7. Printer name appears in print menu.

If you want to define a font not supported by the driver, you can use a PRINTER FONT command. This is usually needed with printers such as HP LaserJets, which can use different font cartridges. The example below sets an 8-point font for a LaserJet printer.

```
PRINTER 2 = HPLAS100.PR2 NAME "HP Laserjet" DEVICE COM1
PRINTER 2 FONT 1 = {Esc}(8U, {Esc}(#@ NAME = " 8 point normal"
```

To set a default printer, use the PDRIVER keyword. Note that the PDRIVER keyword should follow all PRINTER and PRINTER/FONT commands. The command below sets GENERIC driver printer as the default.

```
PDRIVER = GENERIC.PR2
```

---

dBASE IV does not support POSTSCRIPT printers.

Memory Variable Usage. The memory setup can be altered to meet special conditions by setting special memory oriented keyword commands in the CONFIG.DB file. The amount of memory allocated for memory variables is controlled by the MVMAXBLKS (memory variables maximum blocks) and the MVBLKSIZE (memory variables block size) keywords.

The total number of memory variables that can be defined is set at 500 because the default MVMAXBLKS is set at 10 and the MVBLKSIZE is set at 50. This means there are 10 blocks, each capable of holding 50 variables for a total of 50 times 10 = 500. Since each memory variable uses 56 bytes of memory, the 500 variables are allocated 28,000 bytes.

The CONFIG.DB file allows you to set the MVMAXBLKS to a value from 1 to 150, and the MVBLKSIZE to a value 25 to 100. If you wanted to be able to define more than 500 variables, you would enter a command line, such as *MVMAXBLKS = 20* in the CONFIG.DB file. This would raise the number of slots for memory variables to 1000.

Memory is allocated for variables based on the MVBLKSIZE. For example, the default memory variable block size is 50. This means when memory is used for variables, it is allocated in blocks of 50. Since each variable uses 56 bytes, the memory size is 2800 bytes per block.

When the memory is clear no variables defined the memory list shows zero bytes used for variables. As soon as you define a memory variable, dBASE IV uses the first memory block, 2800 bytes, for storage. The 2800 bytes will remain allocated to variables until you define more variables than can fit into that block. When defining the 51st variable, dBASE IV allocates a second block of 2800 bytes, making the total memory used 5600 bytes.

In addition to memory variables, dBASE IV allocates space to *runtime symbols*. These symbols are used to help the program keep track of memory variables created during program execution. Each runtime symbol uses 17 bytes. In order to allocate memory for 500 runtime symbols, the number of variables allowed, two settings, RTMAXBLKS and RTBLKSIZE, allocate the blocks and block size for runtime symbols. The default values of RTMAXBLKS =10 and RTBLKSIZE = 50, match the settings for memory variables. Because each runtime symbol uses only 17 bytes, a single block, enough for 50 symbols, uses 850 bytes. When the 51st variable is defined, a second block of 850 is allocated to bring the total amount of runtime memory to 1700.

Arrays are treated a bit differently. Each array takes up one memory variable and one runtime symbol. The memory needed for the elements in the array is listed under a separate item, *array element memvars*. Each element in an array allocates 56 bytes of memory for that array. For example, an array of 10 rows and 5 columns uses 2800 bytes for its elements. An array of 11 rows and 5 columns would use 3080 bytes, not 5600, since only the exact amount of memory needed for the array is allocated. Recall that an array also counts as a memory variable. Creating a 10 row by 5 column array will allocate 2800 bytes for the elements and 2800 bytes as a memory variable, and 850 for runtime symbols, 2800+850+2800 = 6450 bytes.

Starting dBASE IV

All versions of dBASE, including dBASE IV, allow you to specify a command line option when starting the program. The command line option is the name of a dBASE IV program you want to execute as soon as the program is loaded. The command below automatically executes the program ACCOUNT.PRG (or ACCOUNTS.PRS for an SQL program) as soon as the program is loaded.

```
dbase accounts ↵
```

Note that the command line option takes precedence over the COMMAND= keyword, if one exists, in the CONFIG.DB.

You can also use a command line option, /T, to suppress the display of the Ashton Tate graphics logo at the beginning of the program. Example:

```
dbase/t ↵
```

You can combine both the command line argument with the /T. Example:

```
dbase accounts/t ↵
```

Summary

The dBASE IV system can be customized to meet your needs by changing settings on a temporary or permanent basis.

- **Temporary Changes.** You can use the SET menus or the SET commands at the Dot Prompt to change settings for the current session of dBASE IV. SET options exercised within a dBASE IV program will remain active after the end of the program, unless you include commands that specifically reset the settings to the original values.

- **Permanent Changes.** The CONFIG.DB file contains commands that can change the default settings of dBASE IV. You can set all the same options as the SET commands in dBASE IV through the CONFIG.DB file. In addition, there are special commands involving memory allocation, text editors, and printers that can only be set through CONFIG.DB. The DBSETUP program provides a menu driven way of making changes to the CONFIG.DB file. CONFIG.DB can be edited manually with any text editor.

Index

Abbreviations,
  in Dot Prompt mode, 155
Accept Value When option, 300
ACCESS( ) function, 714
Accumulators, 619-23
ACTIVATE MENU command, 606
Activating a database, 46-48
Aggregate functions, SQL, 763-65
Alias names, 423-24
[Alt], general information on, 21
[Alt-character], to select a
  menu item, 18
ALTER TABLE command
  (SQL command), 739, 741
AND relationships, 116-18
APPEND command,
  in Dot Prompt mode, 157
APPEND FROM command, 524, 533
APPEND FROM file
  TO memo command, 43
APPEND MEMO command, 531-33
Append mode, 63-64, 325
Applications generator, 546
Arithmetic calculations, 179-80
Arithmetic operators, 179
Arrays, 11
Arrow keys, moving the
  highlight with, 13-14
ASCII coding, 122
ASCII sort, 121-22
ASCII text file, importing/exporting
  text to/from memo fields, 531-33
AT clause, 558-59
AUTOSAVE, 75
AVERAGE command, 189, 190

Backup, in Help system, 24
Backup files, 502
Backward search, in Goto menu, 60
BALANCE query, 335-36
BALANCE report, 335-45
  calculating the balance, 335-37
  IIF( ) function and, 337-45
Bands, 211-13. See also
  Group Bands
BAR( ) function, 604-5
Bell settings, 77-79
BETWEEN predicate, in SQL, 754
Binary coded decimal numbers, 40
Binary tree, 91
Blank field command, 69
Boxes, 591-95
  drawing,
    for custom screens, 271-72
Browse mode, 64-70
  adding new records in, 67-68
  in Dot Prompt mode, 157-58
  FIELDS clause in, 159-60
  Fields menu in, 68-72
  keys used in, 66
  LIST or DISPLAY commands as
    faster than, 173

CALCULATE command, 191-93,
  560-61
Calculated columns, 251-55
Calculated fields, 135-41, 183

Character and Date, 138-41
  in linked databases, 436-38
Calculations
  arithmetic, 179-80
  mathematical, 191-93
  summary, 189-91
  in column reports, 225-29
Capitalization, selecting records by
  character fields and, 175
Carry Forward option, 299
Carry settings, 77
CASE command, 608
Case insensitive expressions, 176-77
Case insensitive search, 143
Catalog files, 9
Catalogs, 16, 26-29, 31
  creating new, 27-28, 371-76
  in Dot Prompt mode, 393-95
  keeping track of, 29
  structure of, 394
  switching, 29
Centering items, 570-72
Century settings, 77
CHANGE( ) function, 706, 714-18
Character fields, 38
  selection of records by, 107-11, 175
CHECKS query, 329-34
CHECKS screen form, 330-34
CHKSTATS program.
  See Programming
CHR( ) function, 568-69
CLEAR command, 180, 550-51
CLOSE command (SQL command),
  778
Closing a file, 73-74
Column headings, 219-20
Column reports, 209-65
  BALANCE, 335-45
  calculated columns, 251-55
  column headings, 219-20
  creating, 213-19
  with Group Bands, 345-55
    closing a band, 353-55
    menu, 346-47
  in index order, 234-46
  inserting a field in, 237-41
  logical fields and, 255-56
  memo fields, 257-59
  memo fields in, 241-44
  with multiple databases, 441-44
  numeric calculations, 255
  page numbers and dates, 221-22
  printing, 229-31
  from Query files, 250-51
  quick, 244-50
  reconciliation, 355-65
  report generation process, 233-34
  revising, 237
  saving a report form, 232
  selection of records for, 259-62
  summary, 345-50
  summary calculations in, 225-29
  templates, 222-25
Columns
  freezing, 70-72
  unfreezing, 72
Combining files, 524

COMMAND keyword, 806
Command Language, 149-50
Command level.
  See Dot Prompt mode
COMMAND program, 518
Commands, shortcuts for entering,
  162-63
Command sentences, 149-50
Command verbs, 153-54
Compilation Error,
  screen format file, 314-16
Compiler, 545-46
Compiling errors, 563-67
Conditional operations, 337
Conditional structures, 607-10
Condition boxes, 141-45, 183
CONFIG.DB, program, 13
CONFIG.DB file
  editing, 804-5
  settings, 806-9
Configuration. See also Settings
  and default values
Confirm settings, 77-79
Contents, in Help system, 23
Control Center, 11, 30
  display, 12, 13
  exiting, 150-205
  file operations from, 492-97
  panels, 13
  SET DESIGN option, 791
Controlled break, 349
CONVERT command, 706-7
Converting files, 706-18
COPY command
  (dBASE IV command), 522-23
COPY command
  (DOS command), 517, 520-22
COPY FILE command, 520-22
Copying files, 498, 502-3, 520-22
COPY MEMO command, 43, 531
COPY TO command, 533
COUNT command, 189, 191, 466-67
Counters, 619-23
CREATE REPORT command, 401-2
CREATE TABLE command
  (SQL command), 739, 740
CREATE VIEW FROM
ENVIRONMENT command,
  480-82
Creating a database, 33-83
  activating a database, 46-48
  adding records, 52-64
  Browse mode, 64-70
  closing a database, 73-74
  Ditto function, 57-58
  in Dot Prompt mode, 395-96
  entering a field, 38-42
  Fields menu, 68-72
  freezing a column, 70-72
  memo fields, 42-43
  number of fields that
    can be entered, 44
  printing the file structure, 50-51
  settings, 75-79
  in SQL, 737
  structure, 34-45
  undoing changes in records, 72-73

[Ctrl], general information on, 21
[Ctrl-End], to save a structure, 44-45
[Ctrl-w], to save a structure, 44-45
Cursor, SQL, 736
Cursor movement, input areas with @/GET command, 583-84

Database
  activating a, 46-48
    creating a. *See* Creating a database in SQL, 735
Data entry
  in Dot Prompt mode, 396-97
  with multiple databases, 457-58
  SET commands, 791-92
  in SQL, 741-44
Data Entry mode, 52-64
Date
  in column reports, 221
  SET commands, 796-97
Date fields, 39, 41
  selecting records by, 172-73
Date functions, 173-74
Date Order settings, 77
Date queries, 112-14
  ranges in, 114-16
Date Separator settings, 77
dBASE II, 534
dBASE IV
  changes from dBASE III, 8-11
  command line option, 809
  dual character of, 4
  installing, 12-13
  levels of, 6-7
  loading, 30
  loading 11-1a, 11
  memory requirements, 489
  philosophy of, 3
  quitting, 29-30
dBASE IV SQL. *See* SQL_DBASELOCK field, 706-7
DBDEFINE command (SQL command), 749-50
DBF files, 490
DBMEMO3, 535
DBSETUP program, 13, 797, 799-804
DBT files, 43, 490
DEACTIVATE MENU command, 606
Decimal places, 589-91
  number of, 36
DECLARE CURSOR command (SQL command), 777, 778
Default Value option, 299
DEFINE POP-UP command, 603, 611-15
DELETE command (SQL command), 776
Deleting
  fields, in custom screens, 292-93
  files, 498-501
  records, 527-31
  rows, in SQL, 776
DELIMITED, 534
Delimited files, 37
DELIMITED WITH BLANK, 534
DELIMITED WITH char, 534
Deposits, 317-29

DEPOSITS query, 318-19
DEPOSITS screen form, 319-29
  entering records, 325-29
Descriptions of databases, 48-50
Design Database mode, 15
Detail band, 212, 403-7
Dialog, programs that carry on a, 572
Dictionary sorting, 121-22
DIF (Data Interchange Format), 534
DIR command, 518-19
Directories, 518-20
DISPLAY command, 169-73, 199
  as faster than Browse mode, 173
  with memo fields, 180-81
  STATUS display, 196-97
Display Data option, 52
Display-only commands, 169-72
Display. *See* Screen display; Screen forms, custom
Ditto function, 57-58
Dividing a file, 523
DO CASE/ENDCASE structure, 607-10
DO command, 605-6
$ Dollar sign
  in SQL, 754
  in sub-string examples, 110-11
$ED files, 492
$VM files, 492
DOS, quitting to, 30
DOS Utilities option, 488, 492-97
Dot Prompt mode, 11, 31, 150-205
  adding records in, 156-57
  capitilization not necessary in, 154
  catalogs in, 393-95
  clearing the display, 180
  command shortcuts, 162-63
  correcting mistakes in, 163-64
  creating a database in, 395-96
  date functions, 173-74
  displaying data in, 169-70
  display-only commands in, 169-72
  ending a Dot Prompt session, 205
  entering a command in, 152-53
  exiting the Control Center and activating, 150-205
  exiting to, 30
  file operations in, 518-33
  four letter abbreviations in, 155
  indexes in, 194-96
  list of files in, 155-56
  memo fields, 180-89
  printing lists, 201
  printing reports and labels from, 408-10
  quitting from, 415
  report forms in, 401-3
  selection of files in, 155-56, 159-61
  selection of records in, 161-62
    case insensitive expressions, 176-77
    character fields, 175
    by date, 172-73
    by memo fields, 183-85
    by number values, 177-80
  sequencing in, 159-60
  SET commands, 201-4
  summary calculations, 189-91
  syntax and structure

of commands in, 153-54
Dot Prompt mode (command level), 6
DO WHILE/ENDDO loop, 615-17
Drive, default, 519-20
DROP TABLE command (SQL command), 776
Duplicate databases, 520-23

EDIT command, fields clause with, 160
EDIT FIELDS command, 467-69
Editing
  CONFIG.DB file settings, 806
  files, 499
  on networks, 678-80
  in SQL, 740
Editing options, for custom screens, 299-306, 321
Editing Permitted option, 299, 321
Edit mode
  in Dot Prompt mode, 156
  freezing a column and, 71-72
Editor, 42-43, 54-56
  commands available in, 55
Ejecting the page, 50-51
Encrypted files, 652-56
ENDCASE command, 609
Enhanced video, 15
Entering data. *See* Data entry
ERASE command, 516-18
Erasing. *See* Deleting
ERROR( ) function, 701
Error handling, 701-5
Errors
  compiling, 563-67
  logical, 566
  runtime, 566
[Esc], to exit a mode, 15
Exclusive access, 660-61, 672-74
Exclusive use, 635, 697-701
EXIT command (DOS command), 17, 516
  loops and, 616-17
Exit menu, 21
Exit-Save command, 44
Explicit record locking. *See* Record locking, explicit
EXPORT command, 533

[F3], moving the highlight with, 14
[F4], moving the highlight with, 14
[F10], as menu key, 17, 18
FETCH command (SQL command), 777
Field access, 637-38
Field names, 36, 38
Field number, 35
Fields, 34-44
Fields
  entering, 38-42
  number of fields that can be entered, 44
  protection of, 656-59
  width of, 36
FIELDS clause, 159-60
  with DISPLAY command, 171-72
  with LIST command, 172
Field types, 36, 38-40
  selection of, 40-41
File access, 637

File descriptions, 48-50
File dump, 169
File extensions, 490-93
File header, 490
File locking, 635, 661-62, 677, 697-706
  lock system functions, 705-7
  record locking versus, 667-70
FILELOCK program, 698-701, 726-28
Filenames, 48
File operations, 488-504
  from Control Center, 492-97
  copying, 498, 502-3
  dBASE IV language commands for, 515-36
    combining files, 524
    default drive, 519-20
    deleting records, 527-31
    directories, 518-20
    dividing a file, 523
    DOS commands compared to, 516-17
    duplicate databases, 520-23
    exchanging data, 533-36
    special memo operations, 531-33
    summary files, 524-26
  deleting, 498-501
  DOS commands for, 516-17
  editing, 499
  moving, 498
  in networks. See Networks
  renaming, 498
  viewing, 499
Files
  backup, 502
  protection of, 648-56
  SET commands, 793
  size of and space used by, 485
  sorting sequence of, 497
File skeleton, 99
Filtering, 106-7. See also SET FILTER TO command
FIND command, 198-200
Find operator, 133-34
Fixed length structure, 37
Float fields, 39, 40
FLOCK( ) function, 697
FMO files, 278, 491
FMT files, 278, 491
FOR clause, 166-68
  with DISPLAY command, 171
Form feed, 50-51
Form reports, 214. See report forms
Forward search, in Goto menu, 60
Framework II (FW2), 535
Freeze field option, 69-72
Freezing a column, 70-72
FRG files, 491
FRM files, 491
FRO files, 491
Full Screen formatting, 572-75
Full-screen modes, 168
FUNCTION command, 624-25
FW2 (Framework II), 535

@/GET command, clauses and functions with, 587-89
Goto menu, 59-63
Graphic characters, 287

Graphics, in custom screens, 286-91
Group Bands, 345-55
  closing a band, 353-55
  menu, 346-47
Group By operator, 131-32
Group Summary Band, 351-53

Header, file, 490
Help system, 23-26, 79-81
Highlight, moving the, 13-14
Highlighted item, selecting a, 14-15
History, 162
History buffer, 552
  in SQL, 740

IF/ELSE/ENDIF structure, 607
IIF( ) function, 337-45
IMPORT command, 533
Indexes, 36
  ascending order vs. descending order, 94, 95
  column reports and, 234-46
  creating additional, 91-98
  displaying names of, 196-97
  in Dot Prompt mode, 194-96
  listing records by index order, 86-91
  multiple, 87
  NDX, 87
  production, 37, 490
  for reports and labels, 411-12
  sorting distinguished from, 88
  in SQL, 759-62
  unique, 95-96
  multiple, 8-9
  searching, 198
Index key search, in Goto menu, 60
Index key searches (indexed searches), 89-91
Index tags, 87, 196
Initialization of variables, 578-80
IN predicate, in SQL, 754
Input areas with @/GET command, 577-95
  character input areas, 580-81
  cursor movement, 583-84
  decimal places, 589-91
  initialization of variables, 578-80
  lines and boxes, 591-95
  multiple, 581-83
  options, 587-89
INSERT command (SQL command), 742, 743
INSTALL.BAT, 13
Installing dBASE IV, 12-13

Keystroke macros, 10
Keystroke macros, 10, 488, 504-15
  defined, 504
  keys to which macros can be assigned, 505-6
  keywords within, 514
  modifying, 510-15
  with pauses, 507-10
  ps compared to, 542
  saving, 515
Keywords, CONFIG.DB file, 806-9

Labels, 376-93
  columns of, 379

fields, 380-85
  indexing, 411-12
  printing, 386-88
    from Dot Prompt mode, 408-10
    ? option with, 412-15
  selecting records for, 410
  size of, 376-78
  suppressing blank fields, 389-93
Largest Allowed Value option, 300
LBG files, 491
LBL files, 491
LBO files, 492
Like operator, 109
LIKE predicate, in SQL, 754
Linear programs, 544, 547-50
Lines, 591-95
Linked databases. See Multiple databases
LIST command, 169, 170, 172, 194-96
  as faster than Browse mode, 173
  FIND command compared to, 199-200
  with memo fields, 181
List of examples, 111-12
List of fields, multiple database, 469-72
LIST USERS command, 663
Literals, 144, 154
LKSYS( ) function, 706, 707, 710-14
LOAD DATA command (SQL command), 742, 745-47
Lock fields on left, 68
LOCKREC program, 685-92, 721
LOCKREC1 program, 691-97, 721-23
LOCKREC2 program, 711-12, 723-24
LOCKREC3 program, 715-17, 724-26
Logical combinations, 116-19
Logical errors, 566
Logical fields, 39
  column reports and, 255-56
  in custom screens, 293-94
Logical operations (mathematical inequality symbols), 114-16
  SQL, 753-56
Logical selection of records, 161-62, 166
Logins, 645-47
  forced, 647
LOOP.PRG, 616-19, 628-29
Loops, 615-19
  Counter and Accumulator memory variables inside, 620-23
LOWER( ) function, 176-77
LUPDATE( ) function, 284-85

Macro keywords, 514
Macro substitution, 488
Mailing labels. See Labels
Mailmerge reports, 214, 445-56
  creating, 447-53
  wraparound text in, 453-56
Master (parent) database, 421
  creating, 424-31
Match capitilization, in Goto menu, 60
Mathematical calculations, 191-93

MDX files, 196-97, 490
Memlines( ) function, 185-88
Memo fields, 9, 40, 42-43,
    54-56, 180-89
  in column reports, 241-44
  column reports and, 257-59
  in custom screens, 294-98
  functions that operate on, 185-89
  importing/exporting text to/from,
    531-33
  selection of records by, 183-85
  width of, 181-83
    in column reports, 242-44
Memory, 489
  types of, 75
Memory variables, 553-56
  counters and accumulators,
    619-23
Menu bar, 16-23
Menus, 31
  pop-up. See Pop-up menus
Menu system, 6
Message option, 299
Milne( ) function, 185, 187, 188
Modes, 31
MODIFY COMMAND command,
    548
Moving fields, in Query mode, 104-5
Moving files, 498
Multiple databases (linked
databases),
    419-82
  alias names, 423-24
  benefits of, 419-20
  calculating using linked databases,
    436-38
  column reports using, 441-44
  creating a field list, 469-72
  creating a view from the
environment,
    480-82
  creating the master (parent)
database,
    424-31
  custom screen forms with, 473-80
  data entry with, 457-58
  editing fields, 467-69
  linking databases, 420-22, 431-36
  multiple links, 440-41
  selecting records, 438
  setting relations, 463-66
  sorting, 438-40
  Work Areas, 458-63
Multiple indexes, 87
Multi-user databases.
    See Networks
MVBLKSIZE keyword, 808
MVMAXBLKS keyword, 808

Natural computer languages, 167
Natural order, 86, 98
  return to, 198
Net Present Value calculation, 193
Network lock system database, 706
Networks, 7, 33, 633-728
  components of, 634-36
  exclusive access, 672-74
  list of users, 663
  programming on, 677-728
    converting files, 706-18

editing, 678-80
error handling, 701-5
explicit record locking, 677-97
file locking, 697-706
lock system functions, 705-7
user ID messages, 708-10
security of.
    See Security system
    (protection system)
SET commands, 793-94
SET LOCK command, 670-72
shared mode, 659
NOCLEAR clause, 165
NOINIT clause, 164-65
Norton Commander, 489
NPV( ) calculation, 193
Num, 35
Numeric fields, 39, 40
  REPLACE command used to store
    calculated date in, 399-400
  selection of records by, 177-80
  width of, 41-42

Object-code files, 103, 545-46
Object-oriented commands
    or operations, 364
OPEN command
    (SQL command), 777
OR relationships, 116-19

Packing, 527-28, 530-31
Page breaks, inserting, 407-8
Page Footer band, 213
Page Header band, 212
Page numbers, in column
    reports, 221-22
Panels, 31
PARAMETERS command, 624-25
Passwords, 638-41
PDRIVER keyword, 808
Permit Edit If option, 299, 321
PFS File format, 536
Physical selection of records, 161-62
Picture function, 556-58
Picture functions, 225
Pointer, 198-99
POP1.PRG, 604, 627
POP2.PRG, 612-14, 628
Pop-up menus, 17, 601-15
  commands used to create, 602-3
  conditional structures, 607-10
  selection of a menu item, 603-6
  special features, 611-15
Preprinted forms,
    mailmerge reports and, 456
Print, in Help system, 24
Printer drivers and fonts,
    CONFIG.DB
    file settings, 807-8
PRINTER FONT keyword, 807
PRINTER keyword, 807
Printing
  column reports, 229-31
  database structure, 50-51
  labels, 386-88
    from Dot Prompt mode, 408-10
  reports
    from Dot Prompt mode, 408-10
  SET commands, 794
  SQL information on pages, 783-84

unformatted, 201
Procedures, 605-7
Production index, 37, 490
Program level, 6-7
Programming (programs),
    31, 541-95
  adding more information
    to the report, 560-61
  calculation program using
    Full-Screen commands, 584-87
  centering items, 570-72
  compiler, 545-46
  compiling errors, 563-67
  dBASE II and III, 542
  deferred execution of, 543-44
  dialog, 572
  formatting displayed items, 556-58
  with Full Screen formatting, 572-75
  horizontal location of displayed
    items, 558-59
  input areas with
    @/GET command, 577-95
    character input areas, 580-81
    cursor movement, 583-84
    decimal places, 589-91
    initialization of variables, 578-80
    lines and boxes, 591-95
    multiple, 581-83
    options, 587-89
  linear, 544, 547-50
  memory variables, 553-56
  modular approach to, 544-45
  on networks, 677-728
    converting files, 706-18
    editing, 678-80
    error handling, 701-5
    explicit record locking, 677-97
    file locking, 697-706
    lock system functions, 705-7
    user ID messages, 708-10
  printing on the same line, 561-63
  replicating a character, 568-70
  on the same line, 561-63
  screen display, 550-60
  SET commands, 794-95
  status and scoreboard
    displays, 576-77
  vertical spacing, 567
PROMPT( ) function, 611-13
PROTECT command, 626-38.
    See also Security system
    (protection system)

QBE files, 103, 490
QBO files, 490
Queries. See also SQL
  processing of, 103
  unique, 132-33
  update, 355-58
Query by Example file, 103
Query by Example mode, 9, 98-146
  Calculated fields in, 135-41
  calculated fields in, 183
  condition boxes in, 141-45, 183
  controlling fields in, 99-106
    moving fields, 104-5
    removing fields, 100-3
  date queries, 112-14
  find operator in, 133-34
  list of examples in, 111-12

logical combinations in, 116-19
quick reports in, 244-50
ranges in, 114-16
removing files in, 126-27
saving a query in, 123-26
selection of records in, 106-7
  by characters, 107-11
sorting in, 120-23
sub-string examples in, 110-11
subtotal groups in, 131-32
summary displays in, 127-32
unique lists in, 132-33
variable names in, 136-38
writing a query as a file, 124
Query files, 98, 123-26
  reports from, 250-51
? (question mark) option
    (or command), 169
  AT clause with, 558-59
  with labels or reports, 412-15
  programming and, 550, 551
  as streaming-output
    command, 572-73
Quick reports, 244-50
QUIT command, 415
Quitting dBASE IV, 29-30
Quotation marks, selecting
    records by character fields
    and, 175

Ranges, 114-16
RapidFile (RPD), 535
RecLock, 33
RECNO( ) function, 283-84
Reconciliation report, 355-65
Record locking, 635, 662-63
  converting files, 706-18
  explicit, 677-97
    LOCKREC1 program, 691-97
    LOCKREC program, 685-92
    multiple records, 690
    RLOCK( ) function, 681-85
    SET REFRESH TO
      command, 680-81
    SET REPROCESS
      command, 680, 684
    turning off the lock
      message/pause, 684
    unlocking a record, 684-85
  file locking versus, 667-70
  user ID messages, 708-10
Record number, in
    custom screens, 282-85
RECORD NUMBER command,
    in Goto menu, 59
Records
  adding, 52-64
    in Browse mode, 67-68
    in Dot Prompt mode, 156-57
  deleting, 527-31
  displaying previously
    entered, 58-63
  selection of
    case insensitive expressions,
      176-77
    by character fields, 107-11
    character fields, 175
    for column reports, 259-62
    by date, 172-73
    for labels and reports, 410

linked databases, 438
logical, 161-62, 166-68
physical, 161
Query mode, 106-7
undoing changes in, 72-73
Records Undo command, 72-73
Related Topic, in Help system, 24
RELEASE command, 606
Removing files, in Query by Example
    mode, 126-27
Renaming files, 331, 498
REPLACE command
    (dBASE IV command), 398-401
REPLACE command
    (DOS command), 517
REPLICATE( ) function,
    286-88, 568-69
Replicating a character, 568-70
Report form file, 210
Report forms, 210-13
  Detail band of, 403-7
  inserting page breaks, 407-8
Report Intro band, 212
Reports
  column. See Column reports
  indexing, 411-12
  mailmerge, 214, 445-56
    creating, 447-53
    wraparound text in, 453-56
    ? option with, 412-15
  selecting records for, 410
Report Summary band, 213
Retrieving data, 85-147
  with indexes, 86-98
    creating additional indexes, 91-98
    listing by index order, 86-91
    multiple indexes, 87
    search techniques, 91
  in natural order, 98
  Query by Example mode. See

  Query by Example mode
SET commands, 792-93
  in SQL, 744-45
RETURN command, 552
RLOCK( ) function, 681-85
ROUND() function, 177-78
Routines, 544-45
RPD (RapidFile), 535
RTBLKSIZE keyword, 808-9
RTMAXBLKS keyword, 808-9
RUN command, 516
Runtime errors, 566
Runtime symbols, 808-9

@/SAY com, 581
@/SAY command, 573-77
@/SAY/GET command, 581-82
SCAN/ENDSCAN loop, 616, 619
Scans, 199
Scoreboard display, 576-77
Screen displays. See also Input
    areas with @/GET command
  pop-up menus, 17, 601-15
    commands used to create, 602-3
    conditional structures, 607-10
    selection of a menu item, 603-6
    special features, 611-15
  programming and, 550-60
  SET commands, 795-96

status line, 576-77
Screen format files, 278
Screen form files, 278
Screen forms, custom, 267-316
  adding non-field
    information, 279-82
  adding text to, 269-71
  Compilation Error, 314-16
  copying a screen from a file, 291-92
  creating, 268
  deleting fields, 292-93
  for deposits, 319-29
  drawing a box, 271-72
  editing options for specific fields,
    299-306, 321
  graphics, 286-91
  logical fields, 293-94
  memo fields, 294-98
  with multiple databases, 473-80
  with multiple pages, 306-11
  placing fields, 272-79
  record number in, 282-85
  returning to the default display,
    311-12
Screen memory, CONFIG.DB
    file setting, 806
SCR files, 278, 490
SDF (Standard Data Format), 535
Searches. See also Indexes
  case insensitive, 143
  indexed, 89-91
Security system (protection system),
    634-59
  field protection, 656-59
  file protection, 648-56
  logins, 645-47
  modifying a protected
    database, 654-56
  passwords, 638-41
  user profiles, 641-45
SELECT command (SQL command),
    744-45, 750-51
  for multiple table selections, 766-70
  with ORDER BY clause, 757-59
SELECT DISTINCT command
    (SQL command), 763
Selection
  of a menu item, 603-6
  of fields, in Dot Prompt
    mode, 159-61
  of files, in Dot Prompt
    mode, 155-56
  of highlighted item, 14-15
  of records
    case insensitive
      expressions, 176-77
    by character fields, 107-11
    character fields, 175
    for column reports, 259-62
    by date, 172-73
    for labels and reports, 410
    linked databases, 438
    logical, 161-62, 166-68
    physical, 161
    Query mode, 106-7
Sequencing, 159-60. See also
    Indexes; Sorting
Sequential searches, 91
SET( ) function, 797-99
SET AUTOSAVE command, 75

SET CATALOG ON/OFF
command, 394
SET CATALOG TO command, 394
SET commands, 75-79,
201-4, 790-97
Control Center, 791
data entry, 791-92
files, 793
networks, 793-94
output devices, 794
printing, 794
programming, 794-95
retrieving data, 792-93
screen display, 795-96
time and date, 796-97
SET DEFAULT command, 519-20
SET DESIGN option, 791
SET ENCRYPTION
command, 654-56
SET FIELDS TO
command, 202, 469-72
SET FILTER TO
command, 202-4, 410-11
SET LOCK command, 670-72
SET MEMOWIDTH TO
command, 182
SET ORDER TO
command, 194, 196, 198
SET REFRESH TO
command, 680-81
SET RELATION TO
command, 463-66
SET REPROCESS
command, 680, 684
SET TALK command, 551-52
Settings and default values, 789-809
permanent changes in, 797-809
starting dBASE IV, 809
temporary changes in, 789-97
Shared mode, 659
[Shift-Tab], moving the
highlight with, 14
Size field option, 69
Skeletons
file, 99
view, 99, 101
moving fields in, 104-5
Skip command, in Goto menu, 59
Smallest Allowed Value option, 300
Sort command (DOS), 497
Sorting
ASCII vs. dictionary, 121-22
with linked databases, 438-40
in Query mode, 120-23
Source-code files, 545
Source document, 396-97
SQL, 35, 731-86
CONFIG.DB file settings, 806
creating a database, 737
data entry in, 741-44
dBASE IV compared to, 732-33
dBASE IV expressions as column
specifications, 751-52
dBASE IV used for
SQL data, 747-48
deleting rows, 776
displaying data, 744-45
distinct selections of

records, 762-63
dropping tables, 776
entering commands, 739-41
importing databases, 749-50
indexes, 759-62
indirect totals, 765-66
information about the current
database, 756-57
introduction to, 731-32
loading data from a file, 745-47
logical operators, 753-56
multiple table selections, 766-70
new tables, 774-75
printing SQL information on pages,
783-84
programs using SQL
databases, 776-82
reasons for using, 732
selecting data from tables, 750-51
selecting specific columns from a
table to list, 751
sequencing selections of records,
757-59
starting, 736
summaries with multiple
tables, 770-71
summary queries, 763-65
tables, 735, 738-39
terms used in, 735-36
uses of, 735
views, 772-74
WHERE clause, 752
Sqlcode, 778
SQL_CUR program, 778-82, 786
SQL Server, 734
Standard Data Format (SDF), 535
STATUS display, 196-97
Status line, 14, 576-77
Streaming print system, 10
Structure
creating a, 34-45
delimited, 37
display, 35
fixed length, 37
printing, 50-51
STRUCTURE clause, 194
Structured Query
Language (SQL), 7-8
Structure saving a, 44-45
Submenus, 19-21
Subroutines, 544
Sub-string examples, 110-11
Sub-string match, 90
SUM command, 189-91
Summary calculations, 189-91
in column reports, 225-29
Summary displays, in Query by
Example
mode, 127-32
Summary files, 524-26
Summary operations, 129
Summary queries, in SQL, 763-65
Summary reports, 345-50
SYLK (Symbolic Link) format, 535
Syntax errors, 563-67
System's tables, SQL, 756-57

[Tab], moving the highlight with, 14

Tables, SQL, 735, 738-39.
See also SQL multiple
selections, 766-70
new tables, 774-75
selecting data from, 750-51
summaries with multiple
tables, 770-71
Tags, index, 87, 196
Talk, 93
Templates, 222-25, 556-58
Temporary files, 492
Time, SET commands, 796-97
@/TO command, 591-95
Tools, 17
Tools Settings command, 75-79
TO PRINTER clause, 201
TOTAL command, 524-26
TPA (Transient Program Area), 489
TRANSFORM( ) function, 561-62
Transient Program Area (TPA), 489
Trim function, 253

Unaccepted Message option, 300
Undoing changes, in records, 72-73
Unfreezing a column, 72
Unique indexes, 95-96
in SQL, 761-62
Unique queries, 132-33
Unlocking a record, 684-85
UNTITLED.CAT, 27
UPDATE command
(SQL command), 742
Update queries, 355-58
UPPER( ) function, 176-77
USE A DIFFERENT CATALOG
Command, 372
USE command, 152
USE EXCLUSIVE command, 673-74
USER( ) function, 714
User-defined functions, 623-25
User ID messages, 708-10
User profiles, 641-45

Variable names, in Query
mode, 136-38
Variables. See also
Memory variables
initialization of, 578-80
Vertical spacing, 567
View files, 480-82
Viewing files, 499
Views, in SQL, 772-74
View skeleton, 99, 101
moving fields in, 104-5

WHERE clause (SQL), 752
Width of fields, 36
Wildcards, 109-10
DOS (file specification), 496-97
Windows, 15
WKS, 535
Work Areas, 394, 458-63
Wraparound text, in mailmerge
reports,
453-56
XCOPY command
(DOS command), 517